SCHOOL FINANCE

The Economics
and
Politics
of Public Education

SCHOOL FINANCE

The Economics and Politics of Public Education

Walter I. Garms, *University of Rochester*

James W. Guthrie, *University of California, Berkeley*

Lawrence C. Pierce, *University of Oregon*

PRENTICE-HALL, INC., *Englewood Cliffs, New Jersey 07632*

Library of Congress Cataloging in Publication Data

Garms, Walter I
    School finance.

    Includes bibliographical references and index.
    1. Education—United States—Finance. 2. Education
and state—United States. 3. Federal aid to education—
United States. I. Guthrie, James W., joint author.
II. Pierce, Lawrence C., joint author. III. Title.
LB2825.G35   379.1'0973   77-9100
ISBN 0-13-793315-0

Prentice-Hall International, Inc., *London*
Prentice-Hall of Australia Pty. Limited, *Sydney*
Prentice-Hall of Canada, Ltd., *Toronto*
Prentice-Hall of India Private Limited, *New Delhi*
Prentice-Hall of Japan, Inc., *Tokyo*
Prentice-Hall of Southeast Asia Pte. Ltd., *Singapore*
Whitehall Books Limited, *Wellington, New Zealand*

CONTENTS

PREFACE

Public education in America is facing declining enrollments and increasing resistance to additional educational expenditures. To the extent that this continues, many conventional solutions to educational problems, such as spending more money or adding new programs, will no longer suffice. Resources for schools will become scarce. Programs added during the period of growth will be consolidated. To improve the quality of public education at a time when resources for schools are shrinking will require new approaches. We hope this book will assist policy makers in making the financial and political decisions required to revitalize public education.

This book encompasses three subjects or categories of analyses. Part of the book is concerned with the economics of education. Specifically, we address questions such as: What types of educational services should be publicly produced? What proportion of public budgets should be allocated to education rather than to other services? What combination of resources can produce educational services most efficiently? How are the benefits of education distributed among different classes of citizens? At what level and by what means can educational improvements be sought?

The second topic is the politics of educational finance. How funds are raised to pay for schools and how those funds are allocated by legislatures and local school boards are political concerns of the highest order. Citizens have a variety of points of view on these questions; yet they typically must accept the collective decision of school officials. Being unable to change their residence easily or freely to choose the educational programs they want, most citizens can only express their dissatisfaction with public schools by complaining and pressuring officials to change. The sections of this book devoted to the politics of educational finance analyze means by which individuals and policy makers can apply pressure to bring about change. Here we discuss school budget elections, lobbying, and citizen participation. We also assess the internal politics of education by examining struggles for control of educational decision making. State versus local control, management versus union control, and district versus school site control are examples of such political tensions.

The third subject is the "new political economy" of education. This analytic tool employs economic methods to study those governmental institutions responsible for educational policy. Just as economists attempt to predict economic results by analyzing market structure, social scientists attempt to predict policy outcomes by analyzing the decision-making arrangements of public institutions. According to this perspective, the most important task of social theory is not to dictate what is equitable and efficient policy, but to specify the institutional framework in which equitable and efficient policies will be chosen.

"Political economy" has become a popular phrase for describing a number of approaches to social issues. Sociologists and political scientists frequently describe patterns of dominance in American society as the study of political economy. They are interested in the power of the military–industrial elite and argue for a radical redistribution of power. Others concerned with the politics of economic affairs call themselves political economists. We define the new political economy more narrowly to mean the use of economic methods to analyze governmental institutions.

This book is intended for students, policy makers and their staff members, educational administrators, social scientists, and interested lay people. In addition to its general information and analyses about public education, the book contains sections of particular interest to each audience. For example, educational administrators and students of educational administration can find current information on federal support for public schools, new state aid formulas and how they affect local school districts, new school budgeting procedures, administrative implications of teacher unionism, management of capital, enrollment projections, and ways to increase school efficiency.

Political scientists have in the past ignored education largely because it was organized as an independent or special unit of government and kept clear of local politics. But education's ability to stay above politics is eroding. Education consumes a larger share of state and local tax dollars than any other state or local activity. Furthermore, as competition for tax dollars increases, educators themselves have become more politically minded in order to protect their share of state and local governmental budgets. Political scientists are becoming more interested in the governance and financing of education both because it is becoming more political, and because the high costs of education impinge on other areas of political interest such as land use, transportation, welfare, and prison reform.

Economists, particularly those with an interest in public policy, will also find portions of the book useful. Economic theories based on the assumptions of individual rationality, competition, complete knowledge, and the independence of the government from private activities are inadequate for describing and predicting public policy outcomes. Individuals do not always behave rationally, knowledge of the educational process is uncertain, and the relationships between government and the private sector are highly interdependent. An empirically sound theory of educational policy making must take into account the constraints imposed by the limited capacities of individuals and organizations responsible for public education, and by the procedures and mechanisms used to anticipate and respond to educational problems. This study of educational policy making should help economists understand the complex relationship between policy making and educational outcomes. Economists will also find the chapters on taxes, the management of capital, and the technology of school finance reform of specific substantive interest.

The consumers of public education are perhaps the most important potential audience. Historically, it was assumed that professional educators alone knew what was best for schools and could make decisions in the public interest. Recently, educators have been faced with increasing uncertainty about the goals of education and the means to achieve them, and in many cases are asking citizens to join them in making school decisions. This book is written so lay people can understand it. Conscientious parents and citizens can use much of the following information to prepare themselves for more active roles in education.

This book is divided into four parts and 17 chapters. The first part sets the policy environment of public education. Chapter One discusses policy issues and the policy approach used in this book. Chapter Two analyzes the desired outcomes of public policy. In particular it examines the tradeoffs between the achievement of greater equality and efficiency in education, and the desirability of making our educational institutions more responsive to their clientele. Chapter Three addresses the role of government in public education and the difficult question of how much education is enough.

Part II describes the current organization and patterns of financing public education in the United States. Chapter Four deals with the organization of public schools and some of the organizational problems facing them. Chapter Five analyzes the implications of teacher unionism on the decision-making processes in public education. Chapter Six examines the question of who pays for public education and the effects of current taxes on the provision of educational services. Chapter Seven describes the patterns and politics of federal support for public schools, and Chapter Eight analyzes current systems for distributing state school aid dollars to local school districts.

Part III describes several proposals for reforming the governance and financing of public education in the United States. Chapter Nine looks at state school finance reform and presents a radical proposal for restructuring public education at the state and local levels. Chapter Ten examines the strengths and weaknesses of the most frequently mentioned accountability proposals. Chapter Eleven presents an accountability scheme which shifts major responsibility for decision making and budgeting to local school sites. Chapter Twleve discusses the technical problems of state school finance reform, while Chapter Thirteen analyzes the politics of reform at both local and state levels.

Part IV covers three special topics of educational finance. Chapter Fourteen discusses the management of capital in public education, a topic often omitted from texts on school finance, but now becoming more important as a result of declining school enrollments. Chapter Fifteen applies much of what has already been said to the particular problems of urban schools, and Chapter Sixteen makes the linkage between the financing of public schools and the financing of various types of postsecondary public educational institutions.

The concluding chapter asks the question, "Where Does this Leave Us?"; it summarizes the major policy proposals interspersed throughout the text.

There are a number of people who have contributed to the publication of this book. We would like to acknowledge the finacial support of the Ford Foundation, which enabled the three of us to work together in Berkeley, California during the 1975–76 academic year. The School of Education at the University of California provided office space and an unusually fine group of educators with whom to discuss our proposals. Many individuals read parts or all of the text and deserve our appreciation. In this regard we wish particularly to thank Charles Benson, James Kelly, Michael Kirst, Allan Odden, and Louise Stoll for their patient reading and their suggestions on early drafts of the manuscript. Though they remain anonymous, we wish also to thank the professional reviewers arranged for by Prentice-Hall.

Jo Ann Mazzarella did a superb job of smoothing out the inconsistencies and stylistic awkwardness created by our combined authorship. George Ann Garms is responsible for the index. The task of typing drafts of the book was ably and cheerfully done by Joann Brady, Jane Beaumont, Kathy Dickenson, and the Secretarial staff at the College of Education, University of Rochester.

There exists another dimension of appreciation. At various points in our professional careers, each of the authors received instruction, counsel, and encouragement from one or more of a remarkable group of colleagues and friends. Whatever we are judged to have done well in this book is in large measure attributable to their assistance. We wish particularly to thank Charles Benson of the University of California, Berkeley, for his generosity in sharing ideas and giving advice; William Mitchell of the University of Oregon for his theoretical perspectives on the relationship between economics and politics; H. Thomas James of the Spencer Foundation for his prominent role in the professional development of two of us; James Kelly of the Ford Foundation for his continued encouragement during this project; and Michael Kirst of Stanford University for consistently reminding us that school finance is a field filled with choices between competing values.

It is customary to thank family members for all they endured during the preparation of a book. The truth is that we all had a delightful year in the San Francisco area and are pleased that our families were able to share the sights and tastes of that fine part of the country.

I

Public Values
and
Policy Issues

1

INTRODUCTION

The history of public education in the United States has been one of growth and success. For more than a century and a half public schools grew in terms of students and resources expended. Since World War II public schools have also been asked to solve many social problems as well as provide traditional educational services. During the 1960s, for example, schools were expected to play a role in creating an integrated society and were expected to be dynamic instruments of social change.

The path-breaking role of American public education seemed to be coming to an end in the early 1970s, however. Enrollments leveled off and then began to decline. Pressures for other governmental services meant greater resistance to additional educational spending. Schools were not successful in significantly integrating American society or bringing about social change. Unfulfilled expectations led to a recognition of the limitations of formal schooling. Unable to solve intransigent social problems and faced with tighter budgets, educators began retreating to the safer grounds of reading, writing, and arithmetic. In coming years society will in all probability demand less of public schools and educators will be slower to promise results. Falling expectations, stable or declining school enrollments, and financial competition from other public services portend many changes in American public education.[1]

---

[1] For a similar assessment of the state of public education see James G. March, "Commitment and Competence in Educational Administration," in *Educational Leadership*

Educators and many political leaders have had difficulty adapting to declining enrollments and falling expectations, in large part because they had become accustomed to just the opposite. From early in the nineteenth century through World War II, public education grew rapidly and the public faithfully supported this expansion. During those years there was widespread agreement on the goals of public education. If the country was to grow, prosper, and defend itself, it needed a trained and literate population.

The public school system, having accepted this challenge, actually surpassed most people's expectations. Public schools melded peoples with different languages and cultures into a literate, well-trained, and responsible citizenry. Public education was also credited with providing an informed electorate necessary for the development and stability of our democratic political institutions. Educated Americans created a highly complex and technological society, and the benefits of our industrial progress spilled over our borders to people in other countries as well.

Public education assumed an even more diversified role after World War II. Largely because of their success, and the confidence Americans had in public education, public schools assumed additional responsibilities besides providing basic skills and citizenship training. Schools were singled out as the appropriate institution for bringing about an integrated society. Special courses for handicapped and gifted children were added to the curricula, often under the prodding of the courts. Compensatory education was touted as a panacea for reducing social and economic inequalities in America and strengthening social cohesion in the process.

The results were disappointing. The consensus that had formerly prevailed over the goals and methods of public education gave way to interminable conflicts over the proper role of public schools and the appropriate methods to obtain educational objectives. Debates on whether schools should transmit the older, time-tested values or lead us to new ones raged during the early 1970s. Ironically the lack of agreed-upon objectives did not slow but seemed to stimulate the production of educational innovations. Closed circuit television, teaching machines, team teaching, open classrooms, performance contracting, and busing all offered great hope. But the innovations were no match for the problems they were designed to solve. Programs to solve one problem often created new and worse problems. Decentralization to promote greater community control, for example, also increased the likelihood that schools would be differentiated by class, ethnicity, and race. Rather than revise a program to eliminate an unintended result, the tendency was to redefine the program's objectives to conform with actual results.[2] The most intense controversies have

and Declining Enrollment, ed. Lewis B. Mayhew (Berkeley, Calif.: McCutchan Publishing Corporation, 1974), pp. 131–41.

[2] See Aaron Wildavsky, "The Strategic Retreat From Objectives," working paper #45, Graduate School of Public Policy, University of California, Berkeley, California, December 1975.

surrounded programs designed to help one group but which inadvertently impose restrictions on another. Busing, for example, has not improved the educational opportunities of blacks so much as it has provoked disruptive reactions from whites to busing programs. Recent innovations have languished for a variety of reasons, and few of them have had lasting impact in classrooms.

One should not conclude, however, that trends toward the stabilization of enrollment and financial resources and the lowering of expectations means that education will become less important. To the contrary, education and public schools will continue to play vital roles in our increasingly complex post-industrial society. Education will absorb enormous amounts of money; new jobs will require new and more specialized educational programs; and new social and political problems will require a more educated and sophisticated citizenry. The shift from a period of growth to one of stability or decline, however, means that traditional solutions to educational problems—spend more money or add a new program—may no longer suffice. New approaches will be required to meet future problems. And solutions to some problems will be difficult and will come more slowly than before, as education finds itself farther back in the line of public priorities.

These new circumstances present policy makers with some previously unavailable opportunities. Public schools, like other bureaucracies, now exhibit many symptoms of too rapid growth: waste and inefficiency, and the uncritical acceptance of conventional ways of doing things.[3] Relieved of the pressures of continually devising new programs for ever greater numbers of students, educators can work to bring about more efficiency in the schools. They will have time to reexamine teaching methods and priorities and to choose the most effective. Programs that have been successful in the past can be consolidated, and new ideas can be subjected to careful thought and longer trial periods before they are finally incorporated into the curriculum.

The purpose of this book is to analyze the dual problems of educational governance and finance and to examine the solutions that will in all likelihood be proposed during the 1980s. We start with the premise that public school policy is in transition. This transition from growth to decline creates new policy problems for educators and policy makers. Just as the prescriptions for a period of economic growth are inappropriate during a recession, so any solution to educational problems based on the assumption of growth will not suffice under conditions of decline. Likewise, as the problems facing economic managers are most difficult at the turning points of the business cycle, so the problems now facing educational policy makers promise to be the most ticklish.

In this text we shall attempt to give the reader a new insight into the policy issues in American education during this critical transitional period. From past and current research on the economics and politics of public schools, we shall sift out those approaches that may prove useful to future policy makers.

---

[3] A similar point is made in March, "Commitment and Competence," p. 136.

In line with its policy focus, this book places important restrictions on the themes discussed. The chapters focus on the governing and financing arrangements over which policy makers have some control. While many topics, such as the impact of declining birth rate on school attendance, changing tastes for education, and the declining lifetime economic value of education are of interest to educators and economists, policy makers can do little to alter these variables. Consequently, we shall mention them only briefly as part of the context in which educational policy is made. Before addressing that topic, however, we need to make explicit the policy perspectives of the authors.

Policy Perspectives

As we began organizing the material for this book, it became clear that we shared a variety of biases affecting our analysis of educational finance problems and their solutions. These biases reflect our experiences as academics as well as our successful and, more often, unsuccessful experiences as the advocates of policy reform. In order to make our analysis more understandable, therefore, we briefly describe our underlying assumptions or biases.

THE ROLE OF PUBLIC SCHOOLS

Perhaps the most important assumption underlying our analysis is our belief that public schools are productive, necessary, and understandable. It has become popular among social critics to lay the ills of the world on schools and suggest that if public schooling were abolished or radically changed the ills would go away.[4] Others suggest that schools are only a reflection of the society at large and that the social structure itself must be changed.[5] We do not subscribe to so radical or pessimistic a view. Schools do have problems. Nevertheless, they continue to provide most American children with basic reading, writing, and computation skills. Perhaps most important, public opinion polls reveal that people believe that public schools are doing a better job than most other major public institutions.

We do not mean to imply, of course, that public schools cannot be improved. Many schools, particularly in large urban school districts, have severe problems and need major reform. We believe meaningful reform will only be possible, however, when the limitations of formal schooling are recognized. One of the biggest problems of public schools is that they have been oversold.

[4]Ivan Illich, *Deschooling Society* (New York: Basic Books, 1972).
[5]Martin Carnoy and Henry M. Levin, *The Limits of Educational Reform* (New York: David McKay Company, Inc., 1976).

They have been asked to do more than they possibly can. We believe that schools are good for some things but not for all things. They cannot solve all the problems of the country. When they have been asked to do so, they have failed, not only in their new responsibilities but also in many of their traditional responsibilities. Reform of public education must begin by agreeing upon what schools can and should do and then limiting their responsibilities to those goals.

THE CONTROL OF PUBLIC SCHOOLS

Fundamental to a democracy is local control of public institutions. Following this principle, early schools were organized at the community level and placed under the direction of popularly elected school boards. Local control of community schools has been gradually weakened during the twentieth century, however. In an attempt to encourage professionalism and efficiency in public education, school districts were consolidated and subjected to increasing central control from district, state, and federal education agencies. Local control of schools was further weakened by the introduction of collective bargaining. These changes permitted greater direction of public education by professional educators.[6]

We believe that the trend toward professional control of education has gone too far in the United States. The tension between expertise and popular control that underlies many areas of public policy in a democracy has become unbalanced in favor of professional educators. The balance needs to be restored by reasserting the right of the public to control its schools. We also have an even more fundamental commitment to the principle that except where there is a clear state interest in financing and controlling schools, local citizens should support and run their own schools. Providing equal educational opportunity, for example, clearly calls for state involvement in financing of schools. Outside of this area, however, we believe that equality of opportunity and efficiency can be better pursued without the burdensome domination of educational decisions by professionals at both the district and state levels. Another reason for returning to popular control of schools is disillusionment with educational technology. Professional educators have promised improved performance from a variety of "scientific" educational techniques that for the most part have not worked. Faced with weak technology and no answers, we believe choices of educational programs should be left to the people most affected by public education; parents, students, and citizens of local communities who pay for and benefit from public education.

[6]Tyll Van Geel, *Authority to Control the School Program* (Lexington, Mass.: D. C. Heath and Co., 1976).

REFORMING PUBLIC SCHOOLS

Political reform requires a careful balancing of many competing values. Many of the educational reform proposals during the last three decades have been designed to equalize educational opportunity. In general we agree with the idea of using the public education system to improve the life opportunities of children from disadvantaged backgrounds. We are well aware, however, that schools cannot do the entire job. Income maintenance programs, health programs, housing programs, and employment programs must also do their share.

While pursuing the goal of equality we must also take care to use educational resources efficiently. In some cases equality and efficiency are competing values. In others, however, an inefficient use of resources may cripple programs for the disadvantaged. Furthermore, the efficient management of the schools is necessary for the continuing support of the American public.

We also believe that parents and students should be given as much choice of educational programs as is practicable and consistent with the values of equality and efficiency. In the past, policies to promote equality and efficiency have led to unnecessary uniformity in educational programs. Freedom to select a program best suited to a child's individual educational requirements is not necessarily inconsistent with the desire to have a fair and efficient school system. It is neither equitable nor efficient to instruct a slow learner and a precocious child in the same way. We believe diversity and choice in education should be encouraged and can be made consistent with the goals of equal educational opportunity and efficiency.

The process of reforming public education is not easy since many entrenched interests are involved and there is lack of agreement on what should be done. We believe social scientists can assist educational policy makers to overcome the difficulties in at least two ways. We can analyze problems and provide knowledge and information policy makers need to make informed decisions. Enrollment and revenue projections and state school finance formulas are good examples. We can also assist policy makers in using the political policy-making process to improve the chances that policies will be acceptable to the public. Devising mechanisms for increasing public access to the policy-making process is one way to accomplish this task.

Finally we also believe that policy makers should move deliberately in reforming the educational system both to ensure that what is presently good remains and thoroughly to evaluate the impact of changes. While we certainly advocate caution in not moving too quickly, we do believe that the problems of public schools, particularly in the cities, must be remedied soon. We cannot wait until everyone agrees on the nature of the problems and what to do about them. In other words, we recommend taking small steps in the right direction, even if policy makers do not know precisely where they are going.

The Policy Context of Educational Policy Making

Individuals who become principals, superintendents, school board members, members of a state board of education, or legislators bring with them experiences and ideas about public education which affect their policy choices. These previously formulated ideas are derived from an understanding of the history of public education, from current conditions in American public life possibly quite unrelated to any specific educational issues, and from general cultural perspectives about the role of government. This experiential and ideological legacy is important because it structures a policy maker's thinking about educational issues. The ideas policy makers bring with them into their positions are not easily susceptible to change. Moreover, many of the same ideas and experiences tend to be widely shared by policy makers. Not all of these external or uncontrollable influences on educational policy making will be discussed here. However, since they will not be given further attention when our focus turns to controllable factors, a select few are worth mentioning.

THE DECLINING POLICY IMPORTANCE
OF PUBLIC EDUCATION

Support for public education probably reached a peak in the 1960s. For a while, at least, public education will be unable to claim an increasingly larger share of public sector resources and, indeed in all likelihood, will probably have to live with a smaller proportion of the public budget.

DEMOGRAPHIC FACTORS

The turnabout in the fortunes of schools has a variety of causes. Part of the problem is simple demographics. The fertility rate has fallen steadily since the late 1960s resulting in fewer school-age children. From 1950 through 1970 the number of children 5 to 19 years of age in the United States increased from 35,263,000 to 59,989,000, or by more than 70 percent.[7] Between 1970 and 1972 members of this age group decreased by 382,000 to 59,607,000 persons.

The rate of decline may be altered temporarily. Between 1975 and 1985 an unusually large number of women, born in the post World War II baby boom will reach their prime child-bearing years. However, assuming the fertility rate remains below 2.0 per woman of child-bearing age as most demographers predict, the long-term prospect is for the number of school children to continue to

---

[7] *U.S. Statistical Abstract, 1975* (Washington, D.C.: United States Bureau of the Census, 1975), Table 3, p. 6.

decline gradually. The proportion of the population in schools and the proportion of families with school-age children will decline even more. There simply
will not be the same need for additional buildings and teachers as during most of
the twentieth century.

The converse of the declining school enrollment situation is an increasing
non-school aged population. While the proportion of the population between the
ages of 5 and 19 is expected to decline from 24.38% to 21.78% during the
1980s, the proportion of the population over 65 years of age is expected to increase from 10.84% to 11.61% during the same period.[8] Older people have their
own particular needs for public services. They want better health programs,
more public transportation, expanded income maintenance, and adequate police protection—and not necessarily better schools. Moreover, if senior citizens
continue to vote in larger proportions than any other age group, their demands
will receive disproportional attention. It is easy to understand why educators
have been encouraging political coalitions with senior citizen representatives
in recent years. The expected rate of growth of programs for senior citizens
is many times that of educational programs.

ANTI-GOVERNMENT SENTIMENT

The changing demographic situation accounts for only part of the plight
of public schools. Public education is also likely to suffer from a more general
weakening of the public's confidence in government. For most of our history,
government limited its activities to such things as defense, roads and dam construction, and internal security. Performance in such traditional functions was
generally satisfactory. During the 1950s, and even more intensely in the 1960s,
state and federal government expanded its role to deal with problems of poverty,
racial injustice, special education, and urban decay. It achieved some limited
successes in all of these areas. However, for many Americans the costs of doing
so, both in terms of increasing taxes and increasing infringements on the liber-
ties of some citizens, often outweighed benefits. There occurred a generalized
reaction against new government programs. The popularity of fiscal conservatives such as Governor Brown of California in the last half of the 1970s was
widely viewed as a shift in political attitudes away from government solutions
to social problems.

Public schools may escape some of the disenchantment with big government because local school districts are relatively small and close to the electorate.
On the other hand, schools may suffer from public dissatisfaction with government performance in general. Expressions to the effect that most government
programs do not work and that money spent on them is money down the drain

---

[8]This is a series F. prediction, which assumes that the fertility rate is 1.8. A higher
fertility rate produces a somewhat smaller decline in the 5 to 19 age group during the
1980s. *U.S. Statistical Abstract, 1975,* Table 3, p. 6.

are voiced just as frequently about education as about any other governmental activity. This feeling of dissatisfaction with schools is supported by evidence that racial imbalance is not decreasing in urban school districts as promised, that test scores of high school graduates are falling, and that many social problems continue despite government action. A few social scientists fueled the discontent by emphasizing the strong correlations between students' socioeconomic backgrounds and test performance, and the relative inability of schools to break the linkage.

CHANGING BUDGET PRIORITIES

Finally, public schools may have to live with the fact that they have enjoyed a period of substantial growth but that that period is now over. Between 1950 and 1972, for instance, spending on public primary and secondary education in the United States increased from $5.88 billion to $48.7 billion, or by 728%.[9] The proportion of government budgets used for public schools increased from 8.4% to 12.27%. Average teacher salaries increased from $3,608 in 1955 to $9,624 in 1973, bringing them from 92.9% to 108.1% of the salaries of comparable personnel in the private sector.[10] It may be that now other interests will claim whatever extra public dollars are available.

Declining enrollment, competition from other public programs, public disenchantment with government services, and retrenchment from a prolonged period of growth foretell lean years ahead for public education. Public schools will not receive the attention or the budgetary support they enjoyed in the past.

Yet public schools will survive. To continue their effectiveness, however, will require important changes. The transition from the management of growth to the management of decline will require a careful rethinking of state laws and regulations covering such factors as collective bargaining, tenure, and course requirements, as well as major changes in school finance. Instead of solving problems by adding new programs and spending more money, solutions will have to take place by reallocating existing resources.

CULTURAL VALUES IN AMERICAN EDUCATION

We must also not forget that policy makers are part of the general cultural system that shapes the values and beliefs we as Americans hold in common. It is from the cultural system "that decision-makers acquire the basic categories of thought by which they perceive and attach significance to external social reality,

[9] *U.S. Statistical Abstract, 1975,* Table 398, p. 242.
[10] The figures were compiled by the Advisory Commission on Intergovernmental Relations and reported by Neal Peirce, "Federal-State Report/Public Worker Pay Emerges As Growing Issue," *National Journal,* August 23, 1975, p. 1199.

the values and norms in terms of which they formulate goals, the rules governing their efforts to achieve them, and the standards for judging their performance."[11] The outcomes of public policy can be predicted to some extent by
careful examination of the cultural system in which they are made.

Values generally refer to standards of desirability. They are used to evaluate the goodness or badness of specific actions, objects, or goals.[12] Citizens'
evaluations of educational programs are based largely on the shared values held
about education. Few scholars agree completely in their description of American
values. Nevertheless, a review of influential writings on the American national
character reveals a number of persistent themes.[13] Among them are progress,
science, efficiency, equality, liberty and freedom, individuality, secular rationality, humanism, and patriotism.

Three values stand out as the basis for much of the educational policy
making in this country: equality, efficiency, and liberty or responsiveness.
Curiously, these values often conflict. Policies in pursuit of egalitarian objectives
often conflict with policies to maximize results from each educational dollar
spent. Attempts to eliminate inequalities often necessitate a loss of liberty. As
will be further explained in Chapter Two, each value must be constantly counter-
balanced against the other two in the policy-making process.

EQUALITY

The pursuit of equality in education underlies almost every debate in public education. Schools were established in part to provide a mechanism by which
children from lower income families could improve their economic and social
status. The Fourteenth Amendment to the Constitution guarantees every citizen
equal protection of the laws, and most state constitutions require the provision
of a "general and uniform" or "thorough and efficient" education to all children. In the 1970s courts began to apply the equal protection clause and state
education clauses to overturn legislation denying equal treatment.[14]

The exact meaning of equality in education, and how to implement it,
have been much debated by educators. In Chapter Two we elaborate upon

---

[11] Theodore Geiger and Roger D. Hansen, "The Role of Information in Decision
Making on Foreign Aid," in *The Study of Policy Formation,* eds. Raymond A. Bauer
and Kenneth J. Gergen (New York: The Free Press, 1968), p. 331.

[12] Robin M. Williams, Jr., *American Society,* 2d ed. (New York: Alfred A. Knopf,
Inc., 1968), p. 24.

[13] Williams, *American Society,* chap. 11; Henry S. Commager, *The American Mind*
(New Haven: Yale University Press, 1950); Alexis de Tocqueville, *Democracy in
America* (New York: Alfred A. Knopf, Inc., 1945; originally published in 1835);
Daniel J. Boorstin, *The Genius of American Politics* (Chicago: University of Chicago
Press, 1953).

[14] For a summary of the major school finance cases see "Future Directions For
School Finance Reform," *Law and Contemporary Problems,* 38, No. 3 (Winter-
Spring, 1974).

three possible meanings—ensuring equal educational outcomes, equal access to education, or equal treatment of students.

EFFICIENCY

An educational program is usually considered efficient if it produces the most goods and services for the least possible money. To achieve this end, policy makers will accept the possibility that some people will actually lose rather than gain as the result of a policy decision. The program is still efficient if winners outnumber losers. Here the assumption is that a larger quantity of goods and services is always better than a smaller amount. A difficulty with this form of efficiency is that policies to produce more without spending more often increase income inequalities. For example, attempts to extend educational programs to more districts by requiring local matching money may in effect preclude some communities from receiving grants.

LIBERTY AND POLITICAL RESPONSIVENESS

For Americans, liberty means the freedom to choose. In the economic sphere, this belief underlies the profit-inspired market economy. Theoretically, at least, individuals are free to choose what goods or services they will produce in accordance with their talents and ambitions. Other individuals are free to choose whether or not to purchase these goods or services. But liberty to pursue economic rewards often produces unequal results as those with superior knowledge, wealth, or social position are able to bargain more effectively. Americans have traditionally looked to education to equalize the opportunities for material rewards. A good public education, it was believed, would reduce, or at least mitigate, the disadvantages of poverty or minority status, opening up life's rewards to anyone regardless of race, sex, wealth, or religion. For many people, and many generations, public schools made it possible to realize a standard of living surpassing that of their parents.

In the political sphere, liberty means self-government, or a representative form of government responsive to the people's wishes. For much of the history of public education in the United States, it was assumed that the combination of elected school boards and the professionalism of educators adequately protected the public's interest. Beginning in the 1960s, citizens demanded greater personal participation in the affairs of schools. Legally unable to express their dissatisfaction by altogether removing their children from school, parents demanded a right to voice their concerns directly. Few would disagree about the desirability of responsive schools; however, implementing responsiveness is more difficult. Often only a few citizens make an effort to express their opinions, and it is usually unclear whether they represent a majority of the district's constituents. In addition, citizen demands are usually too general to assist in the most important allocative decisions. Even if client demands are precise and widely representative, government finds it difficult to make radical departures from current patterns of resource allocation. To do so produces intense opposition from the losers, and any innovation, of course, risks being greeted by indifference from those cynical of government programs.

POLITICAL ACCEPTABILITY

Finally, although policy makers may try to maximize equality, efficiency, liberty, and responsiveness, their efforts are always tempered by political acceptability. This rather conservative criterion modifies demands that programs be more egalitarian, more efficient, or more responsive. If too many policy decisions are made that are not politically acceptable, the public loses faith in the ability of political institutions to make future decisions. An institution that outreaches its constituency risks being rejected. Incremental change ensures against major mistakes and prepares the public for policy changes to come. Of course, those who are too cautious risk being labelled unresponsive, but an institution that responds too quickly may lose public support and its ability to respond in the future.

The Policy-Making Process in Public Education

Policy makers have a variety of tools at their disposal. Some instruments involve direct policy actions, such as spending more money or adding new programs. Others operate indirectly by altering the institutional framework in which policy is formulated. If, for example, legislators want to improve performance in urban schools they might appropriate additional state money for compensatory education programs, or they might introduce an urban density factor into the state school aid formula. Another strategy might be for the legislative leadership to appoint urban legislators as chairmen of education or appropriation committees.

PROBLEM-SOLVING ANALYSIS

The first step in policy making is problem-solving analysis. Before tackling a problem, policy makers need to understand it, find out what the public wants done about it, decide whether their organization is the appropriate one to handle the problem, and assess whether there is anything they can do to solve it. District, state, and federal educational policy makers spend much of their time attempting to understand educational problems.

After a problem has been identified, the next step is the development and analysis of proposed solutions. Proposals must be evaluated on a variety of criteria and the tradeoffs between different outcomes must be made explicit. For example, will a proposal to equalize access to fiscal resources reduce incentives for wealthy districts to provide high quality education? Would the same policy, which provides tax equity to all citizens, guarantee equity in education for all students? Time is another important variable that problem solvers consider. How long will it take for a proposed solution to alleviate a condition? Will a gradual solution be more or less acceptable than a radical one?

All of these activities—identifying a problem, developing alternative solutions, analyzing tradeoffs, and evaluating the pace for resolving a problem—are tools of the problem solver's trade.

INSTITUTIONAL ANALYSIS

Policy makers also determine *how* policy decisions will be made. The constitutional and statutory formulas outlining who makes decisions, the procedures to be followed in policy formation, and the rules governing policy implementation can have as great an impact on the decisions themselves as can policy analyses. By changing the rules of the game, policy makers may often achieve the outcomes they want more effectively than by developing a specific proposal. For example, the redistricting of state legislatures to comply with the one-man-one-vote judicial rulings of the courts may have done more to improve government services in urban areas than specific program proposals such as compensatory education. The decision-making activities to be discussed now have nothing to do with any specific problem, but with the institutional context with which future problems will be handled.

There are several reasons for devoting attention to institutional analysis. If one is primarily interested in altering the total package of government programs rather than merely proposing specific remedies, it is more important to consider what can be done to affect groups of decisions over the long run. Specifying the precise conditions of efficiency or equality for one program may have little bearing upon the equity and efficiency of a total package of government programs. A major task of policy analysis, therefore, is to *identify institutional frameworks* which facilitate enactment of efficient, equitable, and responsive programs.

Attention to the institutional arrangements for achieving desired outcomes is also made necessary by the transience and uncertainty of public issues. Although we predict that public education has entered a period of stability or even decline, analysts' inability in the past to foresee problems, even a year or two in advance, renders us less than fully confident. For example, there was no widespread prediction in the late 1950s of a drop in the birth rate that would reduce enrollments. No one foresaw the possibility that high school test scores would drop significantly in the mid-1970s. It is clear that any policy decisions we make now cannot possibly take into account all the uncertainties of the future. What we can do is make decisions about *how* policy can be made and implemented with all due speed in response to a variety of unforeseen issues. Most basically, institutional analysis will compel us to evaluate the state of our institutions themselves.

INSTITUTIONAL ARRANGEMENTS

Institutional analysis ranges from relatively abstract concerns about the role of government and appropriate forms of governmental action to very specific proposals for improving political competence. In our market-oriented economy there is a presumption that government intervenes to improve or correct for deficiencies in the private provision of services. Although public education has been around for a long time, there remain many questions about government's legitimate educational responsibilities. How much education is enough? What kinds of education are public responsibilities and what are private? Defining the government's educational limits provides a general constraint on public education decisions. Deciding whether to treat educational problems at the local, state, or federal level further clarifies the decisional framework.

PROCESSES OF COLLECTIVE CHOICE

The persons elected or appointed to key positions in decision-making bodies directly influence educational policies. Less clear are the ways the alternative procedures for reaching decisions influence these policies. Institutional analysis involves examining these decision-making procedures. In collective decision making, agreement on policy is reached through a variety of methods. For example, political bargaining occurs when individual participants with different preferences are willing to exchange some of their demands for the support of others in reaching agreement. No group obtains everything, but neither does any party to the bargain lose everything. Knowledge of these processes and how to manipulate each of them can greatly enhance the power and success of decision makers.

Summary

Although the financial prospects for public education are not favorable, there are still many possibilities for improving public education if problems are approached intelligently and with a clear understanding of the workings of the political process. The chapters of this book are arranged to enable the reader to understand the problems of public education. In some cases current knowledge and information permit broad generalizations about solutions and their effects on the public. In many areas, however, uncertainty and the absence of a scientific base of knowledge force us to rely upon procedural suggestions. If public schools are intended to serve the interests of children and their parents, then it is best to let parents and children participate in decisions about education. Pessimism about the financial future of public education, recognition of the limits of what schooling can be expected to do, and commitment to the proposition that public institutions should serve the public are themes which entwine themselves throughout this book.

2

PUBLIC VALUES
AND
PUBLIC SCHOOL POLICY

American culture contains three strongly held values that significantly influence public policy; *equality, efficiency,* and *liberty.* Government actions regarding national defense, housing, taxation, antitrust regulation, racial desegregation, and literally hundreds of other policy dimensions, including education, are motivated and molded by one or more of these three values. Equality, liberty, and efficiency are viewed by an overwhelming majority as conditions that government should maximize. These three values are considered "good," "just," and "right." The belief in them has historical roots that are deeply embedded in our common heritage. This belief permeates the ideologies promulgated by political parties, religions, schools, and other social institutions.

Despite widespread public devotion to these values as abstract goals, their ultimate fulfillment is well-nigh impossible. At their roots, the three desired conditions are inconsistent and antithetical. Exclusive pursuit of one violates or eliminates the others. For example, imagine that government, in an effort to increase equality, nationalized the construction industry and mandated that production of housing be standardized. Presumably all citizens above a specified age would be guaranteed a government-produced home. Only one kind or perhaps variations upon that type of building would be manufactured. Consequently, all eligible consumers would be provided with identical products and would by definition have equal housing. An added degree of efficiency would be achieved by the high volume of manufacture possible with extraordinarily uniform products. Unit cost of houses might possibly be reduced. However, liberty would be sacrificed. The absence of variety in housing would severely restrict or totally prevent choice. In the absence of choice, there is no liberty.[1] Moreover, in time, lack of competition might discourage the search for new production techniques and thus impair economic efficiency. Would the absence of horrid slums be worth the presumed loss of freedom and efficiency? These are illustrative of the tradeoffs constantly faced by policy makers.

What emerges is that pursuit of equality exclusively will restrict or eliminate liberty and efficiency. Conversely, complete attention to either liberty or efficiency will diminish the other values. Consequently, efforts to rearrange society so as to maximize one of the three values are constrained by forces desiring to preserve the status quo. This dynamic equilibrium among the three values constantly shifts, with the balance at any particular point being fixed as a consequence of a complicated series of political and economic compromises.

It can be argued that liberty is the highest of the three values. Efficiency for its own sake has little meaning. The justification for desiring that an endeavor be undertaken efficiently is to conserve resources that could then be used for other endeavors, thus expanding *choice*. Similarly, equality qua equality appears hollow. Few if any persons desire absolute parity with their peers. Rather, equality of wealth and circumstance can be viewed as a desirable means to the end of greater *choice*.

Education is one of the prime instruments through which society attempts to promote all three values. Educators and officials involved in educational policy making are well advised to be informed about and alert to the interactions among these value dimensions. Our purpose in this chapter is to describe practical consequences of elevating any one of the three values and to illustrate tradeoffs involved when policy makers attempt to maximize liberty, equality, and efficiency.

Democratic Government and a Market Economy[2]

Nowhere is the tension among equality, efficiency, and liberty better mirrored than in the practical conflicts between democracy and a market-oriented and profit-inspired economy. American political ideology champions equality and freedom. In reacting to the social rigidity and inherited system of privilege which dominated seventeeth- and eighteenth-century Europe, Thomas Jefferson proclaimed in the Declaration of Independence that "All men are created

---

[1] See John E. Coons and Stephen D. Sugarman, "A Case for Choice," in *Parents, Teachers, and Children: Prospects for Choice in American Education* (San Francisco, The Institute for Contemporary Studies, 1977).
[2] This is the topic of an extraordinarily thoughtful volume by Arthur M. Okun, *Equality and Efficiency: The Big Tradeoff* (Washington, D.C.: The Brookings Institution, 1975).

equal. . . ." Subsequently, a constitution was adopted containing an elaborate system of governmental checks and balances to discourage the accumulation of unequal political power and thus to preserve individual liberty. Private ownership of property was seen as an important additional protection against political tyranny.

In the formative years of the United States, the relative absence of inherited social position, liberty for individuals to own the means of production, and freedom to choose one's occupation encouraged the pursuit of private profit. Profit-seeking was justified partly on grounds that it contributed to economic efficiency. The ability to reap returns from personal efforts and retain the benefits of new ideas and methods motivated entrepreneurs to pioneer increasingly better products often at lower prices. Both consumers and producers were held to benefit from such increased efficiency. The prospect of benefiting from profit inspires manufacturers to expand the range of products. The resulting proliferation of choice reinforces the possibility of liberty. However, social approval of profit promotes economic disparity. If political power accrues with the compilation of capital, a private property, profit-motivated economy contains the potential to contradict the democratic idea of political equality. The absence of political equality jeopardizes liberty. Again the three values are inextricably linked.[3]

A major portion of governmental reform for the last two hundred years has been directed at adjusting tensions between social equality and economic efficiency. Antitrust legislation, personal and corporate income taxes, social security, unemployment insurance, medicare, food stamps, housing subsidies, and inheritance taxes are intended to protect against the extremes of wealth, either its absence or its accumulation.

Where these reforms touched the economy, they may have contributed to inefficiency. Perhaps the economy would grow more rapidly if capital were permitted to pyramid perpetually rather than being dispersed through transfer payments for welfare purposes. Perhaps there would be greater productivity if the work force did not benefit from a minimum standard of living provided by minimum wages, social security, unemployment insurance, medicare benefits, and food and housing subsidies. Perhaps agricultural production would be greater if farmers did not enjoy the advantages of a complicated parity system of food price supports.[4] However, against the potential loss of economic inefficiency,

---

[3] A philosophical analysis of the interaction between equality and liberty is contained in John Rawls, *A Theory of Justice* (Cambridge: Harvard University Press, 1971), particularly chaps. 2 and 4, and Kenneth J. Arrow, "Some Ordinalist-Utilitarian Notes on Rawls' Theory of Justice," *Journal of Philosophy,* 70 (May 10, 1973), 245–63.

[4] In 1976, the total dollar cost of all levels of U.S. government required that the average employed person work 2 hours and 39 minutes of each 8-hour day, or almost four months out of each year, to pay his taxes. The largest portion of the tax burden supports transfer payments. For the 1976 federal budget, 47 percent was devoted to welfare purposes, 29 percent to defense, 10 percent to interest on the national debt, and 15 percent for all other purposes.

one must weigh the value of social equality and the increased political stability that this fosters.[5] The above-mentioned reforms may represent a tradeoff between short-term economic inefficiency and long-term political stability. The absence of stability can contribute mightily toward economic failure of a government. Of course, political stability in itself is no guarantee of personal liberty. Many repressive governments have been "stable." However, the lack of stable government may lead to the loss of liberty as the weak or unprotected are overcome by the powerful.

Education as a Policy Variable in the Pursuit of Equality, Efficiency, and Liberty

Among the eighteenth-century leaders of the new republic, education was viewed as a means to enable the citizen to participate as an equal in the affairs of government,[6] and was thus essential to ensure liberty.[7] It was not until the nineteenth century that education began to assume significance in economic terms. The increasing demands of an industrial technology necessitated an educated work force; henceforth schooling was taken as an important contributor to economic efficiency. By the twentieth century, intensified technological development and economic interdependence made formal preparation a *sine qua non* for an individual's economic and social success. Consequently, education assumed new importance from the standpoint of its role in maximizing equality.

Beginning with the 1954 United States Supreme Court decision in *Brown v. Board of Education,* and continuing with the increase in federal government education programs of the 1960s and the school finance reform efforts of the 1970s, a major portion of mid-twentieth century education policy has been directed at achieving greater equality. Consequently, we begin our discussion of values and school policy by concentrating on "equality."

Education and Equality

Translation of the value "equality" for educational policy purposes has almost always meant "equality of educational opportunity." Few have seriously

---

[5] The economic basis for political revolution has been the subject of substantial research. James Davies speculates that instability is intensified if, after a period of progress toward equality, there is an interruption and a slide toward greater inequality. This contention emphasizes that it is not the absolute level of disparity which provokes revolution but rather the level of expectation about equality.

[6] See Frederick Rudolf, ed., *Essays on Education in the New Republic* (Cambridge: Harvard University Press, 1969).

[7] For added discussion of this topic see chap. 1 in John W. Gardner, *Excellence: Can We Be Equal and Excellent Too?* (New York: Harper & Row, 1961).

argued that for each individual, education should itself be absolutely equal. Such an objective would make outrageous assumptions regarding genetically endowed abilities, the possibility of standardizing instruction, and similarities of environmental effect upon human tastes. Consequently, most policy debates center on semantic interpretations of "equal educational opportunity." Over time, this concept has evolved through several major stages.[8]

EQUAL ACCESS TO EDUCATION

Equal access assumes that providing students with at least a minimum level of school resources suffices to ensure equality of educational opportunity. This approach which has been operational far longer and in a far greater number of states than any other, initially implied that schools, of whatever quality, be made available to all students. The fact that a school was provided was taken to be equal educational opportunity.

Subsequently, the definition evolved to mean more than simple access. The quality of the services available also was taken into account: Every child should be provided with at least the same minimally adequate school services. Typically this was translated into a policy whereby the state guaranteed a minimal education expenditure level. Local school districts were then expected to transform these dollars into minimally adequate programs.

Equal access to a minimally acceptable level of school service is reflected in the language of most state school finance statutes, e.g., "Foundation Program," "Basic Aid." If localities choose to add their own resources to the state-guaranteed minimum, they are free to do so. One outcome of local discretion, explained more fully in Chapter Eight, is a wide variation of per-pupil expenditure prevailing among school districts in most states.

The probability is high that wide expenditure differences, at least at the extremes, represent actual disparities in the quality and kind of school services available to students. All other things being equal, it is hard to image that students from poorly funded school districts with large classes, inadequately prepared teachers, and limited course offerings have the same opportunity to learn as their more fortunate counterparts in districts spending two or three times the state average. What historically was an adequate minimum, available equally to all students throughout a state, has been transformed over time into a low level of service exceeded substantially by districts either with greater wealth to tap, greater willingness to tax themselves, or both. Some states, for

---

[8]The historical development of the concept of equal educational opportunity is described by James S. Coleman in "The Concept of Equality of Educational Opportunity," *Harvard Education Review,* Winter 1968. A detailed discussion of varying definitions of equality of educational opportunity is provided by John D. Danner in an unpublished University of California, Berkeley, M.A. thesis entitled "Equality of Educational Opportunity: The Search for the Meaning of the Motto," School of Education, 1974. See also Arthur Wise, *Rich Schools: Poor Schools* (Chicago: University of Chicago Press, 1970).

example New Hampshire and Connecticut, did not attempt until the 1970s even to guarantee such a minimum.

Whatever the reason for these inequalities in educational expenditures and services, they have triggered a series of lawsuits questioning the legality, under both state and federal constitutions, of the school finance arrangements in over 40 states. Because these legal maneuvers substantially influenced school finance reform throughout the late 1960s and 70s, at the conclusion of this chapter we trace the chronology of the "equal protection" cases and explore the legal logic upon which they rest.

EQUAL EDUCATIONAL TREATMENT

This definition of equal educational opportunity is based on the premise that learners have widely varying characteristics and abilities, from which it logically follows that available school services should be highly tailored to each student's specific circumstances. Minimally adequate school services, by this definition, are insufficient because what is adequate for some children does not put less fortunate children at the "starting line" in the race for life's rewards. Under ideal conditions, an assessment would be made of each student's school-related strengths and weaknesses. Subsequently, additional services would be supplied those who, for whatever reason, were judged to be in a deficit situation with regard to some learning abilities.

This definition is reflected in efforts to provide special educational services to students who are physically or mentally handicapped. The drive for so-called "compensatory education," initiated in the mid-1960s with enactment of the federal Elementary and Secondary Education Act (ESEA), also reflects this definition of equality of educational opportunity. Under ESEA, states and school districts are eligible for federal funds in proportion to the number of students they enroll from low-income households. The added funding is justified on grounds that such students are likely to be disadvantaged, by way of their environment, in their ability to benefit from schooling. Federal funds are intended to provide compensatory school service.[9] This attempt to balance any potential learning deficit theoretically results in equal treatment for all pupils but clearly demands unequal resources.

EQUALITY OF EDUCATIONAL OUTCOME

Beginning in the early 1970s, a number of social theorists and policy analysts began to construct a new definition of equal educational opportunity.[10]

---

[9]This program will be described in substantial detail in Chapter Seven.

[10]The "equal outcome" definition is suggested and explained by authors such as Charles S. Benson in *The Cheerful Prospect: A Statement on the Future of Public Education* (Boston: Houghton Mifflin Co., 1965); Henry S. Dyer in "The Measure-

Their position stemmed from the observation that academic achievement had become crucial for personal success. Consequently, they proposed that the measure of equality be equal student learning, at least in terms of minimum or basic skills. Presumably, the objective would be fulfilled if, upon graduating from secondary school, for example, every student were able to perform at least at an eighth-grade level in reading, mathematics, and composition. Schools would be held responsible for achieving such equal minimal outcomes regardless of the resource level necessary.

On occasion, this equal outcome concept is extended further to include the schools' responsibility for "equal life chance." By this definition, school services and resources should be deployed so as to assure every normal child, upon graduation from secondary school, an equal opportunity to compete with any other student. Success in achieving this goal could be measured by the degree to which race, socioeconomic status, ethnic origin, and similar social measures were no longer predictive of adult income or occupation. However, even if one assumed that pedagogical techniques could be so refined and applied as to make such an objective realizable, the resource level necessary to implement it would undoubtedly be staggering.

Efficiency

American culture's substantial attachment to the concept of efficiency is borne out not only in age-old homilies such as "a penny saved is a penny earned," and "a stitch in time saves nine," but also by a number of practical applications. Appeals to frugality are widespread in advertising, and exhortations to become more productive are commonplace in work settings. Efficiency as an ideal stems from components of the Protestant work ethic and is continually reinforced by the profit motive.

In simple terms, economic efficiency is the striving for added units of output per unit of input. This can occur either by holding output constant and decreasing input, or by deriving greater production from the same level of input. Laymen frequently label the first condition as "greater effectiveness" and the second as "added productivity." From the viewpoint of economic analysis, the two are similar.

Efficiency is often achieved by the creation and implementation of new techniques of production, such as those effected, for example, by new tools. Creation of the steel plow, internal combustion engine, electronic computer, and the so-called "miracle grains" are dramatic examples. However, gains in efficiency

ment of Educational Opportunity," in *On Equality of Educational Opportunity,* Frederick Mosteller and Daniel P. Moynihan, eds., (New York: Vintage Books, 1972), pp. 513-21; and James W. Guthrie et al., *Schools and Inequality* (Cambridge: MIT Press, 1971).

are not solely dependent upon creation of new material items. New "techniques" may simply involve workers' adopting new patterns of action or interaction. For example, through experience, better training, or both, a wood carver or bricklayer may be able to accomplish more during a workday. Similarly, the manufacture of many material items has become more efficient not only because of new equipment made available during the industrial revolution but also because of new manufacturing techniques. The concept of interchangeable parts permitted assembly lines and promoted greater output per worker. By becoming a specialist in a narrow part of the production process, each worker became able to perform functions more rapidly, with greater precision, or both.

Schools are no exception to the American desire for efficiency. There have been repeated efforts to increase educational efficiency. For example, during the first half of the nineteenth century, an elaborate British system of tutors and monitors, the so-called "Lancasterian system,"[11] was used to boost school output. Under this method, a single headmaster instructed the older and presumably, most able students who then reinforced their learning by transmitting it in turn to younger students. Elaborate seating arrangements corresponding to this hierarchical pattern were supposed to facilitate the supervision of the master and the instructional efforts of student "monitors." Similarly, near the turn of the twentieth century, American schools were greatly influenced by the scientific management movement which swept the manufacturing sector at the time. This was the era of "cheaper by the dozen," time and motion studies, and efficiency experts.[12] The hope was that schooling could be reduced to a series of scientific principles that could be implemented by trained experts, professional school administrators. The implementation of such managerial principles was expected both to enhance learning and reduce costs. The heated competition for public sector resources that accompanied government-sponsored social programs in the 1960s triggered another cycle of concern for efficiency. This time "accountability" became the fashionable label under which to seek added school productivity.[13]

Despite repeated efforts, schools have remained remarkably resistant to attempts to increase efficiency. Between 1940 and 1970, per-pupil school expenditures for U.S. public schools increased 500 percent, even when discounting for inflation. School costs outstripped growth in Gross National Product (GNP).[14] Yet it was not immediately evident that such increases were accompanied by

---

[11] For an added explanation of this and other techniques of instruction introduced at the time to enhance school efficiency, see David B. Tyack, *The One Best System* (Cambridge: Harvard University Press, 1974).

[12] See Raymond Callahan, *The Cult of Efficiency* (Chicago: University of Chicago Press, 1962).

[13] See Chapter Ten for a discussion of this approach to efficiency.

[14] Total expenditures for education as a percentage of Gross National Product increased from 2% in 1943 to 8% in 1975. Source: U.S. Department of Health, Education, and Welfare, National Center for Educational Statistics.

TABLE 2-1

Achievement Test Results in 1960 and 1975

| | Males N(1975) = 871 | | | Females N(1975) = 926 | | |
| | Raw Score | | Tenth Grade Percentile | Raw Score | | Tenth Grade Percentile |
	1960	1975	Difference	1960	1975	Difference
Vocabulary	18.5	15.7	−17%	17.3	15.5	−11%
English	77.3	73.4	−12%	84.5	79.7	−16%
Reading Comprehension	28.8	28.4	−1%	29.8	29.1	−2%
Creativity	9.1	10.0	8%	8.4	10.1	16%
Mechanical Reasoning	12.4	12.2	−2%	8.5	9.2	7%
Visualization	8.9	8.8	−1%	7.8	8.1	4%
Abstract Reasoning	8.7	9.5	11%	8.7	9.4	8%
Quantitative Reasoning	8.5	7.8	−8%	8.0	7.2	−8%
Mathematics	10.5	10.7	2%	9.9	10.3	3%
Computation	25.7	18.7	−17%	30.8	26.9	−11%

Source: John C. Flanagan, "Changes in School Levels of Achievement: Project TALENT Ten and Fifteen Year Retests," *Educational Researcher* Vol. 6, No. 8 (September 1976), Table 1, p. 10.

elevations in productivity. Students did not complete schooling any more quickly and measures of academic achievement were, at best, mixed. In fact, if one were to judge by the rather narrow criterion of student scores on various achievement tests administered between 1960 and 1975, as shown in Table 2-1, school performance actually declined.[15]

IMPEDIMENTS TO SCHOOL EFFICIENCY

CONFLICTING EXPECTATIONS AND WEAK INCENTIVES

A host of conditions inhibits attempts to make public schools economically more efficient. First, in order to bolster productivity, there must exist agreement about the expected product. What is it that the system is to produce? There are no easy answers to this question when it comes to America's public schools. The fact that school districts have become larger, more bureaucratized, and possessed

[15] Although many tests show similar declines in student achievement, testing experts have been unable to agree on the causes of test score declines.

of less decision-making discretion than before further inhibits efforts to decide upon common goals. The virtual monopoly public schools have over the education market impedes the expression of consumer choice, a mechanism that otherwise might reveal public preference for school outputs. Moreover, a response to the question of what schools should produce is made substantially more complicated by the previously discussed widespread concern for equality. In ways we will illustrate, attempts to maximize equality frequently conflict with efforts to increase economic efficiency.

Also, the educational techniques and materials of "production," when compared to standard manufacturing processes, are extraordinarily primitive. Fundamental pedagogical processes have changed little since the time of Socrates. Moreover, the relative absence of rewards for improving instructional techniques and technology renders dramatic breakthroughs unlikely. There may well be a "better mousetrap" for schools, but it is improbable that the inventor will much benefit economically from its creation. There is no stimulus in public schooling equivalent to the profit motive in the private sector. The standard reward for successful educators is to be removed from close proximity to students. This has proven too modest a motivation to provoke pedagogical breakthroughs. In fact, it has probably acted to dampen school productivity by inducing able instructors to leave classroom teaching.

VALUE CONFLICTS

An intent to achieve equality frequently decreases school efficiency. For example, whether it be court-mandated or voluntary, racial integration usually entails added transportation costs. If contact with students of other races promotes mutual understanding and social cohesion, then the expenditure may be cost effective. If such outcomes do not result, then funds spent for busing are simply added school costs.[16]

Let us examine a less ambiguous example of conflict between equality and efficiency. In the late 1960s, an effort was made to increase school productivity by utilizing "performance contracting."[17] Private entrepreneurs were

[16] The effectiveness of racial integration as a strategy for improving the performance of minority group students has been the subject for substantial argument among social science researchers. Early interpretations of Coleman Report findings suggested that integrated schooling had a beneficial effect upon the school performance of black students; for example, see James S. Coleman, Ernest Q. Campbell, Carol J. Hobson, James McPartland, Alexander Mood, Frederic D. Weinfeld, and Robert York, *Equality of Educational Opportunity* (Washington, D.C.: U.S. Government Printing Office, 1966), pp. 330–33. This general conclusion was subsequently challenged by the research of David Armor, which asserted that integration was associated with no positive outcomes for minority children; David J. Armor, "The Evidence on Busing," *The Public Interest*, 28 (Summer 1972), 90–126. Armor's position has itself been subject to serious criticism. See Thomas F. Pettigrew et al., "Busing: A Review of the Evidence," *The Public Interest*, 30 (Winter 1973), 88–114.

[17] This experiment is described in Edward M. Gramlich and Patricia P. Koshel, *Educational Performance Contracting: An Evaluation of An Experiment* (Washington, D.C.: Brookings Institution, 1975).

encouraged to contract with local school districts to provide specified educational instructional services—most often in reading. Contractors were to be paid in proportion to measured reading achievement gains. For many reasons the experiments were eventually halted; prominent among the reasons was the revelation that a few contractors had concentrated their efforts on selected students who demonstrated the greatest propensity for large-scale improvement and neglected the instruction of others. For the contractors, this was economically efficient—so long as the output was measured in terms of *average class gains*. However, concern for "equal" treatment of all students contributed strongly to the demise of performance contracting as a federal government sponsored experiment.

Our second value conflict pits economic efficiency against a concern for liberty. Compulsory attendance statutes and the strong monopolistic quality of public schools limit individual liberty. This is mitigated not only by the availability of private schooling but also by a limited range of options within the public school system. Particularly in secondary schools, students are usually not confined to a single program of study; they can choose among so-called elective courses. Frequently, the range of electives is broad, including music, languages, sciences, drama, art, business courses, etc.

The provision of electives is consistent with the value of liberty or freedom. But school officials, in attempting to respond to the public's desire for services, can only offer as wide a choice as their budgets permit. The delicate balance between range of offerings and tax rates is decided by elected officials, usually school board members.

Clearly it would be less costly to provide only a modicum of electives. One could delete expensive options such as vocational training courses or advanced foreign language classes with typically small enrollments. Under such restricted arrangements, unit costs of schooling would be reduced. However, the tradeoff might prove sufficiently unattractive and unresponsive to parents' and students' needs to arouse public ire. In such circumstances, efficiency gives way, at least in part, to liberty.

PRIVATE SECTOR SPILLOVERS

Conventional wisdom holds that gains in economic efficiency are shared by labor and investors. If an invention enables labor to produce twice as much in the same amount of time, new-found gains are transmitted to workers in the form of higher wages, or more leisure time, and to owners in the form of added profits. Most productivity gains occur in the private sector. Public sector endeavors, particularly education, are highly labor intensive. They do not lend themselves easily to added efficiency through new technology. Nevertheless, because the public sector competes with the private sector for labor, it must match salaries and working conditions if it is to attract employees. Thus, public sector labor costs increase even in the absence of gains in economic efficiency. This renders the unit costs of "producing" education even higher—that is to say, it makes schools more inefficient.[18] However, if schools could not compete with the private sector for talent they could become even less attractive to their clients and thus might be even more inefficient. It is probably already the case that public schools are at a competitive disadvantage when compared with the total hiring market in obtaining the services of talented individuals.

REDEFINING EFFICIENCY

In the face of conflicting expectations for school output, competing values, weak incentive systems, and private sector spillover effects, how can public schools attempt to become more efficient? For reasons described in detail in Chapter Ten, "School Efficiency," we view efforts to apply purely economic methods and techniques of efficiency to public schools as relatively useless. However, efficiency need not be defined in strict economic terms. It is possible to expand the definition of efficiency to signify maximal consumer satisfaction at minimum costs. By this definition efficiency would result from an ingenious blend of politics and economics.

Public schools could be structured to offer a wider range of choice to direct consumers, households of parents and children. Dissatisfaction because of disagreement over educational goals is substantially lessened by permitting households to select among schools. Presumably they would select schools stressing whatever objectives they believe to be important. By requiring a minimum standard curricular offering at each school, the state could ensure an adequate amount of education is provided, reduce the likelihood of undesirable levels of inequality in school output, and encourage social cohesion. Meanwhile, individual schools could simultaneously be encouraged to be responsive and efficient. They would stand to lose clients if they did not meet parent and student expectations. Presumably the more "efficient" a school in deploying available income, the broader the range or the higher the quality of services it could offer. By constantly attempting to outperform other schools in its sector, a school would not only retain but possibly increase its enrollments.

Such a plan for maximizing consumer preference might evolve through several different avenues. It could take the form of a voucher plan wherein families are provided with a warrant in the amount spent per pupil within their district for public schools.[19] The warrant would be redeemable at a school of their choice, private or public. Restricting parent choices to the public school system would be a less drastic change and thus might be politically more feasi-

---

[18]The relationship between private and public sector efficiency is explained by William Baumol, "Macroeconomics of Unbalanced Growth: The Anatomy of Urban Crisis," *American Economic Review,* June 1967, p. 57.

[19]There have been many varieties of proposed "voucher" plans. The acknowledged twentieth-century forerunner is described by Milton Friedman in *Capitalism and Freedom* (Chicago: University of Chicago Press, 1967).

ble.[20] The tradeoff would be a dimunition in competition. A still milder reform is merely to encourage greater consumer participation by establishing parent advisory councils at each school and empowering them with decision-making discretion over program offerings and personnel.[21] These and other strategies are analyzed in detail in subsequent chapters. Our purpose in listing them here is to indicate that even though there are no perfect solutions in the pursuit of efficiency for public schools, it may be possible to construct better answers.

Liberty[22]

The third value we mentioned as deeply affecting the direction of American educational policy is liberty. This value provided a major ideological justification for the revolution which gave birth to the United States as a nation. After the war with England, James Madison wrote:

> In Europe, charters of liberty have been granted by power. America has set the example, and France has followed it, of charters of power granted by liberty.[23]

For Americans, liberty has meant the freedom to choose, to be able to select from among different courses of action. The desire for choice fueled the historical American affection for a market economy. Competition among producers, among other benefits, is held to expand the range of items from which consumers can choose. In the public sector, responsive governmental institutions are taken to be a crucial link in the preservation of choice and liberty.

In the view of those who initially designed the structures of American government, authority was vested in the citizenry who then delegated the power to govern to selected representatives. A measure of representatives' effectiveness was the degree to which they were responsive to the will of those they governed. Remarkably enough, lack of responsiveness is still viewed today as eroding the power of the citizenry and thus constitutes grounds for removal from office.

A second means for preserving liberty was to disperse governmental

[20] There have been many proposed public school parent choice plans. A good description of this movement during the 1960s and 70s is provided by Mario Fantini, "Alternative Educational Experiences: The Demand for Change," in *Public Testimony on Public Schools,* National Committee for Citizens in Education (Berkeley: McCutchan Publishing Corporation, 1975), chap. 7, pp. 160–82.

[21] This is the primary recommendation of the National Committee for Citizens in Education in *Public Testimony.*

[22] See the discussion of F. A. Hayek, *The Constitution of Liberty* (Chicago: University of Chicago Press, 1960).

[23] Found on page 55 of Bernard Bailyn, *The Ideological Origins of The American Revolution* (Cambridge: Harvard University Press, 1967).

authority widely. This accounts for the balance of powers among three branches and over various levels of government. Efforts to inhibit the accumulation of power also account for the deliberate fragmentation of decision-making authority, specific powers accorded the federal government, some to states, and some powers reserved to the people themselves. Historically, the power to make educational decisions evolved in the same fashion. Centralized authority was viewed as perilous because of the prospect of exerting widespread control and uniformity. Formation of literally thousands of small local school districts, portending both inefficiency and inequality, was intended as an antidote to the accumulation of power. Proximity to constituents, coupled with the electoral process, was taken as a means to enhance governmental responsiveness and preserve liberty.

GOVERNMENTAL CYCLES
AND THE DILUTION OF RESPONSIVENESS

American government has evidenced the liberty–efficiency dichotomy in proposals from three groups of citizens: (1) advocates of responsiveness; (2) those favoring greater centralization of authority—a stronger executive; and (3) those espousing the merits of expert, professional management.[24] Early American government as emphasized above, stressed the first value, representativeness. In large measure this was in reaction to the strong authority of the English Crown, the focus of much intense revolutionary hatred. Whatever its advantages for expression of popular will and the preservation of liberty, strong representative government suffers from the drawbacks of being cumbersome, time consuming, demanding of compromise, and possessed of the potential to obscure responsibility. Thus, in an effort to avoid such liabilities and gain greater decisiveness and accountability, the pendulum of American government periodically has swung to favor a strong executive and greater centralization of decision-making authority.

On other occasions, public opinion has reacted negatively to both representativeness and executive authority. The former is accused of being prone to an excess of partisan politics and the latter overly open to persuasion by selfish interests. In such periods, an argument has been made for the advantages of nonpartisan, disinterested governmental officials who perform government tasks in a fashion free from personal bias and narrow interest. The model here is the expert, the professional or technician, who presumably is apolitical and therefore does what is "right." Such arguments formed the basis of the so-called "Progressive Era" reforms at the turn of the twentieth century and accounted for the city manager form of government and the merit systems and civil service arrange-

---

[24] The cyclical nature of governmental forms is described by Herbert Kaufman in *Politics and Policies in State and Local Government* (Englewood Cliffs, N.J. Prentice Hall, Inc., 1963), chap. 2.

ments now existing at all levels of government. Actual mechanisms of government, whether it be at the federal, state, or local level, reflect the constant adjustments being made among these three views of the governing process.

School governance is no exception to the cyclical emphasis placed in turn upon representativeness, executive authority, and professional management. Representativeness peaked early in the twentieth century and centralized authority and professional management subsequently ascended to prominence. Since this shift in the pattern of governance has strongly colored public education and promises to be even more influential during the last quarter of the twentieth century, it appears appropriate to review briefly the historical events which comprise this pendulum swing.

SCHOOL DISTRICT CONSOLIDATION

By 1932, the number of local school districts in the United States had reached its high point, approximately 128,000 separate units. By 1976 this number had been reduced to approximately 16,000.[25] This drastic reduction in the number of units of a specialized form of local government took place in a manner so subtle as virtually to escape the notice of political scientists. Nevertheless, it constitutes one of the most dramatic of all changes in America's patterns of government.

There were several motives for the consolidation of thousands of small rural school districts, many of them with only one school, frequently a one-room school at that. It was argued that small school districts were inefficient. Specifically, it was asserted that they were incapable of providing a sufficiently wide array of services, impeded the ability of teachers to specialize, and generally inhibited the attainment of economies of scale in matters such as purchasing and maintenance. Enticed by the carrot of legislative inducements and driven by the stick of legislative penalties, local districts were combined into larger units.

Consolidation of local districts took place at a time when the U.S. population was undergoing substantial growth. Average school district size increased manyfold. Consequently, whereas each local school board member once represented approximately 140 constituents, by 1976 this figure had risen to one board member per 2,500 constituents. School board members could no longer be responsive to all their constituents. Representativeness had been diluted to an awesome degree.[26]

---

[25] *A Century of U.S. School Statistics* (Washington, D.C.: U.S. Department of Health, Education, and Welfare, 1974).

[26] The evolution of school governance is described in James W. Guthrie, Patricia A. Craig, and Diana M. Thomason. "The Erosion of Lay Control," in *Public Testimony on Public Schools,* pp. 76–121.

PROFESSIONAL MANAGEMENT

Reduction in number of school districts, and the increase in population, resulted in the creation of school district organizations too large to be managed by school boards themselves. Originally, board members were directly responsible for matters such as hiring teachers, purchasing supplies, setting school curricula, establishing school regulations, and listening personally to citizens' complaints. In short, for school matters, they performed the three functions of government—rule making, rule implementation, and rule adjudication.[27] The formation of large districts brought such practices to a close. It became clear that school districts would require full-time managers to administer them. Consequently, beginning in New York in the 1870s and subsequently spreading across the nation, elected school boards began to employ professional school superintendents and turned over to them the day-to-day operation.[28] In the process, representativeness was further diluted.

The professional school administrator movement was bolstered substantially in the early portion of the twentieth century by the growth throughout the United States of "scientific management." Beginning in the private sector, the philosophy and methods of the efficiency experts—time and motion analysts—spread to the public sector.[29] The argument was made that government, school government included, could be made more efficient and less prone to the excesses and corruption of the political process if managed by experts. The operation of schools would be entrusted to those skilled in education, those capable of making scientific judgments regarding school management. Schools of education began preparing "scientifically trained" administrators who were imbued with the philosophy that while school boards might make policy, there was a strict line between policy and practice, and only the administrator was responsible for the latter.

The scientific management movement was abetted by the uncovering of widespread political scandal, particularly in large cities, during the early part of the 1900s.[30] This provided an added boost to those who argued that representativeness only led to an "excess" of politics, pettiness, and corruption. Thus, by reducing the number of school board members, centralizing authority in

---

[27] For further elaboration of this threefold means for viewing the functions of government see David Easton, "An Approach to the Analysis of Political Systems," *World Politics*, No. 9 (1957), pp. 383–400, and by the same author, *A Framework for Political Analysis* (Englewood Cliffs, N.J.: Prentice Hall, Inc., 1965).

[28] Theodore L. Reller, *Development of the City Superintendency of Schools* (Boston: The author, 1935).

[29] See Callahan, *The Cult of Efficiency*.

[30] See Joseph M. Cronin, *The Control of Urban Schools* (New York: The Free Press, 1973).

fewer persons, and handing over many of the management reins to trained professionals, schools could be run more efficiently.

COLLECTIVE BARGAINING

Beginning in the 1950s, teachers began to organize unions to engage in collective bargaining with school boards. This development was initiated in large cities and subsequently spread to almost every school district in the United States. Increases in organizational size, bureaucratization, and the proliferation of administrative levels probably accounted, in large measure, for teachers' feelings of inefficacy and alienation and prompted them to unionize. Though it frequently is the case that teacher representatives come to the bargaining table with concerns for the welfare of students and respect for the interests of the broader public, their primary allegiance is to teachers' welfare. They cannot legitimately claim to represent the larger public. Nevertheless, duly elected public representatives, school board members, must share decision-making authority with them. The outcome is further to centralize school policy making and to erode the ability of the general public to participate in the process. (See Chapter Five.)

ESCALATING STATE POWER

Though state government has always held the ultimate legal responsibility for school decision making, historically state governments have delegated substantial policy discretion to local units of government. However, in the period since World War II, state-level participation has increased because of three things: increasing school costs, politicization of school decisions, and intensified efforts to achieve greater equality of educational opportunity and more efficient use of school resources.[31] This has removed a large measure of decision-making discretion from local educational authorities; for example, such areas as school curriculum, teacher salaries and working conditions, graduation requirements, and school architecture have been incorporated into state specifications. More decisions regarding schools are now determined by fewer persons. Choice is restricted, the ability of local officials to respond to constituent preferences is constrained, and at least in a legal sense, local autonomy and liberty—and probably efficiency—have been diminished.

REACTION

By the latter half of the 1960s, a reaction to the diminished status of representativeness had begun. Requests for change stemmed initially from ethnic

---

[31] See James W. Guthrie and Paula H. Skene, "The Escalation of Pedagogical Politics,"

enclaves in large cities, who perceived themselves as relatively impotent in affecting the operation of their children's schools. They demanded what was then labeled "community control."[32] For example, several community control experiments were undertaken in the New York City schools. The state legislature ultimately recognized the growing political momentum by fractionating New York City into 32 elementary school districts. Since each of the 32 averaged 30,000 students, approximately the size of the entire school district of the city of Syracuse, the system could not realistically be characterized as "community control." Nevertheless, each of New York City's local districts was authorized to elect a nine-member local board of education. Thus, New York City's elected school policy makers grew from nine to 297.[33]

Reaction to the dilution of representativeness also reached Congress. Federal education acts were amended in the early 1970s to mandate parent participation in the making of decisions about the use of federal program funds. Also, by the mid-1970s, several state legislatures were requiring the formation of parent advisory councils at school sites.[34] Numerous local school districts were voluntarily implementing plans for wider involvement of citizens in the decision-making process.

Reforms intended to increase public participation in educational planning were justified on grounds that schools had fallen too far under the dominance of professional experts and, as a consequence, were insensitive to the public's tastes. Those opposed to the reforms were quick to threaten the recurrence of past political horrors and corruption. Also, arguments regarding the inevitable inefficiency accompanying widespread participation were roundly repeated.

It is difficult to predict the outcome for school governance. However, at the present writing, the scales appear tipped in favor of professional control, and against representativeness. In other chapters throughout this volume, we advocate policies that would inject a larger element of public choice into school decision making. However, in doing so, we are aware that the pendulum of change is constantly in motion and that the present generation's zealously sought reforms can be transformed into tomorrow's insufferable social ills. Continued adjustments between alternative forms of government and the competing values of equality, efficiency, and liberty will undoubtedly persist. We suffer no delusion that our reform recommendations will prove appropriate indefinitely.

Phi Delta Kappan, No. 54, February 1973, pp. 386–89, and Les Pacheco, "The Politicization of Education at the State Level: A Case Study of California, 1947–72," unpublished Ed.D. dissertation, School of Education, University of California, Berkeley, 1975.

[32] See Henry M. Levin, *Community Control of Schools* (Washington, D.C.: Brookings Institution, 1970).

[33] See Melvin Zimet, *Decentralization and School Effectiveness* (New York: Teachers College Press, 1973).

[34] For example, by 1975, both California and Florida had enacted statutes requiring school site advisory councils.

Equality, Efficiency, Liberty: Resolving the Tension

As we have stressed, it is impossible to pursue one of the three values with which we are concerned here without placing the other two in jeopardy. Thus, governmental bodies are engaged in an almost constant readjustment. A new governmental program, a new economic policy, a new technological invention, or any number of other changes can trigger an imbalance in the practical relationships among the three values and provoke government action to establish a new equilibrium. Moreover, government action to maximize one of the three values in one sphere may provoke disequilibrium in another sphere. For example, attempts to achieve greater equality for the poor by public provision of low-cost housing can impair the income base of a local school district and thus frustrate its ability to provide equality of educational opportunity. All three branches and all levels of government are engaged in this balancing and unbalancing process. However, the judicial branch offers particularly dramatic examples of the continual search for stability. More than either executive officers or legislators, judges must explain their actions. Their actions, judicial opinions, are visible and available for examination. Court decisions are also particularly apt as illustrations of the tradeoffs between equality, efficiency, and liberty, because— as noted by Alexis de Tocqueville in the middle of the nineteenth century—there is a tendency in the United States for questions of deep political significance eventually to be settled by the judicial branch.[35] Consequently, we move to a discussion of court decisions revolving around schools and equality.

EQUAL PROTECTION AND SCHOOL POLICY

In 1868, the Fourteenth Amendment was formally accepted as a provision of the U.S. Constitution. Known at the time as the "Reconstruction Amendment," it prescribed conditions for the South's renewed participation in the Union. The last sentence of the amendment's first clause states: "No state shall . . . deny to any person within its jurisdiction the equal protection of the laws." This is the so-called "equal protection clause" which has served as the federal constitutional basis for seeking judicial redefinition of equality of educational opportunity.[36] As we will describe, court cases have also rested on state constitutional provisions, both equal protection clauses and education sections.

[35] Alexis de Tocqueville, *Democracy in America* (New York: Mentor, 1965; originally published in 1835).

[36] For added detail see Michael W. LaMorte, "The Fourteenth Amendment: Its Significance for Public School Educators," *Educational Administration Quarterly*, 10, No. 3, pp. 1–19.

SERRANO V. PRIEST[37]

In 1967, John Serrano, a father in a Los Angeles area school district, complained to the principal of his son's school regarding the quality of services available. The principal informed the parent that the school district simply could not afford more or better instruction and counseled the father to move to one of the wealthier nearby districts. The senior Serrano viewed this advice, no matter how well intentioned, as worthless; he was not able to move. Instead, he joined with others and brought suit against state officials.[38] This suit, *Serrano v. Priest*, questioned the constitutionality of the manner in which California financed its schools.

Complicated judicial procedures extended the case until December of 1976, when the California Supreme Court issued a final ruling. Court actions in this case declared California's schools finance arrangements to be in violation of the state constitution's "equal protection" provision and specified a deadline by which the legislature was to arrive at a judicially acceptable reform plan.

Attorneys for Serrano argued that education is a "fundamental interest," the availability of which cannot be conditioned on wealth. They reasoned that individuals must be educated in order to pursue rights explicitly guaranteed them in matters such as voting, free speech, and religion. Consequently, in the absence of a compelling justification, the state could not discriminate in the quality of school services made available to students.

Throughout various stages of the court proceedings, plaintiffs' counsel cited information and statistics to demonstrate that children residing in property-poor school districts tended to have less money spent upon their schooling. This was the case, despite the fact that residents of such districts frequently were willing to tax themselves at higher rates than high wealth districts. (The evidence on this dimension is similar to the conditions described in Chapter Four.)

In order to dramatize the disparities permitted, perhaps even encouraged, by the extant California school finance system, it was pointed out at trial that in 1968-69 the Beverly Hills school district, with property wealth totaling more than $50,000 per pupil spent $1232 per pupil at a tax rate of only $2.38. Conversely, nearby Baldwin Park, with property valued at $3,706 per pupil spent

[37] The initial California Supreme Court decision was upon a demurrer. The Court held that, if facts were as alleged by plaintiffs, the state's equal protection provision was being violated. The Court remanded the case to the court of original jurisdiction for a trial on the facts. The initial Supreme Court decision was *Serrano* v. *Priest*, 96 Cal. Rptr. 601, 437, P.2d 1241 (1971) known as Serrano I. The subsequent decision favored the plaintiffs and was itself appealed to the State Supreme Court where it was upheld.

[38] Reasonably, the defendant should have been the state legislature. However, one needs the legislature's consent to sue it. Therefore, plaintiffs named state officials as defendants. Priest in this instance is Ivy Baker Priest, then California State Treasurer.

only $577 even though it taxed itself at $5.48, a rate more than twice as high as Beverly Hills. State aid offset the difference somewhat—Beverly Hills received only $125 from the state whereas Baldwin Park received $307 per pupil. Nevertheless, there remained an expenditure discrepancy between the two in excess of $450 per pupil. School superintendents and other experts attested that a dollar difference of this magnitude translated to differences in the quality and services of schooling.

No argument was made that the state can never discriminate in the delivery of services. For example, certainly there can be compelling reasons for treating adults differently from juveniles, criminals differently from non-criminals, drivers differently from pedestrians, and so on. However, plaintiffs in *Serrano* contended that it was unfair to discriminate simply because of an "accident" of location, residence in a property-poor school district. Residence in such a school district was argued to be a "suspect classification," one in which discriminatory treatment was unjustified.

After having heard the legal arguments, California's high court decided in favor of *Serrano*. The court commented:

> . . . affluent districts can have their cake and eat it too; they can provide a high quality education for their children while paying lower taxes. Poor districts, by contrast, have no cake at all.[39]

The court subsequently ruled that differences in school spending, within a tolerance of $100 per pupil, could not be wealth-related and allowed the legislature five years in which to comply.

During the decade in which the *Serrano* suit was winding its way through the courts, a number of other equal protection school finance suits were filed and reached fruition.[40] A brief review of several of these cases, some of which were decided in favor of plaintiffs, some not, aids in understanding the translation of public values into public policy.

McINNIS V. OGILVIE[41]

This was one of the earliest decisions handed down on equal protection as applied to school finance. Plaintiffs, children from a property-poor Illinois school district, requested, as a remedy for the inequity they alleged, that public school revenues be allocated in proportion to student "needs." The plaintiffs'

[39]*Serrano* v. *Priest,* 96 Cal Rptr. at 611–12 as reprinted in Betsy Levin, "Recent Developments in the Law of Equal Educational Opportunity," *Journal of Law and Education,* 4, No. 3 (July 1975), 429.

[40]In fact, simply between 1971 and 1973, 52 court actions were cited in 31 states. *Ibid.,* p. 430.

[41]*McInnis* v. *Ogilvie,* 394 U.S. 322 (1969). Originally *McInnis* v. *Shapiro,* 293 F. Supp. 327, 331 (N.D. Ill. 1968).

position was ultimately denied for, among other reasons, the court ruled that no standards could be developed which would make a decision judicially manageable. The court could not construct a sufficiently objective measure of a child's or group of children's educational "needs." In effect, the court affirmed "equality" as an abstract value, but refused to accept "equal treatment" or "equal outcomes" as definitions of educational equality.

Counsel for plaintiffs in subsequent equal protection cases modified their position on remedy in order to avoid the *McInnis* problem of unmanageable standards. They now sought to persuade courts to adopt the so-called principle of fiscal neutrality. This standard devised by Coons, Clune, and Sugarman in their book, *Private Wealth and Public Education*,[42] holds that "The quality of a child's schooling shall not be a function of wealth, other than the wealth of the state as a whole." This is essentially a negative yardstick. It does not prescribe what a school finance system should be; rather it specifies what it should *not* be. In those instances where courts have invoked fiscal neutrality, legislatures are free to redesign school finance arrangements in whatever manner appears reasonable. The only judicially imposed constraint is that the reform system not exhibit disparities related to school district, and presumably household, wealth. Coons and his colleagues attempted to design a judicially manageable principle which, while furthering the value of equality, would not unduly infringe on liberty.

RODRIGUEZ V. SAN ANTONIO[43]

In 1973, the United States Supreme Court, in a 5-to-4 decision, overturned a Federal District Court ruling in a Texas school finance suit similar to *Serrano*. Plaintiffs were students and residents in a property-poor school district. They had questioned the legality of Texas' school finance system and had cited state officials for acts in violation of the Constitution's equal protection clause. However, upon appeal, the nation's highest court failed to concur. The court majority, in the absence of a specific constitutional reference, concluded that education did not comprise a fundamental right. Thus, the state was not obligated to demonstrate a "compelling interest" in defense of the fiscal disparities which accompanied its school finance plan. The Court held that the Texas distribution plan was legal as long as it complied with a "rational basis test." This meant simply that, as long as the state had a reasonable justification for its system of distribution of school dollars, it would be permitted to stand. In applying this test, the Supreme Court stated that existing interdistrict expenditure disparities were balanced off against the state interest in maintaining local control. Though acknowledging the Texas school finance arrangements might be unjust,

---

[42] John E. Coons, William H. Clune, Stephen D. Sugarman, *Private Wealth and Public Education* (Cambridge: Harvard University Press, 1970).

[43] *San Antonio Independent Sch. Dist.* v. *Rodriguez*, 36L. Ed. 2d16, 93S.Ct. 1278 (1973).

the Court concluded that they were not unconstitutional. A measure of inequality even though distasteful, was permitted to persist in order to protect a measure of liberty.

Plaintiffs' position in *Rodriguez* was found wanting on two other dimensions. The Court held that students of property-poor school districts were not sufficiently homogeneous to comprise a "suspect classification." Such students were not uniformly from low-income households nor were they of any particular racial or ethnic group. Also, the Court was not persuaded that expenditure disparities resulted in damage to students. In the Court's view, the evidence was insufficient to conclude that state-imposed minimum expenditure levels throughout Texas had failed to assure children an adequate level of schooling. In effect, the Supreme Court accepted "equal access to minimally adequate resources" as the definition of equal educational opportunity.

The Rodriguez decision brought to a close, at least for the short run, any hope of a national school finance reform strategy based on the federal Constitution. If reform was to take place nationwide, it would have to occur state by state.

ROBINSON V. CAHILL [44]

Five weeks following the Court's decision in *Rodriguez,* the hopes of school finance reformers received a boost from the New Jersey Supreme Court ruling in *Robinson* v. *Cahill.* This decision, the most pervasive school finance reform ruling to that time, declared New Jersey's distribution formula to be in violation of the state constitution's education clause. That clause charges the legislature with providing a "thorough and efficient" system of education. When provided with testimony regarding the funding and school service disparities then present throughout the state's local school districts, the New Jersey Supreme Court found that the education clause was being violated and mandated that the state legislature redefine the constitutional directive "thorough and efficient." [45]

The case is significant for at least two reasons. It emphasized that school finance reform could take place on state constitutional grounds even though the avenue to nationwide reform had been closed, at least, in the short run, by the negative decision in *Rodriguez.* However, the Robinson ruling also demonstrated that a court mandate is not always sufficient. The New Jersey legislature did not comply with the judicial edict. Legislative action would have inevitably either raised taxes, lowered expenditures in high-spending school districts, or both. These alternatives apparently were judged as politically more costly than whatever gains would have accrued from achieving greater equality. The court eventually closed New Jersey's public schools in order to force legislative compliance with its ruling.

[44]*Robinson* v. *Cahill,* 62 N.J., 473, 303 A.2d 273 (1973).
[45]N.J. Constitution, Article VIII, Section 4, paragraph i.

HOBSON V. HANSEN[46]

So far we have discussed school finance cases that adjudicated problems of *inter*district disparities. Julius Hobson, a Washington, D.C. resident and school board member, took note of the fact that, even within the same district, schools which served predominantly white populations appeared to have a disproportionate share of high-paid teachers and supplies. Consequently, he filed suit against the Washington, D.C. school district, alleging racial discrimination in the distribution of school services.

In defending itself, the school district claimed it had no specific policy accounting for discrimination. Senior teachers, those highest on the salary schedule, held the prerogative of working in the school of their choice. Many chose to teach in white neighborhoods. When they invoked their transfer privilege, they carried with them their higher salaries. The result was an educationally unjustifiable expenditure disparity. In his ruling, Judge Skelly Wright held that the "arbitrary quality of thoughtlessness can be as disastrous and unfair to private rights and the public interest as the perversity of a willful scheme."[47]

Wright ruled that the school district had to redistribute resources, particularly teacher salaries, in an equitable manner. The district attempted to comply but encountered extraordinary technical difficulties in the process.[48] By 1970, the original plaintiff, Julius Hobson, became convinced that substantial disparities persisted. He filed a second suit,[49] and in 1971 Judge Wright issued an even stronger opinion. This case coincided with the discovery of substantial *intra*district resource disparity in many large school districts throughout the nation. The attention focused on the problem prompted the U.S. Office of Education to issue so-called "comparability" regulations demanding that school districts distribute resources equitably in order to remain eligible for federal funds. The Hobson decision and "comparability" policy reinforced the "equal access to minimal resources" view of equality of opportunity, but simultaneously permitted more liberal definition. The court ruling demands simply that minimal school services be distributed at least equally. If there exists an educationally justifiable reason for shifting added resources so as to favor one or another group of students, that is permissible. This latter condition edges closer to the "equal treatment" definition of equality of education.

A final note. The implementation difficulties in attempting to comply with *Hobson* provoked the Washington, D.C. schools to decentralize many budget decisions. The central board assures an equal dollar distribution per

---

[46] *Hobson* v. *Hansen*, 269 F. Supp. 401 (1967). (Known as Hobson I.)

[47] Hobson I, P. 497.

[48] See Joan Baratz, *A Quest for Equal Educational Opportunity in a Major Urban School District: The Case of Washington, D.C.* A report prepared for D.C. Citizens For Better Education by the Education Policy Research Institute of the Educational Testing Service, June 1975.

[49] *Hobson* v. *Hansen*, 327 F. Supp. (D.D.C., 1971). (Known as Hobson II.)

pupil. Thereafter, decisions regarding the best use of money are in substantial measure made by those at the school site.[50] This method of budgeting gives promise both of assuring equality, expanding choice, and inspiring efficiency. (We describe the concept in detail in Chapter Eleven.)

As was suggested earlier, courts are by no means the only branch of government concerned with resolving the conflicts between forces advocating actions consistent with equality, efficiency, or liberty. It is difficult to conceive of a government regulation or piece of programmatic legislation which does not in some way involve a compromise between two or more of the values we have emphasized here. Indeed, arriving at means by which there is greater equality and greater efficiency so as to provide each individual with greater liberty, and doing so in a fashion which minimizes conflict, is what we believe to be the purpose of a government. Governing education is no exception.

Summary

This chapter has described the tension among equality, efficiency, and liberty, three values central to American public policy both in general and to American educational policy in particular.

The value of "equality," when applied to educational policy making, usually revolves around the concept of equality of educational opportunity. In the United States, educational equality first meant equal access to education, or that every child should be provided with at least the same, minimally adequate school services. Equality later came to mean equal educational treatment, or that the educationally handicapped should receive special treatment to remediate the handicap and put them in a position equal to that of other students. Most recently, educational equality has referred to equality of educational outcome, or that schools ought to produce students who all have the same minimum or basic skills.

Although U.S. schools constantly strive for greater efficiency, most recently the cost of education has skyrocketed while student achievement appears to have decreased. Impediments to educational efficiency are our diverse and conflicting expectations about what education ought to do, our lack of an incentive system for promoting efficiency, and the educational labor costs that must rise to compete with the private sector, even though education does not benefit from private sector productivity gains. Too, educational efficiency conflicts at times with educational equality and liberty.

The value of "liberty," when applied to education, often refers to the freedom to choose, and is ensured by governmental responsiveness. Responsiveness, at first strengthened in the United States by large numbers of local school dis-

---

[50] See Baratz, *A Quest for Equal Educational Opportunity.*

tricts, was later eroded by school district consolidation and professional management in the interests of efficiency, and by the increased influence of the state government acting in the interest of equality. Currently, many citizens, including the authors of this book, are reacting to this erosion of governmental responsiveness and are advocating greater public participation in educational planning.

The chapter concludes with a series of court cases concerning schools and equality. These cases illustrate the tradeoffs between the values of equality, efficiency, and liberty.

3

THE ROLE
OF GOVERNMENT
IN FINANCING EDUCATION

Thomas Jefferson wrote that no nation could remain both ignorant and free. In order to protect our freedom as well as to provide a trained work force, Americans gradually developed an elaborate system of free, public schools. In 1974 approximately 45 million children attended public primary and secondary schools. An additional 9 million students enrolled in public institutions of higher education.[1] From modest beginnings, public education has grown to consume $108.7 billion in 1974, or 7.8% of the total goods and services produced that year.[2] Free public education is an integral part of American life.

However, broad political and economic support for public education has not immunized schools against criticism. Throughout the years political conservatives have argued that public provision of schooling is an unnecessary extension of government responsibility.[3] Recent attacks on public education have eroded its political support; in fact, since the late 1970s school bonds and operating budgets have increasingly met defeat at the hands of local voters. Many school programs are attacked by conservatives as being costly luxuries and by

[1] National Center for Educational Statistics, *The Condition of Education* (Washington, D.C.: U.S. Government Printing Office, 1976), pp. 16 and 184.
[2] National Center for Educational Statistics, *The Condition of Education,* p. 180.
[3] As an example see Milton Friedman, *Capitalism and Freedom* (Chicago: The University of Chicago Press, 1962), pp. 85–107.

liberals and radicals as being infringements on student and parent rights. Rapidly increasing costs of higher education are pricing many middle-income families out of the college market, yet we have not found enough places for the under-educated in our industrial society.

A crescendo of public criticism is forcing a reexamination of assumptions about public education. Where does the public responsibility for education end? Who benefits from public education? How much education is enough? This chapter explores these and other questions regarding the role of government in education.

Public Responsibility in Education

Educating young people is a major responsibility of adult society. At birth children depend on parents for many necessities: food, shelter, protection, af-fection, etc. This dependence continues for many years, until children have ade-quate experience and education to function independently in society.

Education, of course, is not free. It requires an expenditure of consider-able time and resources which could be used to produce other things valued by society. The costs of formal schooling (which is only part of the total educa-tional experience of children) amount to billions, making schooling one of the most important economic and social activities in the United States.

While everyone recognizes the importance of education, there is some debate about whether its provision is a public or private responsibility. On the one hand, the family, which is still our basic social unit, is recognized as having the greatest concern and responsibility for educating the young. No other social unit is better able to care for a child's well-being, listen to a child's concerns, or be small enough to be responsive to a child's interests.

On the other hand, the predominance of the family in education has been gradually diminished by government assumption of new areas of educational responsibility. Originally, schools provided a minimum basic education needed by an individual to function in society. Schooling has expanded, however, to include vocational education, special education for the physically and socially disadvantaged, and many higher educational experiences. Even moral education, long regarded as a function of the family and church, is being recommended for public school curricula. All of these accretions have been justified on grounds of their public benefits, or of the failure of the family and private institutions to provide the proper educational experience in question. But when does public responsibility end? Because of a rising divorce rate, will young people be re-quired to earn a family responsibility certificate in school before they are al-lowed to marry? Will disillusionment with politicians lead someone to suggest that aspiring politicians enroll in political science courses before they can run for political office? Even more perplexing is the problem arising when public schools do a poor job of providing services better provided privately. Private failure is a ready excuse for public activity. Is public failure an equal justification for returning responsibility to individuals?

The tension between private and public responsibility in education can be clarified somewhat by examining the private and public benefits of education. Private benefits are those which accrue to a child or a child's family. Public benefits of education are those which are received by individuals outside the family of the child being educated. Public financing and provision of education is usually rationalized, at least from an economist's point of view, in terms of supplementing private education to ensure that societal benefits are forthcoming.

PRIVATE BENEFITS OF EDUCATION

There is clearly an element of pure consumption in many of the benefits of education. Although not all children like going to school, there are obvious advantages, including learning new things, meeting friends, engaging in sports and, in some cases, having a good meal. The consumption component of education probably increases the longer an individual attends school, reaching its height in the many adult how-to-do-it courses offered by community colleges and many school districts.

Most of the literature on the private benefits of education emphasizes future economic returns of educational investment. A high school education is now necessary to ensure good prospects in the job market. Currently, advanced training in business or medicine promises the likelihood of higher than average future earnings. Many studies have compared the expected lifetime earnings of individuals who have completed different amounts of schooling.[4] Those with four or more years of college on the average are likely to earn more than those with only a high school degree. They, in turn, can expect to earn more than those with only an elementary school experience.[5] During the 1970s the economic value of college education declined partly because of a surplus of college graduates.[6] Nevertheless, most economic analyses have found that education, particularly primary and secondary education, is a good investment.

Studies of the economic returns of education concentrate on monetary returns and thus often ignore educational values difficult to measure in dollars. Most people change jobs several times during their working years. A well-educated

[4] For a general review and bibliography on the concept of investment in human capital, see Mark Blaug, *Economics of Education,* Vol. 1 (Baltimore: Penguin Books Inc., 1968), pp. 13–134.

[5] See Gary S. Becker, *Human Capital* (New York: Columbia University Press, 1964).

[6] Richard A. Freeman, "The Declining Economic Value of Higher Education and the American Social System," An Occasional Paper of the Aspen Institute for Humanistic Studies (New York: The Aspen Institute for Humanistic Studies, 1976).

person can adapt more easily to new job situations and opportunities, thus providing a hedge against future unemployment. The same studies find it difficult to measure economic benefits which accrue to individuals as a result of education but which are not exchanged for money. For example, one value of a high school education is the opportunity to go to college or to be selected for on-the-job-training in business or government. Finally, although women who pursue education and then choose to raise families often cannot point to an economic return to their education, it is likely, however, to improve their families' cultural and social opportunities and enhance their children's educational prospects. The economic value of education for those who do not enter the labor force, in other words, is not necessarily lost. Educated parents tend to motivate their children to obtain an education and to excel in school. Education of one generation is passed on to the next, and thus plays an important part in the perpetuation of an educated citizenry.[7]

PUBLIC BENEFITS OF EDUCATION

In addition to conferring benefits on students and their families, education also benefits others. These benefits are frequently called external benefits, or externalities. Educational services that result in considerable public, or external, benefits are viewed by politicians quite differently from services that confer only private benefits. Individuals can, of course, be expected to continue purchasing a service until the cost of an additional unit of that service exceeds the additional benefits received. Since the private benefits of education accrue solely to the individuals involved, the level of services resulting from individual decisions should theoretically produce an optimal level of service. When, on the other hand, public benefits that normally would not be considered in purely private decisions are involved, government intervention is justifiable.

The public, as opposed to the student and his or her family, benefits from that student's education in at least two ways. First, one person's education may change the *economic* situations of others. For example, a trained engineer may improve the productivity of his or her co-workers. Second, education may improve the *social* environment of a community, making it a better place for everyone to live.

The external economic benefits of education are closely related to the increasing interdependence of modern industrial society. Most work processes today, whether in industry or in government, require the coordination, cooperation, and interaction of many people. Consequently, the training and skills of each worker rub off on other workers. Just as the presence of good students in a classroom appears to enhance the performance of their classmates, so ad-

---

[7]Theodore W. Schultz, "Education and Economic Growth," in *Social Factors Influencing American Education* (Chicago: National Society for the Study of Education, 1961), pp. 74–75.

vanced training of a worker or supervisor is reflected in the productivity of his or her colleagues.[8] The process of transferring benefits to other workers can be very simple. A better educated person may set an example for others to emulate. Education may make a person more aware of recent technology, or more flexible and adaptable in applying new technology or ideas to work situations. To the extent that a manager's education, for example, improves the performance of subordinates, both owners and other employees benefit directly from the manager's education.

Another important external economic benefit of education is the long-term cost savings to a community which result from education. There is a fairly strong relationship between lack of education and criminal activity. By providing education for all its citizens, a community reduces the costs of dealing with crime and delinquency. Furthermore, education reduces the likelihood of un-employment, thereby lowering welfare costs and, conversely, increasing total taxable income. The effects may even be greater than the simple increase in a community's tax base, however, since higher income families may also consume fewer public services.

Perhaps the most common external benefit attributed to education is its contribution to economic growth. The idea here is simple although its implications for public policy are hardly unambiguous. According to the argument, education contributes to the productivity of an economy. Investment in educa-tion, or in "human capital"—a term preferred by educational economists—should be considered on the same basis as physical investment in a country's economy. If, for example, investment in education leads to greater economic productivity than investment in roads, then educational investment should be increased until the marginal productivity of investing in education is equal to that of investing in roads. Furthermore, if private educational investment is inadequate to produce the desired total level of educational investment, then government should inter-vene to close the gap between private and public investment. According to this schema, economic growth—that is the opportunity for higher per capita income in the future—is equivalent to investing in education to reduce the social costs of potential unemployment.[9]

It is important to identify a particular type of externality called "spillover effects."[10] Spillover benefits are the benefits persons carry from the community in which they received an education to another community. For example, the

[8] See J. Ronnie Davis, "The Social and Economic Externalities of Education," in *Economic Factors Affecting the Financing of Education,* eds., Roe L. Johns, Irving J. Goffman, Kern Alexander, and Dewey H. Stollar (Gainesville, Fla.: National Educa-tional Finance Project, 1970), p. 66.

[9] See Mary Jean Bowman, "Education and Economic Growth," in *Economic Factors Affecting the Financing of Education,* eds., Roe L. Johns et al. (Gainesville, Fla.: Na-tional Educational Finance Project, 1970), pp. 83–120.

[10] This term refers to the costs and benefits of governmental services which accrue to people in another political jurisdiction.

state of Illinois may contribute $20,000 to the education of a doctor who sets up practice in Ohio. The citizens of Illinois pay the costs but receive no benefits because they have spilled over into Ohio. If Illinois-trained doctors consistently moved to Ohio, voters in Illinois would become increasingly reluctant to support medical training. However, from the point of view of the family whose child is studying to become a doctor, that the benefits of a medical education spill over into another state would be irrelevant to their educational investment decisions.

In addition to improving the economic well-being of a community, education produces important noneconomic benefits. Democratic government requires a citizenry with a common fund of values and an understanding of commitment to the rules of democratic government. Inculcating an understanding of history, geography, and of the cultural heritage of nation and community is an often overlooked task of education. Learning how and why the Revolution, the Civil War, and the social reforms of the 1930s and 1960s came about helps to give a common perspective on current political problems. Knowledge of other languages, athletic skills, and interpersonal proficiency enable children better to communicate and interact in community settings. Finally, and perhaps most important, education passes on from generation to generation the rules by which social and political discourse is conducted. In a democracy a large proportion of actions are voluntary. Individuals are not required to participate in community affairs, to vote, to work, or do many other things that are essential to the functioning of a democracy. Education helps perpetuate the norms and values which guide citizens' behavior in a free society.

Education also helps maintain social cohesion by providing a mechanism for reducing social inequalities. A famous, nineteenth-century educator, Caleb Mills, believed that public schools could do much to ameliorate class conflict. In the colorful language of the time he argued that public schools:

> . . . contribute more than any other one agency, to mould and assimilate the various discordant materials to be incorporated into the body politic and render them homogeneous in character and sympathy. How often have we all seen in those nurseries of knowledge, aristocratic pride humbled, plebeian roughness refined, rustic conceit corrected, haughty insolence rebuked and repressed, gentle modesty emboldened, unobtrusive worth encouraged, and the many asperities of character give place to lovelier traits, all contributing to swell the aggregate of human happiness, domestic peace and civil freedom.[11]

Furthermore, to the extent that people still believe the amount and kind of education plays a significant role in determining the distribution of income in the United States, the availability of free public education may dampen de-

---

[11] Charles W. Moores, ed., *Caleb Mills and the Indiana School System* (Indiana: Historical Society Publications, Vol. III, no. VI, 1905), p. 585.

mands for more rapid redistribution of wealth and privilege. The ability of each new generation to rise above its social and economic beginnings, in other words, encourages tolerance of remaining social and economic inequalities.

PUBLIC BENEFITS
AND GOVERNMENT INTERVENTION IN EDUCATION

From an economist's point of view, government's role in education is justified in terms of the public or external benefits of education. If educational benefits were limited to those receiving education and their families, then there would be no good economic reason for government to become involved.[12] Individuals would purchase an optimal amount of education in the private market. Those who could not afford to pay the full cost of schooling could theoretically borrow what they needed since the rate of return would be more than enough to justify private loans.[13]

As we have indicated above, however, education contributes not only to the well-being of the student and his family, but to the general society as well. External benefits are therefore important for two reasons: First, from an equity point of view, if the costs of private or public services are to be borne by those who benefit from them, then those who receive external benefits should contribute to the costs of education; second, an optimal level of educational expenditures will result only if external benefits are included in the determination of educational spending. If they are omitted, too little education will be consumed from an economic efficiency perspective. Educational spending must be more than that resulting from equating only private benefits and costs.

The quest for a socially equitable way of distributing the costs of education is discussed in detail in Chapter Six. The remainder of this chapter examines alternative ways government can intervene to ensure that efficient levels of educational services are provided.

When external benefits are desirable (as we assume for any progressive society), government can intervene in at least three ways to provide a more efficient level of educational services.[14] The simplest is for government, while not providing education, to require that every citizen obtain a minimum amount

---

[12] There are undoubtedly exceptions to this general statement. For example, citizens may vote against property tax increases for schools even though they still stand to benefit as private citizens. Their reasoning is probably that state or federal funds will become available to supplement or replace local property tax support for schools.

[13] Under current capital market conditions lenders may be reluctant to make loans for education in the absence of a physical asset as collateral for the loan. In a free society we are not likely to permit lenders to bind (or indenture) students to future service. Such imperfections in capital markets could be dealt with, however, without government financing or provision of education per se. For example, federal loan guarantees or income deductions might solve the problem.

[14] Friedman, *Capitalism and Freedom*.

of education. Government can also subsidize education to reduce its private costs and thereby increase the amount demanded. A third possibility is for government to actually provide the service itself. We will examine each of these alternatives.

GOVERNMENT-ESTABLISHED CRITERIA

Suppose education were provided privately. Some families would purchase technical training. Others would send their children to religious schools. Some might opt for apprenticeships in business after a few years of basic education. Still others would invest not only in basic education but also in higher education and professional training. Each family would obtain as much education as it felt it wanted and could afford.[15] From a social point of view, too little education might be purchased, however, if the community agreed upon a minimum of 10 or 12 years of basic education as yielding a minimum level of citizenship. Less than that amount might leave students ill prepared to find employment or to participate in community affairs. This would put the economic burden upon others and increase social tensions in the community. In the presence of such externalities, government could require each student to receive a minimum number of years of basic education. It could go further to require that basic skills in reading, writing, and arithmetic and citizenship training be included in the basic education programs. As Milton Friedman writes:

> What kind of governmental action is justified by this particular neighbor-hood effect? [external benefits] The most obvious is to require that each child receive a minimum amount of schooling of a specialized kind. Such a requirement could be imposed upon the parents without further government action, just as owners of buildings, and frequently of automobiles, are required to adhere to specified standards to protect the safety of others.[16]

Friedman further suggests that the costs of the required minimum level of education be borne by parents, and that government subsidy be available only to low-income families. The argument for placing the burden of financing education on parents is based on efficiency and does not consider whether it is equitable for those receiving external benefits to avoid contributing to the costs of education. Friedman maintains that private financing would eliminate the administrative costs of public collection and distribution of taxes. It would mini-

---

[15] Many argue that such a system would deprive working people of an adequate education. E. G. West points out, however, that before public support of education in England, working-class parents were paying directly for their children's education and that literacy among working-class children was high. E. G. West, *Education and the State* (London: The Institute of Economic Affairs, 1965), chaps. 10 and 11.

[16] Friedman, *Capitalism and Freedom,* p. 86.

mize the tendency of government budgets to grow as personal incomes and tax receipts increase, even though the need for government programs may have remained the same or even declined. Private financing of basic education would also place the cost of children directly on parents, and thus promote a more rational determination of family size.[17]

GOVERNMENT SUBSIDY

Government subsidy or financing is another method of ensuring an adequate supply of basic education. The premise of this method is that individuals and families will purchase more of something at a lower price than at a higher price. The utility of subsidies in promoting an efficient level and type of educational performance depends upon the source of the subsidy and the method by which it is distributed. A head tax on school-age children which is then redistributed to parents according to the number of children would have little or no effect on the purchase of educational services. (The administrative costs of collecting and distributing the tax leave families with slightly less for education than they had before the tax.) A general property or sales tax, on the other hand, would reallocate the costs of education among all households. In fact, the larger the amount of subsidies from the general public, the more money those families with children would have to purchase additional education.

The actual effect of subsidies in reducing a family's educational costs, and thereby determining the level and kind of education purchased, depends also on the kind of subsidies used. Suppose a community decided that all students should have 10 years of basic education, including citizenship and moral instruction. A subsidy distributed to families in the form of equal dollar amounts per school-age child would not be an efficient way of accomplishing the community's objective. Families would tend to use the public funds to purchase vocational and professional training which have high private benefits. To achieve the desired public benefits, it would be necessary to restrict the use of public subsidies to particular programs and, perhaps, particular schools. If a community, in addition to desiring minimum citizenship training, also wanted to reduce income inequalities, they might decide to provide larger subsidies for children from low-income families. Other things being equal, the more highly subsidized families would purchase relatively more education and improve their children's chances of earning higher lifetime earnings.

GOVERNMENT PROVISION

Public provision of education is a third means of ensuring that individuals take account of the external benefits of education. This is the method currently used in the United States along with the requirement that all children between

[17]*Ibid.*, p. 95.

the ages of 5 and 17 attend school. If a socially desirable level of educational services that makes provision for public as well as private benefits can be ensured through the use of minimum standards along with subsidies, why is it necessary to create a $109-billion public educational industry? One argument is that public schools are necessary to maintain a common core of values and thus to promote social cohesion and political stability. A system of private schools, even if supported with public funds and required to adhere to minimum standards, would not provide a sufficiently uniform educational experience. Instead, private schools would emphasize their own individualistic values and transform education into a divisive rather than a unifying force.

This argument, while persuasive, seems inconsistent with many facts about public and private education in the United States. In the first place, public schools are noteworthy for their differences as well as their likenesses. Even though the physical features of schools and the organization of the school day appear similar, there is great variety in the educational climate among schools. The tensions and hostility permeating many urban high schools are not found in middle- and high-income suburban high schools. Even within a large urban high school the educational experiences of children taking a black studies program tend to be very different from those enrolled in a vocational education program or a college preparatory program. It is not at all clear, in other words, that public school children are acquiring a common core of values, or that the values they are acquiring enhance social cohesion. In fact, the necessity of maintaining uniformity may produce conflict in large urban communities with diverse ethnic and social populations. Confronted with demands for greater emphasis on bilingual education, vocational education, compensatory education, basic education, and a myriad of other demands, school boards reach compromises which frequently satisfy no one.[18]

Similarly, it is not clear that a system of private education would be as divisive as some believe. The case against private schools is that they increase class differences and emphasize sectarian values rather than patriotic values. Under our current educational system, private schools do foster class differences since they are available only to the rich who can afford both public school taxes and private school tuition. But if parents were not penalized by having to pay twice for sending their children to private schools, and particularly if public financial support of both public and private schools were weighted in favor of low-income families, then wealth would be a less important determinant of private school enrollment. Children preferring an educational program organized around the arts, for instance, would be brought together regardless of income or social backgrounds.

The second claim that private schools do not instill values supportive of democratic government is not supported by survey results on this question.

[18] See Mancur Olson, *The Logic of Collective Action* (Cambridge: Harvard University Press, 1965).

Greeley and Rossi found that Catholics in parochial schools were slightly less rigid and intolerant and more socially conscious than Catholics attending public schools.[19]

Another possible way to finance education is through voluntary contributions. The problem here is one of lack of incentives, because the enjoyment of external benefits by one person usually does not diminish the ability of others to enjoy those benefits. If, for instance, an additional two years of public schooling increases the expected rate of economic growth, reduces juvenile delinquency, or in any number of ways creates a more enjoyable community, those benefits are shared by everyone. Nevertheless, any single individual in the community would be reluctant voluntarily to pay for the added amenities. In other words, people will refuse to express their true educational philosophy if it means they will have to pay for something they can benefit from without paying. The only solution is a system in which people must reveal their educational preferences or *nobody* will receive any benefits and in which revealing preference means agreeing that everyone will help pay for it.[20]

Under what conditions, therefore, is government intervention in education desirable? Clearly, to the extent that education produces public or external benefits for families other than that of the student, government should intervene both (1) to ensure that those who receive the external benefits share the educational costs, and (2) to ensure that the external benefits are considered in a community's decisions about the supply of education. Minimum standards, subsidies, or public provision can be used.

As a general rule the greater the public or external benefits of a particular type of education, the stronger the case for government financing and provision of education. A good case can be made, therefore, for government support of the minimum basic education required for citizenship. The case for government support of vocational education and higher education is weaker, but not entirely absent. There may be, for instance, substantial public benefits from vocational training for handicapped children and for many students who have difficulty in traditional classrooms, since such preparation may make these individuals more employable and reduce the costs of various social services. Similarly, while many of the benefits of higher education are private, activities such as university research projects increase economic productivity and growth. In cases where both private and public benefits are substantial, government should prorate its support in terms of the proportion of external to private benefits. For example, medical students agreeing to study family medicine and practice in rural communities lacking adequate health services should receive public support for a higher proportion of their medical school costs than those whose specialty already suffers from an oversupply of qualified physicians.

[19] Andrew M. Greeley and Peter H. Rossi, *The Education of Catholic Americans* (Chicago: Aldine Publishing Company, 1966), pp. 136–37.

[20] For a more detailed discussion of this problem, see Davis, "The Social and Economic Externalities of Education," pp. 76–80.

Measuring the Benefits of Public Education

So far we have examined the theoretical arguments supporting government's role in public education. We must now ask a crucial question—How can we *measure* the benefits from education? Are the theoretical justifications for public education confirmed by the actual distribution of societal benefits? Spending for education, as for every other public program, has redistributional consequences. In the case of education there is clearly a redistribution of resources from taxpaying adults to school-age children. Education involves a transfer of resources from families without school-age children to those with school-age children. Many feel that public education involves a transfer of resources from working people to business, since education clearly reduces the costs of on-the-job training. While it is obvious that the distributional effects of education are not neutral, it is quite a bit more difficult to assess those effects.

We have already mentioned several reasons for the difficulty of measuring educational returns. Many of the external benefits of education are nonexclusive; their enjoyment by one person does not reduce the enjoyment of others. Therefore, we cannot say that the group carrying the burden benefits more than any other group. Then, of course, many of the benefits of education are long-term and can only be hypothesized. In addition to these considerations, government has not been very helpful in identifying the beneficiaries of education, partly because not enough research has been done on the distributional consequences of education.

PRIVATE RETURNS TO EDUCATION

Despite the difficulties of identifying and obtaining information on the beneficiaries of education, there is information which casts some light on this question. For example, economists have analyzed the increases to lifetime earnings which accrue to additional increments of education. One approach is to assume that the income earned by persons of various ages who have completed, say, four years of high school, represents the expected income of high school graduates. Adding up the average incomes of different age groups with high school educations provides an estimate of the total lifetime earnings of someone graduating from high school. Since future income is not as valuable as current dollars, the estimate of future income is usually discounted by some market rate of interest.[21] But even if the effects of additional education on lifetime

[21] In general the procedure estimates the total lifetime earnings of someone completing a given amount of schooling and then compares the present value of those earnings with the costs of the education provided. The present value of earnings means the current value one attaches to future earnings. More specifically, one would prefer $1,000 immediately rather than the assurance of $1,000 in five years. There are a number of reasons for this: money in hand can be invested now at interest; there may be an urgent need for the money in the next five years; and there is al-

earnings are properly discounted, not all of the additional earnings should be credited to education alone. Some of the credit is probably due to intelligence and/or the parents' education and income, both of which are highly correlated with the length of time a child remains in school as well as future income. The specific effect of formal education on lifetime earnings is undoubtedly smaller, therefore, than most returns to education studies suggest.

The results of Walter Garms' study of the returns to education are presented in Table 3-1. The magnitude of lifetime earning depends on the discount rate assumed, with the value of education declining as the rate of discount increases.

A second approach for estimating the value of education is to compare the rates of return on investments in varying amounts of education. The methodology of computing rate of return is much like that used to compute the present value of education. The rate of return is simply the discount rate which, when applied to the increase in a life-long stream of expected income from each level of education, equals the cost of education. The higher the expected increments of income and the lower the costs of education, the higher the rate of return.

In 1970, Theodore Schultz, who pioneered much of the research on the human capital approach to education, compared the rate of return of various kinds of education to rates of return in the U.S. private economy, which range from 10 to 15 percent.[22] He concluded that the returns for investment in elementary and high school educations are very high. His estimate for elementary school was about 35 percent. Other studies put the rate of return of elementary schooling at over 100 percent.[23] For high school graduates, Schultz estimated the rate of return at approximately 25 percent. Because of labor market discrimination, the rate of return for the education of blacks was somewhat lower than for whites.

Schultz, and more recently Roger Freeman, have found that the rate of return for college education is lower than for elementary and secondary education. Their estimates range from 15 percent in Schultz's study to only 7 percent in Freeman's study.[24] Also, instead of increasing, as returns to primary and

---

ways some uncertainty about receiving the money in the future. These reasons are captured by the economist's concept of "present value discounting." An amount of money to be received in the future has a present value that is less than that amount in hand. Present value can be calculated by assuming a compound interest rate known as the discount rate.

[22] Theodore W. Schultz, "The Human Capital Approach to Education," in *Economic Factors Affecting the Financing of Education,* eds. Roe L. Johns et al. (Gainesville, Fla.: National Educational Finance Project, 1970), pp. 47–54.

[23] W. Lee Hansen, "Total and Private Rates for Return to Investment in Schooling," *Journal of Political Economy,* 71 (April 1963), 128–40, and Giora Hanoch, "An Economic Analysis of Earnings and Schooling," *Journal of Human Resources,* 2, No. 3 (Madison: University of Wisconsin Press, 1967), 310–29.

[24] Freeman, "The Declining Economic Value."

TABLE 3-1

Value of Lifetime Income Associated with Education

| | Total | Present Value at | |
Category	Income	5 Percent	10 Percent
White males			
1–3 years high school	$427,633	$132,262	$60,488
4 years high school	478,280	147,951	66,940
1–3 years college	534,013	153,187	63,151
4 or more years college	699,771	184,831	68,902
White females			
1–3 years high school	94,693	28,872	13,377
4 years high school	125,428	35,072	14,780
1–3 years college	147,986	40,580	16,729
4 or more years college	276,640	70,769	27,043
Nonwhite males			
1–3 years high school	268,268	86,543	40,636
4 years high school	309,765	99,817	46,323
1–3 years college	355,265	106,002	44,850
4 or more years college	423,395	116,268	44,622
Nonwhite females			
1–3 years high school	111,041	35,027	16,539
4 years high school	139,863	40,277	17,213
1–3 years college	176,101	49,494	20,515
4 or more years college	361,002	94,639	36,357

Notes: The assumption is made that real incomes in 1967 dollars at any given age will increase at 1.62 percent per year as a result of expansion of the economy.

Amounts shown are present values at age 16 of incomes from age 16 to 65, before taxes. Basic data are from U.S. Bureau of the Census, *Current Population Reports,* Series P-60, No. 60, "Income in 1967 of Persons in the United States" (Washington: U.S. Government Printing Office, 1969). Incomes during periods individuals are students are from Robert G. Spiegelman, *A Benefit/Cost Model to Evaluate Educational Programs* (Menlo Park, Calif.: Stanford Research Institute, 1968).

Median incomes were used, to help correct for the upward bias caused by using income rather than earnings data. Data, given by the Bureau of the Census at 10-year age intervals, were positioned at the midpoint of the interval and values for other years were determined by linear interpolation. A mortality correction is included.

Figures shown are for incomes *associated* with education. They include the effect of noneducational causal factors correlated with education.

Source: Walter I. Garms, "A Benefit-Cost Analysis of the Upward Bound Program," *Journal of Human Resources,* VI, No. 2 (Spring 1971), p. 213.

secondary education have since World War II, the returns of college education have been falling.[25] One interesting finding in Freeman's research is that the general conclusion about the lower rates of return to college education do not

[25] See Richard B. Freeman, *The Overeducated American* (New York: Academic Press, 1976).

apply for blacks or women. In both of these categories, returns of further college education are increasing.[26]

Schultz concludes from his review of the human capital studies that there is a serious underinvestment in elementary education, particularly in the rural areas of the south, the southwest, and in the Appalachia region, as well as in central cities. Associated with inadequate resources is neglect for the quality of elementary schooling throughout the country. The rate of return for high school education has been rising but is only slightly above the domestic economic rate of return. Improvements in the quality of high school education are called for, but the economic case for greater investment is less compelling than for elementary schooling. Studies on the rates of return to higher education suggest a possible over-investment in this area. Certainly, given scarce educational resources, a good economic argument can be made for reallocating money from higher education toward elementary education. Schultz suggests that the financing of higher education be rearranged so that those who receive the benefits of higher education pay a higher proportion of its costs.[27]

PUBLIC RETURNS TO EDUCATION

The public or social returns to education are much more difficult to measure. To the extent that public benefits are available to all, there is really no economically feasible way of determining how much value each person acquires. If a course in moral education, for example, reduces a community's crime rate, how much does each individual in the community benefit?

Since economic growth is offered as a reason for public investment in education, we might look at the contributions of education to growth. Table 3-2 provides estimates made by Edward Denison of the contributions of education to the growth rates of nine Western countries. The table reveals a number of interesting facets of the determinants of economic growth. The most glaring observation, that revealed in column 8, is the high percentage of growth unexplained by any input in the table. Another observation is the wide variation in the effects of education in different countries. Education seems to be much more important in the United States, Belgium, and the United Kingdom than in Germany or France. Although the government is obligated under the Employment Act of 1946 to maintain an adequate rate of economic growth, it is not clear how much the public should pay for a half a percentage point of growth a year.

Perhaps we can most accurately measure some of the noneconomic externalities of education, particularly the effects of public education on the dis-

---

[26] Richard B. Freeman, *Black Elite: The New Market for Highly Educated Black Americans* (New York: McGraw-Hill, 1976).

[27] Schultz, "The Human Capital Approach," p. 53.

TABLE 3-2

Sources of Economic Growth in Nine Western Nations: 1950–1962

| Area | Total Growth* (1) | Contributions of Factor Inputs | | | | Increased Output per Unit of Input (6) | Proportion of Total Growth Explained By | |
		Physical Capital (2)	Employment (3)	Education (4)	Other Labor Adjustments** (5)		Education (7)	Output per Unit of Input (8)
United States	3.36	0.83	0.90	0.49	-0.27	1.41	15	42
Italy	5.95	0.70	0.42	0.40	0.14	4.29	7	72
Northwestern Europe:								
Total	4.70	0.86	0.71	0.23	-0.11	3.01	5	64
Belgium	3.03	0.41	0.40	0.43	-0.07	1.86	14	61
Denmark	3.36	0.96	0.70	0.14	-0.25	1.81	4	54
France	4.70	0.79	0.08	0.29	0.08	3.46	6	74
Germany	7.26	1.41	1.49	0.11	-0.23	4.48	2	62
Netherlands	4.52	1.04	0.78	0.24	-0.15	2.61	5	58
Norway	3.47	0.89	0.13	0.24	-0.22	2.43	7	70
United Kingdom	2.38	0.51	0.50	0.29	-0.19	1.27	12	53

*All growth rates are in percentage points per annum.
**Adjustments are for mean hours worked and changes in the age and sex composition of the labor force.

Source: Edward F. Denison, *Why Growth Rates Differ* (Washington: The Brookings Institution, 1967), Tables 21–1 through 21–20, reprinted in Mary Jean Bowman, "Education and Economic Growth," *Economic Factors Affecting the Financing of Education* (Gainesville, Florida: National Educational Finance Project, 1970).

tribution of personal income. In general, and contrary to the widely held belief that public education tends to equalize income differences, it appears that more education (and the earning power that goes with it) is distributed to higher income than to lower income families. Evidence comes from a variety of sources.[28] If we measure education in terms of educational outputs, the evidence clearly shows that children from low-income and socially disadvantaged families do not perform as well as their middle- and upper-income classmates. According to the National Advisory Commission on Civil Disorders, "in the critical skills—verbal and reading ability—Negro students are falling further behind whites with each year of school completed."[29] Many other studies report the same findings.[30]

Evidence that more education is distributed to higher than to lower income families is also available if education is measured in terms of educational inputs, that is, the opportunity to become educated. In most states, property taxes pay the largest share of local school costs. High-wealth districts, those that boast more high-income families, are able to spend more per pupil at equivalent tax rates than property-poor districts.

The tendency for public education subsidies to favor high-income families is even stronger in higher education. In a study of higher education in California, Hansen and Weisbrod concluded:

> Some low income persons have benefitted handsomely from the availability of publicly subsidized higher education. But on the whole, the effect of these subsidies is to promote greater rather than less inequality among people of various social and economic backgrounds by making available substantial subsidies that lower income families are either not eligible for or cannot make use of because of other conditions and constraints associated with their income position.[31]

They found that a greater proportion of children from high-income families attended California's institutions of higher education than from low-income families; that those from high-income families tended to enroll in the more prestigious and expensive University of California while the children of low-income families frequently attended junior colleges; that students from high-income backgrounds stayed in school longer—thus were receiving state subsidies longer;

[28] See W. Lee Hansen and Burton A. Weisbrod, *Benefits, Costs and Finance of Public Higher Education* (Chicago: Markham Publishing Company, 1969).

[29] *Report of the National Advisory Commission on Civil Disorders* (New York: Bantam Books, 1968), p. 25.

[30] See James S. Coleman et al. *Equality of Educational Opportunity,* U.S. Department of Health, Education, and Welfare, Office of Education (Washington: Government Printing Office, 1966).

[31] Hansen and Weisbrod, *Benefits, Costs and Finance,* pp. 77–78.

and that because of their superior education, students from high-income families could look forward to higher lifetime earnings than those from low-income families.[32] Hansen and Weisbrod go on to generalize their findings to other states:

> What we have found to be true in California—an exceedingly unequal distribution of subsidies provided through public higher education—quite probably is even more true for other states. No state has such an extensive system of local Junior Colleges as does California, and for this reason, no state has such a large percentage of its high school graduates going on to public higher education. As a result we can be rather confident that California has a smaller percentage of its young people receiving a zero subsidy than do other states.[33]

Public education provides a number of external benefits which, although difficult to measure, justify public intervention. The current methods of funding and rationing education do not, however, seem to reduce income inequalities in the United States. If government intends to use education to promote income equality, it should then change many of its methods of funding and distributing education. Even with more equitable financing it may be necessary to increase public investments in housing, early childhood education, and compensatory education in order to make much progress toward greater social equality. In higher education, a greater proportion of government support should be allocated *directly to students,* with those from low-income families receiving the lion's share. As we noted in Chapter Two, however, equality is not the only value deserving attention in public policy making.

Supply and Demand for Public Education

Assuming there is a system of free, public education, the question remains, How much public education is enough? Are there some guidelines to assist the American people in deciding when to stop public spending on education— or when to increase it? Ultimately, the decision as to how much education is enough is made politically, a topic we will discuss at length in Chapter Thirteen. In this section we examine the economic factors which affect the supply and demand for educational services. After we have clarified the term *supply and demand,* we will examine the special problems of measuring the market for public education. Finally, we will point out some other factors, in addition to supply and demand, which affect the price and quantity of education provided.

[32]*Ibid.,* chap. 2.
[33]*Ibid.,* p. 78.

SUPPLY AND DEMAND

Economists have a proclivity to think about problems in terms of alternatives. Furthermore, they analyze human behavior from the point of view of an individual and assume that individuals do things to improve their well-being. Third, economists believe that everything worth having or doing is costly. It either costs money, takes time, or requires that something else be given up. We can now add another building block to the economist's model of human behavior. Since individuals attempt to improve their situations, and actions involve costs, other things being equal, people prefer less costly alternatives to more costly ones. Why? Because the cheaper they can obtain some good or service, the more money they have left to do the other things they enjoy.

These assumptions can now be formulated into a simple model of the supply and demand for education. We begin by observing that people desire education. Education, whether it is primary and secondary education, vocational education, or higher education, is something that people want and are willing to pay for. Consequently, there is a certain amount of it produced, which because it is costly has a price. The concepts of economic supply and demand can help us understand how much education is produced and how much it costs.

The relationship between demand and supply of education is illustrated in Figure 3-1. The demand curve, DD', depicts a relationship between the price of education and the quantity consumed. The demand curve slopes downward to the right indicating that as the price of education falls, the quantity consumed increases. Similarly, the supply curve, SS', shows the relationship between the price and the quantity which will be made available for consumption. The supply curve slopes upward to the right indicating that as the quantity of schooling increases we must pay a higher price for each unit of it. Assuming decisions about the supply of education were left to the private market, such that only the private benefits of education are considered, an equilibrium would be reached at S_1. OA_1 of education would be produced at a price of A_1S_1 (or P_1). A decline in price from P_1 to P_3 increases the quantity demanded to OA_2. Since the marginal costs of producing OA_2 (that is, the cost of the last unit of education at OA_2) is A_2S_2, which is more than the amount consumers are willing to pay, A_2D_1, the quantity provided will decline and an equilibrium would eventually be reestablished at S_1. The actual response to changes in price depends on the steepness of the demand curve. If it is very steep (or inelastic),[34] then it would require a large decline in price to produce a small increase in quantity demanded.

---

[34]Elasticity refers to the responsiveness of the quantity demanded to a change in the price with the demand schedule unchanged. Demand is inelastic when the percentage change in quantity demanded is numerically less than the percentage change in price.

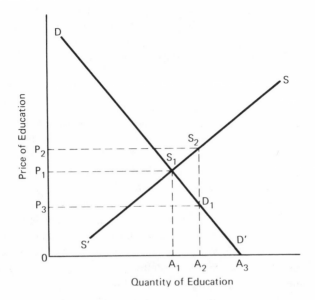

FIG. 3-1. Price and quantity of education.

Conversely, if the demand curve were almost horizontal (or elastic) then a small decline in price would result in a large increase in the quantity of education demanded.

Suppose now that the public or external benefits of education are sufficiently large that the community decides to increase the quantity of education being supplied by the private market. If it felt that education produced $A_1 A_2$ of public benefits, then the price would have to be lowered to $A_2 D_1$ (or P_3) to entice individuals to consume that much. In order to persuade suppliers to produce OA_2 of education they would have to receive a price of P_2, and the community would have to subsidize the suppliers by the amount $D_1 S_2$. If a community wanted to increase the quantity of education to OA_3 it would have to make education free for the consumer and subsidize the entire amount from public sources.

PROBLEMS IN MEASURING DEMAND FOR EDUCATION

This simple model of the supply and demand for education can provide some useful insights into the way education is provided in our society. Interpretation of such an analysis, however, is made unusually complicated by many peculiarities of education.

A major problem in measuring the quantity of education is describing what education is. There are really two answers to the question. Education can be defined as either the amount of knowledge or education a student receives, or as the amount of opportunity a student is given to become educated.[35] We have already discussed this problem in terms of alternative measures of equal educational opportunity, that is, whether you define education as equal outcomes or equal access to education.

We often measure education differently depending on whether we are talking about primary or secondary and higher education.[36] Assume that a teacher spends an equal amount of time teaching two students, one of whom is precocious and the other average. At the end of a period of instruction, the precocious child will probably be able to perform better than the average child. The question is whether the two have received the same amount of education. If you use an output definition of education they have not; the precocious child has received more education. If you use an opportunity to become educated measure, they have. Which of the two definitions is appropriate depends on what is considered to be the educational demand that exists at the time. If we are talking about learning basic abilities to read, write, and compute, skills the community believes absolutely necessary for minimum citizenship, then the appropriate measure is minimum performance, and extra attention for the slower student is expected and provided. In secondary school and higher education, however, no one expects that every student will achieve the same results, so the opportunity to learn is an acceptable measure of educational output. Again the demands are different at the two levels. The external benefits in primary education accrue to others only if most children achieve minimum literacy. In higher education the external benefits accrue if a few students become engineers or researchers who carry out socially beneficial research. Who achieves the level of useful skills depends more on inherent ability and individual motivation than on the number of years spent in a classroom. Despite these distinctions, we usually measure education by the amount of time spent being educated. Knowledge gained or education received, it is hoped, bears some relationship to the amount of time spent in the classroom.

COSTS OF EDUCATION

The direct costs of education depend on many factors, including the number of students to be educated, the type of education they receive, the distribution of students over an area, the number of years of education provided, and the quality of educational services. Total costs of education in the United States have increased dramatically since 1960 in part because of the increasing school population. There have been more school-age children, they have stayed in school longer, and more of them have gone on to college—particularly more

[35] Carl S. Shoup, *Public Finance* (Chicago: Aldine Publishing Company, 1969), p. 129.
[36] *Ibid.*

blacks and women. Many younger and older people who were traditionally excluded from school are now being provided public educations: mentally and physically handicapped children, children with learning disabilities, preschool children, pregnant girls, and many adults. Since the early 1970s a declining birth rate has relieved some of the pressure on public schools, yet this has to some degree been offset by the larger proportion of children and adults attending school.

If the number of persons educated remains constant, costs are likely to increase as additional requirements are added to school curricula, particularly if minimum achievement standards are required. Teaching students the rudimentaries of reading, writing, and arithmetic, and then permitting them to choose among a wide variety of electives and vocational skills, requires more classes and more teachers. School costs are largely made up of teacher salaries. The smaller the classes, the more teachers are required and the higher the costs. Costs are also likely to rise, assuming numbers of students remain constant, if remedial instruction is needed for slow students and average students from socially disadvantaged families to bring them up to minimum standards. A look at almost any large city in the United States would show unusually large expenditures for remedial or compensatory education. Even the wealthiest among the cities, however, is not spending enough to assure that every child meets minimum requirements to complete primary school.

Educational costs are affected by the geographic distribution of children. With a given number of students and a given level of achievement, costs increase with the dispersion of students. Small inefficient buildings, small class sizes, and high transportation costs are inevitable. Total costs are reduced when students are more concentrated, although the optimal number of students is smaller than one would think. Large school districts, those with more than 15,000 to 20,000 students, suffer from higher per student costs resulting from additional administrative burdens, increased allowances for maintenance and vandalism, higher security costs, etc. (See discussions of this topic in Chapters 4 and 15.)

The indirect, or opportunity, costs of schooling vary depending on the level of schooling and family background. The opportunity costs of higher education are substantial since a student must forego an adult income to attend college. Opportunity costs at the secondary level are much less, and for primary school children they are close to zero. Low-income farming families probably lose more from sending their children to school than do middle-income urban families.

PRICE AND QUANTITY OF EDUCATION

If education were provided on a free market basis, the price and quantity of education would be determined by the intersection of community demand and supply curves. However, since most education is provided publicly, decisions about how much education is enough are shifted from the marketplace to the political process. School boards and state legislatures, and ultimately the voters, establish the level of school services.

The separation between consuming education and providing education (paying taxes) creates an interesting situation regarding the supply of education. If we assume that the demand for education increases as price falls, then the practice of providing "free" education may result in relatively too many resources being devoted to public education. This occurs, some argue, because politicians generally attempt to be responsive to constituent demands. Such a conclusion, however, overlooks the important fact that many consumers of public services are also taxpayers. They must make decisions not only about how much education they want, but also about how much they can afford. In this dual role a taxpayer is likely to vote for a lower level of educational services than that dictated by expressed needs alone.[37] Assume that an individual is well informed and can make a reasonably accurate estimate of the tax costs of alternative levels of education. That individual is likely to vote for a tradeoff of taxes and services to suit his or her own preferences. As a participant in a political decision-making process, however, the individual cannot choose independently of the rest of the community. Thus the rational taxpayer will not vote to extend services to the point at which the community's marginal benefit from more education is near or close to zero—a position a consumer would choose if education were truly free. Rather he or she would vote for a level of service at which the marginal benefits at least equalled the marginal costs of additional school taxes.

Whether the equilibrium established by taxpayers weighing both the benefits and costs of education produces a level of services less than or greater than would be purchased privately depends on many factors. For instance, much depends on the proportion of families in a community with children in public schools. If we assume that school budgets require the approval of a majority of taxpayers then the per pupil expenditure is likely to be above the private equilibrium so long as more than a majority of voters have school-age children.[38] Furthermore, as the proportion of families with school-age children declines, but is still more than a majority, per pupil expenditures will increase. This occurs, of course, because as the number of families with children declines toward 50 percent, the tax price of education declines leading to greater demand. In other words, as the proportion of families with school-age children approaches 50 percent, a larger share of the total costs is passed on to taxpayers without

[37] For an interesting analysis of the difficulties created when the demand for a public service exceeds the willingness of taxpayers to pay for it, see James M. Buchanan, "The Inconsistencies of the National Health Service," in *Theory of Public Choice,* eds., James M. Buchanan and Robert D. Tollison, (Ann Arbor: The University of Michigan Press, 1972), pp. 27–45.

[38] Private equilibrium is the amount that would be provided if education were a private activity.

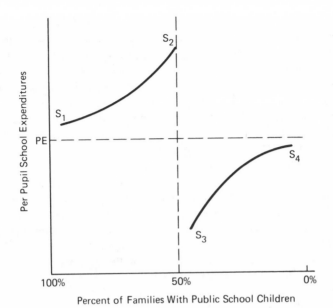

FIG. 3-2. School expenditures and percentage of families with school-age children.

school-age children. The relationship between per pupil school expenditures and percentage of families with school-age children is illustrated in Figure 3-2.

The situation is different when the number of taxpayers receiving private benefits from education (those with children in school) drops below 50 percent. In this case, provision of public schooling is likely to be below the private equilibrium. The average voter now receives only external educational benefits and is likely to vote for a school budget which only provides schooling to cover minimum standards. Again, the per pupil school expenditures are likely to increase as the proportion of families with schoolchildren declines below 50 percent. This occurs because even the demand for external educational benefits is likely to increase as tax price falls.[39]

This analysis of the effects of majority voting on school budgets overlooks many financial and organizational factors which smooth out the curves depicted in Figure 3-2. It does help explain, however, the difficulty of passing school budgets in many large cities. Typically, the proportion of families with schoolchildren is much lower in the cities than in rural or suburban school districts. It is almost impossible to obtain budget overrides or special levies because so few people have a direct interest in school programs. As a consequence, school tax rates in urban areas are generally below average. Most remedial and compensa-

---

[39] As the number of children declines, the average tax price of receiving the public benefits of education also declines thereby increasing the demand for those benefits.

tory programs are paid for from federal or state funds, and even they have been inadequate to ensure the achievement of minimal educational performance.

Another factor affecting the price and quantity of education is the relationship between school boards, which generally approve budgets, and the school bureaucracy. William Niskanen has analyzed this relationship and theorized that there is a tendency for legislative bodies, such as school boards, to approve budgets that are larger than would result from equating marginal benefits (both private and public) and marginal costs.[40] The following paragraphs translate Niskanen's argument into a school district setting.

A school bureaucracy does not normally sell its services to consumers. Instead, it offers a proposed set of programs to a school board in return for a budget.[41] The school board, in turn, obtains its money from tax revenues. The primary financial constraint facing a school bureaucracy is the size of the budget it receives. A less direct constraint is the proportion of personal income the public is willing to turn over to the school board for education. A school bureaucracy has no alternative source of funds except those provided by the school board. Consequently, the personal preferences of the officials on the school board are more likely to be considered in preparing a district's budget than are the preferences of the school clientele.

The relationship between school board and school bureaucracy is not a typical superior-subordinate relationship, however. In fact, the school bureaucracy is in a good position to dominate the relationship and to obtain benefits for itself in the process. School boards, it is true, are elected, exercise control over budgets, monitor the bureaucracy's procedures and performance, and select the school superintendent. The power of the bureaucracy over the school board, however, arises from the board's legal responsibility to provide educational services, and dependence on the district staff as the only supplier of educational services. According to Niskanen, the monopoly position of the bureaucracy gives it a clear bargaining advantage:

> Under many conditions it gives a bureau [superintendent and administrative staff] the same type of bargaining power as a profit-seeking monopoly that discriminates among customers or that presents the market with an all-or-nothing choice. The primary reason for the differential bargaining power of a monopoly bureau is the sponsor's lack of a significant alternative and its unwillingness to forego the services supplied by the bureau. Also . . . the interests of those officers of the collective organization responsible for reviewing the bureau are often best served by allowing the bureau to exploit this monopoly power.[42]

From the viewpoint of the school bureaucracy, the preferences of the

---

[40]William A. Niskanen, Jr., *Bureaucracy and Representative Government* (Chicago: Aldine Atherton, Inc., 1971).

[41]*Ibid.,* p. 25.

[42]*Ibid.*

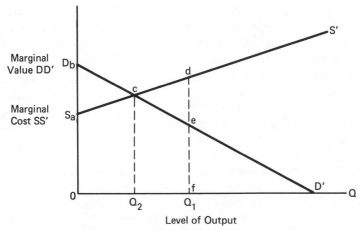

FIG. 3-3. Equilibrium output of a bureau.

Source: Derived from William A. Niskanen, Jr., *Bureaucracy and Representative Government* (Chicago: Aldine Atherton, Inc., 1971), p. 47.

school board are summarized in a budget-output function. "Any point on this function represents the maximum budget the sponsor (school board) is willing to grant to the bureau for a specific expected level of output."[43] The budget-output relationship is such that the school board is willing to provide a larger budget for a higher level of expected output. As output increases, however, the amount of budget increase a school board is willing to provide decreases. This means that the school board's marginal budget-output function (or demand curve) declines as output increases. The important point is that the school board's demand for schooling may not be entirely congruent with that of the community being served.

Assuming that bureaucrats are primarily motivated to maximize the size of their budgets,[44] it is then possible to illustrate how the budget review process limits the budget and output of a school bureaucracy. According to Niskanen, a school bureaucracy will submit to the school board a budget "which maximizes the expected approved budget subject to the constraint that the approved budget must be sufficient to cover the costs of the output expected by the sponsor at the budget level."[45]

The expected level of output is illustrated in Figure 3-3. The school board's marginal valuation of the school bureaucracy's services is represented by DD'. Assuming a marginal cost function SS', the approved budget and output

[43] *Ibid.*
[44] For a defense of this assumption, see Niskanen, *Bureaucracy*, chap. 3.
[45] *Ibid.*, p. 46.

will be Q_1, the point which provides the maximum balanced budget. At this level of output, Q_1, the total budget O_{feb} (amount preferred by the school board) just covers the minimum total costs of producing the same output, O_{fda}. The district will be providing services for which the marginal benefits to the school board, fe, are less than the marginal costs, fd, or at a level above the optimal output level where marginal value equals marginal cost, Q_2. Bargaining will continue up to a point where all the net benefits (acb) which would accrue from an optimal level of service are wiped out by the net costs (ced) of operating above the optimal level, Q_2.

In terms of an efficient allocation of resources, the public budget constraint on the supply of education may be even less adequate than it appears, because school boards are likely to overrepresent both those groups in the community that prefer high levels of educational services *and* those groups sympathetic toward teachers. To the extent that this happens, the marginal valuation function shown in Figure 3-3 will be higher than would a function reflecting the average citizen's demand for educational services.

This analysis of the supply and demand for education has taken into account a variety of peculiar features of education. Determination of the price and quantity of education depends on the definition of education, on the interests of adults in the education of their own and others' children, and on a variety of institutional factors through which education is financed and provided. We have examined the dual role that citizens must play as both consumers of education and as taxpayers, and concluded that the level of services provided by taxpayers is less than they would demand as the recipients of free, public education. We also noted that the interaction between school bureaucracy and school boards tends to produce a level of services in excess of that which equates marginal benefit and cost.

Summary

This chapter has examined the role of government in education. In providing educational experiences from the kindergarten level through graduate school, government confers benefits on those in school, as well as on many who are not. These private and public benefits of education provide justification and support for government financing and provision of education. They do not, however, provide policy makers with a clear rule for deciding when to stop spending for public education.

"How much education is enough?" is actually politically determined. This political decision depends on the forces of demand and supply for education. We have examined factors affecting educational demand and supply, noting in particular several political impediments to decisions that would be optimal from an economic perspective. Even if these impediments were removed, actual decisions on how much to spend for education will also be affected by purely external factors, such as changing population characteristics. Declining birth rate will reduce pressures for expansion of public education. This conclusion, however, masks many other developments which are likely to take place within constrained educational budgets. For example, since birth rates have declined most sharply among high-income, well-educated groups, school children are likely, on the average, to be less well prepared than their peers in the past. This will increase pressures for more preschool education and for more remedial and compensatory education. The increasing proportion of older people in the society may also affect education in unforeseen ways. They may demand some educational benefits for themselves in the form of adult education programs. Most likely, the needs of older people for transportation, welfare services, and police protection may crowd education out of first place on the political agenda.

Education is financed largely out of public budgets. Consequently, education will be affected by the structure of public spending in the future. Our ability to predict future events is not very good so we should expect the unexpected. If, for example, military expenditures were reduced as a result of international treaties limiting the production of military equipment, substantial amounts of money would be released, for which education would make a claim. If, on the other hand, the international situation worsens, military expenditures would increase and education might lose some of its share of public monies. Somewhat more certain is the effect the underfunding of our social security system, veterans benefit programs, and state and local employee pension plans will have on the allocation of public dollars. Billions of future dollars have already been legally spent—dollars that will not be available for education regardless of future needs.

The prospects for major technological breakthroughs in the field of education are difficult to estimate. Many suggestions have been made for rearrangements in the processes, organization, and financing of education. Educational vouchers, banks that would loan money to students in return for a percentage of future income, may substantially change public education. These and other innovations may catch on because of demonstrated successes—or more likely because of dramatic failures in traditional financing arrangements. Without major crises, however, it is not unreasonable to expect inertia and bureaucratic resistance—leaving education much as it has been in the past.

II

The Structure and Financing of Public Schools

4

THE ORGANIZATION
OF PUBLIC SCHOOLS

Knut Wicksell, a noted nineteenth-century political economist, wrote that the task of social theory is not to dictate what is equitable and efficient policy, but to specify the institutional framework in which equitable and efficient policies are likely to be chosen. In Chapter Two we examined the equity and efficiency implications of government involvement in education. In the next two chapters we describe the institutional framework in which decisions affecting the financing of education are made. This chapter examines the formal organization of public education and the sources of fiscal strain affecting it. Chapter Five analyzes the implications of collective bargaining in public education. In both chapters we will be concerned primarily with the institutional framework of public education and how it can be changed to produce equitable and efficient educational policy.

An Economist's Approach to Organizational Analysis

This chapter views the organization of public education from the point of view of an economist. An economist's trademark is a predisposition to think about issues in terms of alternatives.[1] We assume there are many ways to organ-

[1] The centrality of alternatives to an economist is aptly described in the following comment by James Buchanan:

ize public schools, and that different organizational arrangements are likely to create different educational experiences and outcomes. Organizations in themselves are neither good nor bad. They can, however, be evaluated in terms of their likely effects on desired outcomes. Much of economic analysis is concerned with questions of efficiency—whether a particular form of organization is more or less efficient than another. Economic concepts and approaches may also be used to ascertain the consequences of alternative organizational arrangements on the equity and responsiveness of public services.

This perspective contrasts with that frequently held by educators. Many educators assume that choices about the governance and financing of schools are made externally, presumably by legislators or others who do not participate in the day-to-day operation of schools. As a result, most of the literature by and for educators on the organization of education lacks analysis of the incentives or biases toward specific results built into different kinds of educational organizations. Actually, educators do have influence over the organization of education and can benefit from analyzing it.

Several economic concepts are instrumental in understanding organizations. Foremost in the study of economics is the individual. Only individuals possess values, make choices, and take actions. We frequently hear that "the legislature enacted a bill" or "the school board decided to do something." In fact, only individuals take actions. It is important to know what individuals are involved, how they arrived at their joint decisions, and the consequences of their joint decisions on those individuals and on future decisions of the group. Throughout the chapter we will focus on educational organizations as collections of individual decision makers and on the constraints and incentives the organization provides them.

A related concept is that individuals act with a purpose. That purpose is to improve their well-being; to change from a situation that is less desired to one that is more desired. The assumption that individuals act with a purpose, or act rationally, does not mean they are selfish or are free to do as they like. It means that given a choice, they will choose to improve their situation, or avoid or reduce something they do not want. Organizations can be viewed as a set of opportunities to and restrictions on the ability of people to improve their well-being. We try to emphasize how current and alternative educational organizational arrangements allow individuals to improve their situations. In particular,

---

The economist's stock-in-trade—his tools—lies in his ability to and proclivity to think about all questions in terms of alternatives. The truth judgment of the moralist, which says that something is either wholly right or wholly wrong, is foreign to him. The win-lose, yes-no discussion of politics is not within his purview. He does not recognize the either-or, the all-or-nothing, situation as his own. His is not the world of the mutually exclusives. Instead, his is the world of adjustment, of coordinated conflict, of mutual gain. ["Economics and Its Scientific Neighbors," in *The Structure of Economic Science: Essays on Methodology,* ed. Sherman Roy Krupp (Englewood Cliffs, N.J.: Prentice Hall, Inc., 1966), p. 168.]

we are concerned about the ability of the public—parents and citizens—to achieve their interests in public education.

Equally central to economics is the notion that every action is costly. "There is no such thing as a free lunch," as economics professors have been known to warn their beginning students. Estimating the costs of alternative forms of action is an important step in any decisional process. Too frequently people unfamiliar with economic concepts assume that if private actions are too costly, government should take over. They overlook the costs of government action which may be more than the private costs they hope to eliminate.[2]

In public activity there are two important costs that must be kept in mind. Since public choices, once made, are binding on every member of a community, they impose costs on those members of the community who disagree with the decision. These are external costs of collective choice.[3] Public actions also impose decision-making costs on those involved in the decisions. Decision-making costs are the time, energy, and resources needed to reach a joint decision.

We assume there are alternatives to the current structure of public education that may be more efficient, equitable, and responsive. Furthermore, we assume that individuals who are involved in public education take actions, both within the current organizational structure and to change that structure, which are purposive. Finally, public activity imposes both external costs and decision-making costs which must be considered when selecting the appropriate form of educational organization. We view educational organizations as an arrangement of more or less stable rules and procedures designed to produce results that benefit the participants in public education. Sometimes the rules favor parents and students. Sometimes they favor administrators and teachers. Organizations are the result of conscious choices which the designers of the organizations believed would promote their interests. Or in the words of Cohen, March, and Olesen,

> . . . an organization is a collection of choices looking for problems, issues and feelings looking for decision situations in which they might be aired, solutions looking for issues to which they might be the answer, and decision makers looking for work.[4]

The next section of this chapter describes the organization of American schools and analyzes its important features. Subsequent sections examine problems

---

[2] For an analysis of this point see James M. Buchanan, "Politics, Policy, and the Pigovian Margins," in *Theory of Public Choice,* eds. James M. Buchanan and Robert Tollison (Ann Arbor: The University of Michigan Press, 1972), pp. 169–82.

[3] The costs of collective action are analyzed in great detail in James M. Buchanan and Gordon Tullock, *The Calculus of Consent* (Ann Arbor: The University of Michigan Press, 1962).

[4] Michael D. Cohen, James G. March, and Johan P. Olesen, "A Garbage Can Model of Organizational Choice," *Administrative Science Quarterly,* 17 No. 1, (March 1972), 2.

facing public schools and several major issues underlying proposals for reforming the structure of public education.

Public Schools in The United States

Primary and secondary education in the United States is by almost any measure a large endeavor. For example, in 1975–76 public primary and secondary education ranked third only to defense and income security as a consumer of public funds. In that year, $67.1 billion was spent to educate an estimated 44.8 million children enrolled in public schools.[5] An additional $6.3 billion was spent to educate approximately 5 million children enrolled in private primary and secondary schools.

To serve the public school population, approximately 2.4 million teachers and other educational professionals are on the public's payroll.[6] Teachers' organizations now are among the most organized and influential political lobbies in the country. They are a major source of campaign funds at the state and local levels in many states, and they are one of the most active lobbies during most state legislative sessions. Many teachers now serve on school boards and in state legislatures. Educators and their families now account for a larger segment of our population than the historically powerful farm bloc.[7]

THE GOVERNANCE OF AMERICAN PUBLIC SCHOOLS

Although the management of most large industries is centralized and specific, the management of American public education is decentralized and diffused. Public schools are governed within a federal structure in which local, state, and federal governments each have important and overlapping roles.

LOCAL SCHOOL DISTRICTS

Because of the belief that individual freedom can be best protected if government is in the hands of small, self-governing communities, and the generally high regard Americans have for local government, every state except Hawaii has

[5] National Center for Educational Statistics, *Statistics of Public Elementary and Secondary Day Schools, Fall, 1975* (Washington, D.C.: U.S. Government Printing Office, 1976), pp. 22 and 36.

[6] *Ibid.,* p. 14.

[7] The growing power of the educational lobby, particularly at the state level, is discussed in a number of books. See Frederick M. Wirt and Michael Kirst, *The Political Web of American Schools* (Boston: Little, Brown and Company, 1972), chap. 7; Harmon Ziegler and Michael Baer, *Lobbying* (Belmont, Cal.: Wadsworth Publishing Company, 1969).

delegated the major responsibility for operating and financing public schools to local school districts. They are the basic administrative unit in the organization of schools and are the means through which local communities control their schools.

Most school districts are units of special government, created and empowered by state law to administer public schools.[8] They have the power to tax, the right to enter into contracts, and the right to sue and be sued. Independent school districts are legally controlled by elected governing boards. These governing boards generally employ a superintendent to implement the decisions of the school board. Despite the formal independence of school districts, there are many informal ties between school districts and local government. These ties are growing increasingly close as cities become aware of the importance of good schooling to the survival of the cities themselves.

School district relationships with state government are both legal and financial. State laws and regulations specify who shall attend schools, the length of the school year, the rules for establishing and changing district boundaries, required courses, and numerous other aspects of local school operations. State governments also provide a substantial proportion of local school district revenues, accounting for 43 percent of total public school revenues in 1974-75. The bulk of the remaining revenues is raised from local sources, but state laws specify the form of taxes school districts may use and in many states restrict the amounts raised from local sources.

Local school district relationships with the federal government are minor. Districts with children working on federal facilities or living on federal property receive direct financial assistance through federal impact aid programs.[9] Urban school districts also receive some funds directly from the federal government for special programs. Federal funds account for only about eight percent of school district revenues in 1975-76, although in a few states (Mississippi, 21.2 percent; New Mexico, 20.6 percent) they are much greater.

STATE ROLE IN PUBLIC SCHOOLS

State government is the focal point in educational policy making. In fact, education is the responsibility of the states or the people, since it is not one of the functions specifically delegated by the Constitution to the federal government. At the state level several groups have important roles in the governance of public schools. State constitutions, statutes, and considerable practical experience make the state legislatures ultimately accountable for public education.

---

[8] Approximately 10 percent of the school districts are fiscally dependent upon municipal governments and do not share all of the powers of their independent counterparts.

[9] Federal impact aid programs PL 815 and PL 874 will be described in more detail in Chapter Seven.

They have final authority to create and empower school districts, counties, and in some cases, regional agencies, to provide educational services. They justly deserve the appellation, "the big school board."[10] Within the legislature, education committees generally are responsible for bills involving educational policy.

Most of the day-to-day administration of public education, and much of the staff work needed by the legislature for policy making, is carried out by state executive agencies. Governors, state boards of education, chief state school officers, and state departments of education all participate in educational governance at the state level. The importance of each, however, varies among states.

Governors influence educational policy by heading a political party, developing legislative programs, and controlling the state budget. In 1970, for example, Governor Wendell Anderson of Minnesota ran on a platform promising reform of the state's school finance system. Once elected, he used the power of the governor's office to steer his school finance proposals through the state legislature.[11] Perhaps a governor's most potent means of control is the budgetary process. A chief state school officer or a state teachers' organization may recommend bills and have them considered by the legislature. Unless provision for the legislation is contained in the governor's budget, however, its chances of passage are slim. Finally, a governor influences educational policy through the right to veto legislation and the right to appoint members of state boards of education.

In almost every state, a state board of education is given general supervision of the public schools. Members are usually unpaid laymen, appointed by the governor, and tend to have little actual influence in policy making.[12] The State Board of Regents in New York and the State Board of Education in California are exceptions that play active roles in educational policy making in the two states.[13] The state board of education delegates most administrative matters to the chief state school officer and the professional staff of the state education department.

The top professional educator in each state is the chief state school officer. In more than half of the states the chief state school officers are appointed by

---

[10] Roald F. Campbell, Luvern L. Cunningham, Roderick F. McPhee, and Raphael O. Nystrand, *The Organization and Control of American Schools* (2nd ed.) (Columbus, Ohio: Charles E. Merrill Publishing Company, 1970), p. 55.

[11] Anthony Morley, "Minnesota," in Education Commission of the States, *A Legislator's Guide to School Finance* (Denver, Colo.: Education Commission of the States, August 1972), pp. 33–35.

[12] For an analysis of how state boards of education could strengthen their policy-making role, see Michael W. Kirst, "Strengthening and Improving Relationships between State Boards of Education and Legislators," in National Association of State Boards of Education, *The Imperative of Leadership* (Denver, Colo.: NASEBE, October 1975), pp. 5–15.

[13] The role of the State Board of Regents in New York State is discussed in Stephen K. Bailey et al., *Schoolmen and Politics* (Syracuse: Syracuse University Press, 1962).

the state board of education. In about 20 states, however, they are elected by a statewide constituency. The chief state school officer is the nominal top executive of the state education department and serves the state board of education much as a school district superintendent serves the school board. However, he or she is also expected to advise the legislature and the governor on matters of educational policy. This advisory role is complicated in states electing their education executive because the governor and the chief state school officer may be chosen by constituencies with conflicting expectations.

Finally, the administrative functions of the state are carried out by the state department of education. In most states, state education departments are small and involved mainly in administering state education programs. The state education bureaucracies in New York, Illinois, and California, however, are larger than those in most other states, and play active and influential roles in the development of state education policy.

THE FEDERAL ROLE
IN EDUCATIONAL GOVERNANCE

The federal role in public education is a relatively minor one, but certainly not one that is likely to disappear in the foreseeable future. When the Constitution was drafted, education was not one of the functions delegated to the federal government—there was no system of public education—and thus under the terms of the Tenth Amendment, it was reserved for the states and the people.[14] Despite these factors the federal government has always had a hand in public education, and whenever the national interest was involved has not been reluctant to act vigorously. The Morrill Act in 1862 establishing the land grant colleges, the Smith-Hughes Act in 1917 providing support for vocational education, and the Elementary and Secondary Education Act of 1965 providing financial aid to low-income students are just a few examples of federal initiatives in public education.

Federal courts have also intervened in the area of public schooling. No single judicial decision has affected public schools more than the 1954 Supreme Court decision mandating racial desegregation. More recently, federal court rulings on student rights and the rights of handicapped and non-English speaking students have led to changes in the conduct of local schools.[15]

[14] Amendment X of the Constitution states, "The powers not delegated to the United States by the Constitution, nor prohibited by it to the States, are reserved to the States respectively, or to the people."

[15] On due process for students, see *Dixon* v. *Alabama Board of Education,* 194 F2d 150 (5th Cir, 1961); on the constitutional rights of exceptional children, see *Mills* v. *Board of Education,* 348 F. Supp. 866 (D D C, 1972); on rights of non-English speaking students see *Lau* v. *Nichols,* 483 F2d (9th Cir, 1973).

IMPORTANT FEATURES
OF PUBLIC SCHOOL ORGANIZATION

ABSENCE OF PLANNING

At the federal level there is almost no systematic educational planning. The federal government reacts to crises; witness, for example, its funding of science programs after the Russian Sputnik launching. For the most part, there is no national educational policy that works its way down to local school districts.

Although the states have legal responsibility for the establishment and operation of public schools, they have delegated most of the financial and operating responsibilities to local school districts. States legislatures do, of course, enact laws and issue regulations affecting local school districts, but they do not normally develop comprehensive education plans to guide allocation of state resources or development of program criteria. What little ad hoc educational planning exists is totally unrelated to other areas of social policy such as housing, income maintenance, or land use. A flagrant example is the lack of coordination on both state and federal levels between plans to integrate schools and urban housing policies, which tend to resegregate these same areas. Then, too, school building programs seeking the cheapest land outside the urban fringe conflict with land-use plans to control the dispersion of metropolitan populations. Part of the problem is that most state departments of education do not collect, analyze, or publicize data that are needed for educational planning. Even if such information were available, there are few incentives in the political system to encourage comprehensive, long-term planning of educational programs.

What little coordination there is in public education occurs at the local level. A few large school districts have offices of planning and attempt to forecast needs and develop programs to meet them. Most districts, however, operate on a year-to-year basis. Compulsory attendance laws and attendance areas eliminate most of the incentives for schools to be responsive to changing community preferences for education. What has occurred in the past largely determines the trend of future offerings.

DIVERSITY

A newcomer to public education must be struck by the uniformity and, at the same time, the diversity of public primary and secondary education. Most districts are uniformly organized with school boards, superintendents, primary schools, secondary schools, principals, department heads, and classroom teachers. Whether you are in New York City or Amity, Oregon, classrooms, curricula, and the school day appear remarkably similar.

This semblance of uniformity cannot hide the vast differences among school districts, however. The nation's largest school district, New York City, has over a million students, whereas the average school district enrolls fewer than 3,000 students. The median school district is smaller yet. Over 95 percent of the school children in Washington, D.C. are black, while in neighboring Fairfax County, Virginia, blacks account for only 3.3 percent of the student population.[16]

The diversity among school districts is particularly noticeable when school district finances are compared. These differences occur both among states and within states. Table 4-1 provides 1975-76 data on the fiscal dimensions of public schools in the 50 states. The federal share of state educational costs varies from a high of 21.2 percent in Mississippi to a low of 3.8 percent in Michigan. Since most federal aid is distributed according to the number of children eligible for ESEA Title I and impact area programs, there is little a state or school district can do to increase the amount of federal aid it receives. A number of state governments provide more than 60 percent of local school costs, among them Delaware, Hawaii, North Carolina, and Alabama. The state share of the fiscal costs of schools in New Hampshire, South Dakota, Massachusetts, and Nebraska, on the other hand, is less than a quarter of the total. The total school expenditures per child varies from a high of $2179 in New York to a low of $881 in Arkansas. Average teacher salaries are more than twice as high in Alaska as in Oklahoma.

There is also considerable variation in the tax structures among the 50 states. Some states such as Washington, New Hampshire, and Florida have no state personal income tax. Others such as Oregon and Missouri have no sales tax. Perhaps the best picture of the diversity in state and local tax structure can be seen by comparing the distribution of state and local tax burdens relative to family income. Table 4-2 provides these data for six states in 1974. On the average, state and local taxes decrease as a percentage of family income as income increases. In Washington and Texas a family with an income of $50,000 pays about a third as high a percentage of its income as does a family earning only $5,000, which means that these states' tax structures are more regressive than the national average. In Oregon, on the other hand, state and local taxes increase as a percentage of family income as income increases, making their tax structure progressive. States such as New York, Minnesota, and Connecticut have relatively high overall state and local tax burdens. In Texas the rates are well below average. (See Chapter Six for extensive discussion of tax burdens.)

Within states there are also wide disparities among school districts in the wealth, school tax rates, and revenues raised per pupil. Property taxes are the largest source of revenues for public schools. Consequently, the property wealth of each school district largely determines its ability to finance public schools. Table 4-3 compares the 1968-69 assessed property valuation, tax rates, and expenditures per ADA (average daily attendance) in Beverly Hills and Baldwin Park, California, two districts made famous by the Serrano case, discussed in

---

[16]National Center for Educational Statistics, *The Condition of Education*, p. 171.

TABLE 4-1   A Statistical Profile: Education in the States, 1975-76

| State | Revenue Sources for Public Elementary and Secondary Schools | | | | Expenditure per Pupil (ADA) | Average Salaries for Classroom Teachers | Pupil/Teacher Ratio in ADA |
	% Federal	% State	% Intermediate	% Local			
UNITED STATES	8.0	43.7	.5	47.8	$1,388	$12,448	18.8
Alabama	16.1	63.5	—	20.4	1,090	10,597	19.5
Alaska	15.1	64.9	—	20.0	2,096	19,312	18.4
Arizona	10.5	47.8	.4	41.2	1,415	12,394	20.0
Arkansas	15.5	52.2	—	32.3	881	9,648	19.4
California	9.2	40.4	—	50.4	1,320	15,200	20.9
Colorado	6.8	39.8	NA	53.4	1,422	12,000	19.7
Connecticut	4.1	27.7	NA	68.2	1,659	11,874	16.9
Delaware	8.0	67.7	—	24.3	1,606	12,545	18.5
District of Columbia	17.8	—	—	82.2	1,954	15,297	17.6
Florida	6.2	54.6	—	39.2	1,381	10,496	20.1
Georgia	12.1	51.9	—	36.0	1,114	10,622	20.9
Hawaii	7.3	92.7	—	—	1,545	15,209	20.7
Idaho	10.9	49.5	2.9	36.7	1,112	10,212	20.4
Illinois	6.2	46.2	.1	47.6	1,452	NA	17.9
Indiana	5.7	40.6	.4	53.3	1,160	11,165*	20.5
Iowa	4.6	38.0	—	57.4	1,455	11,570	17.0
Kansas	11.6	43.8	—	44.6	1,475	10,710	16.3
Kentucky	14.6	54.3	—	31.1	986	9,770	20.1
Louisiana	17.5	55.7	—	26.8	1,082	10,092	18.5
Maine	8.1	44.6	—	47.3	1,197	10,620	18.5
Maryland	5.7	39.5	—	54.8	1,516	13,709	18.7
Massachusetts	4.1	23.5	—	72.4	NA	11,900	NA
Michigan	3.8	51.7	—	44.4	1,366	15,540	21.9
Minnesota	5.5	54.7	.4	39.3	1,516	12,261	18.9
Mississippi	21.2	55.0	—	23.8	997	9,314	20.1
Missouri	8.2	35.0	5.9	51.0	1,186	10,490	17.6
Montana	6.1	57.6	7.2	29.1	1,554	11,000	18.0
Nebraska	7.4	17.6	3.2	71.8	1,302	10,017	16.6
Nevada	5.5	40.4	—	54.2	1,261	12,716	22.1
New Hampshire	6.0	9.4	—	84.6	1,175	10,500	18.4
New Jersey	4.1	29.4	—	66.5	1,892	13,375	16.3
New Mexico	20.6	63.4	—	16.0	1,261	11,005	20.3
New York	4.6	39.9	—	55.5	2,179	15,950**	16.1
North Carolina	13.1	66.3	—	20.6	1,099	11,165	21.2
North Dakota	7.2	48.8	8.6	35.4	1,207	9,888	16.7
Ohio	5.9	36.6	—	57.5	1,264	11,400	19.8
Oklahoma	11.1	50.0	4.9	34.0	1,130	9,600	18.6
Oregon	5.9	29.0	17.2	48.0	1,501	12,400	17.9
Pennsylvania	8.7	48.1	—	43.2	1,660	12,350	17.7
Rhode Island	7.9	35.9	—	56.2	1,481	13,381	17.3
South Carolina	14.7	58.8	—	26.5	1,030	9,904	20.5
South Dakota	14.5	14.2	.8	70.6	1,094	9,314	17.8
Tennessee	11.1	53.0	—	35.9	969	10,299	20.8
Texas	10.4	50.2	.2	39.2	1,094	11,373	17.7
Utah	7.4	57.9	—	34.8	1,084	11,360	24.4
Vermont	6.0	29.5	—	64.5	1,398	9,975	15.5
Virginia	11.0	30.6	—	58.4	1,197	11,300	17.3
Washington	8.3	51.5	—	40.2	1,443	13,615	21.6
West Virginia	12.3	56.3	—	31.4	1,071	10,480	18.8
Wisconsin	7.5	32.1	.1	60.3	1,618	12,816	16.6
Wyoming	6.9	32.9	21.6	38.6	1,489	11,100	15.1

*Data are for 1974-75 school year.   **Salary data reported as median salary.
Source: National Center for Education Statistics, *Statistics of Public Elementary and Secondary Day Schools, Fall 1975* (Washington D.C.: U.S. Government Printing Office, 1976), pp. 29, 34, and 36.

TABLE 4-2

Distribution of State and Local Tax Burdens Relative To Family Income, 1974
(Tax Burdens as Percentage of Income)

States	Adjusted Gross Income, Family of Four, 1974					
	$5,000	$7,500	$10,000	$17,500	$25,000	$50,000
All States	11.3	10.0	8.9	8.5	8.1	7.8
Oregon	6.6	8.3	8.4	9.0	9.4	10.6
New York	11.6	11.2	10.6	10.7	11.5	15.0
Minnesota	12.7	12.7	12.1	11.9	12.0	11.8
Connecticut	18.4	15.1	12.3	11.9	9.8	7.6
Texas	9.3	7.5	6.1	5.6	4.6	3.5
Washington	10.4	8.3	6.8	5.8	4.7	3.5

Source: Stephen E. Lile, "Family Tax Burdens Compared Among States and Among Cities Located within Kentucky and Neighboring States," (Bowling Green, Kentucky, Western Kentucky University, December 15, 1975), Table 8, pp. 46-47.

TABLE 4-3

Comparison of Wealth, Tax Rates, and Expenditures in
Two California Districts 1968-69

District	Assessed Value per ADA	Tax Rate	Expenditure per ADA
Beverly Hills	$50,885	$2.38	$1,232
Baldwin Park	3,706	5.48	577

Source: *Answers to Inequity*, ed. Joel Berke (Berkeley: McCutchan Publishing Corporation, 1974). Reprinted by permission of the publisher.

Chapter Two.[17] Because property wealth per pupil was much lower in Baldwin Park than in Beverly Hills, parents in Baldwin Park had to tax themselves at two and a third times the tax rate of Beverly Hills to raise less than half the revenues per pupil. In many states the top 20 percent of school districts, in terms of property wealth, have four to five times as much property wealth per pupil as do the districts in the bottom 20 percent. Revenues generated per pupil in these high-wealth districts typically exceed those of the property-poor districts by ratios of two to one, or more. The fact that revenues are unequal (although not as unequal as wealth) is the result of imperfect state attempts to equalize. State inter-

[17]The 1971 California State Supreme Court decision in *Serrano* v. *Priest* is reprinted in Joel S. Berke, *Answers to Inequity* (Berkeley, Cal.: McCutchan Publishing Corporation, 1974), pp. 179-205.

vention in this aspect of school financing will be discussed more fully in Chapter Nine.

While it is common to speak of *the* system of funding and providing public schooling, we have seen that this is far from accurate. There are really 51 different systems of public education in America with wide variations in the sources and amounts of revenue available to school districts within each of those 51 systems.

Organizational Features Contributing to Fiscal Problems

Even to a detached observer, public education in the United States exhibits many signs of strain. Despite declining enrollment, expenditures for education continue to rise at rates greater than inflation.[18] At the same time resistance builds against increased tax payments to meet these rising costs. As discussed in Chapter Two, parents who perceive their children as being discriminated against or as being inadequately educated have resorted to legal action to overturn state finance systems and state education laws. During the 1970s educational problems seem particularly acute in urban school districts which, because of financial problems, have laid off teachers and closed schools. Teacher strikes have been increasing and, with children at home, so also have the frustrations of parents.

What are the reasons for these apparent strains and problems? Why has a long history of successes in public education suddenly turned sour? Some argue that those in control made mistakes that could have been avoided by wiser educational leaders. They point to incompetent politicians, administrators, or union leaders as the source of problems. Educators often encourage this view by saying that schooling is a matter of people working with people; that if you have good people then the education system will be good.

Another view is that public education's difficulties can be attributed to the institutional structures through which schooling is provided; a problem which can only be solved by reforming educational institutions. We assume that the second explanation is more accurate than the first. From our research and personal experience, we can find little evidence to support a view that educators are less competent or more foolish now than in the past, or that, as a group, they are less concerned about the welfare of their clients than professionals providing other public services. Even if it were true, we know of no way to guarantee that future educators will be more competent or wiser. On the other hand, we believe there are institutional reforms which can alleviate many of the strains and problems facing public education. We move now to several structural prob-

[18]Public school expenditures in constant 1973–74 dollars are expected to increase from $56.9 billion that year to $63.6 billion in 1977–78. National Center for Educational Statistics, *The Condition of Education,* p. 148.

lems and then, in this and subsequent chapters, to an analysis of organizational reforms.

THE INADEQUACY OF LOCAL TAXES
TO MEET LOCAL SCHOOL COSTS

It is frequently alleged that there is a serious fiscal imbalance in public education.[19] Local school costs cannot adequately be met with local property taxes. Yet the most productive sources of revenue, personal and corporate income taxes, are controlled by state and federal governments and are generally unavailable locally to meet rising school costs.

The fiscal imbalance argument is raised in support of perennial proposals to increase the state and federal share of local educational costs.[20] Fiscal imbalance between state and national governments was given as a justification for passage of the initial revenue sharing program. It was also behind the proposal floated by former President Nixon for a national value added tax to replace local property tax support of public schools.[21] In the 1970s the National Education Association demanded the federal government fund one-third of the costs of public schools for the same reason.

Underlying the notion of fiscal imbalance in public schooling is the assertion that the demand for public schooling increases faster than the supply of funds from local property taxes. The argument typically made is that education costs rise relatively rapidly, both because public education is labor intensive[22] and because people demand more of it as their incomes rise. Consequently, school budgets rise more rapidly than inflation and more rapidly than the growth of personal income. Property taxes, on the other hand, tend to increase more slowly. At a given property tax rate, the receipts from property taxes are proportional to the increase in assessed property values. Since assessed valuation has increased more slowly than educational expenditures in the 1960s and 1970s, school tax rates have generally increased, and public resistance has been strong.

[19] See James M. Buchanan, *Public Finance in Democratic Process* (Chapel Hill: University of North Carolina Press, 1976), p. 65; and Michael Reagan, *The New Federalism* (New York: Oxford University Press, 1972), p. 38.

[20] The Advisory Commission on Intergovernmental Relations has ranked in order of quality, state fiscal systems by the proportion of local school costs borne by the state. See John Shannon and Michael Bell, "A Preliminary 'Report Card' on the 50 State-Local Fiscal Systems," Advisory Commission on Intergovernmental Relations, December 9, 1975.

[21] A value added tax is like a sales tax that producers and distributors pay on the value added at each stage of the production process.

[22] Productivity gains in the private sector result largely from technological improvements. In education there are few inventions. Consequently, if teachers' salaries are to keep pace with salaries in the private sector, the unit costs of education will have to rise faster than general prices.

The result is that the demand for increased school budgets grows more rapidly than do property tax receipts. According to those who advance the fiscal imbalance argument, local school districts must turn to the more responsive sources of revenues at the state and national levels to recoup the deficit.

From the point of view of the rational taxpayer, this argument is illogical.[23] It presumes that local taxpayers are willing to increase public school expenditures if they can be funded with more responsive state and national revenue sources, but will not support an expanded public school program if it requires raising local property tax rates. This suggests that people care more about their local tax rates than their total tax bill. It appears more reasonable to assume that it is the total tax price of public service which determines the level of service demanded.[24]

If it is the tax price of public education that determines the demand, then it might be argued that the time and costs of enacting new tax rates tend to slow down the responses of government to increasing demand for public schooling. If this were so, the supply of public schooling would be too small.

On the other hand, the apparent willingness of taxpayers to approve increased state and federal support for education but oppose higher property tax rates, may result from being unaware of the real tax costs of greater state and national support. The "fiscal illusion"—that they are getting something for nothing—may result from ignorance[25] or from the belief that someone else pays the costs of better services when state and national taxes are used.[26] "Fiscal illusion" tends to produce an oversupply of public schooling.

It is entirely plausible, and we believe likely, that resistance to local property tax increases is a direct result of individual decisions that enough is being spent on public education. It is to be expected that as school costs rise, a point is reached at which a majority of voters is no longer willing to vote additional taxes for schools.[27] Voters may, of course, decide against purchasing additional education for a number of reasons—a stronger desire for other public services, dissatisfaction with school services or government services in general, or changing economic conditions. Nonetheless, if school districts want to increase school budgets they must either increase the quality of services provided (thus increasing the tax price people are willing to pay for them) or reduce the tax price through internal efficiencies.

[23] An excellent analysis of the "fiscal imbalance" issue is contained in Wallace E. Oates, "'Automatic' Increases in Tax Revenues—The Effect on the Size of the Public Budget," in *Financing the New Federalism*, ed. Wallace E. Oates (Baltimore: The Johns Hopkins Univeristy Press, 1975), pp. 139-60.

[24] Tax price refers to the unit cost of a public service which is paid for from taxes.

[25] See Anthony Downs, "An Economic Theory of Political Action in a Democracy," *Journal of Political Economy*, 65 (April 1957), 135-50.

[26] Mancur Olson, Jr., *The Logic of Collective Action* (Cambridge, Mass.: Harvard University Press, 1965).

[27] Michael Boss, "Revolution or Choice? The Political Economy of School Referenda," unpublished paper from the department of Political Science, Indiana University.

INTERSTATE AND INTRASTATE DIFFERENCES
IN FISCAL CAPACITY

A second source of strain in our federal school finance system is the disparity in fiscal capacity among school districts within states, and the wide differences among states in per capita income and property wealth. As we noted before, it is not uncommon for one district in a state to tax itself at twice the rate of another and produce less than half the revenues of its wealthier counterpart. Similarly, residents of Mississippi would have to tax their personal income at twice the rate of citizens in New York or Connecticut in order to have the same level of public service.

On equity grounds, most states attempt to equalize educational opportunities by providing more state money to poor districts than to wealthy ones. Title I of ESEA also distributes federal dollars to states in proportion to the number of students from low-income families. Despite these efforts, there still exist large variations in the fiscal capacities of districts and states.

District wealth and income disparity, besides being inequitable, creates problems of allocative efficiency.[28] From an efficiency point of view, underinvestment in education in some areas hurts the entire economy. The inefficiencies are compounded when families migrate to wealthier districts so that their children can receive a better education. This results because the right to live wherever one chooses may motivate both high-wealth and low-wealth districts to reduce eduational spending. When low-income familes or families from low-income communities move to high-wealth school districts, the amount spent per child in the high-wealth district declines. Given a normal demand curve for education, as the quality declines, the demand for education at a given tax price also declines. The possibility of migration also creates an incentive for low-wealth districts to underinvest in education because they assume educational services are available in higher wealth districts at lower tax prices. Optimal levels of educational services would be more likely if the states and the federal government redistributed resources to make the amounts of education available to school districts independent of district or state wealth.

THE HIGH COST OF URBAN EDUCATION

A third source of strain is the deterioration of many urban school systems. Urban schools' problems are well documented: declining enrollment, poor academic performance, high levels of truancy, violence, teacher militancy, etc.[29]

[28] There is a lively debate among the experts on the relationship between amount spent and quality of education received. For an analysis of the debates, see John E. McDermott and Stephen P. Klein, "The Cost-Quality Debate in School Finance Litigation: Do Dollars Make a Difference?" in *Law and Contemporary Problems,* 38, No. 3 (Winter-Spring, 1974), 415–35.

[29] James B. Conant, *Slums and Suburbs* (New York: McGraw-Hill Book Company, 1961).

Some of the problems are financial. It costs more to provide similar educational services in urban school districts than in suburban and rural settings. Higher costs of land, buildings, teachers, and maintenance mean less education per dollar spent than elsewhere. Second, cities have relatively large numbers of school children requiring expensive special education programs. These include both poor and disadvantaged children, as well as the handicapped. Also, a larger proportion of urban students opt for vocational training programs that are more expensive than the traditional college preparatory programs. Third, competition for the taxpayers' dollars is greater in the cities than elsewhere, making it more difficult to raise funds for schools.[30]

City schools also suffer from political or jurisdictional problems. Many state legislatures are controlled by either rural or suburban legislators unsympathetic to urban problems. Furthermore, states are reluctant to allow the federal government to assist the cities without going through state agencies, although increasingly, federal programs contain "pass-through" provisions permitting direct assistance to cities. Whether federal aid will be adequate to save urban schools, or whether it provides an excuse for continued state neglect is uncertain. The viability of our federal system of school finance depends on finding solutions to the problems of urban schools. Our failure to do so continues to place a strain on American education.

Size and Organization of Public Schools

Many suggestions have been advanced for adjusting the size of educational organizations to make them more efficient, equitable, and responsive. Proposals range from consolidating school districts into larger jurisdictions to making individual schools the basic unit of school management. The remainder of this chapter attempts to shed some light on the issue of the optimal size of educational units.

THE SIZE OF EDUCATIONAL UNITS

The determination of appropriate size of political units is one of the most frequently recurring issues in the theory of democracy. Political scientist Robert Dahl has written that determination of the optimal size of democratic political units involves an inescapable dilemma. The larger government is, the more it can

---

[30] Factors contributing to the higher costs of urban education are analyzed in depth in The Potomac Institute, *Equity for Cities in School Finance Reform* (Washington, D.C.: The Potomac Institute, Inc., 1973); and Betsy Levin, Thomas Muller, and Corazon Sandoval, *The High Cost of Education in Cities* (Washington, D.C.: The Urban Institute, 1973).

regulate those aspects of the environment its citizens want regulated. The larger the unit, however, and the more complicated its machinery, the less its citizens can participate in its decisions. Conversely, the smaller the unit, the greater the chance for citizen participation, but the more limited its range of control over the environment. In centralized government citizen participation is minimal; in decentralized government citizen participation runs the risk of being trivial.[31]

Economists emphasize the importance of tradeoffs in determining optimum unit size. A more centralized organization of public education, or any public service for that matter, reduces the disparity among services provided by individual units. An egalitarian distribution of income requires a transfer from the wealthy to the poor. In a highly decentralized society, it is difficult to redistribute income. If a single, small unit of government adopts a redistributive set of taxes and subsidies, it creates incentives for the rich to move out and for the poor to migrate into the community. Even if all members of a society believed in a more equal distribution of income, there would still be a tendency for people to pass the burden of eliminating inequality to others.[32] And no individual community would undertake such a utopian goal simply because of the migration problem. If communities begin with unequal resources, only centralized action can substantially reduce the inequalities.

Whereas the pursuit of economic equality favors centralized government, the pursuit of resource efficiency generally favors decentralized government.[33] The task of resource efficiency is to match resource use with consumer preferences. Centralized government provides uniform service for its members. This may be efficient if the preferences of individuals being served are similar. If they are different, however, then centralized provision may be inefficient. Decentralized units of government, on the other hand, can provide a variety of service levels to match the particular preferences of a community. Decentralized government thus offers the prospect of increased efficiency through a greater range of services more nearly satisfying the differing tastes of consumers—even though there may be some diseconomies of small scale.[34]

---

[31] Robert A. Dahl, "The City in the Future of Democracy," *American Political Science Review*, 61 (December 1967), 953-70.

[32] James M. Buchanan, *The Demand and Supply of Public Goods* (Chicago: Rand McNally, 1968), chap. 5.

[33] An exception is in the case of a pure public good. A pure public good is one that is consumed jointly and in the same quantity by all consumers. For example, national defense or clean air benefit everyone regardless of whether a particular individual pays for it or not. Consequently individuals will understate their preference for a public good, believing that someone else will provide it for them. Left to individuals or local government, in other words, pure public goods would be underproduced. See Paul Samuelson, "The Pure Theory of Public Expenditures," *Review of Economics and Statistics*, 36 (November 1954), 387-89; and John Head, "Public Goods and Public Policy," *Public Finance*, 17, No. 3 (1962) 197-219.

[34] Economies of scale refers to the declining per unit costs of production arising from increasing the number of units produced.

Decentralized government may also increase efficiency by encouraging greater experimentation and innovation in the production of goods. Local control of schools is often supported on the grounds that communities are good laboratories for new educational techniques. If a program fails, only a few children are disadvantaged. If it succeeds, then it will be copied by other school districts.

Related to this argument is the claim that alternatives increase with the number of units producing a public service. When each community offers its own program of services, citizens have the opportunity to choose the combination of desired services by deciding where to live. One community may offer excellent schools and parks, while another provides relatively more services for senior citizens. As this argument would have it, citizens are better off deciding their own priorities rather than acquiescing to a uniform level of services provided by a centralized government.[35]

Efficiency may also be enhanced in decentralized units because expenditure decisions are more likely to be made by the same people paying for them. If a school district has to pay for the construction of a new school, it is more likely to consider carefully the costs and benefits of the new building than if construction money is provided by state or federal governments.

Even assuming that the goal of equality can be pursued through the transfer of funds from richer to poorer units of government, and that some degree of decentralization facilitates resource efficiency, we still need to determine the optimal size of the consumer group. We will first discuss this problem abstractly and then consider the empirical evidence on the optimal size of school districts.

In determining the optimal size of a group to receive educational services, whether it be a classroom, school, or school district, several factors need to be considered.[36] First, by organizing in groups people can obtain goods more cheaply. Unit costs are lower, all other things being equal, when there are 20 students per teacher than an individual tutor for each child. Similarly, the per pupil costs of public education in a district with 1,000 students is likely to be less expensive than in a district with only 20 students. Curve OC in Figure 4-1 illustrates the aggregate cost savings from increasing the number of individuals who jointly consume a public good—that is, the resulting lower cost services because of joint consumption. Cost savings rise rapidly at first, as the first few members of a community join together, and then level off as the advantages of having additional people join the group is lessened. At N, all members of the community jointly consume the service.

There is, however, a welfare cost to joint consumption resulting from some

<hr>

[35] The option to "vote with one's feet" is known as the Tiebout hypothesis. See Charles M. Tiebout, "A Pure Theory of Local Expenditures," *Journal of Political Economy*, 64 (October 1956), pp. 416–24.

[36] The following analysis draws primarily from Wallace E. Oates, *Fiscal Federalism* (New York: Harcourt Brace Jovanovich, 1972), chap. 2.

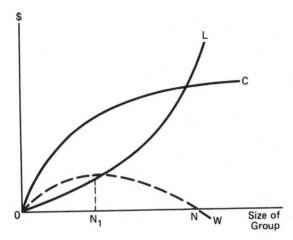

FIG. 4-1. Determining Optimal Unit Size

Source: Wallace E. Oates, *Fiscal Federalism* (New York: Harcourt Brace Jovanovich, Inc., 1972), p. 39.

members of the community having to consume other than the desired level. Such external costs increase with the size of the group. The amount of welfare loss resulting from external costs, represented by curve OL, depends on the range of preferences represented in the group. If everyone prefers the same amount, the loss will be small and OL will lie closer to the horizontal axis. If there are wide differences in preferences, then the loss will be great, and OL will rise more rapidly as group size increases. As expected, the welfare loss increases as the size of the group increases. This results because the influence of individuals on their own level of consumption diminishes as the number of people in a group increases.

Determining the optimal size of a group of consumers of a public good, in other words, involves a tradeoff between the increased cost savings from joint consumption in larger groups (OC) and losses that result from some individuals consuming other than what they desire (OL). The curve OW in Figure 4-1 represents the net welfare from joint consumption for each group size. OW is obtained by subtracting OL from OC and reaches a maximum at N_1, which represents the optimal sized group in the illustration. Increasing the size of the group beyond that point will reduce the net welfare from joint consumption.

This analysis, which has focused on the tradeoffs between the cost savings and welfare gains or losses from collective consumption, overlooks several other factors likely to affect optimum unit size. For example, the analysis ignores the possibility that quality of service in one area may affect the welfare of individuals in another area. With migration, the quality of education in one district spills over into other districts. The smaller the individual units, the more difficult it is to internalize these externalities. Conversely, the larger the group size, the greater the increase in individual welfare resulting from internalizing external costs and benefits. Since the gains from internalizing externalities will increase with group size, curve OW in Figure 4-1 would move upward, and N_1 would move to the right. Existence of interjurisdictional externalities increases the size of the optimal sized group for joint consumption.[37]

STUDIES OF COST-SIZE RELATIONSHIPS
IN PUBLIC EDUCATION

Many studies have been conducted on the cost-size relationship among different sized school districts, although most are poorly done and inconclusive. In general, they conclude that there are significant economies of scale up to about 1,500 to 2,000 students in a district and significant diseconomies of scale when districts are comprised of more than 20,000 students.[38] G. Alan Hickrod, in a study of the cost-size relationship among school districts in Illinois, in 1974 found that the greatest efficiency was achieved in districts with approximately 2,432 ADA.[39] We should probably avoid a fixation on any particular numbers since many factors, including the definition of optimum being used, affect the analysis of optimum sized school districts. The most important considerations are what to do with very small schools and school districts, and what to do with very large ones. The per pupil costs in small school districts are generally higher than in average sized districts. Some economists believe that small district consolidation increases efficiency.[40] Others contend the disadvantages of bigness more than outweigh the high costs of smallness and argue against further consolidation of small districts.[41] We believe that some efficiencies are to be gained by consolidating very small districts, particularly those with fewer than 1,000 students. The greatest gains in efficiency, however, are likely to come from decentralizing those districts with more than 20,000 students. Decentralization within the school district is more fully discussed in both Chapter Eleven on

[37] The problem of interjurisdictional externalities is just one complicating factor. The costs of collective decision making and congestion costs should also be considered when analyzing the most efficient size of an organizational unit.

[38] For bibliographies on school district size, see Robert E. Stephens and John Spiess, "What Does Research Say about the Size of a Local School District?" *Journal of State School System Development,* 1 (Fall 1967), 183–99; and Educational Research Service, *Size of Schools and School Districts,* ERS Information Aid No. 8 (Washington, D.C.: ERS, 1971).

[39] G. Alan Hickrod, "Cost-Size Relationship Among School Districts in Illinois, 1974," Research Paper 2-HCYH-75, Center for the Study of Educational Finance, Illinois State University, 1975.

[40] Elchanan Cohn, *Economics of State Aid to Education* (Lexington, Mass.: D. C. Heath and Company, 1974).

[41] See Jonathan P. Sher and Rachel B. Tompkins, "Economy, Efficiency, and Equality: The Myth of Rural School and District Consolidation," in Jonathan P. Sher, ed., *Education in Rural America: A Reassessment of Conventional Wisdom* (Boulder, Colo.: Westview Press, Spring 1977).

school district management and budgeting and Chapter Fifteen on the political economy of city schools.

Summary

The financing of public education is affected directly by the organization of public schools. This chapter has examined the relationship between school organization and finance, emphasizing the federal structure in which educational choices are made and educational services provided.

Public primary and secondary education in the United States is a large endeavor serving 45 million children and consuming approximately 67 billion dollars. Although states are becoming increasingly involved in school finance, collective bargaining, and school curriculum, both the provision and financing of public schools is still predominantly local. The federal role is a relatively minor one, although important in improving the educational opportunities of disadvantaged, handicapped, and non-English speaking students.

Public school organization is characterized by its lack of planning and its diversity. This seemingly ad hoc manner in which schools operate in our federal system creates numerous financial problems for schools. For example, local school districts are constantly demanding that state and federal governments assume a larger share of local school costs. Many educators believe that relief from heavy local property tax burdens for schools will reduce resistance to larger school budgets. The argument is based on the assumption that taxpayers and voters are less sensitive to higher state and federal taxes than to local property taxes. Another problem arises from the wide variation in local property wealth among school districts. This creates numerous inefficiencies and inequities in public school finance. Finally, the plight of America's urban centers and urban school systems is intensified by state finance systems that do not adequately accommodate the special educational problems of city schools.

The chapter concludes with an analysis of school district size. For most of the twentieth century, reformers believed that consolidation of small schools and small districts would make schools more efficient and more equal. This chapter challenges this conventional assertion and argues that the costs of much consolidation outweigh its potential benefits. The goals of efficiency and equity may be better achieved by providing greater choice and community control over public schooling.

5

COLLECTIVE BARGAINING
IN PUBLIC EDUCATION

Collective bargaining has produced dramatic changes in the political economy of public schools. Approximately 85 percent of public school teachers are now covered by contracts negotiated by teacher union representatives and representatives of school district management. Before unionization, teachers were poorly situated to challenge the dominance of professional administrators in educational decision making. With collective bargaining they are now gaining control over many aspects of school operations. The importance of this shift in the power of teachers resulting from collective bargaining is described by David B. Tyack, a prominent historian of American education:

> From the late 1950s, when teachers had little influence, to 1970, a power-ful new alignment of forces took place in urban schools, one comparable in potential impact to the centralization of control in small boards and powerful superintendents at the turn of the century . . . at the very least, teachers were the group with the greatest power to veto or sabotage pro-posals for reform. No realistic estimate of strategies for change in Ameri-can education could afford to ignore teachers or fail to enlist their sup-port. . . .[1]

The most important change that has accompanied the unionization of

[1] David B. Tyack, *The One Best System* (Cambridge, Mass.: Harvard University Press, 1974), pp. 288-89.

teachers is in procedures for making educational decisions. Prior to unioniza-tion, most decisions at the district level were made unilaterally by a district superintendent or staff member subject to the ratification of a popularly elected school board. Under most collective bargaining statutes, decisions affecting the wages, benefits, and working conditions of teachers as well as many educational matters are now made bilaterally. On many issues it is mandatory under state laws that school managers and teacher representatives reach agreement in a contract.

The shift from unilateral to bilateral decision making reverses the intent of many early twentieth-century reforms in education. Independent local school districts, nonpartisan election of school board members, and professional super-intendents were created to take politics out of education. Although education and politics were never completely divorced, the introduction of collective bar-gaining has quelled any talk of a separation. Collective bargaining is, in many ways, the epitome of the political decision-making process. It establishes a pro-cedure whereby teachers can influence decisions by expressing themselves di-rectly to management. Rather than having to quit in order to register protest, teachers can now voice their dissatisfaction in a straightforward way.[2] Public employees have transplanted from the private sector a political procedure for increasing their power in public organizations.

Despite almost 20 years of experience with a variety of collective bar-gaining arrangements, there is little agreement on their impact on schools, with respect either to costs or to formation of educational policy. Opinions, of course, vary widely. Sylvester Petro claims that:

> Among the numerous, grave, and perhaps critical threats to the survival of civil order in the United States, one more ominous than the rest stands out: the movement in all the states and in the federal government to com-pel collective bargaining between our governments and unions acting as representatives of government employees. Although this movement rests upon a series of incredible distortions and misrepresentations of fact, is propelled by premises, theories and arguments which cannot withstand serious examination, and creates chaos in every branch and sector of government where it takes hold, it is nevertheless gaining ground year by year, even day by day, in all our governments—federal, state, and local.[3]

---

[2]Hirschman coins the terms "exit" and "voice" to distinguish between economic and political methods of registering complaints. "The customer who, dissatisfied with the product of one firm shifts to that of another, uses the market to defend his welfare or to improve his position, . . . one either exits or one does not . . . In all respects, voice is just the opposite of exit. It is a far more 'messy' concept because it can be graduated, all the way from faint grumbling to violent protest; it implies articulation of one's critical opinions rather than a private 'secret' vote in the anonymity of a supermarket; and finally it is direct and straightforward rather than roundabout. Voice is political action par excellence." Albert O. Hirschman, *Exit, Voice and Loyalty* (Cambridge, Mass.: Harvard University Press, 1970), pp. 15–16.

[3]Sylvester Petro, "Compulsory Public-Sector Bargaining; The Dissolution of Social Order," *The Freeman*, 25, no. 8 (August 1975), 494.

Other critics are less apocalyptic than Petro about the consequences of collective bargaining. Nevertheless they point out that the problems municipalities and school districts face grow substantially with the introduction of collective bargaining. It takes more time, energy, and resources to make decisions. Furthermore unionization may distort the political decision-making process. School board members find it more difficult to be reelected following a long strike by school teachers. Perhaps most worrisome to the critics of collective bargaining is the possibility that unionization will limit the role of government in education. Their worry is that both the high costs of negotiated settlements and the loss of public control over educational decisions may force elected officials and the public to seek alternatives to publicly provided education programs.[4]

Most observers, however, have come to accept the extension of collective bargaining rights to teachers. They argue that collective bargaining results from the growing impersonality of large school organizations and, if structured properly, can be a positive force for the improvement of American public education. In particular, they point out that collective bargaining can reduce unrest by establishing an agreed-upon procedure for resolving management–labor disputes. In addition, proponents believe students can learn how problems are solved in democratic political institutions by observing teachers and administrators resolving disputes via negotiations. A third benefit claimed for collective bargaining is that it will improve teacher morale. Today teachers are blamed for the failures of an educational system over which they have little or no control. Collective bargaining promises to give teachers more say about what is taught in the classroom, and this greater control should foster a renewed commitment to the teaching profession. Finally, the supporters of collective bargaining believe it, more than anything else, will force school districts to develop more effective management.[5]

The purpose of this chapter is to describe educational collective bargaining and the issues it raises. We begin by acknowledging that collective bargaining is a reality in most large school districts and is likely to remain an important part of the educational decision-making process. The issue therefore is not whether teachers should have the right to organize and bargain collectively but how collective bargaining should be structured so that both the teachers' right to participate in decisions affecting their working conditions and the right of the public to control their public institutions are preserved. We are interested, to borrow a phrase from the previous chapter, in specifying the institutional framework in which equitable and efficient educational decisions are most likely to be chosen.

---

[4]These and other concerns are discussed in Harry H. Wellington and Ralph K. Winter, Jr., *The Unions and the Cities* (Washington, D.C.: The Brookings Institution, 1971).

[5]For a generally supportive analysis of public sector unionism, see Felix A. Nigro, *Management–Employee Relations in the Public Sector* (Chicago: Public Personnel Association, 1969).

The Existing System of Collective Bargaining

For the sake of simplicity it would be convenient if there were a federal public employee collective bargaining act covering all public school teachers in the United States. Such is not the case, however. There is a wide variety of state laws, opinions of attorneys general, and policy guidelines governing collective bargaining by public school teachers. To complicate matters further, laws in the 28 or so states that require collective bargaining are being amended, and those that presently have only permissive legislation or no legislation are in the process of enacting mandatory collective bargaining bills.

Notable is the rapidity with which state public employee collective bargaining laws have been enacted. In 1962 only two states had legislation permitting public employee bargaining. By 1976, 28 states required that various aspects of management–labor relations in the public sector be negotiated and agreements set down in a contract. Sixteen states permitted collective bargaining although a formal agreement was not mandatory. Four states prohibited collective bargaining and the remaining two states had no guidelines at all.[6] One likely reason for the rapid adoption of state collective bargaining statutes is that the lack of a statute has not stopped public employees who desired to bargain collectively from doing so, or from striking. Consequently, in order to ensure orderly management–labor relations among public employees and to provide a third-party procedure for resolving disputes before strikes occur, states have rushed to establish collective bargaining structures.

It is difficult to find much uniformity in the structure of state public employee collective bargaining statutes. Some cover all public employees. Others such as California cover only teachers in primary–secondary schools and community colleges. Similarly, the administration of teacher collective bargaining laws varies among the states. In states such as Massachusetts and Michigan, public employee collective bargaining is implemented by a state administrative body for general labor relations. In Florida, Minnesota, New York, and New Jersey as well as six others, there is a separate public employee relations board. California and Indiana have separate educational employee relations boards, while Connecticut, Kansas, and Maryland use the state boards of education to administer collective bargaining statutes. A few states have no state boards and several others have delegated the administration of collective bargaining laws to local boards of education.[7]

Collective bargaining statutes typically include regulations covering not only the procedures for collective bargaining but also provisions for establishing union representation, grievance procedures, impasse procedures, and strike

---

[6]Lorraine M. McDonnell, *Teacher Collective Bargaining and School Governance,* working note prepared for the Department of Health, Education, and Welfare (Washington, D.C.: The Rand Corporation, 1976), pp. 5–6.

[7]*Ibid.,* p. 11.

or arbitration rights. To assess the likely impact of a collective bargaining statute, therefore, all of its provisions must be considered together. For example, the right to strike for some nonessential public employees may be an acceptable provision if the issues settled through bargaining are limited, with some issues reserved for management. On the other hand, if the scope of bargaining is virtually unlimited, then the public's right to control policy decisions through their elected representatives requires some alternative to strikes for settling disputes. Despite the complexity of state laws and the variations that occur among states, states have encountered many of the same problems in drafting and administering public employee bargaining statutes. The following sections discuss five major issues that occur in public employee labor relations, particularly with respect to teachers.

THE ORGANIZATION OF COLLECTIVE BARGAINING

In designing a collective bargaining statute, policy makers must consider the entire range of variables affecting the outcomes of public sector bargaining. The intent, of course, is to create a framework of laws that sets up an orderly process for settling labor–management issues in the public sector. Policy makers want a procedure that ensures a continuous flow of public services in a manner and at a price that is politically acceptable.

Policy makers also want a law that is fair, that gives neither public employers nor public employees too much power in the bargaining process. However, there are no agreed-upon measures of the current balance of power between employers and employees in the public sector and no consensus on what a fair balance should be. One might argue that policy makers should accept the current power balance and try to write a neutral law leaving both parties with the same powers as before. Such a goal, however, is likely to be both technically and politically impossible. States where labor is strong tend to write laws more favorable to employees than states where labor is weaker. One of the primary purposes of the National Labor Relations Act was to strengthen the bargaining position of industrial workers by creating a collective interest capable of negotiating from strength with industry leaders. The question in the public sector is whether public employers have too much or too little power relative to public employees. Determining the proper balance requires both political judgment and knowledge of the existing rules and practices affecting public sector labor-management relations.

In the past, public sector collective bargaining laws have been closely patterned after similar laws in the private sector. Such precedents are probably as good a place to begin as any. There are many differences, however, between the rights and responsibilities of management and labor in the two sectors which should be considered.

Public managers, for example, are not motivated to make a profit. Because of the inelasticity of demand for public services, public employee representatives can bargain for higher wages without fear of major employment cutbacks.

The task facing lawmakers is to establish a fair and workable balance of power between public management and labor. In creating a legal framework for public sector negotiations, policy makers possess a variety of resources for distributing power between management and labor at the bargaining table.[8] Lawmakers can allocate *legal powers* such as the right of employees to organize and bargain collectively. To protect the public they can make it illegal to discuss certain topics or to strike. A second resource that lawmakers can manipulate is the *power to organize.* They can specify who is eligible to join a bargaining unit and the procedures of employees for selecting a bargaining representative. *Power over money* is also important in producing a proper balance across the bargaining table. Legislation can establish a dues check-off procedure or fair-share requirement to support union negotiators and finance political lobbying efforts. Regulations may also establish who pays for the services of third parties during impasse proceedings. A fifth source of power available to lawmakers is the power to bring *sanctions* to bear on contending interests. The law may permit boycotts, strikes, lockouts, and public demonstrations as means of forcing a settlement from a contending party. Similarly, government may apply sanctions to discourage such activities as firing employees for striking illegally.[9] Finally, the power of *expertise* can be provided to increase the bargaining effectiveness of all parties to collective negotiations. This may entail allowing the parties to be represented by professional negotiators, or permit the use of professional mediators, fact-finders, and arbitrators to help parties reach agreement. In sum, lawmakers have several resources to write into laws to produce a balance of power among the interests involved in public sector collective bargaining.

THE BARGAINING UNIT

One of the first problems confronting policy makers is determining the membership of a bargaining unit. Deciding who should bargain with whom on what issues involves in itself a complex process in the public sector. Consequently, legislators have as a rule left determination of bargaining units to employee relations boards. Typically state boards establish a procedure whereby

[8]See Douglas E. Mitchell, "The Impact of Collective Bargaining on Public and Client Interests in Education," paper presented at the American Educational Research Association meeting in San Francisco, April 1976, pp. 20-23.

[9]For instance, in New York, employees are fined two days' pay for each day they strike illegally. This has not stopped New York teachers from striking, however. "Teacher Strikes, 1973-74," National Education Association *Negotiation Research Digest,* 8, No. 4 (December 1974), 14-15.

bargaining agents petition them to represent a specified group of employees. Other agents and public managers are permitted to express their preference regarding the organization of the bargaining unit. A final decision is then made by the board after considering such factors as community of interest, wages, hours, and working conditions of the employees involved, the history of collective bargaining for similar organizations, and the desires of employees and employers.

Among the specific problems in many public service cases is what to do with supervisory personnel. In the private sector, supervisors are considered a part of management and are generally excluded from the bargaining unit. In public education, department heads are more likely to consider themselves colleagues of the other teachers in the department and rarely have much control over department hiring, firing, or compensation decisions. As a result department heads are frequently included in the bargaining unit. Middle level administrators, those above department head but below superintendent, on the other hand, have not been included in most teacher bargaining units. Finding themselves without representation and their jobs threatened by teacher union demands for fewer administrators at lower pay, they have petitioned and won bargaining rights of their own in many states. By 1976 there were over 1200 unions of school administrators in 24 states.[10]

Deciding at what level of educational organization to organize units is a special problem in collective bargaining in higher education. In primary–secondary education, all teachers in a school district are usually included in a single bargaining unit. In higher education, bargaining units may include faculty in all public institutions of higher education; or units may be segmented into faculty from all four-year teaching colleges or all community colleges—or even comprise faculty from individual campuses. The political influence of a faculty union on a state legislature is likely to be greater if its organization is statewide. On the other hand, faculty desiring a stronger role in the governance of a university can accomplish their goals more effectively with a single campus unit.

A third issue surrounding unit determination is whether to give the majority union exclusive bargaining rights. The arguments for exclusive representation are that it saves time because management deals with only one union, that it reduces intraorganizational conflict, and that it develops a clear line of accountability.[11] Those opposed to exclusive representation argue that it violates individual rights to freedom of association or nonassociation, and that it may conflict with the notion of academic freedom. Multiple bargaining agents and proportional representation in bargaining teams have not been very successful, however. Consequently, most state statutes provide for an exclusive bargaining agent.

---

[10] Bruce S. Cooper, "Collective Bargaining Comes to School Middle Management," *Phi Delta Kappan*, 58, No. 2 (October 1976), 202–4.

[11] Nigro, *Management-Employee Relations*, pp. 88–90.

IDENTIFYING THE PUBLIC EMPLOYER

Identifying the public employer has been one of the most troublesome issues in public sector bargaining. It is not a problem created by collective bargaining. It is instead a problem of public administration highlighted by the collective bargaining process. In private sector negotiations, management is clearly established by law as the group of officials selected by the owners to run a company. Private managers have both the right and the power to sign a negotiated contract and can be held accountable for meeting the terms of the contract. In the public sector this is not always the case. Public management is not delegated to one group of officials, but is usually shared by elected executives, legislators, and the public. For example, in primary–secondary education the elected school board is almost always considered the employer for purposes of collective bargaining. Actual negotiations, however, are carried out either by members of the administrative staff or by lawyers hired by the board to conduct negotiations, neither of whom can legally reach an agreement. Not even the school board, however, can be held to the terms of a contract it signs since the governor and state legislature determine how much state money the district will receive and may even regulate the amount of local tax support it can raise. Furthermore, if the contract requires a tax increase to be approved by voters, it is the public collectively who ultimately must agree to the terms of the contract.

Union representatives prefer to bargain with whomever controls the public purse strings. As states assume a larger proportion of school funding, or limit the local district's options to fund schools from local tax sources, more union effort will be directed toward governors and state legislators. Regional or statewide bargaining is likely to follow state assumption of school costs. Short of this, unions will direct more energies into lobbying, or "end run" bargaining, to secure benefits they are unable to negotiate at the bargaining table.

The problem of identifying the public employer is further complicated by the fact that in a community there may be several public employers—city council, county commissioners, sewer district officials, as well as school board members, each of whom makes claims against the local property tax dollar. A raise in teacher salaries that increases local taxes may reduce resources to pay county employees. In most communities there is no mechanism for resolving such distributional problems. The choice is left to local tax payers.

THE SCOPE OF BARGAINING

The scope of bargaining refers to the items which may be discussed at the bargaining table. As was true during the early years of negotiations in the private sector, the scope of bargaining has been a source of disagreement and litigation in the public sector. In general, state statutes and employee relations board decisions classify items that are prohibited, permitted, and required to be discussed. Increasingly, state statutes are including language that prohibits certain matters from being discussed on the grounds that they are management rights.[12] Among the items more likely to be prohibited are matters of educational policy, such as class size and teacher-training programs. Other matters such as classroom discipline, teacher aides, and substitute teachers are often permitted to be discussed but neither side is obligated to discuss them or to include them in a final agreement. Usually, employees cannot legally strike, where strikes are permitted, over items that are only permissible items of negotiation, nor can management or labor be charged with an unfair labor practice for its unwillingness to discuss such items. Items required to be discussed—commonly, wages, hours, and working conditions—must be included in a final agreement. Failure to reach agreement on these issues results in an impasse.

Determining the appropriate scope of bargaining is not an easy matter. Public unions, particularly teacher unions, aim for a very broad interpretation of the scope of bargaining. For them, topics like class size, curriculum, and discipline are all matters affecting teachers' working conditions. Management generally prefers a narrow interpretation of the scope of bargaining. An extremely limited scope of bargaining runs the risk, however, of being ignored by powerful unions, who will attempt to bring up excluded issues or use political channels to seek benefits that cannot be negotiated at the bargaining table. On the other hand, an unusually permissive scope may delegate to the bargaining table matters that should be decided by accountable public officials. As with so many aspects of public sector bargaining, a balance must be struck which protects both employees' rights to participate in decisions affecting their working conditions and the people's right to control public institutions.

IMPASSE PROCEDURES

Most union officials believe that collective bargaining without the right to strike is meaningless because the union is denied the only effective means for enforcing its demands. Opponents of public union strikes argue that public strikes endanger the health and safety of citizens and conflict with the public's right to receive services they have paid for. The debate over whether public sector unions should be permitted to strike will continue for some time. Approximately 11 states permit strikes when the public health and safety are not endangered while 33 states make strikes illegal.[13] Most important, however, is that despite the prohibition against strikes, public employees have become increasingly willing to participate in illegal strikes. In 1974 alone there were al-

---

[12] The implicit assumption is that certain subjects are so central to public policy and the public decision-making process that they cannot be determined bilaterally by management and labor, but must be dealt with only by the elected representatives of the people.

[13] Neal R. Peirce, "Employment Report/Public Employee Unions Show Rise in Membership, Militancy," *National Journal*, 7, No. 35 (August 30, 1976), 1244.

most 400 strikes by state and local employees, with over 150 of these by primary and secondary school teachers. Neither economic sanctions, such as New York's loss of two days' pay for each day on strike, nor court injunctions and fines have been effective in stopping strikes.

Since strikes are difficult to stop, most states have devised procedures designed to aid in the resolution of bargaining problems before strikes occur. There are three basic methods of impasse resolution short of a work stoppage. They are mediation, fact-finding, and binding interest arbitration. Mediation involves the participation of a third party who tries to bring about a voluntary resolution of the disagreements between the two principal negotiators. The mediator makes no decisions and must rely solely on persuasion to bring the two parties together.

Fact-finding is a process in which a neutral third party listens to both parties and on the basis of their testimony and independent research issues findings and recommendations considered to be a fair resolution of the disputed matters. The fact-finder's findings and recommendations are usually publicized and the parties are then given a period of time to accept them. The fact-finder's recommendations may be binding but usually are not.

Binding interest arbitration consists of a neutral third party or panel that hears arguments of both sides and then formulates what it considers to be a fair settlement. The decision of the arbitrator or panel of arbitrators is final and binding on both parties. Arbitrators may be permitted to recommend any solution that seems reasonable or be restricted to selecting one of the last offers presented by the parties to the dispute.

All three of these techniques have been useful in resolving disputes. Many public officials oppose arbitration, however, because it delegates final authority to an unaccountable third party. If a school board has limited funds or believes the public opposes increased school expenditures, can it in good conscience allow an arbitrator to encumber the district with new fiscal responsibilities? Many also argue that arbitrators, who are usually trained in the law, are not equipped to make decisions on class size and curriculum because these are educational decisions. Compulsory arbitration takes away from elected officials the right to set public priorities and public policy.

We believe that public school teachers should be permitted to strike after attempts by mediators and fact-finders and a cooling off period have been exhausted. Public disapproval of strikes and the already tight budgets available to school districts are likely to reduce the number of strikes in the future. As one New York teacher commented, "Why strike? Nobody has any money."

FEDERAL COLLECTIVE BARGAINING LEGISLATION

Early in 1975 most congressional observers agreed Congress would pass a federal statute that year guaranteeing bargaining rights for state and local public employees. Such legislation was supported by the three major public employee unions, The American Federation of State, County and Municipal Employees (AFSCME), the AFL-CIO, and the National Education Association (NEA). Furthermore, two different bills mandating collective bargaining were scheduled for hearings in Congress. The first bill, supported by the AFL-CIO would have simply removed the exemption of public employees from the National Labor Relations Act (NLRA), thus bringing them under the jurisdiction of the National Labor Relations Board. The second bill would have established a new National Public Employee Relations Board to supervise labor-management relations in the public sector. This bill, called the National Public Employee Relations Act (PERA), was supported by NEA and would have granted broader bargaining rights to public employees than they would receive if brought under the umbrella of the NLRA. Under PERA, the agency shop would be mandated rather than permitted. The scope of bargaining would include "conditions of employment and other matters of mutual concern," rather than the narrower NLRA definition of "wages, hours, and working conditions." PERA would also give the union sole right to make the fact-finder's recommendations binding if they chose to forego the right to strike.[14]

Union arguments in support of a federal statute are several. They assert that public employees should have the same right to bargain collectively as do employees in the private sector. This right has not been uniformly granted because of the variety of state laws and local ordinances governing collective bargaining for state and local employees. Proponents also maintain that a federal statute would reduce the number of public employee strikes since many result over attempts of unions to seek recognition.

Federal legislation is opposed by a variety of groups representing public management, e.g., the United States Conference of Mayors, National League of Cities, and National School Boards Association. They are not so much opposed to collective bargaining as to federal intervention in bargaining at the state and local levels. Opponents argue that a federal collective bargaining law would ignore the differences among units of state and local government and thereby interfere with local legislative and budgetary processes. They go on to say that since a majority of the states now have their own statutes, and more are passing them every year, there is no need for a federal statute. Finally, the opponents believe that a federal statute would give unions too much political power. Unions already use their political muscle to obtain benefits from state and local legislatures that they are unable to negotiate at the bargaining table. A federal law would enable unions to pressure Congress for legislation favorable to their bargaining position.

Despite union support and favorable prospects early in 1975, no legislation was passed. By the end of 1975 both public opinion and most of Congress had turned against federal collective bargaining legislation. Part of the prob-

---

[14] For a more detailed description of proposed federal legislation, see McDonnell, *Teacher Collective Bargaining,* pp. 23-30.

lem was the reluctance of Congress to act until the Supreme Court had ruled on a case challenging the constitutionality of the 1974 amendments to the Fair Labor Standards Act. This case, *National League of Cities* v. *Usery*, challenged the amendments extending minimum wage and overtime requirements to nonsupervisory state and local government employees as exceeding the permissible limits of the power given to the federal government by the commerce clause. An unconstitutional finding would raise grave doubts about the constitutionality of federal legislation governing public sector collective bargaining.

A more important deterrent to passage of a federal law, however, was an adverse public reaction to public employee strikes. The San Francisco police and firefighters strike and the Kansas City firefighters strike in 1975 are dramatic examples of strikes that turned public opinion against unions. Furthermore, many citizens blamed New York's public employee unions for New York's fiscal crisis during the fall of 1975.

Finally, the unions themselves could not agree on the kind of law they would support. While publicly supporting federal legislation, union officials admitted privately that they already had their hands full organizing public employees in the many states enacting state collective bargaining statutes. Hearings before the House Special Labor Subcommittee brought out more anti-union testimony from right-to-work groups than union testimony.

On June 24, 1976 the Supreme Court ruled in *The National League of Cities* v. *Usery* that state and local governments need not adhere to the Fair Labor Standards Act; it thereby undercut the most likely legal basis for a federal collective bargaining statute, the commerce clause of the Constitution.[15] Interest in a federal collective bargaining law is likely to reemerge. Success will depend on the ability of federal lawmakers to find a new legal access for regulating state and local employees, on the efforts of the major unions to find an acceptable bill, and on a softening of public criticism of public employee unions.

POLITICAL ACTIVITIES OF TEACHER UNIONS

As we noted earlier, managerial authority in public education is shared among several levels of government and the public. This division of authority means that more than two parties are involved in school board–teacher negotiations. Unions have seized on this division of managerial responsibility to enhance their bargaining position. Union officials put pressure on elected officials to weaken the position of the management negotiator—in effect, by coercing city and state officials to intervene in negotiations between school boards and teachers.

Realizing the potential benefits of "end run" bargaining, as it is called, both the American Federation of Teachers (AFT) and the National Education

[15] *National League of Cities* v. *Usery, Secretary of Labor,* No. 78–878, U.S. S. Ct., June 24, 1976.

Association (NEA) have committed large amounts of resources to the pursuit of political objectives. In 1972 the NEA, for example, formed a national political action committee (NEA-PAC) for the purpose of supporting candidates for national office. In that year the committee made political contributions in the amount of $27,000.[16] By 1974, this sum had increased to $240,000 for congressional races alone, plus an additional $3.5 million spent by NEA state political affiliates on federal, state, and local races. In 1974, the California NEA political organization spent $444,965, and all public employee groups contributed a total of $1.7 million to election campaigns, more than any other group in the state.

In 1976 the NEA endorsed Governor Carter for President and again contributed large sums of money to federal, state, and local races. Its major goal was to maintain educational budgets in the face of declining enrollment by having states and the federal government assume larger shares of the costs. NEA maintains that the federal government should increase its support from approximately eight percent to 33 percent.

Whether teacher unions should become involved in political action raises a number of difficult normative questions. Is there not a conflict of interest when union members or politicians with union support win seats on local school boards or participate in decisions as legislators affecting the benefits of teachers? Can politicians who are indebted to teacher unions adequately represent the public interest in legislative deliberations? Regardless of the answers to these questions, increased use of political means to obtain union benefits weakens the relationship of trust between management and labor negotiators at the bargaining table. A more important consequence of teacher unions' increased emphasis on political action at the state level is a distortion of the political process at the local level. Decisions that should properly be made by the elected representatives in local school districts are increasingly being made by governors and legislators under political pressure from the unions.

One of the reasons for organizing is to increase the political strength of teachers in the bargaining unit. Whether the right to bargain collectively and the increased political power of teacher unions have created the right balance or a power imbalance between public management and employee unions is difficult to determine. Time and further research are needed to make a final judgment whether the interests of public employees and the public are being adequately protected.

The Economic Consequences of Teacher Bargaining

Many teachers joined unions to improve their salaries or at least to protect salaries from being cut as a result of declining enrollment and voter resistance to higher school levies. Analysts have attempted to determine the impact

[16]Peirce, "Employment Report," p. 1246.

of collective bargaining on teachers' salaries. The usual procedure is to compare increases in teachers' salaries in districts that bargain collectively with those in districts that do not.

Several problems arise in assessing the economic consequence of collective bargaining. First, since almost 85 percent of public school teachers are now organized, the question of the impact of collective bargaining on salaries may soon be moot. There simply will be no way of distinguishing between the effects of collective bargaining and the many other variables that affect public sector salaries. Second, most of the studies have not tried to assess the effects of collective bargaining on salaries in nearby nonbargaining districts. It may be true that there is little difference between salary increases in bargaining and nonbargaining districts precisely because districts which do not bargain raise salaries of teachers to meet those negotiated in nearby districts. They may do this to reduce the chances of a union successfully organizing their employees or to remain competitive with bargaining districts in terms of their ability to hire and retain good teachers.[17]

EFFECTS OF BARGAINING ON TEACHERS' SALARIES

Table 5-1 presents the findings of seven studies of the effects of bargaining on teachers' salaries. Each of the studies has limitations, making it inconclusive by itself. Together, however, the studies, covering a variety of educational environments and using different techniques, produce a general finding that teachers' unions do increase salaries but not as much as critics of unions are likely to believe.

The studies included in Table 5-1 estimate the increases in salaries due to collective bargaining to range from zero to 16.8 percent greater than salary increases in nonbargaining districts. With the exception of Chambers' results, the others generally support Kasper's original estimates of differences that range from 0 to 4 percent. Baird and Landon (4.9 percent), Hall and Carroll (1.8 percent), and Lipsky and Drotning (0-3 percent) all fall within the approximate range of Kasper's results. Thornton's finding for increases at the lower salary ranges is also similar, while his high estimate for the top salary step is out of line with other estimates.

Only Chambers' estimates show a consistently higher impact of bargaining, an average 7.5 percent increase in unified districts and 16.8 percent in elementary districts. The higher estimates are explainable because he took into account both district and regional effects of bargaining. He found that when regions comprised entirely of districts that bargained were compared with regions where bargaining was either nonexistent or negligible, the effects were much higher.

[17]The effects of collective bargaining in adjacent nonbargaining districts are explored at length in Jay G. Chambers, "The Impact of Collective Bargaining for Teachers on Resource Allocation in Public School Districts: The California Experience," *Journal of Urban Economics* (July 1977).

TABLE 5-1

Studies of the Impact of Unionization on Teacher Salaries

	Findings	Research Design
Kasper (1970)	0–4% increase in average salaries*	Teachers 1967–1968 50 states & D.C. Sample size 51
Thornton (1971)	1–4% increase first 3 steps 23% increase in highest step	Teachers 1969–70 Cities over 100,000 in pop. Sample size 83
Baird & Landon (1972)	4.9% increase in minimum salaries	Teachers 1966–67 Districts 24,000–50,000 students Sample size 44
Hall & Carroll (1973)	1.8% increase in mean salary	Teachers 1968–69 Districts in Cook County Sample size 118
Lipsky & Drotning (1973)	0–3% increase in salary level	Teachers 1967–68 All school districts in N.Y. state Sample size 696
Frey (1973)	–0.4–1.4% increase in salaries	Teachers 1964–70 All school districts in New Jersey Sample size 298
Chambers (1975)	7.5% increase in unified districts 16.8% increase in elementary districts	Teachers 1970–71 89 districts in California in 6 SMSA's

*Percent of increase indicates how much more salaries increased in bargaining districts than nonbargaining districts.

Sources: Hirschel Kasper, "The Effects of Collective Bargaining on Public School Teachers' Salaries," *Industrial and Labor Relations Review,* 24 (October 1970), 57–72.

Robert Thornton, "The Effects of Collective Negotiations on Teachers' Salaries," *The Quarterly Review of Economics and Business,* 2 (Winter 1971), 37–46.

Robert N. Baird and John H. Landon, "The Effects of Collective Bargaining on Public School Teachers' Salaries: Comment," *Industrial and Labor Relations Review,* 25 (April 1972), 410–17.

W. Clayton Hall and Norman E. Carroll, "The Effects of Teachers' Organizations on Salaries and Class Size," *Industrial and Labor Relations Review,* 26 (January 1973), 834–41.

David Lipsky and John Drotning, "The Influence of Collective Bargaining on Teachers' Salaries in New York State," *Industrial and Labor Relations Review,* 27 (October 1973), 18–35.

Donald E. Frey, "Wage Determination in Public Schools and the Effects of Unionization," Working Paper 42E, Princeton University, Industrial Relations Section, 1973.

Jay G. Chambers, "The Impact of Collective Bargaining for Teachers on Resource Allocation in Public School Districts: The California Experience," *Journal of Urban Economics* (July 1977).

He went further to suggest that "the greater the fraction of teachers covered by bargaining contracts, the larger will be the gains from bargaining and the greater the tendency for nonbargaining districts in the same region to match the gains in bargaining districts."[18] To support this conclusion he showed that in regions where 100 percent of the teachers were covered, increases ranged from 7.5 percent in unified districts to 16.8 percent in elementary districts *above those* in regions without collective bargaining. When the percentage of union membership dropped to 70 percent, the salary differentials fell to 5.7 percent for unified districts and 12.2 percent for elementary districts.

Because he controlled for regional effects, Chambers' estimates are probably more accurate for the period he studied than the earlier studies for their respective periods. However, the impact of unionization on salaries has surely declined from Chambers' estimates because of the spread of collective bargaining and because of the increasing scarcity of resources available for education. The important questions now are not the consequences of bargaining on salaries, but rather the consequences of bargaining for the allocation of resources within the educational budget and among education and other public services.

OTHER ECONOMIC EFFECTS OF TEACHER BARGAINING

Concentration on the effects of bargaining on salaries has diverted attention from other economic consequences of collective bargaining. For example, administrative salaries in a district that bargains with teachers are likely to increase along with those of teachers. Chambers found this to be the case in his study in California, although average administrative salary increases in bargaining districts tended to be somewhat less than the teacher increases. Furthermore, the greater the proportion of unionized teachers in a region (and the higher their salary increase differential), the larger were administrative salary increases.[19] While Chambers finds that some kinds of administrators benefit more than others, in general his study supports the conclusion that administrators have something to gain personally from teacher collective bargaining.

Fringe benefits and pension costs have also been rising as a proportion of public school budgets. Research is inconclusive as to whether these costs can be attributed to collective bargaining. Since most teacher contracts include provisions for improved fringe benefits and pensions, one may presume that unions are responsible for at least a part of the increases.

In addition to bargaining for added pay and benefits, teacher organizations are obliged to preserve what has previously been gained. One of the largest concerns in this regard is protecting employees against loss of jobs. A few figures regarding the magnitude of the professional education work force illustrate the significance of the situation.

[18] *Ibid.*, p. 28.
[19] *Ibid.*, p. 29.

In 1869-70 there were 200,515 teachers employed in U.S. schools, one educator every 34.4 pupils By 1974 the number of professional educators had increased twelvefold to almost 2.5 million, approximately 1 educator for every 17 pupils. The awesome growth in absolute numbers has been accompanied by a remarkable proliferation of non-teaching education positions, e.g., guidance and psychology personnel, administrators, consultants, librarians, and supervisors. In 1974, such non-teaching positions accounted for 270,000 employees, a number larger than the total educator work force a century before.[20]

In a period of declining enrollments and limited resources, educator organizations will defend these positions tenaciously; jobs may be the most important item on their bargaining agenda. From the perspective of management, the number of employees is the variable that most directly determines district costs. The potential for intense conflict is obvious.

Many districts have incurred substantial cost increases as a result of educational provisions negotiated in teachers' contracts. Reduced class size, lighter teaching loads, and shorter hours all cost extra money. Often teacher representatives trade such benefits as reduction of class size, teaching load, or hours in return for larger salaries. Although such trades have been made, bargaining does not merely increase class size and leave the budget unchanged. The net result of bargaining has been to increase educational spending. This suggests that the demand for education is relatively inelastic, or that unions have also been successful in persuading decision makers to increase their preferences for education.

Finally, bargaining increases administrative costs of school districts, although the dollar costs of hiring a negotiator and of administering a grievance procedure are relatively small in comparison to the salary component of a school budget. Increases in administrative costs are also likely to be higher in the early years of bargaining. As managers become accustomed to bargaining with unions, the amount of time required will decline. There will be fewer disagreements over scope of bargaining issues, fewer charges of unfair labor practices, and fewer impasses as both management and labor learn what can and cannot be negotiated. Similarly, the large number of grievances which accompany the first years of bargaining in a district tend to decline as the backlog of complaints diminishes and as employees learn what constitutes a legitimate grievance.

The Implications of Collective Bargaining for School Governance[21]

Over the past decade, collective bargaining has triggered a shift of control from school board and school administrators to teachers. Teachers are

---

[20] These data are derived from the National Center for Educational Statistics, *A Century of Public School Statistics* (Washington, D.C.: U.S. Government Printing Office, 1973).

[21] This section summarizes points made by Lawrence C. Pierce, "Teachers' Organ-

asking not only to help determine salaries and fringe benefits; they are asking for, and in some states receiving, the right collectively to determine class size, intradistrict teacher transfer policies, pupil-teacher ratios, subject matter content, student expulsion rules, and other important matters of educational policy.

This shift in decision-making authority has further diminished the power of school boards and the public's ability to express its preferences regarding school policy. The adoption of the private-sector model of collective bargaining has evoked questions about the role of interest groups in the formulation of educational policy. What is the proper balance between the public, the school board, administrators, teachers, and students in educational decision making? Do the present collective bargaining laws establish equitable balance? Does the wholesale adoption of the private-sector model facilitate the cooperation and compromise necessary to accomplish the public purpose in education? If power has shifted too much, how should the proper balance be restored?

THE APPROPRIATENESS
OF THE PRIVATE BARGAINING MODEL IN PUBLIC EDUCATION

EFFECTS OF COLLECTIVE BARGAINING
ON CONSUMERS OF EDUCATION

In discussing the applicability of the private-sector bargaining model, we must look both at what collective bargaining involves and at the institutional assumptions underlying it. Collective bargaining is a process by which employees negotiate with employers over the terms and conditions of their employment. Wage settlements clearly affect the price of goods or services, since labor costs are an important component of production costs. In education, where 70 to 80 percent of total costs are salaries and personnel benefits, collective bargaining settlements are closely related to the price of schooling.

Private sector bargaining is based on several important assumptions about the relationship between the parties at the table and the final consumers of the goods and services produced.[22] Specifically, the model assumes that both employers' and employees' bargaining behavior is constrained by the marketplace.

In the private sector, a change in the price of an organization's services may provoke a variety of responses. The consumer may pay the higher price, realizing that it may be spread over a number of months or years. On the other hand, the consumer may postpone buying the product because it is too costly. Or the consumer may choose another brand or a cheaper substitute. The fact

---

izations and Bargaining Power Imbalance in the Public Sphere," National Committee for Citizens in Education, *Public Testimony in Public Schools* (Berkeley, Cal.: McCutchan Publishing Company, 1975), pp. 122-59.

[22] Myron Lieberman and Michael H. Moskow, *Collective Negotiations for Teachers* (Chicago: Rand McNally, 1966), contains a useful discussion of alternative models of collective bargaining.

that the consumer has the choice of buying or not buying imposes a constraint on the bargaining strategies of both management and labor. Employers want to maximize profits, so they attempt to hold down costs as much as possible. Unions are faced with a similar constraint.

> A price rise of [the] product relative to others will result in a decrease in the number of units of the product sold. This in turn will result in a cutback in employment. And an increase in price would be dictated by an increase in labor cost relative to output, at least in most situations. Thus, the union is faced with some sort of rough tradeoff between on the one hand, larger benefits for some employees and unemployment for others, and on the other hand, smaller benefits and more employment.[23]

Consumers, in other words, have an important role in private-sector collective bargaining. Their role in the economics of public-sector bargaining is less clear. There is no direct link to indicate the consumer's reaction to an increase in the tax price of public goods resulting from a negotiated settlement. In public education, students seldom have the option of changing schools, postponing schooling, or consuming a smaller quantity of education. Management and union representatives are constrained in negotiations on economic matters only by the relatively distant threat of withdrawal of public support in budget elections or by public protests.

Collective bargaining, instead of leading to a change in price, may result in a decline in the quality of services being provided. The compulsory nature of public education and its reliance on taxation for revenues make it extremely difficult to reverse a process of decline. If parents are dissatisfied with the quality of educational services, for instance, they usually cannot move their children to other schools without substantial costs. Nor can they express their dissatisfaction by withholding school taxes. Public schools receive tax support even when they are closed by strikes. The only feasible recourse for dissatisfied citizens is to complain to the school board or any other group of officials who will listen. Parents frequently believe that the impact of such complaints is extremely low.

Thus, although market competition serves as an effective constraint on collective bargaining in the private sector, it fails to restrict public management or labor because of the virtual monopoly enjoyed by most public services and the separation between the revenue raising and product distribution processes. The direct link between consumers and producers in the private market is replaced by uncertainty over who the final consumers of public goods are and how their preferences are communicated.

EFFECTS OF STRIKES ON PUBLIC AGENCIES AND PUBLIC EMPLOYEES

There is another important difference between private- and public-sector decision making that affects collective bargaining in the two spheres. If the

[23]Wellington and Winter, *The Unions and the Cities,* p. 15.

parties involved in private-sector bargaining cannot reach a settlement, labor will strike or management will lock out the employees. This result is an economic hardship for both sides. The employer loses sales and profits, and a prolonged strike may force the company to close. Workers, on the other hand, lose wages. Consumers are also inconvenienced, but only to the extent that they may have to wait to purchase a particular product.

A strike against a public agency has little or no effect upon the agency's continued income. Some states withhold state aid if schools are not open a specified number of days. Generally, however, taxes will be collected and apportioned to an agency despite the curtailment of its services. A strike by public employees, therefore, must be aimed at the consumers of public services rather than management. By withholding public services, the unions pressure the consumers. While consumers may do without new cars or new housing for some time, the loss of mail delivery, electric power, schools, or police protection creates an immediate hardship. Since clients usually cannot purchase public services elsewhere, they can only apply political pressure on elected representatives or the managers of the public agency to settle the strike and restore services.

Strikes in the public sector are also less likely to lead to economic losses for employees than in the private sector. Knowing that most public services are essential for the health and safety of a community, public employees are not likely to suffer a long period without wages. The fear of lost wages is even less among teachers, since most states require schools to be in session for a minimum number of days each year. Wages lost due to a strike are almost always made up by adding additional workdays through the year or at the end of the year.

As a result of these conditions, public sector strikes are heavily politicized. Their effect is not to create economic hardship for either of the bargaining parties, but to inconvenience the consumers of public services and create political pressures for a quick settlement. To the extent that public employees substitute political for economic sanctions, the private-sector model may have to be altered to allow management to apply political pressure in the form of public hearings or referenda to air its objectives as well.

POSSIBLE REFORMS
IN EDUCATIONAL COLLECTIVE BARGAINING

The essential need today is to create a new balance of power among those responsible for educational policy. Steps must also be taken to increase greatly the public's say about educational decision making. Since there is no inherent consumer sovereignty in public education, public control of schools can only be reestablished by revitalizing the legislative process of educational governance and opening channels for direct citizen participation in school government. To accomplish these purposes, reform of the collective bargaining system must be accompanied by reform of the system of educational governance.

As a response to the fears of citizens that their interests are not being protected in public-sector bargaining, a number of attempts have been made to increase public participation in collective bargaining. Parents in Philadelphia formed a parents union and sought the right to negotiate directly with school officials. In Florida collective bargaining negotiations were opened to the press and the public. After more than a year's experience negotiating "in the sunshine," most administrators and many union representatives and labor mediators reported liking the process.[24] Article 8 of the educational collective bargaining statute in California requires that both sides publicize their bargaining positions and that a public hearing be held to evaluate public reaction to those positions prior to collective bargaining.[25] In Oregon, three students were permitted to attend all bargaining sessions in higher education. Although students were designated as nonvoting third parties, they were allowed to put proposals on the bargaining table and address any item during negotiations.[26] The intent of all these experiments is to find mechanisms to protect the public consumer's interests at the bargaining table.

Summary

This chapter has described the variety of issues surrounding collective bargaining in public education. Particular attention is given to problems of determining bargaining units, identifying public employers for purposes of bargaining, defining the scope of bargaining, and designing workable impasse procedures. The arguments for and against a federal collective bargaining statute are analyzed. The likelihood of a federal law has been substantially reduced by the Supreme Court's ruling in *National League of Cities* v. *Usery,* which exempted state and local governments from certain provisions of the Fair Labor Standards Act.

Despite these legal issues, teacher unions continue to exercise considerable political and economic power. Teacher unions are among the largest contributors to political campaigns and spend more than any other lobbying group in many state capitols. They have also contributed to the rapid rise of educational costs, although their precise economic effect has been difficult to measure.

Finally, we have examined the implications of collective bargaining for school governance. Collective bargaining in education raises fundamental questions about the organization of public schools and who controls them. The

[24] Roger Dahl and Marge Shapiro Varney, "Bargaining in the Sunshine; The Experience of Florida Local Governments," Institute of Management-Labor Relations, Washington D.C., February, 1977.

[25] Chapter 10, Section 3547 of Division 4, Title 1 of the California Government Code.

[26] House Bill 3043 passed in 1975 allows three students to attend all negotiating sessions between faculty and state board representatives.

private-sector collective bargaining model would assign determination of educational policy exclusively to teachers and school administrators. The major loser in this realignment of powers is the public.

We believe that in a democracy the people should control their institutions. Since the "consumers" of public education are virtually excluded from exercising control through the marketplace, they must exercise that control by participating in the decision-making process.

Parent unions, "fishbowl" bargaining, public notice and discussion of bargaining positions, and consultative or third-party bargaining are possible ways of restoring public influence over educational decision making. However, educators should not end their search for new mechanisms to enable the public to communicate their concerns cheaply and effectively. Efforts should be expended on designing educational programs to increase the choices available to students and parents and to make educational institutions more responsive to diverse needs and demands. Above all, the guiding principle should be responsiveness. Collective bargaining for teachers challenges the traditional form of administrative government in schools. It will serve education well if it brings about a new balance of power permitting greater participation by the public as well as by teachers.

6

PAYING FOR
PUBLIC EDUCATION

There are three dimensions to educational finance: raising, distributing, and spending money. This chapter is concerned with raising money for public education, and with the taxes primarily used to do so.

Education is supported chiefly by broad-based taxes, but other methods of financing are conceivable. User charges (known as tuition when applied to education) come to mind. If education is primarily a personal investment or consumption good—that is, if it does not have important social consequences—it would appear that students or their families should bear the major burden. If, however, the benefits of schooling are mainly to society rather than to the individual, society should pay the cost through taxes. In Chapter Three we explored this question of the private and public benefits of education, and in Chapter Nine we will recommend a method of financing public education that recognizes both social and private benefits and combines state financing with user charges. At present, however, the public elementary and secondary schools of all states are tuition-free, supported primarily by local and state taxation. Thus, this chapter will concentrate on taxation.

A number of states have dedicated a particular tax source for support of education. However, these narrowly based tax sources have been found insufficient to meet the revenue needs of this largest single object of governmental expenditure. As a result, educational finance has rested primarily on broad-based taxes such as income, sales, and property taxes. In this chapter we first describe the characteristics of taxes in general, and then examine how they apply to each of the three most general taxes.

Characteristics of Taxes

It is important to understand taxes' basis, equity, yield, administration and compliance costs, and their economic, social, and political effects.

BASIS

There are four bases, or criteria for levying a tax: wealth, income, consumption, or privilege. These all involve money; the first three directly, the fourth indirectly.

A tax on wealth is based on the ownership of property. The most common example is a property tax, with the amount of tax paid based on the amount of property owned. Another example is the federal estate tax, based on the size of the estate of a deceased person. Note that the size of the tax bears no relation to the income generated by the property owned, but is based only on the value of the property.

A tax on income is based on the taxable income of individuals (or corporations). Taxable income is income after allowable expenses and deductions. One of the virtues of an income tax is that the amount of the tax is related to the income used to pay it.

A tax on consumption is usually called a sales tax, particularly if it applies to all or most sales. If it applies only to the purchase of a particular class of items (such as a tax on theater admissions), it is called an excise tax. Import duties on particular kinds of goods are also excise taxes.

A tax on privileges is a tax levied on the privilege of engaging in some sort of conduct regulated by the government. It usually takes the form of license fees. These license fees may be directly related to the making of money, as is a retail store license, a medical license, or a license to operate a taxicab. On the other hand, they may have no direct relation to money, as a dog license, a driver's license, or a hunting license. The number of licenses required by state and local governments is large, and the money collected in fees is a substantial portion of all taxes. The imposition of license fees is usually defended as a regulatory function of government, rather than as a tax, with the license fees paying for the bureaucratic costs of regulation. This is only partially true; fees are often much greater than costs.

EQUITY

Since taxes are a burden imposed on all by the will of the majority, they should treat all in an equitable manner. This may conflict with other considerations, as indicated later, but it is a worthy goal. How should we decide whether a tax is equitable?

First, the tax should treat equals equally. Two persons who are equal with respect to the basis of the tax should pay equal amounts. For example, two individuals with the same amount of taxable income should pay the same amount of income tax. Two persons who own property of equal value in the same neighborhood should pay the same amount of property tax. This is a relatively simple criterion, and easy to judge. Most taxes are relatively equitable based on this criterion, although we will particularly discuss exceptions regarding the property tax.

Unfortunately for those establishing tax criteria, not all persons are equal. It is thus necessary to establish rules for the tax treatment of unequals, a more difficult task. The most obvious criterion is that persons should pay taxes in proportion to the benefit received, or in proportion to their contribution to the cost of whatever is supported by the tax. For example, those who use electricity generated by a municipal power company pay taxes for its support in the form of a charge for the electricity used. The charges are not in proportion to benefit received, for there is no way of measuring the benefit a given amount of electricity provides in most cases. However, charges are closely related to the contribution of the user to the costs of operation. For example, some costs of operation are the same regardless of the amount of electricity used, such as costs of meter reading and billing, whereas other costs (e.g., fuel) are proportional to usage. The fee schedule usually recognizes this by placing a larger charge on small amounts of electricity usage than on additional amounts. Other examples of taxes based on cost or benefits include gasoline taxes for the construction and maintenance of highways, and charges by the "front foot" for street improvements.

Taxes based on benefit received or on contribution to cost seem so eminently reasonable that there is a temptation to endorse this as a basis for all taxation. Unfortunately, it is not that simple. It is often difficult to assess either the benefits received or the contribution to cost. Should the cost of police be charged to the person saved from robbery or murder, on the basis of benefit received, or to the felon, on the basis of his contribution to the cost of the department? Or are there benefits to the average citizen for safer streets and homes that cannot be allocated on any strict accounting basis? There is general agreement that the cost of police cannot be allocated on a benefit or cost basis.

What about the cost of national defense? There is a different problem here. Given the choice, no individual operating purely on self-interest would pay taxes for national defense. The reason is that there is no way for the government to defend citizens who pay for national defense without also defending those who do not pay. In addition, there is no rational way of calculating either the individual benefits or costs of national defense. Allocation of taxes on this basis is not feasible. Rather, the total budget is decided on a representative basis through congressional action, and the money raised through taxes based on other than benefit received.

Welfare costs present yet a third problem. Here, individual benefits are clear, consisting of welfare payments to persons. However, the folly of charging individuals a tax equal to the amount of welfare benefits received is obvious. Welfare has as its principal goal the redistribution of income. Taxation based on benefit received would directly contradict this goal.

For these reasons, most taxes cannot be allocated on the basis of benefit received or contribution to cost. An alternative equity criterion must be found. That criterion is the "ability to pay" principle discussed below.

PROGRESSIVE AND REGRESSIVE TAXES

Regardless of the basis for levying a tax (wealth, income, expenditure, or privilege), taxes are mostly paid out of income. If we are to judge the equity of a tax by whether it is consistent with the principle of ability to pay, we must compare the amount of tax paid with income. Suppose we find that, for a given tax, people with incomes of $10,000 pay an average of $100 in tax, and people with incomes of $20,000 pay an average of $200 in tax. Each income group is paying an average of 1 percent of its income in tax. Such a tax is said to be a *proportional* tax. Note that we may be talking about a property tax or a sales tax, rather than an income tax. It makes no difference; we compare the amount of tax paid with the *income* of the payer of the tax. A proportional tax would on the surface, appear to meet the ability to pay standard, for each person pays the same percentage of his income in tax.

Suppose instead that those with $10,000 income continue to pay $100 in tax, but those with $20,000 income pay $150 in tax. Now the lower income group is paying 1 percent of its income, but the higher income group is paying only three-quarters of 1 percent. Note particularly that, although the higher income group is paying *more dollars,* it is still paying a smaller percentage of its income than the lower income group. A tax with this characteristic is called a *regressive* tax.

Finally, suppose that the $10,000 group continues to pay $100, but the $20,000 group pays $400. Those with higher incomes are paying 2 percent of their income, while those with lower incomes are paying only 1 percent. Such a tax is called a *progressive* tax (because the rates progress toward higher percentages at higher incomes).

Which of these types of tax (regressive, proportional, or progressive) most closely meets the ability to pay criterion? In considering this, we must realize that there is a basic amount households need to establish a minimum standard of living. Families whose incomes are at subsistence level must spend all of their income for the necessities and have none left over to pay taxes. At the other end of the scale, extremely rich families find that they are unable to spend all their income on goods and services. They clearly have excess income which could be used for investment, or for paying taxes. Under these circumstances, it is evident that a regressive tax is not based on ability to pay, and that actually a proportional tax is not either. A progressive tax, at least theoretically, leaves untouched monies that are necessary for a minimum standard of living. However, there is no agreement on how progressive a tax must be in order to be equitable. If it is close to being proportional, it is probably unfair to poor people, if it is extremely progressive, it is probably inequitable for rich people. The broad band of disagreement between these extremes results partly from lack of consensus on how much it costs to pay for necessities.

Another reason for belief in the equity of progressive taxation is the unwritten tenet of the American public that government should intervene to reduce extreme income inequalities. One way to do this is to tax a greater percentage of the income of the rich than of the poor.

IMPACT AND INCIDENCE

We have implied in our discussion thus far that the burden of taxation falls on the person who physically pays the tax. This is not necessarily true. Business firms of all kinds are taxed, but ultimately, of course, individuals bear the burden of taxation. If we are to discover whether a tax is progressive or regressive, we must find out who shoulders the ultimate burden of the tax. The actual taxpayer —individual or firm— is said to bear the *impact* of the tax. Those individuals who ultimately feel the burden of the tax are said to bear its *incidence*. In judging progressivity or regressivity we are concerned with incidence.

Discovering the impact of taxes is a trivial matter, for it is easy to record who actually pays. Discovering the incidence is much more difficult. There are no firm guidelines, and economists can only make reasonable assumptions. For example, suppose an excise tax is levied on the production of cigarettes. On which individuals does the burden of this tax ultimately fall? There are three main possibilities. The tax may be shifted forward to the cigarette purchasers in the form of higher prices. It may be shifted sideways to the employees of the cigarette manufacturer in the form of lower wages. Or it may be shifted backward to the owners of the manufacturing corporation (its stockholders) in the form of lower dividends. What will happen in any individual case depends upon the specific circumstances. Shifting the tax backward is a last resort when other shifts fail. To some extent manufacturers may be able to shift the tax sideways (probably not by a reduction in wages, but by a reduction in work force, or by not granting such a large increase the next time wages are negotiated). This may be possible where the tobacco company is the principal employer in a community, for the costs of moving are large, and workers are not apt to leave the employ of the company unless the difference between what they are able to earn there and what they are able to earn elsewhere is sufficient to offset the economic and psychic costs of moving.

The chances of shifting the tax forward to the consumer are good. The demand for cigarettes is relatively inelastic. Regardless of price, people continue to smoke approximately the same amount. As a result, manufacturers will promptly increase their prices by an amount sufficient to cover the tax; they know this will have little or no effect on the number of cigarettes sold. It would be different in the case of a tax on peas, for example. Faced with a higher pea price, many people would shift to beans or carrots. Under these circumstances producers would be able to shift little of the tax forward, and might ultimately shift it back to the owners in the form of a lower return on their investment.

Whether a tax is shifted backward or forward depends upon individual circumstances. However, we are not here concerned with individual cases of shifting taxes. We want to know the overall general effect of tax incidence—whether it is progressive or regressive—and we find that there is no general agreement among economists. Assumptions must be made about what will happen on the average, and economists differ on which are the most reasonable assumptions. There is, however, a modest amount of agreement, and it will be reported in connection with our discussion of specific taxes later in this chapter.

There have been attempts to discover the progressivity or regressivity of the United States tax system as a whole. One example is a study by Joseph Pechman for the year 1965.[1] He calculates that the sum of all federal, state, and local taxes in the United States has an incidence roughly proportional throughout a wide range of incomes, with most people paying about 27 percent of their incomes in taxes. At the lowest incomes, the sum of all taxes tends to be regressive, with very poor people paying more than 27 percent of their income in taxes. At the other end of the scale, taxes of all kinds tend to be progressive, with rich individuals also paying more than 27 percent of their income in taxes.

As pointed out earlier, it is generally impossible to assign benefits of expenditures from tax monies to individuals. The exception is cash payments to people for welfare, unemployment compensation, social security, etc. Among economists these are called *transfer payments,* for they represent neither income nor expenditure in the economy as a whole. They are simply taking money out of the pockets of some individuals and putting it into the pockets of others without the provision of goods or services. Pechman calculates the amount received in transfer payments by different income classes, and subtracts this from their tax burden, to obtain a net amount that they are out of pocket as a result of taxes. He finds, not surprisingly, that the lowest income groups receive more in transfer payments than they pay in taxes. When the effect of transfer payments

---

[1] Joseph Pechman, "The Rich, the Poor, and the Taxes They Pay," *The Public Interest,* 17 (Fall 1969), 21–43.

TABLE 6-1

Taxes and Transfers as Percent of Income, 1965

Income Class	Federal Taxes	State and Local Taxes	Total Taxes	Transfer Payments	Taxes Less Transfers
Under $2,000	19	25	44	126	-83*
$2,000-$4,000	16	11	27	11	16
4,000- 6,000	17	10	27	5	21
6,000- 8,000	17	9	26	3	23
8,000-10,000	18	9	27	2	25
10,000-15,000	19	9	27	2	25
Over 15,000	32	7	38	1	37
All classes	22	9	31	14	24

*The minus sign indicates that the families and individuals in this class received more from federal, state, and local governments than they, as a group, paid to these governments in taxes. They paid 44% of their income exclusive of transfer payments in taxes, but received 126% as much in transfer payments as in other income, leaving them with a net of 83% more after taxes and transfer payments than before either. (Totals vary slightly because of rounding.)

Source: Reprinted with permission of Joseph Pechman *The Public Interest,* No. 17, Fall 1969. Copyright © 1969 by National Affairs, Inc.

is analyzed across all income levels, he finds that our total tax system is progressive at the lowest income levels, proportional in the middle incomes, and progressive again at the higher incomes. If the assumptions on which his calculations are based are correct, our tax system as a whole may be a relatively equitable one. Pechman's findings are summarized in Table 6-1.

This is not to imply, however, that the system is equally equitable in every state or community, or with particular individuals. The tax laws of each state are different, with some states relying heavily on income taxes while others use the sales tax to a greater extent. The burden of the property tax varies substantially from one community to the next. Particular individuals must pay based on their liability for each tax, which may bear little relationship to their income. We can really only talk about progressivity and regressivity in overall terms, not in individual ones.

YIELD

The yield of a tax is its ability to generate revenue. In evaluating a tax it is useful to compare its yield to those of alternative taxes, and to the cost of administering the tax. Some taxes are incapable of large yields. For example, the dollar volume of paper clip sales is so small that even a 100 percent excise tax on paper clips would yield relatively few dollars. On the other hand, the federal individual income tax yields an amount sufficient to cover more than half of federal operating costs. In general, the broader based a tax, the greater its potential yield. Thus, excise taxes are generally not capable of as great a yield as is a general sales tax. The cost of administration of a tax is discussed in the next section, and there the yield and administration costs are compared.

Of interest in connection with a tax's yield is the rate at which the yield increases if average personal income increases. A tax whose yield increases at a greater rate than incomes is said to be *elastic;* one whose yield increases at a slower rate than incomes is said to be *inelastic.* For example, let us suppose there is an excise tax on soap of one cent per bar. If the average income of individuals increases, is the yield of this tax apt to increase, and if so, how rapidly? The demand for soap changes only slightly with changes in income. If the incomes of all people doubled, they would probably only use a little more soap. Thus, one would expect the yield of a tax on soap to increase less rapidly than incomes, and we would thus term the tax inelastic.

We can formalize the measurement of elasticity by defining the "income elasticity of yield" as follows:

$$E = \frac{\text{percentage change in tax yield}}{\text{percentage change in national (or regional) income}}$$

If the percentage change in tax yield is equal to the percentage change in income, elasticity will equal one. An elastic tax has an elasticity greater than one; an inelastic tax has an elasticity less than one. The elasticity of yield of a tax on soap of one cent per bar might be expected to be very low, perhaps in the neighborhood of 0.2.

On the other hand, the elasticity of yield of the income tax is in the range of 1.5, making it a remarkably elastic tax.[2] Elastic taxes are of significant advantage to governments in a period of expanding income, whether the expansion is a real one, or only caused by inflation. The reason is that the tax income of the government increases at a more rapid rate than income in general, while the expenses of the government (given a constant level of services) will tend to increase at about the same rate as incomes in general. This means that in such a period of expansion the government has a continuing excess of income which it may use to finance new programs. The ramifications of this are discussed later under the political effects of taxes.

COST OF ADMINISTRATION AND COMPLIANCE

The cost of administering a tax is the cost to the government of levying and collecting the tax. The cost of compliance refers to the cost to the taxpayer of complying with the requirements of the tax. A federal tax of ten cents a pack

[2] Joseph Pechman, *Federal Tax Policy,* 3rd ed. (Washington, D.C.: The Brookings Institute, 1977), p. 12.

on the manufacture of cigarettes would have a relatively low cost of administration. The reason is that there are only a few manufacturers of cigarettes. It is easy to require these manufacturers to report monthly to the government the number of packs of cigarettes produced during the previous month. The number is multiplied by ten cents per pack, and a check for the total accompanies the report. At relatively low cost the government can audit to ensure correct reporting of the number of packs produced.

The cost of compliance with taxes varies greatly. Usually this cost should be low. Perhaps the tax with the lowest compliance cost is the property tax. The individual receives a tax bill yearly or semiannually, writes a check for the amount, and sends it in. No additional effort on his part is required. At the other extreme is the individual income tax (or the corporate income tax). Careful sets of books must be kept, supporting evidence must be filed, accountants must often be hired to prepare the tax return, and occasionally time and expense are necessary in substantiating the return to the IRS.

ECONOMIC AND SOCIAL EFFECTS

If a tax is designed only for the purpose of raising money, its economic and social effects should be as neutral as possible. That is, the imposition of the tax should not affect the economic decisions made by people, nor should it affect social well-being. (Note that we are discussing the effects of the imposition of the tax, not the effects generated by spending that tax money for governmental purposes.) Some taxes have more substantial economic effects than others. An excise tax on a particular commodity will serve to increase its price (if the tax is passed forward), or decrease profit (if the tax is passed backward). Either situation is apt to result in a decreased consumption of the commodity, an economic effect.

An important alleged social effect of the property tax has been the abandonment of low-rent housing in cities because property taxes (on top of other expenses) exceed rental income. The result is an increasing shortage of adequate housing for the city's poor.

Of course, a tax may be levied mainly for its economic or social effects. For example, an import tax is levied to protect a domestic industry.

POLITICAL EFFECTS

Taxes are at once the nemesis and the lifeblood of public officials. Without tax revenues they are unable to provide governmental programs that attract votes. However, officials' votes to raise taxes can be unpopular and perhaps politically fatal. Consequently, in a period of increasing incomes, such as the U.S. had for the majority of the years since World War II, an elastic tax is greatly favored by politicians. As incomes increase, the yield of the tax increases even faster, providing excess money for new programs without the necessity of raising the tax rate. Politicians can have their cake and eat it. This has been generally true of the federal government's tax structure, which has an elasticity greater than one. Many new programs have been undertaken by the federal government in the last thirty years, although tax rates have been virtually unchanged since shortly after World War II. This has also been true in a few states, notably New York, where constantly expanding tax revenues helped the Rockefeller administration to stay in power for 16 years.

Many states have had a combination of taxes that on the whole is inelastic, forcing frequent increases of tax rates just to keep the existing level of services.[3] This is a no-win proposition for politicians, and it is understandable that they have been anxious to enact state income taxes, which are generally elastic. Although there are still nine holdouts, forty-one states now have broad based personal income taxes, compared with only thirty-one in 1963. For the same reason, state officials have enthusiastically embraced federal revenue sharing, which has enabled simultaneous extension of programs and reduction of state and local taxes.

Of course, elasticity is not a one-way road. An elasticity of greater than one implies that as income decreases, the yield of the tax will decrease even faster. We have been blessed with more periods of expansion than of contraction, but when a recession occurs the results can be disastrous for a government that has based its operations on the expectation of ever-increasing tax revenues. An example is New York, where the halcyon days of the 1960s became the nightmare of the 1970s. Governmental commitments to new and extended programs had been made with the expectation that tax revenues would increase to cover needs. When recession hit, revenues were grossly insufficient. A state which had based much of its governmental finance on borrowing against future revenues suddenly found access to the capital markets severely restricted. Some agencies and political subdivisions of the state were in even worse shape, with New York City trembling on the brink of bankruptcy for months that stretched into years.

Alternative Taxes

In this section we will attempt to compare several important taxes on the basis of previously described characteristics. Because the property tax, rightly or

[3] For 1970, ACIR lists 18 states with tax structures of low elasticity (0.80 to 0.99), and 23 states with medium elasticity (1.00 to 1.19). Only 9 states had tax structures with high elasticity (above 1.20). Lowest was Ohio, with an elasticity of 0.80; highest was Alaska at 1.47, followed by Wisconsin at 1.41. Advisory Commission on Intergovernmental Relations, *State-Local Finances: Significant Features and Suggested Legislation,* 1972 ed. (Washington, D.C.: U.S. Government Printing Office, 1972), p. 49.

wrongly, is the tax most closely connected with education, we devote the most attention to it.

PERSONAL INCOME TAX

The federal personal income tax produces more revenue than any other U.S. tax. In addition, forty-one states have income taxes, and a few also allow local income taxes. While these state and local income taxes vary somewhat, they tend to be similar to the federal tax, and most of the remarks here will apply to them too.

The basis of the income tax, of course, is income. Since income is what people mostly use to pay taxes, this is important. The income tax is more nearly based on ability to pay than any other tax. However, let us examine the issue of equity more closely. Does the federal income tax treat equals equally? That depends upon how we define equals. If equals are people who have the same net income, the same deductions, the same marital status, and the same number of dependents, then their taxes will be equal. Similarly, we can say that, of two persons who differ only in the amount of taxable income, the person with higher income will pay a greater percentage of his or her income in tax. The income tax is thus a progressive tax. However, each of the qualifications above is important, for they mask differences among individuals which many think are used as "loopholes" to avoid taxation. Two individuals with the same gross income will not necessarily have the same taxable income. Capital gains are treated differently from ordinary income. Some expenses, such as moving expenses, can be deducted from income. Some income is not included at all, most notably interest on municipal bonds.

Two individuals may have very different deductions. One can increase deductions (and thereby decrease taxable income) by having large medical bills, by paying taxes (since the local taxes are deductible), by borrowing money and paying interest (interest paid is deductible), by making charitable contributions, by having a casualty or theft loss, or by having expenses connected with income (such as a safe deposit box to store stock certificates). People who are married can pay tax at a lower rate than unmarried individuals, and people with children can deduct $750 of income for each child as well as subsequently deducting $35 per child from the tax due.

There are, of course, many other adjustments to income, deductions, and exceptions, and all of them, at one time or another, have been referred to as "loopholes." Whether they are or not depends upon one's perspective. One frequent complaint is the fact that interest on municipal bonds is nontaxable. It is possible for a person to have an income of over a million dollars a year, all of it in interest on municipal bonds, and pay no income tax at all. While this seems grossly inequitable from the individual point of view, it is defended as a subsidy by the federal government of state and local governments; they are enabled to sell their bonds at a lower interest rate because the interest is nontaxable. If the decrease in interest received exactly balanced the tax which would have been paid, there would be no benefit to individuals. However, the decrease in interest received is equal to the tax paid by the marginal purchaser. High-income tax-payers find that their reduction in income as a result of buying the bonds is substantially less than the tax they would have to pay if the money were in-vested elsewhere. For example, suppose it is possible to purchase a corporate bond at 8 percent interest, or a municipal bond at 6 percent interest. If the individ-ual buying the bond has a tax rate of 50 percent, half of the interest on the corpo-rate bond would be taken away. The individual would be receiving the equivalent of 4 percent return on the corporate bond, compared with 6 percent on the nontax-able municipal bond.

Most other adjustments to income, deductions, and exemptions are also defended as being desirable on some economic or social basis, or simply on the basis of equity to the individual. There is some justification for each. The result, however, is a law so complex that it is difficult to state that it treats equals equally. It has been proposed that all of these adjustments, deductions, and exemptions be abandoned, with people simply taxed on their gross incomes. However, when this proposition is examined in detail, it is clear that it is not equitable either. Obviously, for example, people who operate a small business at home should not report gross receipts as income, for they have expenses connected with the busi-ness. However, defining which expenses are legally deductible brings us back to the complications we are trying to avoid. Other examples could be drawn. Even so, it is possible that the income tax could be simplified, and it is clearly our most complicated tax.

Since the income tax is paid by individuals who are usually unable to shift the burden to others, its incidence and impact are essentially identical. Thus its incidence can be measured more accurately than that of most other taxes. Based on adjusted gross income of families (which is the usual basis for judging inci-dence), the income tax is definitely a progressive tax. This is true not only be-cause the first $750 of income per person is untaxed, but also because the higher the income, the higher are the tax rates. The personal income tax is generally conceded to be our most progressive tax and its progressiveness offsets the regressivity of many other taxes. The result, as mentioned earlier, is a total U.S. tax system remarkably proportional across the majority of incomes.

The yield of the income tax is large and accounts for the majority of fed-eral government revenues. Many states also receive substantial amounts of money from state income taxes. In addition to being a prolific source of revenue, the income tax is an elastic tax. As national (or state) incomes increase, the yield of the income tax increases faster. This is true even if the increase in incomes is caused by inflation. For example, in Column A, a male head of household with a wife and two children has an income of $14,000 and uses the short form to calculate his tax. In column B the conditions are the same, except that the tax-payer's income has increased to $16,800. The increase in income is 20%, but the increase in tax is 37 percent. At this level of income the elasticity of tax is 1.85. The reason for this is twofold: The exemptions are a larger percentage of the lower income, and the rate on taxable income over $10,000 is higher than on that below $10,000. Of course, this elasticity only applies to this particular set of circumstances. The national income elasticity of the federal income tax is about 1.5.

	A	B
Adjusted gross income	$14,000	$16,800
Standard deduction (16% of adj. gross inc.)	2,240	2,688
Exemptions ($750 per dependent)	3,000	3,000
Taxable income	8,760	11,112
Income tax (A): $1551 less 2% of taxable income	1,205	
(B): $2068 less $180 maximum		1,881

It should be noted that this increase in income may simply reflect inflation and the purchasing power of the income of $16,800 may be the same as the $14,000 received earlier. However, the elastic income tax does not distinguish between increases in money wages (which include inflation) and increases in *real* wages (which do not). Thus, our hypothetical family actually suffers a decrease in real income as a result of the elasticity of the income tax.

The cost of administering the income tax is high, for the tax is complicated. Many examiners, auditors, and computer operators are necessary to verify the accuracy of the returns and investigate questionable ones. However, the yield of the tax is so great that the cost of administration as a percentage of yield is acceptably low.

The cost of compliance with the income tax is also high, for the taxpayer must account for income and deductible expenses, keep adequate records, and either spend time preparing the tax return or pay someone else to do it. This high cost of compliance is one of the reasons for calls to simplify the income tax.

The social and economic effects of the income tax are many and varied. Some are unintended, such as the tax shelter for the very rich provided by the nontaxability of municipal bond interest. Many of the effects, however, are intended. The deductibility of charitable contributions is intended to encourage charitable giving, and churches, hospitals, and colleges would be in difficult straits if the deduction were repealed. Deduction of half of the cost of medical insurance regardless of income (other medical expenses are not as liberally treated) is intended to encourage such insurance. In addition to such specific economic and social effects, the federal income tax is used to affect the overall business cycle. Several times, in periods of inflation, a surtax has been added to the tax, to reduce the amount of money in circulation and thus cool off inflation; at other times there has been a temporary tax cut to speed recovery from recession.

The income tax has been a politician's dream because of the elasticity which provides ever-increasing revenues without the necessity of increasing taxes. Not since World War II has there been a significant increase in the income tax rates. However, the percentage of income that the average person pays in income tax has increased substantially in that period of time because inflation has put everyone in a higher tax bracket. But because it has not been necessary to increase the rates there has been very little public outcry. Interestingly, during a recession, the federal government does not experience the same problems as states with elastic tax structures. The federal government simply budgets for a larger deficit, rather than raising tax rates. Only the federal government can continue to do this indefinitely because it controls the money supply. The main result is more inflation.

GENERAL SALES TAX

There are forty-five states with general sales taxes, and for a number of these it is the principal source of state income. In addition, many states allow local governments (usually counties and municipalities—rarely school districts) to "piggyback" a local sales tax on the state tax. The state collects both taxes simultaneously and rebates the local proportion to the appropriate government. The basis of the sales tax, of course, is expenditures. All retail sales are taxed at the point of sale. To avoid double taxation, sales from wholesaler to retailer are not taxed. The retailer actually pays the tax to the state. It need not be collected separately from the customer nor stated separately from the price. Most retailers do this, however, to make clear that they are to pay to the state a tax based on the price alone, and not on the price including the tax. That is, if the merchant sells an item for $100 and states the 5 percent sales tax separately as $5, he pays the state $5. If he simply raises his prices to reflect the tax, he charges the customer $105, and must pay the state $5.25 in tax (5 percent of $105).

There are usually exemptions from the sales tax for certain kinds of sales. Many states exempt food used for home preparation, on the basis that food is a necessity for poor people. Drugs are also exempted in many states because such taxes would unnecessarily burden the sick.

The sales tax treats equals equally, since people who spend the same amount pay the same amount of tax. (This should be modified slightly to note that people who spend a greater part of their income on food pay less tax, which is presumably desirable.)

While the impact of the sales tax is on the retailer, the incidence is almost entirely on the purchaser. Because of the general nature of the tax, it is not apt to cause shifts in the pattern of consumer purchases. Not only are all retailers of the same product subject to the same percentage of tax, but all other products to which individuals might shift are also subject to the same tax. This means that retailers are apt to be subject to the same competitive pressures after imposition of the tax as before, and they do not suffer from passing on the entire tax to the consumer. (Again, exceptions would have to be made regarding food and drugs in most states.) We can thus ask, in order to evaluate the incidence of the sales tax, how individual expenditures compare with income. In general, poor people spend a greater percentage of their income than do rich people. Since this is so, the sales tax appears regressive. It is alleged, however, that the exemption of food, drugs, and rents, which constitute a large part of the expenditures of poor people, actually makes this a roughly proportional tax. As usual, when talking about incidence, we cannot be sure, because of the assumptions necessary in the analysis.

The cost of administering and complying with the sales tax is low. Administration is less expensive than the administration of an income tax because it is easy to deal with a limited number of retailers. The state must, of course, perform occasional audits to ensure that the sales reported are correct. The firm has a slight additional cost for the time taken to add sales tax to the price of the product. It is not necessary to keep the money paid for sales tax separate; firms simply total all sales at the end of the month, multiply by the appropriate sales tax rate, and send a check to the state.

The yield of the sales tax is substantial. In 1974–75 it produced 29.5 billion dollars nationwide. This was 20.6% of total state–local taxes, making it second only to the property tax as a revenue source below the federal level.[4] The economic and social effects of the tax may be rather small in most cases. The tax is paid in small amounts, and on most products, and thus is not apt to exert much influence on purchases. There are geographic effects, though. The New York City sales tax is 3% (on top of the state sales tax of 5%). While this does not cause casual shoppers to leave town to shop, major purchases may be made outside the city. Automobile dealerships have almost been driven out of the city as a result of this tax, for the city sales tax on a $5,000 car is $150, and it is worth a drive to the suburbs to save that amount. Similarly, residents of the Northwest are attracted to the north shore of the Columbia River, where they may live in Washington, with no income tax, and shop in Oregon, with no sales tax.

The elasticity of the sales tax has been estimated at around 1.0, which means that its yield rises at the same rate as personal income in a state. Since expenditures of government have tended to rise faster than incomes, those states that rely on the sales tax have been forced, from time to time, to raise the sales tax rate, a politically unpopular step.

PROPERTY TAX

The property tax is a principal support of the public schools in 49 of the 50 states. The exception is Hawaii, in which statewide income, sales and excise

---

[4] *State Tax Review*, 37, No. 8 (February 24, 1976), 1.

taxes amount to 85 percent of public school funds. Just as the income tax is the principal revenue source for the federal government, and the sales tax for the state governments, the property tax has been the mainstay of local government.

THE BASIS OF THE PROPERTY TAX

The property tax is the most important example of a tax on the ownership of wealth. The only other significant example is the estate tax. However, the property tax does not tax all wealth. Wealth can be divided into real property, tangible personal property, and intangible personal property. Real property consists of land and those improvements firmly attached to the land. Such improvements are mostly buildings, but also include fences, power lines, and improvements such as landscaping. Tangible personal property includes items of intrinsic value not attached to the land. Automobiles, clothing and furniture, and the inventories and machinery of businesses are examples. Intangible personal property consists of evidence of wealth with no intrinsic value of its own, such as bank deposits, stocks and bonds, and mortgages. Most real property is taxed, some tangible personal property is taxed, and almost no intangible personal property is taxed.

THE ASSESSMENT PROCESS

Before property can be taxed, its owner must be located, and the value of the property established. This is the duty of the assessor, an elected or appointed official of the town, city, or county. The assessor prepares maps of his or her area of jurisdiction, showing each separate parcel of land. Dimensions of the land, a description of its boundaries, and the name of the owner are easy to obtain because all states require that any transfer of ownership of real property be recorded, usually by an official known as the recorder. Through the use of these maps, the assessor ensures that every piece of real property in his or her jurisdiction is accounted for. Each piece of property is given an identifying number, and its owner of record is determined from the recorder's files.

The next problem is to assign a value to the property. This is an extremely difficult job and the source of many complaints about the property tax. Usually only the property subject to taxation will be valued. This means that streets, public buildings, and other governmental property will not be valued. Neither will the property of churches and other tax-exempt private institutions. Tax-exempt property can be a large part of the total: in New York City approximately a quarter of all property is tax-exempt.

The usual standard is market value. This is generally defined as the sale price that would be agreed upon by an informed buyer and a seller who were not in collusion. The problem of the assessor is to assign such a value to each piece of property. The easiest place to do this is in a subdivision of similar houses where there are a number of sales during the year. It is easy to take an average of these sale prices and assign the rest of the houses in the subdivision the same value, with minor adjustments for differences such as the installation of a swimming pool. It is more difficult to assess the value of an older home in an area of homes of widely differing styles and sizes. More difficult yet is assessing a small business. Valued as a going concern, the business may be worth much more than if one were to sell the property for a different use. However, the assessor is to value property at its "highest and best" use, and this would normally be the present business use. Since small businesses infrequently change hands, and tend to be quite different from one another, basing the valuation on a comparison of property sales may not be feasible. Frequently an assessor will *capitalize* a business' income. That is, on assuming that a 10 percent profit is reasonable, the assessor multiplies profit figures (which the assessor can require the owner to supply) by 10 to get the assumed value of the business as an investment.

Valuation of a large factory is even more complicated. The factory may be only one of many properties of a large corporation, and it may be impossible to obtain an accurate estimate of the profit of this one property. There is a third basis of valuation that is frequently used in such cases. It is replacement value less depreciation. Each part of the factory (land, buildings, machinery, and inventories) is appraised for an estimate of the cost to replace it at today's prices. These appraisals are then reduced by depreciation based on the assumed useful life of the item. Machinery might have a useful life of only 10 years, whereas a building might have a useful life of 50 years. Land is never depreciated, for its useful life has no limit. The depreciated replacement values for various parts of the property are added together to get a total property value.

Utilities present yet another problem, because of the extensive distribution network associated with them. The power lines of an electric utility are of no value (other than salvage value) except as they are parts of the overall distribution system of the company. If a few miles of high-tension line consists of the entire property of a utility in an assessor's jurisdiction, it is difficult to value. For this reason many states assess utilities themselves. Some states use a combination of capitalized earnings and replacement value less depreciation to assess utilities. The total value of the utility system is determined by capitalizing earnings of the system. The parts of the system are valued using replacement value less depreciation (RVLD). The RVLD of the part of the system within each assessor's jurisdiction is expressed as a percentage of the RVLD of the entire system, and the total value of the utility based on capitalized earnings is multiplied by this percentage to determine the value of the portion of the utility in each assessor's jurisdiction.

Another type of property that is difficult to value is farmland. The farmer who lives well away from centers of population may find that his farmland, based on its income-producing ability, has a value of only $500 an acre. The farmer on the outskirts of an expanding metropolitan area may find that his farmland, with exactly the same crop-producing ability, is valued by the assessor at $5,000 per acre. This is because the assessor must value the land at its highest and best use (meaning the use for which one could realize the highest sale price), and this is as subdivision land. The resulting taxes may be so high that the farmer may be driven to sell the land to developers. In effect, the assessor has constructed a self-fulfilling prophecy. This appears unfair to the farmer who wishes to continue farming, but it is not unfair at all to the farmer who is only waiting for the best offer from subdividers. A way around this problem has been adopted in a number of states, where farmers can place their land into an agricultural reserve. They guarantee that the land will not be used for purposes other than agriculture for a specified number of years, in return for which the assessor must value the land based solely on its value for farming. If the land is sold during the agreement period for a different use, the owner is subject to back taxes based on the difference in assessment between that for farmland and that for its "highest and best" use.

EFFECTS OF ASSESSMENT

This farmland example should serve to illustrate that the assessment process has important economic and social consequences. In the case of the highly taxed farmer referred to earlier, the economic consequence is that land near cities and suburbs is forced into housing development sooner than it would be otherwise. Small farmers are forced out of businesses they had expected to leave to their children. Land on the fringes of the city becomes less expensive to the developer than land closer to the city, encouraging spread-out development, with considerable expense in terms of longer sewer and water lines, utility lines, roads, and travel time of residents. Of course, the economic and social consequences do not hit all evenly, as is evident from the fact that developers will usually fight such special exemptions as that for farmland.

In California, golf courses were subject to the same kind of assessment adjustment described for farmland. The reason was that they are usually located near populated areas, and assessing them for their value as subdivision land was driving them out of existence. However, there was no provision for paying back taxes if the land was converted from golf course use, and a large number of golf courses suddenly came into being as developers realized that this was a way of avoiding taxes on land they were holding for future development.

One of the greatest concerns about the economic and social impact of the property tax has been the adverse effect of the tax on poor people, who pay a larger share of their income in housing costs than do richer people. One way of remedying this, in use in the southern states (and a few others) for many years, is called the homestead exemption. In Florida, for example, the first $5,000 of assessed valuation of an owner-occupied house is exempt from taxes. This clearly favors individual ownership over rental housing. It is also a subsidy available only to those financially able to own a house and not available to those who must rent. The "circuit-breaker" (discussed later) is a more reasonable way of accomplishing the same thing.

ASSESSING PERSONAL PROPERTY

We have discussed the process by which a value is attached to all real property by the assessor. The assessor may also assess personal property, but the extent to which this is done varies widely from one state to another. One of the problems with assessment of personal property is discovering it. Real property transfers must be recorded, and construction of buildings usually requires a building permit. Personal property, though, may be acquired and sold without any public notice. Most assessors make little attempt to assess accurately the tangible personal property of homeowners. If they assess it at all, they simply use a percentage of the value of the residence as the presumed value of the personal property in it. Of more importance is the assessment of machinery and business inventories, for the amounts involved are large. An example of the problems involved with this kind of property occurs in California, where the value of inventories is assessed as of the first Monday in March each year. In February all businesses attempt to reduce inventories to a minimum. Retail businesses have inventory sales. Oil companies cease pumping oil from the ground, and allow their tanks to go dry. In general, each business attempts to sell as much inventory as possible and to buy as little as possible. On the day following assessment day, everyone is madly scrambling to rebuild inventories again.

Intangible personal property is an even greater problem, for the stocks and bonds (which, along with bank deposits, constitute most intangible personal property) can be hidden away in safety deposit boxes, or stored outside the assessor's jurisdiction. The result is that little intangible personal property is assessed, with the exception of bank deposits in a few states. In a few states all personal property is exempt from assessment. An interesting consequence of this occurs in New York. In-ground swimming pools are assessed as real property; they are vastly outnumbered by above-ground pools, which are personal property and not assessed.

DETERMINING ACTUAL ASSESSMENTS

Having attached a value, which is presumed to be a market value, to each piece of property, the assessor must attach an *assessed* value to it. The assessed value is, in most cases, a fraction of the market value. This is true even in those 23 states where constitutions or statutes require assessors to assess property at full market value. The reason for fractional assessment is a practical one. Assessment, by its very nature, is an inexact process. Because it affects the pocketbooks of people, they will protest if they feel that their assessment is too high. An assessment at full market value is much more conspicuous to public scrutiny than an assessment at some unknown fraction of market value. In addition, taxpayers who complain about their fractional assessment being higher than their neighbor's fractional assessment may get a response from the assessor that the law requires full market value assessment, and be asked if they wish their property valued at that. Courts in some states have supported assessors in this practice.

There are more insidious reasons for fractional assessments. As pointed out earlier, assessment of large properties (factories, for example) is extremely complicated. The assessor frequently does not have the expertise to assess such properties accurately. In such a case, the assessed value of the property is frequently negotiated between the assessor and the property owner. The large property owner finds it much more difficult to try to convince a number of boards and councils to keep taxes down than to arrange a private deal with the assessor to keep the assessment low, and this leads to opportunities for illegal transactions.

The law usually requires all classes of property to be assessed either at full value, or at the same percentage of full value. Again, this is followed more in the breach than in the observance. Assessors know that individuals vote and businesses do not, for example. In San Francisco for many years, residences were assessed at less than 10 percent of full value, while businesses were assessed at 50 percent of full value. In a few states fractional assessment at different rates for different classes of property is permitted or required. In Arizona, for example, railroads, mines, and timber are assessed at 60 percent, utilities at 50 percent, commercial and industrial property at 27 percent, agricultural and vacant land at 18 percent, and residential property at 15 percent of full value.

CALCULATING THE TAX RATE

After an assessed value has been attached to each piece of property, the assessor's work is done. It is then up to the counties, cities, towns, school districts, library districts, mosquito abatement districts, and other taxing entities to adopt budgets. The budget of a governmental unit, less its income from other sources, leaves the amount to be raised by property taxes. This amount, divided by the assessed valuation of property within the geographical boundaries of the unit, gives the tax rate to be applied to that property. For example:

School district budget	$ 10,000,000
Other income	5,000,000
To be raised by taxes	5,000,000
Assessed valuation	250,000,000
Tax rate	0.020

This tax rate is customarily expressed in one of three ways, depending upon the state: 20 mills, $20 per $1,000 of assessed valuation, or $2 per $100.

It is not possible, however, simply to add together the tax rates for each of the governmental units within the assessor's jurisdiction to get the total tax rate for that jurisdiction. Each unit usually covers a different geographical area from other units, with much overlapping. The overlapping boundaries create areas in which the total tax rate differs from adjoining areas. *Within* each area, however, the tax rate is the same for all property. Each of these areas of uniform tax rate is known as a tax code area. A typical county in some parts of the country may have hundreds of such tax code areas. On the other hand, there are a few places, mostly in the South, where all functions have been centralized under a single county government, with the tax rate the same countywide. An example is Dade County, Florida, where the county operates everything except the school district (including the municipalities of Miami and Miami Beach), and the school district is coterminous with the county. The same tax rate applies to all property in Dade County.

Fractional assessment creates a number of problems whose discussion was delayed until now. First, of course, if different properties (or different classes of property) are valued by the assessor at different percentages of market value, they will be unevenly subject to the property tax. If, however, the assessor values *all* property within his jurisdiction at the same percentage of market value, there appears to be no difficulty. A low total assessed value would only mean a higher tax rate, since the tax rate is obtained by dividing budgeted tax needs by assessed valuation. However, there are two main problems. First many states have statutory maximum tax rates. By assessing property at less than market value, the assessor is limiting the access of governmental units to the full tax amount they would otherwise be able to levy. Second, states allocate aid to school districts based on the wealth of the district. An underassessed district creates the illusion of a poor district entitled to more state aid. In the past this has led to competitive underassessment among districts in some states. A solution to the intergovernmental aid problem is a state Board of Equalization, which determines for each school district the ratio of assessed to full value, enabling the aid to be based on full value. This, however, does not solve the problem of differences in assessment ratios *within* the district.

In addition to fractional assessment of all property, and differential assessment rates for property of different classes, there is the problem of *intra-class* discrepancies. Properties of identical value are often assessed quite differently. Part of this results from the subjectivity inherent in appraisal. Part of the problem, though, is that many assessors revalue property infrequently. They are understaffed and revalue only that property which comes to their attention, either because of a sale, or because a building permit has been issued. This means that the new owner of an old home may find the assessment roughly equal to 90 percent of its value, while the long-time owner of an identical home next door, not assessed for 30 years, may have an assessment less than 50 percent of its market value. These kinds of intra-class differences are particularly visible and cause much of the unhappiness over the property tax.

In spite of complaints about assessment practices, in most states little reform has occurred. A few states have made major improvements through state action. Examples are Oregon, Maryland, Arizona, and Florida. In Arizona, for example, there is an independent Department of Property Valuation with power to regulate assessment standards and local assessors. Each Arizona assessor's office is provided with a set of asssessment manuals so that the assessor may conform with the statewide uniformity requirements. The State Department of Property Valuation has also provided a uniform parcel numbering and mapping system, along with uniform tax code area maps and uniform procedures for handling exemptions under Arizona statutes. No assessor may establish or change any valuation without approval by the Department. Electronic data-processing equipment is used extensively wherever possible. Current sale prices are stored in the computer and any deviation of appraised value below 80 percent or above 96 percent of the sale price is noted by the computer. County assessors are provided with printouts so they can review and update appraisals to bring their tax rolls into conformity with the standard.

THE EQUITY OF THE PROPERTY TAX

The first concern of equity is whether equals are treated equally. The property tax is probably more at fault in this respect than most taxes. The problem, of course, lies in assessment practices. The inter- and intra-class discrepancies in assessments described above mean that properties of equal value in the same tax code area may pay very different taxes. In addition to these assessment problems, tax exemptions diminish the equity of the property tax as well as its revenue-raising capacity.

THE INCIDENCE OF THE PROPERTY TAX

Consideration of whether the property tax treats unequals equitably involves the tax's incidence. It is trivial to discover the impact of the tax, for tax bills are individually addressed, but analyzing incidence is another matter.

The conventional view is that the property tax is a regressive one, perhaps the most regressive of our major taxes. To examine the reasoning behind this conclusion, we must divide the property tax into three parts: taxes on land, taxes on improvements (both of these are real property), and taxes on personal property. Of total state and local property tax collection, approximately 30 percent comes from land, 50 percent from improvements, and 20 percent from tangible personal property (including utilities).

It is agreed by all that property taxes on land fall on the owner of the land at the time the tax is initially levied or increased. The tax cannot be shifted because under equilibrium conditions the only way to increase price is to increase demand or decrease supply. The landowner has no control over demand, and there is no way that supply can be decreased in the aggregate, because the supply of land is almost perfectly inelastic. Landowners could decide to hold their land off the rental market, thus reducing supply. But to do so does not reduce their tax liability and is thus an unacceptable solution.

Alternatively, the landowner could sell the land to someone else. This has not, however, changed the total supply of land, and the new owner faces the same problems as the original owner. For this reason, the buyer will be unwilling to pay as much for the land as before the tax was levied or increased. The result is that the original owner has suffered a loss as a result of the imposition of the tax. The original owner must either continue to rent at the same rate as before, finding profit decreased by the amount of the tax, or must sell the property at a lower price than obtainable without the tax.

Rich people, who have more disposable income than poor people, own proportionately more land. Since the incidence of the property tax on land falls entirely on the landowner, this portion of the tax is presumably progressive.

The tax on improvements (and on personal property) can be divided into three categories. First is owner-occupied housing. Again, all agree that the burden of this falls entirely on the owner-occupant, who is both capitalist and consumer, with no one to whom to pass the tax liability. Since this was already true for the land on which owner-occupied houses stand, the incidence of the property tax on these properties is exactly the same as the impact. (One should not be confused by the existence of mortgages into thinking that banks own much of our housing stock. The individual who owns the house, and has merely borrowed money with which to purchase it, must pay the taxes, not the bank.) The incidence of the property tax on single-family owner-occupied housing is indeed regressive, as is shown in Table 6-2. While the extent of the regressivity differs from region to region (as does the average burden of property taxes), everywhere the tax is clearly regressive. At each higher income level the percentage of current income paid in property taxes decreases. It bears repeating here that it is not dollars paid in taxes that determine whether a tax is regressive, but taxes paid as a percentage of income. For example, in Table 6-2, the average rate of tax for incomes of $2,000 to $2,999 is 9.7% for the U.S. as a whole. If the average income for this class is $2,500 this amounts to a tax payment of $243. For the $15,000 to $24,999 income class the average tax rate is 3.3% and the average tax payment, $660. The dollars of tax paid by the higher income family are more than twice as great as those paid by the low-income family, but the low-income family pays almost three times as great a *percentage* of its income in residential property taxes. Although Table 6-2 is for 1970, percentages from 1980 census tables are likely to be similar.

The analysis is more difficult in the case of rental housing, for it is not clear to what extent the burden of the tax can be passed on to the renter in the form of higher rents, and to what extent it must be absorbed by the landlord in the form of a diminished return on his investment. The traditional view has all of the property tax on rental *housing* (not land) passed forward to the renter. Since poor people pay a greater proportion of their incomes in rent than do rich people (and assuming for the moment that property taxes are a relatively constant percentage of rents), incidence of the property tax on rental housing must also be regressive.

Finally, the traditional view of the incidence of the property tax on commercial and industrial buildings and business machinery and inventories is that

TABLE 6-2

Real Estate Taxes as a Percentage of Family Income, Owner-Occupied Single-Family Homes, by Income Class and by Region, 1970

Family income*	United States Total	Northeast Region	Northcentral Region	South Region	West Region	Exhibit: No. and Distribution of Homeowners	
						No. (000)	% dist.†
Less than $2,000	16.6	30.8	18.0	8.2	22.9	1,718.8	5.5
$2,000– 2,999	9.7	15.7	9.8	5.2	12.5	1,288.7	9.7
3,000– 3,999	7.7	13.1	7.7	4.3	8.7	1,397.8	14.1
4,000– 4,999	6.4	9.8	6.7	3.4	8.0	1,342.8	18.5
5,000– 5,999	5.5	9.3	5.7	2.9	6.5	1,365.1	22.8
6,000– 6,999	4.7	7.1	4.9	2.5	5.9	1,530.1	27.8
7,000– 9,999	4.2	6.2	4.2	2.2	5.0	5,377.4	45.0
10,000–14,999	3.7	5.3	3.6	2.0	4.0	8,910.3	73.6
15,000–24,999	3.3	4.6	3.1	2.0	3.4	6,365.6	94.0
25,000 or more	2.9	3.9	2.7	1.7	2.9	1,876.9	100.0
All incomes						31,144.7	
Arithmetic mean	4.9	6.9	5.1	2.9	5.4		
Median	3.4	5.0	3.5	2.0	3.9		

*Census definition of income reported received in 1970.
†Cumulated from lowest income class.

Source: Advisory Commission on Intergovernmental Relations, *Financing Schools and Property Tax Relief–A State Responsibility* (Washington, D.C.: U.S. Government Printing Office, 1973), p. 36.

the tax is passed on to consumers in the form of higher prices for goods purchased. Through the same reasoning as with rental housing, this tax is also regressive. Thus, we have a tax on land that is probably progressive (because rich people own proportionately more land than poor people), and a tax on improvements and personal property that is regressive. The conventional view is that the total result is regressive. Dick Netzer, who has been most prominently identified with this viewpoint, has said,

> . . . the component of the property tax that falls on housing amounts to the equivalent of a very stiff sales tax on consumer expenditures for housing. We tax housing more heavily than any other item of consumer expenditure in the United States with the exception of liquor, tobacco, and gasoline. I think it is a grotesque social policy to tax something we all agree is a good thing—more heavily than almost anything else a consumer chooses to spend money for.
>
> The property tax on housing in American cities is probably the most seriously regressive aspect of the entire American fiscal system. Other taxes that can be said to be more regressive are only minor revenue producers. Of the *major* taxes, this one is by far the most regressive.[5]

It is generally agreed that a regressive tax is a bad tax, at least on that account. It offends our notions of equity involving ability to pay. Many of the proposals for reform or elimination of the property tax stem from this alleged regressivity. Thus, it is of considerable interest to find that a group of "revisionist" economists conclude that the property tax is actually progressive![6] Their reasons have several bases.

First, they note that the short run supply of housing is almost as inelastic as land. This means that it will be impossible for landlords in the short run to pass the property tax forward to renters. But neither will they end by absorbing it all. The reduced rate of return on rental housing will induce some capital to be employed elsewhere, where the returns are greater. This will reduce the return to capital in these other parts of the economy, until an equilibrium is again reached where the return to capital in all parts of the economy is again commensurate with the risks. Under this view, the property tax on rental housing is spread back to the owners of all capital. Since rich people own proportionately more capital than poor, this part of the property tax is progressive, just as the tax on land is.

Second, the revisionists note that even if the property tax on rental housing is passed forward to the renter it may not be regressive, because property taxes are not a constant percentage of rents, as the traditionalists assume. The

---

[5] Dick Netzer, "Property Taxes," *Municipal Finance*, 44, No. 2 (November 1971), 36.

[6] See, for example, Henry J. Aaron, *A New View of Property Tax Incidence* (Washington, D.C.: The Brookings Institution, 1974), and Mason Gaffney, "The Property Tax is a Progressive Tax," *Proceedings of the National Tax Association*, 64 (1971), 408–26.

proportion of rent that represents a return to capital in low-rent housing is considerably smaller than it is in high-rent housing. Most of the rent in inexpensive housing pays for current costs of the housing. (In the extreme case, landlords find that their return on capital has decreased to zero—current costs equal rents —and they then abandon the building.) Since property taxes are supposed to be proportional to value, they will presumably be a smaller proportion of the rent of low-rent housing. The traditionalists counter this argument by noting that some low and middle-income housing in many cities is assessed at a higher percentage of market value than is higher priced housing.

Third, the revisionists point out that it is an illusion that truly poor families are paying high property taxes. Among those with very low incomes are a disproportionate number of people who have low incomes only temporarily. Among these are young families who can reasonably expect to rapidly increase their incomes, retired people who have accumulated substantial wealth even though their current income is low, and individuals who have been able to offset income against business expenses or otherwise reduce their adjusted gross income. Looking again at Table 6-2, it does seem probable that the 15 percent of people who earn less than $3,000 a year yet own houses are not all permanently poor. Revisionists argue that one should not use *current* income as the measure in judging regressivity, but *permanent* income. They define permanent income as that income that individuals expect to earn on the average over the long term. They argue that when permanent income is used, even the tax burden on owner-occupied housing is progressive. Again we must note that we are talking in the aggregate. Some permanently poor people own houses, and for them the property tax is onerous. However progressivity and regressivity are only defined in terms of what happens on the average.

It is not at all clear whether the traditionalists or the revisionists will win the property tax argument. Anyone who reads carefully the analyses of both sides is struck by the number of assumptions that must be made because of lack of data. Economists are fond of making assumptions, for it simplifies conditions and renders them more amenable to analysis. Unfortunately, it also abstracts from reality, and often it is difficult to determine the extent to which an assumption is justified, or how it will upset the conclusion if it is not correct. In the case of the property tax, it appears that the most we can say at present is that it is by no means certain that the tax is regressive. We should be careful not to condemn it solely on that account.

If the property tax is regressive, its greatest burden is on poor people. A way of selectively reducing this burden has now been adopted in one form or another by many of the states, and is called the "circuit-breaker." The circuit-breaker excuses all or a portion of the property taxes a family pays on its residence above a specified percentage of its income. For example, the law might provide (as in Michigan) that 40 percent of the excess of taxes over 6 percent of family income will be forgiven. Suppose a family has an income of $10,000 and pays property taxes of $1,000. Six percent of its income is $600, and the excess of property tax is $400. Forty percent of this is $160. The family would report this fact on its state income tax return, and deduct the $160 from the income tax. If the deduction exceeded the tax, the state would refund the difference. In order to make this applicable to rental property also, it is assumed that 20 percent of the rent constitutes property taxes paid.

The circuit-breaker has been adopted in one form or another by 27 states in an exceedingly short period of time since its first appearance in Wisconsin in 1964. The reason for its popularity is that it is a tax exemption tailored to the income of the taxpayer. Thus it is less costly to the state than a homestead exemption, which benefits rich and poor homeowners alike in dollar terms (although a larger proportion of the total rebates go to poor than to the rich). However, the circuit-breaker has certain drawbacks. It tends to benefit most those who spend a high proportion of income on their homes, including those with higher incomes who choose to invest in extravagant homes. Another problem is the assumption that a uniform percentage of rent is property tax, for this is patently false even if we agree that landlords pass the entire burden of the property tax on to tenants. Yet this notion, too—that the incidence of the property tax is upon renters—has come under challenge, as we have indicated in the last section.

THE YIELD OF PROPERTY TAX

The property tax is a very potent generator of money. In 1970-71, property taxes were 15 percent of total taxes at all levels (federal, state, and local), 40 percent of combined state-local taxes, and 85 percent of local taxes.[7] Well over 60 billion dollars is raised each year in property taxes nationwide. In New York State alone, in 1974-75, the property tax raised more than 7 billion dollars (see Table 6-3). This is far more than was raised by any other tax in this most highly taxed state.

The property tax has usually been thought of as an inelastic tax. The reasoning is that assessed values do not tend to increase as rapidly as personal incomes, mainly because assessments are not kept constantly updated. The result is that a constant tax rate will produce revenues that do not increase as rapidly as incomes. However, the analysis is not that simple. It is not necessary to assume a constant tax rate. The demands of governments for money have increased faster than incomes. Those governments that depend heavily on the property tax (that is, almost all local governments) have been forced to increase property tax rates, and they have been surprisingly successful in doing so. The results are shown in Table 6-4. From 1922 to 1927, a period of prosperity, receipts from the property tax increased from 3.3 billion dollars to 4.7 billion, a

---

[7]Calculated from data in Tables 2 and 3, p. 16, in Advisory Commission on Intergovernmental Relations, *Financing Schools and Property Tax Relief—A State Responsibility* (Washington, D.C.: The Commission, 1973).

TABLE 6-3

Total Estimated State and Local Taxes (in billions)
New York State, 1974–75

Tax	State	Local	Total
Property	—	$7.20	$7.20
Income	$3.80	.57	4.37
Sales	1.99	1.35	3.34
Other Taxes*	3.09	1.04	4.13
Total	$8.88	$10.16	$19.04

*Includes motor vehicle, motor fuel, cigarette, beverages, licenses, highway use, New York City general business, stock, transfers, occupancy, etc.

Source: *Educational Finance and the New York State Real Property Tax* (Albany: Education Study Unit, New York State Division of the Budget, 1976).

42 percent increase. They increased from 4.5 percent to 4.9 percent of the Gross National Product, making the tax clearly elastic during this period. From 1927 to 1946 property taxes stayed remarkably constant, raising between 4 billion and 5 billion dollars per year. A long period of prosperity (interrupted by several minor recessions) began in 1946 and continued for 25 years. During this time property tax yields increased eight-fold, and yield as a percent of GNP rose steadily from 2.4 percent to 4.0 percent. The property tax, then, has shown in this century a remarkable characteristic: it is elastic in periods of prosperity, increasing in yield faster than the economy, yet very inelastic during depression, with the yield decreasing scarcely at all even when the economy takes a terrible beating. From the point of view of governments that depend upon the property tax, this is the best of all possible worlds. From the point of view of the taxpayer, particularly the one with no children in school, the picture is, of course, not as rosy.

COST OF ADMINISTRATION AND COMPLIANCE

The administrative cost of the property tax is usually quite low when expressed as a percentage of yield. Part of the reason for this, however, is the fact that in most states assessments are so poorly done. Proper assessments might double or triple the cost of administration. The general effect of this would be to improve the equity of the tax (through reducing inter- and intra-class discrepancies), but it would probably not improve the yield at all in most cases. The reason is that the yield of the property tax is determined by local government revenue needs, which are translated into a tax rate. Evasion of taxes actually levied is rare, for governments can collect back taxes that are not paid. There is significant evasion of taxes through abandonment of property in a few cities, such as New York, but it can be argued that where this occurs the assessed value

TABLE 6-4

Federal, State and Local Taxes in Relation to Gross National Product,
Selected Years, 1902-1972

| | | Tax Collections (in millions) State and Local Taxes | | As Percent of GNP State and Local Taxes | | |
Year	Federal Taxes	Total	Property Taxes Only	Federal Taxes	Total	Property Taxes Only
1971-72*	$156,400	$106,000	$41,500	14.9%	10.1%	4.0%
1969-70	146,082	86,824	34,083	15.7	9.3	3.7
1964-65	93,710	51,243	22,583	14.8	8.1	3.6
1962	82,262	41,554	19,054	14.7	7.4	3.4
1960	77,003	36,117	16,405	15.3	7.2	3.3
1954	62,409	22,067	9,967	17.1	6.0	2.7
1950	35,186	15,914	7,349	12.4	5.6	2.6
1946	36,286	10,094	4,986	17.4	4.8	2.4
1944	40,321	8,774	4,604	19.2	4.2	2.2
1942	12,265	8,528	4,537	7.8	5.4	2.9
1940	4,878	7,810	4,430	4.9	7.8	4.4
1936	3,882	6,701	4,093	4.7	8.1	5.0
1932	1,813	6,164	4,487	3.1	10.6	7.7
1927	3,364	6,087	4,730	3.5	6.3	4.9
1922	3,371	4,016	3,321	4.6	5.4	4.5
1913	662	1,609	1,332	1.6	4.0	3.3
1902	513	860	706	2.1	3.6	2.9

*1971-72 figures are estimated.

Source: Advisory Commission on Intergovernmental Relations, *Financing Schools and Property Tax Relief—A State Responsibility* (Washington, D.C.: U.S. Government Printing Office, 1973), p. 16.

of the property was too high, otherwise the property would not have been abandoned.

The cost of compliance for the property tax is probably the lowest of that for any major tax. The property owner receives a tax bill and pays it in one or more installments. The time and effort involved in doing so are nil.

ECONOMIC AND SOCIAL EFFECTS

As should be evident from the foregoing discussion, the economic and social effects of property taxes are important. There is no general agreement among economists on the overall or specific effects of the tax, but many would agree with the ideas expressed below.

First, the property tax is, in effect, an excise tax on consumption of housing, as noted earlier by Netzer. In other words, although it is a tax on the ownership of a particular kind of wealth (primarily real property), to the extent that it is levied on residential housing it has an effect similar to a sales tax on the expenditures associated with home ownership. If the average property tax, expressed as a percentage of average expenditures for housing, is greater than the general sales tax rate (and it usually is), the result will be to discourage the consumption of housing—that is, people will choose to live in smaller, less expensive houses. While this is probably true as an abstract statement, it is not necessarily bad. Americans are the best housed individuals in the world, and it may not be necessary or desirable to encourage overall increases in the consumption of housing. There may be specific instances where high taxes discourage housing, primarily in city ghettos, but this is mostly a result of assessed values that are unreasonably high considering the return on investment of the landlord. Proper assessment can correct these abuses.

Second, the fact that property taxes are higher in some places than in others has an effect on the value of property. An interesting example occurred in Rochester, New York, in the mid-1970s. Several small "free" school districts existed there, the result of an agreement many years before that brought some valuable industrial property into the city, in exchange for which the city agreed to educate the students of the small districts at no cost in perpetuity. As a result, the residents of the free districts paid no school taxes. A house in a free school district would sell for $10,000 more than its identical counterpart across the street in the city school district. The cost of borrowing the money needed to make this additional $10,000 investment was approximately equal to the school taxes paid by the owner of the house in the city. When the legislature abolished these districts by annexing them to others, the homeowners suffered a loss of roughly $10,000 in the value of their homes.

This problem is not confined to such unusual situations, however. In most states there are "tax islands," school districts with large concentrations of industrial or commercial property and few students. The burden of school expenses is low and the assessed value high, resulting in a very low tax rate. This encourages location of more industry, exacerbating the situation. Probably the most egregious example is Teterboro, New Jersey, with an assessed value in 1971 of $62,600,000 and only one pupil. Other examples are Emeryville in California and Lackawanna in New York. Businesses locating in these tax islands effectively escape most school property taxation, which is typically more than half of the total property tax bill. It has been proposed by many that commercial and industrial property be taxed by the state for schools at a uniform rate, thus leaving only the residential tax base available for local discretion. Presumably this would have several desirable results. Businesses would not be able to escape taxation by locating in tax islands. Decisions on business location would be made on bases other than avoidance of taxes. Furthermore, local taxes would be paid only by those who made the decision on rate: local voters. In spite of its attractiveness, this proposal has not yet been adopted by any state. This is partly because of the political power of industries situated in tax islands. It is also partly because the short-range problems seem to outweigh long-range benefits. For one thing, the necessary statewide tax rate would in many cases be more than industry is currently paying in large cities. In other words, large cities, whatever their other problems, are to some extent tax islands with regard to schools. The fact that industry could relocate in the suburbs without incurring a tax penalty might hasten the exodus of industry and commerce from the city, increasing urban decay.

A third effect of property taxes springs from the *exemption* of certain types of property. The exemption of such property as government buildings, streets, churches, hospitals, private schools, and other nonprofit agencies seems desirable. There is no point in government taxing itself, and the encouragement of religious and eleemosynary institutions is considered important by most people. However, this can result in a serious problem for cities (especially state capitals) and school districts having large concentrations of these properties.

There are a number of other economic effects, but it is possible that to some extent these effects merely balance the effects of other taxes. Netzer has noted, for example, that the income tax gives favorable treatment to capital gains, and that land transactions are a principal generator of such gains. The property tax tends to offset this favorable treatment of real property by the income tax. Similarly, the income tax encourages the consumption of housing through deductions of interest paid on mortgages. Sales taxes are never applied to rents. Both of these taxes, then, tend to encourage spending on private housing, although the property tax may act as a deterrent to home buyers.[8]

The social effects of the property tax are also important, although it is often difficult precisely to differentiate these effects. A combination of factors, among them lower taxes at the time suburban land was being developed, have contributed to the urban sprawl that has made us into a nation of commuters. Resistance to property taxes has made its impact more on the schools than on other arms of government; the long-range effects of possible poorer education for many children are yet to be felt.

POLITICAL EFFECTS

The political ramifications of taxation are of great practical importance, and unfortunately are often ignored in treatises on the subject. Because they are intimately connected with the politics of revenue distribution, we defer the discussion until Chapter Thirteen.

Summary

The American system of public education is the largest single enterprise of state and local government, and even nationally it is rivaled only by defense and

[8] See Dick Netzer, *Economics of the Property Tax* (Washington, D.C.: The Brookings Institution, 1966), p. 69.

welfare expenditures. Supporting the costs of education is a system of general taxes, consisting primarily of local property taxation supplemented by state grants-in-aid coming mainly from sales and income taxation. The percentage of each tax used for school support varies from one school district to the next, and from state to state.

This chapter has identified and explained five characteristics of taxes:

1. The basis of the liability for payment of the tax. The basis is either wealth (as in the property tax), income (the income tax), expenditure (the sales tax), or a privilege conferred by the government (license fees of various kinds).

2. The yield of the tax; that is, its capability for raising money. A property tax has an inherently greater yield than a tax on theater admissions.

3. Cost of administration and compliance, usually expressed as a percentage of the yield.

4. Economic and social effects. Although a tax ought to be free of unintended economic and social effects, unfortunately our most important taxes are not.

5. Political effects. Each of the major taxes also has important political effects that must be taken into account.

In explaining the basis of taxes, equity of taxes was also discussed. Equity requires that equals be treated alike, and, in general, that unequals be taxed based on the ability to pay. Progressive taxes are more equitable than regressive taxes which cost low-income persons proportionately more than those with high income. When assessing the equity of a tax, it is not sufficient merely to look at the *impact* of the tax, or at those who initially pay it. Rather, in assessing the burden of a tax we must look at the *incidence* of the tax or at who ultimately pays. Determining the incidence of taxes is a complicated economic exercise. There are two schools of thought regarding the incidence of the property tax, one determining it to be progressive, the other concluding that it is regressive.

The three most important taxes (personal income, sales, and property) were compared on the basis of each of the characteristics above. Each has advantages and disadvantages. One of the major problems of the property tax is in determining its value through the assessment process. This process was described in detail, and potential solutions to some of the problems of assessment were discussed.

The property tax raises more money than any other tax for schools, and in addition it is the only tax on which citizens regularly have an opportunity to express their disapproval; they express such dissatisfaction through voting for school budgets and school board members. This fact, plus the inequities in assessing property that lead to inequities in taxation, has made the property tax appear to be our most unpopular tax. An analysis of this tax, and a comparison of its characteristics with those of the income tax and the sales tax, shows that some of this antipathy may be misdirected.

More important, we are not likely to abandon the property tax as a source of school support in the foreseeable future for the simple reason that it raises such a massive amount of money. To shift this to another revenue source would be politically difficult, as the only taxes broadly based enough to provide the necessary money are the sales tax and the income tax. In most states these taxes would have to be doubled, tripled, or quadrupled to match the amount now provided for schools by the property tax.

In addition, there is a great deal to be said for a balanced tax structure involving taxes based on income, wealth, and consumption, for those who manage their affairs in such a way as to minimize one tend to be hit by another. Those who espouse a single tax (whether it be an income tax or a land tax) tend to ignore this. In addition, it should be noted that the higher a particular tax is, the greater is the incentive to find ways to avoid or evade it.

All of this implies that we should not attempt to abandon the property tax as a principal means of support for the public schools, but should be seeking ways to improve its operation. This chapter provides some suggestions for improvement, including proper assessment practices to prevent inter- and intra-class inequities in taxation, and circuit-breakers to relieve the excessive burden of property taxation on low-income individuals and families.

7

THE POLITICS
AND ECONOMICS OF
FEDERAL EDUCATION POLICY

Historically and constitutionally, responsibility for school policy and operation in the United States has resided with state and local government. Nevertheless, in the 1976-77 school year, the U.S. Office of Education distributed in excess of $7 billion to support various facets of American education.[1] This approximated 7 percent of total estimated school expenditures. When compared with the national government contributions of nations with centralized education systems, England, France, U.S.S.R., etc., this is a paltry proportion. From the perspective of a strict constructionist, however, the $7 billion represents an awesome example of the federal government's tendency to exceed its constitutional authority.

What is the federal education policy and what justification exists for federal government participation? How has the federal role in education evolved? How is federal education policy made and administered? What political controversies and interest group forces affect federal school policy? What are federal dollars intended to accomplish, and how effective are they? What changes should be made in the federal government's education role? This is the sequence of questions addressed in this chapter.

[1] National Center for Educational Statistics, *The Condition of Education, 1976 Edition* (Washington: U.S. Government Printing Office, 1977), p. 66.

Federal Policy and Purposes

There is no consistent or coherent federal school aid policy.[2] Instead, there is a complicated web of education related policies, a web spun of federal statutes, executive orders, regulations, guidelines, and judicial rulings. Present policies have resulted from the political demands of numerous and varied interest groups and individuals. Federal programs assist both low-achieving and academically gifted students. The purposes for which federal funds can be used are narrowly prescribed in some education statutes. Federal funds can be used for building educational facilities under some programs and not under others. A 1976 federal publication listed 131 separate programs administered by the U.S. Office of Education.[3] Dozens of other education related federal programs are administered in other executive branch departments and agencies, Commerce, Labor, HUD, and Defense. The variety is simply a reflection of the remarkable diversity characterizing our nation and permeating federal policy-making bodies.

Despite its crazy quilt nature, it is possible to deduce three underlying purposes of federal education policies and programs: (1) extension and promotion of equal educational opportunity, (2) stimulation of greater efficiency and prevention of under-investment in important education related endeavors, and (3) preservation of diversity and choice in higher education institutions. No single federal program may fit any one purpose exclusively, and practical steps taken toward fulfillment of a particular objective may, on occasion, bring benefits to proponents of one of the other goals. Consequently, federal efforts in pursuit of equality, efficiency, and liberty seldom emerge as clear and distinct in practice as we treat them here for purposes of illustration.

EQUALIZATION

As described in Chapter Eight, there are substantial inequities both among and within states with regard to school spending and tax effort. Numerous proposals have been placed before Congress for the use of federal funds to alleviate such unequal conditions.[4] In 1973, for example, Walter F. Mondale, then a

---

[2]This should not be taken as a critical comment. Few if any states or local school districts can claim to have education policies which are coherent and internally consistent.

[3]*American Education,* 12, No. 6 (July 1976), 27–34.

[4]Frank J. Munger and Richard F. Fenno, Jr., *National Politics and Federal Aid to Education* (Syracuse: Syracuse University Press, 1962), provide an excellent history of the evolution of federal school aid and the political controversies which have accompanied it. More recent works on the same dimension include Stephen K. Bailey and Edith K. Mosher, *The Office of Education Administers A Law* (Syracuse: Syracuse University Press, 1968), Harry L. Summerfield (author and editor), *Power and Process: The Formulation and Limits of Federal Education Policy* (Berkeley: McCutchan Publishing Corporation, 1975), and Norman C. Thomas, *Education in National Politics* (New York: David McKay Co., 1975).

U.S. Senator from Minnesota, and Senator Adlai Stevenson of Illinois submitted bills to provide federal monies to those states enacting distribution formulas that substantially reduced interdistrict spending differences. Other proposals had previously been submitted to equalize the ability of states to pay teachers, construct buildings, and purchase instructional materials. The greatest gain came in 1975 when Congress authorized a minimum of $100,000 for each state to fund studies of school finance and to devise mechanisms to achieve greater fiscal equalization.[5] As is discussed later, equalization schemes providing aid to states or districts have become entangled in one or more political controversies and have fallen short of congressional enactment. The only legislatively successful federal equalization efforts have been those to provide aid to students, rather than to state or local school districts.

The prime example of federal efforts to equalize individual educational opportunity consists of the 1965 Elementary and Secondary Education Act (ESEA, PL 89-10). This legislation continues to be the most important federal school aid authority, and we will pay substantial attention throughout this chapter to its origins, provisions, and administrative problems. In its original form, this legislation provided federal funds to assist in compensating for those educational deficits that frequently accompany poverty. Subsequently, the act was amended to include funds for purposes such as educating bilingual or non-English speaking students, children of migrant agricultural workers, and students residing in various overseas U.S. Trust Territories such as Guam. Federal legislation was enacted in 1975 for educational support of the handicapped (Education for all Handicapped Children Act, PL 94-142). Also, federal funds have been provided school districts to assist in racial desegregation (Emergency School Assistance Act, PL 92-318), a program consistent with equalizing educational opportunity. In addition, federal funding is prohibited in districts or programs where racial or sexual discrimination is practiced. Lastly, the frequently amended Higher Education Act provides federal subsidies to pay the college costs of students from lower income families at the college of their choice. These are known as Educational Opportunity Grants.

EFFICIENCY

Federal aid funds are also intended to promote greater educational efficiency. This objective is pursued in most instances by efforts to prevent underinvestment in areas such as research and manpower development.

EDUCATIONAL RESEARCH AND DEVELOPMENT

The view that schooling can be made more effective by discovering more about learning and developing new methods of instruction is buttressed by

[5] Public law 93-380, Section 842.

analogy to the astonishing technological successes of U.S. industry and agriculture. However, in the absence of federal incentives, states, local school districts, and private firms are unlikely to spend significant amounts of money on educational research and development. For the private sector, returns to such investments are generally viewed as too slender to warrant the effort. Only instructional materials and audiovisual aids are profitable private sector items in education, and these do not entail high development cost.

There is little enthusiasm for research and development among local school districts and states because costs may be prohibitively high and new techniques often are not successful. Furthermore it is much easier to wait for others to develop and perfect new techniques and choose those that seem most successful. As a consequence, almost no state or local resources are devoted to educational research and development.[6] The function falls logically to the federal government.

Federal support for educational research and development takes several forms. The initial pattern was for the U.S. Office of Education to subsidize university-based social scientists. In 1965, Title IV of the ESEA increased the amount of federal research money and also expanded the scope of institutions involved. It established a national network of Research and Development Centers and Regional Education Laboratories. During the early 1970s, this system was drastically reduced and partially replaced with a comprehensive research and development agency, the National Institute of Education (NIE). In addition to specific education research progams such as these, other federal agencies, like the National Science Foundation (NSF) and the National Endowment for the Humanities, distribute millions in support of educational research and development.

MANPOWER DEVELOPMENT

Federal aid has played a central role during times when the nation has experienced shortages of skilled persons in various occupational categories. The Morrill Acts of 1862 and 1890, for example, provided incentives for education and training of mechanics, engineers, and military and agricultural experts. The 1917 Vocational Training Act was motivated by the need for skilled technicians to assist in the World War I production effort. Similarly, in 1958, Congress enacted the National Defense Education Act (NDEA) as a stimulant to the schooling of scientists, mathematicians, and linguists.

Benefits from the preparation of individuals to fill sorely needed occupational categories, especially benefits from research and development, clearly transcend the borders of any particular state. State and local governments

---

[6]This is not to claim that no state or local funds are utilized in this fashion. However, most state and local "Education Research" efforts are in reality "assessment" efforts, attempting to measure how well students learn under existing programs. They are not directed at developing new techniques and products.

are reluctant to risk expensive investment for training when the high mobility rate of the U.S. population means they may be deprived of the benefits of such training. While this is understandable from the point of view of any one state, in the aggregate such behavior is detrimental to all states. Thus, it often devolves upon the federal government, in the national interest, to stimulate the preparation of skilled individuals.

The consequences of poor manpower development are not confined to the state or district with a poor education program, for the failure of one school system can become a welfare expense to another state. Federal aid for manpower development is justified to guard against the risk of any particular state underinvesting in schooling.

LIBERTY

Policies directed at preserving or expanding educational choices are notably lacking in federal education programs. Of course, efforts to equalize educational opportunity can be interpreted as extending liberty. For the children they affect, successful compensatory education programs probably expand choices for careers, jobs, and life style. However, only a few federal programs at the primary or secondary level have had the explicit intent of extending educational choice.

For five years, the U.S. Office of Education subsidized the efforts of local districts in providing "alternative schools" in the public sector. This Experimental School Program was terminated in 1976.[7] In 1973 the Office of Economic Opportunity initiated a voucher project in Alum Rock, California.[8] Despite moderately high evaluation ratings, the project was not expanded. Efforts to begin similar experiments in other local school districts and for the entire state of New Hampshire were unsuccessful.

Federal higher education policies have been substantially more mindful of "choice" as a policy objective. For example, the benefits provided veterans following World War II and the Korean and Vietnam wars took the form of direct tuition aid to the student rather than a network of federal subsidies to institutions of higher education. This congressional decision accomplished two objectives: support of many colleges and educational agencies and motivation of individuals to choose from a broad band of different kinds of institutions. The provisions of various higher education acts since the 1960s have sustained the federal interest in promoting diversity. Educational Opportunity Grants aid students in attending the college of their choice, and several federal programs directly aid small colleges and preserve the spectrum of choice.[9]

---

[7]The Experimental Schools Project districts were Berkeley, California; Gary, Indiana; and Minneapolis, Minnesota.

[8]See Chapter Nine for greater detail.

[9]These programs are outlined in the 1965 Higher Education Act and in its 1968 amendments.

TAX LOSS COMPENSATION

A fourth and altogether separate purpose for federal school aid is the compensation of states and local school districts for the loss of tax revenues resulting from federal functions. For example, many local school districts have federally owned facilities within their boundaries or serve children of federal employees. Because federal facilities, and frequently the facilities of private firms engaged in fulfilling federal contracts, are exempt from taxation, local school districts lose property tax revenues. Yet such facilities often send their children to local schools. Federal funds are appropriated annually to compensate school districts for such conditions. This aid has also become a very important source of revenue to districts serving children from Indian reservations. These "in lieu of tax monies," sometimes known as Impact Aid, are authorized under Public Laws 815 and 874.

Historical Evolution of Federal School Aid Policies

Although the Constitution does not specifically enumerate an educational role for the federal government, liberal judicial branch interpretations of the Constitution's general welfare and interstate commerce clauses have allowed the federal government to play a significant role in the development of U.S. education.[10] This role emerged slowly, but in the years following World War II it expanded at a remarkable rate. World War II is a good dividing line between historical and modern federal school aid proposals and programs.

PRE-WORLD WAR II FEDERAL AID

In 1773, Colonel Henry Dickering proposed that surplus lands in the Ohio territory be sold and the proceeds divided among the states to support a variety of public services, education included. Dickering's plan was not passed, but only a few years later the Continental Congress enacted the Land Ordinance of 1785 and then the Northwest Ordinance of 1787.[11] The first of these acts stipulated

---

[10]The following court cases are generally viewed as conveying constitutional legitimacy to federal government education programs: *United States* v. *Butler,* 297 U.S. 1; *Steward Machine Company* v. *Davis,* 301 U.S. 548; and *Helvering* v. *Davis,* 301 U.S. 619. For a discussion of these cases in a contextual framework, see Michael S. Sorgen, Patrick S. Duffy, William A. Kaplin, and Ephraim Margolin, *State, School, and Family: Cases and Materials on Law and Education* (New York: Mathew Bender, 1973), pp. 14-4 to 14-14, and Jay D. Scribner, "Impacts of Federal Programs on State Departments of Education," in *Education in the States: Nationwide Development Since 1900,* eds. Edgar Fuller and Jim B. Pearson (Washington, D.C.: National Education Association, 1969), pp. 447-54.

[11]See R. F. Campbell, L. L. Cunningham, and R. F. MacPhee, *The Organization and*

that "there shall be reserved the lot No. 16 of every township for the maintenance of public schools within said townships." The 1787 Act set forth somewhat more explicitly the rationale for reserving resources to education. The legislation said in part, *"Religion, Morality, and Knowledge, being necessary to good government and the happiness of mankind, schools and the means of education shall forever be encouraged."* When California became a state in 1850, the number of sections allocated for the support of education was increased to two, and later was expanded to four for Utah, Arizona, and New Mexico. This land and the income derived from its sale or lease provided resources for education in what otherwise would have been constrained economic conditions. Perhaps an even greater legacy from these Acts than the land and income was the general mandate for public support of education and the more specific precedent for federal involvement in that support.

Following the Land Acts and after ratification of the Constitution, numerous proposals were made for federal support of educational activities.[12] It was almost three-quarters of a century later, however, before Congress took effective action. In 1862, Abraham Lincoln signed the first Morrill Act into law. As mentioned earlier, this legislation provided an endowment to states for colleges to teach "agriculture and mechanical arts." Revenues received from lands granted to states under this authority were instrumental in founding many prestigious institutions of higher education (e.g., Cornell University, Massachusetts Institute of Technology, and the University of California). The Act was amended in 1890, the second Morrill Act, to include federal support for a broader range of subjects and to preclude racial discrimination toward those receiving the services of land grant institutions.

The next major federal concern for education and manpower development came with passage of the 1917 Smith-Hughes Vocational Education Act. This legislation established a Federal Board for Vocational Education and authorized an annual appropriation of $7 million to be distributed to states for promotion of vocational education in agriculture, trade, industrial arts, and home economics. The Smith-Hughes Act was amended in 1937 and was accompanied by a complete package of education legislation intended to alleviate the Great Depression. Thus, by the time World War II began, the federal government was spending in excess of $20 million annually on vocational education and $100 million on elementary and secondary education altogether. A small amount in today's terms, but sufficient to create an interested constituency among educators and whet their appetite for more.

Control of American Schools (Columbus: Charles E. Merrill Publishing Company, 1965), p. 21. The land area involved in the Northwest Territory contained all or part of what are now the states of Indiana, Illinois, Michigan, Ohio, Wisconsin, and Minnesota.

[12] See Frederick Rudolf, ed., *Essays on Education in the Early Republic* (Cambridge: Harvard University Press, 1965).

MODERN FEDERAL SCHOOL AID PROGRAMS:
WORLD WAR II AND THEREAFTER

IMPACTED AREAS LEGISLATION

At the onset of World War II, it became evident that opening a new military base could instantaneously place almost insurmountable burdens on adjacent schools. Enrollments would skyrocket overnight, yet the local property tax base did not expand. Congress' answer was the 1941 Lanham Act. Public Laws 815 and 874 are the result of a mid-century revision of the Lanham Act following the Korean conflict. These laws have become immensely popular, in part because they authorize funds for almost 4,000 U.S. school districts[13] with few restrictions on how the money is used.[14] This "impact aid" has been controversial, however, because some very rich school districts (especially near Washington, D.C.) are notable recipients. Such inequities have led to efforts to repeal the program.

THE NATIONAL DEFENSE EDUCATION ACT

Following the various vocational education acts, the federal government's next major step into manpower development was taken in 1958 with passage of the National Defense Education Act. This legislation followed in the wake of public reaction to the 1957 launching of Sputnik, the Soviet space success that caught the American public by surprise. It was shocking that the United States could be outdone in any area of technology, but to run second to our primary international rival was particularly disconcerting. An explanation had to be found, and in this instance schools provided a convenient, and defenseless, scapegoat. Critics of American education such as Admiral Hyman Rickover held that U.S. schools had become too easy, their standards too low, and, particularly in mathematics and the sciences, that we were teaching little more than intellectual mush.[15] It was clear, then, that U.S. education would have to be improved if we were to overcome the Soviet challenge. It was this climate of concerned opinion that stimulated Congress to pass the National Defense Education Act.

[13] Figures provided by the National Center for Educational Statistics in the U.S. Office of Education.

[14] Every president from Truman to Ford attempted, unsuccessfully, to reduce the appropriation level of PL 874. A ploy attempted periodically by the executive branch was simply not to release all PL 815 and 874 funds appropriated. This procedure, known technically as "impounding," is of dubious constitutionality and provoked powerful political pressures against the president. The Budget Reform Act of 1974 attempted to clarify the President's impoundment powers.

[15] For a general summary of Rickover's views on education see his book *American Education: A National Failure* (New York: Dutton, 1963).

The NDEA authorized federal funds for a wide variety of educational activities, including loans designed to induce college students to enter the teaching field; funds for local districts to use in the purchase of instructional equipment for mathematics, science, and foreign language courses; money for the preparation of guidance and counseling personnel; and resources to encourage research with educational television and other audiovisual materials. Eventually the Act was expanded to allow federal matching funds to be used to assist in the purchase of instructional materials for almost all subject matter areas.

THE 1964 ECONOMIC OPPORTUNITY ACT

This was one of the larger programs initiated during President Lyndon B. Johnson's "War on Poverty." The Economic Opportunity Act authorized unusual educational programs, several bypassing conventional educational channels. They were not only not administered, initially, by the Office of Education, but also not operated through local school districts. The Office of Economic Opportunity (OEO) was established as a separate agency within the federal executive branch to administer the legislation. However, by 1972, all OEO programs had either been terminated or transferred to other administrative agencies. For example, Headstart and Upward Bound were ceded to the U.S. Office of Education. The Job Corps was not refunded. The Office of Economic Opportunity itself was dismantled.

THE 1965 ELEMENTARY
AND SECONDARY EDUCATION ACT

This landmark piece of legislation in the field of federal aid to education appropriates the largest amount of federal funds, covers the broadest spectrum of educational functions, and contains the greatest potential for exciting political controversy of any federal education act. In its original form, the ESEA authorized in excess of $1.2 billion. By 1977, Congress was appropriating more than $2 billion for this Act. The primary purpose, addressed in Title I of the Act, is to provide educationally disadvantaged children with remedial and compensatory services. The remainder of the Act also embodies a number of important programs, many of which had no precedent.

THE 1968 VOCATIONAL EDUCATION ACT

This comprehensive piece of legislation amends the 1963 Vocational Education Act to encompass almost all previously existing federal vocational education programs. In addition, the 1968 amendments authorized a number of new programs and significantly increased the amount of federal funds authorized for vocational education. In fiscal year 1977, funds appropriated under this Act approximated $600 million.

EDUCATION
FOR ALL HANDICAPPED CHILDREN ACT

Enacted in 1975, this federal program of extraordinary breadth authorizes funds to aid state and local school districts in the schooling of handicapped individuals from ages three to twenty-one. Distribution of funds is dependent upon federal approval of state plans and local school district compliance with many federal program regulations. By 1982, this act will authorize payments to states for each handicapped pupil equal to 40 percent of the state's average annual expenditure per pupil. This act has the potential, in time, to convey as much money to states and local school districts as any other federal program, even ESEA.

In summary, from a modest colonial beginning, federal school aid has expanded to encompass a wide variety of purposes and programs. The absence of a specific constitutional mandate is no longer taken as a limitation. Teachers' salaries, school construction, student loans, food services, compensatory education, research and development, vocational training, and purchase of textbooks are all permitted under the modern mantle of federal aid to education.

Passage of a school aid bill is still far from automatic; political support is still a prerequisite. However, school bills today face nowhere near the traditional level of congressional controversy and interest group resistance. There exist two possible exceptions to this statement: (1) bills to provide federal funds to nonpublic schools, and (2) so-called "general aid" legislation, bills to permit federal funds to be spent at the discretion of state and local education officials. The first of these concerns, aid to nonpublic elementary and secondary schools, increasingly appears to be outlawed by Supreme Court decisions. Also, advocates of such aid are inhibited by the fear that it might benefit segregated "white academies." Nevertheless, this topic and the second, "general aid," continue to provoke political conflict.

Federal Education Policy

The following is an attempt to describe and analyze the process of formulating a federal school aid policy, but this process is infinitely more complex and convoluted than words can capture. We begin with a description of policy formation, progress to the enactment and appropriations stages, illustrate the steps involved in implementing a major piece of federal education legislation, and end by formulating several general propositions regarding the federal aid political process.

GENERATING EDUCATION LEGISLATION

In order to be enacted, a legislative idea must be politically popular, or at least not too politically controversial. The idea may stem from any number of sources—a book, a speech, a cause of some organized group, or an old proposal previously ignored. Indeed, the roots of most major pieces of legislation, whether planted in Washington, D.C. or at any other level of government, are so varied and diffuse that they are virtually impossible to trace. There are three major points from which an idea can take shape as a legislative proposal: (1) in the federal executive branch; (2) in Congress; or (3) in an interest group or a coalition of interest groups. Sometimes, if the idea is a popular one, legislative proposals may emanate from all three sources. More generally, however, the impetus necessary to frame a bill emanates from only one source.

Since the 1920s, the locus of initiation for major social welfare proposals has rested with the executive branch. This trend began under the aggressive leadership of Woodrow Wilson and gained momentum under FDR. For the most part, Roosevelt's successors have followed suit.

EXECUTIVE BRANCH INITIATIVES

Emergence of the executive branch as the principal initiator of federal policy proposals has come about for reasons such as the following: (1) the uniquely national political power base of the president, (2) the extraordinary expertise at the president's disposal, (3) the executive's almost unmatched ability to command mass media attention, and (4) the ability, particularly when the president's political party controls both houses of Congress, to coordinate legislative branch efforts.

Except for the vice-president, whose role though increasingly active is still largely ceremonial, the president is the only public official elected from a national constituency. Certain senators, and more rarely a few representatives, may periodically appeal to a national audience, but each must revert from time to time to the more homogeneous and highly parochial cares of his or her home base constituency. The president is the only public official who speaks for all citizens. As such, he incurs responsibilities which stimulate him to seek national programs. For example, he makes campaign promises that frequently necessitate legislative proposals, or he perceives a national need, the filling of which may possibly accrue more popular votes to him and his party, and he proposes relevant legislation. Regardless of motivation, the president, by virtue of his nationally elected position, is an unmatched focal point for initiating legislation dealing with matters of national significance such as education.

In addition to the president's nationwide political base, the executive branch has been moved to the role of prime legislative initiator by virtue of its vast expertise. Legislation of a major sort is a remarkably complex phenomenon. Arriving at the formula in Title I of the ESEA, for example, was a process which occupied literally months of time for several experts in school finance, and even then their various proposals had to be analyzed further by dozens of computer simulations. Social problems toward which such legislation is directed seldom lend themselves to simple answers, and complex solutions demand time and knowledgeability. These requirements are found in greatest measure in the executive branch.

A congressman's staff, even the largest senatorial staff, is no match for the expertise at the disposal of the president. It is true that a congressman has access to the Legislative Reference Services of the Library of Congress and the legal staff of Congress' own Legislative Counsel's office. However, these tend to be composed of overworked, though highly competent, generalists who seldom have an opportunity to match the specialized skills of their executive branch counterparts. It is also true that congressmen can call on the skills of executive branch experts; this is known as requesting "technical assistance." But, should a congressman desire information or advice on a matter contrary to the president's position, "technical assistance" can dry up. In the same vein, interest groups, though sometimes possessing crucial information on a narrow dimension, have difficulty amassing the range of expertise and other resources to compete with the executive branch in framing broad-scale policy proposals.

A third explanation for executive branch policy initiation stems from the public attention commanded by the president's actions. No other single human being is so consistently the focus of mass media coverage. The president need only make a gesture to trigger a press conference; any major policy announcement immediately receives national publicity. The president is thus automatically able to stimulate greater public concern for his ideas than are other individuals in policy proposing positions. In addition to the attention given his actions by virtue of his office, he is granted opportunities to form and influence public and congressional opinion. For example, his campaign platform, State of the Union address, and budget message are three formal and highly visible opportunities granted almost completely to the president.

Finally, by cooperating with leaders of his political party, the president can frequently coordinate the actions of Congress in a unique fashion. This is especially the case when the president's party constitutes a majority in both houses. An individual congressman or senator, at best, may be able to facilitate a flow of business so as to gain favorable action in his or her own House. However, only with the cooperation of party leaders can actions of both House and Senate be coordinated closely. This cooperation is more readily available to the president because he controls the greatest number of relevant rewards and sanctions.

We do not wish to leave the impression that all educational policy proposals originate in the executive branch. However, of those groups situated in policy proposing postures, the president is in the best position.

"**Percolation.**" How are education policy proposals constructed within the executive branch? The legislation generation process appears to have two directions or routes within the executive branch. The first path is the one most frequently followed for minor legislative proposals, usually technical amendments to existing legislation. This is a bureaucratic "percolation" process wherein a "call" for new legislative ideas is sent out regularly each year, usually in mid-summer, from the president's staff to executive branch departments and agencies. The "call" gradually filters to the levels of bureaus, divisions, branches, and sections. In time, ideas begin to bubble back up through the hierarchy until they reach what approximates a policy "filter." At this point they are examined closely for their consistency with the president's directives and fiscal guidelines and are also "packaged" for assessment by significant decision makers. For example, within the Office of Education, the office of the Assistant Commissioner for Legislation is where ideas are assembled for approval by the operating bureau Associate Commissioners and by the U.S. Commissioner of Education. Following the latter's approval, proposals are then evaluated by the Secretary of the Department of Health, Education, and Welfare, with assistance from the legislative and analytic staff. From there, proposals flow to the Office of Management and Budget (OMB), where staff analysts assemble recommendations from the entire executive branch and prepare them for presidential evaluation. This process is not as orderly as depicted by this narrative, and probably never happens the same way any two years in a row. Different people occupy positions; different economic and social conditions provoke varying priorities. Nevertheless, the process applies in its most general outline to the great mass of education legislation proposals formulated in the executive branch.

"**Trickle down.**" Major bills like the ESEA are exceptions to the process just described. The tendency in these instances is for the instrumental idea or framework for a bill to originate high in the executive branch hierarchy, with the Commissioner of Education, the Director of NIE, the Secretary of HEW, members of a high-level presidential task force assigned to a problem,[16] or, perhaps, with the president himself. In these instances, proposals may flow back through the executive branch educational bureaucracy to be fleshed out and to enlist the support of the bureaucrats involved. The essence of the bill, however, will have been established at high levels.

---

[16] In large measure, the legislative substance of the ESEA was the creation of a secret LBJ Presidential Task Force chaired by John W. Gardner, then President of the Carnegie Corporation and subsequently appointed as Secretary of HEW. The ingenious political strategy involved in gaining enactment of the ESEA was primarily devised by then Commissioner of Education, Francis Keppel, and Samuel Halperin, then Assistant USOE Commissioner for Legislation. See James W. Guthrie, "A Political Case History: Passage of the ESEA," *Phi Delta Kappan,* 49 (February 1968), 306–9.

At some point after presidential approval is gained for an idea, but usually before the bill is introduced in Congress, representatives of relevant interest groups will be informed. This preview serves a number of reciprocally beneficial functions. For the executive branch, it provides an opportunity to enlist support from influential organizations. Moreover, the preview exposes the bill's controversial "rough edges" and gives executive branch staff an opportunity to polish them and bring about compromises before having to appear in public with the bill. The preview enables interest group representatives to appear particularly effective to their organization's members. They obtain the "inside dope" on forthcoming legislation likely to effect their members, and they can demonstrate their effectiveness to their clients by virtue of being "consulted on legislation by the president."

At a point late in the legislation generation cycle, usually in December, a sufficient agreement has been reached on the president's education program to enable a team of attorneys to begin drafting bills. This is an arduous task and involves immense technical skill. At the same time bills are being drafted, the president's program is being prepared for public unveiling. This may take place in a general way in the State of the Union address, but it will usually appear in considerably more detail in the president's message on education, if he has one. Once this is done, arrangements are made with relevant committee chairmen, or ranking minority members if the president's party is out of power, in the House and Senate to introduce the bills.

This concludes what we have labeled the "legislation generation stage," and momentum subsequently shifts to the actions of the Congress. This is not to imply that the executive branch is now out of the picture; rather, it assumes an active posture as an advocate for the president's program. Nevertheless, it is now the legislators' turn to take up the action and the president's team is, for the moment at least, cast more in the role of reactor.

CONGRESSIONAL LEGISLATIVE INITIATIVES

Generally speaking, most bills are the product of congressional legislative initiatives, and only major bills emanate from the White House. There are exceptions. On occasion, a social policy item that has been neglected by the president may be of sufficient interest to motivate congressional bills. In these instances, a committee staff or the staff of one or more representatives or senators constructs the substance of the bill. In so doing they obtain assistance from the Legislative Reference Service, an arm of the Library of Congress. Once the bill's outline is formed, the bill itself is usually drafted by the Legislative Counsel's Office. Unless such a bill has the support of the majority party and the president, however, it is unlikely to pass. By utilizing his reservoir of power, the president can try to kill a bill in Congress rather than have it enacted and then have to exercise his veto power.

THE ENACTMENT PROCESS

Much has been written regarding the tendency of Congress and its procedures to frustrate rather than facilitate the passage of legislation. This reluctance to enact laws applies particularly to education legislation. The negative attitude of Congress toward education legislation became legendary. For the best typical example for his book on the "footdragging" phenomenon in Congress, Robert Bendiner[17] chose education bills. At least until 1965 when ESEA broke the legislative logjam, the problem was that decisions about education must seemingly involve conflicting values like those surrounding race, religion, or the role of the federal government in correcting social ills. We will shortly discuss the major political controversies that have shaped federal school aid policy. First, however, we describe the path a school aid bill must follow in order to reach fruition.

THE LEGISLATIVE ROUTE

We do not intend to describe in detail the path by which a bill becomes a law since that is a task performed admirably in a number of other places.[18] Rather, what follows is an effort to note the significant congressional decision points for education bills.

Regardless of where a bill is generated, whether in the legislature, executive branch, or elsewhere, it must be introduced in Congress by a member. It is not particularly difficult to obtain introduction of a bill; literally thousands are submitted during each session, many of which have no hope of becoming law. Members of Congress are particularly glad to introduce a major bill because, should it be enacted or even gain great positive acclaim, it will reflect well politically upon the person or persons who "sponsored" it. When the proposal is a part of the president's program, he usually arranges for a prominent member of his party to introduce the bill. The hope is to draw positive attention to the bill by attaching to it the name of a well-known and respected "sponsor." Frequently if the president's party is in power, the House sponsor will be the chairperson or subcommittee chairperson of the Committee on Education and Labor, and in the Senate, the chairperson of the Committee on Labor and Public Welfare, or its Education subcommittee.

A majority of education bills start in "hearings" in these committees. The committee's majority approval is crucial if the measure is to proceed to the

---

[17] Robert Bendiner, *Obstacle Course of Capitol Hill* (New York: McGraw-Hill Book Company, 1964).

[18] Among the best are Daniel M. Berman, *A Bill Becomes a Law* (2d ed.) (New York: The Macmillan Company, 1966), and Stephen K. Bailey, *Congress Makes a Law: The Story Behind the Unemployment Act of 1946* (New York: Columbia University Press, 1950).

"floor" for consideration by the entire body. Thus chairpersons of these committees and their component subcommittees are key figures in a bill's career. A negatively disposed chairperson has the power to jeopardize severely the survival of a bill. In the past, anti-federal aid chairpersons, such as Graham Arthur Burden (D., Georgia), were able to "kill" hundreds of school aid bills. Conversely, early champions of an expanded federal aid to education role such as Senator Robert Taft, Sr. (R., Ohio) and Representative Adam Clayton Powell (D., New York) were able to exercise powers of the Chair to facilitate passage of federal aid legislation.

Open hearings are usually held in which committee members receive testimony from the bill's proponents and opponents. The schedule of witnesses is heavily influenced by the committee or subcommittee chairperson and thus those who speak may over-represent one point of view. However, any individual or speaker for an organization who desires strongly to be heard has a good chance of so doing.

The importance of hearings is not clear. There are those who contend that members' minds are typically made up in advance of hearings and change little in the process. Hearings serve only to present a facade of rational deliberation and a platform from which interest groups can publicly proclaim their political positions. Conversely, there is evidence to suggest that significant decisions are stimulated by committee hearings. Sections of the ESEA were revised following testimony by several witnesses that the bill contained unconstitutional transgressions of the church–state boundary. Also, in the course of ESEA hearings, Senator Robert Kennedy (D., New York) became convinced of the necessity for a provision to evaluate ESEA's effectiveness, and this resulted in important amendments to the bill.

Following committee hearings, the bill and possible amendments are voted upon in committee. In the House, if a favorable majority is sustained, the bill is then cleared for floor debate, if granted a "rule" by the powerful House Committee on Rules. Historically this has been a big "if" for education bills. In theory, the Rules Committee is supposed to function as an impartial "traffic cop," directing an orderly flow of business to the House floor. In fact, the Rules Committee on occasion becomes embroiled in the substantive controversies associated with proposed legislation. For years, prior to 1965, the Committee's membership was biased against school aid bills, and on a number of occasions refused to grant a rule allowing a bill onto the floor for debate. Parliamentary procedures whereby the Rules Committee can be overcome are now less difficult to invoke than before the ESEA.[19] The Senate has no formal equivalent of the House Committee on Rules. Senate scheduling for floor consideration of bills is handled in an informal manner between the majority and minority leaders.

---

[19] In 1961, President John F. Kennedy placed a restructuring of the Rules Committee high on his political agenda, and in a tightly fought battle his congressional allies managed to expand the membership on that committee to tip the voting scales to favor school aid legislation. For this reason, and because its legislative authority has been curtailed, the Rules Committee is no longer the threat that it once was.

On the floor, the House again presents more obstacles to passage than does the Senate. Because of its large size, the House frequently employs a special parliamentary procedure to enable it to operate with a quorum substantially smaller than the normal number, 218 members. This procedure, meeting as the "Committee of the Whole House of the State of the Union," requires that only 100 members be on the floor and, in addition, allows for suspension of cumbersome parliamentary procedures. Though the "Committee of the Whole" may expedite legislative business, it may also subject bills to double jeopardy. Any measures passed by the Committee of the Whole must ultimately be ratified in a regular session of the full House; thus, frequently a school aid bill must be approved twice on the floor of the House of Representatives. The Senate considers matters only once.

Framers of the Constitution provided for indirect election of Senators in the belief that to do so would create a more conservative body less prone to persuasion by "precipitous passions of mob action," than the directly elected House. Contrary to these beliefs, the Senate, now directly elected also, has proven to be more liberal on matters of domestic social welfare legislation, education included, than the House.[20] Prior to enactment of the ESEA, the Senate, for example, had passed a broad-scale aid to education bill on eight separate occasions whereas the House had done so but twice. (In no instance had the two bodies passed the same bill.)

If a bill survives obstructions awaiting it in the legislative pathways of both houses, chances are good that through amending the original bill, each has enacted a slightly different version. Then a "Conference Committee" composed of equal numbers of members from each body meets to resolve differences. This usually necessitates compromises by both sides, and the resulting bill must again be approved by both houses. Conference Committees frequently have been a graveyard for important school aid proposals; that is, either a majority in the Senate, the House, or both was not sufficiently moved to ratify the compromise bill. Knowledge of this danger prompted proponents of the 1965 ESEA to strive to gain passage of an identical bill in both houses thus avoiding the necessity for a Conference. Their tactic, though complicated and rarely tried, proved successful, despite the Kennedy evaluation amendment to which we referred earlier. Once enacted in final form by both House and Senate, the bill is delivered to the White House for presidential action.

THE FLOW OF FEDERAL FUNDS[21]

Few persons understand that the process by which federal dollars are appropriated is different from the procedures for constructing and enacting

---

[20] The 17th Amendment, enacted in 1913, provides for direct election of Senators. For an explanation of why the Senate is more "liberal" than the House, see Lewis Froman's *Congressmen and Their Constituencies* (Chicago: Rand McNally, 1963).

[21] This topic is explained in greater detail in James W. Guthrie, "The Flow of Federal Funds for Education," chap. 3 in Summerfield, *Power and Process*, pp. 249–94.

substantive bills. In order to have a federal school aid program, the Congress must enact both an "authorizing" and an "appropriations" statute. Authorizations establish purposes for which federal funds can be used, provide detail regarding the act's administration, and frequently specify the upper limits of federal funding. However, the appropriations process determines the precise dollar amount, for an authorized purpose, to be drawn from the Treasury in any particular fiscal year. The two steps are closely connected but rely upon different machinery for passage.

Federal funding depends upon actions in both the executive and legislative branches. Each year, the president submits a proposed budget to Congress containing recommendations for congressional funding action. This budget reflects the president's spending priorities and his policies for managing the national economy. The president may recommend deficit spending to stimulate recovery from a recession or a surplus to slow inflation.

Compilation of the president's budget is coordinated by the Office of Management and Budget (OMB). Since 1974, a comparable agency in the legislative branch, the Congressional Budget Office (CBO), has made budget recommendations to Congress. This office acts primarily to assist the Congressional Budget Committees in establishing overall congressional spending limits. These limits, and Congress' advocacy of deficit or surplus budgeting, are established consistent with Congress' view of the nation's economic needs. It is too early in the life of the CBO to discern whether or not it will develop a pattern of nonpartisan expertise or be subject to the political will of a strong majority party. Also, the degree to which CBO and the Budget Committees will concur or conflict with OMB overall spending levels remains to be seen.

Upon receiving the president's budget and economic guidelines established by the Congressional Budget Committees and approved by Congress, Appropriations Committees in both houses begin deliberations.[22] Appropriations committees rely heavily upon subcommittees, one of which in each house is responsible for analyzing budget requests for the Department of Health, Education, and Welfare. The total appropriation recommended for HEW must be consistent with the congressional spending ceiling. However, within that figure, appropriations subcommittees, and ultimately the full committees, have discretion to determine how much will be allocated for things such as USOE, NIE, Food and Drug Administration, and Social Security Administration.

Appropriation subcommittees make recommendations to their parent appropriation committees. From there, bills proceed to the floor of the respective bodies. Amendment at this stage is possible, but historically it is improbable. The exception took place during the Nixon administration when a coalition education lobby, the Committee on Full Funding (discussed in more detail

---

[22] For an insightful description of congressional appropriations politics, see Richard F. Fenno, *The Power of the Purse: Appropriations Politics in Congress* (Boston: Little Brown and Company, 1966).

later), continually succeeded in persuading a floor majority of both houses to override not only the president's recommended level of education spending, but also the recommendations of the appropriations' committees. Barring such unusual circumstances, appropriations committees historically have seldom exceeded presidential recommendations, and the Senate and House usually accept the proposed spending levels of their respective appropriations committees, with the Senate typically appropriating more than the House. After passage on the floor, bills proceed to conference to resolve differences between House and Senate versions, and subsequently, to the president for his action. If vetoed, congressional deliberations begin again, either to override the veto or to frame a new bill. However, eventual passage of appropriations bills at some level of funding is assured. On occasion, the entire procedure is repeated in a budget year to adjust for spending overruns in an agency. These bills are known as "supplemental appropriations." The final bill, when signed by the president, permits the Treasury to expend federal funds consistent with the purposes of the authorizing legislation.

Fiscal 1977, beginning October 1, 1976, marked the first operational year for the 1974 Budget Reform Act. Consequently, it is too soon to assess the effects of joint action by the CBO and Congressional Budget Committees. However, it appears that the new procedures will inhibit further the ability of education interests to obtain their desired levels of funding. Under the new procedures, Congress assumes greater responsibility for the nation's total economy; no longer will the president alone shoulder the entire burden of fiscal management. Thus some contend that Congress will scrutinize expenditures more carefully and that education appropriations, since they must be consistent with an overall congressional spending ceiling, will be placed in substantially greater competition with other public sector services, particularly those administered by HEW. The outcome could be a tighter school aid purse.

IMPLEMENTING FEDERAL LEGISLATION

There is no sharp demarcation between enactment and implementation. Where and how a bill will be administered is given substantial consideration both in planning legislation and in congressional considerations. Indeed, at times questions about administration can provoke the hottest political controversies about a bill. Political controversy does not cease with enactment. Implementation and operation of a federal program involve many accommodations, as the executive branch administering agency takes into account desires of Congress, pressures of interest groups, views of clients the program is designed to benefit, and an administrator's own thoughts regarding what is educationally most sound. Because useful suggestions may come from any of these four groups, subsequent shifts in administrative format are possible, even likely, over time. What follows is a brief description of the steps taken as the United States Office of Education (USOE) prepares to administer a new piece of federal aid legisla-tion.[23] We also cite examples of political considerations entering this process.

Administration of a bill is generally specified in the bill itself. In educa-tion bills, the Commissioner of Education or the Director of the National In-stitute of Education is typically charged with administrative responsibility. Here we consider the Commissioner exclusively because most elementary and secondary bills fall under the jurisdiction of USOE. When a bill is passed, the Commissioner and his staff begin a two-pronged process: (1) interpreting new legislation to the "field"—those persons in education who will be affected by it; and (2) identifying the staff and bureaucratic locus within the Office of Educa-tion to operate the program. The first prong is necessary because of the gen-eralized language in which a piece of legislation is usually couched. A bill does not contain details, such as how a local school district applies for funds, due dates for submitting project proposals, or the form that such proposals should take. These and hundreds of other questions are anticipated in the USOE drafting of two documents: (1) administrative regulations, and (2) program guidelines.

Shortly following passage of a bill, a task force of USOE personnel is assigned to draft regulations and guidelines. They also may seek advice of ex-perts outside of USOE. Administrative regulations contain a more detailed ex-planation of the new law and the way it is to be administered. Those drafting the regulations depend heavily upon the legislative history of the act (what was said in congressional committee hearings, reports, and in the course of floor debates). Regulations are reviewed by the substantive congressional committee involved, revised accordingly, printed in the *Federal Register,* and incorporated in the Federal Administrative Code. For some purposes, regulations have the weight of law.

Guidelines, written in much less technical language, are aimed at ex-plaining the new program to educators; they are generally written by those who have been designated by the Commissioner to administer the program. Local educators may have read about the new program in newspaper articles and in publications from educational organizations but federal guidelines usually provide the most complete and accurate information.

Depending on the nature of the new program, it will be assigned to one or another of USOE's various bureaus. In order to administer the many new pro-grams associated with the 1965 ESEA, the USOE underwent a major adminis-trative reorganization. This rearrangement was an effort to devise functional administrative categories to encompass all old and anticipated new programs. It was not long, however, before interests outside of USOE were dissatisfied with the new arrangements and exerted presssures to change them. For example,

---

[23] A description and analysis of the implementation process is provided in Stephen K. Bailey and Edith K. Mosher, *ESEA: The Office of Education Administers a Law* (New York: Syracuse University Press, 1968).

interest groups and members of Congress concerned with handicapped children regretted that their cause had not been granted bureau status under the new structure. Accordingly, political pressures resulted in reestablishment of such a bureau. The USOE, like many federal executive branch agencies, is in a constant state of change.

At the time of the 1965 reorganization of the USOE, regional offices were formed. Considerable controversy surrounded this decentralization. Behind the move was an attempt to make administration of programs more efficient and faster by closing the distance between state and local clients and federal administrators. In fact, it is not clear that this has or will come about. One problem was initial confusion regarding whether regional office personnel would have decision-making authority or whether such power would be retained in Washington. Moreover, local educators sometimes do not wish to deal with regional offices, even when those offices are empowered with decision-making authority. There is higher status and prestige associated with dealing directly with Washington, and, given modern rapid communication, a phone call to Washington to clarify a matter may be as fast as a phone call to a regional office. In fact, if regional personnel must first consult Washington, the likelihood is great that regionalization impedes efficiency. The topsy-turvy administrative world is exemplified by the following. In the latter part of 1968, the U.S. Office announced that regional administrators of ESEA Title I, II, and III would be returned to Washington. This was reversed in 1970.

A further example of the manner in which political considerations pervade operational components is the struggle to elevate the U.S. Office of Education to department status in the executive branch. From its inception in 1867, the Office has been situated in a number of executive branch settings. Since 1953 it has been one of the components of the Department of Health, Education, and Welfare, although various education organizations and individuals have constantly argued that it be given departmental status. The explicit justification such advocates frequently give is that education is today such an important function it must be accorded national significance by creating a cabinet level position. An informal motivation for such proposals comes from the increased prestige that would accrue to those associated with USOE, not only to educational interest groups but also to congressional committees.[24] Status of a congressional committee or subcommittee is generally perceived as higher if it has operational oversight and legislative jurisdiction over a department rather than a component agency. Up until 1977, presidents, once in office, have opposed such a move, primarily on grounds that education is not slighted and thus there is no need to proliferate the number of departments and increase the size of the federal government. Former HEW

---

[24] For details, see *Study of the United States Office of Education,* Report of the Special Subcommittee on Education, 90th Congress, 1st Session (Washington, D.C.: U.S. Government Printing Office), House Document No. 193.

Secretary, John W. Gardner, further contended that contemporary social problems do not divide themselves neatly into compartments labeled "health," "education," and "welfare." Systematic attack on domestic crises depends upon a coordinated effort and this is easier when education is administered jointly with other relevant services. President Carter, however, advocated department status for education in his 1976 campaign.

Financial Distribution

How federal funds are distributed to local school districts is an area of controversy frequently accompanying federal aid proposals.

The distribution controversy contains at its core a conflict between educational desirability and political feasibility. It is generally conceded among educators that federal school finance formulas should in substantial measure be based upon the principle of "equalization"; that is, federal revenues generated in wealthy states should be distributed in a compensating fashion to less wealthy states. However, congressional spokesmen for wealthy states have tended to oppose school aid bills that returned proportionately less to their constituents than they contributed in taxes to the federal treasury. Conversely, members of Congress from poor states have seldom been favorably disposed toward school aid bills that did not allow their constituents proportionately more than their federal tax contribution. For several decades prior to 1965, no politically acceptable and educationally sound rationale could be found for an equalization formula.

In arriving at the elimination of poverty as the justification for distributing federal funds, it was possible to construct a distribution formula that met the classic political test of "something for everyone" while still retaining substantial value for education. The original Title I formula components, number of children from low-income and welfare-assisted families multiplied by one-half a state's average annual per pupil expenditure, represent an ingenious mix. It is estimated that 90 percent of all U.S. counties receive federal assistance under this formula. At the same time, however, the particularly heavy educational needs of poverty-stricken large city and rural children are also served. The result is an educationally sound and politically acceptable federal aid distribution formula.

CHANGING THE FORMULA

Since its initial passage, there have been numerous efforts to alter the Title I distribution formula. What is perhaps the most dramatic attempt took place in 1974 when Congressman Albert Quie, the ranking Republican on the House Education and Labor Committee, proposed an amendment to distribute Title I funds on the basis of student achievement rather than measures of household income. Quie contended that the act was directed at assisting low-achieving students; thus, what could be more logical than to allocate funds to states and districts based on achievement test scores. Also, he argued, the then employed measures of household income, decennial census data and Aid for Families with Dependent Children (AFDC) status, were inaccurate, untimely, and lacking in uniformity across state and school district boundaries. Quie's opponents asserted that use of tests might encourage federal control of school objectives, would enable local districts to manipulate conditions so as to inflate the number of eligible students, and would become a reward for low performance on the part of school districts.

The Secretary of HEW commissioned a study to assess the distribution consequences of a Title I formula revision. By using a computerized simulation model of the general type described in Chapter Twelve, it was possible to predict that a test score-based formula would trigger substantial shifts in the flow of Title I funds.[25] Specifically, a test score formula would place proportionately more money into suburban school districts and less into large urban districts. This is the case because, though high, the correlation between poverty and low school performance is not perfect. Consequently a conversion to test scores moves money out of districts where poverty is concentrated. The simulations also demonstrated a shift of funds among states, with the South and Northeast being the beneficiaries. This redistribution effect is not so easily explained but probably is a consequence of the fact that these sections of the nation administer welfare funds (AFDC) in a fashion that does not reflect the true level of poverty.

The Quie bill was defeated but the Title I distribution formula debate continues. For example, in an effort to meet Quie's criticisms regarding inadequacy of census measures, the formula's original low-income component was altered in 1975 to utilize the Orshansky Index. This is a more complicated measure of family economic circumstances which adjusts absolute income level for cost differences associated with size of family and rural-urban geographic location.[26]

DISTRIBUTIONAL EFFECTS: INTRASTATE

Another premise at the time Title I was passed was that the newly authorized federal funds would help to equalize financial disparities between central

---

[25] James W. Guthrie, Ann S. Frentz, and Rita M. Mize, *The Use of Performance Criteria to Allocate Compensatory Education Funds* (Menlo Park: Stanford Research Institute, 1974), and Nadine M. Lambert and Carolyn S. Hartsough, "Models of Performance: Economic Criteria for the Allocation of Compensatory Education Funds and Their Relationship to Student Outcomes," paper prepared under contract to the National Institute of Education, Compensatory Education Study, 1976.

[26] For a complete description of the Title I formula see the *Federal Register* for Tuesday, September 28, 1976, pp. 42894-42923.

cities and wealthier school districts on their perimeters. Evidence on the matter suggests that Title I *does* exert an equalizing influence, but it is too small to off-set the inequities provoked by state and local funds and other federal statutes. The most complete evidence on this was compiled in a 1972 study directed by Joel S. Berke of Syracuse University and Michael W. Kirst of Stanford University. Relying on survey research information and case studies from six states, Berke and Kirst offer the following general conclusions regarding the intrastate distribution of federal aid funds:

1. Non-metropolitan areas, largely rural and small town in character, tend to receive more federal aid per pupil than do metropolitan areas.

2. While central cities get more total federal aid than their suburbs, the amount of federal aid is too small to offset the suburban advantage in local and state revenues. Suburbs averaged $100 more per pupil in total revenues than their core cities in four of the five states in the study.

3. With the exception of ESEA Title I, federal programs frequently provide more funds to suburban districts than to central city districts. Large cities appear to receive less money from programs such as ESEA II, ESEA III, NDEA III, and Vocational Education than their proportion of state-wide enrollment would suggest.

4. Districts with lower income tend as a general rule to get somewhat more federal aid than districts with higher income, but there are numerous glaring exceptions. With regard to property valuation, federal aid shows no overall equalizing effect.

5. Somewhat more federal aid goes to districts with higher proportions of non-white students. However, the amounts are not in proportion to the magnitude of the added costs in educating the educationally disadvantaged.

6. During the four-year period under study, the amounts of aid received by local districts varied erratically. Almost half the metropolitan areas in the sample reported an actual decrease in revenues during the last year of the study.

7. ESEA I has channeled needed funds to districts with the greatest educational and fiscal problems. However, its use is frequently applied to after-hours or summer programs rather than to the core curriculum presented to the educationally disadvantaged. The failure to expend these funds on pupils most in need of compensatory education and ESEA's improper use as general aid for system-wide purposes have diluted its educational impact.

8. The amounts of federal aid are simply too small to avail anything but marginal help to financially imperiled educational systems. In comparison with total revenues from all sources (which ran from $475 to $1,000 per pupil in the five states), we found total federal revenues averaging only $22 to $50 per pupil, or from 3.3 to 10 percent of statewide average district revenues.[27]

[27] Joel S. Berke and Michael W. Kirst, *Federal Aid to Education: Who Benefits? Who Governs?* (Lexington, Mass.: D.C. Heath & Co., 1972), pp. 22–23.

At present we have little knowledge regarding the extent to which federal funds equalize across state boundaries. In a 1969 study, a comparison was made of the proportion of all federal aid funds received by a state to the proportion of all federal personal income tax revenues contributed by that state.[28] Comparing the various proportions of funds received to funds disbursed, the interstate transfer of federal funds was found to be as follows: On balance, dollars flow from northeastern, midwestern, and West Coast states to states located in the Rocky Mountains, along the Mason-Dixon Line separating North and South, and the deep southern states. In particular the last benefited. However, ESEA Title I was found to have the greatest equalization effect. Most other federal education statutes were either neutral or anti-equalizing. These calculations were repeated for 1971 data, and the findings were substantially similar.

The Influentials: Educational Interest Groups

One of the accommodations enabling the American political system to remain representative in spite of a large and geographically far-flung population is the social invention of the organized *public interest group.* Education is not lacking in its share of such groups; there are at least 100 educational organizations that maintain offices and staff in Washington to keep their membership informed about relevant federal actions and to communicate the views of their organizations to members of Congress and other public officials.[29] The effectiveness of these organizations, shown by ability to influence federal policy decisions, varies.

Interest groups are generally thought to wield influence in proportion to the number of individuals they can legitimately claim to represent, degree to which their policy interests are focused rather than diffused, and extent to which they can supply public officials with "expert" information and advice rather than simple opinion. The cartoon stereotype of the lobbyist as a shady character with abundant money with which to grease the palm of legislators is exaggerated. There no doubt exist less than totally open lobbyists, but "buy-

[28] James W. Guthrie and Stephen B. Lawton, "The Distribution of Federal School Aid Funds: Who Wins, Who Loses?" *Educational Administration Quarterly,* 6, No. 1 (Winter 1969), 47–61. For added evidence on this point, see Joel W. Berke and Michael W. Kirst, "How the Federal Government Can Encourage State School Finance Reform," *Phi Delta Kappan,* December 1973, pp. 241–44.

[29] An interesting analysis of education-related interest groups is provided by Harland G. Bloland in "The Role of Associations in a Decentralized System of Higher Education" (unpublished doctoral dissertation, University of California School of Education, Berkeley, 1968). See also, Stephen K. Bailey, *Education Interest Groups in the Nation's Capitol* (Washington, D.C.: American Council on Education, 1975) and Harry Summerfield, *Power and Process.*

ing" legislators is rare. This is especially the case for education lobbies, most of which have small, overworked, and under-financed facilities and staff.

In education, as one might expect, interest groups are characterized by differing points of view. It is difficult to be against education per se, but the disagreement accompanying consideration of such matters as when and how the federal government should be involved in education seems endless. The positions of interest groups on these questions run the gamut from those contending that the federal government has no right at any time to be involved in the education sector to those advocating that the federal government operate the nation's entire educational system. The number and diversity of these educational interest groups is so extensive as to preclude our describing each in detail, so we provide a simplified summary.

SERVICE AND BENEFIT-SEEKING ORGANIZATIONS

The National Education Association (NEA). The NEA has in excess of 1.7 million members and maintains a well staffed office for congressional relations. Through its state and local components it is sometimes able to generate astonishing grass roots communication with Congress when a particular NEA cause is involved. In terms of membership, money, and staff, the NEA is the largest educational interest group. In fact it may be the largest interest group of any kind.

The AFL-CIO. As can be readily recognized, this organization is primarily concerned with those matters that affect labor, but one of the most central of the matters is education. The AFL-CIO is a firm and influential proponent of an expanded educational role for the federal government and lobbies in behalf of such legislation. The American Federation of Teachers (AFT) is an AFL-CIO component.

The U.S. Catholic Conference (USCC). This organization speaks for the Roman Catholic Church on matters of social welfare. In that it purports to represent the nation's 40 million Catholics, the USCC has the potential for substantial influence.

Committee for Full Funding (formerly, Emergency Committee for Full Funding). Organized in April 1969 by representatives of the AFL-CIO and other interest groups, it was founded in response to deep concern over budget cuts in education in President Johnson's final budget and in President Nixon's early proposals. Charles W. Lee, a professional staff member of the Senate Education subcommittee from 1962 to 1969, was named director of this committee and charged with the responsibility of gathering interest groups into a coalition supporting greater education appropriations. The committee was overwhelmingly effective until disbanded in 1975.

OPPOSITION GROUPS

Not all groups support a larger federal role in public education. A few have been effective in limiting this role. Their primary strategy has been to split apart potential supporters of school aid bills by capitalizing upon and playing up tensions between them. For example, the U.S. Chamber of Commerce, once an ardent opponent of federal aid legislation, was successful in its opposition by feeding the church-state controversy that typically transpired between the U.S. Catholic Conference and the NEA. Divide and conquer was the Chamber's strategy and it worked well until 1965, when an executive branch team brought the USCC and NEA into a coalition by constructing a series of compromises in the ESEA.

The U.S. Chamber has been accompanied in its opposition from time to time by the Daughters of the American Revolution, the National Association of Manufacturers, and the American Farm Bureau Federation.

One of the more severe problems limiting the effectiveness of educational interest groups is a tendency to fragment, both within and among themselves. For example, the National School Boards Association (NSBA) has long been handicapped by the frequent inability of its state affiliates to reach a consensus sufficient to allow the national organization to take a strong stand. Worse yet, the conflict between the teacher groups, NEA and AFT, on the one hand, and "management" organizations such as the American Association of School Administrators (AASA), on the other, severely restricts the effectiveness of the "school aid lobby." The Committee for Full Funding was a dramatic exception.

Effects of Federal School Aid Policies

It is difficult to determine conclusively whether or not major federal school aid programs have been effective. This indeterminacy stems from problems such as: (1) ill-defined legislative objectives, (2) inept administration, and (3) inadequate research and measurement techniques. Each of these impediments can be illustrated by referring to experiences with ESEA Title I.

CLOUDY LEGISLATIVE OBJECTIVES

Is ESEA Title I meeting its legislative objectives? Perhaps, or perhaps not. What are its objectives? Is it intended to increase reading and mathematics test scores of low-achieving or low-income children? During the bill's enactment phase, many members of Congress argued that the purposes were substantially broader than simply improving school achievement. In their view, the bill was intended to interrupt the intergenerational cycle of poverty. If that entails striving to improve children's health, emotional stability, or self-image, then those are the appropriate objectives of Title I. All of these are admirable goals but successful evaluation depends upon an understanding of a program's specific objectives. ESEA Title I offers no such understanding.

Absence of legislative precision in forming program objectives may be a problem inherent in the political process. Frequently, sponsors of a bill add objectives to the legislation, expand the scope of those already included, or deliberately cloud the outcomes expected. Tactics such as these are intended to attract or retain support and to neutralize opposition. What works to gain enactment, however, may subsequently inhibit successful administration.

INEPT ADMINISTRATION

In order to attract political support for ESEA enactment, Johnson Administration officials occasionally implied that the bill was general aid—that it could be used as local school officials decided. The U.S. Office of Education initially did not audit program use of funds. By the late 1960s, poverty organizations were claiming that Title I funds were not reaching children for whom they were intended. The Lawyers Committee for Civil Rights Under Law and the NAACP Legal Defense Fund revealed research results suggesting strongly that local school districts were using federal funds as general aid.[30] In effect, Title I's effectiveness could not accurately be assessed because there had yet to be a Title I program.[31] Subsequently, in 1971, Congress enacted the so-called "comparability" requirements whereby school districts must first ensure equal distribution of local and state revenues to Title I eligible students.[32] This began to ensure that Title I would be special aid for low income students over and above local and state aid. It did not, however, clarify the purposes of the program.

INADEQUATE RESEARCH METHODS

The technical difficulties of assessing school programs are described in Chapter Ten on school efficiency. We note here that problems of research design and measurement apply to federally funded school programs as much as or more than they do to local and state funded services. However, it should be noted that

---

[30] *Title I of ESEA: Is It Helping Poor Children?* (Washington, D.C.: Washington Research Project of the Southern Center for Studies in Public Policy and the NAACP Legal Defense and Education Fund, 1967).

[31] W. W. Charters, Jr., and John E. Jones, "On the Risk of Appraising Non-events in Program Evaluation," in *Educational Researcher*, November 1973, pp. 5-7.

[32] See PLANAR Corporation report to HEW, "The Silken Purse: Legislative Recommendations for Title I of the Elementary and Secondary Education Act," Contract HEW-OS-72-224, 1973.

the federal requirements of program evaluation have greatly aided in the development of research techniques that promise greater rigor and sophistication.

Despite political, administrative, and technical problems, increasingly defensible research is taking place regarding federal program effectiveness. Initial evaluation findings, particularly for ESEA Title I, were discouraging. Report after report concluded that program results were nonexistent to negligible. By the mid 1970s, however, both program directors and evaluators were becoming more sophisticated.

UNANTICIPATED FEDERAL PROGRAM OUTCOMES

Frequently, both planned and unplanned outcomes result from public policy. Unexpected outcomes can be both positive and negative, and such appears to be the case for federal school aid programs.

POSITIVE OUTCOMES

In addition to the possibility of improving the achievement of low-income students, of retraining large numbers of teachers, and of widely distributing instructional materials associated with federal programs, teachers and administrators report other benefits. For example, many schools now have a coherent instructional program linking subjects such as reading and mathematics from one grade to the next. Title I requires that federal programs be well planned. However, a spillover is that now schools frequently plan their total program, not simply the Title I component. The happy outcome is better schooling for all students. Similarly, Title I Parent Advisory Councils have had the unexpected outcome of motivating many low-income parents to return to school and extend their own education.

POTENTIAL NEGATIVE OUTCOMES

Some school officials assert that federal funds frequently distort spending and program priorities of local school districts. Distortion of program priorities can occur overtly. Even if the federal program is unimportant or inappropriate, a district, no matter what its priorities, must spend the funds in compliance with federal regulations, or forego the money. Although the district is not forced to accept funds, to refuse them may be virtually impossible. In times of declining enrollments, increased resistance to school taxes, and shrinking revenues, school districts badly need marginal funds. They must apply for and use federal funds whether or not they desire the program involved.[33]

[33] For evidence on this point see Iris Polk Berke, "Administering Federal Education Policy in a State with Different Priorities," paper submitted to the Institute for Educational Leadership, September 1976.

It is alleged that distortion can be more subtle than that imposed by compliance with federal regulations. A few school districts report that the administration of federal programs costs more than the dollar amount of administrative overhead allotted. Consequently, the district must tap local and state general funds in order to subsidize the administration of federal programs.

Another subtle, unexpected outcome is the proliferation of educational specialists. Beginning with the National Defense Education Act and bolstered mightily by the ESEA, categories of licensed professionals such as counselors, guidance workers, and skills specialists expanded at an astonishing pace. There is little evidence that such specialists have assisted in increasing student achievement. In fact, the rise of this cadre coincides closely with the great slide in pupil performance of the 1960s and 1970s.[34] One must be cautious not to confuse correlation with causation, however. What is clear is that the increase in such staff did not stem declining achievement; in fact, it may be that the federally inspired specializations contribute to the negative system of performance incentives.

Summary

Underlying purposes of federal education policies include extension and promotion of equal educational opportunity, stimulation of greater efficiency, preservation of liberty, and tax loss compensation.

In the absence of a specific constitutional mandate, federal education policy evolved slowly. However, the activist social intervention of Franklin D. Roosevelt during the depression greatly stimulated enactment of federal school aid programs, and this momentum was sustained after World War II. By the mid-1970s, federal funds were authorized for almost every conceivable school-related function. However, proportionately federal funds account for only a small percent of U.S. school expenditures when compared with state and local contributions.

Federal programs have had consistent effects on at least two major educational dimensions, expanding equal educational opportunities for previously neglected groups such as low-income, handicapped, and non-English speaking students, and stimulating educational research and development.

This chapter has described the manner in which federal school aid policy formation originates in the federal executive branch, in Congress, or in interest groups. Federal legislation is then administered by the U.S. Office of Education.

Educational legislation is influenced by special interest groups such as the National Education Association, the AFL-CIO, and the U.S. Catholic Confer-

---

[34] See Annegret Harnischfeger and David E. Wiley, *Achievement Test Score Decline: Do We Need to Worry?* (Chicago: CEMREL, 1975).

ence. By the early 1970s education interest groups rose to a new high level of organization and influence.

The effectiveness of specific federal school aid programs is difficult to document. However, research findings increasingly uncover positive evidence in support of federally sponsored programs. On the other side of the ledger, however, school officials increasingly voice a concern that federal funds distort local and state spending priorities and usurp decision-making prerogatives of local and state officials.

Complaints regarding federal programs, the social science controversy surrounding the effectiveness of school generally, and increasing competition for funding among federal social welfare programs may provoke a new form of federal school aid in the 1980s.

8

DISTRIBUTING
STATE EDUCATION DOLLARS

Education is Primarily a State Responsibility

Among the three levels of government in the United States, prime responsibility for public schooling rests with the state. This has not always been so.
During colonial days, schooling was an individual responsibility. Formal education took place in private schools, with attendance generally limited to those
whose parents could afford the tuition. This form of private education began in
the New England colonies, where two schools had been established by 1635. In
1642 the Massachusetts "General Court," the legislative body of the time,
decreed that "ye chosen men" should have the power to punish by fines all
parents and masters who were neglectful in "training up their children." This
law proclaimed state authority over parents, but not over the operation of
schools. Five years later, the Massachusetts Law of 1647 required every town of
50 or more families to appoint a teacher. Every town of 100 or more families
was further required to appoint a schoolmaster to give instruction in Latin gram-
mar to prepare boys for college. With the passage of this act the "New England
pattern" had been established.

The New England pattern consisted of four principles: the state could require children to be educated; the state could require towns to establish

schools; the civil government could supervise and control schools by direct management in the hands of public officials; and public funds could be used in the support of public schools.[1]

In the southern colonies, administration of schools became the responsibility of parish and county officials. In the middle colonies, public authority was early used to promote education, but private control was dominant. Nonetheless, in the 1770s, when both the middle and southern colonies drafted their constitutions, the principles of public support and lay control of education were explicitly stated. Indeed, middle and southern colonies enacted strong constitutional provisions regarding education and did so earlier than the New England colonies, in spite of the leadership shown by the Puritans and their immediate heirs.[2]

As population spread westward and new states were established, each state wrote into its constitution language expressing state responsibility for education. At present, every state constitution authorizes the legislature to establish and maintain a "uniform" or "thorough and efficient" system of education. In addition to this, there are usually more specific provisions.

How is it, then, that we have in all but one state (Hawaii) a system whereby the public schools are operated by local school districts? Do not local districts operate essentially like municipalities, and cannot we then say that the primary responsibility for education is local? The answer is "no." In most states, municipalities have a constitutional position as a separate arm of government with clearly stated powers and responsibilities. School districts, on the other hand, are administrative units of the state. As such they may exercise a measure of decision-making discretion, but the decisions must be within boundaries delegated by state authorities.

Because it is usually a state responsibility to provide education on a uniform basis, numerous suits have been brought in state courts challenging the constitutionality of school finance laws. The legal logic of these cases has been explained in greater detail in Chapter Two.

Because there is no reference in the federal constitution to education, it is one of the powers "reserved to the states respectively, or to the people." The *Rodriguez* case (see Chapter Two) attempted to shift the burden of uniform provision of education to the federal government.[3] Its failure left us with the current manner of finance through a state-local partnership, an arrangement we analyze in this chapter. In Chapter Nine we will examine proposals to diminish problems arising from the state–local finance partnership.

---

[1] R. Freeman Butts and Lawrence A. Cremin, *A History of Education in American Culture* (New York: Henry Holt & Co., 1953), p. 103.

[2] Charles S. Benson, *The Economics of Public Education* (Boston: Houghton Mifflin Co., 1961), p. 314.

[3] *Rodriguez* v. *San Antonio Independent School District,* 337 F. Supp. 280 (W.D. Tex., 1971); and *San Antonio Independent School District* v. *Rodriguez,* 411 U.S. 28.

Types of State School Finance Systems

In financing public schools, states traditionally have been concerned with adequate provision of education, efficiency, and equality, in roughly that order.

ADEQUATE PROVISION

From 1940 to 1970, the major concern of state school finance officials was to provide the money necessary to meet the rapidly increasing demands on schools. Not only were enrollments burgeoning, but also the public was demanding more services. Programs such as vocational education increased average cost per student at the same time that the number of students was also increasing rapidly. The result was that state governments felt under persistent pressure for new money. While there was also concern with efficiency and equality during this time, those goals often had to be subordinated to a continuing need to finance expansion.

This period of growth was accompanied by a manpower shortage as well as a money shortage. Teachers were in short supply and the economic system responded, as is typical, by increasing the price, thus encouraging more people to enter the profession. Teacher salaries increased faster than salaries of workers in general. Some saw this increase as raising salaries from grossly inadequate to a decent living wage, while others believed the new salary levels exorbitant.

Increased labor costs were added to the other costs incurred from growing numbers of students and expanding program demands. Average cost per student increased tenfold, from $100 in 1940 to $1000 in 1970; total elementary–secondary public education costs increased 18-fold, from $2.26 billion to $40.27 billion during the same period.

Legislatures responded to increasing costs in a variety of ways, but these ways seldom promoted efficiency. Because of difficulties in defining and measuring school efficiency, the pressures for efficiency usually took the form of expenditure restrictions. During the years from 1940 to 1970, previous expenditure restrictions were relaxed or eliminated, either by legislatures or by direct vote of the people. For example, many states had tax rate limitations, but local elections to permit school districts to tax above this limit regularly passed by large margins.

Legislation increasing costs seldom increased equality either. Although most states had equalization programs—and most were spending more on education than ever before—these higher disbursements did not lessen expenditure inequities within states.

Large increments of state money were injected into education in the 1950s and 1960s, and this was generally matched or exceeded by increases in local revenues. Most of the state money and almost all of the local money was in the form of additional *general aid*, money which could be used for any district purpose (as opposed to *categorical aid,* which can only be used for specified purposes).

In addition to general aid, states provided categorical aid for a variety of special programs such as education of mentally retarded and physically handicapped children, and several states even attempted to alleviate environmental handicaps such as poorly educated parents or proverty and ghetto living conditions.

Other categorical aids were for the construction of many badly needed new schools, particularly in suburbs in the fast-growing states. These suburbs frequently were unable to raise enough money locally, and state help became crucial. Florida annually provided each district a set number of dollars per student for school construction, whether the district needed it or not. The district was expected to invest the money until construction was required. This was inequitable if it is assumed that money from the state should only cover unmet needs. It was inefficient both because money was being provided to some districts with adequate schools and because money was being taken prematurely from taxpayers, to be invested by school districts. It is a basic principle, not always observed, that government should not take money from taxpayers before it is needed merely to invest it, even though private businesses frequently raise funds in anticipation of future investment. Rather, government should allow taxpayers the use of their money as long as possible, and only collect taxes to meet current budgets.

Other states, such as California and New York, had more sophisticated systems of state aid for school construction, providing more money per student in poor districts than in rich districts, and limiting aid to necessary construction. These states made a bow in the direction of efficiency by limiting the number of square feet that could be constructed per student and by specifying maximum cost per square foot that could be state financed.

Some states also established formulas that would in effect act as incentives to district spending. For example, New York, Pennsylvania, and Rhode Island had "percentage equalizing" formulas (about which more will be said later) that rewarded high-spending districts by providing more state aid.

EFFICIENCY

Efficiency as we noted in Chapter Two, has long been a goal of those who finance education. This is expressed as a desire to obtain adequate education for as little money as possible. The goal is laudable, but difficult to attain. The problem, of course, is that there is little agreement on what education is to accomplish, how to accomplish it, and how to measure accomplished performance. Usually those concerned with school efficiency merely advocate imposing spending limits, on the theory that if restricted in the amount of money available, educators will use it more wisely. During the post-war period of rapid school expansion, the goal of efficiency was muted, but the enrollment decline in the 1970s coupled with the continued rapid rise in expenditures per student, provoked the reinstitution of limits. Often, school finance reforms to achieve greater equality have necessitated spending restrictions in some districts. The limits have generally taken one of three forms: direct revenue or expenditure limits, tax rate limits, or annual budget votes.

DIRECT REVENUE OR EXPENDITURE LIMITS

In this form of budget restriction, the state limits the amount each district can spend per student. This is the most direct form of control and, pursued to its logical extreme, it would result in uniform expenditures per student statewide. However, there are two reasons why uniformity does not occur. First, it is not politically possible to establish a standard expenditure limitation because to do so would either result in some districts being forced to reduce their expenditures drastically (if the limit were established only slightly above the median expenditure), or would be no real limitation (if established near the level of the highest spending district). As a result, when legislatures institute such limitations, they usually set each district's current rate of expenditure as its ceiling and provide for a yearly increase to allow for inflation. However, if each district were allowed to increase its annual limit by, say, 7 percent, the dollar spread between low-spending and high-spending districts would continue to increase. Thus, there is usually a provision preventing high-spending districts from inflating their expenditures as rapidly as low-spending districts. This eventually would result in equalizing expenditures statewide, but it would take a long time. In any case, it should be realized that expenditure limits are not always instituted for the purpose of equalization, but to limit the rate of increase of school expenditure. They are an "efficiency" measure, not an equality measure.

Another reason for expenditure limits not automatically effecting equalization is that usually there is an escape provision. Individual districts are allowed to hold an election to determine whether they can exceed their expenditure limit. To the extent that districts are successful in passing such elections, the ceiling concept is unsuccessful. As of the mid-1970s, the states of Arizona, California, Colorado, Iowa, Kansas, and Oregon had expenditure or revenue limits of the kind described here. In addition, Montana and Wisconsin had adopted such limits but later repealed them.

TAX RATE LIMITS

Except in the Northeast (where budget elections are the rule), most states without expenditure or revenue limits have tax rate limits. These have not proved as confining as expenditure limits because a rapid increase in assessed valuations coupled with enrollment declines has increased the dollars per student available from local taxation at the same tax rate. The tax rate limit, a rate which the local district may not ordinarily exceed, will obviously not result in equalization. A rich district can raise more at any given tax rate than can a property-poor district. Like expenditure limits, tax rate limits can usually be exceeded by a vote of the district's electorate. Where these limits have been confining, this has meant a change from control by tax rate limits to de facto control by budget election. In only a few states (New Mexico and Florida, for example) are the limitations inviolate.

ANNUAL BUDGET VOTES

In the northeastern states, annual votes on the school district budgets have long been a custom. Like the other two methods, this is not a device for equalizing expenditures, but simply for limiting them. Theoretically, this direct vote should be a useful mechanism for adjusting expenditures to voters' desires. However, sometimes it does not work: Even voters who want to inform themselves thoroughly before voting usually find it extremely difficult and thus may not vote intelligently.

Also, elections are sometimes delayed until autumn, thereby threatening voters with a delayed school opening. In New York the law provides that a district that fails to pass a budget election can go on an "austerity" budget. This budget is austere only in excluding auxiliary programs of particular interest to parents: interscholastic athletics, non-required transportation, and school lunches. On the other hand, whatever the district agrees, in collective bargaining, to pay the teachers is automatically included in the budget, and taxes are raised to pay these salaries. Thus the budget is austere for the public but not necessarily for educators.

EQUITY

The last goal of school finance has been that of equity. This is usually expressed as "equality of educational opportunity." There are many possible definitions of equality of educational opportunity, but in practice it has been limited to assuring equal dollars per student or to assuring enough money to provide comparable programs for students when their different needs and the the costs of providing them have been taken into account. To meet the second goal, three separate kinds of inequalities among school districts must be taken into account: differences in wealth, differences in educational need, and differences in educational cost. Separate remedies are appropriate for each, and the three must be combined in constructing a school finance program that is truly equitable. Each of them will be discussed at some length below.

WEALTH EQUALIZATION

The original public schools in the United States were for the children of paupers who could not afford private schools or tutors. These schools were paid for exclusively with local property tax revenues. While this was equitable among local taxpayers (ownership of property, at that time, was a good measure of ability to pay taxes), it was inequitable among communities. A property-rich community could, with lower taxes, finance a better education than could a property-poor community with higher taxes.

The flat grant program. When states began to appropriate money to local communities to assist with the cost of schooling, grants took the form of equal amounts of money to each community, regardless of the number of children or the ability to raise money locally. Subsequently, funds were distributed on the basis of equal dollars per pupil to each district. At the turn of the twentieth century, 38 states distributed so-called "flat" grants using the school census as a basis for apportionment. Other states used enrollment or average daily attendance.[4] Since the school census basis (a count of all school-age children in a district) provided districts with state money whether or not children attended school, there was no incentive for districts to retain children in school.

Ellwood P. Cubberley, in 1906, was the first to write persuasively of the problems of school finance.[5] He was concerned with the manner in which flat grant formulas favored cities and other areas, where they could afford to operate schools longer, and where larger class sizes were possible. School costs were higher in rural areas where it was frequently necessary to employ a teacher to instruct ten or fewer children. Cubberley's solution was to allocate to each district an amount for each teacher employed. This, of course, still did not equalize wealth. It can best be described as another variety of flat grant, with the teacher as the unit of measurement instead of the child. Today, no state depends only upon flat grants as a means of financing the state share of educational cost. The last state to rely upon such a method, Connecticut, adopted an equalizing plan in 1975.

Each of the methods of wealth equalization we will shortly explain contains an implicit philosophy. The flat grant approach assumes that a specific minimum of schooling should be guaranteed to every citizen. Presumably the minimum is that amount necessary for the proper functioning of a citizen in society. It is further assumed that the state in its wisdom can determine the costs of this minimum education and will allocate that dollar amount as a flat grant. Schooling in excess of this minimum is held to be of benefit only to the individual recipient or to the community in which he or she resides. It is therefore a local luxury to be indulged in as each community sees fit, but not to be subsidized by the state. Under this philosophy, the flat grant is a satisfactory wealth equalizer. It does not equalize for differences in need or cost, but that is a different matter, to be discussed later. Since the amount of the flat grant is presumed to be sufficient to cover the level of education the state

---

[4] Ellwood P. Cubberley, *School Funds and Their Apportionment* (New York: Columbia University, Teachers College Press, 1906), p. 100.
[5] *Ibid.*

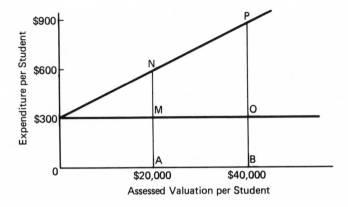

FIG. 8-1. A Flat Grant Program

believes to be minimally necessary and, furthermore, since it is provided to all students equally and is raised by taxes levied at a uniform rate on all residents of the state, there is nothing inherently unequal about it.

There are, of course, practical problems with the way flat grants are administered. The principal difficulty is that there is no way of knowing how much education is minimally necessary. Consequently, there is no way to determine how much it costs. Instead, the size of the flat grant is determined by the political process, and, because there are many other demands on the state treasury it is inevitably lower than the level at which even flat grant proponents believe a minimal education can be purchased. Another problem we have already alluded to is that the flat grant typically lacks any consideration of the special needs of atypical children. Nor does it account for the fact that it costs more to provide a minimally adequate education in some school districts than in others. However, these are relatively technical problems that can be remedied. When the remedies are invoked there is nothing basically wrong with the flat grant as a wealth equalizer if one adheres to the philosophy implied by it.

In order to facilitate our explanation of wealth equalization programs, a diagram is offered for each. Figure 8-1 illustrates the operation of a flat grant program. The vertical axis is dollars of expenditure per pupil; the horizontal axis is district wealth, expressed as assessed valuation per pupil. Districts A and B on the chart represent, respectively, a district with an assessed valuation of $20,000 per pupil and one with an assessed valuation of $40,000 per pupil. We assume, for purposes of comparison, that each district decides to levy a local property tax of 15 mills (which can also be stated as $1.50 per $100 of assessed valuation, or $15 per $1000).[6] There is a state flat grant of $300 per pupil. Line AN repre-

---

[6] A mill is an old English coin, no longer in use, the value of which is a tenth of a cent, or $0.001. A tax rate of 15 mills is a tax of 1.5 cents (15 mills) per dollar of assessed valuation.

sents the amount of money per pupil District A has at its disposal, in this case
$600 per pupil. District B, also receiving $300 per pupil from the state, would
however raise $600 per pupil in local taxes (OP), providing a total of $900 per
pupil. One could select a district with any other level of wealth and calculate
how much per pupil it would have to spend under this system. Note that the flat
grant has absolutely equalized the first $300, but not any further expenditure.
In terms of total expenditures, it has not reduced the dollar difference between
the districts from what it would have been had they levied a 15 mill tax and received no state money. However, it has decreased the percentage difference in
expenditures. District B's expenditures are now only 1.5 times those of District
A, rather than twice as much.

The foundation program. One practical problem with flat grants is that
states seldom have sufficient revenue to finance a flat grant program that provides an adequate amount per student. For example, Connecticut, in the last
year in which it used the flat grant (1975), provided $235 per student (plus
some categorical aids), while the average expenditure per student in Connecticut
at the time was $1507.[7] A solution to this problem was described in 1923 by
George D. Strayer and Robert M. Haig. In a report to the Educational Finance
Inquiry Commission, based on a study of New York State, they proposed a system that has the effect of capturing a portion of the local property tax for state
purposes, without that being openly evident.[8] Their proposal has since become
known as the "foundation program plan," or the "Strayer-Haig plan." Just as
with the flat grant, the state specifies a dollar amount per student that each
school district is to receive. Implicitly, this is the amount of money that is necessary to guarantee a minimally adequate education. The state computes each
district's contribution at a fixed tax and provides only the difference between
the amount computed and the guaranteed expenditure level. Thus, a property-
poor district will raise very little with the tax at the specified rate, and the state
will provide generously. A district richer in property will raise almost as much as
the dollar guarantee and will receive very little equalization aid from the state. A
very rich district will raise more than the guarantee and will receive nothing from
the state.

If the state requires each district to levy a property tax at a specified rate
in order to receive state money, and counts the proceeds of that local tax as part
of the guarantee, the required property tax is, in effect, a state tax. If the required local tax rate is relatively high, a substantial amount of money will be
raised. This, combined with state money, enables the legislature to establish a
guarantee level sufficient for a minimal education. Some states do not require
the district actually to levy the tax at the specified rate, calling it instead a

[7] Marshall A. Harris, *School Finance at a Glance* (Denver, Colo: Education Commission of the States, 1975), p. 1.
[8] George D. Strayer and Robert M. Haig, *Financing of Education in the State of New
York* (New York: The Macmillan Co., 1923), pp. 173-74.

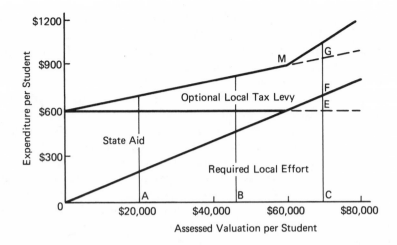

FIG. 8-2. A Foundation Program

"computational tax." It then is a device used only in determining the amount of state aid. A few property-poor districts may then levy a lower tax than this, raising less money per child than the guarantee and subverting the intent of the equalization plan.

The operation of the foundation program is illustrated in Figure 8-2. The horizontal line depicts the dollar amount of the foundation guarantee, supposedly representing the cost of a minimal program. The section labelled "Required Local Effort" is the amount raised by the local property tax at a required rate of 10 mills. The section labelled "State Aid" is contributed by the state, with a foundation level of $600. For District A, the required local effort (RLE) raises little money and the state contribution is high; for District B the district raises more of the guarantee than the state; and for District C the district raises more than the guarantee and receives nothing from the state. The solid line at the top is the dollar increment that would be raised if all districts chose to levy an optional local tax at the rate of 5 mills on top of the required tax. District B can raise more than District A, and District C can raise more than District B. The line becomes steeper at point M because the districts beyond that point already raise more than the guarantee by using only the required rate, thus making the total amount they collect that much higher.

It may be argued that it is unfair that some districts, because they happen to be rich in property, have more money to spend from levying the required tax rate than do property-poor districts. If the required tax is indeed a state tax, then the amount raised above the guarantee should be returned to the state to be used elsewhere. This concept is called "recapture," or "recycling," and the effect of it is shown by the dashed lines on Figure 8-2. District C would raise, at the required rate, the amount shown by the line CF. It would return to the state the amount EF, leaving it exactly as much as every other district. Because of this, if it levied an additional optional tax at the same rate as the other districts, it would raise the amount EG. With recapture on the 15 mills of RLE, the amount raised by any district is shown by the dashed diagonal line.

A system such as this would provide complete wealth equalization if one believed in the underlying philosophy and if the foundation guarantee were established at an amount that would pay for a minimal education. States, however, have been reluctant to employ the recapture concept. To do so is to admit publicly that the required property tax is a state tax rather than a mechanism open to local option. In addition, the amount of taxes exported from the district is highly visible. It is thus not surprising that this idea is not politically popular. Districts prefer to think of the property taxes they raise as belonging to local government and are reluctant to part with them. Recapture has only been tried in a few states (Utah, Maine, Montana, and Wisconsin). An alternative, of course, would be simply to levy a statewide property tax at this rate, and use the proceeds to finance a flat grant system. Looked at this way, it can be seen that the flat grant is simply a special case of the foundation program, in which the required local tax rate is zero. The reason states have not done this is that almost all of them have apportioned the property tax to local governments, while claiming the income tax and the sales tax mainly for themselves. These distinctions may be dissolving. States with sales taxes frequently allow local governments to levy a sales tax also. The tax is collected with the state sales tax and rebated to local governments. A few states (Maryland, for example) allow local government to "piggyback" income taxes on the state income tax. Conversely, a few states, e.g., Washington, are beginning to levy state property taxes.

As with the flat grant (and indeed with all school finance schemes) there are practical problems with the foundation plan. There is an assumption that the foundation amount is the amount necessary for a minimally adequate education, although there is no way of determining this with accuracy. Because of additional money made available through required local effort, at least this guarantee may be set higher than with the flat grant. However, there is still no substitute for setting it politically, and controversy will always occur over whether it has been set sufficiently high.

A second problem has to do with the tax rate mandated for the required local effort. If this is set low (for example, if it were specified at the rate required by the richest district to raise the foundation amount), the money required from state sources may be more than the state can afford. On the other hand, if the required rate is higher, so that less money is required from the state, there will be a substantial number of districts that will raise more than the foundation guarantee at the required rate and will not be eligible for state aid. This is unpopular; it is usually politically desirable to appear to give everyone something. As a result, states frequently give districts a minimum state amount per student regardless of how much they raise locally. This is the equivalent of a flat grant for rich districts only (or a lowered foundation, with a flat grant on top for all, which amounts to the same thing). Such a foundation program combines the worst features of both programs, but economically it is less costly than the flat grant, and politically less costly than the unaltered foundation program.

Percentage equalizing. Both the flat grant and the foundation plan have the same philosophical underpinning: The state has an interest in seeing that each student receives a minimum education, and it undertakes to guarantee this on an equal basis. Percentage equalizing has a different philosophical base. Essentially, it defines equity as access to education on the same terms, and it also holds that the amount of education to be purchased by a community should be determined by that community.

Percentage equalizing has frequently been explained in terms that make it seem more complicated than it really is. The usual explanation is that the state will share in the financing of education by providing a fixed percentage of each school district's expenditures. The district determines the size of its budget, and the state provides a share of that budget determined by the district's "aid ratio." This aid ratio is defined by means of a formula usually written in the form

$$(1 - f\frac{y_i}{\bar{y}})$$

where y_i is the assessed valuation per pupil of the district,

$\bar{y}$ is the assessed valuation per student of the state as a whole, and

f is a scaling factor that is usually set somewhere between 0 and 1.

For example, if assessed valuation per pupil of the district were \$10,000 and that of the state \$40,000, and the scaling factor were .5, the aid ratio for the district would be

$$(1 - .5 \times \frac{10,000}{40,000}) = .875$$

This means that the state would provide 87.5 percent of the budget of the district, with the district expected to raise the remaining 12.5 percent from local taxes. (Note that the "budget" being discussed here is only that portion of the budget financed from local taxes and general state aid. It does not include federal funds, categorical grants from the state, or miscellaneous revenues.) If the district had instead had an assessed valuation per pupil of \$40,000, the aid ratio remaining at .5, the state would have provided 50 percent of the budget. It is easy to see that, with this particular scaling factor, when a district's assessed valuation per pupil becomes twice that of the state, the aid ratio becomes zero. Above that point it becomes negative, the implication being that the district should instead export tax money to the state. This is recapture, the same idea as discussed in connection with foundation plans, and it has proved no more popular in percentage equalizing states than in foundation states.

Despite the somewhat confusing use of the term *aid ratio,* the fact is that percentage equalizing is the mathematical equivalent of guaranteeing each district the same assessed valuation per student. The district calculates the tax rate necessary to raise its budget, using as an assessed value for the purposes of calculation the guaranteed valuation per pupil times the number of pupils. It then levies this calculated rate against the actual assessed valuation. The state compensates for the difference between the amount actually raised and the amount that would be raised at the guaranteed valuation. In our example, the guaranteed valuation of $80,000 per pupil can be verified by the reader by calculating state aid for some hypothetical examples.[9]

[9]Let us define the following symbols:

A_i = state aid to the ith district
r_i = tax rate of the ith district, in mills
y_i = assessed valuation per pupil of the ith district
$\bar{y}$ = assessed valuation per pupil of the state as a whole
s_i = number of students in the ith district
E_i = budget of the ith district which is to be guaranteed by the state, consisting of local taxes plus state equalizing aid
f = the scaling factor of the percentage equalizing formula
V = the guaranteed assessed valuation per pupil

The percentage equalizing formula for state aid is as follows:

$$A_i = \left(1 - f\frac{y_i}{\bar{y}}\right)E_i$$

If instead we were to express state aid as a guaranteed assessed valuation per student, we would say that the state would provide to the district the difference between the district's tax rate applied against the guaranteed assessed valuation and its tax rate applied against the actual valuation. This would be written as follows:

$$A_i = \frac{Vs_i r_i}{1000} - \frac{y_i s_i r_i}{1000}$$

where Vs_i is the guaranteed assessed valuation and $y_i s_i$ is the actual assessed valuation. The divisor of 1000 is necessary because we expressed the tax rate in mills instead of dollars. We can find the conditions under which these two formulas would be equivalent by setting them equal to each other:

$$\left(1 - f\frac{y_i}{\bar{y}}\right)E_i = \frac{Vs_i r_i}{1000} - \frac{y_i s_i r_i}{1000}$$

The budget we are guaranteeing in percentage equalizing is the same budget that is to be raised through the operation of the guaranteed valuation plan, so

$$E_i = \frac{Vs_i r_i}{1000}, \text{ and}$$

$$1 - \left(f\frac{y_i}{\bar{y}}\right)\frac{Vs_i r_i}{1000} = \frac{Vs_i r_i}{1000} - \frac{y_i s_i r_i}{1000}$$

Expanding,

$$\frac{Vs_i r_i}{1000} - \frac{f y_i Vs_i r_i}{1000\,\bar{y}} = \frac{Vs_i r_i}{1000} - \frac{y_i s_i r_i}{1000}$$

Percentage equalizing, in effect, makes all districts equally able to raise tax revenues, that is, a mill on the tax rate, combined with state aid, will raise the same amount in any district.

Adoption of the percentage equalizing concept was first urged by Harlan Updegraff and Leroy A. King in 1922, about the same time that Strayer and Haig were recommending the foundation plan.[10] However, it was popularized by Charles Benson in 1961, and most of the eight states that enacted it did so shortly thereafter.[11] It is interesting that the Strayer-Haig plan became part of the school finance plan of the majority of the states, whereas the percentage equilizing plan was never widely adopted. Only Iowa, Massachusetts, Maine, New York, Pennsylvania, Rhode Island, Utah, and Wisconsin adopted a form of percentage equalizing, although it will be noted in the next section that a number of states have more recently adopted an equivalent and labelled it power equalizing.

Like other plans, percentage equalizing has suffered from practical problems. One of them is that, since its philosophical underpinning emphasizes that the local district should decide the size of its budget and the state should thereafter guarantee equal access to funds, there should be no restriction on the size of the budget. This is not a problem with the flat grant and foundation plan, which differ in philosophy, However, to guarantee that the state will share in any budget, no matter how large, is a frightening prospect for lawmakers and state officials, who fear the possibility of wholesale raids on the state treasury. Consequently, states that have adopted percentage equalizing have placed limits

---

Subtracting $\dfrac{Vs_ir_i}{1000}$ from both sides and multiplying by -1, we have

$$\frac{fy_iVs_ir_i}{1000\,\bar{y}} = \frac{y_is_ir_i}{1000}$$

Solving for V,

$$V = \frac{\bar{y}}{f}$$

In other words, if we will set a guaranteed assessed valuation per pupil equal to the ratio of the state assessed valuation per pupil divided by the scaling factor, we will achieve the same result as with the percentage equalizing formula. In the case of the example given earlier in the text, where the state-assessed valuation per pupil was $40,000 and the scaling factor was .5, the guaranteed assessed valuation per pupil that would accomplish the same thing is $80,000. This is in accord with the earlier observation that at $80,000 the state aid ratio became zero.

[10] Harlan Updegraff and Leroy A. King, *Survey of the Fiscal Policies of the State of Pennsylvania in the Field of Education* (Philadelphia: University of Pennsylvania, 1922), chap. 2.

[11] Charles Benson, *The Economics of Public Education* (New York: Houghton Mifflin Co., 1961), pp. 242–46. Prior to the publication of this book, only Wisconsin and Rhode Island had plans that were percentage equalizing in form.

on the expenditure per student that will be equalized by the state. So long as this limit is substantially above the average expenditure, there is little cause for concern. Frequently it is set much lower. In New York, in the last year before that state abandoned percentage equalizing (1973), the maximum expenditure in which the state would participate was $760 per student. At the time the state average expenditure per student was more than twice that amount. For most districts the percentage equalizing plan had become a foundation plan, with a foundation guarantee of $760 and a required local effort tax rate of $12.92 per $1000 of assessed valuation.[12]

A second problem with the percentage equalizing formula is that, like the foundation plan, it carries the possibility that some districts will get no equalization money at all (or worse, be forced to contribute to the state instead). This has been politically unpalatable, and the remedy has been to see to it that all districts receive some state aid, either by setting a minimum amount per pupil to which each district will be entitled, or by specifying a minimum aid ratio. In New York in 1973, the minimum aid ratio was .36. Since almost all districts, particularly wealthy ones, were spending more than $760, this amounted to the equivalent of a flat grant of .36 × $760 = $273.60 per pupil to each district as a minimum.

A third problem is the political risk that a district with a very high aid ratio will spend a large amount of money simply because it knows that an additional dollar of local taxes will bring in an additional $10 or $20 of state money. This was diluted in New York by specifying the maximum state aid ratio at .90. This is a greatly exaggerated fear. A poor district desiring to spend a large amount would have to tax itself at the same rate as a rich district that wished to spend that amount. Establishing a maximum limit to the state's participation is a restriction therefore that has a certain political attractiveness, but that saves little money and harms a few very poor districts substantially.

Just as it was noted that the flat grant is a special case of the foundation plan, it should be noted that the foundation plan is simply a special case of the percentage equalizing plan in which the budget to be participated in by the state is set at a particular figure instead of being allowed to fluctuate.

The percentage equalizing plan is illustrated in Figure 8-3. Shown are the results of two different tax rates (one with solid, the other with dashed lines). The actual tax rate of a particular district, of course, could be anywhere, but the principle is the same. Note that in each of the two instances, the lines represent-

---

[12]This tax rate is obtained by calculating the guaranteed valuation given the formula $V = \frac{\bar{y}}{f}$, where $\bar{y}$ in 1973 was about $30,000 and f was .51. Then the guaranteed assessed valuation was $58,824, and the tax rate necessary to raise $760 from this assessed valuation was $12.92 per $1000. (See footnote 9 for development of the formula.)

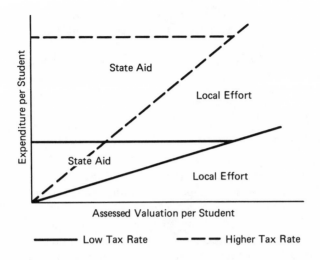

FIG. 8-3. Percentage Equalizing

ing state aid and local effort are graphically the same as those in Figure 8-2 for the foundation plan.

Power equalizing. Power equalizing is a wealth equalization concept described by John E. Coons, William H. Clune, and Stephen D. Sugarman in their book entitled *Private Wealth and Public Education.*[13] They do not concern themselves with equalizing expenditures per pupil, but with equalizing the ability of local districts to support schools. They argue strongly for the virtues of "subsidiarity," by which they mean the making of decisions at the lowest level of government feasible. This implies that decisions on school expenditures should be made by the local district. (Indeed, they argue that these decisions should even be made by the individual family, leading to a concept called "family power equalizing." This will be discussed in Chapter Nine.) Coons, Clune, and Sugarman put forth their "Proposition 1," which states that public education expenditures should not be a function of wealth, except the wealth of the state as a whole. This formed a substantial part of the legal reasoning exhibited in *Serrano* and other school finance "equal protection" cases.[14]

The philosophy behind power equalizing is the same as that behind percentage equalizing: the ability to raise money should be equalized, but the decision as to how much money to raise should be left to the local district. Under power

[13] John E. Coons, William H. Clune III, and Stephen D. Sugarman, *Private Wealth and Public Education* (Cambridge: Harvard University Press, The Belknap Press, 1970).

[14] *Serrano* v. *Priest* and similar school finance cases are discussed in Chapter Two.

equalizing, the state establishes a schedule of tax rates, with an amount per pupil guaranteed to a district for each level of tax. Such a schedule might look like this:

Tax Rate (Mills)	Guaranteed Revenue per pupil
5	$ 400
10	$ 800
15	$1200
20	$1600

(The guarantee at other tax rates is obtained by interpolation.) The schedule illustrated above is the simplest power equalizing schedule, and amounts to a guarantee of a certain number of dollars per pupil per mill levied. It is interesting that this form of power equalizing is identical with percentage equalizing, and percentage equalizing thus becomes a special case of power equalizing.[15] Thus we find that each of our types of wealth equalization is simply a special case of the one that follows it.

---

[15] It has already been shown (footnote 9) that percentage equalizing can alternatively be expressed as a guaranteed assessed valuation. A linear power equalizing schedule that begins at zero can also be expressed as a guaranteed assessed valuation. We use the same definitions as before, with the addition that

J = power equalizing guarantee per mill of tax rate per student. Then the power equalizing formula declares that the state aid will be the amount guaranteed per student per mill times the number of students times the millage, less the amount raised by the local tax at that tax rate:

$$A_i = Jr_i s_i - \frac{r_i}{1000} y_i s_i$$

The formula for state aid under a guaranteed assessed valuation system is

$$A_i = \frac{Vs_i r_i}{1000} - \frac{y_i s_i r_i}{1000} \text{ (see footnote 9)}$$

If these are equivalent, we can set them equal to each other:

$$Jr_i s_i - \frac{r_i}{1000} y_i s_i = \frac{Vs_i r_i}{1000} - \frac{y_i s_i r_i}{1000}$$

Reducing

$$J = \frac{V}{1000}$$

From footnote 9, $V = \dfrac{\bar{y}}{f}$ and thus

$$J = \frac{\bar{y}}{1000f}$$

However, power equalizing is more general than percentage equalizing because it is not necessary to have the linear schedule that is implied by the guarantee of an amount per mill per student. Several additional possibilities are discussed in Chapter Nine.

A diagram for power equalizing is not shown here because it would duplicate the diagram for percentage equalizing.

Coons, Clune, and Sugarman were influential. A 1975 count revealed that twenty-two states had adopted some form of power equalizing, whereas years earlier no state had.[16]

Full state funding. A third philosophical position regarding equalization was first espoused by Henry C. Morrison in 1930.[17] This position contends that education is a state responsibility and it must be made available to all the state's children on an equal basis. The flat grant and foundation plan allow variations in local expenditure per child, although these are unassisted by the state. They are thought of as luxuries that are not the business of the state. Percentage equalizing and power equalizing not only allow differences in expenditure, but actually encourage them. Full state funding, on the other hand, permits no geographical

---

We have shown that the power equalizing guarantee can be expressed in terms of two numbers which are constants in the percentage equalizing formula, neither of them having anything to do with an individual district.

Let us take a specific example. We will take two districts, each with 500 students, each wishing to spend $1800 per student. District A has an assessed valuation of $20,000 per student, District B. $60,000. The average assessed valuation of the state is $40,000, and the scaling factor used in the percentage equalizing formula is 0.5. Then the budget of each district is $1800 x 500 = $900,000. Setting up the following chart:

	District A	District B
Budget to be guaranteed	$900,000	$900,000
State aid, based on percentage equalizing formula	675,000	225,000
To be raised locally through taxes	225,000	675,000
Tax rate necessary, in mills	22.50	22.50

Now our proof states that if the state adopts a power equalizing program that guarantees an amount per mill per student equal to $\frac{\bar{y}}{1000f}$, each district will receive the same state aid as under percentage equalizing.

$$\frac{\bar{y}}{1000f} = \frac{40,000}{1000 \times .5} = \$80$$

Since each district is levying 22.5 mills, it is guaranteed 22.50 x 80 = $1800 per student, or a total budget of $900,000. District A raises $225,000 at this tax rate and receives $675,000 from the state, and District B raises $675,000 and receives $225,000 from the state. This is the identical result obtained under percentage equalizing.

[16] Marshall A. Harris, *School Finance at a Glance*, pp. 1–2.

[17] Henry C. Morrison, *School Revenue* (Chicago: University of Chicago Press, 1930). For an explanation of the legal principles that can be used to support full state funding, see Arthur C. Wise, *Rich Schools, Poor Schools* (Chicago: University of Chicago Press, 1967).

variation in school expenditure. It does not, however, preclude adjustments for differing educational needs or differences in the cost of producing education of equivalent quality. It does mean that, *other things being equal,* students will be recipients of equal monetary provision. The only means by which this can be accomplished operationally is for the state to mandate the expenditure level, and equity demands that the expenditures be supported by statewide taxation. (The state could mandate an expenditure level but require it to be supported solely by local taxation. The resulting large differences in tax rates would be manifestly unfair, and would not constitute wealth equalization.) Therefore, this method of financing the schools has become known as full state funding, or full state assumption.

The philosophical basis of full state funding is much closer to that of the flat grant and foundation plans than it is to the percentage and power equalizing plans. For this reason, it is possible to have full state funding as a limiting position for a flat grant or a foundation plan. One merely specifies that no local taxation is allowed (in the case of the flat grant program), or that the district may only tax at the required rate (for the foundation program).

Full state funding does not necessarily imply state operation of the schools, but merely state guarantee of equal amounts of money per pupil to each district.[18] As of 1976, only four states approach full state funding. Since Hawaii has only one school district, all schools are operated by the state. New Mexico has a foundation-type plan with a required local effort of 8.925 mills and a prohibition from levying more than this amount. The required millage becomes, then, a statewide property tax, and New Mexico would have the equivalent of a full state funding plan—with equal tax rates and equal expenditures—except that there is a range of approximately 60 to 1 in assessed valuation per pupil among New Mexico districts. This makes it possible for one rich district to stay out of the foundation program and raise much more than the amount guaranteed by the state at less than the required millage. By staying out of the program, this district forfeits only the state aid it would not have received anyway. Except for this one district, New Mexico's system can be characterized as full state funding.

Florida is the third state in which the finance system approaches de facto full state funding. Florida has a foundation plan with a required local effort tax rate of 6.3 mills and a ceiling of 8 mills. Almost all districts are at 8 mills. A provision was added in 1976 permitting districts to override the 8 mill limit, but none has done so. Florida has only 67 districts, each of them a full county, which results in a relatively small difference in taxable wealth. The foundation is thus established at an amount greater than even the richest district raises with its required effort.

---

[18] It should be noted, however, that full state funding will probably lead to statewide collective bargaining, with a further dilution of the options for decision-making by local districts.

Minnesota is the fourth state that approaches de facto full state funding. In 1976 it had a foundation of $910, with a required effort tax rate of 29 mills. Districts were not allowed to exceed the required rate without a vote, and few districts did so. However, the existence of wealth discrepancies similar to those in New Mexico prevented complete equalization.

Full state assumption would appear to solve most of the problems previously discussed in connection with the other formulas. The marks of a true full state funding plan are that all educational funds will be raised by statewide taxes (which could include property taxes) and that the money will be spent equally on similarly situated students. Disallowing any local supplementary aid eliminates the problems of tax and expenditure discrepancies that haunt the practical application of the other plans. Such a high degree of equity has a price. The legislature providing all of the revenue for education from state sources will want to see to it that money is spent judiciously. It is almost inevitable that full state assumption will bring increased state control over education. In Florida, for example, where de facto full state assumption was enacted in 1973, the state at the same time enacted a requirement that the funds generated by the presence of students in a school must be spent on those students in that school. Since students in different programs (mentally retarded, physically handicapped, career education, etc.) generated different amounts of state money, this requirement mandated a school-by-school, program-by-program accounting system, with auditing by state officials. The result is to take some of the initiative away from local school officials.

NEED EQUALIZING

During the foregoing discussion of wealth equalization, we have made the "other things being equal" assumption, i.e., that all students are alike in their needs for education. This is manifestly untrue. Many students have unusual learning problems that require costly special teaching methods. The mentally retarded, emotionally disturbed, blind, deaf, and crippled are only a few of the categories. In addition, there are many normal children who can benefit from a program that is more expensive. This is particularly true in the area of career or vocational education. Fortunately, these differences in needs can be incorporated into a wealth equalizing scheme as part of a comprehensive state aid plan. There are four ways in which this is done.

Weighting systems. Imagine a foundation plan that guarantees a given number of dollars per student. Implicit in such a plan is that all students should have the same basic amount spent on them. If we wish to spend different amounts on students with special needs, we can do so by counting each of them as more than one student. For example, educable mentally retarded students might be weighted 1.5 as compared with the 1.0 weighting of so-called normal students. The weighting presumably represents the ratio of the cost of providing a basic special program to that of providing a basic normal program. A weight can be attached to each category of special student: handicapped, vocational, high school, or kindergarten students. Usually the normal student in the elementary grades is weighted 1.0 and all other weights are related to this standard. The sum of all weighted students is obtained, and this weighted student count is used as the basis for calculating state aid. Simply by substituting weighted students for actual students, this method can be used with any of the wealth equalizing plans that have been discussed. This means that practically, as well as conceptually, it is possible to separate need equalization from wealth equalization.

As is the case with wealth equalization methods, there is a philosophic assumption embedded in each of the need equalization methods. The philosophy of the weighting schemes is that the cost of special programs bears a fixed cost relationship to the cost of normal programs. This is held to be true both within districts and among districts. It is further assumed that the state should compensate districts on this basis, but without otherwise dictating the content of programs.

If a weighting plan for need equalization is to be equitable, it is necessary to have an accurate determination of the program cost for special categories of students relative to the program costs for normal elementary students. This constitutes a major difficulty in the use of weighting plans. Because we do not yet have an agreed-upon technology for educating each student category, it is impossible to agree on the extra cost involved. In the late 1960s and early 1970s, the National Educational Finance Project made a large-scale attempt to establish appropriate weights.[19] They defined special areas, ranging from kindergarten to emotionally disturbed to vocational education. They identified "exemplary" programs in each of the special student areas. In each area they determined the program costs, and compared them with the cost of a program for normal elementary students in the same district. The ratio of the costs was determined, and the average of these ratios was reported as a weight that could be used with such a program. Unfortunately, there are several flaws in this procedure. First, as explained earlier, there is no agreed-upon educational technology. Consequently, the sample programs were selected simply on a reputational basis by asking state directors of special education to identify exemplary programs. Second, even if a program is especially good in one district, there is no assurance that an identical program would be effective in another. Third, there is no reason to believe that a comparable program could not be operated at a reduced cost. These problems all arise from the fact that there is no agreed-upon instructional technology.

Fourth, assuming appropriate programs have been selected, obtaining reliable cost data is extremely difficult. Local district cost-accounting methods are undeveloped. Although business has utilized sophisticated cost-accounting procedures for many years, school districts have not adopted the techniques, possibly because of a lack of pressure to demonstrate a profit. In general, investigators

---

[19] See Roe L. Johns and Kern Alexander, *Alternative Programs for Financing Education* (Gainesville, Fla.: National Educational Finance Project, 1971), Chap. 6.

may find that, given available data, it is impossible to separate program costs adequately. This troublesome condition forced the NEFP to state that their published weights were only "examples," and that any state wanting to use such a system should establish its own weights on the basis of adequate cost studies. In spite of this caveat, the NEFP weights have been adopted unchanged by some states.

Another difficulty with pupil or program weights is that they need frequent revision in order to remain consistent with actual cost differences. But this is where circular reasoning enters the arguments, for this year's weights will depend on the amount spent last year. However, the amount spent this year will depend on the money available, and therefore on the weights used.

In addition to such technical problems, there are practical difficulties with weighting. A major one is that of misclassification. A weighting system places state money into a district's general fund in an undifferentiated manner, unwittingly encouraging misclassification. If, for example, districts can operate handicapped or vocational programs more cheaply than the state allowance, this may encourage placement of students into these programs whether or not they are eligible. Money saved can then be diverted to other programs, including the education of normal students. During examination of Florida's comprehensive weighting system, it was revealed that some small rural districts have placed a majority of their students into either mentally retarded or vocational programs. The remedy for such abuses is either state quotas, directing what proportion of the students of the district may be classified into any program, or a state audit of the classification decisions. Either implies an element of state control that is foreign to the philosophical basis of weighting.

Actually, this problem occurs mainly where the state subsidy is equal to or greater than the special program costs. In states with flat grant and foundation programs, of course, this is not apt to be the case because districts must finance at least a portion of the extra cost of the special programs.

A similar misclassification problem occurs when the special program weight is based on the cost of operating *separate* programs, but districts are allowed to "mainstream" students. That is, they place students in regular classes most or all of the day, but provide them with special help. Weighting systems encourage mainstreaming because of the lower costs. Mainstreaming is generally thought to be educationally desirable, but it is doubtful that this kind of financial incentive should be involved.

Approximately 26 states use weighting schemes in their state aid program. Perhaps the best example of extensive use of weightings is Florida, where there are 26 separate programs. Table 8-1 lists these programs and gives the applicable weights for the 1975-76 school year. Other states use many fewer weights; the majority weight only kindergarten and normal high school students. They prefer to fund special programs in one or more of the ways we will now discuss.

Excess cost reimbursement. An alternative to weighting is to provide districts grants to cover the excess cost of educating special students. Districts

TABLE 8-1

Weights for Various Educational Programs in Florida, 1975–76

Basic Programs

Kindergarten and Grades 1, 2, and 3	1.234
Grades 4 through 9	1.00
Grades 10, 11, and 12	1.10

Special Programs for Exceptional Students

Educable mentally retarded	2.30
Trainable mentally retarded	3.00
Physically handicapped	3.50
Physical and occupational therapy, part-time	6.00
Speech and hearing therapy, part-time	10.00
Deaf	4.00
Visually handicapped, part-time	10.00
Visually handicapped	3.50
Emotionally disturbed, part-time	7.50
Emotionally disturbed	3.70
Socially maladjusted	2.30
Specific learning disability, part-time	7.50
Specific learning disability	2.30
Gifted, part-time	3.00
Hospital and homebound, part-time	15.00

Vocational-Technical Programs*

Vocational Education I	4.26
Vocational Education II	2.64
Vocational Education III	2.18
Vocational Education IV	1.69
Vocational Education V	1.40
Vocational Education VI	1.17

Adult Education Programs

Adult basic education and adult high school	1.28
Community service	0.675

*Vocational-technical programs are put into one of six categories depending upon the relative cost of providing the program. Most expensive are certain shop courses using a great deal of expensive equipment; least expensive are secretarial courses.

Source: Jack Leppert, Larry Huxel, Walter Garms, and Heber Fuller, "Pupil Weighting Programs in School Finance Reform," in *School Finance Reform: A Legislators'Handbook,* eds. John J. Callahan and William H. Wilken (Washington, D.C.: National Conference of State Legislatures, 1976).

account for special program expenditures, deduct state-defined costs of educating normal students, and receive state reimbursement for all or a portion of extra costs.

Excess cost programs are based on the philosophy that the state should reimburse districts for the extra costs of operating special programs. However, these expenditures should be made only for specified purposes, and districts should be held accountable for such expenditures.

A major advantage of this approach is that districts are reimbursed only for the actual extra cost of the programs, and this eliminates the misclassification incentive. Another advantage, particularly from the legislature's and the state education department's view, is that money is restricted to categories for which the grants are given. This necessitates state definition of types of reimbursable expenditures, a cost accounting system, and a reliable state audit, all of which are restrictions on the district's freedom to spend as it sees fit.

Another advantage of the excess system is that the amount granted is tailored to a district's expenditure pattern. This is better than the assumption, as in a weighting system, that costs in all districts are the same proportion of normal costs. There is, however, a disadvantage connected with the categorical method. The state grant does not arrive until the close of the year, after expenditures have been incurred. This often leaves poor districts in a bind, for they must hire teachers and pay them from the beginning of the year, resulting in a cash flow squeeze. Periodic state apportionments throughout the year, based on estimates of attendance and cost, can alleviate this problem.

Approximately 24 states have excess cost aids at least for instructional programs. Many of these states also use weights for some programs, particularly for high school and kindergarten.

Flat grants for special programs. About seven states fund one or more special programs through a flat grant of a specified number of dollars per pupil in the program. This is the equivalent of a weighting applied against a flat grant or foundation guarantee, but the grant is usually restricted to use in the special program, and this is not necessarily true for weighting.

Intermediate districts. A fourth manner of providing services for special students is by assigning special program responsibility to an intermediate education district. The main advantage of the larger district is organizational. Because of economies of scale, intermediate districts can afford to provide programs for students with special handicaps that individual districts might find too costly. Experts in special fields can be hired. A disadvantage is that it is not practical to use this approach for all special programs. Students must be taken away from their usual schools, and this inhibits mainstreaming. Also, additional transportation costs may outweigh economies of scale gained by concentrating handicapped children in intermediate district programs. Finally, local district authorities may fear loss of control over an important part of the education of their children.

COST EQUALIZATION

Equalization may be needed to balance differences among districts in the cost of providing educational services of similar quality. There are several reasons for cost differences. They divide rather well into two categories: (1) differences in the amount and cost per unit of supplies and services that must be purchased by the school district, and (2) differences in the amount the district must pay to attract and retain employees of comparable quality.

Supplies and services may differ in cost for various reasons. The school district in mountain areas may have to pay a large annual bill for snow clearance. The mountain district may also use more fuel for heating and find that its unit cost for fuel is higher. A sparsely settled rural area may be unable to avoid small classes and the resulting inflated costs per pupil. A ghetto school may have high vandalism costs. Schools in sparsely populated areas have high busing costs, as may urban districts that bus for racial balance. Land cost for school sites is much higher in cities. Thus there are many ways in which costs of supplies and services may differ from district to district. In general, extra costs tend to be higher in rural and highly urbanized districts, and lower in suburban areas.

Salaries constitute 70 to 80 percent of the average school district's budget. Thus, differences in the cost of hiring and retaining employees of equivalent quality is even more important than differences in the cost of supplies. There may be differences in the cost of living in districts, resulting from variation in rents or housing prices, food costs, and so on. More important, however, are differences in the attractiveness of a school as a place to teach and a community as a place to live. It is possible that one must pay more to get a teacher of comparable quality for a ghetto school than in a part of town with expensive homes. The same thing is probably true to an even greater extent among districts. In an upper-middle-class suburban district there is no danger of being moved to a ghetto school. Not only are ghetto schools frequently perceived as undesirable places in which to teach, but also many ghetto neighborhoods and their surrounding areas are undesirable places to live. The teacher in an urban area may have a large choice of residences (although with extra commuting costs to some of them). However, a teacher in a rural area or factory town may be unable to find a place where there are people with similar interests or a suitable house. These conditions give rise to the concept of "combat pay" for ghetto teachers and "isolation pay" for rural teachers.

It is easier to recognize the existence of cost differences than it is to measure and subsequently compensate districts for them. The most important attempts have been in the areas of pupil transportation and necessary small schools. All states compenstate districts for the costs of bus transportation. This is because such costs vary widely, and because they weigh heaviest on rural school districts (which prior to reapportionment in the 1960s had disproportionately strong representation in legislatures). The usual means of compensation is on a cost reimbursement basis. A district records transportation cost of eligible students. This typically excludes students who live less than a mile from school and optional transportation such as field trips. Record keeping for such purposes is usually complicated; in fact, accounting for the transportation reimbursement, a small part of total state payments, is frequently more complicated than all the rest of the district's cost accounting combined. The state then reimburses the district for a portion of these transportation costs.

In New York, state reimbursement is 90 percent of the costs; in Oregon it is 50 percent, and in California the state reimburses the difference between actual costs and revenue that could be raised by a specified computational tax levied on the assessed valuation of district property. An alternative is used in Florida. Each district's transportation costs are estimated by means of a regression equation and the district is paid the estimated cost.[20] If the district manages to transport students for less than estimated, it may use the extra funds for other purposes; if it spends more than estimated, it must pay the difference from its own sources. The method is only as good as the equation used in the estimation. The Florida approach encourages transportation efficiency, whereas New York's 90 percent reimbursement has exactly the opposite effect.

States also subsidize cost differences for necessary small schools, schools that must exist because transportation distances to larger schools would be too great. Students may be weighted, with those in the smallest schools (or classes) given the highest weightings. These students are counted like those weighted for need differences. Alternatively, "small school" students may be treated separately, with a special formula specifically for them.

Although these are two areas of cost variation, the major difference is in salaries necessary to attract teachers and other employees of equivalent quality. It might appear that a number of states have attempted to deal with this problem through adjusting the amount of state aid a district receives by means of a state salary schedule on which the district's teachers are placed. Actually, this may be an anti-equalizing measure, as is discussed in Chapter Nine. The only state (as of 1976) that has made an attempt at a solution is Florida. Each district is assigned a cost-of-living index, and its foundation aid level is adjusted by this index. Districts with lower costs of living have lower foundation levels. A cost-of-living index is a poor indicator of the actual cost differences in hiring employees of comparable quality. In addition, it is expensive, and probably quite inaccurate, to try to conduct cost-of-living analyses for each district. In Florida, where there are only 67 districts, cost-of-living studies are actually conducted for only a few districts in the state, and from this the index position for other districts is inferred.

---

[20] See pp. 230–31 for a discussion of regression equations.

The Present State of School Finance

In almost all states school finance is badly in need of reform. The inequities of our finance systems are denying some students an adequate education while providing handsomely for others. They force some taxpayers to pay more than others while receiving less education for their money. School finance systems are so complicated that few completely understand them. The provisions of these systems frequently work against one another. Major problems of state school finance systems in the 1970s are outlined in this, our concluding section of Chapter Eight.

INADEQUATE WEALTH EQUALIZATION

The conceptual basis for wealth equalization has been well formulated. Once a philosophical position has been decided upon, there are appropriate wealth equalization plans for implementing it. But these plans are never implemented in their ideal form, and the aberrations result in substantial departures from complete equalization.

First, only a few states have instituted the concept of recapture, or recycling. In most states, wealth differences among districts are so great that the only way to achieve complete equalization is by capturing for the state, money raised by districts above the state guarantee. Until states find a politically acceptable way of accomplishing recapture, property-rich districts will continue to fare better than property-poor districts.

Second, most states, far from taking money away from rich districts, have guaranteed them a minimum amount of state money per student regardless of their wealth. These provisions appeal more to political exigency than to equity.

Third, the philosophy of flat grant and foundation programs, that the state should guarantee only a minimum education to all children on an equal basis, has been successfully attacked in the courts of a number of states. This means that ultimately another philosophical position must be chosen—either equal provision of education, or equal access to wealth.

INAPPROPRIATE
AND INSUFFICIENT NEEDS EQUALIZATION

The means of compensating for varying educational needs in a school finance plan are not as well developed as those for wealth equalization. Weighting plans suffer from an inability to define appropriate programs or to measure their costs accurately. Circular reasoning is involved in the establishment of weightings, for these are usually based on the cost of programs that are themselves influenced by the weightings provided. Misallocation of students to programs is encouraged. Excess cost plans frequently define reimbursable costs in such a way that only traditional programs are encouraged, and experimentation is discouraged. Small bureaucratic empires flourish around each special program in state departments of education. The uncompensated differences in educational need have not yet been successfully challenged in court, but attempts are being made. If a legal principle is found for need differences that is equivalent to the successful principle in the Serrano wealth equalization suit, there will probably be a rash of lawsuits to force better need equalization in a number of states.

COST EQUALIZATION IS ALMOST NONEXISTENT

Aside from minor programs of aid to necessary small schools, and major but peripheral aids for transportation cost, little has been done about differences among districts in cost of delivering equivalent educational services. The major cost differences are those connected with salary level differences necessary to attract teachers of equivalent quality. However, not all salary schedule differences result from actual cost differences. Some districts simply wish to attract higher quality teachers and are willing to pay more for them. These are usually property-rich districts, and it is a dubious kind of equalization that would reward such districts with more money because they are able to pay higher salaries. Thus, if there is to be appropriate equalization for cost differences, a method must be developed for differentiating actual differences in cost from differences that result from demand for higher quality. This is high on the list of priorities in school finance reform, for a substantial part of the crisis of the city school districts can probably be traced to lack of equalization for cost differences.

URBAN SCHOOL FINANCE PROBLEMS

Urban school districts once could afford the best in education, but today most have very serious problems. Not only are the higher costs in cities largely unrecognized in school finance formulas, but also there is frequently inadequate compensation for the extra costs associated with educating children of poor and minority parents. In terms of wealth, cities appear well off, for they usually have a higher assessed valuation per student. However, this measure may well be specious, since the already high tax rate levied for municipal purposes—municipal overburden—effectively reduces access of cities to the property tax. Thus, cities are frequently suffering from improper equalization of wealth, needs, and cost simultaneously.

SPECIAL INTEREST LEGISLATION

Regardless of the simplicity and equity of school finance legislation when it is first passed, it soon is amended by provisions designed to foster the interests of particular groups. These special provisions are frequently disequalizing, and at the least complicate the finance system so much that scarcely anyone (including state officials who administer it) completely understands it. As an example, various "save-harmless" provisions were added to the New York law over time. These were intended to keep districts from receiving less money under a new law than under a previous law. The result was that there were 36 different ways to calculate a district's state aid, and each district was entitled to use whichever calculation brought the most money.

DECLINING ENROLLMENTS

The period of declining enrollments that began in the mid-1970s brought new complications to educational finance, for such a decline had not occurred before. Although this reduction in numerical pressure was welcomed by some, there was not a concomitant cost reduction. Cost per student went up, at least partly because declining enrollments left districts with teachers under contract who had fewer students to teach. Equitably providing for extra costs associated with declining enrollments is a priority item in many states.

INADEQUATE PROVISION
FOR KEEPING FORMULAS CURRENT

In a period of inflation, flat grants or foundation amounts pegged to a specific dollar amount rapidly became inadequate. The same is true of dollar guarantees per mill of tax rate under power equalizing formulas. Yearly legislative battles to raise the guarantees seem a poor way of handling needed adjustments.

There has also been a rapid increase in assessed valuations in most states. Combined with the declining enrollments, this has resulted in a rapid increase of district property wealth per student. Since under most wealth equalization plans, increasing assessments reduce state contributions, this trend ultimately increases disequalization.

Few states have adequate provisions for keeping school finance formulas current. One of the challenges of school finance reform is to find ways to accomplish this.

POOR ADMINISTRATION OF THE PROPERTY TAX

Administration of the property tax in most states ranges from inadequate to atrocious. Assessments on which taxes are based are improperly set, out of date, and inconsistent among districts and among classes of property. Assessors are poorly trained, have inadequate tools at their disposal, and sometimes find it impossible to resist illegal special pleading. The property tax is widely believed to be a regressive tax, and some poor people certainly find the burden of the property tax beyond their ability to pay.

The indictments above clearly indicate a need for reform of most state school finance systems. A few states have made progress; much remains to be done. Chapter Nine will discuss some ways in which our school finance systems might be improved, although we must keep in mind the property tax problems that have already been presented in Chapter Six.

Summary

This chapter discusses the development and present status of the school finance systems of the states. The early concern of the states for adequate provision of education has been diminished by near-universal schooling. The concern with efficiency or ensuring that the educational dollar is well-spent has usually taken the form of restrictions on the ability of school districts to raise money, through direct revenue or expenditure limits, tax rate limits, or annual budget votes.

The concern to which the greatest attention is currently being paid is that of equity, ensuring that equally situated children of the state are treated equally, and that those with special needs receive the increased expenditure that those needs require. There are three reasons for a lack of equity in the present school finance systems: differences in the ability of school districts to raise money, the existence of pupils with special needs, and differences among districts in the cost of providing equivalent services. Ways in which each of these is dealt with are explained.

Wealth equalization schemes can be grouped into three categories. Full state assumption includes schemes that ensure the same expenditure on all pupils of the state (or at least on all normal pupils). Percentage or power equalizing plans include schemes that equalize the ability of districts to raise money while leaving it to each district to decide how much to raise. Flat grants or foundation plans are those that guarantee an equal number of dollars per student for all students, but allow districts to raise additional money through unequalized local taxation.

Need equalization, to take care of differences in educational needs of pupils, is accomplished by weighting the count of such pupils for state aid purposes, by state reimbursement of the excess costs of providing programs for these pupils, by flat grants per pupil for the programs, or by providing the programs through intermediate districts.

Cost equalization, to take care of differences in the cost of education, is in a rudimentary state. The only cost differences that are equalized by more than one state are those connected with transportation and with the high cost of providing small schools in isolated areas.

The chapter has discussed in detail the methods and problems of each of the three methods of equalizing.

III

Reforming
Public School Finance
in the United States

9

SCHOOL FINANCE REFORM
AT THE
STATE AND LOCAL LEVELS

Chapter Eight noted that states have traditionally been concerned with adequate provision of education, efficiency, and equality, in roughly that order. In recent years priorities have changed. Pressure for adequate educational provision during the 1950s and 1960s resulted from the post-World War II baby boom. This demographic problem has now abated, with falling birth rates in the late 1960s and lowered public school enrollment in most states in the 70s.

The need for increasing quantities of education has thus effectively come to a halt, and states have been able to turn to other concerns. This is fortunate because other needs have come to the fore. The 1954 Supreme Court decision in *Brown* v. *Board of Education* was the first of a series of decisions in state and federal courts guaranteeing the rights of racial, ethnic, and economic minorities. As we discussed in Chapter Two, since 1968 a series of court cases has challenged the extent to which states were providing equal educational opportunity in school districts differing greatly in property wealth. The most famous of these was the California case, *Serrano* v. *Priest,* which established the legal precedents for subsequent cases. *Rodriguez* v. *San Antonio,* a Texas suit, was appealed to the Supreme Court, which ruled that the equalization demanded was not a federal problem. This shifted attention to the state courts, where a series of cases is still pending. Other court cases, based on different premises, also challenged the traditional ways in which the schools were financed and operated\ *Hobson* v. *Hansen,* in Washington, D.C. attacked intradistrict disparities in educational provision. *Lau* v. *Nichols,* in San Francisco, declared that Chinese children who did not speak English were being effectively excluded from education when it was conducted solely in English. The result was the institution of bilingual education in many, if not most, school districts of the United States.

The courts were not the only arena for action. The Johnson Administration's War on Poverty produced many federal pressures for reform of the schools. It also produced the massive Elementary and Secondary Education Act of 1965 (ESEA). Title I of that act provides over $2 billion yearly for the education of the disadvantaged. The money is distributed to school districts based on the number of pupils from low-income households and is thus an important equalizing force. The civil rights movement produced advocates who fought for equal rights not only in the courts but also in the legislatures and in the bureaucracies of executive departments. Teacher unions became an important force. Simultaneously, the old PTA-NEA coalition disintegrated and was no longer able to be an important influence on legislation. The result of all this was a massive attack on the status quo, affecting the way schools are financed, staffed, and operated.

At the same time, signs appeared of what was widely interpreted as a taxpayer revolt. In 1962, 72.2 percent of school district bond elections resulted in voter approval of the bonds. In 1972, only 47 percent of these elections were successful.[1] Similarly, in those states where the school budget must be voted on every year, increasingly large numbers of districts saw the first proposed budget voted down, and had to return (often several times) for voter consideration. There was much talk about "accountability" and similar ideas that reflected a general dissatisfaction with the amount of money the public was spending for schools.

These conflicting pressures produced important changes in school financing in about half of the states in the first half of the 1970s. In some cases, the action was in response to court cases; California, Minnesota, and Michigan are examples. In some states other pressures were sufficient to bring about change even in the absence of a court case. Florida, Maine, and New Mexico, for instance, accomplished meaningful reform without significant pressure from the courts. In a few states (e.g., Oregon and Washington), adverse decisions in court helped to forestall reform. As discussed in Chapter Two, in at least one state, New Jersey, a court case (*Robinson* v. *Cahill*) led to a constitutional confrontation between the courts and the legislature.

Satisfactory *Serrano* Alternatives

{ The primary objective of school finance reform has been to equalize differences in educational expenditure that result from differences in taxable

---

[1]Phillip K. Piele and John Stuart Hall, *Budgets, Bonds, and Ballots* (Lexington, Mass.: D. C. Heath and Company, 1973), p. 3.

wealth per student among a state's school districts. Our first task will therefore be to examine possible responses to the Serrano suit and others like it.

In its 1971 decision (now called *Serrano I*), the California Supreme Court invoked a principle of compliance: The quality of public education may not be "a function of the wealth of . . . [a pupil's] parents and neighbors." This so-called "principle of fiscal neutrality" had been first put forth by Coons, Clune, and Sugarman to circumvent barriers raised by the McInnis case.[2] Because it does not specify any particular state school finance program, it is essentially a negative principle—it would allow any arrangement so long as district spending is unrelated to district wealth. While the court was not specific, it apparently would allow differences in spending based on particular educational needs, and on differences in the cost of obtaining equal services. It is particularly important to note that the Serrano decision did not outlaw the property tax as a means of school support. Either a local property tax properly equalized by state aid, or a state property tax would be allowed.

The Serrano case adopted the Coons, Clune, and Sugarman proposition that expenditures should not be a function of the wealth of the district. Nevertheless the power equalizing formula proposed by these authors to implement the court's decision allows and even encourages differences in expenditure associated with tax rate. However, the trial judge who reheard the Serrano case in April 1974 declared the following provisions of the California school finance system unconstitutional:

> (1) the basic aid [flat grant] payments of $125 pupil to the high-wealth school districts; (2) the right of voters to each school district to vote tax overrides and raise unlimited revenues at their discretion; (3) disparities between school districts in per-pupil expenditures, apart from the categorical aids of special-need programs, that do not reduce to insignificant differences, which means an amount considerably less than $100 per pupil, within a maximum period of six years; and (4) variations in tax rates between school districts that are not reduced to nonsubstantial variations within [six years.][3]

Regardless of a school finance program's formal structure, if local school tax rates are the same and expenditures equal, it amounts to full state funding, with local property taxes being the equivalent of a state property tax. In spite of this apparently clear statement, some of the judge's other findings seem to indicate confusion and perhaps a willingness to allow expenditure variations that are not wealth-related.

The California legislature responded to the 1971 Supreme Court decision by substantially altering the school finance system. The most important innovation was the imposition of a revenue limit. School districts were restricted in

[2] John Coons, William H. Clune III, and Stephen D. Sugarman, *Private Wealth and Public Education* (Cambridge, Mass.: Harvard University Press, Belknap Press, 1971).
[3] *Serrano v. Priest*, Civil No. 938, 254 (Cal. Super. Ct., April 10, 1974). at 102-3.

the amount of revenue they could raise through a combination of state aid and local taxes. The limit was their actual revenue per pupil in 1973–74, increased each year by an amount that was permitted for inflation. However, districts with revenue limits below the state average are allowed to increase their limits faster than districts with limits above the average, and over a period of time (estimated at from fifteen to thirty years) this would result in equal revenues per pupil in all districts. While this response reveals the legislature's willingness to address the problem, the equalization in expenditures takes far longer than the six years allowed for by the judge, and because the foundation plan remains in effect, there is no equalization of tax rates.

In its decision of 1976 (now called *Serrano II*), the California Supreme Court affirmed the trial judge's ruling in all respects, thus leaving stand the confusion in the trial court decision. However, the California Legislature appears to have assumed that expenditure differences not wealth-related will be allowed.

The Serrano criterion merely requires that the quality of education (usually defined as amount spent per child) shall not be a function of community wealth, but only of the wealth of the state as a whole. This would seem to eliminate flat grant or foundation programs, for they allow unequalized local taxation; however, any form of school finance program can be made to conform with the principle through appropriate modifications. Suppose, for example, that a state establishes a foundation program, specifies a foundation sufficiently high so that no district is able to raise the foundation amount with its required local effort, and then forbids additional local school taxation. Although the form is that of a foundation program, the actuality is one of full state funding, with spending per child in all districts equal, and the required local effort being the equivalent of a state tax. Florida has enacted a plan similar to this. The foundation is greater than the amount raised by any district with a required local effort of 6.3 mills, making recapture unnecessary. There is unequalized local taxation allowed, but it is limited to less than two mills. The result is a system in which spending differences per student are small, and almost all districts are levying eight mills. New Mexico's program is similar.

POWER EQUALIZING

Two important questions have been raised regarding whether power equalizing meets the Serrano criterion. The first is based on the presumption that people who live in property-rich communities have a greater taste for education than those in property-poor communities. If this is so, in a completely power equalized system we might find that property-rich communities tax themselves at a higher rate to provide higher expenditures.

Then, with school spending correlated with wealth, would the fiscal neutrality principle be satisfied? To answer, one must choose between *ex post* and *ex ante* concepts of fiscal neutrality. The *ex post* interpretation is that the actual level of educational support must not correlate with wealth. On that basis, a system that resulted in both higher spending and higher tax effort in wealthy districts would not be acceptable. The *ex ante* formulation is that the *ability* of a district to support schools should not depend on wealth. This means only that a unit of effort must produce the same support everywhere. In that case a correlation between expenditure and wealth might be acceptable.[4]

Coons, Clune, and Sugarman clearly have formulated their plan with the *ex ante* notion in mind, and so have those states that have adopted power equalizing.

In the quotation above, Stephen Barro assumed that property-rich communities might want to spend more on education than property-poor communities. Martin Feldstein has questioned this, and suggests that, on the contrary, power equalizing in the form usually recommended might result in *poor* communities spending more than rich ones.[5] He points out that the propensity to spend is determined both by the wealth of the community and the price it must pay for educational services. Prices being equal, wealthy districts will spend more than poor ones, but the state attempts to equalize this with matching grants, thus reducing the price the poor community must pay. Only if the price effect exactly counterbalances the wealth effect will the propensity to spend be neutralized. Feldstein shows that for Massachusetts in 1971, the price effect of the percentage equalizing system outweighed the wealth effect, predisposing poorer districts to spend more. This finding, of course, applies only to one particular state at one particular time.

These problems point out that if we use an *ex post* definition of wealth neutrality we are almost forced to full state assumption, or some similar way of guaranteeing equality of expenditure. To achieve a system in which communities are free to choose their level of expenditure yet without a correlation between wealth and expenditure is probably beyond our present ability. On the other hand, use of an *ex ante* definition avoids these problems. We will assume an *ex ante* definition in the rest of our discussion.

There are several ways power equalizing might be used to implement school finance reform. Power equalizing need not guarantee a fixed number of dollars per student per mill of tax rate, as was discussed in Chapter Eight. A virtue of power equalizing is its flexibility. Figure 9-1 depicts some examples. Figure 9-1a is the power equalizing formula discussed in Chapter Eight, in which districts are guaranteed $80 per student for each mill of tax levied. (Note that the graph is not the same as used in Chapter Eight. Here, the hori-

---

[4]Stephen M. Barro, "Alternative Post-Serrano Systems and Their Expenditure Implications," in *School Finance in Transition,* ed. John Pincus (Cambridge, Mass.: Ballinger Publishing Co., 1974), p. 32.

[5]Martin S. Feldstein, "Wealth Neutrality and Local Choice in Public Education," *The American Economic Review,* March 1975, pp. 75–89.

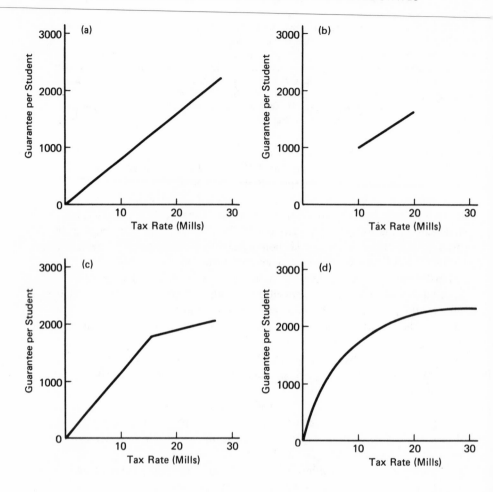

FIG. 9-1. Power Equalizing Formulas

zontal axis is tax rate, rather than assessed valuation per student.) Figure 9-1b
contains a different scale, represented by the following:

Tax Rate	Guarantee
Less than 10 mills	$ 0 per student
10 mills	$1000 per student
15 mills	$1300 per student
20 mills	$1600 per student
Above 20 mills	$1600 per student

This schedule has several distinguishing features. First, a minimum tax rate
must be levied before there is any payment. This enables the state to express
a value regarding the minimum amount of education offered. In other words,

it is a way of combining the features of the flat grant and foundation plans with those of power equalizing. Second, even if extended, the line does not pass through the origin. Third, there is a maximum allowable spending amount. Since the district receives this amount regardless of its tax rate above 20 mills, no district will tax higher than 20 mills, and the line on the graph ends at this point.

Figure 9-1c illustrates a schedule with a "kink" in it. Up to 15 mills, there is a rather steep increase in the guarantee; after 15 mills the increase is less steep. This provides a financial incentive for districts to move toward the kink point. Districts with tax rates below the kink find that with a modest increase in their tax rate they can gain substantial revenue increases. Districts with tax rates above the kink find that they can reduce tax rates substantially while suffering only a modest loss in income. A schedule of this sort has been proposed in California and Oregon, but has not been adopted anywhere.[6]

Finally, Figure 9-1d depicts a curved schedule. It expresses the economist's idea that the marginal utility of additional expenditures decreases and finally becomes zero. No state has adopted such a schedule, at least partly because of the technical difficulty of interpolating for tax rates not shown in the schedule.

FULL STATE FUNDING

Full state funding would also be acceptable under the Serrano criterion, since expenditures per student would by definition be a function of the wealth of the state as a whole. Full state funding, of course, would eliminate local power to set expenditure levels, permitted but not required by the Serrano criterion. A formal recapture mechanism is unnecessary with full state funding, for the system is completely supported by state taxes. These are levied at a uniform rate and the money thus raised is used where it is needed. The effect is exactly the same as produced by a foundation program with recapture, for the excess money raised through taxes in one community is taken by the state and used elsewhere. Redistribution of state-levied taxes is unlikely, however, to disturb people as much as a formal recapture program, which conveys the image of taking away from the community local revenues it regards as its own.

VOUCHER PLANS

Another alternative, properly implemented, would satisfy the Serrano criterion. This alternative, commonly known as a voucher plan, was originally

---

[6]See Charles S. Benson, *Final Report to the Senate Select Committee on School District Finance* (Sacramento, Cal.: California Office of State Printing, 1972), and Lawrence C. Pierce, Walter I. Garms, James W. Guthrie, and Michael W. Kirst, *State School Finance Alternatives: Strategies for Reform* (Eugene, Ore.: Center for Educational Policy and Management, University of Oregon, 1975).

proposed by Milton Friedman, economist formerly at the University of Chicago, in 1955.[7] It is a "radical" concept in that it proposes dismantling the present system of publicly operated schools. It is conservative in an economic sense in relying on the private market rather than on government. Friedman described his plan thus:

> Governments could require a minimum level of education which they could finance by giving parents vouchers redeemable for a specified maximum sum per child per year if spent on "approved" educational service. Parents would then be free to spend this sum *and any additional sum* on purchasing educational services from an "approved" institution of their own choice. The educational services could be rendered by private enterprises operated for profit, or by nonprofit institutions of various kinds. The role of the government would be limited to assuring that the schools met certain minimum standards such as the inclusion of a minimum common content in their program, as it now inspects restaurants to assure that they maintain minimum sanitary standards.[8]

As originally developed by Friedman, the voucher system might not meet the Serrano criterion, since it would allow parents to supplement the government voucher with their own money. There are ways to remedy this, however. One could, for example, require that participating schools accept vouchers in full payment of tuition. Even under the most restrictive rules suggested in the court cases, there has been no thought of forbidding parents to supplement their children's schooling with private lessons in music, art, sports, or even reading Thus, private schools faced with accepting vouchers in full payment of tuition could provide only a basic program for that amount. A separate school, not accepting vouchers, could be established next door to provide any enrichment for which parents were willing to pay.

Voucher proponents assert that the plan has a number of advantages. Parents would be allowed to place their children in schools of their choice, instead of being forced to use schools and teachers for which they had no enthusiasm. The injection of a greater amount of private enterprise would make schools more efficient and promote a healthy variety. Salaries of teachers would become more responsive to market forces. On the other hand, there would clearly be more segregation by economic class, and probably also by race, than at present. The few public schools that remained might become the dumping ground for pupils private schools were unwilling to accept.

In fact, an equivalent of the voucher plan has been operating in higher education for more than 30 years. The G.I. Bill, enacted immediately after World War II, provided a higher education subsidy for any veteran who could

---

[7]Milton Friedman, "The Role of Government in Education," in *Economics and the Public Interest,* ed. Robert A. Solo (New Brunswick, N.J.: Rutgers University Press, 1955).

[8]*Ibid.,* pp. 127-28. (Emphasis in original.)

gain entrance to a program. It paid full tuition, regardless of the tuition being charged by the institution, and subsistence for the veteran and his family. Social security entitlements perform the same function for families whose principal provider has died, and many states have provided scholarships for higher education, with the amount of the scholarship based on family income.

In spite of this, voucher plans have not been accepted in elementary–secondary education. Far from being adopted in any state, the system has not even had a real trial on an experimental basis. For several years during the 1960s and early 1970s the Office of Economic Opportunity and the U.S. Office of Education attempted to promote a trial of a voucher system somewhere in the United States. The closest they came to achieving their goal was a limited experiment in the Alum Rock School District, near San Jose, California, involving no private schools. Approximately half the district's public schools developed differentiated programs, and parents were allowed to choose their child's school. The absence of private sector involvement seriously blunted competition that is supposed to be a major factor in voucher programs. Nowhere else has there been a serious voucher system trial, although a number have been proposed.

FAMILY POWER EQUALIZING

Coons, Clune, and Sugarman recognized a problem with their proposed system of power equalizing.[9] While it met the Serrano criterion that the amount spent on a child's education should not depend upon the wealth of his or her neighbors, expenditures might still depend upon the *decisions* of those neighbors. A rural family desiring and willing to pay for an excellent education for its children might find its neighbors less interested, preferring to have low taxes and low school expenditures. To remedy such conditions of forced inequity, Coons, Clune, and Sugarman proposed "family power equalizing." In this modified voucher plan, several levels of educational quality would be available in a community's schools. Each family is then free to choose the level of quality it wants for its children, and is taxed accordingly. The child attends the school whose per pupil expenditures are linked to his parents' choice of tax rate. For example, parents willing to pay an income tax of 5 percent for support of schools could enroll their children in a school that provided a minimum basic education. Those willing to pay 10 percent could have their children in a considerably better school, while those willing to pay 15 percent of their income in school taxes could enroll their children in a school with many extras. Of course, a poor household would pay less than the cost of education at each level, and substantially less at the 15 percent level. On the other hand, a wealthy household would pay more than the cost of educating its children at the 5 percent level,

[9] John Coons et al., *Private Wealth and Public Education*, p. 200–42.

and substantially more at the 15 percent level. Under such circumstances, the poor might opt for higher tax rates in order to ensure their children an excellent education, whereas the rich might opt not to send their children to public school at all, thus reducing their school taxes to the lowest level, whatever was required of households without children.

Family power equalizing has had no warmer political reception than Friedman's voucher plan, and it seems highly unlikely that it will be implemented.

The problem to which we alluded, of the possible different patterns of choice between poor and rich in family power equalizing actually haunts ordinary power equalizing.[10] Suppose a state installs a power equalizing system (with recapture) that guarantees $100 per student for each mill of tax levied. A district with only $20,000 assessed valuation per student would raise $20 for each mill of tax, and the state would supplement this with $80 per mill per student. If the district had 1,000 students and decided to levy a 20 mill tax, it could spend $2,000 per student. It would raise $400,000 in local taxes and receive $1,600,000 from the state. A community with an assessed valuation of $200,000 per student, however, would raise $200 per mill of tax for each student, and would be forced to return $100 per student to the state. At the 20 mill tax rate it too would be able to spend $2000 per student; however, it would export to the state $2,000,000 in locally raised taxes and would receive nothing in return. Under these circumstances, parents and taxpayers of the wealthy district could hardly be blamed for deciding to support their schools at a minimum level, transferring all possible school functions (e.g., libraries, art and music classes, and athletics) to unequalized municipal tax rolls.

MANDATED EXPENDITURE LEVEL

There is yet another arrangement that would possibly meet the Serrano criterion, although it may not have been anticipated by those who filed the original suit. A mandated expenditure level could equalize expenditures. The state could require all districts to spend the same number of dollars per child, even though allowing all money for education to be raised from local taxes. This would result in very different tax rates, with poor communities struggling under heavy tax burdens while rich ones had low rates. This would be unfair to taxpayers, but since expenditures were the same everywhere it would not be unfair to students.

It seems unlikely that this blatantly simple form would be politically feasible, but states could both mandate and guarantee an expenditure level at a given tax rate. This would be the equivalent of a foundation plan with a

---

[10]See Charles S. Benson, "The Transition to a New School Finance System," in *School Finance in Transition,* ed. John Pincus (Cambridge, Mass.: Ballinger Publishing Co., 1974).

prohibition on additional expenditures. State money would supplement local taxes in poor districts; rich districts could continue to levy low rates to support the mandated level. A number of states appear headed in this direction; they have adopted revenue or expenditure limits that will ultimately tend to be equal across the state. Of course, this solution will be tested in the courts, and it is too early to predict the outcome.

FOUNDATION PROGRAMS AND FLAT GRANTS

As pointed out in Chapter Eight, the philosophy of the flat grant and foundation programs is that a certain amount of "basic" education should be provided on an equal basis to all. Any amount beyond that provided by the flat grant or the foundation guarantee is a local luxury, not to be aided by the state.

The Serrano criterion appears to say that any education undertaken by a public school district must be provided on an equalized basis. It would not touch the right of individual parents to purchase additional education for their children as they wished. Nor would it prevent other branches of government from providing services (such as recreation) on an unequalized basis that, if provided by a school district, would have to be provided on an equalized basis. Thus, the Serrano criterion appears to prohibit the use of the foundation program or flat grant if unequalized local taxation is allowed. An interesting suit was brought to the state of Washington in 1976 challenging the foundation program on a different basis. Washington had a foundation program that was completely equalized up to the amount of the foundation, for it was supported by a statewide property tax. However, the remaining third of the school districts' revenue derived from unequalized taxation. In *Seattle School District* v. *Washington*,[11] the plaintiffs relied on a provision of the Washington constitution that states, "it is the paramount duty of the state to make ample provision for the education of all children. . . ." They argued that, in the absence of research that clearly indicates how much should be spent on education, ample provision is the average of what school districts in the state actually decide to provide for their schools, and that the state should guarantee this amount through the foundation program. Any additional expenditures would constitute more than ample provision and might be supported out of unequalized local taxation. This criterion, somewhat less restrictive than the Serrano formula, would allow the continuance of flat grant and foundation programs.

Of course, any unequalized taxation in one year would increase the average state expenditures that must be guaranteed by the state in the following year. Special levy elections are governed by provisions that make them ex-

---

[11] *Seattle School District No. 1* v. *Washington,* Thurston County Superior Court No. 53950. The trial court judge ruled that the state was not making ample provision (whether the criterion used here, or a criterion based on required staffing ratios was used), and declared the school finance system unconstitutional.

tremely difficult to pass in Washington, so this should not be an overwhelming problem. Only if the foundation guarantee were allowed to slip to a low level (or if inflation raised the cost of service appreciably) would local elections raise a great deal of additional money. This would then be reflected in the foundation program for the next year, as it appropriately should.

Correcting Other Inequities

Expenditure differences resulting from differences in school district property wealth are not the only inequities that have been the target of reformers. A series of court cases has focused attention on the plight of the handicapped, and the federal government has undertaken to encourage all school districts to provide an adequate education for each child, regardless of mental or physical handicaps, by the early 1980s. Similarly, *Lau* v. *Nichols* has established the right of non-English speaking minorities to a bilingual education. It is clear that every one of these programs will cost more than the standard program for the average child. School finance reform guaranteeing equal expenditures per child can thus be inequitable to those districts having a higher proportion of children requiring special programs. These differences, of course, relate to the theme of equalization of need.

The third type of disparity described in Chapter Eight is that resulting from cost differences. A solution providing only equal dollars or equal access to wealth ignores cost differences. Thus, districts incurring higher expenditures may provide an education inferior to that provided by their more fortunate neighbors.

Another problem is that the measure of wealth (assessed valuation per student) used in most school finance programs may not be the best measure of ability to pay taxes. If not, wealth equalization based on this measure will be inaccurate.

It is not necessarily desirable that these inequities be taken up by the courts. Judicial remedies are frequently blunt instruments. Application of the rule generated by the court may provoke other inequities. By contrast, the legislature, through political give and take, can design a finance system that balances inequities, fine-tuning it so that no group bears the brunt of discrimination. Legislatures can change laws as conditions change and can make exceptions for special cases. Courts, in general, are unable to exhibit such flexibility. Of course, legislatures will not necessarily act in the enlightened manner described. They have frequently not acted at all, or acted in ways that do nothing to correct inequities, and this has made resort to the courts a necessity. The legislative process of school finance reform is discussed in Chapter Thirteen.

In the three sections immediately following, we describe a selection of possible solutions for these inequities.

NEED EQUALIZATION

Need equalization has usually been handled in one of five ways: no specific allowance for need, weighting, excess cost reimbursement, flat grants, and having services performed by an intermediate district. The advantages and disadvantages of each approach have been discussed in some detail in Chapter Eight. The most sensible alternative is probably to choose the best approach for each situation as it arises.

The weighting method is heavily dependent upon arbitrary cost factors, inviting misclassification of students or a failure to offer specific programs. It is probably best used where there is little or no possibility of either type of subversion—for example, when weights are used for various levels of education. Obviously these levels must be offered, and students cannot be arbitrarily classified into a different grade level. Many states weight high school students at approximatley 1.25 (compared with 1.00 for elementary grades). This reflects the fact that more is usually spent on high school students, although this need not be so. Florida, however, reverses the typical procedure and weights high school students 1.10, but kindergarten through third grade at 1.234. The fact that these weights are arbitrary is not important from an equity standpoint (as it would be for special programs) because all students experience each level of schooling.

Certain special programs such as those for the multiply handicapped or severely mentally retarded are probably best handled by an intermediate education district. These services usually require a large investment in tools and equipment, and the intermediate district can spread these costs over a large pupil population.

Districts should also be allowed to contract with intermediate education districts for special programs. Such services will then be offered by the intermediate education district only if it can convince local officials that it can offer better services than they can. The state would offer a cost reimbursement to local districts for special students who are, say, multiply handicapped. There would be a maximum allowable reimbursement per student. If a district has enough handicapped students to operate a special program with regular funding and state excess cost reimbursements, it will do so. However, intermediate education districts, because of economies of scale, usually can offer a better program for the same or a lesser amount, and local districts would save money by contracting for it.

Most special needs should be handled through programs providing cost reimbursement for excess costs. With such programs there is little incentive to misclassify students into programs or not to offer the programs, as there is with weighting. Districts can spend different amounts to meet needs without being rewarded or penalized. The biggest problem is that the state must establish a maximum allowable reimbursement to prevent districts from operating needlessly expensive programs. There is no better basis for setting this maximum than by specifying weights, yet the maximum, since it costs the district no more, will frequently become the actual expenditure for most districts. An alternative is to partially reimburse excess cost, forcing local districts to share the cost of expensive programs. However, where the district has more than an average number of students with special needs, it will suffer an extra tax burden, even where the regular program has been wealth equalized.

Finally, there can well be some special needs that the state will simply ignore in its financial scheme, allowing districts to provide for them out of money to which they are entitled for regular students. This would be the case for experimental or inexpensive programs.

A particularly important special need about which much has been written is that of "socioeconomically deprived" students. These students appear to require added services in order to succeed in school. This has been recognized in weightings or categorical programs for such students in a number of states. Two difficulties frequently accompany such "compensatory" programs. One is that guidelines for student selection are uncertain. IQ tests classify mentally retarded students, and physical examinations do the same for physically handicapped. However, if students are selected for compensatory programs by socioeconomic status some will be helped who do not need it, and others who need the help will be ineligible. If low pupil performance on standardized tests is used to determine eligibility, there is a risk of rewarding schools for doing a poor job. In addition, if schools use the money effectively, the improvement in test results brings a decrease in state aid.

The other problem is that there is no generally agreed-upon technique for educating "compensatory" students. Since there is no agreement on program, weightings are probably no more arbitrary than cost-reimbursement, and they may provide more freedom to experiment. Alternatively, a state that installed a successful *cost* equalization program (to be discussed shortly) might find substantial aid provided in the same districts where compensatory programs are now operated, and separate provision for compensatory education might be unnecessary.

One possible way to determine the amount of money districts should receive for compensatory education has been proposed by Walter Garms and Robert Goettel, who found that much of the variation in percentage of students in a school performing poorly in standardized tests could be explained by variables measuring non-school factors thought to influence achievement.[12] These factors included the percentage of children in the school from broken homes, those who live in overcrowded housing, those for whom English is a

---

[12]Walter I. Garms and Robert Goettel, "Measuring Educational Need: Developing a Model for Predicting Achievement Levels from a Composite of Socioeconomic Characteristics," in *Financing Equal Educational Opportunity* eds. Joel Berke et al. (Berkeley, Cal.: McCutchan Publishing Corporation, 1972).

second language, and the average number of schools attended in the last three years. These variables are used in a multiple regression to predict percentage of low-achieving students. (For an explanation of multiple regression, see the section entitled "Cost Equalization.") This *predicted* percentage can then be used in a state aid program. For example, each district could be given a specified number of dollars per predicted low achiever. This method does not identify the individual low achievers—its value lies in predicting the percentage of low achievement based on factors not controllable by schools, thus eliminating the possibility of schools being rewarded for poor performance.

Schools should then be allowed to spend this money as they see fit. Periodically the predicted percentage of low achievement would be compared with the actual results. When a district performs significantly better than predicted, there should be some reward for the staff, if only recognition of a job well done. Aid, of course, would not be reduced, since it is based on the prediction. If the school does significantly poorer than predicted, the state could provide help in seeking the causes. Thus, this proposal provides an element of efficiency along with equity.

COST EQUALIZATION

As noted in Chapter Eight, the few existing attempts at cost equalization occur in budget categories involving large and obvious cost differences among school districts. The major cost difference among districts takes the form of higher salaries paid teachers and other employees to recruit and retain them in less desirable school districts. The present surplus of teachers does not change the problem, for at the same salary the most attractive district will be able to hire the best teachers, regardless of supply.

There have been proposals, usually by urban public officials, that the state should simply consider higher average salary rates to be the cost difference necessary to hire equivalent quality teachers. These proposals have been opposed by others who contend that the richest districts typically pay the highest salaries in the state, although these districts are usually desirable places to live and teach. Obviously, these districts simply want teachers of higher quality and are willing to pay for them; it is dubious public policy for the state to reward them for this. Similarly, teacher unions may negotiate skillfully and thus increase salaries in a district above what they would otherwise be. State subsidy in such a situation would be a self-reinforcing process.

One approach to such cost differences which has been implemented by several states uses a state salary schedule to determine the district's state aid. Each district hires the teachers it wants. The maximum number of teachers it may hire is specified as a ratio to the number of pupils, e.g., one teacher for every 25 pupils. The teachers actually hired are then placed on the state salary schedule according to the training and experience of each, and total district entitlement for teacher salaries is determined. To this is added an additional dollar amount per teacher for non-personnel expenses, such as supplies, resulting in a total district entitlement. If a foundation plan is used, the yield of a required local effort tax rate is then subtracted, and the difference paid to the district by the state. The state salary schedule is used only for computational purposes, however. The state may insist that teachers be paid at least as much as the state schedule, but does not prohibit them from paying more. Most of the states using this method are in the South, although there are a few others (New Mexico, Utah, and Washington, for example).

Unfortunately, this approach, as it is usually implemented, can make inequalities stemming from cost differences even worse. Property-rich districts can afford to hire teachers with more training and experience, for they can offer higher salaries. They then receive more for these teachers from the state. Even under a completely wealth equalized system, which would eliminate the advantage of high assessed valuation, some districts, at the same salary levels, will still be more attractive to teachers than others. These districts will be able to attract teachers with more training and experience, and the state will subsidize them. Thus the state salary schedule is disequalizing in the cost sense even where there has been wealth equalization. This is less true in a situation of declining enrollments, where there is little movement of teachers; a district may be burdened with many teachers near the top of the salary schedule.

Obviously, what is needed is a means by which to separate legitimate cost variations from differences in tastes for educational services. That is, we must separate supply influences from demand influences on the price of teachers and other employees. A pioneering attempt at this was made in 1974 by Harvey Brazer.[13] He gathered data on a number of variables for Michigan school districts. Measures were taken both of a community's desirability as a place to live, and its desirability as a place to teach. Both sets are "supply" variables. Similarly, he gathered proxy measures of a community's "demand" for high quality education, such as assessed valuation per pupil, extra voted mileage, and percentage of households with incomes over $15,000. All of the variables were used in a multiple regression analysis.

Multiple regression is a statistical procedure in which a number of "independent" variables are employed to predict a single "dependent" variable. The variable to be predicted in Brazer's study was *average teacher salary*. The regression technique assigns a weight to each independent variable. When one multiplies each variable's value for a district by its weight and sums the products, the result is a prediction of the dependent variable's value. In effect, each product represents the influence of that variable on the predicted variable when all other variables in the equation are held constant. The predicted value of a dependent variable will not equal its actual value for any specified school dis-

[13] Harvey E. Brazer, "Adjusting for Differences Among School Districts in the Costs of Educational Inputs: A Feasibility Report," in *Selected Papers in School Finance 1974* (Washington, D.C.: U.S. Dept. of Health, Education and Welfare, 1975).

trict. However, the average difference between actual and predicted values for all districts will be smaller than for any other set of weights that might have been derived.

These products represent the effects of variables on average teacher salaries. Thus, it is theoretically possible to separate the effects of supply and demand. New predictions are made, using *actual* values for supply variables but using *average* values for demand variables. This provides predictions of average teacher salary levels allowing for variation in district attractiveness, but holding constant demand for teacher quality. Brazer used the ratio between this prediction and average teacher salary for all districts as an index of district cost for hiring teachers of equal quality. For example, if a district had a predicted teacher's salary (holding demand constant) of $11,000 and the average salary for all districts was $10,000, the ratio would be 1.10. This district would have to pay 1.1 times as much as the average district in the state to obtain teachers of average quality.

Like many investigations that break new ground, Brazer's effort had flaws. Nevertheless, it is important that attempts be made to measure interdistrict cost differences. Other researchers are continuing this line of investigation and are developing more sophisticated measures.[14]

Of the three equalization goals, wealth, need, and cost equalization, the last is least understood, and little has been done about it in school finance formulas. Florida is the only state in which a general cost adjustment has been attempted. The state undertakes a cost-of-living survey, and derives a cost-of-living index for each school district.[15] The amount of the state foundation per student is then adjusted by this index, with the result that districts like Dade County (Miami) have an increased state aid allowance, while low-cost North Florida counties suffer a reduction. The system is notable mainly as a first attempt to take cost differences into account. Living cost differences are only one component of school district cost differences, however. The desirability of a district as a place to live and to teach, ignored in the Florida adjustment, may be considerably more important.

DECLINING ENROLLMENT

It is seldom that a school district attains stability of enrollment for more than a few years. The number of students is either increasing or decreasing, and

[14] See for example Jay Chambers, "Educational Cost Differentials: The Conceptual Framework and an Empirical Analysis for School Districts in the State of Missouri," prepared for the Educational Finance Committee of the Governor's Conference on Education in the State of Missouri.

[15] For a brief description of the Florida school finance system, see Jack Leppert et al., "Pupil Weighting Programs in School Finance Reform," in *School Finance Reform: A Legislator's Handbook* eds. John J. Callahan and William H. Wilken, (Washington, D.C.: National Conference of State Legislatures, 1976), pp. 21–23.

sometimes at alarming rates. By the mid-1970s a majority of districts were experiencing significant declines or were anticipating impending declines, notably a number of large, central city districts. Enrollments in Seattle, for example, declined more than 30 percent between 1970 and 1976. There is no way of knowing how long this trend will continue. Population trends on a national basis have baffled even the U.S. Bureau of Census. It made four projections of population for the decade 1970–1980 based on assumptions it felt would bracket the possible alternatives. However, actual population increases were even less than its lowest estimate. Predicting individual school district populations, where migration is much more of a factor, is even more uncertain.

In any case, an enrollment decline poses short-term school district budgetary problems. Typically, such declines result in one or two fewer students in each class; this makes consolidation of classes difficult. The district continues to use the same number of teachers and classrooms, resulting in an increase in per student cost. Over time, a district can make reductions, remedying the short-term problem.

A number of states have made efforts to provide additional aid to districts suffering enrollment declines. One alternative is to permit a district to choose either last year's or this year's enrollment as a basis for claiming state aid. The growing district uses the current year's enrollment figure; districts with decreasing enrollments use last year's figure. A variation allows districts to use either current enrollment or a moving average of the last three, four, or five years. Either method provides temporary relief for a district faced with enrollment declines, but does not put off the day of reckoning indefinitely.

In New York, districts are offered a "save-harmless" provision guaranteeing no less total state aid than received in any previous year. There are districts that have been declining in enrollment for 15 years, yet they still receive as much state aid as they did at their maximum enrollment. The result is much as if "phantom students" were enrolled, and these phantom students may constitute as much as a third of total enrollment for some districts.

Alternative Measures of Ability to Provide Education

Ability of local school districts to provide educational revenue has usually been measured by property valuation per student. This is logical, because the local revenue of a school district comes almost exclusively from property taxes, and the amount of property value is a measure of ability to raise such taxes. Similarly, number of students is a measure of the task to be performed by the schools. However, the methods for measuring property valuation and number of students have been challenged as being inaccurate or inappropriate. In addition, the entire concept of using property valuation to measure wealth has been questioned.

THE STUDENT MEASURE

Number of students is usually measured by average daily attendance (ADA) or average daily membership (ADM). The ADA is calculated by counting those in attendance or legally excused each day during the school year and dividing by the number of school days in the year. This is a measure of the average number of children actually being taught. The ADM is calculated by totaling the number of children enrolled in school on each day (whether or not the students are actually in attendance), and dividing by total days. Average daily membership will thus be higher than ADA. If there is a fixed amount of state aid available, use of ADM instead of ADA will only make a difference if some districts have higher absence rates than others. Urban districts have many more unexcused absences, and a switch to ADM from ADA is helpful to them. These districts claim, with a measure of justification, that teachers must be provided on the basis of total children eligible to attend whether they are there or not. Suburban districts, which suffer from the switch to ADM, claim that this provides no incentive to districts to enforce compulsory attendance laws.

A third alternative is to use total enrollment as a measure. This is simply all students enrolled in each school during the year, regardless of how long enrolled. It is a poor measure in that form. It can be converted to average enrollment by totaling the number of days of enrollment and dividing by the number of days in the school year. This makes it equivalent to ADM.

A fourth possibility is to use "census" children as the measure. This is the number of children of school age residing in the community, regardless of whether they attend public school. This measure has been proposed in Massachusetts, a state with many students in nonpublic schools. The presumed advantage is that it provides added money per public school student to districts with large private school enrollments, enabling those districts to reduce the burden of local school taxes on parents paying private school tuition. Aside from this advantage, it has little to recommend it.

All of these arrangements become inapplicable when used for measuring students in special programs. If students are in special programs all day all year, there is no problem. However, if they attend these programs only part time, the foregoing measures do not provide a prorated record of relative time spent in regular and special programs. Florida, which has a comprehensive pupil weighting system, adopted a sophisticated means of coping with the problem. The number of students in a program is determined by computing pupil-minutes of time in each program for the whole year, and dividing by the number of minutes in the school year. The result is the number of full-time equivalent pupils (FTE). The total FTE for all programs in the district is equal to the average daily attendance of the district. Use of this method ensures that a student will not be counted twice for weighting purposes. An FTE system is not as cumbersome as might first appear. A reasonable approximation can be obtained by measuring student-minutes once or twice a month, rather than every day. The FTE concept is particularly useful for situations where students do not attend school for a full day or a full school year, as in adult education and summer session.

THE TOTAL WEALTH MEASURE

Assessed valuation per student is usually an unsatisfactory measure of wealth because most assessors do not value property at its full market value. (See Chapter Six for a discussion of the problem of property taxation.) If two districts have the same *market* value of property per student, they are, in that sense, equally wealthy; however, if the assessor for one district values property at half market value, and in the other district it is valued at one-fourth market value, the first district appears to be twice as rich. There is thus an incentive for assessors to undervalue property, giving a district the appearance of being poor and therefore eligible for more state aid. To counteract this, most states have "equalization" boards, whose duty is to survey, for each assessing jurisdiction, the average ratio of assessed value to full market value. This ratio can then be used to inflate assessed values for all municipalities and districts to full market value. This *equalized assessed valuation* becomes the standard for measuring district wealth. This procedure is substantially better than using uncorrected assessed valuation, but it is only as good as an equalization board's ratios, which may be based on small samples. Requiring assessments to be at full value is more satisfactory, with both assistance and penalties as inducements to comply.

There will still be large differences in the market value of property per student from one district to another, partly because of differences in the value of commercial and industrial properties. This has been particularly true in a few districts in each state that are "tax havens" for industry. Students in a tax haven can be educated entirely with local taxes at an extremely low rate. The low rate of taxation attracts more industry to the district, lowering the tax rate even further. Effectively, industry, by settling in such tax havens, has insulated itself from full responsibility for supporting schools through taxes.

A serious proposal has been made (but not yet adopted anywhere) that school districts be allowed to tax only residential assessed valuation. Use of residential assessed valuation per student renders all districts poorer, some of them substantially so. Equalization would then require added state money. Presumably, the state would raise this with a uniform statewide property tax on nonresidential property. This would allegedly have two salubrious effects. School tax havens would be eliminated, for industry would be subject to the same tax rate anywhere in the state. Industry's location decisions would then be based on considerations other than tax rate. There would be less competition among communities for "ratables," i.e., additional corporate assessed valuation to help pay tax bills. Additionally, lower property wealth per student would make it possible for the state to operate an equalization program without resorting to the unpopular concept of "recapture." (Actually, of course, recapture is in effect for nonresidential property subject to the statewide tax, but it is not as evident.)

Enticing as this idea is, it has so far foundered on a hard political fact. The uniform tax rate on nonresidential property necessary to support this sytem would presumably be about the average of tax rates levied under the current system. This would be lower than the current rate in some districts, *but it would be higher than the current rate in many of the largest cities,* and these cities have a great deal of nonresidential property. The combination of higher school taxes plus already high property taxes for municipal purposes could well hasten the exodus of industry from the cities, exacerbating the urban financial bind.

Another alternative for measuring wealth of a district is to use personal incomes instead of property value. This idea is frequently advanced by the cities, which have a high proportion of poor people despite a high assessed valuation per student. However, so long as districts collect property taxes rather than income taxes and do this on nonresidential as well as residential property, this approach is obviously omitting an important variable. If parents of the few students who live in an industrial area were poor, the district would qualify for substantial state aid even though the schools could be supported by a low property tax rate. Income would not be a reasonable measure of ability to pay except perhaps in districts taxing only residential property. Of course, income as a measure of wealth would be particularly appropriate if school districts were allowed to raise money locally through the individual income tax. Such a local income tax for schools is in use in some Maryland districts, as a supplement to property taxes.

Cities have also complained of a condition called *municipal overburden.* They allege that the property tax for schools is only one of the competing claims for the tax dollar, and that non-school property taxes are much higher in cities than they are in other jurisdictions. They feel, therefore, that the valuation of property per student should be reduced by the ratio of non-school property taxes to total taxes. This would produce a much lower valuation per student in the cities, and therefore more state aid. As discussed in Chapter Sixteen, we specifically reject this argument, on what we consider to be solid public finance grounds.

Phasing in Formulas

Some districts undergoing school finance reform encounter problems. An abrupt transition to a new system may result in financial distress for some districts which receive less state aid yet have made commitments under the present system that are difficult to change on short notice (e.g., tenured teachers with high salaries). On the other hand, some districts might find the bonanza of increased state aid more than they could effectively spend immediately.

The easiest way to institute school finance reform is to have sufficient state money available so no district need receive less state aid than previously. Those that benefited under the former system would receive minimal increases; those that had fared badly before would receive larger increases in state aid. This "leveling up" method is politically the easiest way to institute reform; no district is actually harmed in the sense of getting less than formerly. Unfortunately, states seldom have sufficient extra money to pursue this strategy. A successful example occurred in Florida in 1973. Unexpectedly large receipts from federal revenue sharing provided a $300 million budget surplus. This enabled the state to institute one of the most thorough reforms of school finance in the nation, without less money flowing to any district.

Because there is seldom enough new money to level up (this is particularly true when the bulk of revenues was formerly dispensed in the form of flat grants), alternatives are necessary. To prevent a once deprived district from suddenly receiving a windfall gain it cannot handle, the law may provide that additional aid shall not increase any district's revenue per pupil by more than 15 percent in a year. For some districts, this limitation may mean that several years will elapse before they achieve their normal entitlement under the law. Nevertheless, the provision seems reasonable as a way of preventing unwise use of a sudden flood of new money.

For districts faced with lower entitlements under a new law than under the old one, the usual device is a "save-harmless" clause, often also referred to as a "grandfather" clause. This specifies that the district will not receive less money than at present. Sometimes, such provisos specify no fewer total state dollars than at present, sometimes no fewer dollars per pupil, and sometimes no fewer dollars than would be received under the old formula applied to present district data. As indicated earlier, guaranteeing the same total state dollars as at present can result in large unwarranted bonuses to districts that are steadily losing students. The other two save-harmless guarantees can also result in some districts continuing to receive more money than the new system allots them. For example, a wealthy district might receive no money under a new formula were it not for a save-harmless clause which indefinitely provided the flat grant per student formerly received.

One way to prevent save-harmless clauses from persisting indefinitely is to permit inflation to take care of the situation. As money amounts in the new formula are increased year by year, the percentage value of aid under the old formula becomes negligible. The save-harmless grant will never disappear completely, though. A more positive means for ensuring that such inequities do not persist forever is the "disappearing save-harmless." District entitlements are calculated under both the old and the new formula. If entitlements under the old formula are greater, the disappearing save-harmless comes into play. If the benefit is to disappear in five years, in the first year the district is entitled to its allowance under the old law. In the second year it is entitled to its allowance under the new law plus four-fifths of the difference between its new and old entitlement. In the fifth year, the district is entitled to its new allowance plus one-fifth of the difference between the allowance calculated under the old and that under the new law. In the sixth year, it would receive only its entitlement under the new law. Disappearing provisions of this sort would have saved New York from the clutter of save-harmless clauses present in the mid-1970s. At that time, all but 8 of the state's 709 districts were receiving aid based on save-harmless clauses rather than on the regular formula.

Keeping the Formula Current

One of the problems in the design of school finance formulas is that of reflecting changes over time in expenditures per student and in local fiscal ability. These changes produce similar effects, but for different reasons.

Expenditures per student will probably continue to increase both because of general inflation, and increases in relative productivity of the economy's private sector. The first is self-explanatory. The reason for the effect of the second is that in the economy as a whole, productivity (output per person, or per man-hour) continues to increase. Since labor tends to be paid in proportion to its productivity, real wages (i.e., inflation aside) of the labor force in the private sector tend to increase over time. In the public sector, which largely produces services instead of products, increases in productivity are harder to achieve. The public sector is labor-intensive, whereas increases in productivity in the private sector have come about largely in capital-intensive industries. However, the public sector does not have the option of leaving real wages the same (reflecting no increase in productivity) while they are increasing in the private sector. Consequently, the public sector tends to raise the real wages of its employees by roughly the same percentage as they are raised in the private sector. Since there has been no increase in productivity, the net result is an increase in cost per unit of output. In public education, this is reflected in an increase in the real cost per student educated.

Most state school finance formulas are designed to limit total cost to the state. Otherwise, independent actions of local districts would provoke a raid on the treasury. The limitation in a foundation formula is stipulated by the amount of the foundation guarantee and the required local tax rate. In a percentage or power equalizing plan, the open-ended nature of the state commitment is usually foreclosed by a limit on the amount per student equalized by the state. As average expenditures per student in a state begin to exceed the foundation guarantee or maximum reimbursement, the state aid percentage decreases and a consequent increase in revenue from local sources is required. Since the amount from local sources above the guarantee is unequalized, the result is less equalization throughout the state.

While there has been a general increase in local fiscal ability (expressed as assessed value per student) in the past, it has not presented as persistent a problem to state aid formulas as increases in expenditures per student, and has not been given the same attention. However, rapid increases in property valuation in the mid-1970s, combined with a decline in number of students, created a rapid increase in assessed valuation per student. The result of this is similar to the situation above: the percentage of state funds decreases and the percentage of local money increases. It is difficult to tell which of the two—increase in expenditures per student or increase in local fiscal ability—causes the most difficulty. Both are a serious source of obsolescence in state aid formulas.

The most frequent solution has been to legislate a formula which implicitly assumes that expenditures and fiscal abilities will remain stable, and then do nothing until political pressure necessitates change. At this point, the legislature increases the foundation guarantee, or the maximum guarantee in a power equalizing plan. Alternatively, the state can temporize by instituting various categorical aids. A virtue of increasing the guarantee is that all districts spending more than the guarantee (and that is usually most of them) receive more money, which is politically palatable. Categorical aids, on the other hand, may provide little or nothing to many districts.

As another possibility, both foundation guarantee and required local effort may be increased. This aids poorest districts most. The effect on other districts depends on the changes in guarantee and tax rate. However, there generally is no assurance that some districts will not get less money. Thus, this measure is usually combined with save-harmless guarantees.

Yet another possibility is to attempt to design a formula that keeps up with the times, making it unnecessary to legislate changes every year or two. Oregon's formula in the mid-1970s represented a rather sophisticated attempt to do this. It enabled the basic formula to remain stable for over 20 years. The foundation guarantee is not determined by the legislature; rather it automatically escalates each year based on the increase in average school district expenditures per student. Specifically, the amount of the guarantee per student each biennium is set equal to the foundation in 1955–56 times the ratio of average expenditures per student in the immediate past year to those in 1955–56. For example:

Foundation guarantee in 1955–56 = \$230 per weighted ADM
Statewide average expenditures in 1973–74 = \$971.63 per weighted ADM
Statewide average expenditures in 1955–56 = \$270.37 per weighted ADM

$$\text{Foundation guarantee for 1975–77 biennium} = \$230 \times \frac{971.63}{270.37} = \$826.55$$

Allowing the foundation guarantee to increase in this fashion without changing anything else would jeopardize the state treasury; therefore, an ingenious safety device was used. Total money to be spent each year for general state school aid was determined by legislative appropriation. This aid was distributed by calculating a computational tax rate sufficient to distribute all equalization money.[16] That is, given the foundation guarantee, one particular rate of required local effort distributes all of the money. Any higher tax rate requires less money; any lower rate necessitates more money. The method of calculation is complicated, but need not be explained here.

The Oregon system is one in which the foundation guarantee is adjusted by allowing the increase in educational expenditures to drive it, and in which amount of state aid is independently determined by the legislature. It is easy to see that the determination of the amount of money to be distributed is independent of the foundation guarantee so long as the computational tax rate is not fixed. If the amount allocated by the legislature is high, the computational tax rate will be set low, and equalization aid will be distributed to many districts. If the amount appropriated by the legislature is low, the computational tax rate will be set high, and fewer districts will receive aid.

Another Way of Thinking About School Finance Formulas

Enough has been said in this chapter and the preceding one to make it clear that school finance formulas are far from uncomplicated. Not only are there a number of different goals to take into account, but also states often use more than one way of attacking problems such as wealth equalization. Many states provide a flat grant to all districts, along with a foundation program that equalizes poor districts but not wealthy ones. Maine, among others, provides a foundation plan with a power equalizing add-on. Combine this with varying types of weighting or cost reimbursement programs for need equalization, provision for cost differences, different ways of measuring wealth and students, and other variations, and the program is extremely complicated. Put on top of this expenditure or tax rate restrictions, save-harmless provisions, and phase-in provisions, and the task of describing a state school finance program becomes well-nigh impossible. There are usually only a few people in each state who thoroughly understand how its school finance program actually works. Also, to categorize a particular state's school finance formula as one type of program or another is to ignore the fact that the label may indicate little about how the money is actually distributed. In 1973 New York changed from percentage equalizing to a foundation program, but save-harmless provisions of the law eventually affecting 701 of the 709 districts of the state vitiated the new program.

What is needed is a new way of evaluating school finance systems that makes it possible for states to be compared to each other. Although such a way has not yet been completely developed, we would like to propose that the method look at the *actual* distribution of revenues among the districts of the

[16] Lawrence C. Pierce et al., *State School Finance Alternatives*, pp. 20–21.

state, rather than use such terms as *power equalizing* or *pupil weighting* that imply some ideal distribution. The structural characteristics of the school revenue distribution of a state would be described by a set of statistics that would distinguish states from one another on a realistic basis. Some of these descriptors might be:

1. Total state aid (including categorical aid) as a percentage of total state-local school revenue. Like the other descriptors, this would be a single figure for the state, calculated from readily available data. Often the percentage of state aid may be more important than the form of the formula. If the percentage is high, there will probably be a significant amount of equalization regardless of the form of the program. This is not necessarily true, however. Therefore, it is necessary to have other descriptors.

2. Amount of unequalized local taxation as a percentage of total state-local revenues. This gives an idea of the extent to which inequality may be the result of unequalized local taxation. In particular, it indicates the effectiveness of expenditure or tax limits, as well as of the equalization program. California, for example, would show a sizable percentage of unequalized local taxation because of the ease with which expenditure controls can be overridden by local vote. New Mexico, on the other hand, would show a very low percentage. The local tax rate for all school districts is 8.925 mills; no district may levy more nor less. In all but one district the foundation guarantee is greater than the amount raised by the 8.925 mills, and thus local taxes are completely equalized. The unequalized taxes for New Mexico would consist of the amount above the foundation guarantee raised by that one district.

3. The coefficient of variation (standard deviation divided by the mean) of equalized expenditures per weighted student. If this were large, it would indicate an effective power equalizing program. A pure foundation state would presumably show no variation on this measure.

4. The coefficient of variation of equalized expenditures per unweighted student. In combination with the preceding measure, this would gauge the extent to which weighting programs are actually effective.

5. Coefficient of variation of school tax rates. This would be a measure of differences in effort among school districts. In New Mexico this coefficient would be zero; in other states it would be fairly large.

6. State categorical aid as a percentage of total state-local revenue. This helps to measure the extent to which states attempt to target funds instead of providing general aid.

7. Tax price of education: the average revenue associated with a mill of local school tax rate. This is an important measure of the extent to which the state relies on local taxation for support of the schools.

8. Coefficient of variation of tax price. This is an important measure of equalization.

These are not all of the descriptors of the structural characteristics of school revenue distributions that might be used; they are intended only to be illustrative. The important thing is that each of them is applicable to any system of financing education through a state-local system, and the data are probably readily available at the state level. Thus it should be possible to develop a profile of the school finance system of each state based on these uniform characteristics. We do not at present have any such way of comparing state school finance systems.

A New System of School Finance

In this chapter we have attempted to present the pros and cons of alternative ways of reforming school finance distributions. (Alternatives for raising the money have been discussed in Chapter Six.) While we have indicated a preference for some methods, we have not outlined a comprehensive program. The alternatives for wealth equalization, need equalization, cost equalization, and measurements of ability to support education, can be put together in a variety of ways. There is no one right answer, and the combination used in a particular state will depend upon that state's traditions, its fiscal ability, and the political situation at the time.

However, we believe it possible to outline a potential system that seems more fair and more responsive than any currently in existence. It is recognized that the criteria against which a system of finance should be appraised depend upon the values of the judge. Our values frequently conflict with each other, as do those of most people; nevertheless, we feel strongly that:

1. All children should have the right to a basic education without respect to wealth or place of residence.
2. The best way to encourage school efficiency is by leaving as much choice as possible to consumers of education.

These are not unusual beliefs; many people would support them. We believe our plan achieves a better balance between them than most.

First, the right to an equal basic education for all children is necessary for the proper functioning of a democracy, and is therefore a proper state responsibility. It is not easy to decide what the basic education is that should be guaranteed to all. Ambivalence exists within and among the states. A state may have a foundation program that is supposed to provide a minimum basic education on an equal basis, but at the same time it mandates a variety of curricula that appear not to be basic (because they are not required in all states), such as music, art, and physical education.

Our definition of a basic education is considerably more restricted. It consists of those things necessary for minimal effective functioning in a democracy. This includes the ability to read, write, and do basic arithmetic, and knowledge of our democratic government. These goals are relatively clear-cut, and accomplishment is more easily measured than in other curricula. Most people would agree that they form the core of education, while few would agree on other curricular objectives. It should be possible to complete this basic education by the end of the eighth grade.

This basic education would be guaranteed on an equal basis to every child through full state funding. The amount of money to be provided for each child would depend upon measures of need and cost differences, so that districts whose children have learning difficulties would receive more money per student, as would districts having to pay more to provide the same quality of education. Of course, full state funding implies no difference in revenues as a result of district wealth, nor any required local effort.

Since the program involves the coercion of mandatory attendance, it would be kept as flexible as possible by allowing children to attend any public school selected by their parents, whether in their own school district or any other. The school district of residence would be responsible for transportation to any school within a 15-mile radius; parents would be responsible for transportation to schools beyond this radius. (A provision like this already exists in New York, where school districts must transport private school children to any school within a 15-mile radius.)

For the rest of the elementary education, we would provide much more freedom than currently exists. We propose a system based on "educational coupons." These are a form of voucher, with some interesting twists. The coupons could be purchased by parents from the local school district in any amounts desired. The cost of the coupons would depend upon family income and number of school-age children of the purchaser. A poor family with several children would be able to purchase coupons at as little as 10 cents on the dollar; a rich family with one child would have to pay as much as 90 cents on the dollar. The excess cost of the coupons, above that paid by the purchaser, would be fully state funded. The progressivity of the schedule for purchase of the coupons would depend upon other factors in a particular state. If a state has an adequate income maintenance program, for instance, it would not be necessary to make the schedule as progressive as in a state lacking such a program.

The coupons could be used to purchase additional educational services for children of the purchasers, either at a public school or through any private institution certified by the state. Parents could spend these coupons on any kind of additional education they wished for their children: foreign language instruction, music, art, or swimming lessons, remedial reading, vocational instruction, flying lessons, study of medieval architecture, or baton twirling. While the intent is to encourage the diversity provided by private entrepreneurs, the public schools would not be excluded from providing these educational services. And the local electorate that wished to provide even more services could supplement the value of the educational coupons purchased at local schools through power equalized local taxation.

Compulsory education would end with the eighth grade. However, each person would be provided with a portable grant that could be used at any time during the remainder of his or her life. It would entitle the individual to a maximum of six additional years of education at any school, public or private, that offered the subjects covered by the entitlement. The amount of the entitlement in any one year would be equal to the average expenditure by the state on basic education in the elementary schools in that year, possibly multiplied by a factor such as 1.2 to take care of the additional costs of secondary education. The state would provide the money to both public and private schools for this education, at the specified rate. The courses would be those on a list approved by the state, and the individual using the entitlement could enroll to take 6 years of such courses at the rate of 15 hours a week during the school year.

Through the use of these grants, individuals could put off education until they had learned more about the world and had decided what they really wanted to study. In addition to this entitlement, individuals could continue to buy educational coupons throughout their lives, to be used for learning enrichment activities of various sorts. These coupons, for use by adults, would be issued by the state, and purchased by individuals at a discount dependent upon family income. The excess cost of them, above the purchase price, would be paid for though state taxes.

We believe this proposal strikes a reasonable balance between equity and efficiency by providing an equal basic education for all, and providing for additional education based on ability to pay, with the sort of responsiveness built in that can come only with free choice by parent or student. There are a number of implementation questions. We will consider a few of them here.

First, the free choice of public schools for basic education would leave some schools with crowded classrooms, and others with excess space. This is a natural result of the operation of the marketplace. From the viewpoint of those who favor a planned economy it is inefficient, but a market economist would state that allowing parents to choose promotes efficiency. The state could help solve crowding problems by making relocatable buildings available for rent to school districts. When no longer needed at a particular location, the state could move them elsewhere.

The fact that some parents would be able to buy educational coupons cheaply, while others would pay almost full price, would encourage a black market in cheap coupons, with poor parents tempted to sell them to rich parents at a discount. Preventing this is a relatively simple bureaucratic exercise involving writing the pupil's name on the coupons, and ensuring through occasional audits that redeemed coupons are for children actually enrolled in the school.

How are private schools to be certified to receive educational coupons? If these institutions were held to the same standards required of public schools, a large certifying bureaucracy would be formed, and the requirements established would result in squelching the diversity this program is designed to encourage. Thus, certification should be limited to three areas:

1. The schools (or individuals) receiving the coupons should not be operating fraudulently.
2. The facilities used should not be dangerous to the health or safety of the students.
3. Students should not be denied admittance on any basis unrelated to the purpose of instruction. In most cases this would prohibit discrimination on the basis of race, religion, or sex. In the case of public schools offering enrichment subjects it would also prohibit discrimination on the basis of residence.

There is a danger that school districts in some areas might attempt to drive private institutions and individuals out of the market by supplementing coupons redeemed with money from local taxation. But there is a natural curb on this tendency because the public school cannot deny attendance to children from other districts, and local voters will be unwilling to subsidize the education of children of nonresidents. On the other hand, the opportunity to supplement education in this way should be left open, particularly for the rural districts, where there may be few private opportunities available.

There is no doubt that this plan would substantially transform public education. We believe most of the changes would be desirable. The public elementary schools, relieved of their present charge to be all things to all children, could concentrate on basic instruction in reading, writing, arithmetic, and citizenship. Of course, some additional subjects would still be offered because the school could do a better job than private institutions or individuals. This should certainly be possible in many cases, since the fixed costs of offering additional instruction are minimal: classrooms and administrators already exist for the basic program.

Parents would, in many cases for the first time, be given the opportunity to make choices about their children's education. They would be able to choose the public school attended for basic instruction and could choose among a variety of enrichment courses. Parents would, of course, have to pay for a portion of this additional instruction, but the poorer they are, the larger the amount contributed from the public purse.

A particularly important part of the plan is the fact that mandatory attendance ceases after the eighth grade. High schools would no longer play the custodial role they now have, and the result should be substantially fewer discipline problems. (It would be necessary to reduce the minimum working age in some states.) The provision of the portable grants would encourage lifelong learning, and a fair number of older students in the high schools would probably also bring a more serious tone to studies there. Finally, the ability of all adults to buy educational coupons on a more or less equal basis (again because of state subsidies) would also encourage lifelong learning.

A particularly difficult task involved in fleshing out this proposal is defining what constitutes approved subjects eligible for the portable grant. Our suggestion is to limit the use of four years of the portable grant to courses in organized schools that are designated as basic or vocational by the school and are on a list of such courses approved by the state. Two years of the portable grant could be applied toward any kind of courses. Probably the majority of students would use the first four years of the grant to take basic and vocational courses in a conventional high school, supplementing their program as desired with courses paid for with educational coupons. They might then use the final two years of the grant in a college or university, community college, vocational-technical school, or with individual tutors. Some, who found that eight grades of formal education were sufficient, might opt to use only the two years of the grant which are not restricted to organized schools and designated courses. For the electives-type courses designated by these two years of the grant, normal tuition might well be more than the state guarantee. The school (or tutor) would claim the guarantee from the state, and then charge the student the difference, payable in educational coupons.

Immigration into and out of the state should not be a problem. Residents of the state are entitled to the portable grant for six years of education after eighth grade and to buy educational coupons as adults so long as they are residents of the state. When they leave the state they forfeit the privileges so long as they are gone. Immigrants to the state (and former residents returning) would be entitled to the six years of additional education, less any already obtained elsewhere, and the right to purchase coupons.

It will be noted that most of this proposal is fully state funded. Only enhancement of local public school efforts to furnish enrichment activities is supported with local taxation. This plan, then, achieves the tax equity of state taxes while preserving local and individual options as to the amount and kind of education to be obtained. The public cost of this program would be less than the present system, because the state would be fully funding only the basic and vocational education, plus a portion of the cost of enrichment education. Nevertheless, the cost would be substantial, and it would probably be necessary for the state to finance it at least partially with a statewide property tax. We do not consider this bad, as we noted in Chapter Six.

Perhaps the strongest objections to this proposal will come from those who feel that it dismantles the public schools as we have known them. It takes away the music, art, physical education, and other subjects that have been added to the mandatory list in most states during this century. Our reply is that we feel there is a certain amount of education that is the direct interest of the state. It is clear that reading is the *sine qua non* of educated, functioning, and productive citizens. We have probably diluted our efforts in reading as we have added other programs to the curriculum. The same thing can be said about the ability to communicate through writing and to do ordinary arithmetic, and to understand the way in which our government functions.

Unless music, art, and other subjects are necessary for all students (which we do not believe), to require them of all students not only takes away from the effort to provide all students with the ability to read, but also smacks of big-brotherism. We feel that the decision as to which of these subjects, and how much, should be studied by each student should be left to students or their parents. Most public schools would still continue to offer courses other than the basic ones, financed partly by local taxation and partly by educational coupons provided by parents. However, an artistically gifted student would not have to spend time being bored in music classes or physical education. If this student's parents desired, he could spend several hours a day in the art class of the public school, or could study art at a private school or with a tutor.

We offer this plan not as a blueprint, but as an illustration of the possibilities that exist for school financing if one casts off some of its traditional constraints. We hope that perhaps some of the ideas may be found useful.

Summary

Chapter Nine has taken the Serrano case in California as being representative of a number of state school finance cases resting on equal protection clauses of state constitutions. Such cases assert that the quality of a student's education should not depend upon the wealth of the community in which he or she lives. A number of alternative finance plans that would satisfy this criterion are discussed.

The most frequently adopted response is power equalizing, which equalizes the ability to raise dollars per student at equal tax rates, but does not mandate the rate or the resulting expenditure level. A second alternative, more frequently discussed than implemented, is full state funding. This scheme guarantees expenditures that do not depend upon local wealth (although not necessarily equal per pupil expenditures), and because all of the money is raised through statewide taxation, it also guarantees equal tax rates.

A completely different way to meet the criterion would be to abandon state operation of the schools, leaving this to private entrepreneurs paid by vouchers provided by the state to parents. Another alternative, called family power equalizing, would allow parents to choose the quality of the school their child would attend by choosing the rate at which they desired to be taxed for school purposes.

Yet another alternative that would meet the Serrano criterion would be a mandated expenditure level. This would equalize expenditures, but would allow continuation of unequal tax rates.

The chapter also has discussed ways in which other inequities could be corrected, in the areas of need equalization, cost equalization, and declining enrollment. The technical, but important, questions of the appropriate measure of local district fiscal ability, phasing in formulas, and keeping them current are discussed.

Finally, we have presented our conception of a completely new school finance system. This voucher system would simultaneously provide equity, give parents more choice regarding where, with whom, and what their children would study, and put increased emphasis on the basics of reading, mathematics, and citizenship. It constitutes a radical yet reasonable way of financing and operating the schools.

10

SCHOOL EFFICIENCY

How can students be educated most efficiently? How can schools produce the most learning for the least money? In the face of declining school enrollments and shortages of tax dollars, what is the most effective way to educate students?

Questions such as these have been asked of public education since its inception. However, periodically, the inquiries are posed with greater intensity. Raymond Callahan, in his book, *Education and the Cult of Efficiency,* describes the early twentieth-century efforts of educational administrators to apply industrial techniques to schools in order to make them more efficient.[1] A movement in some ways similar began in the late 1960s.[2] Fueled by growing school costs and increasing competition for public sector dollars, policy makers at all levels of government began to inquire how schools could be made more effective. This quest came to be known as the "accountability" movement.

Accountability has almost as many meanings as it has champions, but in its broadest sense, accountability means *responsibility.* Followers of the accountability movement attempt to establish specific educational goals, clearly affix

[1] Raymond E. Callahan, *Education and the Cult of Efficiency* (Chicago: University of Chicago Press, 1962). See also David B. Tyack, *The One Best System* (Cambridge, Mass.: Harvard University Press, 1974).

[2] See Jerome T. Murphy and David K. Cohen, "Accountability in Education—the Michigan Experience," *Public Interest,* 36 (Summer 1974), 53-81.

responsibility for reaching those goals, precisely measure whether goals have been reached, and often, calculate the costs of doing so.

Schools are usually asked to shoulder the responsibility for achieving the specified goals. Sometimes administrators are asked to carry the burden, but most often the greatest weight falls on teachers.

Many widely differing methods have been proposed for achieving accountability—just as many different goals have been specified—but one of the most important goals of accountability is to make schools more effective. The aim is not merely to point a finger at those responsible for schools' failures or successes, but by affixing responsibility for achieving goals, to make schools more productive.

The Technical-Industrial Accountability Model

Some of the first and perhaps the most popular methods for making schools accountable came to education via the discipline of economics and the field of business. Schools were expected to be responsible for altering the ratio between useful results obtained (outputs) and the resources expended in obtaining them (inputs). This was the avenue pursued by those in the accountability movement who followed in the footsteps of those in the efficiency movement of 50 years earlier. In order to improve the relationship between school inputs and outputs, policy makers and administrators attempted to use economic concepts and technical-industrial schemes such as "Management by Objectives" (MBO), Planning-Programming-Budgeting Systems (PPBS), systems analysis, Program Evaluation and Review Techniques (PERT), performance contracting, and educational production function analysis. All of these have analogs in efforts to measure and maximize output in manufacturing organizations.

All these attempts to improve school productivity assume existence of the following: (1) one or more agreed-upon "products" or learning outcomes; (2) a "scientific" instrument for measuring student progress toward those outcomes; and (3) research techniques that make it possible to separate schooling effects from out-of-school influences (such as home environment and individual IQ) upon student achievement.

PRODUCTION FUNCTION ANALYSIS

Perhaps the best example of the technical-industrial model of accountability is the attempt to formulate an education production function. This attempt is based on the assumption that one can improve productivity by measuring and comparing, in a mathematical way, the outcomes of various educational techniques.

In the industrial field, production function analyses are frequently conducted to assess the optimum mix of manufacturing materials and techniques in order to minimize production costs and maximize profit. When applied to education, the scientific expression of these analytic components takes the form of the following generalized equation:[3]

$$A_{it} = g\left(F_{i(t)}, S_{i(t)}, P_{i(t)}, O_{i(t)}, I_{it}\right)$$

The subscript i refers to the ith student; (t) refers to an input that is cumulative to time t. The letter g means that A_{it} is a function of all that follows, without specifying that function. The other symbols are as follows:

A_{it} are educational outcomes for the ith student at time t.

$F_{i(t)}$ are individual and family background characteristics cumulative to time t.

$S_{i(t)}$ are school inputs relevant to the ith student cumulative to t.

$P_{i(t)}$ are peer or fellow student characteristics cumulative to t.

$O_{i(t)}$ are other external influences (the community, for example) relevant to the ith student cumulative to t.

I_{it} are initial or innate endowments of the ith student at time t.

This technical–industrial model of accountability was conceived as an attempt to make educational goals explicit and precise. It was based on the conviction that school budgets were being spent, federal grants were being given, and teachers were being hired, all to accomplish vague goals like "educating children." No longer would money or jobs be bestowed on those who could not set specific goals or could not show that goals had clearly been reached. Educational institutions would be forced to be as productive as America's industry.

COST-EFFECTIVENESS ANALYSIS

One of the most useful assessment techniques to spring from the technical-industrial model of accountability is cost-effectiveness analysis. Much of its usefulness arises from the fact that its goals are much more modest and simple than the all-encompassing production function. This attempt to measure and improve school productivity is appropriate when (1) expected outputs are agreed upon and means exist for measuring the degree to which they have been accomplished, and

[3] This equation is from "Measuring Efficiency in Educational Production," by Henry M. Levin, reprinted from *Public Finance Quarterly*, 2, No. 1 (January 1974), 3-24, by permission of the Publisher, Sage Publications, Inc. An extended description of production function analyses is provided by Elchanan Cohn, *The Economics of Education* (Lexington, Mass.: D. C. Heath and Company, 1972), chap. 8, "Input and Output in Education," pp. 235-70. Added criticism of the industrial accountability model is provided in a set of reviews on accountability books by Ernest R. House, "Accountability: An Essay Review of Three Books," *American Educational Research Journal*, 2, No. 3 (Summer 1974), 275-79.

(2) there are at least two competing methods or procedures for accomplishing the desired outcomes.

For example, let us examine the use of cost-effectiveness analysis in foreign language teaching. This is an area where it is rather easy to agree on what a student is supposed to learn and how to measure whether this learning has occurred. To perform cost-effectiveness analysis, it is possible to construct alternative instructional strategies based on varying mixes of teacher time and technology. One can establish a series of experiments to assess, for example, the relative effectiveness of a computer-assisted instruction program, a language laboratory, and a self-contained classroom.

The fact that cost-effectiveness studies are conceivable is not meant to imply that they are simpleminded or easy. Substantial effort is needed in designing the "treatment" to be received by the experimental groups and in ensuring compliance with the canons of experimental science, including such things as proper selection of subjects, sample size, control for outside influence, and avoidance of the so-called "Hawthorne effect."[4] Indeed, such studies are similar to the comparative analyses of instructional techniques that have been conducted for decades by psychologists and educational researchers. The best of such analyses have always attempted to be scientifically rigorous. The added step imposed by cost-effectiveness analysis is to compute and compare expenses involved in delivering alternative instructional "treatments." Systematic comparisons of instructional methods, when performance standards are agreed upon and measurable, could eventually lead to more productive educational systems.

Process Accountability

Other kinds of accountability focus on the "process" rather than the "product" of schooling. Followers of these forms of accountability assert that it is unfair to hold teachers or schools accountable for specific educational outcomes. Students have differing abilities, and environmental factors have extremely strong effects on students' learning. A teacher may be extremely successful with an able group of students and yet with no change in technique, motivation, or ability, fail miserably with a less able group. The rationale behind process accountability is that teachers can only be accountable for "teaching well," for using good "educational practices," or in short, for the "process" that goes on in the classroom.

[4]The classic explanation of educational research designs is contained in Donald T. Campbell and Julian S. Stanley, *Experimental and Quasi-Experimental Designs for Research* (Chicago: Rand McNally, 1963).

An insightful discussion of the technical utility and political implications of these analytic techniques is contained in Charles L. Schultze, *The Politics and Economics of Public Spending* (Washington, D.C.: The Brookings Institution, 1968).

Despite its emphasis on "process," this type of accountability still resembles the technical–industrial model in aiming to make schools more productive. By identifying those teachers who are able to teach most effectively and those who are least effective, and by forcing ineffective teachers to improve or be replaced by better teachers, process accountability is a mechanism for helping schools educate students most efficiently.

COMPETENCY BASED TEACHER EDUCATION

Competency Based Teacher Education (CBTE), one form of process accountability, rests on the idea that it is unfair to hold teachers accountable for educational outcomes. This form of accountability evaluates teachers before they are licensed or credentialed in an effort to prevent ineffective teachers from reaching the classroom.

Like process accountability, CBTE assumes a linkage between particular sets of teacher behaviors and specified student performance. For example, if it is desired that students learn how to add two digit numbers the teacher is expected to follow certain specified instructional procedures. In order to become licensed or credentialed, a teacher trainee must demonstrate proficiency on these and other instructional dimensions. In short, the trainee must illustrate that he or she can competently perform the desired instructional behaviors to move students from learning point A to learning point B. A teacher training and credentialing scheme consists of a long list of prescribed teacher behaviors. Competency based teacher education was adopted in various forms by many states.[5] It is not clear, however, how many are continuing to enforce the provisions.

We have mentioned just a few of the many accountability programs. The ones we have chosen illustrate some of the most important approaches to improving school productivity.

Problems with Accountability Methods

All the accountability methods present problems in implementation. When using technical–industrial accountability methods, three difficult questions must be dealt with: (1) Exactly what educational outcomes are we striving for? (2) How can we measure those outcomes? and (3) How can we separate the effects of schooling from out-of-school influences upon student achievement?

When using process and competency based forms of accountability, we can, on the whole, avoid these questions, but we must deal with others equally

---

[5] Alfred P. Wilson and William W. Curtis, "The States Mandate Performance-Based Teacher Education, *Phi Delta Kappan*, Vol. 56 No. 2 (October 1974), 76–77.

difficult: What *is* the process that ought to go on in the classroom? What *are* the teaching practices in which teachers ought to demonstrate competency? In short, what are the best teaching methods?

PROBLEMS
WITH THE PRODUCTION FUNCTION APPROACH

Almost all the production function studies reveal weaknesses in the collection of data, errors in measurement, or methodological flaws of such magnitude as to render them useless for immediate purposes such as informing public policy.[6] In 1973, a prestigious citizens' committee in New York State attempted to squeeze every ounce of policy utility from the production function studies of that time. After an exhaustive review they concluded only that schools were probably more effective if they employed teachers who were characterized by high ". . . general intelligence, experience and advanced training."[7] Even these three slender reeds were surrounded and almost buried by qualifications and equivocations. Virtually the same conclusion was reached by a 1972 Rand Corporation study conducted for the President's Commission on School Finance.[8]

It was not the case that all these studies were ineptly done. Instead, their lack of findings reflects major problems in the basic assumptions of the technical-industrial model.

Some critics believe that schooling, unlike many manufacturing processes, is at a very low state of technological development and simply does not fit an industrial model for assessing productivity. After having viewed the technical accountability model from many perspectives and after having attempted to employ it for analytic purposes, the economist Henry Levin writes:

> . . . the lack of similarities among the production techniques used by different schools may mean that neither average nor frontier findings can be applied to any particular school. Indeed, in the extreme case, each individual school is on its own production function (which varies according to the outputs being pursued), and evaluation results for any group of schools will not be applicable to individual schools in the sample.
>
> While measurement of educational production may be a useful exercise in itself, it is not clear that such studies can help us to improve the effi-

---

[6]The technical criticisms which undermine the validity of the production function studies are reviewed in James W. Guthrie, George Kleindorfer, Henry M. Levin, and Robert Stout, *Schools and Inequality* (Cambridge: MIT Press, 1971).

[7]*The Fleischmann Report on the Cost, Quality and Financing of Elementary and Secondary Education in New York State,* Vol. III (New York: Viking Press, 1973), p. 183.

[8]Harvey A. Averch, Stephen J. Carroll, Theodore S. Donaldson, Herbert J. Kiesling, and John Pincus, *How Effective is Schooling: A Critical Review and Synthesis of Research Findings* (Santa Monica: The Rand Corporation, 1972).

ciency of the education sector. In particular, our focus on a single and measurable output, student achievement, not only limits the analysis considerably; but it may provide policy recommendations that would reduce the economic efficiency of the educational industry if they were adopted. Perhaps the only generalization that one can make from this pessimistic overview is that the analysis of production of public activities is fraught with difficulties that are unusually severe given the present analytical state of the art. The implications of estimates of public sector production functions for improving social efficiency should probably be stated with far greater modesty than they have been. They may be totally misleading.[9]

Levin's critique was specifically aimed at production function techniques. Yet his conclusions are based on problems that beset all the technical-industrial methods. These problems arise from disagreement over the goals of schooling, the inexactitude of educational measurement technology, and inability to control for outside influences.

DISAGREEMENT OVER THE GOALS OF SCHOOLING

The purpose of schooling has been a topic for philosophical consideration and debate for a long time.[10] Despite the time and effort given to the problem, however, there is no widespread public agreement. Only under the most autocratic national systems of education is there ever a clear pronouncement of the goals of schooling. To be sure, even in a complicated and overlapping set of school jurisdictions such as we have in the United States, there can be a modicum of agreement on the purposes of schooling. However, such a consensus, at least when stated publicly, tends to be too general to be measurable.[11]

For example, most citizens concur that schools should strive to teach basic reading, writing, and counting skills, good citizenship, tolerance of fellow citizens, good habits of health and safety, occupational training, patriotism, life adjustment, physical fitness, and on and on. The difficulty comes when efforts are made to arrive at priorities among these goals or when the objectives are made specific. How much effort should be given to teaching youngsters patriotism? Is this best done by teaching "critical thinking" which might result in students questioning national endeavors such as military involvement in foreign lands? Or, should it be inculcated, particularly at an early age, "My country,

[9]Levin, "Measuring Efficiency," pp. 21-22, by permission of the Publisher, Sage Publications, Inc.

[10]For example, Aristotle once wrote: "At present opinion is divided about the subjects of education. All do not take the same view about what should be learned by the young, either with a view to plain goodness or with a view to the best life possible . . ." [*The Politics of Aristotle,* trans. Ernest Barker (New York: Oxford University Press, 1969), p. 333. First published in paperback, 1946.]

[11]For further elaboration on this point see Aaron Wildavsky, "The Strategic Retreat on Objectives," Working Paper #45, School of Public Policy, University of California, Berkeley, December 1975.

right or wrong"? Or, perhaps more time should be devoted to matters of health and personal hygiene.

The argument over educational priorities and objectives takes place at every level of government.[12] Local and state statutes are filled with confusing and conflicting rhetoric regarding the purposes of schooling, and so are federal government educational provisions.

The point we wish to emphasize is that the objectives held for schools are nowhere clear or simple. In the absence of such a consensus, policy makers typically strike a compromise of either of two sorts. One route is, in effect, to have no goals for schools—or to have them stated at such a high level of abstraction as to render them immeasurable. The second route is to try to accommodate all tastes by having a multitude of school objectives. The outcome here is that many goals are found to be antithetical or internally inconsistent.

Whichever alternative is pursued, technical-industrial methods of accountability become difficult to implement when educators cannot agree on desirable educational outcomes.

THE INEXACTITUDE
OF MEASUREMENT TECHNOLOGY

Even when we do manage to agree on what it is that we expect schools to accomplish, we still have problems in assessing school effectiveness. One reason for this is the inexactitude of educational measurement.

Many accountability programs are standardized norm-referenced tests to measure achievement. Although scores on such tests, expressed in percentile ranks or grade-level equivalents, look like precise measures, almost all experts on testing agree that such scores are only rough approximations. All that can be deduced from norm-referenced tests is that an individual student scored higher or lower than other students.[13]

Using inexact measures to evaluate accountability causes a multitude of problems. A Rand Corporation researcher put it:

> Evaluations that use imperfect information run into both analytical and political problems. Educational accountability systems based on achievement scores are an instance. Such systems frequently turn out to be *irrelevant* to policy decisions, *resisted* by educational groups that fear unflattering

[12]In fact, as a University of Chicago study amply demonstrated, there is also substantial geographic variation in publicly held expectations for schools. See Lawrence W. Downey, *The Task of Public Education* (Chicago: University of Chicago, Midwest Administration Center, 1960).

[13]The technical details of the measurement problems contained in testing are described by Barbara Heyns in "Education, Evaluation, and the Metrics of Learning," a paper prepared for the American Sociological Association meetings held in Montreal in 1974.

comparisons and the misuse of results, and *infeasible* given faulty data and limited time and money.[14]

Many educators have suggested that criterion-referenced tests might solve the problems presented by norm-referenced tests in measuring educational outcomes. Criterion-referenced tests, rather than comparing students to each other, merely indicate whether students have mastered specific skills. For instance, a criterion-referenced test in the area of foreign language would indicate such things as whether students had mastered a certain number of vocabulary words, grammatical rules, idiomatic expressions, and so on.

While criterion-referenced tests do seem more suitable for accountability programs than norm-referenced tests, districts that use them must teach exactly the same skills that the test evaluates or develop their own criterion-referenced tests, a procedure that is time-consuming and expensive. Other problems such tests present become apparent in the discussion on professsional resistance to productivity measurement.

INABILITY TO CONTROL FOR THE "OUTSIDE"

Evaluation schemes with even a modicum of sophistication attempt to take account of the fact that much of a child's learning is beyond the control of schools. For example, though no one is sure of its importance, it is generally conceded that humans vary with respect to their genetically endowed learning capacity. Presumably, innate intellectual capacity is established at the child's conception and is a learning factor beyond the ability of schools to manipulate. Similarly, family and neighborhood environment is consistently held to be

[14] Robert E. Klitgaard, *Improving Educational Evaluation in a Political Setting* (Santa Monica: The Rand Corporation, 1974), p. i.

The logical and technical weaknesses of various research procedures employed by social scientists to "control" for external influences on learning are well described in the following works:

Glen G. Cain and Harold W. Watts, "Problems in Making Policy Inferences from the Coleman Report," *American Sociological Review,* 35, No. 2 (April 1970), 228–42.

James S. Coleman, "Reply to Cain and Watts," *American Sociological Review,* 35, No. 2 (April 1970), 242–49.

Eric A. Hanushek and John F. Kain, "On the Value of Equality of Educational Opportunity as a Guide to Public Policy," in *On Equality of Educational Opportunity,* eds., Frederick Mosteller and Daniel P. Moynihan (New York: Random House, 1972), pp. 116–46.

Robert E. Klitgaard, *Achievement Scores and Educational Objectives* (Santa Monica: The Rand Corporation, 1974).

Robert E. Klitgaard and G. Hall, *A Statistical Search for Unusually Effective Schools* (Santa Monica: The Rand Corporation, 1973).

Andrew C. Porter and Garry L. McDaniels, "A Reassessment of the Problems in Estimating School Effects," paper presented at the American Association for the Advancement of Science, March 1974.

related to children's school achievement.[15] There is probably no stronger social science finding.

When it comes to measuring non-school influence on learning, measurement techniques of social scientists are woefully inadequate. Pure genetically endowed intelligence is almost impossible to measure accurately. Psychologists readily admit they do not know exactly what IQ tests measure. These examinations require a child to manipulate materials or complete paper and pencil tests. Ability to score well on such tests depends profoundly on one's environmental experiences, especially school experiences. Thus, isolating the component for "innate endowments" in the school production function is extremely difficult.

Controlling for a child's social environment outside of school is equally frustrating. The typical procedure here is to select numerical measures which purport to capture the essence of a child's social circumstances, and then apply statistical "controls" for them. Such procedures are very crude. The measures frequently used are parents' occupation, education, and income. These are sometimes supplemented by an index of cultural possessions in the home and an estimate as to the financial value of the home itself. In a few instances, these data are gathered directly from the student or parents. More frequently, they are pieces of information averaged over census tracts. Occasionally these social background data are no more than the best judgments of observers or a school principal. Even when such pieces of information are correctly gathered, they tend to be but fragmentary indicators of a child's social circumstances. It is simply not true that well educated, financially comfortable parents always provide their children with succor and intellectual stimulation, while economically and academically impoverished parents inevitably produce poor scholars. Sufficient numbers of children deviate from the statistical norm with regard to these background proxies that one is led to the conclusion that, at best, they are of limited validity.

PROBLEMS WITH PROCESS
AND COMPETENCY BASED METHODS

It is easy to see why the problems with agreeing on the "product" of schooling or how to measure it led educators to attempt to evaluate the "process" that goes on in the classroom or the "competency" of teachers. The problem with these accountability methods, however, is that there is no consistent body of research revealing what constitutes an effective repertoire of instructional behaviors.

[15] Brent Sheal, "Schooling and Its Antecedents: Substantive and Methodological Issues and the Status Attainment Process," *Review of Educational Research,* 46, No. 4 (Fall, 1976), 463–520.

In fact, there exists no body of scientific findings which links any set of teacher activities with any particular set of learner outcomes. A devastating blow was dealt the CBTE concept by Heath and Nielson who, after having reviewed every conceivable item of related research, state:

> Our analysis of this literature leads us to three conclusions: First, the research literature on the relation between teacher behavior and student achievement does not offer an empirical basis for the prescription of teacher-training objectives.
>
> Second, this literature fails to provide such a basis, not because of minor flaws in the statistical analyses, but because of sterile operational definitions of both teaching and achievement, and because of fundamentally weak research designs.
>
> Last, given the well-documented, strong association between student achievement and variables such as socioeconomic status and ethnic status, the effects of techniques of teaching on achievement (as these variables are defined in the CBTE research) are likely to be inherently trivial.[16]

Thus, the list of "competencies" that teachers should have are either so abstract as to be meaningless or, if precise, rooted in a quagmire of invalid research. Whatever, the end result is the same—CBTE provides no sure short-run hope for effectively increasing school productivity.

PROFESSIONAL RESISTANCE TO ACCOUNTABILITY AND PRODUCTIVITY MEASUREMENT

GOAL CONFLICT

Professional educators, teachers particularly, have been overwhelmingly critical of efforts to measure school productivity that involve evaluating their performance. In part this reticence can be explained by the fear of consequences: if evaluated and found wanting, teachers may be penalized. Given the inadequacies of the current state of the evaluation art, however, this reluctance is substantially justified. Teachers fully understand that there exists little consensus regarding the goals of schooling, and this disagreement makes citizen evaluation sound frightening. For example, teachers reasonably fear being evaluated by one group of citizens for achieving one set of results while others evaluate their achievement of a different or, worse, antithetical set of objectives. The teacher then is in a zero-sum situation: to satisfy some citizens is inevitably to displease others. Teachers have similar fears about the lack of agreement on the best educational processes or required teacher competencies.

---

[16] Robert W. Heath and Mark A. Nielson, "The Research Basis for Performance-Based Teacher Education," *Review of Educational Research,* 44, No. 4 (Fall 1974), 463–84.

GOAL DISPLACEMENT

Another concern of educators is that the necessity of many accountability schemes to focus on measures of achievement will trigger a "goal displacement" process.

If teachers are to be evaluated on the degree to which they have increased average achievement on norm-referenced tests, they may be under so much pressure that they will be tempted to raise scores by devious means. A teacher who focuses on raising the scores of the brightest quartile of students can elevate scores sufficiently to boost the entire class average several points. Meanwhile, less able students may be neglected.

If teachers are to be evaluated by students' performance on criterion-referenced tests, then efforts to achieve easily measurable educational outcomes may effectively displace efforts to achieve equally important outcomes that do not lend themselves to quantification. For example, knowing that they are going to be evaluated in such easily measurable subjects as reading or foreign language, teachers may neglect social studies, health or other difficult-to-measure areas.

Of course, the professionalism and character of most teachers will inhibit such devious methods, but a reward system based exclusively upon narrow measurement of quantifiable learning objectives may pressure even the most ethically minded into distorted behavior.[17]

INFRINGEMENT UPON PROFESSIONAL AUTONOMY

Because teachers are professionals and therefore concerned with their clients' welfare, they will resist pressures to specify both objectives and "treatment." A teacher might reasonably argue that classroom objectives and the means for achieving those objectives can only be formulated to fit individual students' needs. Beneath a teacher's "I am not worrying now about teaching Johnny to read," probably runs some such line of reasoning: "I will not neglect reading, but Johnny has recently undergone a severe personal trauma, and the most important thing I can accomplish for him is to teach self-reliance, restore personal confidence, assist in building a positive self-image, etc. Only after this has been accomplished can he learn effectively. By requiring me to concentrate on reading (or any other substantive area), you are impairing my ability as a professional to facilitate the welfare of my client." Because of the fact that teaching is, to a high degree, an art, teachers argue for freedom and day-to-day

---

[17]In fact, a performance contracting experiment in Gary, Indiana, led to goal displacement of this type; see G. R. Hall and M. L. Rapp, *Case Studies in Educational Performance Contracts: Gary, Indiana* (Santa Monica, Cal.: The Rand Corporation, 1971).

autonomy in establishing standards, or at least in determining them together with clients or public officials.

On occasion, the resistance of professional educators to evaluation schemes takes the form of overt political activity at the state or local school district level intended to defeat an evaluation plan. At other times, it consists of simple foot-dragging to destroy effectively such a plan. This is well illustrated by educators' general refusal to comply with California's 1970 PPBS mandate and with the 1973 Stull Act requiring specification of objectives by which teacher and administrator performance could be assessed. No matter how they show it, professional educators, though usually willing to agree that an enterprise as costly and as important as schooling must be subjected to measurement and evaluation,[18] are generally reticent to approve any practical plan to do so. This is particularly the case when such a scheme has likelihood of financial reward or punishment embedded in it.

Political Accountability

While the accountability movement itself has spurred some contributions toward greater school efficiency, it is clear that the accountability methods we have examined here are beset with difficulties. It is hard to agree on the ends and means of public education or objectively to evaluate the productivity of schools.

A new way to make schools effective might be to formulate another kind of accountability. This type of accountability could be called "political account-ability" and would be based on the belief that performance can best be improved by achieving a better match between client preferences and government services. If "accountability" is defined as increasing the ability of a system to satisfy the preferences of consumers, then it may be that economic concepts such as efficiency are less relevant. What becomes important is whether a school system is responsive to the desires of its clients. If the answer is "no," if schools are insensitive to the demands for change, then the appropriate reforms must be undertaken politically.

Perhaps, in the absence of clearly defined, agreed-upon, objective answers, we will have to substitute subjective answers. Perhaps the best way to organize schools in the face of this indeterminacy is to allow maximum diversity of instructional techniques and permit citizens to choose the techniques they believe are best for their children.

---

[18] In a recent survey of teacher attitudes, 79 percent of those queried reported, that at least in theory, they were in agreement with the idea of "accountability." The study conducted by Thomas L. Good et al., is summarized in the January 1975 *Phi Delta Kappan,* Vol. 56, No. 5, pp. 367–68.

Voucher systems or school site management systems allow parents to choose among several different kinds of schools for their children. In such systems, where there are many different kinds of schools—different in the sense that they not only strive to accomplish different objectives for their clients but also attempt to achieve these ends through a variety of instructional techniques—it is more probable that consumer tastes will be satisfied.

The provision of widely varying school styles not only promises to satisfy a wider range of consumer preferences, but might also result in added productivity. That is, among those schools attempting to accomplish the same objectives, some would use different instructional techniques than others. This eclecticism, if accompanied by suitable experimental efforts, might in time lead to an educational technology.

Summary

In this chapter we have examined problems presented by past efforts to enhance school productivity. Many of these efforts have conceived of public schools as analogous to manufacturing firms and amenable to a technical or industrial model of measurement and analysis. Others have concentrated on the educational process. The relative absence of public agreement on school goals and the weak technology, or base of scientific knowledge, underlying teaching and learning theories makes most accountability models difficult to implement. Consequently, we have proposed that a more appropriate route to productive schools is via the political process. Specifically, we advocate a series of school reforms intended to give the consumer, both parents and students, a greater voice in the operation of schools and a choice of which school to attend. The specifics of our proposal are outlined in the next chapter.

11

REFORMING PUBLIC SCHOOL MANAGEMENT AND BUDGETING

Local school districts came under increasing financial pressure during the late 1960s, with the advent of the so-called "taxpayers revolt." Voters who had usually passed school district budgets and bonds increasingly began to reject them. At first, this widespread rejection of school budgets was blamed on dissatisfaction with local property taxes and the inequities of state school finance systems. Consequently, much effort was exerted to reform state school finance systems during the early 1970s. Spurred by election defeats and judicial prodding, legislatures devised new formulas for distributing state money to local school districts in a more equitable manner. Many states substantially increased their level of state support for public schools as well. These reforms, it was hoped, would ameliorate the financial problems of public schools.

The fiscal problems of schools did not disappear, however. State school finance reform dealt only with the revenue side of school finance; it did little to control the rising costs of public education. In fact, state reform often increased costs by raising minimum standards and mandating new educational programs.

San Francisco provides an example of how rapidly school costs have risen in recent years. From the 1969-70 to the 1975-76 school year, per pupil costs in San Francisco rose from $1,108 to $2,323—an increase of more than 100 percent.[1] Controlling for inflation, this still represents approximately a 55 percent increase in per pupil spending over five years.[2]

The major fiscal problem facing most public schools, in other words, is that costs are rising more rapidly than school revenues. Voters are unwilling to increase local tax rates to meet rising school costs. State and federal governments are unlikely to provide enough funds to completely bridge the gap between rising school costs and the amount local districts can raise for themselves. Since some cost increases (such as teacher salaries) are an automatic result of inflation and wage increases elsewhere in the economy, the gap between school costs and school revenues can only be filled by saving money elsewhere, that is, by increasing school productivity.

At the same time the public began demanding more efficiency in schools, it also began demanding a stronger voice in local school governance. Local control of education, originally envisioned as rendering schools responsive to the people, hindered the professionalization of schools; it also obscured the state's responsibility for ensuring that every child receive a basic education. Thus, in pursuit of greater accountability and higher professional standards, the pendulum of school government swung back toward greater professional autonomy and stronger executive control during the period from 1920 to 1970.[3]

This centralization of public education inevitably tended to increase the distance between educational managers and the public, and at the same time had the unintended effect of making it more difficult for teachers to influence educational policy. As school systems increasingly came under the dominance of professional managers, teachers lost their ability to communicate freely with their superiors. Furthermore, teacher discretion over classroom procedures was eroded by management's efforts to introduce educational innovations. Public dissatisfaction with schools has thus been coupled with the growing alienation of teachers who find themselves being criticized for the failure of programs and policies over which they have very little influence. Recent demands for citizen participation and community schools reflect a desire to nudge the pendulum back toward greater representativeness.

We believe that the improvement of public education requires not only new

[1] During the same period, school attendance in San Francisco decreased by more than 10,000 students, which certainly exacerbated cost inflation in the district. For a complete analysis of the fiscal problems of San Francisco's schools, see James W. Guthrie, Walter I. Garms, and Lawrence C. Pierce, *The Fiscal Future of the San Francisco Public Schools,* prepared for the San Francisco Public Schools Commission, January 1976.

[2] According to the *1975 Economic Report of the President,* the general price inflator increased 35 percent between 1970 and 1975.

[3] See Herbert Kaufman, "Emerging Conflicts in the Doctrines of Public Administration," in *The Politics of the Federal Bureaucracy,* ed. Alan A. Altshuler (New York: Dodd, Mead & Company, 1968), pp. 72-87.

approaches for controlling educational costs, but also renewed commitment to the education of young people by parents and teachers—those who are most responsible for their education. It is particularly important to increase the involvement of parents in the education of their children. Only they can provide a supportive home environment where learning is encouraged and continued after school hours. But we also must develop schools that are coherent and committed to teaching basic skills, yet have enough flexibility to reflect the character of individual communities. We need teachers who care and schools that are understandable.

In Chapter Ten we examined school efficiency and the reasons why attempts to use private industry techniques have not enhanced it. Much of the analysis was theoretical or technical. The concerns of this chapter are more practical. It examines current school management and budgeting methods and offers a proposal for improving the productivity and responsiveness of public schools. We believe this proposal, which shifts much of the responsibility for managing public schools to the school site, affords the best prospect for reducing the fiscal and political problems of local school districts.[4]

Current Budgeting and Management Practices

In most urban and suburban school districts that enroll a vast majority of the country's public school children, management decisions are controlled by a district superintendent and staff. School principals and teachers have little to say about the development of educational policy or how district policy is implemented. The problems of centralized school management are best illustrated by examining school district budgeting.

SCHOOL BUDGETING

Much can be learned about the management of an organization by examining the manner in which it utilizes resources. For school districts, the budgetary process constitutes the primary mechanism for planning and controlling educational activities. Most people understand that budgeting affects teachers' salaries, quantities of supplies available to a school, and the kind of maintenance a school receives. What is not so readily understood is that budgeting also affects important decisions about what is taught, how it is taught, and who teaches it.

[4] An earlier version of this chapter was presented at an education workshop sponsored by The Aspen Institute for Humanistic Studies in July, 1976, and was subsequently published. See Lawrence C. Pierce, *School Site Management,* An Occasional Paper, Aspen Institute for Humanistic Studies, 1977.

The budgetary process not only determines which goods and services will be purchased and for what purposes, but it also reveals the most important decision makers in a school organization. To the extent that individuals or groups participate in the preparation of the school budget they reveal their relative influence on the direction of schooling. Through budgeting, individuals influence when, where, how, and for whom the district's resources will be utilized.

A school district's budget process is much like the central nervous system of a higher vertebrate. Although it is not highly visible, it nevertheless is the mechanism for coordinating and controlling most of the organism's functions. A school district's budgetary process is a logical target for efforts to achieve organizational reform.

DEVELOPING A SCHOOL BUDGET

The budgetary process consists of two sets of activities: (1) budget formation and (2) budget administration. Budget formation includes all the activities that determine how a district spends its revenues; budget administration includes those activities needed to ensure that budgetary decisions are actually implemented. Budget administration affects the efficient use of resources only indirectly, by ensuring that monies are spent as planned. Consequently, hopes for improving resource utilization must rest largely on efforts to improve the methods of *formulating* school budgets.

School budget formation means developing a plan for acquiring and allocating a district's financial resources. This plan is summarized in the school district's budget, which must then be approved by the community's elected representatives and filed with the state in accordance with state law.

A casual glance at the precise language and impressive detail of a finished budget creates the impression that public school budgeting is a highly rational process. Budgets typically discuss a community's educational needs and social objectives and assert that designated educational programs will accomplish those objectives in an equitable and efficient manner. However, this process is not nearly so rational as it looks.

In fact, public school budgeting is part and parcel of an often heated political process. The final budget for a large district reflects choices constrained by state law, previous budgets, negotiated agreements, and the political influence of key actors. Those choices may have little to do with the rational analysis of alternative means to accomplish the stated objectives. It is important to recognize the political nature of public school budgeting and to design the decision-making process to fairly represent those with an interest in education, including citizens, administrators, teachers, parents, and students.

KEY ACTORS IN THE BUDGETING PROCESS

The important decisions in public school budgeting are increasingly being made outside classrooms and school buildings. State legislatures and state departments of education currently exercise much influence and control over the school budget process. Through statutes and regulations, they prescribe budgeting procedures, budget calendars, budget forms, accounting procedures, and auditing requirements. Many states also place limitations on district expenditures, revenues, and indebtedness. A large number of states have collective bargaining laws establishing state supervision of collective bargaining. In some states employing extensive education codes (such as California, New York, and Illinois), many of the substantive budgeting decisions are dictated by the state. Often, state regulations establish the amount to be spent on children receiving categorical aid, and many states even specify the number of teachers required for each special education or early childhood education classroom.

At the district level, school district budgets are constructed by a small group of people in the district office. In most districts the superintendent and the business manager prepare the budget. In very large districts, such as New York and Los Angeles, there is usually a fiscal office with dozens of people involved.

In recent years, some of the superintendent's control over budgeting has been constrained by collective bargaining. Under most collective bargaining statutes, decisions affecting wages, hours, and other conditions of employment must be negotiated. The superintendent or a special assistant hired by the school board negotiates in private with union representatives on a wide variety of matters affecting the district's budget. The public, most teachers, and even school board members are absent from these negotiation sessions. Since as much as 80 percent of a district's budget is spent on personnel, the results of such bargaining sessions greatly affect school budgets. While participation in school budgeting was seldom widespread before the advent of collective bargaining, delegation of important budgetary decisions to the bargaining table has even further diluted the ability of principals, teachers, or parents to influence budget decisions.[5]

TRADITIONAL BUDGETING PRACTICES

The budgetary process begins with an estimate of enrollment and revenues for the budgeted year.[6] Enrollments are relatively easy to predict. Estimates

[5] For an analysis of the implications of public sector collective bargaining on the ability of the electorate to control its institutions, see Lawrence C. Pierce, "Teachers' Organizations and Bargaining: Power Imbalance in the Public Sphere," in *Public Testimony on Public Schools,* National Committee for Citizens in Education (Berkeley, Calif.: McCutchan Publishing Corporation, 1975), pp. 122-59.

[6] Techniques for computing enrollments and revenues are explained in Chapter Twelve.

of the number of new children entering kindergarten or the first grade can be derived from census figures on the number of live births five years earlier. The proportion of children who progress from one grade to the next is relatively constant; a district knows, for example, that 95 percent of current fourth graders will enroll in the fifth grade. Adding new entrants to those who remain in the system produces a fairly accurate prediction of enrollment. This estimate is important because a district's enrollment largely determines the amount of money it receives from the state, and in some states, the amount a district is legally permitted to raise locally.

Revenue estimates depend on enrollments, the growth of assessed property valuation in the district, and a variety of assumptions about sources of funds. Federal revenues are difficult to predict because they can be changed so quickly by Congress; however, funds available through the Elementary and Secondary Education Act and the impact aid programs change only slightly from one year to the next. School district revenues received from the state tend to be more predictable than those received from the federal government. Knowledge of a state's financial situation suggests whether state funds will increase and by how much. Local revenues consist primarily of property tax receipts. These depend on state laws governing the taxes of local property, the growth of local property assessments, and the willingness of voters to support education.

Once enrollment and revenue projections are made, department heads and principals are usually asked to submit budget requests according to their particular needs. Generally, however, this "bottom-up" approach is inconsequential. Since a large share of a school district's budget pays salaries, which are usually negotiated at the district level, there simply is not much money left to respond to the particular needs of individual schools.[7] What money is left is usually controlled closely by the superintendent, subject to the requirements of state laws and local school boards. The result is a budgeting process that is highly centralized, with most decisions flowing from the top down.

Resources are usually allocated to schools in accordance with previously established rules or "norms," such as one teacher for every 25 students. Staffing norms might be adjusted for higher grade levels, for larger numbers of non-English speaking students, for handicapped students, or for compensatory education students. The point is that, no matter how sophisticated the norms, instructional personnel are allocated to schools on a purely impersonal basis. Likewise, the number of administrators, clerks, maintenance workers, counselors, and cafeteria employees is determined in the same manner.

A similar procedure is followed in nonpersonnel budget categories. A line-item account is established for each school, with a number of expenditure categories (e.g., instructional supplies, textbooks, supplementary books, transportation, health supplies, telephone, and office supplies). The amount placed in each

---

[7]For a detailed analysis of school district budgeting, see Donald Gerwin, *Budgeting Public Funds* (Madison, Wisc.: The University of Wisconsin Press, 1969).

school's account by the central office is usually a function of enrollment. In some instances, it may be a function of factors other than enrollment—e.g., the number of square feet covered by school and school yard may determine the number of custodians and the amount allocated for maintenance supplies.

Under such centralized budgeting systems, the most crucial decisions involve the design of the norm tables. Once the norms are designated (usually by top-echelon administrators) and subsequently confirmed by the school board, the rest of the budget process becomes almost entirely mechanical. It takes only a clerk to translate a school's projected enrollment into the specified number of teachers, vice-principals, counselors, and custodians.

Once a school's allocations have been determined, there can be little or no flexibility in resource use at that school. It matters little if the principal and his staff would have preferred to have two teacher aides instead of the one new teacher the norm table assigned them because of an enrollment increase, or if they would rather have purchased supplementary books instead of textbooks.

In the best centralized systems, it may be possible to transfer a percentage of funds from one nonpersonnel budget category to another (e.g., from office supplies to instructional supplies). However, it is extremely unlikely that a principal would be permitted to "trade" an allocated vice-principal for three part-time teachers, an office clerk for a noon-duty aide, or a counselor for three teacher aides.

BUDGET ADMINISTRATION[8]

Budget administration is primarily a record-keeping activity designed to ensure that budget programs are implemented. The records deal with financial transactions: from whom and how much money is collected; to whom and for what purpose money is spent; how much money is required to carry out a specific function. Budget administration or accounting is a particular form of record keeping which classifies financial data so as to provide decision makers information for adequate control and planning.

School budgets consist of many accounts. An account is a financial record containing information about a transaction related to expenditures, receipts, assets, fund balances, liabilities, etc. For example, most schools have a textbook account and a salaries account. School districts have used at least three major budget classifications for expenditure accounting. The most widely

[8] For a more detailed account of budget administration in public schools, refer to one of the standard texts on public school financial administration such as: E. M. Foster and H. E. Akerly, *Financial Accounting for Schools,* circular 204, rev's 1948 (Washington, D.C.: Government Printing Office, 1952); P. I. Reason and A. L. White, *Financial Accounting for Local and State School Systems, Standard Receipt and Expenditure Accounts,* Bulletin 1957, USOE, Handbook II (Washington, D.C.: Government Printing Office, 1957); S. J. Knezevich and J. G. Fowlkes, *Business Management of Local School Systems* (New York: Harper & Row, 1960).

used classification of accounts is called line-item or object-of-expenditure budget. This classifies expenditures on the basis of articles or services purchased. A line-item budget may be very short or consist of hundreds of separate entries.[9] Table 11-1 presents a sample line-item budget. The primary purpose of line-item budgets is accurate control over district expenditures. By increasing the amount of detail in the budget the superintendent and school board can greatly reduce the ability of principals and low-level administrators to exercise judgment over the expenditure of school funds. The obvious disadvantage of such a budget is that it reduces an administrator's ability to respond to new situations or to divert funds where they are most needed.

A second classification scheme is called a functional budget. A functional budget reports data on expenditures in terms of the major purposes for which they are made. In 1972 the U.S. Office of Education proposed five principal headings for major expenditure accounts. Table 11-2 illustrates these functional classifications.

The advantage of a functional classification is that it is clearly understandable to the public. It enables citizens to compare the use of funds in one district with another, for example, in terms of the proportion of funds used for administration, instruction, and pupil services. Classification by major functions may not provide school board members with enough information on the effects of educational expenditures, however. Knowing the amount spent on administration may not reveal exactly how school resources are being expended. Consequently, most districts combine functional and object of expenditure classifications in their district budgets.

District functional budgets may also mask the performance of individual schools within a district. To facilitate comparisons, some districts organize the budget by schools or types of schools using a function-object budget. This provides decision makers with a finer breakdown of expenditures along with information on the effects of expenditures on program objectives.

In addition to expenditure accounts, school budgets also reveal the sources of revenue in a set of receipt accounts. Table 11-3 provides an abbreviated set of revenue accounts.

DEFICIENCIES OF CENTRALIZED SCHOOL BUDGETING

Centralized school budgeting emerged for several reasons. Budgeting is a time-consuming and tedious task, and many districts found it easier and less costly to coordinate budget formulation in a single office. Also, state regulations

---

[9]Many accounting schemes are found in public schools. For illustrative purposes we have followed those suggested in National Center for Educational Statistics, *Financial Accounting: Classifications and Standard Terminology for Local and State School Systems, 1973,* State Educational Records and Reports Series, Handbook II, revised (Washington, D.C.: U.S. Government Printing Office, 1973).

TABLE 11-1

Expenditure Classification by Line Item

Account Code	Major Line Item Category
100	*Salaries*
110	Regular Salaries
120	Temporary Salaries
130	Overtime Salaries
200	*Employee Benefits*
300	*Purchase Services*
310	Professional and Technical Services
311	Instructional Services
312	Instructional Programs Improvement Services
313	Pupil Services
.	.
.	.
320	Property Services
330	Transportation Services
340	Communications
350	Advertising
.	.
.	.
400	*Supplies and materials*
410	Supplies
420	Textbooks
430	Library Books
.	.
.	.
500	*Capital outlay*
510	Land
520	Buildings
530	Improvements Other Than Buildings
540	Equipment
550	Vehicles
600	*Other objects*
610	Redemption of Principal
620	Interest
.	.
.	.
700	*Transfers*
710	Fund Modifications
770	Transits
790	Other Transfers

Source: National Center for Education Statistics, *Financial Accounting, Classifications and Standard Terminology for Local and State School Systems, 1973,* State Educational Records and Reports Series, Handbook II, revised (Washington, D.C.: U.S. Government Printing Office, 1973), pp. 23–24.

TABLE 11-2

Expenditure Classification by Function

Account Code	*Major Functional Categories*
1000	*Instruction*
1100	Regular Programs
1110	Elementary Programs
1120	Middle/Junior High Programs
.	.
.	.
1200	Special Programs
1300	Adult/Continuing Education Programs
2000	*Support Services*
2100	Support Services—Pupils
2110	Attendance and Social Work Services
2111	Service Area Direction
2120	Guidance Services
2130	Health Services
.	.
.	.
2200	Support Services—Instructional Staff
2300	Support Services—General Administration
.	.
.	.
3000	*Community services*
3100	Direction of Community Services
3200	Community Recreation Services
.	.
.	.
4000	*Nonprogrammed charges*
4100	Payments to Other Governmental Units
5000	*Debt services*

Source: National Center for Education Statistics, *Financial Accounting, Classifications and Standard Terminology for Local and State School Systems, 1973,* State Educational Records and Reports Service, Handbook II, revised (Washington, D.C.: U.S. Government Printing Office, 1973), pp. 24-27.

usually require a central controller to ensure that funds are spent and audited properly. Furthermore, having a single budget office makes it easier for a school district to deal with outside funding agencies. The federal government, private foundations, state education departments, and the Internal Revenue Service all require a variety of records and forms that can most easily be completed if all budgetary data are compiled by a single office. However, despite the obvious advantages of centralized budgeting, and the impact of external factors that

TABLE 11-3

Revenue Accounts

Account Code	Revenues
100	*Revenue from local sources*
110	Taxes
111	Ad Valorem Taxes Levied by School System
112	Ad Valorem Taxes Levied by Another Governmental Unit
113	Sales and Use Taxes
•	•
•	•
120	Revenue Received from Local Governmental Units other than School Systems
130	Tuition
140	Transportation Fees
150	Earnings on Investments
160	Food Service
170	Pupil Activities
190	Other Revenue from Local Sources
200	*Revenue from intermediate sources*
210	Grants-in-Aid
220	Payments Received in Lieu of Taxes
230	Direct Expenditures for/on Behalf of the Local School System
300	*Revenue from state sources*
310	Grants-in-Aid
311	Unrestricted Grants-in-Aid
312	Restricted Grants-in-Aid
320	Payments Received in Lieu of Taxes
330	Direct Expenditures for/on Behalf of the Local School System
400	*Revenue from federal sources*
410	Grants-in-Aid
411	Unrestricted Grants-in-Aid Received Directly from Federal Government
•	•
•	•
420	Payments Received in Lieu of Taxes

Source: U.S. Office of Education, *Financial Accounting,* State Educational Records and Reports Series, Handbook II, revised (Washington, D.C.: U.S. Government Printing Office, June 1972), pp. 25–27.

require at least some budgeting at the district level, centralized budgeting has a variety of deficiencies.

ASSUMES SUSTAINED GROWTH

From 1940 through 1970, school enrollments and budgets grew at historically unprecedented rates. Perhaps unconsciously, public school officials developed a philosophy of management built on the assumption of sustained growth. As a result, new, emerging problems, were simply dealt with by adding new school programs.[10]

Many school districts today face declining school enrollments and revenue limitations that have made growth-oriented management and budgeting procedures obsolete. New problems now must be solved not by adding new programs, but by redistributing existing resources to meet new requirements. Obviously, school district budgeting must play an important role in such a redistribution. The question is whether traditional school budgeting procedures are appropriate for this task.

Theorists of public budgeting are dubious about this possibility. Wildavsky's studies of the budget process conclude that each year's budget focuses only on the "add on" to the preceding year's budget, or base, which is considered inviolate.[11] Lindblom also argues that incremental budgeting is inevitable but bases his reasoning on the multiplicity of goals—and alternatives for accomplishing them—that make means-ends analysis of the entire budget impossible.[12] The "add-on" portion of the budget can only be determined by the political process. Good policy is whatever analysts and politicians can agree upon. Old programs, once implemented, are very difficult to eliminate because they have ready constituencies to argue for their continuance.

Other research, however, indicates that the budgetary process may not be so incremental as once believed. Natchez and Bupp in analyzing the Atomic Energy Commission's budgets for a 15-year period, found that while the total budget increased gradually, significant changes in program priorities occurred within the budget. These priorities were not set by the national administrators but were established as "the operating levels of federal bureaus—by program directors sensitive to their own clienteles."[13]

---

[10] An analysis of budgeting in the federal government found that budgeting is largely incremental. See Otto A. Davis, M. A. H. Dempster, and Aaron Wildavsky, "A Theory of the Budgeting Process," *American Political Science Review,* 60, No. 3 (September 1966), 529-47.

[11] Aaron Wildavsky, *The Politics of the Budgetary Process* (Boston: Little, Brown and Company, 1964).

[12] Charles E. Lindblom, "The Science of 'Muddling Through,'" *Public Administrative Review,* 19, No. 2 (Spring 1959), 531-38.

[13] Peter B. Natchez and Irwin C. Bupp, "Policy and Priority in the Budgetary Process," *American Political Science Review,* 67, No. 3 (September 1973), 963.

This study and others[14] suggest that budgets can change "from the bottom up" if operating personnel have sufficient discretion over program decisions and have sufficient funds available to respond to changes in client interests. This kind of discretion is not usually available in public school budgeting. Until more choice at the school site is available, school budgeting will remain incremental and will continue to be poorly suited to handle problems of declining enrollment and resource reallocation.

INCREASES EDUCATIONAL INEQUALITIES

One of the major flaws of centralized budgeting is frequently viewed by proponents of such systems as its primary strength. It is mistakenly argued that depersonalized, standardized norm tables eliminate discretion. With allocations based on an abstract set of decision rules, some argue, no element of racial or ethnic bias can seep into budget deliberations to warp resources and services in favor of a privileged or powerful segment of the school population. Under such a supposedly sanitized allocation system, predominantly black, Chicano, or low-income schools should receive the same treatment as schools populated by middle-class white students.

As persuasive as such logic may be, it has been too frequently proven inconsistent with reality. Findings in *Hobson* v. *Hansen* (discussed in Chapter Two) and various school comparability audits provide evidence to the contrary.[15] Intradistrict expenditure disparities are common and exist for many reasons. In a few instances, no doubt, systematic expenditure disparities within school districts have been a consequence of deliberate and malicious discrimination. In a few other instances, intradistrict expenditure differences have proven to be an unanticipated consequence of naive budget policies. For example, a decision to permit small classes for advanced courses in academic high schools at the expense of large classes in general curriculum and vocational high schools favors college-bound students. In such situations the term "institutional racism" appears appropriate.

However, by far the most common explanation of unjustified intradistrict expenditure disparities stems from a source other than prejudice or naiveté; this explanation is related to teacher salaries. It is the privilege of teachers to transfer from one school to another based upon seniority in the system. Teachers frequently perceive their status to be linked tightly to the social status of the students they instruct. Consequently, the path of upward mobility for teachers is from elementary school in low-income or minority-dominated areas to secondary schools on the district periphery, where there are more middle-class, academically oriented white students. As teachers accrue seniority, they sift toward

---

[14] See John Wanat, "Bases of Budgetary Incrementalism," *American Political Science Review*, 68, No. 3 (September 1974), 1221–28.

[15] *Hobson* v. *Hansen*, 327 F.Supp. 844 (DDC 1971).

"desirable" schools, carrying with them the higher salaries they have earned for longevity in the district and additional course credits. The end result of such a migration can be a substantial disparity in instructional expenditures between races or income groups. And this can take place under the mantle of equity and fair play provided by such supposedly neutral abstractions as norm tables.

Even where centralized budgeting procedures lead to relatively equal expenditures among students and schools within a district, they may still impede or deny the essence of equal opportunity. By utilizing abstract allocation formulas, centralized budgeting discourages individual schools from matching their services to the particular mixture of their students' needs. It is quite possible that while one group of students may benefit from a particular mix of classroom teachers, counselors, vice-principals, and office clerks, another group of students might benefit more from fewer counselors and administrators and more teachers, teacher aides, and tutors.

Decisions about the correct mix of services and personnel for any aggregate of students are difficult to make under the umbrella of standardized, district-wide rules. A centrally determined mix will likely be suited to the majority and will probably not acknowledge that minority groups have systematically different educational needs. Without individually tailored mixtures of services and staff, it is difficult to accomplish anything more than superficial dollar equality among schools and students in a district.

This latter assertion is illustrated by the post-*Hobson* v. *Hansen* anecdote of a senior French teacher who was moved from one Washington, D.C. high school to another because her high salary was contributing to an expenditure imbalance. By shifting her to a school with lower per-pupil expenditures, school administrators were attempting to comply with Judge Skelly Wright's decision calling for dollar equality. However, the end effect of the transfer was to deprive one group of students of a French teacher in mid-semester. Moreover, no students at the school to which the teacher was transferred elected to take French; so she was assigned to clerical tasks and hall monitoring.[16]

CONTRIBUTES TO INEFFICIENCIES

Besides failing to assure equality of opportunity, centralized norm-based budgeting may contribute to serious inefficiencies in the operation of schools. This is true for at least four reasons. First, standardized budget allocation procedures inhibit efforts to tailor school services to the idiosyncrasies of individual students or groups of students. Some students may need extra reading or math instruction. Others may need individualized instruction in order to work their

[16] This anecdote was related to the author by an individual closely involved with *Hobson* v. *Hansen*. For a detailed analysis of the district's compliance with Judge Wright's ruling, see D. C. Citizens for Better Education Report, "Equalization," Final Report NIE Grant #NE–G–00–3–0201, June 1975.

way back into the general educational program. Others may work better in large classes, or on their own in a school library. Educational efficiency is increased when instruction is tailored to fit students' needs.

Second, current, centralized budgeting seldom provides incentives for teachers or school administrators to be efficient. Suppose a teacher develops a new career information system that saves the district the cost of several guidance counselors. Under the usual arrangement, neither the teacher nor the school principal receives a salary increase, bonus, or reward. Moreover, in most districts, savings in one budget area cannot be transferred to another area or carried forward into the school's next fiscal year budget. Consequently, there is no financial incentive to introduce new teaching methods or practices. In fact, if the amount saved is taken away from the school, there may be an incentive to maintain current expenditures.

The absence of diversity under centralized budgeting fosters inefficiencies of another sort. Education is, for the most part, an art; there exists very little scientific knowledge of the best way to teach mathematics or to organize a curriculum. In order to create a firmer technical base for schooling, we need to experiment with a variety of teaching methods. Only by encouraging many instructional styles and strategies can we hope to develop more productive means of schooling.

Inefficiency also results from centralized budgeting because crucial actors are for the most part absent from the decision-making process. By preventing school principals, teachers, parents (and, perhaps, students) from influencing the use of their school's resources, school district administrators transmit the implicit message, "You don't count." When such treatment is prolonged, the almost inevitable result is a diminished desire to succeed and a heightened tendency to blame someone else for failure. Under such circumstances, it is easy to understand the contention of New York City principals that they are not mangement personnel and should therefore be permitted to bargain collectively on the side of teachers (although at latest report, they have not offered to remit their salary differential for the same reason). They assert that most important decisions are made "downtown," and a reasonable observer would have to concur.

STIFLES CITIZEN PARTICIPATION

Another flaw in centralized, norm-based budgeting is the difficulty citizens have in influencing the budget process. Many districts appoint lay members to budget committees and hold hearings on budget proposals developed by staff members however, these procedures still allow access to the budget process to only a few nonstaff people.

Principals and teachers have little voice in most budget decisions, yet when citizens and parents are dissatisfied with the education their children are receiving, they are likely to complain to these selfsame individuals. Of course, these complaints have little chance of influencing budgetary decisions made at the district level.

Even if citizens could participate in budgetary decisions, citizen participation in large districts could conceivably be counterproductive. In these districts, with their enormous range of demands, responsiveness would probably result in giving a little to everyone. Arriving at workable compromises under such circumstances would be extremely difficult. Furthermore, citizen participation in large districts is relatively costly in terms of time and effort expended and in relation to the probability of influencing district policy. The larger the district the smaller that chance becomes. This discourages urban residents from taking part in educational decision making, and prompts many, who can afford to do so, to move to the suburbs.

A Solution to School Budgeting Problems

For some school districts, centralized budgeting and management procedures have worked well in the past and still continue to perform adequately the function of allocating resources at the district level. However, for others, particularly those districts faced with declining enrollment and resources, traditional budgeting methods are no longer adequate. Rather than adding programs and spending more money, many districts have been forced to cut programs and budgets. Lacking effective procedures for relating how much is spent on school programs to the effects of those programs, such districts frequently fall back on such norms as "last hired, first fired," or "one counselor for every 250 students."[17]

Many of the programs adopted in the late 1960s to address the special educational needs of handicapped, bilingual, and disadvantaged children have been the first casualties of district fiscal crises. For example, recent financial shortfalls in the Berkeley Unified School District in California—for many years considered a "lighthouse" school district—have led to severe cutbacks in the district's educational program. Over half of the alternative school programs established in the 1960s have been closed, and many minority teachers hired in the early 1970s have been released.[18]

During periods of stable or falling enrollment, school districts need new budgeting and management mechanisms for controlling resource allocation. To cut costs and maintain program quality, districts must develop procedures for comparing the effectiveness of school programs and weeding out those that are least effective. The most difficult problem is deciding who should make the decisions about what should be kept and what should be deleted.

[17] The second norm was promulgated by the American Personnel and Guidance Association and accepted by many districts without evidence of its validity. There are other equally unsubstantiated norms for the number of librarians in a school, the number of administrators relative to teachers, etc.

[18] Ralph Carib, "Berkeley's Big School Crunch," *San Francisco Chronicle,* March 3, 1976, p. 4.

An alternative to centralized school budgeting is delegation of budgeting and management responsibility to the individual school site. Both school site management and vouchers rest on the assumption that public schooling will be improved if consumers are given greater responsibility for deciding what educational services are provided.

Although it would not offer as much freedom of choice as does the voucher system, school site management would offer consumers a greater voice in school affairs.[19] Even if we accept many liberals' scepticism about the responsiveness of the marketplace and the competence of families wisely to choose educational programs under arrangements such as the voucher system, consumers can still be given greater responsibility in education by increasing their participation in educational decisions. When a school's performance declines, school site management would encourage parents to change the program rather than simply withdrawing their children as they would in a voucher system.

School Site Management—A Strategy for Enhancing School Productivity and Responsiveness

School site management is a decision-making arrangement that would substantially increase the ability of parents and school personnel to influence school policies. School site management is not new. It incorporates many proposals for returning some school decisions to the individual school site while leaving others (such as the auditing function) at the central office. School site management is an intermediate solution between centralized school management and educational vouchers. Public provision of education would continue; however, there would be a major shift in the locus of decision-making responsibilities. State education departments, district school boards, district superintendents, and central district staff would lose influence in educational decision making, while principals, teachers, parents, and students would gain influence.

We believe that school site budgeting would solve many of the problems inherent in centralized budgeting, yet before we discuss these solutions we must explain how a school site management system would function.

THE ORGANIZATION OF A SCHOOL SITE MANAGEMENT SYSTEM[20]

THE SCHOOL SITE AS THE BASIC UNIT OF EDUCATIONAL MANAGEMENT

The essence of school site management is a shift of decision-making responsibility from the school district to the individual school. Under current

---

[19] Albert O. Hirschman, *Exit, Voice and Loyalty* (Cambridge, Mass.: Harvard University Press, 1970).

[20] The original discussions of school site management were held among senior staff

state laws, school districts are legally responsible for providing educational services. They are empowered to raise money and are the recipients of state school support funds. School site management would not remove the district's responsibility for providing educational services or its power to raise money or receive state school support funds. In order to provide families greater control over school affairs, however, important aspects of educational decision making would be delegated to the schools.

The reasons for doing this should be clear. The most important contact between school personnel and families takes place not at the district level, but at the school site. Parents and students are more interested in their particular school than in the district, and consequently, they are more likely to become involved at the school site. Furthermore, by dealing with individual school units, the opportunities for parent participation are increased, while the scope of problems considered and the number of people involved at any one meeting are reduced. It is thus easier to respond to parent preferences, and having to compete against fewer participants increases the chance of any one parent to influence school policy. Finally, school site management gives those educational professionals most familiar with a student's problems—the principal and teachers —greater responsibility for the education of children. The educational needs of children within a school and between schools are not always the same. The principal and teachers in a school are in the best position to respond to those differences.

One might reasonably inquire, "Is not what you say of the school even more true of the classroom? Why not employ the classroom as the basic management unit?" In an earlier era we might have agreed. However, today even at the elementary level, many students are in contact with more than one teacher during the course of a school day or week. Team teaching is increasing, as is the use of specialists, which makes it difficult to identify a group of students as the exclusive responsibility of one instructor. Thus, because the classroom is apparently too small and the district too large, the individual school becomes the most reasonable unit for primary managerial functions.

PARENT ADVISORY COUNCILS

In order to amplify parents' "voice" and to compensate for the over-population and resulting depersonalization of school districts, parent advisory councils (PACs) could be established at all school sites in districts with more than 1,000 students.[21] These councils would select and advise school principals,

members of the New York State Education Commission, most notably Charles S. Benson, James W. Guthrie, Will Riggan, Roger Hooker, and Carl Jaffee. These ideas have also received widespread attention when adopted by the Florida state legislature and frequently are referred to as the "Florida Plan."

[21] The combined forces of increased population and vastly reduced numbers of school districts have substantially diluted the representative nature of school boards. The effectiveness of citizens' "voice" has therefore been badly eroded. This phenomenon

approve school site budgets, and participate in negotiations with teachers on details of the school's educational program. The number of PAC members would be proportional to a school's enrollment. Schools of less than 300 students might have a five-member PAC, while those of 900 or more might have 13 members. Regardless of school size, parent advisory councils should not be larger than 13 members.

The manner in which individuals are selected to serve on PACs is crucial. A first requirement might be that only parents of children presently enrolled in the school can serve on the PAC. Citizens without children do have school-related interests; however, they are probably best expressed at the school district level. Since nominations by principals or district school board members would be open to substantial criticism of professional dominance, nonrepresentativeness, and personal favoritism, those eligible to serve might be nominated by a nonpartisan caucus or through a petition process. For example, any parent obtaining signatures from five percent or 50 parents (whichever is least) in the school would be placed in nomination on the ballot.

Members of parent advisory councils would best be selected by an election. Although the electoral process never guarantees "true" representation and is cumbersome and time-consuming, it is better than any other procedure. Nominations by principals or district school board members are open to substantial criticism of professional dominance, non-representativeness, and personal favoritism. An appropriate term of office would be two years, with members permitted to serve no more than two terms. Terms could be staggered so as to provide membership continuity from year-to-year.

Since the principal appears to be the single most important component of a school's success, one of the most important functions of the PAC, not unlike the board of education at the district level, would be to participate in selection of the school's chief executive officer. It is possible under some conditions to have a capable principal and still end up with a "bad" school, but it is extraordinarily rare to find a "good" school with an incompetent principal. Even though there are few incentives for principals to encourage good teaching, they appear to set the tone of a school and to light the spark of excitement that spurs staff members and students to excel.[22] Therefore, if the schools are going to offer programs in keeping with client tastes, local citizens must participate actively in the selection of school principals.

PAC participation in principal selection could be either from the bottom up or by a "trickle down" process. In the "bottom-up" approach, the PAC

---

is explained in greater detail in James W. Guthrie, "Public Control of Public Schools," *Public Affairs Report* 15, No. 3 (Berkeley, Cal.: University of California Institute of Governmental Studies, June, 1974).

[22] The significance of the principal's position is described in Neal Gross and Robert E. Herriott, *Staff Leadership in Public Schools: A Sociological Inquiry* (New York: John Wiley & Sons, 1965), and more recently by Thomas Sowell, "Patterns of Black Excellence," *The Public Interest,* No. 43 (Spring 1976), pp. 26–58.

would interview applicants and recommend a group of three to five acceptable candidates to the district board and administration, who then would make the final choice. In the "trickle down" approach, the central administration or school board would narrow the field to some limited number of acceptable candidates and then permit the school PAC to make the final choice. Whichever approach is pursued, the principal should be on a three-to-five-year contract, with renewal subject to PAC approval.

THE PRINCIPAL AS EDUCATIONAL MANAGER

Under school site management, school principals would supersede district superintendents as the most influential educational managers in American education. A principal would be accountable both to the school district for operating the school within state and district regulations, and to the PAC for tailoring the school's program to the council's policies.

Initially, there would probably be some confusion as to who controls a school. Clear assignment of responsibilities might prove to be the most difficult part of the transition from centralized district management to school site mangement. The principle is clear, however. If the school is the basic unit of educational management and its staff is held accountable for the service provided, then the principal must have adequate authority to make changes according to the desires of parents and the school council.

The principal, as representative of the PAC, would have discretion over three important areas of school management: personnel, budget, and curriculum. The authority to hire personnel is essential if the principal is to be held accountable for the school's performance.[23] The classroom teacher remains the critical link in the education process. Without the ability to hire and assign teachers, the principal would have little control over school performance. The PAC and members of the existing school staff may assist the principal in screening candidates and developing criteria for selecting among qualified applicants, but ultimately, the decision to hire is the principal's.

The principal would also be responsible for preparing the school budget for approval by the school council, and for the establishment of a school curriculum. School site budgeting will be discussed in a subsequent section. Curriculum decisions would involve negotiations between teaching staff, PAC, and principal. Initially, schools would undoubtedly find that state curriculum requirements and pressures from national accreditation and testing organizations

---

[23] For example, in a 1971 study of a large metropolitan school district Kittredge demonstrated that school sites at which the principal makes personnel decisions experienced noticeably less staff turnover, absenteeism, requests for transfer, and formal grievances. Michael H. Kittredge, *Teacher Placement Procedures and Organizational Effectiveness* (unpublished Ph.D. dissertation, School of Education, University of California at Berkeley, 1972).

leave little room for curriculum innovation at the school level.[24] Over time, however, many of the state requirements might be relaxed to allow schools to develop their own educational curricula. Provisions calling for agreement among teachers, PAC, and principal on the curriculum at each school would be part of the district-level contract with teachers' unions or professional organizations. The principal would be held responsible by the PAC for implementing the school curriculum and any changes it deemed necessary.

SCHOOL SITE BUDGETING

School site budgeting would require a two-step budgeting process. First, school districts would allocate funds to schools and develop an accounting procedure to ensure that district funds were properly utilized. District superintendents and school boards would determine the amount of money available for public schools in each district. A total operating budget for the district would be established, then funds would be allocated to each school in unrestricted, lump sums. Each school would be entitled to a specified amount for each enrolled child. The district might want to vary the amount for different age groups, or for handicapped or otherwise disadvantaged children. Nevertheless, once district revenues and enrollments were established, each school's revenues would be computed by multiplying the number of students in the school by the amount available for each category of student.

The second step of the process, budgeting at the school site, would be more complex than at the district level. Two budget formats would be needed to obtain the best use of funds within a school. First, to ensure that funds are spent properly, the school would need a simple line-item or object budget that would indicate how funds received by the school are actually spent. Both state and district regulations presently require such information to protect against the misappropriation of public funds.

More directly usable for school site budgeting is a second format, a work-flow budget that measures how students are progressing through a course or series of courses toward some defined objective.[25] For example, if improving reading skills is the goal, then information should be collected showing each student's progress through the reading curriculum. Work-flow budgets showing the cost of moving students from one level of reading skill to another would enable parents and teachers to decide when and where to spend resources in the reading program. If it is discovered, for example, that 60 percent of each year's reading achievement is lost during summer vacation, the school staff and PAC

---

[24] For a full explanation of the many forces acting to standardize our nation's school curriculum, see Roald F. Campbell and Robert A. Bunnell, eds., *Nationalizing Influences on Secondary Education* (Chicago: University of Chicago Press, 1963).

[25] An attempt to measure progress through a juvenile rehabilitation program was made by Nathan Caplan, "Treatment Intervention and Reciprocal Interaction Effects," *Journal of Social Issues*, 24, No. 1 (1968), 63–88.

may want to reallocate resources to summer reading programs. Work-flow budgets would help build knowledge of educational processes and provide data for more detailed program budgets. Most important, work-flow budgets would enable teachers and parents to assist school principals and PACs in deciding what programs work best and which do not. If program B moves students toward the goal of reading competence at half the cost of program A, then there is a rational basis for selecting program B over A. Until this kind of technical, work-flow information is available, it will be difficult to reallocate resources in a manner that will assure the maintenance of quality education.

THE STATE'S ROLE IN SCHOOL SITE MANAGEMENT

Shifting responsibility for schooling to the school site would not eliminate the state's role in public education. States would continue to provide a substantial portion of public school resources, particularly for districts that lack the ability to finance their schools adequately, and for districts with large numbers of children requiring specialized programs.

In addition to funding, states need to be involved in setting school standards. Public pressure for higher standards in public schools should encourage states to establish minimum standards for schools and develop procedures for ensuring that the standards are met. This probably would require statewide examinations to assess student achievement in at least the areas of reading and mathematics, since, despite the variety of tasks involved in schooling, reading and computing are commonly accepted as minimum skills for every child. (Individuals may disagree on the relative significance of these skills, but it is difficult to identify a rational point of view that holds that they are of no importance.) Consequently, it is highly probable that an annual statewide assessment of children's achievement in these two areas would be publicly acceptable.

There is no need to specify a single best method of establishing a statewide testing scheme. It is not necessary to test every child every year. By selecting a relatively small sample at each grade level from each school, it would be possible to assess the performance of each school. It is important, however, that the sampling population be sufficient to generalize about each grade level at each school.

ANNUAL PERFORMANCE REPORTS

Whereas a statewide testing program is intended to provide the state with an early-warning system regarding its interests in minimum levels of student achievement, an Annual Performance Report would primarily enhance local client interests. This report would probably appear each spring. The principal should be primarily responsible for overseeing its production; however, it should have sections reserved for exclusive use of the parent advisory council, students (above the ninth grade), and staff. The report should be published in the local newspaper, posted prominently in the school, and, most importantly, sent home to the parents or guardian of each student. The report would be the primary printed instrument by which clients could assess the effectiveness of their local school. In addition, these reports would provide sufficient information to permit clients to choose among schools.

Proliferation of reporting forms and data collection efforts has long been a frustrating fact of life in both the private and public sectors. Well designed Annual Performance Reports should help to reduce some of this burden. For the state, federal government, and local school districts, as well as for the individual school site, the Annual Performance Report should be the primary data-compilation instrument. The school district could aggregate information from individual school reports to meet state reporting requirements for school districts.

The contents of an Annual Performance Report includes topical categories and items similar to those illustrated in Table 11-4.

SCHOOL SITE MANAGEMENT AND COLLECTIVE BARGAINING

In most areas of the country, teacher's representatives negotiate with district school boards over items and conditions of employment. Since districts are likely to continue raising money for public schools, teachers will likely insist on negotiating salary schedules and working conditions at the district level.

For school site management to be effective, current collective bargaining practices would have to be modified. Hiring of personnel and grievance hearings would be conducted at the school site, and if seniority rights are agreed upon, they would apply only within a particular school. The most important change from current collective bargaining practices, however, would be the addition of school site bargaining to the agenda of school site planning. Teachers would sit down with the principal and representatives of the parent advisory committee to develop the next year's educational program. Members of the press and public would be permitted to observe those sessions. Final settlement of the district-wide economic agreement would be contingent upon the signing of local school site program contracts.

Bargaining at the school site would enable parents to influence the kind of schooling being offered. If teachers at one school insisted on shorter class periods, parents could indicate their dissatisfaction directly by complaining to the PAC or indirectly by transferring their children to another school. To keep their jobs, teachers would have to be sensitive to parents' concerns. School site agreements on the content of the school program would help bring the public back into public education.

TABLE 11-4

An Elementary School Annual Performance Report
Illustrative Table of Contents

School Information

Name, location, enrollment, age of building, number of classrooms, number of specialized rooms, school site size, state of repair, amount spent on maintenance in the last year and last decade, library volumes, etc.

Staff Information

Number of staff members by category, age, sex, ethnic background, experience, degree levels, proportion of various license classifications, etc.

Student Performance Information

Intellectual performance data: all information on student performance on standardized tests should be reported in terms of state-established minimum standards. Relative performance of different schools in the district should also be provided. Other performance data might include: student turnover rate, absenteeism, library circulation, performance of past students at next level of schooling (junior high, high school, college), etc.

Areas of Strength

Here the school can describe what it considers its unique or noteworthy characteristics. The purpose is to encourage every school to have one or more areas of particular specialization and competence, to espouse a particular educational philosophy, or to employ a distinct methodology or approach. This section would inform parents about the tone or style of the school.

Areas of Improvement

In this section the school would identify five areas for improvement and would outline its plans regarding them. These problem areas might change from year to year or remain the same as the school mounts a long-term improvement project. This section should encourage schools to be self-critical, to establish specific goals, and to report on subsequent progress.

Parent, Teacher, and Student Assessment of School Performance

Responsible parents, teachers, and students should be permitted an uncensored opportunity to assess school performance. This section would permit various school constituencies to express their opinions of school success or failure with respect to such matters as actual instruction, curriculum development, racial relations, drug abuse, student participation in decisionmaking, etc.

Source: *The Fleischmann Report on the Quality, Cost, and Financing of Elementary and Secondary Education in New York State,* Vol. III (New York: The Viking Press, 1973), pp. 58–59.

PARENT CHOICE OF SCHOOL PROGRAM

So far, only elements designed to increase the voice of school site personnel and the public have been discussed. It is entirely possible that teacher and citizen participation at the school site may generate many suggestions but produce few changes. In this case, it is important that parents be free to transfer their children to another school if their complaints are ignored. Allowing choice of schools is likely to make schools more responsive to parent suggestions.[26]

There are several ways of providing parents more choice among school programs. For example, each school could offer several alternative programs— a traditional program, an arts program, a free school program, a career education program, etc. Parents would select a program for their child, and the school would then allocate personnel and other resources to each alternative on the basis of the number of children enrolled.

Parents would be free to send their children to any public school within the district that offers instruction for their child's age group. Many parents would continue to send their children to the neighborhood school, but others would not. It is possible, therefore, that some schools would be oversubscribed while others would have extra room. Districts could handle this problem in several ways. One way would be to provide mobile classrooms, which could be used in the short run to permit expansion of more successful programs. In the long run, new facilities could be built or leased to accommodate the children who transfer.

However, providing extra classrooms may be too expensive, and parents may regard mobile classrooms as inferior. An alternative approach would be to expand the authority of a successful principal to include some functions of a school that does not attract as many students. For example, if school A attracted more students than it could handle, and school B enrolled only one-half as many as it could accommodate, the principal of school A might be asked to manage some instructional areas in school B to accommodate school A's overflow.

Regardless of the institutional arrangements, a number of characteristics must be present in order for competition to be effective.[27] First, parents must

---

[26] This point is clearly stated by Albert Hirschman:

> Similarly, when an organization arouses but ignores voice while it would be responsive to exit, thought must be given both to making exit more easy and attractive by appropriately redesigned institutions and to making the organization more responsive to voice. The approach to the improvement of institutional designs that is advocated here widens the spectrum of policy choices that are usually considered and it avoids the strong opposite biases in favor of either exit or voice which come almost naturally to the economist and political scientist respectively. [*Exit, Voice and Loyalty,* pp. 123–24.]

[27] A more detailed discussion of these characteristics is found in Anthony Downs, "Competition and Community Schools," in *Community Control of Schools,* ed. Henry M. Levin (Washington, D.C.: The Brookings Institution, 1970), pp. 219–49.

be able to evaluate the performance of programs within a school and among various schools. This is not easy in large school districts, since the performance of students on standardized tests is affected by many factors besides the quality of instruction. Nevertheless, the annual performance reports could provide information which, together with the informal information spread by word of mouth, would be adequate to enable most parents to make an intelligent choice of program.

Second, competition among school programs is possible only if there are realistic alternatives for every family. At a minimum, there would have to be open enrollment within districts. But even this may not provide real options unless transportation is available to each school, particularly for children from low-income families. The possibility that some schools will be oversubscribed will also have to be considered.

Third, schools must be free to offer different educational programs. If district regulations force every school to provide similar services, an open enrollment policy will not produce competitive pressures. School principals must be free to hire and fire personnel and to use resources in different ways to promote different educational products. Finally, allocation of school district resources must reflect parents' choices of educational programs. Schools must receive some reward for attracting more students and some penalty for losing students if competition is to work.

Allowing for free choice among school programs makes school site management look much like a voucher plan in which parents are constrained to use publicly operated programs and money is paid directly to the schools. Taken by itself, this element of the school site management plan is not much different from some voucher proposals. The intent of providing free parent choice of school programs, however, is to increase the sensitivity of schools to greater parent participation. School administrators and teachers must know that if they are not responsive to parent concerns, parents have the option of going elsewhere. To use Hirschman's terminology, the exit option is used to strengthen the voice option.[28]

WILL SCHOOL SITE MANAGEMENT WORK?

Most of the elements of school site management—parent advisory councils, school site budgeting, open enrollment—have been tried singly or in combination in a number of school districts. The experience of these districts provides clues to the likely effects of school site management. In school districts that have permitted individual schools to develop alternative educational programs, a variety of programs has emerged. Delegating educational program

[28] Hirschman, *Exit, Voice and Loyalty*, pp. 123-24.

TABLE 11-5

Expenditure Variations Among Elementary Schools
in Newport-Mesa Unified School District
Using School-By-School Budgeting, 1972-1973

Expenditure Category	District-wide Average Expenditure per Pupil	Range of School-By-School Expenditure per Pupil
Field Trips	$1.15	$0.32-$2.58
Textbooks	0.15	0.00- 1.24
Other Books	0.74	0.00- 1.74
Professional Meetings	0.16	0.00- 1.56
Instructional Supplies	13.35	8.25-33.68
Office Supplies	1.00	0.00- 2.59
Health Supplies	0.10	0.00- 0.26
Telephone	1.49	0.90- 2.36
New Equipment	3.02	0.07-11.07

Source: Diana K. Thomason, unpublished paper, University of California, Berkeley, 1977. Berkeley, 1977.

decisions to the school site will almost certainly produce a broader range of educational offerings than under centralized program management.[29]

An analysis of school site budgeting in the Newport-Mesa Unified School District in California is revealing. When provided with discretion over the use of funds, the schools within the district chose to spend their funds in markedly different ways. Table 11-5 shows the school district average and school-by-school expenditure variation for a school district that used lump-sum school site budgeting. Clearly, some schools within the district chose to forego entirely items such as office supplies, new textbooks, and professional meetings in order to concentrate funds on new equipment and instructional supplies.

Similar variations occurred in the use of personnel under lump-sum school budgeting. When permitted, school administrators selected a wide mixture of teachers, aides, and special service personnel such as counselors, reading teachers, part-time tutors, and assistant administrators. Some of this variation may have been the result of differences in pupil characteristics among schools. Of course, if the allocation of school resources were viewed over a longer period, some of the variation might disappear, yet preliminary information and logic both suggest that school site management and budgeting would produce a much greater variety of educational services.

[29] A summary of educational alternatives in public schools is found in Mario D. Fantini, "Alternative Educational Experiences: The Demand for Change," in *Public Testimony on Public Schools,* prepared by the National Committee for Citizens in Education (Berkeley, Calif.: McCutchan Publishing Corporation, 1975), pp. 160-82.

A more difficult question is whether school site management will help districts adjust to a period of declining resources in a manner that is responsive to community preferences. The evidence needed to answer this question is not readily available.

Under centralized management, cutbacks tend to be made first in the capital outlay and maintenance budgets. Next, programs that are only indirectly related to the purpose of schools (such as driver education or arts programs) or programs that serve small segments of the community (such as adult education programs) are cut. As a last resort, teaching staff are released on a "last hired, first fired" basis.[30]

Under school site management, many of the cutbacks would be made at the school site, and each school might cut something different. Capital outlay, maintenance, and unessential programs would probably still be the first casualties. Staff cutbacks, however, might vary considerably among schools. For example, a ghetto school might decide to retain recently hired minority staff members if those teachers' programs were deemed sufficiently important. Of course, some parents might object to such a decision and decide to send their children elsewhere.

The key question is whether the tyranny of the majority at a single school site would produce better public policy than the tyranny of the majority in an entire district. Our guess is that more people would be more satisfied with school-by-school cutbacks than with district-wide cutbacks—both because they would be able to influence those decisions more easily and because cutbacks would be more carefully tailored to the educational preferences of smaller communities.

IMPLEMENTING SCHOOL SITE MANAGEMENT

Implementing a major reform proposal is never easy. Those people who benefit from the existing order will naturally oppose the reform. Those who are likely to benefit from the new arrangement are often disorganized and only half-hearted in their support. Their lack of enthusiasm for change arises partly from their fear of those in power and partly from their unwillingness to believe in anything new until they have actually experienced it.

OPPOSITION TO SCHOOL SITE MANAGEMENT

The political feasibility of school site management is an important question. Opposition to school site management would come from several areas. Many superintendents and central office personnel would oppose decentralization, because it would diminish their role and influence. Frequently, proponents

---

[30] Gerwin, *Budgeting Public Funds*, p. 148.

of administrative decentralization seek to rally support for their proposals by emphasizing the incompetence of district administrators. This strategy both misses the major reason for decentralization and solidifies administrative opposition to the plan.

The purpose of school site management is to encourage greater program flexibility, which is impossible with centralized administration. Furthermore, school site management would not eliminate the need for a central administration. Rather, it would free the central administration to spend more time on those things it does best, such as carrying on financial transactions with external agencies and ensuring that district activities are being performed properly. Many financial, monitoring, auditing, and testing functions would remain the responsibility of the central administration. Most program and personnel planning, however, would be delegated to the school site.

Another likely source of opposition would come from union leaders. In many districts, unions are in the process of establishing relationships with teachers and district management, and they are likely to oppose any reform that complicates their organizational task. They would particularly oppose the delegation of most personnel functions to individual school sites because it would mean dealing individually with many principals, rather than with the school board or its representative. Finally, unions are likely to oppose school site bargaining on program issues. Their task is easier and their position is stronger if they can bargain on all issues with a single board or its representative.

Union opposition might prove fatal to school site management if most teachers were also opposed to the idea. The question of teachers' attitudes is complicated and is likely to vary considerably among districts. Many teachers today are disillusioned because they are often blamed for the failures of public education, at the same time they are increasingly constrained from doing anything to improve it. A key element of school site management is strengthening the role of the teacher in the classroom. If teachers are given greater control in the classroom and more influence over school policy—in selecting a principal and designing a school's curriculum, for instance—they are likely to support school site management, or at least some parts of it. Teacher support is essential for the plan to work; it is also the key to diluting union opposition.

PHASE ONE: DEVELOPING IMPLEMENTATION PLANS

To minimize professional opposition to school site management and to build public confidence in its ability to improve public education, the proposed reforms might be phased in gradually. During the first year emphasis should be on developing a detailed school site management policy that includes goals, objectives, and an implementation strategy. Principals, teachers, students and parents should be encouraged to participate in development of the decentralization plans. Whenever possible, schools should be permitted to experiment with various forms of school government.

More specifically, a number of innovations could be made without major changes in state or district laws and regulations. Parent advisory committees could be established. Alternative election procedures could be tried, and PACs could be given a variety of responsibilities to find out which tasks they are likely to perform most effectively. Principals could gradually be accorded greater control over school curricula and school budgets. As they became experienced in making curriculum and resource decisions, they could be allowed to reallocate surplus funds and hopefully encourage improved program efficiency and productivity.

Districts could also begin experimenting with open enrollment policies to learn how many and what kinds of students change schools. Principals and advisory school councils could prepare performance reports and distribute them throughout the district. Initially, few restrictions or requirements should be placed on the contents of these reports. Experimentation would help identify those elements of the reports that are of interest to the public.

Major emphasis should be given to creating interest in school self-government, to conducting experiments and discussions of alternative arrangements of school government, and to collecting information on the likely consequences of greater parent, principal, and teacher control at the school site.

PHASE TWO: TRAINING SCHOOL PERSONNEL

During the second year, emphasis would be on training of school site personnel. Of primary importance would be the retraining of principals, since the principal's role is crucial to the success of school site governance. The principal must become a strong educational leader, a good manager, and an accomplished public relations expert. These skills are seldom gained through experience as a classroom teacher, nor are they emphasized in most schools of education. Careful thought and much effort would have to be given to the training of school principals.

A considerable amount of staff retraining would also have to be undertaken to prepare teachers for their expanded roles. They would have to become accomplished in curriculum development and program evaluation. The role of teachers would be particularly important in low-income districts, since they would act as liaison personnel in teaching parents how to choose educational programs and participate in the education of their children.

PHASE THREE: ELIMINATING LEGAL BARRIERS

A third phase, which might take as long as two years, would focus on developing the institutional vehicle for carrying out a school site management policy. Initially, state statutes and regulations would have to be reviewed to uncover requirements that are inconsistent with administrative decentralization. For example, under most state laws, school boards are not permitted to delegate responsibilities to school site committees or councils. State budget or finance laws are also likely to prohibit delegation of budgeting responsibilities below the district level. Such laws would have to be changed to permit greater control over educational policy and budgeting at the school site.

State provisions regarding teaching certification, employment, assignment, etc. would also have to be amended to permit the delegation of personnel functions to individual schools. Particularly troublesome would be tenure or fair dismissal laws and collective bargaining laws. For school site management to be effective, principals should have the authority to hire teachers. Regulations giving teachers seniority rights throughout a district would have to be revised. To increase the program flexibility of local school administrators, certification requirements could be relaxed under certain circumstances. There are many persons without teaching credentials—some with Ph.D.'s and some with "real world" experience—who would make outstanding classroom teachers.

In addition to revising state laws, policies would have to be enacted outlining the specific responsibilities of parent advisory councils, principals, and parents. Attention should also be given to the kinds of support each group needs in order to carry out its responsibilities. PACs would be powerless without adequate information on which to base policy recommendations; necessary information could be supplied by individual principals or by a central office responsible for assisting PACs. It might be useful to empower a broad-based committee at each school site to develop a specific implementation plan. This committee, consisting of the principal, teacher representatives, students and parents, would attempt to thrash out the issues that school site management might engender. This activity of constitution building at the school site would also be good training for principals and potential PAC members.

PHASE FOUR: ALLOCATING FUNDS

During the final implementation phase, district funds would be allocated to each school on a lump-sum basis, and program planning, implementation, and evaluation would be carried out at the school site. At this point an open enrollment policy would go into effect, and provisions would have to be made for intradistrict transportation of students.

PROSPECTS FOR SCHOOL SITE MANAGEMENT

Some elements of school site management have been enacted into law in Florida. The concept is also being discussed in some urban districts, such as San Francisco.[31] School site management is a decision-making arrangement that

---

[31] On January 6, 1976, San Francisco School Superintendent Robert F. Alioto proposed an organizational redesign of the district that included a shift from school district to school site management.

I recommend that we move toward a school site management model that values

enables school districts to make hard economic decisions in ways that are responsive to the consumers of public education. It counteracts the trend toward increasing centralization in public education and is therefore consistent with demands for greater citizen participation in public decision making.

In addition, school site management provides a mechanism for making professional educators more accountable for their performance. Accountability would shift from the district level to the school site. If a school failed to meet the expectations of its constituents, parents could ask that the principal be replaced, or they could try to change the school's curriculum and methods of instruction, or failing all else they could send their children to a different school. School site management would provide citizens with a stronger voice and greater choice in public education than they now possess. Both of these abilities would go far toward restoring confidence in public schools.

Summary

This chapter has examined school district management and budgeting procedures, showing how they fail to be responsive to the interests and concerns of school clientele. More specifically, local school management and budgeting are dominated by district superintendents and central office staff. Typically, resources are allocated by norms, which give local schools little flexibility of resource use at the school building or site.

Centralized norm-based budgeting has a number of deficiencies. While it provides a workable basis for allocating resources during periods of economic growth, it does not adequately cope with the hard decisions required when budgets must be trimmed back or cut. Centralized management and budgeting have also had the unintended consequence of discriminating against children in poor central city schools because of the tendency of more experienced and higher paid teachers to transfer to schools in the district's periphery where there are more students from middle-income families.

Besides contributing to inequality, centralized budgeting may encourage serious inefficiencies in the operation of schools. Finally, this kind of system stifles citizen and parent participation, which is critically important in urban achievement.

We propose a major realignment of management responsibility, focusing it at the school site. This arrangement would increase the ability of parents and

---

staff and community involvement and stresses accountability. We must recognize the principal as the instructional leader of the school. We must expand the budgeting and fiscal control at each school site. . . . We must establish at each school site one active advisory committee which includes parents, students, and staff representatives of the school's ethnic population. . . . [Robert F. Alioto, "An Education Redesign for the San Francisco Unified School District," San Francisco, CA January 6, 1976.]

school building personnel to influence school policies. Specifically, we recommend:

1. making the school site the basic unit of educational management.

2. appointing parent advisory councils to assist principals and teachers in managing the local school.

3. making the principal accountable for the development of a school program and the performance of a school's students.

4. allocating centrally raised funds to schools on a "lump-sum" basis.

5. making the state responsible for administering statewide assessments of local school performance.

6. requiring schools to prepare annual performance reports.

7. insisting that issues concerning a school's educational program be negotiated at the school site with maximum citizen participation.

8. giving parents greater choice among local school programs.

These reforms are designed to increase the responsiveness and efficiency of local schools and, in the process, to provide more equal educational opportunity by ensuring more understandable and effective public schools.

12

THE TECHNOLOGY OF SCHOOL FINANCE REFORM

What Kinds of Technologies?

Developing the information needed for making good decisions in the area of school finance reform necessitates the use of technology for data processing and analysis. In the past, unavailability of computers and lack of knowledge have resulted in guesses more often than analysis, and sometimes the result has been disastrous for a formula based on these guesses. Computers are now widely available, and analytic techniques designed for use on computers are a vast improvement over previous techniques. In this chapter we discuss the usefulness and potential application of these techniques.

The technologies needed for school finance reform come under three general headings. The first is computer simulation. This is a technique for testing alternative plans for financing schools and efficiently handling the mass of data required to analyze each plan's effects on each school district in a state. It is a powerful technique, and a complex one.

In the second group are simpler techniques concerned with projection of enrollments, assessed valuations, and school district revenues.

In the third group of techniques are those concerned with the measurement of inequalities in the provision of educational services. Inequalities in school finance and philosophical positions that underlie the plans to eliminate them are discussed in Chapter Two.

Computer Simulations

Although courts may mandate school finance reform and staff experts provide technical advice, legislators must ultimately write the laws that enact the reforms. Legislators frequently have difficulties anticipating the results of their actions in any area of state funding, but the problems in the case of school finance are compounded by the sheer magnitude of the money involved. Schools are the most expensive single item of state and local government, often consuming more than half the total budget. This makes it critical that legislators make decisions in full knowledge of the consequences, both for the multitude of local school districts in the state, and for the state treasury.

There are several reasons legislators have problems getting reliable information to guide their decisions. First, a typical state has from 100 to over 1,000 school districts. Each district has characteristics (number of students, fiscal ability, special needs, etc.) that distinguish it from every other district, and determine the amount of state money to which the district will be entitled. Simply gathering data on all districts can be a massive undertaking. Calculating the effect of a finance plan on each district using desk calculators may take weeks. Trying several alternative plans may be impossible during a legislative session.

Second, legislators may wish to accomplish a variety of objectives in a finance plan—objectives that interact with each other in unforeseen ways. For example, equalization programs in school finance must deal with wealth equalization, need equalization, and cost equalization.[1] Each of these equalization goals can be dealt with in an almost infinite variety of ways. For example, district power equalizing (a wealth equalizing mechanism) is based on a schedule that specifies the revenue amount each district is guaranteed for each tax rate it wishes to levy. This schedule may be a straight line, or it may be bent in various ways. The local portion of this guarantee, the part not contributed by the state, is based on a calculation of local taxes. These may be subject to certain exemptions, or modified to include only taxes on residential property, and based on assessed valuations of either the current year or a previous year. The prediction of how districts will react to the power equalizing schedule can be based on a variety of assumptions about school district behavior. Thus, the number of possibilities for combinations of alternatives within a power equalizing scheme alone is very large. While no one would want to try all possibilities, legislators would certainly want to be informed about a number of viable alternatives. The other two goals of equalization (equalization of needs and costs) will interact with the

---

[1] These three equalization goals are discussed in detail in Chapter Eight.

equalization of fiscal ability in various ways. Thus, there is almost no end to the complexity.

Finally, devising a school finance plan is not just a technical exercise. No solution, no matter how equitable, is successful if it does not meet the test of political feasibility. This necessitates being able to tell every legislator how the proposed plan will affect his or her district. Moreover, legislators must know with reasonable accuracy how much a proposed plan will cost, and attempt to balance this cost against the other demands on a state's resources.

Considering the complexity and the mass of detail involved in an analysis, it is not surprising that most reforms in state school finance are less than thoroughgoing, in fact, make only minor changes in the present method of distributing funds. It is usually possible to calculate rather quickly and easily the financial impact of these minor changes on districts and their cost to the state. Even so, legislators are frequently in for a surprise when a new program is enacted into law.

Because of inadequate knowledge of consequences, legislators frequently pass laws specifying the way in which each district's allowance will be calculated, but subsequently appropriate a sum that is smaller than the totals of these allowances. District claims are then reduced pro rata so as not to exceed the total appropriation. Frequently these reductions may be a third to a half of the total claims. School districts find it difficult to budget rationally when they do not know how much such reductions may be.

Fortunately, there is a technique that greatly increases the amount of accurate information on school finance reform. The technique is computer simulation. The simulation discussed here is a computerized model of the finances of a state and its school districts. The model incorporates data on every school district, and facilitates design of various state school aid alternatives and assessment of results. Because the computer is almost error-free,[2] and because it can perform in minutes calculations that otherwise would take weeks, numerous alternatives can be tested and the most desirable identified. The computer will perform all the necessary calculations, print out results for every school district, and determine the cost to the state of the whole program.

Why hasn't a tool as useful as the computer simulation technique been adopted by many more state departments of education? Probably for several reasons. Most state education departments use computers almost exclusively for routine data processing. They seldom have a programmer on their staff who is capable of building a simulation, and senior people in the department do not understand computers well enough to realize their potential. There may be an even more powerful reason. State departments of education have a tremendous investment in the status quo. Any change in the school finance law portends

---

[2]Unfortunately, the human beings who operate computers are not error-free; but the number of errors that result from a simulation that has been properly constructed and tested are miniscule compared to those that infest hand-calculation methods.

changes in the distribution of funds, retraining of personnel who must calculate and approve the amounts, and new forms to be designed. Thoroughgoing reform entails massive changes that are frightening to some. It is simpler and easier to limit the availability of information and thus restrict the range of reforms to those that are easy to handle administratively.

Similarly an education department may not really want to investigate a large number of reform proposals. In the absence of a simulation, the typical legislature, and usually everyone else, is dependent upon the state department of education to conduct analyses. In Oregon, for example, the legislature was accustomed to proposing a plan in detail and then requesting a cost analysis from the state department of education. The department responded that they would be happy to do so, and would have the answer in three or four weeks. An alternative plan, unless it was almost identical, would require an additional three or four weeks. At this pace, it is clear that the legislature was severely limited in the plans it could seriously pursue.

School finance simulations have been developed in a number of states, but usually by agencies other than the state department of education. In New York, for example, the Bureau of the Budget performs this task. In Florida, it is the Senate Education Committee, and in Oregon the Legislative Revenue office. California may be one of the few states where a joint effort of the state education department and other government branches has been made toward developing a simulation.

THE COMPONENTS OF A SIMULATION

THE INPUT DATA

A school finance simulation has four components. The first is a set of input data on every district in the state. These data are stored in the computer and are used in making calculations. The data normally include the following kinds of information:

1. Enrollment and/or average daily attendance at each school level (kindergarten, elementary, junior high, high school, adult).
2. Enrollment of students in special high-cost classes for the handicapped or in vocational subjects, or estimates of those eligible for such classes.
3. Predictions of enrollment for future years.
4. Data on current year's (or last year's) receipts from each source, for each program.
5. Data on current expenditures by category.
6. Data on assessed valuation, and predictions of future assessed valuations. Data on the ratio of assessed valuation to full valuation.
7. Other data unique to a particular financing program.

The second component of the simulation is a set of decisions that may be made by the simulator (i.e., the person who wishes to simulate a program). The decisions available in the Oregon simulation are shown in Table 12-1.[3] The first decision is the year to be simulated; the second is the weight to give each category of student. Note that in this simulation, elementary students have been weighted 1.00, kindergarten students 0.50, and high school students 1.30. Alternatively, one could choose to have special categorical programs for certain students, allowing a set number of dollars per student (see the set of decisions beginning with D301 in Table 12-1).

Next, one decides what kind of wealth equalization program is desired. This example uses district power equalizing (called local guaranteed yield in this simulation). The minimum required local tax rate is specified as 10 mills, and $760 per student is guaranteed at this rate. For each additional mill up to 16 mills, an additional $40 per student is guaranteed. From 16 mills to 22 mills, an additional $25 per student is guaranteed for each additional mill levied. The district is allowed to tax above 22 mills, but receives no additional state aid for so doing.

Projections are then made of school district behavior under a district power equalizing plan. This simulation allows the exploration of four alternatives: (1) one may specify separate tax rates for elementary, high school, and unified districts, with all districts of the same type levying the same tax rate; (2) one may specify that districts will continue to levy last year's tax rate; (3) one may specify that districts will levy a tax rate that will enable them to maintain the same receipts as last year (the alternative specified here); or (4) one may specify that districts will levy a tax rate halfway between the present rate and the rate required to maintain present receipts. If there is to be a tax rate limit, it may also be specified.

Two types of regional equalization districts were possible in this simulation. One created three regions within the state, specifying an amount per student to be raised by the equalization district. The simulation would automatically calculate the tax rate necessary to raise such an amount within the equalization district, add the tax rate to the rate of each individual district, and add the specified receipts per student to other receipts for the district. Alternatively (or in addition), one could use intermediate education districts (IED's, which were essentially county units) for equalization, either specifying an amount per student to be raised or a tax rate to be levied.

---

[3]More detail on the Oregon school finance simulation, including a complete list of input and output data and a complete flow chart of the simulation, may be found in Lawrence C. Pierce, Walter I. Garms, James W. Guthrie, and Michael W. Kirst, *State School Finance Alternatives* (Eugene, Ore.: Center for Educational Policy and Management, University of Oregon, 1975), chap. 7.

TABLE 12-1

The Oregon School Finance Simulation
Decisions for Simulation Run

Decision No.	Decision Name	Value
D100	Years to be Simulated	1973–74
D101	Kindergarten Cost Factor	0.50
D102	Grades 1–8 Cost Factor	1.00
D103	Grades 9–12 Cost Factor	1.30
D116	Comp Ed Cost Factor (1st 5% of ADM)	0.0
D117	Comp Ed Cost Factor (5%–10% of ADM)	0.0
D118	Comp Ed Cost Factor (Over 10% of ADM)	0.0
D120	Necessary Small School Cost Factor	0.0
D200	Flat Grant Program	No
D202	Amount of Flat Grant ($/ADMW)	0.0
D210	Foundation Program	No
D212	Amount of Foundation ($/ADMW)	0.0
D215	Fndn Reqd Local Effort ($/1000)	0.0
D220	Local Guaranteed Yield (LGY)	Yes
D222	LGY Required Local Effort ($/1000)	10.00
D225	LGY Amt at Reqd Local Effort ($/ADMW)	760.00
D228	LGY Lower Line Rate ($/Mill/ADMW)	40.00
D231	LGY Upper Line Rate ($/Mill/ADMW)	25.00
D234	LGY Kink Point Tax Rate ($/1000)	16.00
D237	LGY Max Allowed Tax Rate ($/1000)	22.00
D238	Dist Allowed to Tax Above LGY Max Rate	Yes
D240	District Response	Mnt Rcpt
D241	Elementary Specified Tax Rate ($/1000)	0.0
D242	High School Specified Tax Rate ($/1000)	0.0
D243	Unified Specified Tax Rate ($/1000)	0.0
D244	% of 73–74 Unrestr Rcpt to be Maintained	100.00
D245	Tax Rate Limit	No
D247	Amt Raised by Eq Dists ($/ADMW)	0.0
D250	Amt Raised by IED Equalizing ($/ADMW)	0.0
D251	IED Equalizing Tax Rate	Specif
D252	IED Eq Rate if Specified ($/$1000)	0.0
D301	Grant for Kindergarten ($/Student)	0.0
D303	Grant for Special Students (% of 73–74)	100.00
D316	Grant for Comp Ed (1st 5% of ADM)	200.00
D317	Grant for Comp Ed (5%–10% of ADM)	400.00
D318	Grant for Comp Ed (Over 10% of ADM)	600.00
D320	Grant for Necessary Small Schools ($/Stud)	0.0
D330	Transportation Present Allotment	No
D331	Transportation Percent of Reimb Costs	75.00
D338	Debt Service Percent of Present Expend	0.0

TABLE 12-1 (Continued)

Decision No.	Decision Name	Value
D340	Basis for District Type Adjustment	Present
D345	TCV Year Used in Equalization Programs	Previous
D350	Non-Residential TCV Locally Taxable	Yes
D351	Non-Residential TCV Taxable by IED	Yes
D360	State Recapture Allowed	No
D361	Districts Held Harmless	No
D362	Cost of Living Adjustment	No
D363	Max % Increase in Tot Rcpts Over 73–74	Not Used
D364	Use Cherry Factor for Portland	No
D400	Districts Printed	Sample
D401	Print Order	County

Source: Lawrence C. Pierce, Walter I. Garms, James W. Guthrie, and Michael W. Kirst, *State School Finance Alternatives* (Eugene, Ore.: Center for Educational Policy and Management,, 1975), p. 42.

A number of other decisions could be made, as can be seen from Table 12-1, but they will not be discussed in detail here. There were also several alternatives for printing the information generated by the simulation. The information could be printed for a sample of districts. This was the alternative chosen here, and involved a selection of 40 school districts chosen to be most useful to legislators and others. It contained all of the cities of any size in Oregon, the home district of each influential legislator, and a sample of other districts, selected to display the diversity of Oregon districts. Alternatively, all 339 districts could be printed, either by county, by category (elementary, high school, or unified), or arranged by size within category.

THE PROGRAM

The third component of a simulation is the computer program, which specifies how the computer is to manipulate the input data and how it is to print the results. Writing such a program is complicated and time consuming. It generally requires collaboration between a person who thoroughly understands school finance and a skilled computer programmer. The school finance expert must understand enough about programming to be able to work effectively with the programmer. Conversely, the programmer must understand school finance sufficiently to comprehend the problems the school finance expert is addressing. The steps (and pitfalls) in writing such a program are roughly as follows:

1. Develop a rough sketch of the kinds of decisions to be made by the simulation. It is desirable to make the program flexible, so that a wide variety of alternatives may be simulated, but alternatives tend to interact with each other,

and these interactions must be specifically accounted for in the program. Thus, the more alternatives included, the more complicated the program, and the more difficult it is to be sure it is giving accurate, unequivocal results. In addition, the more complicated the program, the more costly it is to operate. If a particular factor is of dubious value (e.g., a cost-of-living adjustment), it should be omitted, simplifying the program.

2. Develop a tentative list of the input data required and the output data desired. Steps 1 and 2 should be done by the school finance expert.

3. Determine whether desired input data are available for all school districts. If they are not, determine whether the missing data can be gathered, or whether substitute data can be used. The work of determining which data are available may be performed by clerks, but the school finance expert must finally approve the categories of data to be used. As soon as this is done, the clerical effort of compiling and keypunching data for each district can begin. It is vital that this be done as accurately as possible. When it is done (keypunched and *verified*), the printout should be examined by persons familiar with state school finance for obvious errors. Even so, a few errors probably will not be caught until a later stage (and a few may never be found).

4. Write a generalized flow chart of the program. A flow chart specifies the sequence of operations to be undertaken. It should be written using conventional symbols. An example of a portion of a generalized flow chart appears in Figure 12-1.[4] This critical step should be undertaken jointly by the school finance expert and the programmer, for it constitutes the basic design of the simulation.

5. Based on the generalized flow chart, a detailed flow chart should be written. This will describe actual formulas and other manipulations to be used in the simulation. This step should be the responsibility of the programmer, but with assistance from the school finance expert. The school finance expert subsequently should verify the logic of the flow chart and the computations involved. A portion of a detailed flow chart is shown in Figure 12-2.[5]

6. Write the computer program from the flow chart. If the flow chart has been well done, writing the program should be easy. The program should be written in a common computer language, such as Fortran, so that it will be simple for others to understand and modify. For the same reason, the program should be written in a straightforward fashion, forfeiting efficiency for easily understandable logic. A simulation is of little value if consumers doubt the

[4]The conventional symbols used in flow charts show the type of operation. The order in which the steps are taken is indicated by arrows. A rectangular box indicates that calculations are to take place; a diamond-shaped box indicates a decision. Thus two or more arrows come from such a box. A circular box indicates that the reader should find the circle with the same letter on a later page to continue.

[5]Figure 12-2 is the detailed flow chart that covers the same part of the program indicated by the two boxes at the lower left of Figure 12-1 labelled "Foundation Program?" and "Compute foundation amounts."

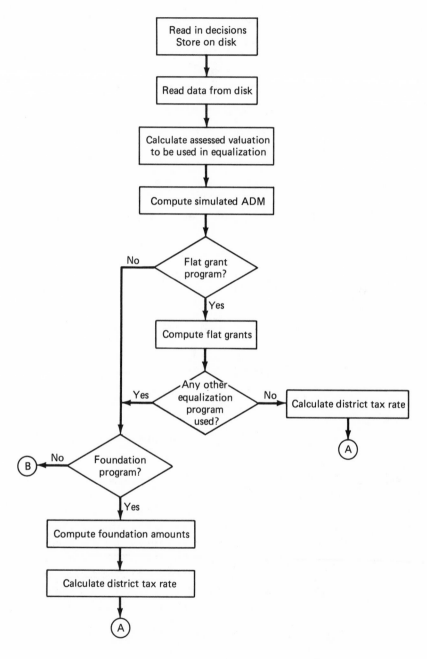

FIG. 12-1. Generalized Flow Chart (Partial) of a Simulation

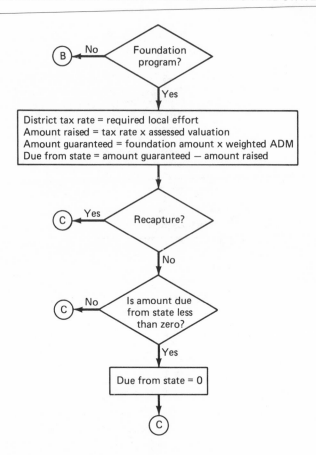

FIG. 12-2. Detailed Flow Chart (Partial) of a Simulation

results, and so the logic of the program should be evident. It is also vitally necessary to document the program thoroughly by means of a precise written description that will supplement the generalized and detailed flow chart. This will clarify the logic of the program and synchronize the program with the flow charts. If the flow charts have been carefully constructed, the remaining documentation is easy. However, this is an important step: *Without documentation the logic of a program is quickly forgotten,* even by the programmer who wrote it. Other programmers encounter difficulty in understanding it. Despite the importance of documentation, most programmers find the task boring, and one must be very insistent that they do it.

7. "Debugging" is a term used by programmers to refer to the identification and elimination of program errors. There are two steps to debugging. The first involves correcting any mistakes in syntax that prevent the program from running or that give meaningless results instead of answers. This is the easier part of debugging, and is done by the programmer.

8. The second step in debugging is uncovering errors in logic. This will be primarily the job of the school finance expert who should examine computer runs that display the results of various alternatives and hand calculate the results for a few districts to ensure that the program is providing expected answers. Finding errors in the logic of a program is extremely difficult, partly because some interactions are not self-evident. They may become evident only when a particular set of decisions is specified. The combinations of possible decisions are large; thus it is necessary to be imaginative in testing the program for logical errors.

9. It is essential that the program be able to simulate the present system accurately. The reason is political as well as technical. If the program will not simulate the present system, legislators and others will have little confidence in its ability to simulate alternative systems. The state department of education will insist that the simulation be tested on the present system. In addition, simulating the present system will reveal many kinds of special situations that the simulation will have to be programmed to handle. It is primarily because of such special situations that a general school finance simulation would be a very complex one. The Educational Policy Research Institute of Educational Testing Service has developed such simulation. However, its complexity makes it questionable whether it can be operated and revised by state personnel after the specialists have left. The authors prefer the development of a simulation for the individual state, which can therefore be substantially less complex.

THE OUTPUT DATA

The last component of a simulation is the output data. These data are calculated from the input data and the set of decisions, and constitute the information desired from the simulation. The output data typically include the following:

1. Estimates of school district revenues in future years from each major source.
2. Estimates for future years of number of pupils in each handicapped or vocational category.
3. Estimates of total cost to the state of equalization programs and categorical programs.
4. Estimates of cost to the state of save-harmless programs, or of foregoing recapture on equalization programs.
5. Estimates of future assessed valuation per student.

Table 12-2 displays a list of approximately one-third of the input and output data available for the Oregon simulation.[6] Of course, not all these data need be

---

[6] In this table, ADMW means weighted average daily membership. Each array contains data on the particular item for each of the 339 school districts in Oregon. The arrays that start with a B are input arrays; those starting with C are ouput arrays calculated by the program.

TABLE 12-2 Partial List of Input and Output Data for Simulation

Array Name			
Total	Per ADM	Per ADMW	Description
B001			District Number
B005			Kindergarten ADM, 1972–73
B006			1–8 ADM, 1972–73
B007			9–12 ADM, 1972–73
B008			Kindergarten ADM, 1973–74
B009			1–8 ADM, 1973–74
(similarly through 1978–79)			
C011			Kindergarten ADM, simulated
C012			1–8 ADM, simulated
C013			9–12 ADM, simulated
C025			Compensatory education students ADM, simulated
C030			Career education students ADM, simulated
C035			Small school ADM, simulated
C400			Total ADM, simulated
C402			Total ADMW, simulated
B047	C090	C093	Assessed valuation, 1972–73
B052	C072	C082	Assessed valuation, 1973–74
(similarly through 1978–79)			
C041	C042	C043	Adjusted assessed valuation, previous year
C044	C045	C046	Adjusted assessed valuation, present year
C048	C091	C094	Previous year residential assessed valuation
B060			District operating levy rate, 1973–74
B064			Bond levy rate, 1973–74
C910			Total operating tax rate, simulated
C911			Total operating tax rate, difference from 1973–74
C403	C404	C405	Total federal receipts, 1973–74
B100	C408	C409	Title I receipts, 1973–74
B101	C414	C415	Impact aid receipts, 1973–74
B103	C424	C425	Other federal receipts, 1973–74
(similarly for 17 other categories of receipts)			
B150	C520	C521	Transportation reimbursable costs, 1973–74
B151			Number transported daily, 1973–74
B170	C624	C625	Debt service interest, 1973–74
B171	C628	C629	Debt service principal payments, 1973–74
B180			Cost of living index
C700	C701	C702	Flat grant receipts, simulated
C710	C711	C712	Foundation equalization receipts, simulated
C720	C720	C722	Guaranteed yield receipts, simulated
C726	C727	C728	Cost of living adjustment receipts, simulated
C730	C731	C732	Total state general purpose receipts, simulated
(similarly for simulated state special purpose receipts, federal receipts, intermediate receipts, and local receipts)			
C900	C901	C902	Cost of recapture negation, simulated
C903	C904	C905	Cost of save harmless provision, simulated
C906	C907	C908	Saving to state from phase-in, simulated

Source: Lawrence C. Pierce, Walter I. Garms, James W. Guthrie, and Michael W. Kirst, *State School Finance Alternatives* (Eugene, Ore.: Center for Educational Policy and Management, 1975), pp. 129–30.

printed on any one simulation run. Rather, desired items from among the input or output data can be printed, at the choice of the simulator. Table 12-3 illustrates for a few districts how the output data are printed. In addition to printing these data, up to eight columns to a page, the simulation automatically calculates the statistical data shown in Table 12-4 for each information item.

Forecasting Techniques for School Administrators

PROJECTING ENROLLMENTS

It is important, if schools are to be at all efficient in their operation, that they anticipate the budget consequences of current expenditure policies, and compare these consequences with anticipated future revenues. It seems prudent for school districts to project future revenues and expenditures for at least five years. Businesses with much more uncertain income and expenditures routinely do so. However, few school districts do more than they are mandated—i.e., to prepare a budget for the coming fiscal year. For example, the San Francisco Public Schools Commission, a citizen group appointed in 1975 to examine the operation of that city's schools, found that San Francisco had never projected revenues, or even enrollments, for more than one year in advance. The reason given was the uncertainties involved, although these uncertainties probably amounted to only a small percentage of the total budget.

The technology for projecting revenue is straightforward, and there is no reason for not doing it for several years in advance. Much of the revenue received from the state is received on a per student basis, and this makes a projection of enrollment vital.[7] Both local school districts and the state need this information. The state must know how many students there will be within its jurisdiction as an aid to projecting revenue demands. The computer programmer must, of course, have a projection of enrollment for each school district in the state in order to anticipate the consequences of alternative school finance schemes for more than the coming year.

There are three commonly used methods of projecting enrollments. The first is to plot past enrollments on a graph, draw a rough curve through the dots, and extend the curve. This rough-and-ready method is insufficiently exact for most purposes and will not be further discussed. The second method is "cohort survival," and the third is "regression line prediction."[8]

---

[7]One may, of course, wish instead to project average daily attendance or average daily membership. The procedure is identical.

[8]For a detailed description of calculations using these methods, see Guilbert C. Hentschke, *Management Operations in Education* (Berkeley, Cal.: McCutchan Publishing Corporation, 1975), chap. 14.

TABLE 12-3

Results of Total Tax Effort Equalization Plan for Selected Oregon School Districts

School District Name	Present Year Adj TCV per ADMW	Weighted ADM Simulated	Tot Oper Tax Rate Sim	Oper Tax Rate Dif	Total State Rept Sim per ADMW	Tot Receipts Simulated per ADMW
Plush No. 18	482994.41	8.05	4.03	-0.99	86.96	2825.84
Olex No. 11	183985.90	39.22	9.74	-1.90	253.99	1839.64
McKenzie No. 68	171386.42	481.05	9.97	-4.98	173.46	1973.46
Sherman UH No. 1	108781.04	231.40	6.28	1.05	120.91	1833.63
Central Linn No. 552	92260.55	1085.50	13.06	-1.03	91.32	1418.07
Harper No. 66	69795.57	110.50	15.75	-1.16	142.96	1274.17
Portland No. 1J	67790.33	70290.56	14.15	0.50	200.66	1318.53
Reedsport No. 105	67098.49	1691.90	12.42	-0.07	187.97	1244.10
Bend No. 1	51026.99	6052.00	11.60	-3.42	419.87	1200.27
Parkrose No. 3	50635.40	5745.77	12.49	-2.43	436.18	1160.80
Klamath Falls No. 1	47821.37	2125.00	10.26	1.67	103.33	1250.04
Beaverton No. 48J	47375.79	21896.59	15.84	-3.10	396.48	1273.49
Corvallis No. 509J	45175.89	8098.09	18.57	-2.05	446.88	1531.29
Eugene No. 4J	44446.17	22260.29	15.16	-4.03	450.12	1270.36
Lake Oswego No. 7J	43765.06	7066.59	13.24	-3.96	444.12	1368.60
Salem No. 24J	43066.86	24494.19	12.22	-4.70	459.29	1232.47
Hood River No. 1	42828.28	3465.07	14.34	-3.83	427.35	1416.46
Burns UH No. 2	42114.67	653.90	10.96	4.06	42.71	1359.73
Medford No. 549	41992.99	10882.59	10.71	-4.55	477.41	1017.98
Oregon City No. 62	41538.87	6538.50	8.37	-5.81	576.57	1026.58
Pendleton No. 16R	41392.41	4006.92	14.08	-4.37	436.07	1103.48

TABLE 12-3 (continued)

School District Name	Present Year Adj TCV per ADMW	Weighted ADM Simulated	Tot Oper Tax Rate Sim	Oper Tax Rate Dif	Total State Rcpt Sim per ADMW	Tot Receipts Simulated per ADMW
Coos Bay No. 9	40373.96	6584.40	14.14	-5.08	541.47	1207.03
Springfield No. 19	39700.19	10889.84	14.05	-4.41	519.94	1232.33
Astoria No. 1	39190.44	2220.00	13.32	0.36	500.02	1438.44
Ashland No. 5	38423.11	3235.00	11.61	-4.82	527.12	1138.14
Falls City No. 57	38109.75	218.00	6.84	-7.29	748.99	1380.86
Baker No. 5J	37152.90	3086.30	7.79	-2.98	508.96	1059.18
North Bend No. 13	36728.62	3751.30	12.32	-5.90	625.88	1226.76
Redmond No. 2J	36175.75	3380.60	12.42	-5.50	587.87	1246.63
Gresham No. 4	35476.60	3400.00	14.75	3.55	281.67	1283.21
Ninety-one No. 91	32226.50	400.00	6.31	-0.47	509.66	1058.38
Creswell No. 40	30679.12	1092.40	9.94	-4.78	679.06	1170.81
Hermiston No. 8	26479.96	2790.80	12.54	-4.02	710.60	1167.14
Scio No. 95C	25369.02	923.10	7.50	-2.29	662.45	1000.31
Reedville No. 29	24810.24	875.00	8.98	1.20	391.55	1029.89
South Umpqua No. 19	24504.82	2554.00	6.26	-2.32	662.14	1139.52
Oak Grove No. 4	23904.33	200.00	12.69	3.54	304.34	1082.86
Cascade UH No. 5	23627.67	1330.00	13.51	4.22	484.81	1255.75
State Total or Mean	47621.84	516233.45			396.33	1239.17

Source: Lawrence C. Pierce, Walter I. Garms, James W. Guthrie and Michael W. Kirst, *State School Finance Alternatives* (Eugene, Ore.: Center for Educational Policy and Management, 1975), p. 48.

TABLE 12-4

School Finance Statistical Summary

Variables	Range	District	Value
Present Year	High:	Brothers No. 15	537760.75
Adj TCV per ADMW	90th %tile:	Helix No. 1R	132135.50
	80th %tile:	Irish Bend No. 24	88677.50
	Median:	North Douglas No. 22	43991.03
	20th %tile:	Sandy No. 46	32054.02
	10th %tile:	Orient No. 6J	27907.15
	Low:	Knox Butte No. 19	16119.33
Weighted ADM	High:	Portland No. 1J	70290.50
Simulated	90th %tile:	Gresham No. 4	3400.00
	80th %tile:	Reedsport No. 105	1691.90
	Median:	Carlton No. 11	335.00
	20th %tile:	Pratum No. 50	81.40
	10th %tile:	Arock No. 81	38.40
	Low:	Flora No. 32	4.92
Tot Oper Tax	High:	Umapine No. 13R	23.71
Rate Sim	90th %tile:	Tillamook No. 9	15.43
	80th %tile:	Lebanon No. 16C	13.67
	Median:	Union No. 5	10.15
	20th %tile:	Lacomb No. 73	7.39
	10th %tile:	North Plains No. 70	6.18
	Low:	Sutherlin No. 130	1.55
Oper Tax	High:	Troy No. 54	12.92
Rate Dif	90th %tile:	Denny No. 78	3.21
	80th %tile:	Hillsboro UH No. 3JT	2.01
	Median:	North Powder No. 8J	−0.62
	20th %tile:	Crook County Unit	−4.27
	10th %tile:	Redmond No. 2J	−5.50
	Low:	Gaston No. 511J	−12.39
Total State	High:	Gaston No. 511J	769.24
Rcpt Sim per ADMW	90th %tile:	Crane UH No. 1J	613.04
	80th %tile:	Ashland No. 5	527.12
	Median:	Molalla No. 35	325.99
	20th %tile:	Paisley No. 11	102.57
	10th %tile:	Three Lynx No. 123	68.96
	Low:	Oakville No. 36	4.45
Tot Receipts	High:	Pistol River No. 16	5145.88
Simulated per ADMW	90th %tile:	Detroit No. 123J	1939.28
	80th %tile:	Condon No. 25J	1639.11
	Median:	Lakeview No. 7	1234.17
	20th %tile:	Scotts Mills No. 73J	1052.24
	10th %tile:	North Howell No. 51	993.82
	Low:	Central Howell 540C	691.21

Source: Lawrence C. Pierce, Walter I. Garms, James W. Guthrie, and Michael W. Kirst, *State School Finance Alternatives* Volume II (Salem, Ore.: Legislative Revenue Office, Oregon Legislature, February, 1975), p. 57.

THE COHORT SURVIVAL METHOD

The cohort survival technique predicts enrollments grade by grade. For example, the enrollment in grade 5 for the coming year is found by multiplying the enrollment in grade 4 this year by the historical percentage survival of fourth graders entering fifth grade. Table 12-5 provides an example. The survival rate for Year 2 is the ratio of fifth grade students in Year 2 to fourth grade students in Year 1. Similarly, the survival ratio of .96 in Year 3 is the ratio of 125 to 130. In other words, the majority of fifth grade students this year were in grade four the previous year. Thus, we use the ratio of one to the other as a basis for prediction. The survival ratio of .953 for Year 6 is the mean of the survival ratios for the four previous years and is used as the basis for prediction from this point foward. Enrollments shown for Years 1 to 5 are actual figures; enrollment (in italics) for Year 6 is predicted from actual grade 4 enrollment in Year 5 by multiplying that number by .953. Predicted enrollment in Grade 5 for Year 7 would be found by multiplying Grade 4 enrollment in Year 6 by .953. Of course, one would first have to predict Grade 4 enrollment in Year 6 from Grade 3 enrollment in Year 5 by this same process.

It should be obvious that some method other than cohort survival must be used to obtain estimated enrollments for the lowest grade. These can be obtained by various methods. A census of preschool children in the district may be the most accurate method. Alternatively, one may be able to obtain records of the number of live births to residents of the school district five years previous to kindergarten enrollment. Lacking both of these, one can make estimates based on the amount of residential construction in the district or similar indicators. If the jurisdiction is a high school district, cohort survival projections of enrollments can be constructed in each of the sending elementary school districts as a basis for projecting freshmen enrollments. Since projections are seldom made for more than five years in advance, they would be based entirely on children already in school. In any case, a major advantage of the cohort survival method is that it permits the inclusion of demographic data. In addition, the method of projection allows for the possibility that enrollments will expand and then contract, or vice versa. Regression line projection always shows a steady increase or decrease.

TABLE 12-5

Sample of a Cohort Survival Projection

Year	1	2	3	4	5	6
Grade 4 Enrollment	120	130	145	135	130	
Grade 5 Enrollment	110	118	125	135	127	*124*
Survival Ratio		.98	.96	.93	.94	*.953*

TABLE 12-6

Student Survival Ratios in San Francisco

Grade	Ratio	Grade	Ratio	Grade	Ratio
1	.90	5	.95	9	1.01
2	.91	6	1.00	10	1.09
3	.94	7	1.06	11	.89
4	.96	8	.93	12	.78

Source: Walter I. Garms, Revenue Projections, 1975–76 to 1979–80 for the San Francisco Unified School District (unpublished, July, 1975), Appendix, p. 12.

The cohort survival method has been criticized for focusing its entire attention on those who are already in public schools in the district, but that is not so. Survival ratios are affected by students who leave or enter the community, who drop out of school, or who transfer into the public schools from private schools. For example, Table 12-6 shows the survival ratios in the mid-1970s in San Francisco. Note that in the seventh and tenth grades survival ratios were substantially greater than 1. This is because many children transfer from parochial elementary schools to public junior high and high schools at Grades 7 and 10. Note also the marked decline of survival ratios in the eleventh and twelfth grades, as students drop out of high school.

REGRESSION LINE METHOD

The other commonly used method is "regression line projection." This technique assumes that at each grade level (or group of grades) the change in enrollments from year to year consists of a constant trend with random variations superimposed on it. One establishes the trend and eliminates the effect of the random variations by the statistical technique known as regression, which consists of drawing a "line of best fit" through the data points. An example is given in Figure 12-3 where the dots represent actual enrollments for Years 1 to 5, the line is the line of best fit, and the circles indicate the projected enrollments for Years 6 through 10.

This method of projection has some advantages. No demographic data are used, since even for Grade 1, projections are made from past data for Grade 1. Also, if data are only available for groups of grades (such as 1-6, 7-9, and 10-12), one can still use this method quite satisfactorily. However, there are drawbacks. It has already been mentioned that the regression method always projects a steady increase or decrease in enrollment, even in a period when enrollment is peaking and then declining. It is not as satisfying theoretically to assume a steady trend in enrollments by grade level as to think that there is a relationship between fourth grade enrollments this year and fifth grade enrollments next year.

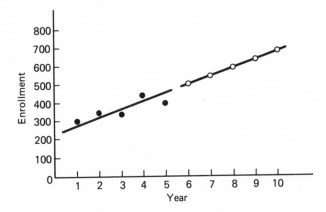

FIG. 12-3. Graph of a Regression Line Projection

If enrollments are being computed for a single school district by either of these techniques, a desk calculator is all that is necessary, but for state purposes, covering every district, the advantages of a computer are obvious. It will accept enrollment and demographic data for each district and automatically compute and print the enrollment projections for each district. At the same time, it can automatically accumulate totals for the state by grade level and for all grades. Fortunately, the mathematics involved in either of the projection methods are simple, and any competent programmer should be able to develop an appropriate program.

PROJECTING ASSESSED VALUATIONS

THE INDIVIDUAL SCHOOL DISTRICT

For an individual school district, projecting assessed valuation is an important operation. This is particularly true in those states where district property tax revenue is limited to a specified maximum tax rate.

An individual school district may project assessed valuation by graphing the assessed valuations for the past several years (five is probably sufficient), drawing a smooth curve that appears to fit the data well, and then extending the curve for as many years as desired. Projecting for more than five years is probably of little value. Alternatively, one may use a regression method, of which more will be said later. An individual district can usually improve on these methods by investigating details. The assessor is a source of valuable information. Because assessors may have reasons for not divulging all they know, however, it is well to check their information through other sources. These are the kinds of information that can be of help in making a projection of assessed valuation more precise:

Is the assessor, voluntarily or under court or legislative mandate, changing the ratio of assessed value to full value? If the ratio is increasing, and if the tax rate limit of the school district is based on assessed value, this may mean substantial additional revenue available to the district.

Is the assessor engaged in a reassessment of the district's real property? A wholesale reassessment, particularly following a long period when there were no reassessments, may result in a large increase in assessed valuation.

Does the assessor make a practice of revaluing property regularly, increasing all or most assessments yearly? If so, assessed valuation increases will come from all property. A more frequent practice is to revalue property only when it is sold. Under these conditions some property will not have been revalued for many years. A few assessors never revalue; assessed valuations change only when new construction takes place.

How many new homes are being built? This information, along with information on the average ratio of assessed valuation to sales price for new homes, provides a reasonable estimate of additions to residential assessed valuation.

What new industry is developing in the community? This is frequently a difficult dimension to estimate. Assessed valuation is frequently negotiated between the assessor and the industry, and actual cost of construction may be a closely guarded industrial secret. Assessed valuation of industry is typically a larger fraction of true value than that of residences, whose owners vote for the assessor—owners of industry are frequently absentee. Regardless of the particular circumstances, an industry can have a major impact on the assessed valuation of a school district, so its effect must be estimated.

Is there a new power plant or other utility being constructed? A power plant can be a major asset to a school district. Its value is high, but it takes few employees to operate, and brings few new school children into the community. Utilities are frequently assessed by a state agency rather than by the local assessor, and it may be possible to obtain the best assessment figure from the state.

REGRESSION LINE PROJECTION

The kind of detailed investigation of assessed valuation suggested here for a single school district is too time consuming for projections of assessed valuation of all school districts in a state. For this, we revert to regression line prediction, which operates on essentially the same principle as the technique for enrollment projection. However, there are three modifications worthy of mention. One is that many districts undergo a major reassessment every few years. A sudden jump in assessed valuation will tilt the regression line upward more than is warranted. A solution is to adjust data for years prior to the reassessment upward, on a basis proportional to the new valuation, before calculating the regression line.

The second modification concerns the fact that the regression line, although it has an upward trend, may lie below the most recent data point. The result is a projection that is initially lower than the present year and then begins an upward trend. The solution is to establish a regression line with the same slope as the true regression line, but which runs through the data point for the most recent year.

A third modification compares the total projected assessed valuation for the state based on individual district data with projections based on statewide data. Because of the level of aggregation, statewide data are probably more accurate. It is appropriate to multiply projected assessed valuations for each district by a factor that is the ratio of the total from statewide data to the total from district data. This will not improve the presumed accuracy of individual district data, but the results of using these data in securing statewide total costs for a projected finance plan should be more accurate.

As with enrollment projections, use of a computer for projecting assessed valuation for all districts in the state is highly recommended. Such a program automatically incorporates all modifications suggested above and prints an adjusted estimate of assessed valuation for each district for each year. As an additional help, the computer can be programmed to print assessed valuations in the form of bar charts, printing the actual and projected valuations for a particular district for all the years for which there are data or projections. This makes it easy to verify results and modify estimates in light of special situations. The same kind of bar chart can also be printed for enrollment projections.

PROJECTING SCHOOL DISTRICT REVENUES

Once projections of enrollment and assessed valuation are made, revenue estimates can be made, based on reasonable assumptions and personal judgment.

FEDERAL REVENUES

Federal revenues are difficult to project. Congress frequently changes laws, and a local school district's eligibility is subject to complicated and changing criteria. Most federal money is categorical, intended for specific programs. It might be assumed that if federal funding is not forthcoming, a district would simply withdraw the special programs. But programs begun as "special" have a way of becoming part of a district's general offering. Thus it becomes all the more important to estimate federal funds as accurately as possible. It is not appropriate, as some districts have done, to estimate federal receipts at zero, with the implicit assumption that all federally funded programs will be eliminated if the funds are not received. Federal funds can be put into categories and estimated separately.

ESEA Title I funds are monies for compensatory education and constitute the largest single federal allocation. Most school districts receive some. Since allocation is based on a dollar amount per eligible child, the first step is to project the number of eligible pupils based on the trend of past eligible children as a percentage of total enrollment. Recent allocations per eligible child can then be multiplied by these estimates to provide total dollar estimates.

Public Law 874 money is the only category of federal general aid money granted to school districts. This "impact aid" has been discussed in Chapter Seven. Although impact aid is rather controversial, districts should probably estimate receipt of impact aid unless the law is formally repealed.

The formal allocation of money under PL 874 is made based on the number of children of parents who either live *or* work on federal land, plus the number of children from parents who both live *and* work on federal land, weighted twice as heavily. Most administrators project a continuation of past trends in PL 874 receipts per student unless they know of changes in federal activity in the district.

Categorical program money (there may be over 100 separate grants in a large district) can be lumped into three groups:

1. Programs for which funds have been appropriated and for which funding can be reasonably anticipated.
2. Programs for which the district has applied for funding but which have not yet been approved.
3. Programs for which the district will apply for funding if pending legislation is approved.

One can then examine past receipts as a percentage of funds applied for in each of these groups, and use this as a basis for estimating future receipts. A recent revenue estimate for the San Francisco Unified School District used 100%, 67%, and 20% respectively, as the percentage of money applied for that the district could expect to receive in each group.

STATE REVENUES

State contributions to a district consist of general aid, major categorical aids, and minor categorical aids. General aid usually takes the form of flat grants or equalizing funds under a foundation or power equalizing program. Knowledge of the present law, plus projections of enrollment and assessed valuation, should enable one to predict general aid with fair accuracy. If substantial changes in the law are considered likely, an alternate estimate should be made based on the provisions of these amendments.

Major categorical aids generally consist of aid for transportation, for the mentally retarded and physically handicapped, and for construction. Each of these categories has its rules for determining district eligibility for compensation, and these do not normally change drastically from one year to the next. Thus, estimates of receipts from these categories can be made by projecting past trends on a per pupil basis.

Minor categorical aids consist of money for special programs similar to those for which federal funds are provided. In some states, the application process for state and federal monies is consolidated. The state programs, like the federal ones, can be divided into three groups (funding approved, funding requested but not yet approved, funding to be requested if pending legislation passes), and receipts from each group separately estimated.

INTERMEDIATE REVENUES

While intermediate revenues are minor or nonexistent in many states, in others they are substantial. Where they are substantial they frequently serve an equalizing function, and this, of course, must be taken into account in any calculations. Where they are not intended for equalization the best method is simply to project past trends on either a total basis or a per pupil basis, whichever seems more appropriate.

LOCAL REVENUES

Local funds consist mainly of tax revenues. In states where there is a tax rate limit, the maximum potential local taxes available (or those available without a vote) can be found by multiplying maximum tax rate authorized by assessed valuation. In states where there is an expenditure limitation, one must estimate the future increase in the expenditure limitation per child, multiply by projected enrollment to obtain projected total expenditures, and then subtract income from other sources. The remainder is to be raised from local taxes, and the required tax rate can be found by dividing this by the assessed valuation. In states where the budget or tax rate is subject to an annual public vote, the best projection procedure is probably to use past tax rates approved, multiplied by projected assessed valuation.

A NOTE ON EXTRAPOLATION

A precautionary note should be sounded about the dangers of extrapolation compared with interpolation. Interpolation is the act of estimating a data point when there are one or more known data points on either side of it. The existence of these data points form natural bounds that limit the inherent inaccuracy of an estimate. Not so with extrapolation, which consists of extending a series of data points into the future. There are no natural bounds. One has no way of knowing whether the line of extrapolation should be straight or curved, and if curved, to what degree. This makes little difference for the first few data points, but the degree of uncertainty subsequently increases until the projected points are of no value. In general, it is probably unwise to make detailed projections for more than five years into the future, and even the grossest of projections are probably worthless more than ten years ahead.

Measurement of Equality

THE RANGE

The last technology needed in school finance reform is a methodology for measuring inequality. The simplest way of measuring inequality is to depict the range of values that exist in a state. To show that there is a range of 46 to 1 in assessed valuation per child (and therefore in local tax-raising capability) among districts—as there is in New York, for example—is to illustrate at least the extent of the problem of equalization. Similarly, a range of school expenditures per child in the state from $1,500 to $6,000 shows real evidence of inequality in the provision of educational services, although whether this inequity truly represents inequity in the ability to provide is another question. For example, if the district that spends $6,000 must levy a tax rate four times that of the district that spends $1,500, those who believe in the principle of power equalizing would declare the system equitable, but those who believe in equal expenditures state-wide would not. This demonstrates two important points. Inequality cannot be measured in the abstract. It must be measured against a criterion based on a clearly defined philosophical position. Single measures of inequality are also like-ly to be inadequate. Since districts have different kinds of students, some requir-ing more expensive educational programs, the existence of expenditure differences does not necessarily mean that there are undesirable inequalities.

Both of these comments apply to any measure of inequality, but the range is a particularly poor measure even if one has taken those comments into account. The reason is that since it measures only two cases, the most extreme ones, it often gives a false impression. For example, an analysis of expenditures per pupil in New York school districts in 1975–76 reveals that the highest spend-ing district spent $6,327 per pupil and the lowest, $1,453. The range is $5,874. However, the second highest spending district spent $4,632 and the second low-est, $1,456. By eliminating only two districts (both of them small, incidentally) the range has been decreased to $3,176, a 35 percent reduction. Despite the fact that the range has been criticized for exaggerating the differences between unrepresentative cases at the extremes, it continues to be extensively used in school finance analyses.

THE INTERQUARTILE RANGE
AND THE STANDARDIZED INTERQUARTILE RANGE

The "interquartile range" is a more stable measure. All of the cases are arrayed from highest to lowest, and divided into four equal groups. The value at the dividing point between groups one and two is the first quartile, that between groups two and three is the second quartile, or median, and that between groups three and four is the third quartile. The difference between the first quartile and the third quartile is the interquartile range. The interquartile range utilizes values in the most highly populated portion of the distribution, where cases are less apt to be unrepresentative. As a result, it is a much more stable measure, in the statistical sense that repeated samples drawn from the same population are apt to show much less variation in interquartile range than in total range. For the same reason, differences in interquartile range of expenditures per pupil of school districts over several years are more apt to vary as a result of real differences in the total distribution and less as a result of random variations than are differences in the range. This useful method is only a little more difficult to measure and to explain to a lay audience than is the range, and is a much more reliable statistic.

A problem with the interquartile range (and with the range, for that matter) is the fact that differences in the scale of the values measured makes it difficult to make comparisons. For example, in one state the interquartile range of expenditures per child may be $750, and in another state it may be $1200. This does not necessarily mean that there is more inequality; the entire level of expenditure may be higher in the second state. A measure that facilitates this comparison is the interquartile range divided by the mean, a "standardized interquartile range." In the case of these two states, if the first is spending an average of $1000 per child, and the second is spending an average of $2000 per child, the first has a standardized interquartile range of 750/1000, or 0.75, while the second has 1200/2000 = 0.60. Based on this measure, the second state shows less inequality.

STANDARD DEVIATION
AND THE COEFFICIENT OF VARIATION

The standardized interquartile range suffers, as does the interquartile range, from the fact that inequality is being measured by selecting only two points from the distribution. "Standard deviation" is a measure that eliminates this criticism by utilizing information on the extent to which all of the data points differ from the mean. In a normal, or bell-shaped, distribution (and many finance-related distributions have approximately this shape), two-thirds of the cases will lie within one standard deviation from the mean, 95 percent of the cases will lie within two standard deviations, and 99.75 percent of the cases will lie within three standard deviations. Because it utilizes information from the entire distribution, the standard deviation is a more stable measure than the interquartile range. As we move to better measures, however, we also find that those measures are more difficult to calculate, and more difficult to explain to the layman.

Standard deviation also suffers from a lack of comparability because of scale. This can be solved in the same way as was done in standardizing the interquartile range, i.e., by dividing by the mean. This provides a standardized standard deviation, and because this is a confusing name, it is usually termed "coefficient of variation."

CROSS-TABULATION

All of the measures of inequality discussed so far have dealt with only one variable at a time, but we are usually concerned with at least two variables simultaneously. We may wish to know whether the variation in expenditures per child is associated with variation in tax rate, for example. Cross-tabulation is a relatively simple means of analyzing such data. It consists of dividing the two variables into appropriate groups, establishing a table in which the groups of one variable are the rows of the table and groups of the other variable the columns, and then placing the cases into appropriate positions in the table. Table 12-7 provides an example. Here, we are interested in the extent to which poor districts spend less than rich districts. The variables have been divided at their mean, so we have "rich" and "poor" districts, and we have "high spending" and "low spending" districts. The table shows that 150 "rich" districts are high spending, while only 50 "poor" districts are high spending. On the other hand, more low spending districts are poor.

Cross-tabulation is frequently used, for if properly done it is easy for lay persons to understand. It has problems however. The primary difficulty is that it is necessary to divide variables in some way. If we divide all districts into "rich" and "poor" we have lost much of the data's depth. Dividing them into "rich," "average," and "poor" is only slightly better. One could divide them into five categories, or ten, but by then the table is too complicated to understand. As a general rule, it is inadvisable to divide variables into more than three categories for cross-tabulation purposes.

Another problem with dividing data into groups is that the results can be affected greatly by the place at which the separation occurs. Suppose, for example, that we are distributing the students of California into a table such as the one in Table 12-7, and that Los Angeles happens to fall between the mean and

TABLE 12-7

Cross-tabulation

	Rich Districts	Poor Districts
High spending districts	150	50
Low spending districts	75	120

the median in assessed valuation per child. If we decide to break the data at the mean, we will obtain a different result than if we decide to break at the median, because a sizable percentage of California's students lives in Los Angeles.

CORRELATION

A more sophisticated measure of the association between two variables, and one which does not suffer from the problems of cross-tabulation, is the "correlation coefficient." Like the standard deviation, it uses all of the information, but it uses data from associated pairs of two distributions. For example, it utilizes pairs of data representing expenditures per pupil and tax rate for each of a number of districts. The result of the calculations is a single number, the correlation coefficient, which ranges between -1 and +1. A coefficient of +1 indicates a perfect positive association between two variables, so that when one increases, the other always increases by a predictable amount. A coefficient of -1, indicates a perfect negative association, so that when one variable increases the other always decreases by a predictable amount. If the correlation coefficient is zero, there is no predictable association between the variables—it is purely random. The relationship will seldom be at any of these extremes, but will lie in between. To determine the importance implied by a correlation coefficient, square it. Thus, if the correlation coefficient is 0.6, its square is 0.36. This implies that one can predict 36 percent of the variation in one variable by knowledge of variation in the other variable, while the remaining 64 percent is random variation or is associated with some unmeasured variable. The correlation coefficient is usually designated by the symbol r, and its square by r^2. If you encounter an r, square it mentally before interpreting it.

MULTIPLE REGRESSION

Finally, the most complicated of the appropriate statistical measures is multiple regression. This is a technique for measuring the extent to which variation in one variable is associated with variation in two or more other variables. The technique allows the statistician to hold all but one of the variables which are thought of as being causes constant while examining the influence of that one on the variable being influenced. In this way the separate effects of several variables can be explored. However, the multiple regression technique contains pitfalls, including the temptation to read into the results more than should reasonably be inferred. In addition, it is difficult to explain the results to laymen. In spite of this, it can be a very useful tool in the hands of competent statisticians.

All of the techniques described so far are covered in basic statistics texts, and will not be described in further detail here.

THE LORENZ CURVE AND THE GINI COEFFICIENT

Another useful technique for measuring inequality has nevertheless seldom been used in connection with school finance. It is a graphical technique called the "Lorenz curve." It has long been used by economists to describe inequalities in income in a country. Like the range, interquartile range, and standard deviation, the Lorenz curve is essentially a univariate technique, examining changes in only one variable without reference to any other. A modification of it, to be described later, enables a second variable to be taken into account.

As used in the measurement of income inequality, the Lorenz technique entails arraying all individuals in order of ascending income. Then at convenient points (for each one percent of the total individuals, say) the cumulative percent of individuals and the cumulative percent of total income is calculated. One can do this for school expenditures in a state in the same way. As an example, hypothetical data on ten districts are displayed in Table 12-8. Cumulative percentages are then plotted on a graph known as a Lorenz chart. The horizontal axis is the cumulative percentage of students, running from 0 to 100, and the vertical axis is the cumulative percentage of expenditure, also running from 0 to 100. The data given in the two columns of Table 12-8 have been plotted on a Lorenz chart (Figure 12-4), and are represented by the curved line. The straight diagonal line represents complete equality of expenditures. That is, if all students had the same amount spent on them, the "lowest" 10 percent of the students would receive 10 percent of the expenditure, the "lowest" 50 percent would receive 50 percent of expenditures, and so on. The extent to which the curved line sags below the diagonal line, then, is a measure of the inequality of expenditure. This measure is summarized in the Gini coefficient, which is the

TABLE 12-8

Data for Lorenz Curve of School Expenditures

District No.	Students	Expenditures per Student	Cumulative Percent of Students	Cumulative Percent of Expenditures
1	1000	800	10	7
2	2000	900	30	21
3	500	1000	35	25
4	500	1100	40	30
5	1000	1200	50	40
6	1000	1300	60	50
7	2000	1400	80	73
8	500	1500	85	80
9	500	1600	90	86
10	1000	1700	100	100

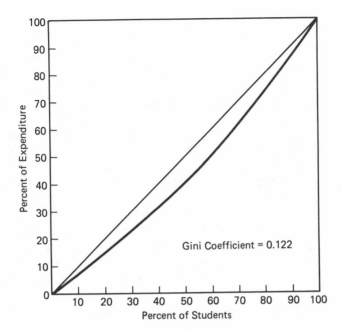

FIG. 12-4. Unmodified Lorenz Chart of School Expenditures

ratio of the area bounded by the diagonal line and the curved line to that of the triangle bounded by the diagonal line, the horizontal axis, and the right-hand vertical line. A Gini coefficient of zero would represent absolute equality, and a Gini coefficient of 1.00 would represent absolute inequality (the situation in which one individual got all of the expenditure and no one else received any). The Gini coefficient for the expenditure data displayed above is about 0.122.

A difficulty with applying the Lorenz curve and other measures of inequality to public school expenditures per student is that not all of the differences in expenditure are undesirable. At the same time that states are engaged in equalization programs to reduce expenditure differences caused by differences in fiscal ability, they are subsidizing programs that result in higher expenditures for special students than for normal students. Unfortunately, the results of these two kinds of subsidization are combined in a single statistic, expenditures per student. Measures such as the range, interquartile range, and standard deviation are incapable of separating desirable from undesirable inequality. The Lorenz curve, as traditionally used by economists, is also incapable of making this distinction. Since there is no way of knowing how much of the expenditure in a particular district is the result of differences in fiscal ability, how much the result of differences in expenditures for special students, and how much the result of differences in community desires for education, the chart as it is now arranged is interesting, but not especially informative.

If, however, the districts are arrayed in order of increasing fiscal ability (that is, assessed valuation per student), the Lorenz chart can then provide information about the extent to which differences in expenditures are correlated with differences in fiscal ability. A possible consequence of this technique is that part of the Lorenz curve may lie above the diagonal line. It is also possible to have substantial differences in expenditure which are unrelated to fiscal ability and yet have the Lorenz curve lie close to the diagonal line. In calculating the Gini index, it is appropriate to think of areas above the diagonal line as negative areas. There could be substantial deviation of the Lorenz curve from the diagonal line, but if this were the result of differences in expenditure that were uncorrelated with differences in fiscal ability, the Gini index would be close to zero.

That expenditures should not be a function of community wealth is one side of the coin of fiscal neutrality. The other side is that tax effort should not be a function of community wealth. The Lorenz curve can be used to examine this in an analogous fashion, though the meaning of a cumulative percentage of tax rates is not as intuitively obvious. One may find in this way that expenditures uncorrelated with wealth may be achieved through tax rates that are highly correlated with wealth. It is clearly necessary to look at both at the same time.

Hand calculation of the Gini coefficient is tedious. It is done by measuring the vertical distance from the diagonal line to the Lorenz curve at equal intervals of, say, two or five percentiles, summing these, and then dividing this result by the sum of the vertical distance from the horizontal axis to the diagonal line for each of the same intervals. An alternative is to construct the Lorenz curve and use a planimeter (a device for measuring areas) to obtain the areas. A second alternative is to use the computer to make the calculation. It can calculate the position of the Lorenz curve for each of as many intervals as desired (100 intervals, one for each percent, seems appropriate), and can automatically do the summations and the dividing necessary to compute the Gini index. Also, the computer can be programmed to print the Lorenz curve.

WHICH MEASURE SHOULD WE USE?

Measurement of educational finance inequalities is still in its infancy. Each of the techniques discussed here has advantages and disadvantages. Those that are technically most useful are in general the most difficult for the lay person to understand. In addition, there are problems of measurement for which there are as yet no solutions.

For example, one is usually interested in three kinds of equalization: wealth equalization, need equalization, and cost equalization. We have been describing measurement of wealth equalization. If we use univariate measures, such as range, interquartile range, and standard deviation, differences in expenditure that are legitimately the result of needs variation or cost variation cannot be distinguished from undesired wealth variation. Correlation of expenditures with assessed valuation, or use of the modified Lorenz technique can separate wealth effects from the need or cost effects only if the latter two are not correlated with the former. Even multiple regression is powerless to separate out the effects when this type of correlation occurs. The most that this technique can do is to reveal the extent to which the expenditure variation is associated with the unique effects of certain variables, and the extent to which it is associated with the joint effects of two or more variables.

Measuring needs inequalities presents another problem. There is no agreed-upon criterion for determining equality. Theoretically, we would have achieved equality in provision for needs when each student, regardless of handicaps, was given the same opportunity to achieve. We do not know how to measure whether that has occurred, and if we did, we do not know how to accomplish it. The result is that the weightings that are used in providing for students with special needs are usually set by custom or by a political process of negotiation, with no one knowing how much these weights coincide with adequate provision for needs. In addition these weights usually apply only to students who are in special programs. Students who have needs but are not in special programs usually are not identified. The result, then, is that we typically have neither knowledge of the total potential need nor of the commitment that should be made to meet that need.

When it comes to cost equalization, available technology is even more primitive. Some of the problems of cost equalization, such as how to separate legitimate cost differences in teacher salaries from those that are a result of differences in community tastes or in the bargaining power of unions, were discussed in Chapter Nine. There is no general agreement, however, on how to measure cost differences for purposes of state school finance.

Summary

This chapter has described the technology that has been involved in school finance reform efforts. The first section of the chapter examined the unique contributions that have been made by computer simulations. With the aid of these complex models of state school finance systems, it has been possible to calculate the effects of a number of new programs on each of a state's districts in a short time, whereas beforehand the calculations for even one program took weeks. And tabulations can be done with greater detail and accuracy than ever before possible.

The second section of the chapter explained some of the more traditional techniques enabling both districts and states to project enrollments, assessed valuation, and revenues. Although these techniques are not as complex as computer simulations, it may be useful to use computers when making calculations for an entire state.

The third section has explored the problems of measuring the extent to which we are providing equality in education, and the kinds of measures that are appropriate for so doing. These range from a simplest of measures, such as the range, to considerably more sophisticated measures like the Lorenz curve and multiple regression.

This chapter has not attempted to survey all of the technical approaches that might be used in studying school finance reform, but has instead presented a sampling of them, in the hope that a few may be of immediate value to those responsible for fiscal affairs in the individual school districts.

13

THE POLITICS
OF SCHOOL FINANCE

The preceding 12 chapters have examined the educational goals pursued by public policy, the resources committed to achieve them, the methods available to distribute educational resources, and who benefits and who pays for public education. We have not specifically focused on the way educational decisions are made. The purpose of this chapter is to explain how educational finance decisions are made in the political process.

Decisions regarding the financing of public schools are political. By this we mean they are made by individuals in accordance with the rules and procedures comprising our political institutions. Citizens may affect educational financing by voting for school board members and state legislators, or by voting on school-related initiatives and referenda. They may petition school agencies and speak out at public hearings. Judges and jury members influence policies by ruling on the legality of governmental actions. Legislators may enact educational programs and impose taxes to pay for them, subject to rules of the legislative process and the willingness of voters to elect them to office. Governors and educational executives propose programs and taxes and exercise some control over educational financing by the way they implement programs. In general, the actions available to individuals are prescribed by constitutions and institutional rules known to everyone. Adherence to predetermined rules increases the predictability of political behavior and makes it possible to reach collective decisions.

Another distinguishing feature of political decisions is that they usually require the agreement of many political actors, and once agreements are reached they are binding on all the members of the political jurisdiction involved, including those who disagree with the decisions. In other words, once decisions are made, the government can force compliance with them.

Political Bargaining

Political decision making can be best described by comparing it to non-political or market decision making. When we decide what to eat, what car to buy, or where to live, we engage in a market exchange with some other party. Usually, market decisions involve only two parties and the consequences of those decisions impinge only on those directly involved. An exchange, called a sale, takes place if both parties benefit. The restaurant would rather have the money than the food offered at that price; and the customer would rather have the lunch than the money. The decision rule in most market transactions, in other words, is unanimous consent. All parties to an exchange must agree to the terms of the exchange or there is no sale.[1] Sometimes when someone is particularly persuasive we say that he or she got a "steal." Nevertheless, if both parties do not believe they are benefiting, no exchange takes place.

Likewise, political decisions result from an exchange process, called bargaining, whose purpose is to produce mutually beneficial outcomes.[2] Bargaining requires that something of value be given up in order to obtain something else that is more valued. However, political bargaining is more complicated than market decision making for several reasons. One reason is the variety of situations in which bargaining takes place and the variety of political resources employed to influence decisions. Someone who wants a car, approaches a car owner and attempts to arrive at a price for which the owner is willing to sell the car. The owner may be a private individual, a used car salesman, or a new car distributor. Generally the possibilities are few and there are only a few types of financial instruments the seller will accept. In politics, many situations and resources are available to influence a decision. For example, parents who want a better reading program for their child can petition the school principal, the school board, the state legislature, or even the federal government. They can use their votes to try to elect school board members and legislators sympathetic to the need for better reading programs. They can

---

[1] For a discussion of the unanimity rule in both market and political decisions, see James M. Buchanan and Gordon Tullock, *The Calculus of Consent* (Ann Arbor, Mich.: The University of Michigan Press, 1962), pp. 85-96.

[2] Bargaining is the subject of numerous political science books. For a general discussion of political bargaining, see Joyce M. Mitchell and William C. Mitchell, *Political Analysis and Public Policy* (Chicago: Rand McNally, 1969), pp. 437-66.

seek support from other parents and interest groups. They can threaten legal action or a recall campaign if other tactics fail. There are many ways and tactics for influencing political decisions.

A second complicating feature is that there are several levels of decision making in politics. There are "constitutional" decisions which may have nothing to do with educational finance, for instance, but which establish the rules by which educational finance decisions are made.[3] For example, many states require the voters in a school district to approve budgets exceeding the previous year's budget or requiring a higher tax rate than before. Or, states may earmark certain revenue sources for education or prohibit the use of specific taxes for education. In addition to constitutional decisions, politicians make policy decisions. These set specific policy guidelines, such as the exact amount of public money to be spent for education. Finally, administrators make operational decisions. These implement policy decisions and frequently determine how educational resources are allocated. These operational decisions, who gets what within the totals available for a program or a district, produce some of the most intense bargaining in education.

Third, different bargaining strategies have different purposes. Litigation, for example, is usually designed to establish some limits on the behavior of policy makers. Courts may declare that a statewide property tax is illegal, or that state funds may not be used in a manner discriminatory against particular categories of students. Referenda, of course, generally establish only general policy guidelines or limitations. Most of the bargaining required to arrive at specific programs for financing schools occurs in state legislatures or local school district board rooms. This is where much of the "fine tuning" on school programs and budgets take place.

The most complicating characteristic of political decision making, however, is the need to obtain agreement, not just between a buyer and seller, but among many people, usually a majority. In referenda this may mean thousands or hundreds of thousands of people. In a state legislature a hundred or more legislators may have to consent to enact legislation. On some issues it is easy to obtain majority support. A resolution to commend someone for an outstanding achievement usually passes easily because everyone is for achievement and words of commendation are politically costless. But finding majority support for a new school finance program or tax reform program is always difficult, because citizens in the various legislative districts will be affected differently and legislators will attempt to negotiate programs which benefit their districts the most.

What then does political bargaining involve? It requires that individuals involved in making political decisions be able to persuade others of the merits

---

[3] James M. Buchanan, *Public Finance in Democratic Process* (Chapel Hill, N.C.: The University of North Carolina Press, 1967), pp. 287–93.

of their proposals and, in most cases, be able to convince them to settle for less than they really want. Persuasion and compromise are necessary because:

1. people have different ideas about what should be done and how to do it;
2. in most political institutions no one group has enough power to impose its views on all others; and
3. politicians generally share the belief that in most situations, some solution to a problem is better than none.[4]

Persuasion, negotiation, and compromise, in other words, are the characteristic ways in which a democracy solves political problems and maintains social peace.

Politicians who are unwilling to compromise on difficult issues stand properly accused of failing in their political responsibilities. George Bernard Shaw, remembering his own political career, convincingly argued for the necessity of compromising when he attacked a fellow Labour candidate for Parliament, Joseph Burgess, for being unwilling to do so:

> When I think of my own unfortunate character, smirched with compromise, rotted with opportunism, mildewed by expedience . . . dragged through the mud of borough council and Battersea elections, stretched out of shape with wire-pulling, putrified by permeations, worn out by 25 years pushing to gain an inch here, or straining to stem a backrush, I do think Joe might have put up with just a speck or two on those white robes of his for the sake of the millions of poor devils who cannot afford any character at all because they have no friend in Parliament. Oh, these moral dandies, these spiritual toffs, these superior persons. Who is Joe anyhow that he would not risk his soul occasionally like the rest of us?[5]

Our perspective on the politics of school finance, in summary, focuses on the bargaining processes that produce decisions. Since public schools are financed largely from local and state sources, we will limit our discussion to the kinds of political bargaining that occur within school districts and state legislatures over the financing of public schools.

Local Voters and Educational Policy

Although state constitutions hold the state responsible for providing public education, most states delegate a major part of this responsibility to local school districts. Approximately 50 percent of funds for primary and

---

[4]William C. Mitchell, *Public Choice in America* (Chicago: Markham Publishing Company, 1971), p. 126.

[5]Hesketh Pearson, *GBS* (New York: Harper & Row Publishers, Inc., 1942), p. 156.

secondary education are raised by local school districts, and local school boards are largely responsible for planning, operation, and control of public schools.

School districts are highly constrained in the actions they may take, however, particularly with regard to the financing of schools. The federal government places many conditions on grants to school districts. These limitations have already been described in detail in Chapter Seven. Similarly, state legislatures and state education departments have constructed a complex superstructure of regulations local districts must follow in building local school programs. In the 1970s many states enacted collective bargaining measures which further constrained the autonomy of local school officials. The legal and fiscal relationships between states and local school districts have been analyzed in many of the preceding chapters, particularly in Chapters Four, Eight and Nine.

Local school districts are also affected by events over which they have little or no control. The Russians' launching of Sputnik created a wave of interest in education and along with it increased federal funding of science programs. The Supreme Court's decision in *Brown* v. *Board of Education,* linking race and education policies, has had a profound effect on local school decisions. Future events will similarly alter local school policy. Despite these constraints and the vagaries of unknown events, the day-to-day decisions required in America's public elementary and secondary schools must be made at the district level.

DETERMINING THE EDUCATIONAL NEEDS OF A COMMUNITY

Decisions affecting the amount and mix of educational services in a local district emerge from the interactions of many groups.[6] One important group is "professional educators" whose livelihood and well-being depend upon future increases in support for schools. Just like advocates for other public services, professional educators generally argue that more programs and funds are needed. With a declining rate of increase in school enrollments they can be expected to look for new clientele—preschool children and adults. Their advocacy of new and bigger programs needing greater financial support is tempered only by their calculations of what is politically feasible. If they seek too much, their claims may be entirely disregarded and they may end up with nothing.

Another important group are "policy analysts" who provide supposedly objective estimates of educational needs and their costs. The analysts, who are on the superintendent's staff or hired as consultants by school districts, project school enrollments and estimate the costs of providing alternative packages of

---

[6]For a more extended discussion of varying definitions of educational need, see James M. Buchanan, "Taxpayer Constraints on Financing Education," in *Economic Factors Affecting the Financing of Education,* eds. Roe L. Johns et al. (Gainesville, Fla.: National Education Finance Project, 1970), pp. 266–71.

services for the students expected to attend the district's schools. Typically, analysts start with the basic education program, usually the program a district already offers, and then examine the costs and benefits of proposed additions. They employ a variety of analytic techniques designed to provide policy makers with the best estimate of educational need.

Decisions regarding the "need" for education, however, are ultimately made by citizens of the community served by a school district. School board members may support the goals of teachers or have the greatest confidence in the district's policy analysts; nevertheless their goals and analysis are worth nothing unless backed by local citizens. Educational decisions, particularly with regard to finance, are made by those members of the community who elect school board members or approve school district budgets.[7] The individual voting decisions of citizens can only be manipulated or ignored within narrow limits. School board members failing to recognize this fact are not likely to be re-elected. Educational professionals who divorce school policy from community preferences will find many of their plans rejected.

Once the central role of the citizen–voter in educational decision making is recognized, then there is no one correct answer to the question of how much education is enough. The answer emerges from many individual calculations of the benefits and costs of education programs. This answer is expressed by the votes in school board elections or on school finance referenda, and in the arguments presented by concerned citizens in public meetings or communicated informally to policy makers. The rationalizations of the educational advocates and the estimates of the policy experts enter into public decisions as part of the information citizens use to make their judgments. The most important information, however, is every individual's own perception of the benefits and costs of proposed educational programs. This is why it is often easier to obtain funding for a new football stadium or gymnasium than for a school library or music wing. Athletics provides private benefits for many members of the community while a library or music building mostly benefits those in school.

TRANSLATING CITIZEN PREFERENCES
INTO EDUCATIONAL POLICY

Let us see then how individual estimates of educational need are translated into policy decisions via one important mechanism, the electoral process. For the most part, equal educational services are available to all school-age residents in a district regardless of their individual preferences for education. The costs are imposed largely on property owners in proportion to the value of their property, but not in relation to their consumption of education. A property owner with no children pays the same as an owner of comparable

[7]*Ibid.*, p. 270.

property with five children in school. Although citizens cannot affect the supply of education directly through their purchases of education (as they do when they buy a car, for instance), they can do so by voting in school elections.

Since it is required in many school districts, we assume here that any proposal to increase spending for education must be approved by a simple majority of voters.[8] We also assume that voter-taxpayers are able to make a personal valuation of proposed packages of educational services and to estimate their personal tax-cost of proposed spending programs.

This does not mean that voters' knowledge about how much education they want or how much it will cost is precise or exact. On the contrary, taxpayers' attitudes are quite imprecise and subject to manipulation. The campaign propaganda of professional education associations and other pressure groups at the time of elections are effective only if voters are somewhat pliable. Much electoral advertising is designed to provide voters with information about the benefits and costs of measures to be voted upon. Some of it, though, is designed to change opinions through persuasion. For example, the Chamber of Commerce may argue that a proposed school budget should be passed because efforts to obtain new businesses depend upon continued excellence of the public schools.

There are clearly limits to the flexibility of voters' attitudes, however. Ultimately, if only subjectively, the voter-taxpayers estimate the tax-costs (the tax liability of the proposed educational budget), the resultant tax price per child served in the program, and the quantity of education preferred at the estimated tax price. On the basis of these estimates, they decide whether to vote for or against school levies.

Let us suppose that all voters in a school district can be arrayed according to the quantity of education that each prefers (quantity here is the amount per pupil at each individual's estimated tax price per unit).[9] One possible array is illustrated in Figure 13-1. Q_s is the proposed school budget being voted upon. Q_m is the amount preferred by the median voter-taxpayer. Voters lying between O and Q_s along the array believe that the proposed budget would produce an oversupply of education at the required tax price. They prefer less education than is proposed and can be expected to vote against the budget. All those lying to the right of Q_s would prefer to have more than is being proposed. Many of them might be expected to vote against the budget because it is too small. However, since most districts reduce their budget requests if the budget is rejected

[8]There are some states and communities which add certain stipulations to majority approval of school tax and bond levies. For instance, the state of Washington requires that 60 percent of the voters approve budgets and that the total number of ballots cast be at least 40 percent of those cast in the previous general election.

[9]The following analysis draws heavily from Michael Boss, "The Supply and Tax-Cost of Education and the Vote," CASEA Technical Report No. 13 (Eugene, Oregon: Center for the Advanced Study of Educational Administration, February, 1973).

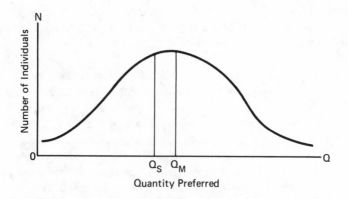

FIG. 13-1. Array of Individual Preferences for Education

Source: Michael Boss, "The Supply and Tax-Cost of Education and The Vote." A CASEA Technical Report, No. 13, (Eugene, Oregon: Center For The Advanced Study of Educational Administration, February, 1973), p. 6.

at the polls, those to the right of Q_s are likely to vote in favor of the proposed budget for fear that they would be offered even less if it is defeated. This hypothetical array of voters, therefore, is likely to approve the proposed budget, or any budget not greater than Q_m, which would just receive a majority vote.[10]

As is clear, there is no direct way for one individual to change the supply of education through voting. The preference of the median voter, however, is one measure of the collective preference of a community for education, assuming of course, that the community agrees that such a decision should be made by a majority of voters.[11] The median preference expresses the maximum amount that will be approved under majority rule.

The median preference may be close to the optimal supply of education for a community. Most voter–taxpayers are likely to be partially disappointed with any proposed education program. They will either prefer more or less than is offered. If, however, the degree of disappointment is measured by the difference between their preference and what is being offered, then the aggregate dissatisfaction in a community is minimized if the supply is set at the median preference.

---

[10] Taxpayers who do not vote are ignored. Presumably, such voters expect that the utility of attempts to adjust supply and tax-cost through voting is less than the expected cost of voting. This assumption is discussed at length in Anthony Downs, *An Economic Theory of Democracy* (New York: Harper & Brothers, 1957).

[11] Analyses of the "median voter" model of local fiscal decisions are found in Theodore Bergstrom and Robert Goodman, "Private Demands for Public Goods," *American Economic Review,* 63 (June 1973), 280-96, and Noel Edelson, "Budgetary Outcomes in a Referendum Setting," in *Property Taxation and the Finance of Education,* ed. Richard Lindholm (Madison: University of Wisconsin Press, 1974).

The bell-shaped distribution of the education supply curve reflects both voter response to varying tax-costs of education and the varying tastes of different individuals for education. Analyses of voter preferences among school districts must be careful to distinguish between quantities of education chosen because of different tax-costs of education and quantities chosen because of different preferences (or tastes) for education. Both are frequently related to personal characteristics such as income and education.

Another implication of the median voter model is that a large percentage of favorable votes in a budget election is *not* a good indicator of a community's satisfaction with the education being proposed. A 75 percent favorable vote means that most of the 75 percent believe too little education is being offered. Districts whose budgets receive barely 50 percent favorable votes are more likely to be providing near optimal levels of education.

THE TAXPAYERS' REVOLT

If our description of the voter–taxpayers' role in the fiscal decisions of local school districts is correct, then what meaning can be given to the so-called "taxpayers' revolt"? The term has been used to describe at least three different situations:

1. when voters turn down tax referenda more frequently than in the past for any of several reasons;
2. when voters reject tax referenda because the conditions surrounding school budget referenda have changed; or
3. when voters reject tax referenda merely because their attitudes toward public schools have changed so much that they would vote against referenda they would have approved in the past.[12]

These possibilities are illustrated in Figure 13-2.

Depicted are two patterns of community voting in response to proposed tax rates. Schedule A represents voter response to various rates under one set of conditions; schedule B represents response under another set of conditions. A shift along schedule A indicates a change in the demand for education resulting from a shift in tax rates; a shift from schedule A to B indicates a change in the demand for education because of factors other than the tax rate.

In order to simplify the discussion, only the effects of a proposed increase in school tax rate are shown. The first interpretation of a taxpayers' revolt is shown by a shift from a higher point to any lower point on either vote-tax schedule. A decline in the proportion of "yes" votes from 2 to 5, from 4 to 2,

[12] Arthur J. Alexander and Gail V. Bass, *Schools, Taxes and Voter Behavior: An Analysis of School District Property Tax Elections* (Santa Monica, Cal.: The Rand Corporation, April, 1974), p. 49.

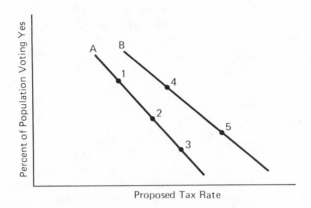

FIG. 13-2. Alternative Views of Voting Behavior in Local School Tax Referenda

Source: Arthur J. Alexander and Gail V. Bass, *Schools, Taxes and Voter Behavior* (Santa Monica, Calif.: The Rand Corporation, April 1974), p. 50.

or from 2 to 3, all would be regarded as revolts. This view assumes that the purpose of referenda is to ratify decisions made by school board members and professional schoolmen. Since voters are expected to approve budgets, any decline in their willingness to do so is interpreted as a revolt. This view of referenda is a curious distortion of the original purpose of referenda which was to increase the participation of citizens in governmental decision making.[13]

In the second way of looking at the taxpayers' revolt, the higher rate of budget rejections is explained by voters responding to a different set of conditions than in the past. A shift from one point on either tax-vote schedule to a lower point on the same schedule (from 2 to 3, or from 4 to 5) would reflect such a situation since the schedule of preferences has remained the same and only the proposed tax rate has increased. A variety of factors might account for declining support for school budgets, besides the proposed tax rate illustrated in Figure 13-2, even though the underlying attitudes toward public education (represented by vote-tax schedules A and B) remain unchanged. Alexander and Bass examined over 50 variables in a study of school taxes and voter behavior in California in the 1950s and 1960s and found that the proposed tax rate and its change accounted for most of the decline in voter support for school budgets.[14] In other words, the higher the proposed percentage tax rate increase, the lower the percent of school budgets passed. This suggests that voters are willing to support gradual increases in school costs but not rapid increases.

Boss took this analysis one step farther in a study of school referenda

[13] Frederick M. Wirt and Michael W. Kirst, *The Political Web of American Schools* (Boston: Little, Brown and Company, 1972), p. 97.

[14] Alexander and Bass, *Schools, Taxes and Voter Behavior,* p. 65.

in Oregon.[15] He developed a simple mathematical model to estimate a community's demand for education by examining their votes. Application of the model to school budget elections in Oregon from 1963 to 1970 indicated that while collective demand for education in Oregon increased continuously, the supply of education increased even more rapidly. As school boards set proposed supplies of education nearer the estimated level of collective demand for education, instances in which the proposed supply of education exceeded the level of actual demand for education increased, thus resulting in budget defeats. These defeats, he concluded, are part of the normal and desirable operation of a democratic system of public finance.

The implication of these studies is that voters use school budget referenda in part to correct the fiscal policies of local school officials. Districts that increase the tax rate too quickly, or that offer more education than the community prefers, suffer higher proportions of budget defeats.

What constitutes too high a tax rate or too much education is not always clear. In New York State, for instance, school expenditures and school tax rates are very high. In Arizona expenditures are much lower, yet in both areas voters must believe they are receiving about the right amount of education at the prevailing tax price, or they would elect officials willing to provide the correct amount of education. The important determinant of how much is enough seems to be how much similar and neighboring districts are spending or taxing themselves for schools.[16] The larger the difference between a district's proposed tax rate increase or per capita school expenditure and that of similar neighboring districts, the greater the voter turnout and the greater the likelihood of voters rejecting the referenda.

We believe referenda play a useful role in correcting the fiscal decisions of school officials. Professional educators want larger school budgets than voters seem willing to support. Consequently, they would like to see educational finance decisions shifted to the state where it is easier for the education lobby to influence policy. To the extent that citizens should control educational decisions, local referendum on school budgets is an appropriate mechanism for ensuring that local voters obtain the education they want.

The term *taxpayers' revolt* actually is appropriate only to describe a situation in which voters reject tax referenda which in the past they would have approved. A shift from 4 to 2 or 4 to 3 in Figure 13-2 would indicate such a change. There is little evidence that a major shift in public attitudes toward public schools has occurred. Public opinion polls reveal that most parents are still satisfied with the performance of schools and localities continue to approve larger school budgets.[17]

[15] Boss, "The Supply and Tax-Cost of Education and The Vote," pp. 9–23.

[16] Jack W. Osman and W. Norton Grubb, "Adjustments from Disequilibrium in Local Finance: School Referenda in California," unpublished paper from The Childhood and Government Project, University of California at Berkeley, 1975.

[17] In the 1976 Gallup poll of the public's attitudes toward public schools, 50 percent

There are a number of factors, however, that are likely in the future to constrain the ability of local school districts to raise school taxes. The growth in the proportion of older people, to whom property taxes are particularly oner- ous, will affect school budgets. This effect will be particularly strong because a larger proportion of older people go to the polls than do younger voters.[18] We have mentioned that the birth rate is declining and with it the proportion of voters with school-age children. This trend will limit a district's ability to in- crease local taxes. Large increases in the costs of other local services are likely to compete with rising school costs for the marginal taxpayers' dollar. All of these factors, however, are rational grounds for limiting the rise in educational expenditures. Older people and families without children value other public services more than education. To the extent that they reflect a shift in median preference away from additional school expenditures, referenda are serving to adjust the mix of public services to conform to a community's preferences.

Shifts of a second type—for example, from vote-tax schedule B to A— can also result from actions by school officials only indirectly related to citizens' demand for education. One instance is forced consolidation of school districts, an action that has been shown to create hostility among unwilling constituents and to reduce their willingness to support future school budgets.[19] Forced bus- ing, violence in schools, and the declining performance of high school students on national achievement tests are also likely to erode the public's confidence in schools and their willingness to spend more for schools.

It is more difficult to predict voters' reaction to the increasing tendency of policy makers to use schools as an instrument for social change. For most of its history, public education has functioned to transmit to young people a set of broadly accepted values. Since World War II, however, schools themselves have become instruments of social change, particularly with regard to racial integration and to wealth redistribution. The point is that the role of social reformer conflicts sharply with the value transmission role. To the extent that voters in a community expect schools to pass the values of the community on to the students, they will react negatively to shifts in the educational program toward social reform. Renewed concern about basic skills may have dampened the social reform movment in public schools, however. During the late 1960s and early 1970s, public education lost some public support by expanding its educational role too far.

In summary, the politics of school finance at the local level are tied close- ly to the behavior of local citizens. The ultimate constraint in many local

---

of those polled with children in public schools gave schools an A or B rating. *Phi Delta Kappan,* 58, No. 2 (October 1976), 189.

[18] Philip K. Piele and John Stuart Hall, *Budgets, Bonds and Ballots* (Lexington, Mass.: Lexington Books, 1973), pp. 44–47.

[19] L. A. Wilson, II, "A Partial Model of Citizen Response to School District Con- solidation," unpublished paper for the Department of Political Science, University of Oregon, Eugene, Oregon, 1974.

school districts is the willingness of local voters to support school budgets, and indirectly, the necessity of school board members to win elections. When school boards seek to expand education too rapidly, or to extend the role of public schools beyond that desired by a community, voters are likely to express their dissatisfaction at the polls. During the late 1960s and early 1970s local voters rejected increasing numbers of school budgets and bond requests largely because they felt that the benefits of additional schooling did not outweigh the additional costs involved. Rather than being a revolt against public schools per se, this was simply an instance of voter participation in decisions affecting the supply of public education. The public should be wary of proposed school finance reforms that reduce voter control over the supply of educational services by shifting financial responsibility to the state or by tying finance decisions to impersonal criteria such as the cost of living. Local voter–taxpayer control at the polls is one of the few mechanisms currently available for making schools accountable to the public.

State School Finance Reform

During the last half of the 1960s and early 1970s, the financing of schools became a major policy issue in most state legislatures. There was a variety of reasons for the upsurge of interest in educational finance. Most of them have to do with the problem of rising cost and falling enrollments.

During the 1950s and 1960s public education grew rapidly in the United States. This rapid expansion created serious problems when the flow of new dollars to public education was slowed in the 1970s. Conflicts emerged as to how much and where to cut educational costs. Such conflict should not have been unexpected. Political theorists have observed that revolutions are most likely to occur when rising expectations, fostered by a prolonged period of growth, are suddenly unfulfillable because of an economic downturn.[20] When public education's period of growth came to an end—because of declining enrollment and increasing voter resistance to school budget increases—competition for increasingly scarce educational dollars produced open conflict among the many interests involved. The coalition between educational administrators and teachers, often known as the education lobby, which had previously worked together to secure additional funds for education began to splinter. School board members and legislators who had previously supported increases for education were confronted by a larger and increasingly vocal constituency demanding more efficiency and accountability in the use of educational funds.

Since states are legally responsible for public schools, it was only a matter

[20] James C. Davies, "Toward a Theory of Revolution," *American Sociological Review,* 27 (February, 1962), 5–19.

of time before conflicts over educational finance percolated up to state legisla-tures. Much of the pressure on the legislators for reform first came from educa-tors seeking new sources of funds for public schools. Acting in their own interest, they chose to interpret taxpayers' resistance in school budget and bond elections as a repudiation of the method of financing schools rather than as a rejection of the need for greater school spending. Consequently, they urged legislatures to shift more of the costs of local schools on to state taxes. At the same time, tax-payers, confronted with rapidly rising costs for all local services, wanted the local property tax burden reduced or shifted to other tax sources. Since a large part of local property taxes are used to support schools, the method of financing schools became an integral part of debates over the appropriate tax structure to pay for all state and local services.

Curtailment of the growth of educational expenditures also highlighted the inequalities in the existing methods of financing schools. As long as all school district budgets were growing, most parents and school officials were satisfied with the resources available to them. When resources became tight, however, educators began to ask if all districts were experiencing similar short-ages. They discovered that there was a wide range of tax rates and expendi-ture levels among school districts in most states.

Awareness that property-poor districts often had to tax themselves at two or three times the rate of property-rich districts in order to raise only a portion of the revenues per student, led to a series of legal challenges to the constitutionality of prevailing methods of financing public education. In Cal-ifornia, Minnesota, Texas, New Jersey, Wyoming, Kansas, Connecticut, and Idaho, judges held that existing finance arrangements violated education or equal protection clauses in state constitutions.[21] Courts did not, however, provide solutions. The task of finding constitutional remedies to court rul-ings, and to possible rulings in states where litigation was being pursued or was threatened, fell to state legislatures.

The most difficult problem facing legislators was how to reform state school finance systems so that the quality of a child's education was not un-duly influenced by the wealth of the school district and at the same time to control or even cut back educational spending. Equalizing educational re-sources would not have been so difficult had additional state dollars been avail-able to increase spending in poor districts. Nor would budget tightening have been so difficult if everyone's budget were squeezed by the same amount. Com-bining reform and retrenchment was politically explosive, however. These be-came the underlying themes of what has come to be known as the school finance reform movement.

---

[21] The most important state school finance cases are reviewed in "Future Directions for School Finance Reform," in *Law and Contemporary Problems,* 38, No. 3 (Win-ter–Spring, 1974).

SCHOOL FINANCE REFORM MOVEMENT

Following the California Supreme Court decision in *Serrano* v. *Priest* in 1971, cases were filed in most states challenging the constitutionality of state finance laws. While the U.S. Supreme Court's ruling in *Rodriguez* v. *San Antonio* slowed down the search for court remedies, many cases were still pursued on the grounds that state constitutional provisions had been violated. In response to these cases and to public demands for property tax and school finance reform, most states created state school finance commissions to propose alternative state finance arrangements. In those states providing for initiative and referendum, some groups put measures before the voters to limit the use of property taxes for schools and to place restrictions on educational spending.[22]

Court actions and citizen concerns moved school finance reform onto the agendas of most legislatures. For the most part, however, there has been little movement toward reform. There are several reasons for this legislative paralysis.[23] One is the repeated attempts to seek reform through the courts. The judiciary is greatly limited in its ability to develop and administer public policy. Judges, for the most part, are not experts on educational finance. Neither do they have the staff, resources, or time to develop a comprehensive understanding of state finance systems and alternative financial arrangements for accommodating the many values pursued in the financing of public schools. Consequently, courts have tended to respond to observed inequities in the distribution of funds by mandating legislative reform, but without setting clear guidelines. For example, in the famous *Serrano* decision, the California Supreme Court held that "the quality of education may not be a function of wealth other than the wealth of the state as a whole," but did not say how the state should meet this negative standard. Similarly, the New Jersey Supreme Court in *Robinson* v. *Cahill,* while requiring the state to define the scope of the educational opportunity specified in its constitution, and to ensure that this is provided equally to all children in the state,[24] did not specify how its decision should be implemented. The courts' decisions, in other words, have not appreciably narrowed the alternatives available to state legislatures. Without specific judicial guide-

---

[22] State constitutional referenda to revise school finance systems are described in Donna E. Shalala, Mary F. Williams, and Andrew Fishel, "The Property Tax and the Voters," occasional paper #2, The Institute of Philosophy and the Politics of Education, Teachers College, Columbia University, November 1973.

[23] Reasons for the failure of states to reform their school finance systems are discussed in Michael A. Cohen, Betsy Levin, and Richard Beaver, *The Political Limits to School Finance Reform* (Washington, D.C.: The Urban Institute, March 1973; and in Arnold J. Meltsner and Robert T. Nakamura, "Political Implications of *Serrano*," in *School Finance in Transition,* ed. John Pincus (Cambridge, Mass.: Ballinger Publishing Co., 1974), pp. 257–85.

[24] Paul L. Tractenberg, "*Robinson* v. *Cahill:* The Thorough and Efficient Clause," *Law and Contemporary Problems,* 38, No. 3 (Winter–Spring, 1974), 330.

lines, legislators must work through the tedious process of constructing a politically feasible school finance law.

Even if the courts were capable of mandating specific school finance remedies, which they are not, they are poorly equipped to administer any such program. There are few actions they can take except negative ones, such as closing down schools or calling in the police, to gain compliance. They cannot enact new taxes, impose expenditure limitations, or create new distribution formulas, all measures reserved for the use of state legislatures. The unsuccessful experiences of the court in integrating public schools highlight the weaknesses of the courts in administering public policy.

Reliance on litigation has also retarded movement toward school finance reform because it provides legislatures an excuse for inaction. The judicial process is very slow. *Serrano* was originally filed in 1969. A final decision in the case was not handed down until 1976. While a case is before the courts, the legislature can postpone action pending clarification of legal points being adjudicated. Then if the court rules against the plaintiffs for any reason, the legislature can argue that the court has given the existing system a clean bill of health.

Another reason for legislative inaction on school finance reform is that legislators simply cannot agree on what is wrong with schools. Some legislators believe educators' complaints of inadequate resources but they are increasingly in a minority. Many more believe that accountability, decentralization, and efficiency are more important educational issues, which—if achieved—would either solve schools' financial problems, or would at least provide better guidelines for reforming school finance. These issues receive substantial support from influential business groups and from citizen groups. Whatever their diagnosis, or the reasons they adduce for their beliefs, many legislators do not think the problems of schools are entirely financial. If schools have problems why give them more money, particularly when enrollment is declining? This common perspective reduces commitment to reform and slows legislative action.

A third reason for legislative inaction is that very few people can estimate the impact of reform proposals on individual taxpayers and individual school districts. State tax structures and educational finance systems are extremely complex. Only a few states have developed the analytic capability to estimate the tax and distributional consequences of reform proposals.[25] Even the best estimates are based on very uncertain assumptions regarding future state revenues, enrollment growth or decline, and the likely rate of inflation of school costs. This lack of knowledge or fear of the unreliability of official estimates impedes the development of a political coalition in support of school finance reform.

[25] See chap. 12 for a discussion of the technical difficulties surrounding school finance reform proposals and for a description of computer simulation techniques to manage these complexities.

A fourth reason for legislative paralysis is that the proponents of reform are weak while its opponents are strong.[26] Support for reform comes from three sources: the school lobby, parents and taxpayers in low-wealth school districts, and school finance experts. None of these groups has been particularly successful in mobilizing support for school finance reform.

The school lobby consists of organizational representatives, administrators, school board members, and larger school districts in most states. These groups are joined on specific issues by such groups as the League of Women Voters, civic organizations and, occasionally, progressive business groups. Despite its size and diversity, the educational lobby has not been a cohesive or influential force behind school finance reform.

The very diversity of the educational lobby has tended to divide it on important educational finance legislation. School board members and local administrators disagree with teachers over local control, accountability, collective bargaining, and tenure. The large disparities among districts in size, wealth, and educational needs breed conflicts. School board members and administrators in wealthy urban districts stand on one side of the political fence on issues of equalization, categorical aid, and shifts in the tax structure, while their colleagues in poor suburban and rural districts are on the other.

In addition to its internal divisions, the school lobby suffers from other problems that reduce its effectiveness. Many legislators distrust the narrow set of concerns that educators bring to the legislature. In testimony before legislative committees, educators are inclined singlemindedly to support measures to increase funds for education and to oppose legislation for additional controls over the educational establishment. Likewise the research provided by educational organizations is often one-sided. This tendency to have a narrow conception of its interest, along with the fact that the educational lobby is one of the best financed pressure groups in most states, makes legislators wary of their advice, even though large compaign contributions guarantee educators ready access to legislators. Some legislators feel that the educational lobby is not really concerned about the people, and that the legislature must protect the public interest against a monolithic educational establishment.

Parents and taxpayers in low-wealth districts stand to gain the most from school finance reform but are poorly organized and represented in most legislatures. Effective participation in the political maneuvering surrounding an issue as complex as school finance requires knowledge and commitment of time. Administrators and school leaders in poor, often small districts, are too busy trying to keep their school programs operating to become informed or to send representatives to state capitols. Furthermore, the complexities of school finance make it extremely difficult to mobilize public interest in reform. Many local voters cannot believe that the proposed reforms will actually provide the

[26] Meltsner and Nakamura, "Political Implications of *Serrano*," pp. 263-85.

promised benefits. Finally, poor districts cannot rely on support from either the wealthy districts who would lose by school finance reform, or from the majority of moderately wealthy districts who would neither gain nor lose by a change in the methods of financing schools. The middle districts prefer the certainty of the existing system to the uncertainties of a new formula that offers them little. Rather than supporting comprehensive reform, they are more likely to seek minor adjustments that offer them specific benefits.

The third group advocating reform are school finance experts. Such experts are found on the staffs of state education agencies and legislative committees, and occasionally in universities. They collect and analyze data on current systems of school finance, and keep various reform proposals before legislative committees. Their problem is that they can provide little or no political support for the proposals they espouse.[27] They frequently are estranged from the educational lobby which resents their interference in issues for which they claim proprietary rights, and they find it difficult to communicate to school district officials who do not understand the intricacies of their statistical models and complex formulas. Their best chance of promoting school finance reform is to tie themselves to an influential legislator in the hopes that he or she can provide the necessary political support to enact the experts' recommendations.

The opponents of reform are usually less numerous but more zealous in guarding the privileges they receive from existing finance systems. Most state school finance laws favor large businesses, farmers, and parents and taxpayers in wealthy school districts. School finance proposals designed to provide equal educational opportunity would increase resources for poor districts at the expense of wealthy taxpayers or taxpayers in wealthy districts. The more comprehensive the reform, that is, the more equitable the proposed system and the more districts to receive equalization, the greater the cost to wealthy districts.

Despite their lack of numbers, those speaking for wealthy school districts are in a particularly advantageous position to oppose reform. In the first place, reform almost always requires additional state funds. Therefore opponents of reform can usually count on the help of well organized interests opposed to tax increases such as taxpayers associations, state industrial associations, the Farm Bureau, and state grange organizations. Large public utilities and manufacturers often have their own lobbies that can be counted on to oppose new taxes on business or proposals to take funds away from the relatively wealthy cities where their offices are located.

Opponents of reform can also rely on the support of the powerful legislators representing wealthy suburbs and cities. While they may not have a majority, reap-

---

[27] An excellent discussion of the role of experts in the public policy-making process is found in Guy Benveniste, *The Politics of Expertise* (Berkeley, Cal.: The Glendessary Press, 1972).

portionment has given urban interests sufficient strength in most states to block measures they oppose. This veto power comes also from holding key committee and leadership positions. Furthermore, it is much easier to block a bill than to ensure its passage. The supporters of a bill must guide it through a succession of committee, floor, and conference votes, winning majority support at each stage. The opponents need only break the chain of favorable votes once. Even if they fail in the legislature, opponents have a reasonable chance of obtaining a governor's veto, since governors are always under pressure to hold down the costs of government. And finally, there is a good possibility of overturning reform by referring it to the people.[28]

Opponents usually have the advantage of agreeing on their objectives. They are against proposals that will cost them more in taxes but will reduce the flow of state dollars to their districts. Proponents, however, must build coalitions of groups, each wanting something a little different. The division typically found among the proponents of school finance reform is seldom found among its opponents.[29] If there is any law in politics, it is that comprehensive reform requires the undivided support of a large and influential coalition. The proponents of school finance reform have frequently had the support of many influential leaders both in the educational community and state government. They have had difficulty, however, building enough support for specific proposals to pass over the many hurdles to legislative enactment. In order to see why school finance reform has so often failed miserably, we will examine the most important issues dividing legislative supporters of school finance measures. We will conclude with a discussion of the strategy for building a winning reform coalition.

POLICY ISSUES IN SCHOOL FINANCE REFORM

Hundreds of school finance plans have been proposed throughout the country. Few have been enacted into law. An analysis of bills before any legislature would reveal that finance plans revolve around a limited number of basic issues. These issues or elements include such things as the scope of state responsibility, reapportionment, local control, equalization, and property tax relief. Each has its supporters and opponents. Only by understanding these issues and being able to identify the actors likely to support each, is it possible for legislators to build a plan with enough support to become law. Political decisions require the agreement of at least a majority of legislators at each stage of the legislative process. In practical terms, this means that more than a majority of

---

[28] Meltsner and Nakamura, "Political Implications of *Serrano*," 265.

[29] See Lawrence C. Pierce, "The Politics of School Finance Reform in Oregon," in *Remaking Educational Finance,* ed. James A. Kelly, *New Directions for Education,* No. 3 (Autumn 1973), 113–31, for an analysis of how division defeated a major reform proposal.

legislators is needed to enact legislation, since a minority of opponents has numerous opportunities to defeat it. No one group can produce a large plurality. Consequently, if a reform proposal is to have any chance of passing, it must involve compromises and tradeoffs among interests favoring each of the basic issues

THE SCOPE OF STATE RESPONSIBILITY

The overarching issue confronting school finance reformers is the scope of state responsibility in education. This issue is basically definable in terms of two subissues. First is the issue of how much public education should be provided by each level of government. The educational lobby will in general support more education at every level. Legislators must balance funds for education with those required for other public services such as prisons, welfare, highways, etc., as well as keep the public sector from taking too much from individual taxpayers. Consequently, legislators must decide explicitly or implicitly, the total amount to be spent for education.

The decision as to actual dollar amount available for schools may be delegated to local school districts by allowing them to ask local voters how much they prefer to spend. Or the legislature may establish a firm revenue limitation per child, like the one in California, with very limited provisions for local district overrides. In general, the educational lobby will oppose limitations on school expenditures or taxes, while taxpayers, representatives of business, farm groups, and senior citizens will favor them.

The second issue is the proportion of total revenues to be provided by the state. Almost every reform proposal and reform group holds that the state should assume a larger responsibility for the funding of public schools. This position necessarily follows from the desire to provide more equal funding. Since property wealth per pupil varies widely among districts, and local school districts must rely on local property taxes to support the local share of school costs, equalization of expenditures can only take place if the burden of school support is shifted to the states.

Larger state funding of schools is strongly supported by county and municipal governments, which argue that schools' insatiable appetite for funds leave them too few property tax dollars for necessary county and local services.

Agreement on the need for a larger state share has not, however, produced agreement on where to obtain the needed additional funds. Increasing state funding requires that the state allocate surplus revenues to public education, that other state programs be cut, or that state taxes be increased. The first possibility is the easiest and probably explains why a number of states passed school finance reforms in 1972–73 when inflation had created surpluses and revenue sharing funds were available to provide extra funds for public schools. Diversion of funds from welfare, highways, or health programs is unlikely, since demand for those services is growing even faster than for education. Increasing state taxes provokes opposition from many groups, even some of those who openly support the need for a larger state share of educational costs.

Consequently, school finance proposals calling for full state funding of schools are unlikely to be enacted, since they would entail major new state taxes, or very large increases in existing taxes. Only the closing down of New Jersey's public schools in July 1976 by the state's supreme court finally forced the New Jersey legislature to enact a modest state income tax favored by the court. In May of 1973 Oregon attempted to pass a statewide property tax on business and to increase the state income tax as alternatives to local residential property taxes that had supported the schools. It was soundly defeated at the polls.[30] The state share of educational costs is likely to increase gradually as pressures for greater equalization increase and as surplus state funds become available. The price for additional state funding, however, will be paid in controls over the growth of educational expenditures, since legislators are all too aware that school districts are more likely to increase expenditures than reduce local taxes.

REAPPORTIONMENT

Reapportionment of state legislatures is a second element in the drive toward school finance reform.[31] Legislators, for the most part, will vote the interests of their constituents on school finance matters. They will support proposals to reduce taxes and distribution formulas that increase state grants to their districts. Since alternative school finance plans have different impacts on different types of districts, legislative reapportionment changing the balance of votes between urban, suburban, and rural districts affects the fate of many school finance proposals.

The process of legislative reapportionment following the Supreme Court decision in *Baker* v. *Carr* has changed the pattern of representation in many states. Whereas in the past rural representatives were dominant, today urban and suburban communities are more heavily represented.

The increasing number of urban and suburban representatives has not necessarily improved the chances of school finance reform. Increased representation of urban interests may exacerbate conflicts in states with a large rural population. In states still predominantly rural and poor, reapportionment has given wealthy cities veto power over proposals to redistribute resources from the rich cities to the poorer countryside. Reapportionment also tends to increase the diversity of representation in state legislatures; generally there will be more blacks, more women, and more highly partisan members, which makes the task of agreeing on solutions more complicated.

The increasing representation of urban areas may also produce a change in the legislature's definition of equal educational opportunity. Urban members will emphasize the importance of providing adequate funds to meet the needs of

---

[30] Pierce, "The Politics of School Finance Reforms," pp. 113–31.

[31] Cohen, Levin, and Beaver, *The Political Limits to School Finance Reform*, pp. 23–28.

different kinds of children. Instead of focusing on providing equal resources for children, they will support plans to equalize the results of public education, particularly if it means spending more on urban children requiring higher cost services.

There is usually a lag between the election of a new group of legislators and the enactment of policies that reflect the interests of that group. Reformers must nevertheless carefully analyze the constituent interests of new legislators and include proposals that can be shown to have favorable effects on those interests. Ironically, this may lead to a substantial rethinking of school finance reform proposals, since many of the traditional solutions require metropolitan areas to provide increased subsidies of education in less populated, rural school districts.

LOCAL CONTROL

The most frequently raised argument against school finance reform is the fear that it will result in a loss of local control. The concept of local control exasperates reformers, who claim that local control is a myth.[32] Legal responsibility for public education rests with the states. They have the power to regulate almost every aspect of public education, even though most states delegate important responsibilities to local school districts. Furthermore, the reformers argue, local control is a privilege enjoyed only by relatively wealthy school districts that can afford enrichment programs and other luxuries in addition to the programs required by state education codes. Poor districts tax themselves to the limit of their ability in order to meet minimum state requirements, and therefore cannot afford optional programs. Finally, school finance reformers generally suspect that local control is actually a euphemism to obscure the efforts of educators to maintain their domination of educational decision making.

There is more to the doctrine of local control than the critics are willing to admit, however. Local school districts—despite their lack of legal authority—are still the basic unit of educational management in America. Many program and personnel decisions are made by local school boards and administrators. Parents and taxpayers are also able to influence these decisions through their periodic votes for school board members and on school budget and bond elections.

The real question is whether school finance reform would weaken local control. The proponents of reform point to a study by the Urban Institute showing no consistent correlation between the percentage of state funding and the degree of local school district autonomy.[33] Those who want to protect local control point to the deeply held belief that control follows dollars. They need

---

[32] Meltsner and Nakamura, "Political Implications of *Serrano*," pp. 278–79.

[33] See Betsy Levin and Michael A. Cohen, *Levels of State Aid Related to State Restrictions on Local School District Decision-Making* (Washington, D.C.: The Urban Institute, 1973).

only describe the regulations tied to most federally funded programs to emphasize their point.

Believers in local control also argue that, as a general principle, government should leave decision making and administration to the smallest unit of government competent to handle them.[34] This argument places the burden on reformers to show that the state can do a better job of managing schools than local districts, something that is difficult for them to prove.

Whether it is fact or fiction, the doctrine of local control has broad legislative and popular support. Attempts by legislators to restrict local spending or redistribute local tax dollars among districts will have to work around the local control argument.

Not all education groups, of course, will adhere staunchly to the local control line. Representatives from wealthy districts will defend the principle at all costs. Representatives from poorer districts will accept some loss of local control for additional state financial support. Similarly, conservatives and republican legislators are more wedded to the principle of local control because it means smaller state budgets and lower state taxes. Liberals and Democrats may agree with the concept but support more funds for equalization and additional restrictions on local district spending. Local control is an important element in debates about school finance reform. Successful reform proposals must acknowledge its symbolic importance if not its reality.

ACCOUNTABILITY

A fourth issue affecting proposals to reform school finance is accountability. Rapidly rising school expenditures with little or no improvement in performance have led taxpayers and their legislative representatives to demand demonstrable results in return for additional educational funding. Demands for accountability may be used to oppose school finance reform. If increasing educational funding makes no difference in the performance of schools, why should we support new educational programs or impose new taxes on our constituents? Accountability has become, in other words, an important political argument against increased support of public education.

Demands for greater accountability are also a direct challenge to the doctrine of local control. To the extent that local control serves to protect the hegemony of educators over educational decisions, accountability moves in the opposite direction by increasing political supervision of public school programs. On one hand, the legislatures themselves are taking a more direct role in the operation of schools. Instead of providing funds and leaving educational choices to educators, they are attempting to define a basic education program and are

---

[34]For a thoughtful defense of local control in education, see John E. Coons, William H. Clune, III, and Stephen D. Sugarman, *Private Wealth and Public Education* (Cambridge, Mass.: Harvard University Press, 1970), pp. 14-20.

likely to support specific programs which are proved effective. California's Early Childhood Education program is a good example of the increasing legislative support of programs whose effectiveness can be demonstrated. On the other hand, legislatures are enacting legislation to increase citizen influence over educational decisions. Open meeting laws, assessment programs, and efforts to devolve educational decisions to the school site are all intended to increase the responsiveness of public schools to the citizens they serve.

Most accountability proposals are vigorously opposed by teacher unions and professional organizations. Fear of teacher evaluations, revision of tenure and fair dismissal laws, and provisions for merit or performance pay mobilize teachers against such proposals. In other words, while provisions to increase educational accountability may be essential to obtain support from business groups and many legislators, their inclusion greatly weakens the probability of support from the educational lobby. A struggle has arisen between educational interests and legislators responding to constituent demands for greater accountability on school finance reform. The effects of this struggle vary from state to state depending upon the strength of the various groups involved. This issue complicates the process of creating a proposal capable of majority support, yet it cannot be ignored. As mentioned before, the proponents of reform are relatively weak in most states; any weakening of the education lobby's support narrows even further the potential coalition for school finance reform.

EQUALIZATION

Most school finance reform proposals contain some element of equalization, that is, proposed changes in the distribution of state funds to reduce unequal expenditures among school districts. Legislators and educational policy makers generally believe that dollars do make a difference in the quality of education a child receives, and that equal educational opportunity is enhanced by a more equal distribution of resources among school districts. These beliefs persist despite contradictory social science evidence on the cost-quality question.[35] Agreement on the goal of equalization is not matched, however, by consensus on how to bring it about.

There are at least four separate questions that arise in developing an equalization program:

1. What should be equalized?
2. How much equalization is required?

---

[35] For a review of the literature on the cost-quality debate, see John E. McDermott and Stephen P. Klein, "The Cost-Quality Debate in School Finance Litigation: Do Dollars Make a Difference?" in *Law and Contemporary Problems,* 38, No. 3 (Winter–Spring, 1973), 415–35. Also Harvey A. Averch et al., *How Effective is Schooling? A Critical Review and Synthesis of Research Findings* (Santa Monica: The Rand Corporation, 1972).

3. What method should be used to provide equalization?
4. How fast should educational spending be equalized?

With respect to what should be equalized, there are three frequently mentioned possibilities: expenditures per pupil, educational resources per pupil, and educational outcomes. Providing equal expenditures per pupil is the simplest measure of equality but unacceptable to most educators. It entirely overlooks the fact that it costs more to provide the same services in some districts than in others, and that the distribution of children who are relatively costly to educate is uneven across school districts. Equalizing educational outcomes would also create problems because it would require improved diagnostic techniques and would involve substantially increased subsidies to slow learners at the expense of more capable students. Policy makers generally agree on the desirability of equalizing resources per pupil by making allowances for educational cost differences among school districts and by providing categorical aid to districts with higher proportions of difficult to educate children. Representatives from high cost, urban districts negotiate for larger categorical programs and cost adjustments. Rural and moderately wealthy suburban representatives generally favor larger equalization grants.

There is also disagreement on how much equalization is desirable, or required by the principle of equal educational opportunity. Those who adhere strictly to the "fiscal neutrality principle," "that the quality of public education may not be a function of wealth other than the wealth of the state as a whole," believe that all educational resources, including capital outlay, should be equalized. Others argue that only the basic education program mandated by state constitutions need be equalized; that what a district does in providing services beyond what is required by the state is its own business. Again, the representatives of poor districts argue for across the board equalization since they must pay for only a fraction of every dollar received as equalization, whereas representatives of wealthy districts try to restrict expenditures to be equalized.

Equalization may be achieved in several ways. Most states have some form of foundation program in which the state guarantees a district a specific number of dollars per pupil or classroom unit. The least politically costly way of increasing equalization is to raise the state's foundation level. The state's funding method thus remains the same, and little or no money is taken away from high-wealth, high-spending districts.

Actually, the political feasibility of raising the foundation floor depends on the source of additional funds needed to meet the higher state guarantee. If the funds come from a statewide property tax, then high property wealth districts suffer increases in property tax rates. If the state draws the extra funds from state income or sales taxes, however, the burden of equalization is better disguised and probably more acceptable. Full state funding and district power equalizing, discussed in earlier chapters, entail both lower expenditures in high-spending districts and a major redistribution of local tax dollars from high-wealth areas to property-poor areas. The "Robin Hood" character of these proposals and uncertainty of impact create strong opposition. Those who would gain won't believe it until they actually experience it; and those who would lose fight to protect their current privileges.

Finally, equalization is more politically acceptable if it can be phased-in over several years. The courts have been generally unspecific on how fast a state must move to equalize educational opportunity. In California, Judge Jefferson gave the state legislature six years. In New Jersey the court specified a date by which the legislature had to comply with its decision, but then backed down when the legislature failed to do so. The courts are not equipped to determine state educational finance policy. Consequently, if the state can show that it has a good reason for moving deliberately but gradually toward an equal distribution of resources the courts are likely to find such a solution acceptable.

PROPERTY TAX RELIEF

Property tax relief is inexorably linked to the prospects for school finance reform. Educational expenditures have risen rapidly since the 1950s and along with them the burden of local property taxes. Property-poor districts generally must tax themselves at much higher rates to raise an amount equal to that raised in a property-rich district. Therefore, state programs to equalize expenditures—or to equalize the resources raised by commensurate local tax efforts— produce property tax relief in poor areas and property tax grief in wealthy ones. In other words, property tax relief and equalization are actually the same thing. The major difference is that equalization attracts relatively little public support (and likely opposition from those fearing a loss of local control), while property tax relief is a politically attractive euphemism.

Just as equalization ultimately requires a redistribution from high-wealth to low-wealth districts, property tax relief also involves not an overall lessening of tax burdens but a shifting of tax burdens.[36] Usually, property tax relief means shifts in existing taxes from elderly and low-income property owners to some other classification of taxpayers. The appeal of property tax relief depends in large part on the ability of the program to disguise who eventually must pay the cost of the relief program. For example, a property tax relief program that shifted the burden onto business property would generate strong business opposition. Corporations would waste no time informing the public that their higher tax costs are likely to drive away new businesses from the area, thus contributing to unemployment, and that higher costs will eventually be passed on to the consumer. Increases in state sales taxes or income taxes, on the other hand, spread the added burden more evenly, even though the same people who benefit from property tax relief end up paying for some of their own benefits.

[36]Meltsner and Nakamura, "Political Implications of Serrano," p. 273.

Property tax relief can actually be accomplished in several ways. Elderly or low-income homeowners may either receive a rebate for a portion of their property taxes from the state, or they may receive exemptions from local property taxes, which monies are then supplied from alternate state revenues to the local taxing jurisdiction. The advantages of direct taxpayer rebates or exemptions are that specific categories of recipients, such as the elderly and the poor, can be identified and benefited, and that state officials can claim credit for the assistance.

Another means of providing property tax relief is to impose limits on local tax rates or school expenditures. Some states have such limitations and others have attempted to impose them. Besides setting a maximum rate in all districts, states can accomplish the same thing by imposing a statewide property tax, the effects of which are to equalize tax burdens across districts.

A third possibility for providing residential property tax relief is to shift some of the tax burden from residential property to business property. The advantages of splitting the tax rolls and taxing business property statewide are that:

1. a major source of wealth differences among districts resulting from the location of business property would thereby be eliminated;
2. the major opposition to raising property taxes comes from homeowners; and
3. property that is income producing would be paying the higher taxes.

Businesses are strongly opposed to this idea and argue with some justification that once their property is legally distinguished from residential property, popularly elected legislators would have little reason not to raise business tax rates with impunity. The technical problems of placing apartment and farm property into residential or business categories have also detracted from the political feasibility of this idea.

Despite the problems in providing property tax relief, it remains a highly popular idea. States finding it impossible to develop politically feasible equalization programs may accomplish much the same result via property tax relief. The benefits may be even more equitable than those of other equalization schemes, since they would go to property-poor families wherever they lived. Property tax relief would also eliminate the unfairness inherent in equalization schemes that increase the tax burdens of poor families living in property-wealthy cities.

CORRELATES OF STATE SCHOOL FINANCE REFORM

That school finance reform has been difficult to accomplish should not be surprising, for it frequently requires major alterations in existing institutions and in long practiced patterns of citizen behavior. Machiavelli warns of the difficulty of creating new institutions in his advice to new rulers:

> So they should observe that there is nothing more difficult to plan or more uncertain of success or more dangerous to carry out than to introduce new institutions, because the introducer has as his enemies all those who profit from the old institutions, and has as lukewarm defenders all those who will profit from the new institutions. This lukewarmness results partly from fear of their opponents, who have the laws on their side, partly from the incredulity of men, who do not actually believe new things unless they see them yielding solid proof. Hence whenever those who are enemies have occasion to attack, they do it like partisans, and the others resist lukewarmly; thus lukewarm subjects and innovating prince are both in danger.[37]

Many states have attempted to reform their systems of school finance, and from their successes and failures we can discern in general which strategies are most likely to work. The task of school finance reformers, of course, is to develop a proposal that can obtain enough support to be enacted by the legislature, signed by the governor, and approved by the voters. Since the supporters of school finance reform are usually weak and disunited, they must actually create a coalition of supporters. Reformers must begin by assuming that opponents greatly outnumber the supporters and by figuring out how to persuade weaker opponents to change sides.

In general the tactics of building winning coalitions are well known and practiced in most state legislatures. Major provisions are added to a proposal to attract potential supporters. Those elements likely to mobilize opposition are deleted or disguised. This requires bargaining with powerful interests, and, as we mentioned earlier, a willingness to settle for less than ideal solutions. Once the basic proposal has been constructed so as to accommodate the major interests required to enact it, sponsors of the proposal enter into negotiations with other possible supporters to gather additional support, and with opponents to weaken their opposition. Minor provisions are added and dropped, and promises of future support are traded off against promises not to oppose the bill openly at some stage in the legislative process. Success in formulating a reform proposal that is attractive to a winning coalition comes from understanding the underlying policy issues involved and how those issues affect different groups of constituents.

PRECONDITIONS FOR REFORM

We can now provide more specific observations about the development of successful school finance proposals.

[37]Niccolo Machiavelli, "The Prince," in *Machiavelli: The Chief Works and Others,* trans. Allan Gilbert Vol. I, Copyright 1965 by Duke University Press.

Those who have observed the politics of school finance reform agree that several conditions greatly favor the passage of reform legislation.[38] First, states passing school finance reforms usually have a history of attempts to change the methods of financing schools. Reform comes about through an evolutionary process rather than suddenly in response to specific events. For example, Berke describes how reform came about in Kansas:

> Kansas was a state in which, since the 1970 session of the legislature, there has been an alternation of standing committees and interim committees (during the off season of the legislature) studying and considering change in the educational funding system. Finally, in the legislative session of 1973, a reasonably significant piece of legislation, a modified power equalizing approach, was passed. When you trace this progression forward you can see the proposals and counterproposals developing, closure slowly coming about, and a continuing of legislative personnel and staff working on the effort.[39]

Similarly, successful reform efforts in Minnesota, Florida, and California emerged only after years of study and the consideration and rejection of numerous proposals.

School finance reform is also sufficiently unpopular and complex that some outside event is often necessary to rouse the legislature to build support for a reform proposal. In a number of states, legal opinions have activated public and legislative concern for school finance reform and even forced a legislative response. Court decisions in themselves are unlikely to produce an acceptable school finance package. Nevertheless, they may act as a catalyst for change. *Serrano* v. *Priest* in California not only forced changes in that state but became the major theoretical justification for reform efforts in other states. Governor McCall frequently talked about the "Serrano principle" in his unsuccessful effort to win voter approval of a full state funding program in Oregon.

Of course, there are other external events that influence school finance reform. The availability of revenue sharing funds for two entitlement periods in 1972-73 made it easier for several states to pass reforms that year. Widespread voter rejection of school district special levies forced legislative action in the state of Washington. Special school finance meetings convened by the Education Commission of the States, the National Conference of State Legislatures, and the National Educational Finance Project produced new ideas that found their ways into successful reform proposals. In most cases these external events are gratuitous. Nevertheless, reformers may consider whetting the public

---

[38] A good example of a participant-observer view of the correlates of school finance reform is Joel S. Berke, "Strategies and Tactics for State School Finance Reform," an address delivered to the National Symposium on State School Finance Reform, November 26, 1973 (Washington, D.C.: Syracuse University Research Corporation, 1973).

[39] Berke, "Strategies and Tactics," p. 3.

appetite for reform by filing lawsuits and encouraging voter initiatives designed to increase the sense of urgency for reform.

Political leadership is a third precondition for reform.[40] Successful proposals require a great deal of bargaining and compromise. Consequently supporters in the legislature must be willing to expend the effort to build a winning coalition. Governors in some states, such as Minnesota, have played an important role in educational finance reform, particularly when they have been elected on platforms calling for such measures. Private commissions and state education departments, on the other hand, have not been close enough to the legislative cloakrooms to be effective. Since school finance proposals are complicated, and the opportunities numerous for a proposal to be derailed, leadership in both houses of the legislature is important. Support of both presiding officers is also helpful. Most important, though, is the attention and guidance of committee chairpersons in both houses who are well informed and are willing to stake their political careers or reputations on the outcome of specific proposals. School finance reform needs all the help it can get from any source, and there are inevitably able people from universities and educational organizations who perform useful services. The point is that their efforts are likely to fail if they do not have the assistance of powerful insiders—legislators who have the respect and political resources needed to persuade uncommitted colleagues to go along.

Finally, school finance reform almost always coincides with the availability of surplus funds to increase expenditures in low-spending districts *without recapturing funds from high-spending districts.* Florida's reform program drew on $300 million of surplus state funds. The Maine legislature was able to use three years of state revenue sharing money to ease the burden of its financial reform program in the first few years. With the recession in 1973–74, state surpluses evaporated and with them passage of many reform bills. As resources for education become more scarce, as we believe they will, reform will become more difficult and less frequent. Future reforms may either have to be more modest in scope or wait for short-run fiscal surpluses created by favorable economic events or federal assumption of state programs such as welfare. The politics of school finance reform is the politics of more. Those who would lose much from reform usually have adequate incentive and resources to block it.

STRATEGIES OF REFORM

Reform of any kind is difficult, as Machiavelli warns. Reform of a state's school finance system is particularly difficult because so many resources, both physical and human, are involved and because educational finance reform by

[40]*Ibid.,* pp. 4–5.

itself is seldom sufficiently attractive to pass. Consequently, careful attention must be given to developing a finance proposal.

Perhaps the most important consideration is the necessity of packaging school finance reform with other more popular measures. Usually, reformers combine finance reform with property tax relief, since the latter is clearly more popular with legislators and local voters. This particular combination involves an interesting set of tradeoffs. Property tax relief means there is less money provided to schools locally. This means the state must assume part of the costs of maintaining current school programs, leaving less available for equalization. The greater the extent of property tax relief, the less there is available for equalization and vice versa. School finance reform may also be tied to programs providing greater accountability. This is the approach Governor Brown in California proposed. Again, however, tradeoffs are involved. Accountability will weaken support for school finance reform among teachers. Accountability, on the other hand, may be necessary to win the support of conservative legislators and the public.

Successful packaging of a reform proposal also requires another kind of tradeoff within the legislature itself. Urban legislators may demand specific categorical programs in return for their support of meaningful equalization provisions. Urban school districts are benefited by counting students enrolled in school rather than those in attendance. Whether to use average daily membership (ADM) or average daily attendance (ADA) may become an important issue in legislative bargaining. In Utah, for example, disagreement on this issue was resolved in a most predictable way. The legislature finally settled the conflict between urban and suburban interests by making the student count ADA plus ADM divided by two.[41]

Political bargaining and compromise can get out of hand, however. Given the uncertainties of the legislative process, some legislators have a tendency to strive for everyone's approval of their proposals. Legislation designed for such a comprehensive coalition becomes unreasonably costly since every interest's special program must be added. Furthermore, Christmas tree bills of this kind provide legislators and voters with more specifics to vote against. Finally, such bills, in trying to satisfy too many interests, often obscure the original goals. Reformers should try to keep their proposals relatively clean by aiming for a minimum winning coalition.[42] Legislators and the public deserve to know what they are being asked to accept.

A second strategic consideration is the scope of the proposed reform. In general, it is best not to aim too high. Large comprehensive changes excite strong opposition from those whose interests are hurt. Modesty in the reformer's goals also reduce the risks of making mistakes. Public policy failures

---

[41] *Ibid.*, p. 5.

[42] William H. Riker, *The Theory of Political Coalitions* (New Haven, Conn.: Yale University Press, 1962), pp. 32–33.

occur too frequently to afford us much certainty that intended goals will be achieved. Modest, incremental changes minimize the changes for major mistakes and provide policy makers the time to correct small errors.

Finally, policy makers should carefully consider the consequences of proposed reforms on the public. The ultimate voice in determining whether a program works is the public's voice. The public pays the necessary taxes and experiences the effects of the changes proposed. In general, the amount of difficulty state government can expect in implementing school finance reforms is a function of the scope of the proposed changes, the number of the population whose behavior would be changed, and the significance of the changed behavior to those being controlled.[43] The corollary of this proposition is that the more modest the changes, the fewer the number of people involved, and the less sensitive the issues included, the more likely the public is to accept the proposed change. Our experience with racial integration illustrates this point. The efforts of both courts and legislative bodies have simply been insufficient to combat the large number of citizens who feel aggrieved by the steps taken to achieve racial balance in public schools.

Finally, legislators should pay particular attention to the rewards for compliance and penalties for noncompliance. Often public policies fail because rewards and penalties are inadequate. A graduated system of rewards and penalties—providing large and increasing rewards for those whose behaviors are most important, and large and increasing penalties for behaviors policy makers wish most to discourage—may work. Most important, however, is to recognize that people generally do not like to be told what to do. School finance reforms that impose strict controls and limitations are bound to be unpopular. Free choice and voluntary compliance should always be considered as a distinct possibility.

A Personal Note

The funding of public schools is a responsibility of the state. For too long, state governments have permitted systems of school finance that discriminate against children living in property-poor school districts. They have become the victims of inferior education for no other reason than the location of their family's home. We believe that steps can be taken to rectify this injustice. The steps may be small at first and it may take years to complete the journey. Furthermore, the path toward reform may be poorly marked, leading to many sidetracks and delays. Nevertheless the effort must be made to provide equal educational opportunity for everyone regardless of background.

The one cautionary note that must be sounded for school finance reform-

[43]William C. Mitchell, *Public Choice in America,* p. 342.

ers is never to underestimate the value of the people's choice. In a democracy, the people not only have the right to participate in public institutions and to control their decisions, but also when allowed to exercise those rights, will produce better collective decisions. As educators we have no corner on the knowledge of what kind or how much education is in the public's best interest. We must learn to encourage citizen choice. By doing so we will not only sharpen their ability to make better choices, but we will also greatly increase their incentive to make maximum use of the educational opportunities provided.

Summary

School finance reform ultimately requires the support of local citizens and members of state legislatures. Local citizens, through their votes for school board members and in local school budget and bond elections, participate in decisions affecting the kind and quality of education provided. The first part of this chapter has examined the procedures through which citizen preferences are translated into educational policy.

Special attention has been given to the meaning of the so-called "taxpayers' revolt." We suggest that the frequent rejection of local school budget and bond proposals reflects a majority belief that the benefits of additional educational spending are outweighed by the additional costs involved, rather than the more widely accepted view that the public has become disillusioned with government and schools in particular.

School finance reform in state legislatures must overcome a wide variety of problems created by many competing values and interests that surround school finance proposals. Legislative inaction often results because of complex legal maneuverings in the courts, disagreement over the problems needing to be resolved, uncertainty about the results of proposed solutions, and widely divergent and competing interests. We have attempted to divide the school finance reform problem into several parts in the belief that the resolution of more specific issues increases the likelihood of more comprehensive reform. These issues —the scope of state responsibility, reapportionment, local control, accountability, equalization, and property tax relief—lie at the heart of most reform proposals.

The chapter concludes with a discussion of the correlates of state school finance reform. In the legislature, the main task is to develop a proposal that can gain enough support to be enacted by the legislature, signed by the governor, and, perhaps, be approved by the voters. This requires a package of provisions that appeals to a majority and at the same time does not arouse the intense opposition of any strong interests. In general, we find that reforms take time, often being enacted after years of unsuccessful efforts. External intervention by state courts may, in some cases, start the school finance reform process moving. Equally important, however, will be the political backing of governors and legislative leaders, and the availability of surplus funds so that most local school districts can benefit from a new method of distributing state funds.

The task of building a successful reform proposal takes much legislative skill and a keen appreciation of the public's interests and attitudes about education and taxes. The more comprehensive the change, the more people who are affected; and, the greater the change required, the greater the opposition proponents can expect. Resistance to change will be less in proportion to how much free choice citizens are given and how much the plan relies on voluntary compliance.

IV

Special Topics in
Public Educational Finance

14

MANAGEMENT
OF CAPITAL

Capital Construction

During the period from World War II to the end of the 1960s an unprecedented number of new schools were built. The rapid increase in student population, combined with migrations from farm to city and suburb, made necessary the construction of thousands of new schools. The decreasing birth rate in the 1970s caused a relaxation in the pressure for new construction, but migration continued, and many school districts are still building new schools and additions to old ones; others are making major repairs or are replacing schools that are outmoded or in poor condition. Money spent for these purposes is classified as a capital expense, and is normally budgeted and accounted for separately from current operating expense. Capital expenses are usually limited to purchase of items of a permanent nature, normally divided into the categories of land and improvements, buildings, and equipment.

An important characteristic of capital expense is unevenness of expenditure. Construction of a school in one year may cost several million dollars, with expenditures in succeeding years being almost zero. Only the largest districts, such as New York and Chicago, can manage to even out these capital expenditures and spend about the same amount each year. This unevenness has important implications. Because construction of a new school is such an enormous investment, it is worth spending a great deal of time and effort to be sure that it is done properly. And because financing capital expenditures completely out of current revenues would mean large fluctuations in tax rate, borrowing is utilized. In the section that follows we discuss briefly the steps involved in constructing a new school. Then we turn our attention to the topics of borrowing and the financing of debt.

HOW IMPORTANT ARE SCHOOL FACILITIES?

The amount of school board and administrative time spent on bond elections and school plant planning is great, and constitutes a burden particularly in medium and smaller school districts on already hard-worked administrators. Unfortunately, there is little to guide us in determining the importance of particular facilities to the education of students. It is clear that if students are to be taught they must be housed, but it is by no means clear how well they should be housed. Should there be an allowance of at least 40 square feet per student in classrooms? Should elementary school sites contain at least 10 acres, and high school sites 25? Should there be a multi-purpose room at each school? These, and many other similar standards are incorporated into the rules of state departments of education and serve as guidelines for school districts all over the country. Yet studies have consistently shown little or no relationship between provision of facilities and educational attainment. Students in old and crowded schools frequently do as well as or better than students in new, expensive schools. It can be argued that new facilities are necessary to operate the more modern instructional programs, particularly the open classroom concept. This is probably true, but we have little hard proof as yet that the open classroom promotes such increased learning that it justifies large expenditures on new school plants.

However, the fact that no close connection between facilities and educational attainment has been demonstrated does not mean that such a connection does not exist. Most studies concentrate on cognitive learning, primarily of reading and mathematics. The attitudes developed in a clean, modern school may be important, even though we are not able to measure them well.

We are in the same position regarding facilities as with the rest of the educational enterprise: we know that minimum provision is essential, but we do not know how much additional provision will yield commensurate returns in increased education. The result is that schools will continue to be designed and built based on community standards and the pressures of concerned teachers, administrators, and parents, rather than on scientific benefit-cost analysis of alternatives.

We are on somewhat less shaky ground in deciding the size of a school. A number of studies have shown that there is a range of size that is reasonable.[1]

---

[1]Cohn, for example, found an optimum size high school in Iowa to be between 1,500 and 2,000 students. Osburn found an optimum high school size in Missouri of

Economies of scale dictate a minimum size. In a school housing six grades, for example, an enrollment of 100 students would mean only about 17 at each grade level. If a teacher is hired for each grade, the cost for teacher salaries per student is greatly increased. There are similar diseconomies of scale in other parts of the operation of a small school. There seems to be a traditional view that an elementary school of fewer than 300 students is uneconomical, as is a secondary school of fewer than 600 students.

At the other end, very large schools may result in financial economies bought at the expense of student and teacher satisfaction. A smaller school usually develops a sense of community that is not evident in a large school. Studies show that a smaller percentage of students participate in extracurricular activities in a large school, and there are proportionately fewer opportunities for leadership.[2] An elementary school of more than 800 students, and a high school of more than 2000 students may encounter these kinds of problems.

BUILDING A NEW SCHOOL

Purchase of land and construction of a new school are major undertakings in any school district. Large districts often do enough of this to have a special staff for the purpose; small districts must usually rely on the business manager to initiate the action. There are a number of books on the subject of construction, and an extended treatment is out of place here.[3] Nevertheless, a brief outline of the steps in a construction project is useful.

The first step is determining the extent of need. Projections of number of students to be served by the district for at least five years are essential (see Chapter Twelve for projection methods). These projections, combined with careful analyses of present building capacity, provide a picture of future needs. The second step is to determine where construction will take place. Additions to present schools may be the least expensive alternative if space is available on the site and if shared facilities (multi-purpose room, playgrounds, etc.) are adequate for the additional student load. However, this lower cost may be balanced by higher busing costs if enough students live in part of the district where there are

2244. Elchanan Cohn, "Economies of Scale in Iowa High School Operations," *Journal of Human Resources,* 3, No. 4 (Fall 1968), 422–34. Donald D. Osburn, "Economies of Size Associated with Public High Schools," *Review of Economics and Statistics,* 52 (February 1970), 113–15. See also Stephan Michelson, "Equal Resource Allocation," *Journal of Human Resources,* 7, No. 3 (Summer 1972), 283–306; Martin T. Katzman, *The Political Economy of Urban Schools* (Cambridge, Mass.: Harvard University Press, 1971); and John Riew, "Economies of Scale in High School Operations," *Review of Economics and Statistics,* 48 (August 1966), 280–87.

[2] See, for example, Roger G. Barker and Paul V. Gump, *Big School, Small School* (Stanford: Stanford University Press, 1964).

[3] Two examples are Basil Costaldi, *Creative Planning of Educational Facilities* (Chicago: Rand McNally 1969) and *Guide for Planning Educational Facilities* (Columbus, Ohio: Council of Educational Facility Planners, 1969).

no schools. Thus, it is vital that the projection include not only the number of students to be served, but also where they live and will live in the future. The necessary data may often be obtained through consultation with the city or county planning department, the electric and telephone companies, and major builders and developers.

Assuming that it is desirable to build a school at a new site, the district must now proceed to purchase land. The simplest solution would be to find a piece of land in the middle of an area about to become a large subdivision and agree with the owner on a price. However, it is much more likely that a suitable site must be assembled from parcels owned by a number of individual owners. A developer ordinarily does this by proceeding in secrecy, obtaining options on each necessary parcel before making any purchases to prevent owners from holding out for a high price. It is difficult for school districts to deal in secrecy, particularly in states with "open meeting" laws. However, the district has an ultimate weapon not possessed by the private developer, the power of condemnation. Districts proceed in different ways on land purchases, with some doing all purchasing through negotiation and others using condemnation exclusively. Condemnation has the advantage of the price being set by a court, which relieves the district of allegations of overpayment or cozy deals. Negotiation, however, is often more appropriate when establishing cooperative arrangements with the developer of a large area, or where special concessions important to the owner and unimportant to the district (such as payments spread over a period of years) would result in a lower price. Each situation must be approached on its own merits. In any case, the district's legal counsel must be involved in every step of the transactions.

Having selected a site, architectural planning must be commenced. A good architect can plan imaginatively and simultaneously save the district money; a poor one can be a catastrophe, with effects that last for the life of the building. Selection of architects should not be on a bid basis. The fees of most architects are standard, and any architect who promises to charge a lesser fee should be viewed skeptically. Rather, an architect should be selected on the basis of past performance in other situations. Firms that have constructed schools elsewhere should be invited to present sample photographs of their work, along with a description of the size of the firm and the kinds of expertise available. After a preliminary screening, district personnel should visit schools designed by the firms under consideration, and talk with administrators, teachers, and maintenance personnel. This will narrow the choice to a few architects, who should then be interviewed regarding preferred method of working, current office workload, and particular employees to be assigned to the project. It is important that the personalities of these individuals be compatible with those of the district personnel who are to be most closely involved with the project.

The school district should next develop educational specifications. These detail the number of students to be housed, and the kind of educational programs offered. The more careful and complete these specifications are, the more likely it is that the architect will be able to design the kind of school the district wants. Avoid an architect who says, "Tell me how many students you want to house, and I will design a school for you with no further worry on your part." Development of educational specifications is one of the most important parts of the job of designing a school and should involve teachers, supervisors, and administrators. It is not a job to be rushed, for time must be allowed for the reconciliation of differing views on the educational program.

With the educational specifications in hand, the architect confers with district representatives to develop preliminary ideas through a great deal of talking accompanied by sketches. At this point it is desirable to have the district delegation small, in order to be able to reach tentative agreement on many aspects of the plan in a reasonable length of time. However, a number of sessions may be necessary, and the district may need to gather additional data or refine its educational specifications. At some point the architect presents preliminary plans, usually consisting of plan views and elevations. When these have been sufficiently modified they will be ready for formal approval by the school board.

The architect can now develop detailed drawings and specifications. It is important that from this point on the district's maintenance supervisor be involved, for the decisions made here can save or cost the district many thousands of dollars over the life of the building. Final detailed drawings should be carefully reviewed by district representatives. Errors found at this point are easy to correct. If found during construction, they result in costly change orders; if not found until after the building is completed they are even more costly to correct.

The district now advertises for bids. Each bidder will obtain a set of plans from the architect, estimate manpower and materials necessary, and obtain commitments from subcontractors. Typically, the general contractor does all carpentry work, some of the other work, and supervises and coordinates all construction. Subcontractors are usually obtained for electrical work, plumbing, site grading, mechanical work, and for a number of other jobs. At the date and time advertised, general contractors' bids are opened and read. The district is generally required to accept the bid of the lowest *qualified* bidder, but this need not necessarily be the lowest bid. The architect should be present, and should carefully review the two or three lowest bids. The financial status of the general contractor should be determined, if possible, and performance on other contracts ascertained. The same is true of each of the subcontractors, who must be listed in the bid. There are many other items that must be assessed by the architect before recommending the award of the bid. (If recommending the award to other than the lowest bidder, the architect should have good reasons, for there will probably be a challenge from the lowest bidder before the school board.) The board need not award the bid to anyone, although it usually will if the lowest acceptable bid is at or below the architect's estimate. Frequently the architect will specify alternatives, with a separate bid on each alternative, in order to be able to adjust the size of the total contract to the funds available in case the bid is above the estimates. This complicates selection of the bidder, for the lowest bidder on the base contract may be high on some of the alternative additions.

Construction now begins, under the supervision of the architect who visits the job site several times a week to ensure that the plans are followed, to resolve problems in interpretation of drawings or specifications, and to develop change orders where these become necessary. However, it is difficult for the architect to be on the site at all times, and shoddy workmanship can occur and be covered up between visits. Thus, it is essential for a district to hire a full-time inspector of its own. This should be a person thoroughly experienced in all facets of the building trades. He or she should be on the job at any time work is underway, and should insist on the opportunity to inspect all work before it is covered. This is a crucial role, for opportunities for concealing poor workmanship or outright fraud are great, and the potential cost to the district is much more than will be paid to the inspector in salary.

The final construction step is formal acceptance of the building after the architect has certified to the school board that construction is complete and satisfactory. Final payment may be made soon thereafter, although a percentage may be held for a legally specified period against the possibility of liens filed by employees or subcontractors for nonpayment by the general contractor.

However, this is not the final step in preparing a new school for students. The most important remaining activity (begun well before completion of construction) is purchase of equipment for the building. This involves careful planning to be sure that everything will be delivered in time. Lists of items must be compiled and cross-checked. Detailed specifications are drawn up, based both on the educational needs expressed by principal and teachers and the desires of the maintenance supervisor. These are frequently in conflict, for maintenance personnel prefer standardized equipment so as to minimize the problem of spare parts and of training repairmen, whereas teachers frequently want something unique, in the belief that it will be more convenient or provide for better instruction. Equipment other than that for a new building (such as additional desks for an existing school) is also a capital expense, but is usually purchased from current revenues instead of from bond funds. These capital expenditures from current revenues are usually minor compared with those from bond funds.

TRANSPORTATION EXPENDITURES

However, there is one capital expenditure usually not financed from bond funds that can be a major problem for districts. School busing has become a major activity of districts, and they maintain large fleets of buses. Because buses do not last as long as buildings, it is usually considered inappropriate to purchase them from bond funds. School districts faced with this problem have several alternatives. One is to set up a schedule for replacement whereby a percentage of the buses are retired and replaced each year. This smooths out the capital expenditures and works well if the district is not faced with the necessity of purchasing a large number of additional buses at one time (as a result, for example, of a court decision requiring desegregation).

A second possiblity is lease-purchase. The agreement is made with a bus company, a finance company, or another governmental agency to lease new buses for a period of years, after which the buses will become the property of the district. This is really an installment purchase agreement with the advantage of spreading costs over a period of time. The concomitant disadvantage is the extra cost, which amounts to the equivalent of interest payments on money borrowed for purchase. Whether leasing will be advantageous depends upon the provisions of the state's transportation aid formula. If it provides aid for current transportation expense but not for capital expenditures, it may be to the advantage of the district to lease-purchase all vehicles.

Another possibility is to contract for all or part of the district's transportation. The contractor then has the responsibility for purchasing, maintaining, and operating the buses, and the district merely pays a contracted price. The principal problem with contracting is that the district loses some control over maintenance, quality of personnel, and scheduling. A secondary problem may be that there may be only one contractor in the area, preventing a competitive bid.

SURPLUS FACILITIES

Many districts, because of enrollment declines or population shifts, have underused or unused buildings. Disposing of these is often more a political problem than a fiscal one. Regardless of how underused a facility is, those families remaining in the neighborhood usually prefer to have their children attend a neighborhood school than be bused to another one. Economic arguments are often ineffectual in such situations, and programs usually remain in force until the district has severe financial problems. District administrators tend to use such facilities to expand special programs, rather than consolidating, and this is one of the reasons that declining enrollment usually accelerates expenditure increase per student.

In some cases, it is possible to convert surplus facilities to other community uses. Since they are frequently in a section of the community that has little in the way of other community facilities, the use of a surplus school may help to bring this area to a par with newer and more affluent areas. The school may be operated as a community facility by the school district, or it may be conveyed (usually without charge) to another local government.

Alternatively, another local government may have a use for the space. It is usually more economical to deed the school to this other government than to attempt to sell it as surplus while the other government purchases land and constructs a new building. Construing the public's interests too narrowly often blocks such action, however. School district officials will have more money to spend on school purposes if they sell the building than if they give it to another government, but if the other government must purchase the building at its full value it may decide that it is more advantageous to construct a new building. Thus the taxpayers who support both governments will ultimately pay more than if the old building were merely transferred.

Another possibility is renting surplus facilities to private individuals and corporations. However, smaller districts in particular are often not practiced in being landlords, and the rents they receive may hardly compensate for the bickering among community leaders and depreciation of the property. The district may also be in the precarious position of trying to decide whether to accept a lucrative rent from a tenant whose business is disapproved of by some members of the community.

If the district decides to dispose of the building and land as surplus, the method is usually specified in the state education code. Typically, it must be advertised and sold to the highest bidder. Sometimes a bid by another governmental agency that is no more than a specified percentage below the highest private bid must be accepted instead.

Debt and Its Management

CATEGORIES OF DEBT

There are three categories of debt, and they apply equally to individuals, school districts, and corporations. The first category is represented by the amount owed for items recently purchased and received, but not yet paid for. For an individual, examples are the charge account at the department store, or the amount owed for current purchases on a credit card. This category of debt, for school districts, would be called "accounts payable." While these are certainly a form of debt, they are normally paid out of current revenues within a month of receipt of goods and invoice. Thus they need not be further considered as part of debt management. Of course, if a district should be unable to pay its accounts on time, it may try to stall its creditors (dangerous if you want to deal with them again), or borrow from the bank. This converts the debt into the second type.

This second type of debt is the sort that individuals incur when they borrow money on a short-term basis to pay for purchases, or do the equivalent by paying less than the full balance on their monthly credit card statement. We can call this type of debt *short-term debt*. One can think of this type of borrowing as being made to take care of a "cash flow" problem, whereby money comes in too slowly at one time of year, and more rapidly than is needed at another time. This is particularly apt to happen with school districts, where tax money is received in large sums once or twice a year, while expenses continue on a more even basis throughout the year. The district faced with this problem will usually borrow money from a bank or other lending institution on a short-term basis, repaying the loan when the tax receipts arrive. The district guarantees to repay the loan at a stated interest rate. Such loans must typically be repaid within 12 months, and this period of time constitutes the dividing line between short-term and long-term debt.

Long-term debt is incurred almost exclusively for the purchase or construction of capital assets. The individual incurs such debt when borrowing from the bank to buy a house, giving the bank a mortgage. The school district borrows also, but special circumstances dictate the use of a different evidence of indebtedness, called a bond. The bond is simply an acknowledgement that money has been borrowed. The district promises to pay a stated rate of interest on the debt, and to repay the principal amount at a stated time. However, there is not one loan. Rather, the bonds are issued in multiples of $1000 or $5000. Since the amount borrowed at one time may be several million dollars, there will be many bonds, and many individuals or corporations can own them. In addition, the bonds can be sold by one person to another. The school district owes interest and principal to whomever owns the bonds at the time payment becomes due.

Another difference between a bond and a loan to an individual is that the individual typically pledges the property as security. If payments are not made, the bank can seize the property and sell it, keeping what it is owed plus expenses, and returning the remainder to the owner. School land and buildings are public property and cannot be seized for sale. Thus, the bond usually pledges the "full faith and credit" of the district. This means that the district must tax its property owners a sufficient amount to pay principal and interest on the bonds, and it can be compelled to do so through court action.

REASONS FOR BORROWING

Should a school district borrow? Some people believe any form of borrowing is wrong, or perhaps even sinful. However, there are several good reasons for borrowing under the right circumstances.

First, it is sometimes simply good business. Frequently, a business will give a cash discount for prompt payment. A typical bill might state, "Discount 1 percent ten days, net thirty days." By paying 20 days sooner than required the district can save 1 percent of the purchase price. Figured on the basis of 360 days per year, this is equivalent to an interest rate of 18 percent per year charged by the vendor. If the school district can pay the bill promptly, it should do so. Even if it does not have the money to pay promptly, it can probably borrow the money for less than 18 percent and it will save money by so doing. Of course, this type of borrowing must be monitored carefully, for if more is borrowed than is necessary, the extra interest costs may negate the saving.

Districts could eliminate the need to engage in short-term borrowing to ease cash flow problems by levying a higher tax than is currently needed, and amassing a reserve fund to meet cash needs during the year. In most states, however, this is illegal. The law requires that the property tax each year be only sufficient to make up the difference between budgeted expenditures and receipts, with receipts including all cash available at the beginning of the year. The reason for this is the basic principle of taxation that a government should not have tax revenues available until it is ready to spend the money. In general, it is felt that individuals should have the right to use or invest cash themselves, rather than allowing a government to do so.

Of course, short-term borrowing can be abused. A prime example was provided by New York State during the 1970s. As a result of political pressure, the legislature voted large increases in state aid for school districts. Each year there was insufficient money in the state coffers to pay for these increases, so from July 1 to March 31 the state only paid 25 percent of the money it owed districts, hoping to pay the rest when revenues were collected from the next fiscal year which began April 1. Since schools were functioning with only 25 percent of their state aid, most of them were forced into short-term borrowing, which they then repaid with interest when the state revenue arrived after April 1. However, when April 1 arrived the state could not immediately pay the money, for its fiscal year had just begun, and it would be some time before tax revenues arrived to cover the payments to local governments. Thus, the state also borrowed and repaid when tax money arrived. All this borrowing was a bonanza for banks, and increased the cost to school districts and the state of doing business. Nevertheless, not much thought was given to it until normal state receipts were insufficient to meet state obligations to local school districts. In the spring of 1976, at the last possible moment, the state was able to borrow the necessary $4 billion, part of it from state employee retirement funds. If the state had been unable to borrow this money, many school districts would have defaulted on their short-term loans, something which did not happen even during the Great Depression of the 1930s.

A reason for long-term borrowing is that school building construction is a costly proposition. To tax property owners enough to pay for the entire construction cost during the year it is accomplished would usually mean prohibitively high tax rates, and in any case would result in extreme fluctuations of tax rates from year to year. By borrowing, the cost is spread over a period of years, giving more stability to tax rates. An alternative, possible in some states, is to pass an election for a special tax levy to be in effect a specified number of years. The trouble with this method for major construction programs is that construction will not be possible until some years after the initiation of such a levy. School districts are seldom able to convince the public to pass such a levy sufficiently in advance of the need (and may in fact not be able to project the need sufficiently ahead). The idea is enticing to some because, with no money borrowed, no interest need be paid. However, the presumed savings are illusory. Taking money away from taxpayers prematurely means they are prevented from using the money for their own ends, which might include earning interest on it. The effect to taxpayers is equivalent to that of borrowing at interest.

Long-term borrowing is also defended as a reasonable way of spreading costs among generations. A school building will last for many years, typically from 30 to well over 60. It seems unfair to force the present generation to pay the entire cost of buildings that will be used by future generations too. If people always lived in the same place, this kind of generational inequity could be excused on the same basis that we defend parents paying for the education of their children. However, since individuals move, while school buildings stay put, it is more equitable to allow the future residents of a school district to pay part of the cost of the building.

MANAGEMENT OF SHORT-TERM DEBT

Short-term debt, usually incurred to take care of cash flow problems, may be a loan from a local bank, as is usual when needs are small or for a limited period. Where needs are more substantial, districts may sell notes. These are similar to bonds, for they are promises to pay, but they have a short life (typically no more than 12 months) and do not pledge the full faith and credit of the district. Because they do not commit the district to tax itself for repayment, electoral approval is not necessary and the borrowing is not subject to bonding limits. As security, notes pledge the revenue to be obtained from some future assured source. If they are secured by a promise to repay from taxes to be received at a later time, they are known as tax anticipation notes. Those secured by future state aid payments are called revenue anticipation notes, while those secured by the revenue to be obtained from the sale of bonds are called bond anticipation notes. While notes are transferable, they are not usually bought by a dealer for resale, as are bonds. Rather, they are bought by the bidder who quotes interest cost, usually a bank.

In addition to notes, which take care of cash shortages expected to last for several months, the district may borrow directly from a bank for periods of one day to several weeks.

The other side of the cash flow coin is that at certain times of year the district may have substantial cash surpluses. Usually, keeping the money in bank savings is the least profitable way of investing it. Large districts typically have an employee whose duty it is to see to the investment of idle funds (and usually to short-term borrowing as part of the whole cash flow problem). This investment specialist estimates the cash position for each day several months in advance, taking into account anticipated revenues and expenditures. Then investments are made in such a way that the necessary amount of money, and not too much more, will be available to meet the district's day-to-day needs. The specialist makes only short-term investments, i.e., those less than a year in maturity, typically investing in Certificates of Deposit, Banker's Acceptances, Treasury Bills, and so forth.

To get the most out of funds, the specialist may even invest any cash left at the end of the business day overnight, and have it back again the next day. This is done through "repurchase agreements" with banks. Banks are required by law to have a certain percentage of their assets available at all times in cash. However, they strive also to be as fully invested as possible. At the end of the business day they may find that their cash position is below the requirement. Because government auditors always appear after business hours and without advance warning, the bank must borrow money overnight to cover its requirements, and it does so by means of repurchase agreements.

Smaller districts usually cannot afford to have a specialist in short-term investments. However, they can usually do substantially better by putting part of their funds in Certificates of Deposit than having it all in a savings account. In many states, the district has no responsibility for the investment of idle funds, for the cash flow problem is taken care of by the county or the state. In other states, however, where a local district treasurer may be in charge, small districts inevitably experience inefficiency because of an inadequate investment policy.

LONG-TERM DEBT

Because long-term debt commits a school district to repayments over a period of many years, it usually must be approved by a vote of the people, frequently by more than a majority (votes of 60 percent and 2/3 are common). In addition, there are usually state restrictions placed on the total debt incurred. This limit is typically 5 or 10 percent of the assessed value of real property in the district. The intent is to prevent present residents of the district from saddling future residents with too large a debt, and to ensure that ability to repay present bonds is not diluted too much by future issues. Long-term debt may usually be incurred only for purchase of land and construction and initial equipping of buildings.

The steps involved in authorizing, approving, and issuing bonds are numerous and complex. Each step must be carried through with complete legality, otherwise bonds will not be salable. For this purpose the district should engage a financial consultant who specializes in bonding. Such a consultant

> (a) Surveys issuer's debt structure and financial resources to determine borrowing capacity for future capital financing requirements.
> (b) Gathers all pertinent financial statistics and economic data such as debt retirement schedule, tax rates, overlapping debt, etc., that would affect or reflect on the issuer's ability and willingness to repay its obligations.
> (c) Advises on the time and method of marketing: terms of bond issues; including maturity schedule, interest payment dates, call features, and bidding limitations.

(d) Prepares an overall financing plan detailing the recommended approach and probable timetable.

(e) Prepares, in cooperation with bond counsel, an official statement, notice of sale, and bid form and distributes same to all prospective underwriters and investors.

(f) Assists the issuer in getting local public assistance and support of the proposed financing.

(g) Keeps in constant contact with the rating services to ensure that they have all the information and data they require to evaluate credit properly.

(h) Is present when sealed bids are opened and stands ready to advise on the acceptability of bids.

(i) Supervises the printing, signing, and delivery of the bonds.

(j) Advises on investment of bond proceeds.[4]

In addition to a financial consultant it is necessary to engage a "bond counsel." This is a specialized law firm that looks into every legal detail of the bonding procedure so as to assure that the bonds are indeed a legal obligation of the district. Each purchaser of a bond expects to find attached to it an opinion by bond counsel (it is often printed on the back of the bond), stating that there can be no reasonable legal challenge to the indebtedness represented by the bond. This function cannot be served by the board's attorney, for purchasers will want an opinion signed by an independent law firm. The same firm may serve the functions of both financial advisor and bond counsel.

The bond election is the moment of truth when the district finds out whether it will be possible to borrow money needed for construction. In the period from 1940 to 1960, over 80 percent of all school district bond elections passed with the required majority, but since that time passage has become increasingly difficult. In the 1970s, fewer than half of these elections were passed by the voters. Obviously, the need must be justified and documented, and then, presented to voters in a convincing manner.

Assuming that the district's voters approve the bond issue, the next step is to find a purchaser for the bonds. School districts do not sell bonds singly to individuals. Rather, they sell the entire issue to a dealer, usually a bank, a brokerage firm, or a syndicate composed of several banks or brokers. Availability of the bonds is advertised and bids are accepted. The bid resulting in the lowest net interest rate to the district is accepted. Frequently, the bids will only differ in the second or third decimal place (6.244% and 6.253%, for example), but this difference of 0.009% on a $10,000,000 bond issue amounts to a difference of $12,700 in interest paid over a period of 20 years (assuming equal semi-annual payments of principal and interest).

[4] Arthur R. Guastella, "Municipal Finance Consultants," in Joint Economic Committee of the Congress, *State and Local Public Facility Needs and Financing* (Washington, D.C.: U.S. Government Printing Office, 1966).

In order to obtain the best bid, at least two things are necessary: a rating of the district's credit by one of the bond rating agencies, and a bond brochure describing the issue. Both have the goal of assuring prospective purchasers that interest and principal will be paid in full and on time. There are two important bond rating agencies: Moody's and Standard & Poor's. They use different codes to express the risk of a bond issue, but both rate issues on a scale from highest quality to extremely risky. If the district has sold more than $1,000,000 worth of bonds in the fairly recent past, it is probably already rated by one or both of these agencies. If it has not, or if the fiscal condition of the district has changed markedly since it was last rated, the financial advisor will approach the agencies with a request to review the rating. A small improvement in the rating can result in markedly lower interest costs over the life of the bonds, and is well worth pursuing. In making a rating, the bond analyst

> . . . tends to look beyond the issue itself to the aggregated local economy and its burden of debt. He is interested in the "debt capacity" of the issuer (the maximum amount of debt that can legally be issued by the governmental unit) and in the untapped margin of debt capacity still available. . . . The analyst is also interested in a quantification of "indirect debt," composed of bond issues for which the issuer may be a guarantor, and "overlapping debt," the sum of all debt issued by all local governments in an area. Usually expressed in per capita terms, overlapping debt includes the individual citizen's proportionate share of city, county, school district, and other special district debts outstanding.[5]

Preparation of the bond brochure is the responsibility of the financial consultant. The district should not attempt to do it unaided. Nonprofessional brochures are immediately apparent to purchasers, and tend to alienate the sophisticated buyer. A professional knows what information is needed by purchasers in making a decision, and knows how to emphasize the most positive facets of the district's situation. A properly prepared brochure may also result in lower interest costs that will repay many times the cost of preparing the brochure.

Economies of scale are immediately apparent in the area of bonding. The cost of the election, of bond brochure preparation, and of printing bonds is almost the same regardless of size of issue. The cost to bidders of the analysis necessary to make a bid (again reflected in the bid) is also almost independent of the size of the issue. The larger the issue, the less will be the cost of all these fixed items per dollar of indebtedness. In addition, it is extremely rare for a small district to receive a high rating by the agencies, and frequently they will not rate the issue at all. A low rating will result in higher interest costs, and no

[5] Alan Rabinowitz, *Municipal Bond Finance and Administration* (New York: John Wiley Interscience, 1969), p. 35.

rating may even mean no bidders. This then usually results in private placement of the issue with a local bank at a substantially higher interest cost.

There is an alternative available for small districts, called the Municipal Bond Insurance Association. The school district can secure a commitment from the Association to "guarantee unconditionally and irrevocably the full and prompt payment of the principal and interest to the paying agent of the bonds," with the result that the rating agencies will give the issue a higher rating than otherwise. The district pays a premium to the Association for this guarantee, with the amount of the premium based on the Association's estimate of the riskiness of the issue. It might seem that the premium would not be much less than the cost of higher interest rates if the issue went to market at the lower rating. The Association, however, by specializing in small, fiscally sound districts, has been able to charge a premium low enough to save money for these districts.

As with all of the other steps in the bonding process, care must be taken in the printing. The financial consultant assists in this. If the bonds are not correct in every detail, the purchasing bank or broker will discover the error, and they will have to be printed again. Bonds are then sold by the bank or broker to individuals or other institutions. The bonds may either have coupons attached, which the bond holders send in each six months to receive their interest payment, or they may be registered, with the interest paid to the registered owner at the time each payment becomes due.

The school district could borrow, say, $5,000,000 for 20 years through sale of bonds, with the interest payable semiannually, and the entire amount of the principal falling due 20 years hence. Such a bond is called a term bond. This places a large repayment burden on the district at that future time, and to meet its commitment to redeem the bonds it would have to establish a sinking fund into which it annually placed sufficient money to add up to $5,000,000 (including interest on the fund) by the end of the 20 years. Most school districts have elected to have varying maturity dates for bonds, so that the sum of interest and principal payments each year is about the same. These are called serial bonds. An example is given in Table 14-1 for $5,000,000 borrowed at six percent interest, with the first payment at the end of the fiscal year, the last payment at the end of 20 years, and annual interest payments on the balance immediately prior to each principal repayment. Note that the sum of principal and interest are not precisely the same each year, for this would require paying a fraction of a thousand dollars in principal each year and the schedule created here assumes that principal repayments are in multiples of $5,000. A given number of bonds mature each year, as shown by the schedule and stated on the face of each bond. Owners of the bonds that mature in a given year present them for redemption and are paid the face amount. Except in the last year, annual payments are between $433,000 and $439,000.

The entire issue of bonds schematized in Table 14-1 has a 6 percent coupon

TABLE 14-1

Schedule of Principal and Interest Payments on a
$5,000,000 20-year Bond Issued at 6% Interest

Year	Interest Payment	Principal Payment	Total Payment	Principal Remaining End of Period
1	300,000	135,000	435,000	4,865,000
2	291,900	145,000	436,900	4,720,000
3	283,200	155,000	438,200	4,565,000
4	273,900	165,000	438,900	4,400,000
5	264,000	175,000	439,000	4,225,000
6	253,500	185,000	438,500	4,040,000
7	242,400	195,000	437,400	3,845,000
8	230,700	205,000	435,700	3,640,000
9	218,400	215,000	433,400	3,425,000
10	205,500	230,000	435,500	3,195,000
11	191,700	245,000	436,700	2,950,000
12	177,000	260,000	437,000	2,690,000
13	161,400	275,000	436,400	2,415,000
14	144,900	290,000	434,900	2,125,000
15	127,500	310,000	437,500	1,815,000
16	108,900	330,000	438,900	1,485,000
17	89,100	345,000	434,100	1,140,000
18	68,400	365,000	433,400	775,000
19	46,500	390,000	436,500	385,000
20	23,100	385,000	408,100	0

rate. This means that the school district will pay 6 percent annually on the principal amount of each bond. The bank or broker, however, will make an independent decision on the effective interest rate for each maturity date that will be necessary to attract buyers. The broker will establish this effective interest rate by selling at a higher or lower price than the par value of the bond. In the case of a discount, for instance, the buyer may buy a $1000 bond for $960. Nevertheless, interest of $60 per year is paid by the school district (6% of $1000), and this amounts to 6.25% interest on the purchase price. In addition, when the bond matures, the owner will receive the full $1000, or $40 more than paid. This further increases the effective interest rate. If the bond matures in 10 years, the effective yield to maturity of the bond will be 6.55%; if it matures in 20 years, the yield to maturity will be 6.36%. The bank will make these calculations for each maturity date, setting a price on the bonds maturing in each year that will yield the effective interest rate it believes necessary to attract buyers. The sum of these will be the anticipated receipts from sale of the entire issue. The amount bid by the dealer may be more or less than the par value of the bonds, and the difference between anticipated receipts and amount bid is the dealer's gross profit. The award of the bid is based on net interest cost to the district.

It is also common for the dealer to adjust coupon rates of the bonds (within limits stipulated by the school district) as another way to establish a yield to maturity that will be attractive to investors. Table 14-2 shows a 10-year bond with different coupon rates.

Table 14-2 also shows the calculations that are made to determine the net interest cost to the district, offering price of the bonds to individual investors, yield to maturity based on the offering price, and calculations necessary to determine the dealer's profit on the issue. A brief explanation should clarify details of the table.

Principal and interest payments are assumed to be made at the end of each year (actually, interest payments are usually made semiannually, but for simplicity annual payments have been assumed). The principal amount due at the end of each year is shown in Column (2), with total amount of the issue being $5,000,000. Column (3) shows a separate "coupon rate" (the rate of interest paid by the district on par value of the bond) for the bonds that mature in different years, ranging from 5.50% to 6.30%. In Column (4) principal amount is multiplied by number of years to maturity. Column (5) multiplies coupon rate times bond years to provide total amount of interest paid during the life of bonds of each maturity. The total of Column (5) is the total interest paid during the life of the bond issue. This amount, less any premium paid by the dealer on the purchase, divided by total bond years, results in net interest cost to the school district. In this case, the dealer offered to buy the bonds for $5,001,000, thus paying a premium of $1,000. The calculations at the bottom of the table show that the net interest cost to the district is 6.0288%.

The dealer decides what yield to maturity must be offered to attract buyers. In general, the longer the maturity, the higher must be the yield of maturity. The dealer will also decide what offering price will be attractive. Knowing these two, plus the years to maturity, makes it possible to calculate the coupon rate necessary for the bond, using a bond table or a special calculator. This rough calculation usually produces an uneven interest rate. For example, it may be decided to sell the bonds with a three-year maturity at an offering price of 100.50. (Price of a bond is always expressed in terms of the percentage of the par value at which the bond is priced. Thus, a $1,000 bond priced at 100.50 will cost $1,005.00.) Using this calculation, a coupon rate of 5.8837% is arrived at. This rate is then rounded off to 5.90% and the offering price recalculated to be 100.54.

"Production," the amount produced through sale of the bonds at each maturity, is shown in Column (7). It is the product of the principal amount and the offering price (divided by 100). The total of Column (7) is the total amount anticipated by the dealer from sale of the bonds, and this, less the amount paid for the bonds, is the dealer's gross profit.

Note that the dealer plans to sell most of the bonds at a premium. However, those with a ten-year maturity have been tailored for a particular customer, who for tax reasons prefers to buy a low-coupon bond at a discount rather than

TABLE 14-2 A Ten-Year Bond at Differing Coupon Rates

Year (1)	Principal Amount (2)	Rate (3)	Bond Years (1) × (2) (4)	Interest Cost (3) × (4) (5)	Offering Price (6)	Production (2) × (6) (7)	Yield to Maturity (8)
1	$350,000	6.00%	$350,000	$21,000	100.38	$351,330	5.60%
2	400,000	6.00	800,000	48,000	100.65	402,600	5.65
3	450,000	5.90	1,350,000	79,650	100.54	452,430	5.70
4	450,000	5.85	1,800,000	105,300	100.35	451,575	5.75
5	500,000	5.90	2,500,000	147,500	100.64	503,200	5.75
6	550,000	6.00	3,300,000	198,000	101.00	555,500	5.80
7	600,000	6.10	4,200,000	256,200	101.13	606,780	5.90
8	650,000	6.20	5,200,000	322,400	101.57	660,205	5.95
9	700,000	6.30	6,300,000	396,900	102.06	714,420	6.00
10	350,000	5.50	3,500,000	192,500	95.92	335,720	6.05
	5,000,000		29,300,000	1,767,450		5,033,760	

$$\text{Net Interest Cost} = \frac{\text{Total Interest Cost} - \text{Premium}}{\text{Bond Years}}$$

$$= \frac{1,767,450 - 1,000}{29,300,000}$$

$$= .060288, \text{ or } 6.0288\%$$

Profit = Production − Amount paid for issue

$$= 5,033,760 - 5,001,000$$

$$= \$32,760$$

a higher coupon bond at a premium. This customer still receives a higher yield to maturity than any other purchaser.

Money to pay principal and interest on bonds is usually set aside by the district in a special bond interest and redemption fund. Each year a tax is levied sufficient (along with any balance in the fund) to pay interest on all outstanding bonds, and to redeem all bonds that mature during the year. Bonds are a legal obligation of the district, and neither the school board nor the voters can refuse to levy the necessary tax. The decision made at the time the bond issue was approved by the voters binds the district as long as there are any bonds of the issue outstanding.

Money from sale of the bonds is received almost immediately (usually within three weeks of the bid date), but is spent over a period of perhaps two or more years as construction progresses. Meanwhile it must be invested in whatever ways are allowed under state statute. Typically, it may be put into other government securities. It is interesting that it is frequently possible to invest the idle funds at a higher interest rate than it is necessary to pay out on them. Doing this is called *arbitrage*. The investment must be carefully planned, of course, so that portions can be liquidated as necessary to make payments on construction contracts.

PRESENT WAYS
OF FINANCING CAPITAL IMPROVEMENTS

The way most school construction is financed presents several problems. Perhaps the greatest problem is the increased difficulty in passing bond elections. As we mentioned earlier, the rate of approval of bonds by the public has plummeted in recent years. It is clear that people are reacting to the general level of taxation by rejecting new taxes on which they have an opportunity to vote. Another problem is that the cost of borrowing has increased substantially. Shortly after World War II, interest rates on muncipal bonds averaged only 1.3%; by 1967 the rate was 4%, and in 1976 the rate averaged 6.8%. Part of this reflects a general increase in the interest cost of all money, for reasons that have to do with the national and the world economy. Part of the increase, however, has been the result of a narrowing of the gap between the interest rates of municipal bonds and taxable bonds. This is mainly due to the fact that some of the major money sources now get tax breaks on ordinary interest, among them life insurance companies, mutual savings banks, and pension funds. The non-taxable feature of municipal bonds thus becomes unimportant to them, and the lower coupon rate then makes them unattractive. The clientele for municipal bonds is now chiefly limited to commercial banks and highly taxed individuals. Restriction of the market has also narrowed the difference in interest rates, and thus the subsidy conferred by the federal government on local governments.

Another problem with the usual way of financing school construction is the limit set by all states on the amount a school district can borrow, usually expressed as a percentage of its assessed valuation.[6] Rapidly growing school districts have found themselves reaching this borrowing limit with no way to satisfy the needs of their unhoused students. Then too, many states do not aid districts with construction, but force them to do it on their own. If it is unconstitutional for a state to discriminate among students in the matter of operating expenses, as established by *Serrano* and other cases, is it not equally unconstitutional to discriminate in the matter of school housing? This issue has not been conclusively tested, although discrimination in capital outlay was declared unconstitutional by an Arizona court.[7]

The most complete answer to the problem of equity is for the state to assume total responsibility for school construction, an experiment that is being tried in Florida and Maryland. This is similar to full state funding for operational expenses, as discussed in Chapters Eight and Nine. The state of Florida conducts a survey of all school buildings and rates each according to the number of students it can house and the condition of the facilities. Combining this information with projections of number of students in each district, the state can predict the need for facilities five years hence. It then allocates funds for approved projects to meet these needs, subject to a maximum allowance per square foot for each type of construction, adjusted for intrastate differences in cost of construction. Since school districts are not allowed to levy local taxes for construction, the state allowance determines the amount spent. At the time this system was installed (1973), some districts had bonded themselves heavily and had provided adequate schools, while other districts had not been able to pass bond elections and suffered from inadequate schools. It would have been unfair to the districts that had already provided schools to pay only for future construction, and therefore the state also pays for the districts' bond interest and redemption costs.

Maryland, although it uses a somewhat different system, is the only other state to provide, in effect, full state funding of school construction. The major problem with full state assumption of construction costs is that it eliminates a great deal of local option. The state will not be content simply to provide the indicated money without strings, for this would be looked upon as improper stewardship of public funds. The result is apt to be a complex maze of state

---

[6] "The amount of a school bond issue is customarily limited to an arbitrary percentage of the local assessed valuation of property, ranging from 2 percent in Indiana and Kentucky to 20 percent in Florida, according to reports by state school officials in 1969–70. Tennessee permitted an unlimited amount, subject to voter approval. Alabama limited bond issues to an amount which could be repaid from a dedicated local debt service tax rate. Alaska relied on a locally approved limit, and Pennsylvania had an approved ratio of debt to income." W. Monfort Barr and William R. Wilkerson, *Innovative Financing of Public School Facilities* (Danville, Ill.: Interstate, 1973), p. 23.

[7] *Hollins v. Shofstall,* Civil No. C-253652 (Arizona Superior Court, June 1, 1972) rev'd 110 Ariz. 88, 515 P.2d 590 (1973).

requirements for approval of plans, specifying number of square feet per pupil, types of buildings and rooms, and even minute details regarding equipment, inspections, and approval of contractors. The goal of choice is substantially overshadowed by the goal of equity.

New York and Illinois provide funds on a percentage equalizing basis. The district decides what it wants to build and how much it wishes to spend. The state shares in the cost of construction, with the percentage share depending upon district wealth. There is a maximum reimbursement rate based either on pupils housed or square feet constructed, to prevent poor districts from erecting monuments at state expense. This system allows much more local discretion in school construction, but is of little comfort to the district that is unable to pass a bond election or has reached its legal bonding limit.

At the other end of the scale is the system used in Mississippi, South Carolina, Tennessee, Alabama, and Kentucky, where a fixed number of dollars per student is provided by the state each year for capital construction whether it is needed or not. Districts with declining enrollment find no need for this money and simply put it into interest-bearing accounts, while districts with increasing enrollments usually find the amount provided grossly inadequate. There is little that can be said in favor of this plan except that it preserves local discretion.

In between is a variety of arrangements, some based on a foundation program, others simply loans from a state fund based on proven need. Forty percent of the states have no provision at all for helping districts with construction needs, or provide emergency loans only.[8] Because construction cost accounts for a smaller proportion of the school budget than operating cost, there have been fewer efforts to equalize it, and it is a fertile field for reform.

ALTERNATIVES FOR IMPROVING FINANCING
OF CAPITAL OUTLAY

The problems of financing construction should decline so long as school populations decline. However, this should be looked at as an opportunity to achieve equity without excessive cost, rather than as an occasion for complacency over the present system. Regardless of the statewide situation, there are still districts that are growing rapidly, and these frequently have low assessed valuations, have reached their debt limits, or find it impossible to pass bond elections. There are several alternatives available to a state to alleviate these problems; each has its advantages and disadvantages.

The most comprehensive method for achieving equity would be complete state assumption of responsibility for school construction, as has been attempted in Florida and Maryland. As mentioned earlier, this tends to achieve equity at the expense of local choice.

---

[8]Marshall A. Harris, *School Finance at a Glance* (Denver: Education Commission of the States, 1975).

Another possibility is for the state to construct a school building for the district on a lease-purchase plan. The district pays rent for a period of years after which it owns the building. This eliminates the problem of passing a local bond election or exceeding local bonding capacity, for the state floats the bonds. However, it does nothing to relieve poor districts of heavy costs. To do this, the state could require the district to make a payment amounting to the yield from taxing at a certain tax rate per million dollars of construction expense for a set number of years as rental. At the end of this time the district would own the building and any unpaid balance would be forgiven. For poor districts this would provide some equalization, whereas rich districts would find it cheaper to bond themselves than to make payments to the state of more than the construction cost. For the state to require districts to make payments amounting to a certain tax rate yield, even if this exceeded that necessary to return construction cost, would be the equivalent of recapture on an operating cost formula, and probably just as unpalatable. It should also be noted that this method, even with recapture, does not provide the same degree of equalization as full state assumption, because some districts will be growing and have to tax themselves at the specified rate, whereas other districts will escape this tax entirely.

It should be mentioned that use of the state's credit for bonding instead of the district's can bring lower interest costs. However, a large increase in state debt as a result of school construction bonds might reduce the safety of all state bonds, and thus increase the interest rate that would have to be paid on all future issues.

Several plans to be implemented at the local level would help decrease the burden of capital outlay, although they would not help with the problem of interdistrict inequity. In some cases state laws would have to be changed to allow these plans. For example, facilities can be designed for use both by school district and community. Good candidates are playgrounds, auditoriums, multi-use rooms, and libraries. A project could be financed jointly by the school district and the municipality, or could be financed by one with the other paying rental for the opportunity of joint use. In New York City, school buildings have been built as part of a commercial building, with the school district leasing the lower floors, and the upper floors rented as apartments. Some of the "new towns" started in the 1960s and 1970s have constructed schools as part of a comprehensive community center. It makes sense to plan for more intensive use of school buildings which now sit idle every evening and all summer.

Another possibility is to put part of the burden for new schools on those who generate the demand. County supervisors have been known to impose a special tax of approximately $1,000 on each new residence constructed, with the money earmarked for new schools. In other areas, land developers have been forced to deed a portion of a new subdivision as a school site.

Year-round use of the schools has been proposed frequently and tried occasionally as a way better to utilize existing school buildings. Under such a plan, each child attends school for nine months, and during each quarter of the school year one-fourth of the children are on their long vacation. Teachers have a similar schedule, but school facilities are used year-round. This would seem to have the potential for increasing school utilization by as much as 33 percent, but the actual savings are much more modest. Partly, this is because maintenance that was formerly done during the summer period now must be scheduled at nights or on weekends, at extra cost. Then too, special personnel (counselors, subject supervisors, some secretaries and clerks, etc.) who formerly served all students during a nine-month period must now be paid additional salary to work 12 months. A comprehensive study of savings under such a plan in Virginia Beach, Virginia, concluded that the savings were almost nonexistent.[9]

Summary

Chapter Fourteen first examined capital construction. Considering the importance that has been attached to it by school boards, administrators, and even parents, it might be assumed that the quality of buildings is very important to the educational process, although there are few research studies indicating this. In any event, the decrease in pupil populations in the 1970s has led to a decrease in interest in construction. Nevertheless, some districts must build new schools, and this chapter has outlined the steps to be undertaken in doing so, along with some of the pitfalls. Separate sections have discussed the financing of school buses and disposing of surplus facilities.

This chapter has also discussed debt and its management. There are sound fiscal reasons for borrowing, both short-term and long-term. Short-term borrowing is primarily used to even out cash flows; long-term borrowing smooths out the otherwise huge expenditures that occur over a short time for construction, and enables future users of facilities to shoulder part of the financial burden. The management of both short-term and long-term debt has been considered in this chapter, as well as the complicated process of the approval, sale, and servicing of bonds.

We conclude this chapter with suggested alternatives for improving the financing of capital outlay. The suggestions include complete state assumption of the financial burden of school construction and debt service, as has been done in Florida and Maryland; and use of the credit of the state through state-issued bonds and state loans to local districts, or through district lease-purchase of state-constructed buildings. At the local level, districts could construct joint-use buildings financed together by district and municipality; or finance needed buildings by a special levy on the construction of new houses, which generate additional demand on the schools. A frequent suggestion for reducing the necessity for new construction is the year-round school, but it appears that the potential savings are minimal, and the idea is frequently rejected by parents because it interferes with their own schedules.

[9]Guilbert C. Hentschke, E. E. Birckell, and Jay C. Mounie, "Year-Round Education: Failure with a Future?" *Educational Economics,* 1, No. 1 (February 1976), 20–23.

15

THE POLITICAL ECONOMY OF CITY SCHOOLS

This chapter describes economic and political conditions that affect public school systems in our nation's largest cities and analyzes proposed solutions. In effect, this chapter is a microcosm of the entire book; most of the topics considered in individual chapters, such as taxation, finance distribution formulas, and political reforms, are blended here with a focus on city schools.

Urbanization

The transition from an agricultural to an industrial economy fostered widespread growth of cities beginning in the United States in the nineteenth century and peaking around 1950.[1] The 1920 federal census marked the turning point when 50 percent of America's population resided in cities. In 1950, 75 percent of the U.S. population were urban residents. Cities themselves even began to fuse which led Jean Gottman, writing about the densely populated

---

[1] See Lewis Mumford, *The City in History: Its Origins, Its Transformations, and Its Prospects* (New York: Harcourt, Brace, and World, Inc., 1961). Also for an excellent technical discussion of U.S. urbanization, see Eric E. Lampard, "The Evolving System of Cities in the United States: Urbanization and Economic Development," in *Issues in Urban Economics*, eds. Harvey S. Perloff and Lowdon Wingo, Jr. (Baltimore: The Johns Hopkins University Press, 1968), pp. 81–139.

northeast corridor stretching from Boston to Washington, D.C., to label the intensive urban development *megalopolis*.[2]

Then 1960 and 1970 census figures revealed a new demographic trend; several core cities declined in population. The suburban movement following World War II constituted a counter migration that finally surpassed the flow into cities. Between 1950 and 1970, net migration from city to suburb averaged 500,000 per year.[3] However, many of those who moved to the fringe were still tied economically to the city and identified themselves with it. Because of these ties, increased transportation costs and the prospect of future shortages of gasoline may eventually inhibit suburban growth. Proximity to the city's core may again become attractive.

Whatever the fate of big cities, even if they go the way of dinosaurs,[4] their present conditions cannot be ignored. It took more than a century for city growth to reach its climax; it may take that long for a new demographic pattern to emerge. Meanwhile, great effort is still necessary to ameliorate urban problems, school problems in particular.

City Problems

The growth of densely settled urban areas resulted in social and economic problems. Cities experience more crime, higher death rates, greater incidence of illness, elevated concentrations of low-income households and unemployed individuals, disproportionate numbers of suicides, intense rates of mental illness, and heightened racial conflict.[5]

It is difficult to assess all the causes for such a disproportionate amount of social malaise. Simple population density may be one factor: Residents per square mile in cities frequently outnumber their rural counterparts by 5,000 to one. One can readily believe that a good deal of the modern city-dweller's tensions and dissatisfactions were unknown to our farm-oriented forebears.[6]

[2] Jean Gottmann, *Megalopolis: The Urbanized Northeastern Seaboard of the United States* (New York: The Twentieth Century Fund, 1961).

[3] Quoted in Dick Netzer, *Economics and Urban Problems* (New York: Basic Books, Inc., 1970). See also Irene B. Taeuber, *Population Trends in the United States: 1900 to 1960*, Bureau of the Census Technical Paper No. 10 (Washington, D.C.: U.S. Government Printing Office, 1964).

[4] Those who adhere to the economics of limited growth would argue for the dismemberment of big cities. See E. F. Schumacher, *Small is Beautiful* (New York: Harper & Row, 1973).

[5] An excellent documentation of city problems is contained in the *Report of the National Advisory Commission on Civil Disorders* (Washington, D.C.: U.S. Government Printing Office, 1968).

[6] Ena-Vesquez Nuttall, Ronald L. Nuttall, Denise Polit, John B. Hunter, "The Effects of Family Size, Birth Order, Sibling Separation, and Crowding on the Academic Achievement of Boys and Girls," *American Education Research Journal*, 13, No. 3 (Summer, 1976), 217–24.

City problems do not spring from population saturation alone, however. Unwittingly, federal government post-World War II transportation and housing policies encouraged middle-class households to leave cities. Public funds made possible the construction of freeway systems that dramatically reduced the time necessary to commute to the central city from outlying areas. Simultaneously, federally subsidized mortgages became available in sufficient amounts to finance construction of suburban housing tracts.[7] Initially, suburban housing promised more open space than cities, homes of modern construction, and mortgage payments within range of a large number of middle-income families.

The availability of reasonably priced, conveniently located, and relatively attractive suburban housing acted as a social magnet to attract thousands of urban inhabitants to move to the city's rim. The migration was dominated by middle-income whites.[8] Their exodus markedly changed the demographic composition of major cities. For example, in 1950, ten percent of central city residents were black. This had increased to 20 percent by 1966 and was projected to be 30 percent by 1985.[9] In particular cities, the statistics are far more extreme. In Washington, D.C., for example, in 1975, 80 percent of the resident population was black. Cities became a refuge for those who could not afford to live elsewhere or for whom suburban housing was denied because of racially restrictive covenants.[10]

The suburban outflow of middle-income households was replaced by an expanded population of low-income individuals, racial and non-English speaking minorities, and the elderly. Such individuals needed expanded public services. Costs of health care, welfare, and low-income housing increased dramatically in cities in the 25 years following World War II. These costs in turn placed a heavier burden upon city sources of tax revenue.

The cycle of change proved self-reinforcing. Large numbers of disadvantaged city inhabitants, and the consequent higher public service costs, encouraged many remaining middle-income households to leave for suburbia. By moving, they could not only enjoy better housing, lower taxes, and a mix of public services more in keeping with their needs and tastes,[11] but also more easily disassociate themselves from the discomfort and despair so visible in cities.

The downward spiral of city finances continued. The provision of added public services required not only more money, but also more land. Public

[7]See Mark I. Gelfand, *A Nation of Cities: The Federal Government and Urban America, 1933–1965* (New York: Oxford University Press, 1975).

[8]See Frederick M. Wirt, Benjamin Walter, Francine F. Rabinovitz, and Deborah R. Hensler, *On the City's Rim: Politics and Policy in Suburbia* (Lexington, Mass.: D. C. Heath and Company, 1972), chap. 2.

[9]Netzer, *Economics and Urban Problem*, p. 15.

[10]Harry Sharp and Leo F. Schnore, "The Changing Color Composition of Metropolitan Areas," *Land Economics*, No. 38 (1967), pp. 1–66.

[11]Charles S. Benson and Peter B. Lund, *Neighborhood Distribution of Local Public Services* (Berkeley, Cal.: Institute for Governmental Studies, 1969).

housing and public institutions such as hospitals expanded. City land that once contributed revenues was removed from the tax rolls. This problem was exacerbated by construction of freeways leading to the suburbs. This vast network of high-speed roads removed thousands of acres of city land from taxation.[12] Also, as described in Chapter Six, property tax policies and, in some cities, rent controls discouraged proper maintenance of property. Potential rent returns on investment did not exceed taxes and other outlays sufficiently to motivate landlords to spend funds on building renovation and upkeep. Consequently, landlords frequently permitted housing to decay, not only depriving the city of needed housing stock but also decreasing assessed valuation for tax purposes. Declining tax bases drove tax rates for most city services higher. Higher tax rates, the outward flow of skilled workers, and the availability of less expensive land provoked many city employers to relocate. Businesses frequently deserted the central city for the suburban periphery. For example, between 1959 and 1963, the number of workers in industrial plants increased approximately one million in all metropolitan areas. However, central cities in the 25 largest metropolitan areas lost nearly 300,000 manufacturing jobs. Also, Netzer estimates that central cities lost 100,000 wholesale trade and 300,000 retail trade jobs between 1950 and 1970.[13] Not only did this economic decentralization result in loss of jobs, it also further eroded the city's tax base, forcing rates even higher. The situation was a self-perpetuating downward spiral.

City School Problems

Urban problems spilled over quickly into city schools. At the turn of the twentieth century, city schools were the pride of the American educational system. Families migrated to cities or sent their offspring to live with relatives so they could benefit from city schools. Standards of academic excellence and worthwhile pedagogical innovations were thought to originate with city schools and diffuse outward. Secondary schooling first developed extensively in cities. Also, teacher certification criteria were initially highest in urban schools.[14]

By 1970, the situation had altered dramatically. The outflow of middle-class children left city public schools with high concentrations of children from low-income households who were frequently handicapped not only by their parents' poverty but also by poor health. City schools were attended by disproportionate numbers of students who did not have English as their native language, many speaking no English whatsoever. Also, perhaps as an accom-

---

[12] See Anthony Downs, *Urban Problems and Prospects* (Chicago: Markham Publishing Company, 1970).

[13] Netzer, *Economics and Urban Problems,* p. 29.

[14] See Willard Waller, *The Sociology of Teaching.* Originally published in 1932, reprinted in 1965 by John Wiley & Sons, New York; Diane Ravitch, *The Great School Wars: New York City, 1805-1973* (New York: Basic Books, Inc., 1974), and David B. Tyack, *The One Best System* (Cambridge, Mass.: Harvard University Press, 1974).

paniment to poverty, perhaps attracted by better services, city schools enrolled a large share of physically and mentally handicapped students in need of special and often costly school services.[15] Consequently, the public perception of city schools began to change. Not only were urban middle-class parents increasingly seeking private schools for their children, most students in city public schools were there because they had no other choice.

Urban problems penetrate city schools in other ways. Violence and racial strife occur with disproportionate frequency. Many city schools bear the extra costs of security personnel in order to protect students and staff from incursions by individuals and gangs bent on illegal actions. Such efforts are only partially successful. In 1976, a U.S. Senate subcommittee reported that city schools suffered extraordinary vandalism costs.[16] Such property destruction adds to the already deteriorating physical condition of many city school buildings.

The coincidence of such intense problems rather understandably is associated with low levels of student performance. National Assessment of Educational Progress (NAEP) reports describe urban school students and graduates as performing lower on almost every measure of school achievement. For example, a 1974 study of functional literacy revealed that 80 percent of 17-year-olds in big cities could not read an insurance policy.[17] Similarly, the National Commission on Civil Disorders reported that city school nonenrollment rates averaged 20 percent for blacks and 6 percent for whites.[18]

These and dozens of other problems provoked former Harvard University President James Bryant Conant, writing in *Slums and Suburbs,* to characterize city schools as a keg of "social dynamite."[19]

City Schools and Governmental Policies

Urban problems escalated, at least in part, because cities long lacked proportionate political influence in state government. Until the 1950s, many state legislatures strongly over-represented rural areas.[20] This lopsided condi-

---

[15]Patricia A. Craig and Norman McEachron, "The Development and Analysis of Baseline Data for the Estimation of Incidence in the Handicapped School Age Population," unpublished draft (Menlo Park: Stanford Research Institute, 1974).

[16]See *The Nature, Extent and Cost of Violence and Vandalism in Our Nation's Schools,* hearings before the Senate Subcommittee to investigate juvenile delinquency, Committee on the Judiciary, chaired by Senator Birch Bayh (D., Indiana), April 16 and June 17, 1975 (Washington, D.C.: U.S. Government Printing Office, 1976).

[17]National Center for Educational Statistics, *The Condition of Education.* 1976 edition (Washington, D.C.: U.S. Government Printing Office, 1976), p. 60.

[18]*Report of the National Advisory Commission on Civil Disorders,* p. 425.

[19]James Bryant Conant, *Slums and Suburbs* (New York: McGraw-Hill Book Company, 1961), p. 2.

[20]For a description of legislative imbalances prior to reapportionment decisions, see

tion was a consequence of legislative reluctance to reapportion and redistrict congressional and legislative districts in order to keep pace with population migrations. Consequently, rural areas retained more legislative representatives than their number of inhabitants warranted. Cities paid a double price. Not only were urban problems neglected relative to matters of concern to agricultural and other extractive industries, but also solutions to non-city problems were frequently funded with revenues generated from city wealth.

In the landmark judgment, *Baker* v. *Carr* (1962), the United States Supreme Court ruled against this version of taxation without representation. In this and in subsequent cases, *Wesberry* v. *Sanders* (1964) and *Reynolds* v. *Sims* (1964), the Supreme Court invoked the "one-man-one-vote" principle and required that congressional and state legislative districts (both for upper and lower houses) be redrawn so as to contain equal numbers of constituents.[21] These rulings triggered a wave of legislative reapportionment.

For cities in several states, reapportionment rulings were either too late or a mixed blessing. By the 1950s, suburban expansion was well underway. Thus, while rural areas lost their representative advantage, cities did not always gain. State legislative bodies became more fairly apportioned, but cities sometimes still constituted a minority vote. The balance of power shifted from rural to suburban representatives. The decline in central city population beginning in the late 1960s and 1970s had thus sealed the political fate of many cities. The result in most states is that cities may control sufficient influence to exercise veto power over potentially damaging state policies, but frequently still lack the political ability to initiate positive solutions.

In addition to suffering from under-representation, cities have long labored under an anti-urban ethos of many state governments.[22] The perception is widely held that cities are a great revenue sink into which must be poured an ever increasing amount of money for services such as welfare, crime, and education. Rural and suburban representatives frequently resent such added urban costs and resist voting for measures to aid cities. This pattern of behavior probably originated during the period of rural dominance. However, the post-World War II migration of minorities to cities and the subsequent exodus of middle-income whites may have exacerbated an already troublesome condition.

Bias against cities and against the poor not only hindered cities in obtaining state government aid, but also intensified their problems in other ways.[23]

Malcolm E. Jewell, ed., *The Politics of Reapportionment* (New York: Atherton Press, 1962). Also, see Andrew Hacker, *Congressional Districting* (Washington, D.C.: The Brookings Institution, 1964).

[21] *Baker* v. *Carr*, 369 U.S. 186 (1962); *Wesberry* v. *Sanders*, 376 U.S. 1 (1964); *Reynolds* v. *Sims*, 377 U.S. 533 (1964).

[22] Wirt et al., *On the City's Rim*, chap. 8, "City-Suburb Attitudinal Differences in the National Population."

[23] Norman Drachler, "The Large City School System: 'It Costs More to do the Same'," chap. 2, in *Equity for Cities in School Finance Reform* (Washington, D.C.: The Potomac Institute, 1973), pp. 15–44.

For example, many suburbs have refused construction of federally subsidized low-income housing within their borders. Consequently, cities were forced to become the residential receptacle for the poor and many of the elderly. Similarly, several state legislatures established intermediate service units to assist schools in rural areas and suburbs but excluded city school districts. For example, in New York State, Boards of Cooperative Educational Service (BOCES) were available to serve almost every school district except those located in the state's five largest cities. Also, those states which assist local districts in serving severely handicapped students frequently exclude city students. Even on the revenue dimension, cities often find themselves subject to different treatment. For example, again in New York, city districts are prevented by statute from raising property tax revenues in excess of two percent of total assessed valuation. Non-city school districts suffer no such limitation.

FEDERAL POLITICS AND CITIES

Federal level politics generally have been more sensitive to city conditions. City residents' voting power was diluted on the state level but not their power to choose U.S. senators and the president. City residents have frequently been the balance of power in presidential elections, particularly for the Democratic Party. Their numbers can tip the electoral vote scale, for a candidate obtaining a simple majority in a number of the highly industrialized states can claim those states' total electoral vote. This is what made it possible, for example, for Mayor Richard Daley in 1966 to phone President Lyndon B. Johnson and resolve a complex dispute over millions of dollars of Chicago's federal school aid funds literally in seconds. The Illinois legislature, by contrast, could afford for many years simply to ignore Chicago's pleas for added school aid.

As a consequence of general responsiveness, federal programs to assist cities began developing in the 1930s.[24] Such efforts included massive funding for renewal of city physical facilities, public housing, new urban rapid transit systems, and federal funds for school programs. The 1965 Elementary and Secondary Education Act (ESEA) contains a funding formula in large part based on measures of poverty. This was deliberately inserted in the bill in order to provide disproportionate amounts of aid for city schools.[25]

Despite substantial generosity, federal programs have by no means solved city problems. In large measure, the authority needed to resurrect cities resides within the purview of state government, yet, as we have described, states have not always faced the problem. Consequently, cities and city schools continue to suffer from extraordinarily intense fiscal and organizational difficulties. The inability to initiate legislative and executive branch action led many reformers

[24] Gelfand, *A Nation of Cities.*
[25] See chap. 7 for a brief history of the ESEA.

in the 1960s to frame a strategy for judicial solution. Early versions of the equal protection court cases were viewed as potential solutions to city school problems.

City Schools and Serrano

Chapter Two describes the legal efforts to promote equality of school finance. Out of such cases emerged the Coons, Clune, and Sugarman principle of fiscal neutrality invoked in the initial Serrano opinion: "The quality of a child's schooling shall not be a function of wealth, other than the wealth of the state as a whole."[26]

The principle of fiscal neutrality, strictly pursued, provokes the specter of substantial resource restriction for city schools.[27] Urban school districts spend more per pupil than the average for their respective states. A study of an eight-state sample revealed that central city school district expenditures per pupil were, on the average, 13 percent higher than state spending figures.[28] Such high spending is defended by city advocates on grounds that services simply cost more in cities and city schools have disproportionate numbers of students in need of high-cost services.

While cities unquestionably spend above average amounts per pupil, they also tend to tax themselves for schools at lower rates than other districts statewide. High expenditures are possible despite relatively low tax rates because "per pupil property values in 34 of America's largest cities are 26 percent higher than state averages."[29] These high per pupil property values are a function not only of the concentrations of high valued property in many cities, but also of the number of school-age children in cities enrolled in nonpublic schools, which substantially exceeds the national average of 10.4 percent.[30] This means that the high wealth base of cities is divided by proportionately fewer pupils than in other kinds of districts producing more wealth per pupil.

Because of the interaction in cities among high spending, low tax rates, and high property wealth, Serrano reform plans must be carefully calibrated if cities are not to be harmed fiscally. Callahan, Wilken, and Sillerman simulated

[26] John E. Coons, William H. Clune, and Stephen D. Sugarman, *Private Wealth and Public Education* (Cambridge: Harvard University Press, 1970); *Serrano* v. *Priest,* 5 Cal. 3rd 584, 96 Cal. Reporter 601, 487, 2nd. 1241 (1971).

[27] See Joel S. Berke and John J. Callahan, *"Serrano* v. *Priest:* Milestone or Millstone for School Finance," *Journal of Public Law,* 21, No. 1 (1972), 42.

[28] Betsy Levin, Thomas Muller, and Corazon Sandoval, *The High Cost of Education in Cities* (Washington, D.C.: The Urban Institute, 1973), p. 8.

[29] John J. Callahan, William H. Wilken, and M. Tracy Sillerman, *Urban Schools and School Finance Reform: Promise and Reality* (Washington, D.C.: National Urban Coalition, 1973), p. 12.

[30] National Center for Educational Statistics, *The Condition of Education,* 1976, p. 6.

the effects of three typical school finance alternatives, each of which would have satisfied the principle of fiscal neutrality, in order to assess their consequences for city school districts. Most city districts, to comply with a strict Serrano ruling, would either have to lower expenditures, raise taxes, or both.[31]

City School Finance Specifics

In order to formulate state school finance policies to treat cities fairly— policies that consider not only fiscal conditions but also pupil characteristics— it is necessary to discuss in detail several dimensions of city schools.

EXCESS COST OF CITY SCHOOLS

School spending in cities is higher than the average for their respective region or state for three major reasons: (1) disproportionate numbers of pupils in need of special school services, (2) higher prices for school-related purchases, both material and personnel, and (3) the apparent necessity of city schools to purchase a large number of non-instructional services.

CITY SCHOOL STUDENTS

There are two major categories of pupils needing extra cost school services. One category consists of the "disadvantaged," those students evidencing the deprivation and low school achievement frequently accompanying economic poverty. Another category consists of the "handicapped," those who are physically, mentally, or emotionally impaired.

"Disadvantaged" and "handicapped" students attend city schools in disproportionate numbers. We have already cited reasons for the high levels of poverty in cities. Finding an explanation for the unusually large numbers of handicapped children in need of special education is not as simple. Historically, city schools were the first to provide services for the handicapped. Some suburban and rural school districts still do not offer services for handicapped children, so that families who cannot afford private schooling still may be forced to move to the city. Also, scientific evidence increasingly suggests that poverty imposes another penalty on the poor. Children born in low-income households appear to suffer inordinately from various physical and mental handicaps. This suggests that the inability to acquire adequate prenatal care and infant malnutrition may provoke a higher rate of malformation among children of cities than among the population generally.[32] Regardless of the causes, deprived and

---

[31]Callahan et al., *Urban Schools,* pp. 7–11.

[32]For details of the relationship between prenatal and infant malnutrition and the incidence of physical handicaps and mental retardation, see J. J. Cravioto and E.

handicapped children in high concentrations must be schooled, necessitating a high level of school expenditure.

DISADVANTAGED STUDENTS

In the 1960s, the federal government began the "War on Poverty" intended to stimulate the nation's economy and weaken the effects of low income.[33] Passage of the 1965 Elementary and Secondary Education Act, particularly Title I, marked the inclusion of public education as a weapon in the "war." As described in Chapter Seven, Congress was impressed by the high correlation between low income and low school achievement, and Title I was intended to sever this connection.[34]

ESEA Title I funds are intended for disadvantaged students regardless of their geographic location. However, such students are concentrated in city school districts. For example, the Urban Coalition report by Callahan and his colleagues revealed that, for 1972, city school districts enrolled almost three times the proportion of Title I eligible students as was the case for their respective states.[35]

Delicardie, "The Effects of Malnutrition on the Individual," in *Nutrition, National Development, and Planning,* ed. A. Berg (Cambridge, Mass.: MIT Press, 1973).

[33] For a description of the "War on Poverty" and an analysis of its failings, see Daniel Patrick Moynihan, *Maximum Feasible Misunderstanding* (New York: The Free Press, 1969).

[34] The linkage between socioeconomic (SES) and demographic measures of poverty, on one hand, and student achievement, on the other, is revealed as significant by a number of correlational analyses. For example, a 1969 study by Walter I. Garms and Mark C. Smith, "Educational Need and Its Application to State School Finance," *The Journal of Human Resources,* 5, no. 3 (Summer 1970), 304–17, reported an explanation of 73 percent of the variance when regressing socioeconomic and demographic variables against student test scores. A 1974 study by Daniel U. Levine and his collaborators carries the analysis a step further. Levine separated family variables from neighborhood poverty, e.g., unemployment, age of residential buildings, density, and occupations, and found that variations in student achievement were more fully explained by neighborhood conditions than by measures of family poverty alone. See Levine, Kenneth R. Mares, Jeannie K. Meyers, and Robert S. Stephenson, "The Utility and Implications of 1970 Census Data in Predicting Achievement and Assessing Effects of Concentrated Urban Poverty in Chicago," a paper prepared under the auspices of the Center for the Study of Metropolitan Problems in Education, School of Education, University of Missouri, Kansas City, 1974.

[35] Callahan, et al., *Urban Schools.* A study conducted by the Stanford Research Institute for the Department of Health, Education, and Welfare employed more recent data to confirm the disproportionate burden in cities of low-income and low-achieving students. This study revealed that California's city school districts in 1974 enrolled only 19 percent of the state's total student population. However, they contained 31 percent of those defined as poverty level and 27 percent of those defined as low achieving (scoring lower than the 18th percentile on a state administered achievement test). See James W. Guthrie and Anne S. Frenz, *The Use of Performance Criteria to Allocate Compensatory Education Funds* (Menlo Park: Stanford Research Institute, 1974), pp. 11–19. See also Betsy Levin et al., *The High Cost of Education,* p. 67.

The 1965 enactment of ESEA Title I marked the beginning of widescale public recognition of the desirability of providing extra resources for disadvantaged students. Since that time, a number of states have supplemented federal monies with state funds for low-income or low-achieving students. At this writing 18 states have seen fit either to incorporate a disadvantaged student weighting scheme into their distribution formulas or to award flat grants to school districts for eligible students.[36] Generally, eligibility criteria bias the funds toward cities. For example, the "Educationally Disadvantaged Youth" (EDY) component of the California distribution formula provides added dollars to districts based on a combination of their concentrations of low-income, non-English speaking, and transient students,[37] three factors that heavily favor large city school districts such as San Francisco and Los Angeles.[38]

There are thousands of young people who do not speak English well enough to comprehend instruction. The largest numbers are from Asia and Spanish-speaking countries. Cities typically have disproportionate numbers of such youth. Prior to 1973, these students frequently were doomed to sit in classrooms in which the language of instruction was English, whether or not they understood it. In a far-reaching decision, *Lau* v. *Nichols,* a federal district court ruled that public school districts are obliged to provide instruction which is intelligible to non-English speaking students.[39] Subsequently both state and federal statutes have begun to recognize the added costs of bilingual instruction.

Whether or not funds are distributed in the form of flat grants or as a consequence of a weighting system, there presently is no scientific evidence on how much added money is needed to compensate for poverty or low achievement. A similar problem exists in the area of handicapped children.

HANDICAPPED STUDENTS

Until the mid-1970s, not every state saw fit to require or provide schooling for pupils with handicaps such as physical, mental, and environmental disabilities. However, in several landmark cases, e.g., *Mills* v. *Board of Education,* and *Pennsylvania Association of Retarded Children* v. *Commonwealth of Pennsylvania,*[40] courts have mandated that handicapped pupils be served. Also, as discussed in Chapter Seven, Congress passed the comprehensive federal aid statute, the 1975 Education for All Handicapped Children Act.[41] The conflu-

---

[36] John G. Augenblick, *School Finance at a Glance* (Denver: Education Commission of the States, 1977).

[37] See California Senate Bill 1641 (1976), Section 15.

[38] Michigan's so-called Chapter 19 program distributes added funds to school districts based on statewide student test scores. See Educational Commission of the States, chart, "School Finance at a Glance: 1975."

[39] 472 F. 2d 909 (9th Cir., 1973). Upheld by U.S. Supreme Court 414 U.S. 563 (1974).

[40] 348 F. Supp. 866 (D.D.C. 1972); 334 F. Supp. 1257 (E.D.Pa. 1971).

[41] Public Law 94-142.

ence of these legislative and judicial actions resulted in substantially greater attention to the schooling of handicapped children.

Despite the concern for special education students shown in recent educational policy, we continue to suffer from a lack of demographic and technical information. Even the most primitive questions regarding the incidence of various handicaps can seldom be answered accurately. No satisfactory nationwide census of handicapped pupils has been conducted as of this writing. Consequently, we must rely upon estimates. In this regard, a 1975 study of the Stanford Research Institute suggests that urban areas (municipalities with populations of 250,000 or more) had substantially greater concentrations of pupils suffering from hearing, visual, orthopedic, and speech handicaps, mental retardation, and emotional disturbance than did either nonurban or rural areas.[42] For example, teacher-identified incidence of mental retardation among 12- to 17-year-olds is estimated in the SRI study to be 2 to 2.5% in urban areas and lower than 1 percent in cities 25,000 or less. Mental retardation is a condition necessitating extraordinary expenditures in order to provide the individual student with proper care and instruction.

Beginning in the 1950s and accelerating with the two previously listed court cases in the early 1970s, state aid formulas paid increasing attention to funding programs for handicapped students. The absence of a solid research base impeded construction of equitable financing mechanisms. There is no body of knowledge that specifies how much *should* be spent upon the schooling of handicapped pupils in order to assure them an equal or adequate educational opportunity. Lacking such information, handicapped aid arrangements are constructed from practice and political reality.

States have pursued three major strategies for dispensing aid to handicapped students: weighting, flat grant, and cost reimbursement.[43]

Financing for handicapped and disadvantaged children, besides being a special problem for cities, is an increasingly important concern of educators and citizens alike. However, regardless of the funding mechanisms involved, seldom is the total burden of such costly services borne fully by the state or federal government. Some portion of the added dollars necessary to provide such pupils with school services must almost always be paid by local taxpayers. This in itself is not necessarily evil. The inequity stems from the disproportionate numbers of such students in urban areas. For this reason, we advocate

[42] Patricia A. Craig and Norman B. McEachron, "The Development and Analysis of Baseline Data."

[43] See M. Thomas, "Finance: Without Which There is No Special Education," *Exceptional Children,* 39, pp. 475–80. For a review of the literature on financing educational services for handicapped children, see Charles D. Berstein et al., *Financing Educational Services for the Handicapped* (prepared for the U.S. Office of Education by the Management Analysis Center Inc., Palo Alto, California, December 1974).

added state attention to adequate reimbursement to cities of the high costs of schooling disadvantaged and handicapped.

VOCATIONAL TRAINING STUDENTS

A third category of expensive students are those receiving intensive vocational training. Added expenses here are not a function of students' characteristics but, rather, a consequence of the specialized equipment and personnel involved. Lathes, presses, computer terminals, and other machines necessary to teach students to perform tasks in a technological economy are remarkably costly when compared to the expenses involved, for example, in teaching a student U.S. History or Latin. Cities typically have a large number of students enrolled in such high-cost training programs. Although as a proportion of enrollment, rural districts frequently have even more, suburbs tend to have the lowest of all. Federal legislation frequently provides funds for vocational programs but state aid is not usually directly available to local school districts. Most states providing financing for vocational training usually do so through intermediate units and regional occupational centers.

MORE SCHOOL SERVICES

A second explanation for higher urban school expenditures is the apparent necessity for cities to purchase a wider range of services than their rural and suburban counterparts. The best available evidence in this regard was assembled in 1973 by Norman Drachler, former School Superintendent for Detroit. In a fact-laden essay, Drachler illustrates the costs attached to providing protection from and repairing the damage of vandals, employing additional attendance personnel to maintain records on a population so mobile that some inner-city schools experience turnover rates in excess of 100 percent in the course of an academic year, and providing non-instructional services, such as lunch and bus transportation, to indigent students.[44] These and other problems explain Drachler's response to a legislator's query as to whether he thought "money made a difference in solving school problems?" Drachler reportedly replied, "I don't know, but I would like once to try 'money' as a solution to see if it works."

An earlier effort by Dr. Frederick M. Fox, former Budget Director for the Los Angeles Unified School District, revealed findings similar to those in Detroit. Fox listed items such as those in Table 15-1 as illustrations of the extraordinary expenditures faced in 1966 by city school districts.

HIGHER CITY PRICES

A third cause of high city school expenditures levels can be traced to the higher prices cities frequently must pay for school-related goods and services, particularly for construction and maintenance of buildings.

[44] Norman Drachler, "The Large City School System" pp. 15-44.

TABLE 15-1

Extra Costs of Los Angeles Schools

Security agents to protect students, employees, and property	$ 450,171
Special "Adjustment Center" schools	1,229,483
Pupil transiency and population mobility accounting	1,127,062
Truancy and child welfare services	1,680,902
Smog control	544,213

Source: Frederick M. Fox, "The Missing Factor," a paper prepared for the California State Legislature (Los Angeles Unified School District, 1966).

Frequently, purchase of school sites in cities is substantially more expensive than in rural and suburban areas. City site acquisition may involve purchase and demolition of existing structures; outside cities this is usually not necessary. Drachler's essay illustrated this situation dramatically. In 1971 Detroit began construction of four new schools. Total land acquisition was 40 acres at a cost per acre exceeding the average price in Michigan by $125,000. The total purchase of the land cost $5 million more than would be the case, on the average, elsewhere in the state. Construction costs, because of the high union wage scale then prevailing in Detroit, accounted for more than $6 million in additional expenses. The total was $11 million more for the four schools than for comparable schools built outside of Detroit.[45] These figures are dramatic; yet a mitigating factor is that building new facilities is not an everyday occurrence for school districts, especially city districts.

The high cost of urban school construction appears to slow down city systems' replacement of outdated facilities. A 1970 survey conducted by the National Education Association revealed that almost 40 percent of the big city teachers worked in school buildings built prior to 1930.[46] Another sur-

---

[45] As reported by Norman Drachler, "The Large City School System," pp. 37–38. See also, The Research Council of the Great Cities, *The Challenge of Financing Public Schools in the Great Cities,* Chicago, Illinois, 1964; and Levin et al., *The High Cost of Education,* p. 42.

An analysis conducted in 1964 by the Great Cities Research Council revealed that the average cost of land per acre in the 14 city school districts surveyed was $68,156. By contrast, the average cost per acre in the nonurban districts in the same states was $3,074. Levin's study also confirms Drachler's analysis. For Michigan, New York, California, and Washington, these three analysts reported school construction costs to be higher in central cities than in suburbs. This is the case regardless of whether the measure is cost per square foot of construction or cost per pupil enrolled. In addition to site acquisition, higher school construction costs are probably a consequence of at least two conditions. First, cities frequently have more complicated and restrictive building code conditions than do other areas. Secondly, wage scales for union laborers tend to be higher in cities and are then passed forward to school districts in the form of higher construction bids.

[46] "Age of School Buildings Where Teachers Teach," *NEA Research Bulletin,* October 1970, p. 82.

TABLE 15-2

Per Pupil Cost—Maintenance of Plant, 1967-68

State		City	
1. New York	(N.A.)	New York	$27.00
2. California	$23.00	Los Angeles	30.00
3. Illinois	22.00	Chicago	21.00
4. Pennsylvania	20.00	Philadelphia	26.00
5. Michigan	20.00	Detroit	31.00
6. Massachusetts	19.00	Boston	25.00
7. Missouri	21.00	St. Louis	43.00
8. Colorado	18.00	Denver	23.00
9. Louisiana	12.00	New Orleans	29.00
10. Maryland	26.00	Baltimore	36.00
11. Minnesota	15.00	St. Paul	28.00
12. Ohio	15.00	Cleveland	24.00
13. Oregon	26.00	Portland	31.00
14. Wisconsin	22.00	Milwaukee	31.00

Source: Norman Drachler, "The Large City School System: It Costs More to Do the Same," Chapter 2 in *Equity for Cities in School Finance Reform* (Washington, D.C.: The Potomac Institute, 1973), p. 25.

vey reported that 13 percent of the school buildings in the nation's 15 largest districts were constructed prior to 1900; 36 percent were constructed prior to 1920. Thousands of city children attend school in buildings constructed before the widespread use of electricity or modern heating and plumbing.[47]

Once constructed, city schools continue to be more expensive to maintain. For example, as displayed in Table 15-2, a late 1960 national survey reported that school maintenance costs in 14 of the nation's largest city school districts exceeded the average for their respective state. The only exception to this pattern was Chicago, which reported a maintenance expenditure one dollar lower than the state mean.[48]

One high-cost factor for cities is somewhat controversial. Urban advocates frequently contend that cities must pay higher salaries to teachers to overcome less desirable city working conditions and to compete successfully with more attractive suburban districts. On balance, it is correct that city school systems pay higher average teacher salaries.[49] However, the causes for higher pay are clouded. City school personnel were among the first to unionize

[47] Ben E. Graves, "The Decaying School House," in *The Schoolhouse in the City,* ed. Alvin Toffler (New York: Praeger, 1968), pp. 61-62.

[48] Drachler's data are from Lynn H. Fox and Gordon E. Hurd, *Finances of Large City School Systems: A Comparative Analysis,* U.S. Office of Education (Washington, D.C.: U.S. Government Printing Office, 1971), pp. 52-53.

[49] Robert O. Reischauer and Robert W. Hartman, *Reforming School Finance* (Washington, D.C.: The Brookings Institution, 1973), p. 62.

and their salaries may not reflect labor market competition so much as they represent union bargaining advantages. Second, with few exceptions, city school teachers tend to have more seniority and higher levels of education than their rural and suburban counterparts.[50] This confounds research efforts to separate competitive labor market conditions and teacher "quality." Whether city teachers' higher salaries are necessary to retain able teachers or, rather, whether big city school boards should be admonished to adopt a stiffer posture at the bargaining table cannot be deduced from available information.

SIZE AND SCHOOL EFFICIENCY

Conventional wisdom suggests that the large size of city school districts should open the possibility for added operational efficiencies. The weight of available evidence argues that this potential, if it exists at all, is not being realized. In the simplest of terms—expenditures per pupil—city schools are more costly to operate than other kinds of school districts. Per pupil current expenses in 1969-70 were found to be higher in central cities than in surrounding areas in 46 of the 70 largest metropolitan areas.[51] Given the excess cost factors we have just described, we are not surprised at the absence of economies of large scale. Nevertheless, within various components of school operation one might reasonably expect to uncover efficiencies. Purchasing of supplies and equipment would appear to be a natural dimension on which size would work to the advantage of city districts. However, there is no conclusive information regarding this point. The viewpoint widely held among school administrators is that a school business administrator's ability to strike a bargain is a more powerful explainer of lower purchase prices than is district size. A preliminary survey in 1971 by the New York State Education Commission revealed no particular advantage to New York City resulting from its mammoth centralized purchasing operation.

It is sometimes held that the size of city schools permits greater administrative specialization and thus lower overhead costs. This too is difficult to assess. Large city school systems sometimes report a lower ratio of administrators to students or to teachers than do suburban school systems.[52] However, this may not accurately reflect costs, since city administrative salaries frequently are higher. Even a per pupil comparison of administrative costs is not sufficient.

[50] Levin et al., *The High Cost of Education*, p. 22.

[51] Seymour Sacks and Ralph Andrew, with Tony Carnevale, "School State Aid and the System of Finance: Central City, Suburban and Rural Dimensions of Revenue Sharing," an unpublished paper cited in Reischauer and Hartman, *Reforming School Finance*, p. 67.

[52] J. H. Freeman and M. T. Hannan, "Growth and Decline Processes in Organizations," *American Sociological Review*, 40, (April 1975), 215-28.

School districts do not always account accurately for administrative expenditures. In 1976, for example, a large city district was revealed to have assigned almost 200 teachers to administrative positions and to have charged the expense to instruction. This substantially overstated instructional costs while paring administrative figures.

In terms of instructional costs, large size should enable city schools, *ceteris paribus,* to afford more specialized forms of instruction. To offer advanced physics to three students in a small rural high school may prove impossible financially. Such a specialized class in a large city system by contrast may draw one or more complete classes and render the unit costs quite low. Indeed, in extraordinarily large systems there sometimes are sufficient numbers of students to justify an entire school given over to a subject. The special schools of science, design, and performing arts in New York City are good examples. Viewed from this perspective, city schools are able financially to offer advantages to their clientele which are the envy of the nation.

Despite these obvious advantages, city school districts appear badly in need of reforms to eliminate inefficient use of personnel. There has been a tendency since the late 1950s to increase the number of non-instructional professional personnel. Nationwide, in 1959–60, 2.17 percent of the public school teaching staff was engaged in non-instructional duties. Fifteen years later, the number constituted 5.43 percent.[53] It is doubtful that the proliferation of such specialized personnel has had any positive impact upon the school performance of students. Nevertheless, it has been a costly item of expenditure.

In New York State, the number of non-classroom professionals employed in grades 7 through 12 grew 140 percent from 1965 to 1970. Meanwhile average class size declined only from 20.2 to 18.2 pupils per instructor.[54] Similarly, a 1976 analysis of San Francisco's schools revealed that one out of every five employees certified to teach was in fact deployed in a position other than classroom teacher.[55] Many of these individuals, of course, perform highly useful, non-classroom functions, e.g., librarians. On the other hand, it is not clear that the proliferation of personnel specializations among educators has added significantly to the effectiveness of schools. Aside from the question of the utility of such non-classroom positions, it appears that large city school districts have a high proportion of their employees in this category.

[53] National Center for Educational Statistics, *The Condition of Education; 1976.* Percentages derived from figures presented on p. 246.

[54] *The Fleischmann Report on the Cost, Quality and Financing of Elementary and Secondary Education in New York State* (New York: Viking Press, 1973), Appendix 13B, pp. 266, 279.

[55] James W. Guthrie, Walter I. Garms, and Lawrence C. Pierce, "The Fiscal Future of the San Francisco Public Schools," a paper prepared for the San Francisco Public Schools Commission, June 1976.

CITY SCHOOL REVENUES

Not only do cities suffer from several conditions that make school operation expensive, but also it is frequently alleged that the revenue-generating capacity of cities is severely eroded. The ability of any district to raise property tax revenues hinges upon (1) "fiscal capacity," wealth available to be tapped, and (2) "effort," the extent to which residents are willing to tax existing wealth. In order to assess the revenue-generating capacity of cities, it is necessary to examine these two conditions.

FISCAL CAPACITY

Standard wealth measures reveal cities, on the average, to be in a favorable position relative to surrounding geographic areas. Table 15-3 displays equalized property values and personal income, both per pupil and per capita, for the central city, suburbs, and rural areas in 14 major metropolitan areas. These are 1969-70 data analyzed by Reischauer and Hartman. In eight of the 14 cases, property wealth *per pupil* is greater in cities. However, in only three instances do city property values exceed those of suburbs on a *per capita* basis. The explanation for this condition is to be found in the last column, "Public School Enrollment as Percentage of Total Population." As we discussed earlier in this chapter, city schools tend to enroll a smaller portion of the total population than is the case elsewhere. This is a function both of the larger number of childless households and higher nonpublic school enrollments in cities, particularly cities on the eastern seaboard.

Another study, utilizing data from the subsequent school year, contains stronger results. This study, by Callahan, Wilken, and Sillerman, covers more cities and encompasses all regions of the U.S. Callahan and his colleagues report that per pupil property values in 34 major cities exceed the average for their respective states by 26 percent. Put another way, according to these data, the average city school district in the United States has a *per pupil* property value 26 percent higher than the average for the state in which it is located.[56]

These researchers also report that *per capita* property values tend to be higher for cities than the average for their states. Here, however, the difference is small, only five percent. The lower percentage of urban school-age children enrolled in public schools again accounts for the difference between per pupil and per capita figures.

What emerges from the analysis thus far is that, on a per pupil basis, cities generally have an ability to support schools comparable or greater than

[56]Callahan et al., *Urban Schools.*

TABLE 15-3

Fiscal Capacity and Public School Enrollment Ratios for Selected Cities, Suburbs, and Rural Areas, 1969–70 School Year (money amounts in dollars)

Area	Equalized Property Value Per pupil	Equalized Property Value Per capita	Personal Income Per pupil	Personal Income Per capita	Public School Enrollment as Percentage of Total Population
Boston	20,661	3,120	20,345	3,099	15
Suburbs	32,520	6,775	18,715	3,899	21
Rural Massachusetts	53,144	12,315	14,021	3,249	23
New York City	47,625	6,546	27,270	3,736	14
Suburbs	37,640	8,131	22,421	4,843	22
Rural New York	20,582	5,139	10,296	2,574	25
Newark	19,815	4,089	11,344	2,498	22
Suburbs	48,443	8,909	25,936	4,629	18
Rural New Jersey	45,780	10,523	14,086	3,238	23
Philadelphia	24,057	3,549	20,614	3,041	15
Suburbs	26,952	5,246	20,085	3,909	19
Rural Pennsylvania	14,279	3,397	10,632	2,529	24
Wilmington	27,899	5,142	16,081	2,964	18
Suburbs	19,165	4,481	15,881	3,713	23
Rural Delaware	12,222	3,009	11,174	2,751	25
Baltimore	15,727	3,331	13,624	2,886	21
Suburbs	19,674	4,080	19,117	3,965	21
Rural Maryland	13,010	3,239	8,925	2,222	25
Cleveland	30,281	6,043	14,276	2,849	20
Suburbs	52,057	9,972	23,004	4,406	19
Rural Ohio	23,788	5,444	8,839	2,023	23
Detroit	16,808	3,271	16,920	3,227	19
Suburbs	15,644	3,990	15,785	4,026	26
Rural Michigan	11,032	3,033	8,977	2,468	27
Chicago	20,798	3,618	19,662	3,420	17
Suburbs	18,381	4,157	19,228	4,348	23
Rural Illinois	21,870	5,399	11,189	2,762	25
Milwaukee	30,875	5,671	17,445	3,204	18
Suburbs	40,176	8,822	18,694	4,105	22
Rural Wisconsin	21,989	5,433	9,519	2,352	25
Minneapolis-St. Paul	14,851	2,349	22,027	3,484	16
Suburbs	10,021	2,719	14,828	4,024	27
Rural Minnesota	8,746	2,276	8,799	2,290	26
St. Louis	15,314	2,825	15,025	2,772	18
Suburbs	14,260	3,024	19,081	4,046	21
Rural Missouri	10,290	2,249	10,143	2,217	22
Denver	13,255	2,474	19,055	3,557	19
Suburbs	7,068	1,920	13,791	3,747	27
Rural Colorado	8,738	2,272	9,554	2,484	26
San Francisco	24,108	3,056	33,832	4,289	13
Suburbs	13,955	3,042	21,307	4,644	22
Rural California	16,991	3,844	13,450	3,043	23

Source: Robert O. Reischauer and Robert W. Hartman, *Reforming School Finance* (Washington, D.C.: The Brookings Institution, 1973), p. 68.

that of other areas. This is slightly less true when fiscal capacity is measured on a per capita basis.

As indicated in Chapter Six on school revenues, whatever the property tax base, taxes themselves must be paid from personal or corporate incomes. Thus, it is also important to examine in income terms the relative ability of city residents to support schools. Table 15-3 reveals that the majority, 9 of 14, of the cities examined by Reischauer and Hartman have higher per pupil personal income than surrounding areas. However, on the dimension of personal income per capita, no city in the table exceeds its suburban neighbors. Again, the relatively low proportion of public school pupils to the total population leaves cities in an advantaged position.

However, wealth per capita is more accurate than wealth per pupil as a reflection of ability to support aggregate municipal services. If cities by necessity must support higher cost public services, there may be little money left for schools, and the advantaged urban fiscal position may not exist. This is a subject to which we will return shortly.

Although cities fare relatively well when their fiscal capacity is compared to that of surrounding areas, the property tax base of some cities may now be declining. When this occurs, it is generally attributable to at least two factors: First, removal of property from tax rolls for purposes such as public housing, freeways, public buildings, and tax exempt institutions (e.g., churches and universities); second, systematic undervaluation of property by city assessors.[57]

Urban renewal programs eventually may assist in inhibiting or reversing the trend toward declining value but, all in all, cities probably do not occupy the same relatively advantaged fiscal condition they did during the first half of this century. They do, however, have at their disposal a fiscal capacity that is comparable with other areas. Our next step is to assess their efforts to tap this wealth.

TAX EFFORT

How does city school tax effort compare to suburban and rural counterparts? Existing evidence suggests that, when educational taxes alone are considered, city districts tax themselves at lower than average rates. A 1968-69 study revealed that central cities have lower measures of effort than suburban, rural, and small city districts as well as states taken as a whole.[58] Judging from

---

[57] For example, a 1966 study by James, Kelly, and Garms revealed that in the three decades from 1930 to 1960, assessment ratios declined in 13 of the 14 major cities they studied. H. Thomas James, James A. Kelly, and Walter I. Garms, *Determinants of Educational Expenditures in the Great Cities of the United States* (Stanford, Calif.: Stanford Unviersity, School of Education, 1955).

[58] Callahan et al., *Urban Schools*, p. 30.

these data alone, it is difficult to sympathize with city revenue problems. One might suggest that cities generally are deserving of more state or federal assistance only when they tax themselves at a level equal to that of other school districts.

MUNICIPAL OVERBURDEN

City advocates argue that straightforward comparison of tax rates is overly simple and disguises important differences between cities and other school districts. They base the major portion of their case on what has come to be labeled *municipal overburden*. This is the condition whereby cities, perhaps as a sheer consequence of the density of their population, are called upon to provide a wider and more costly array of public services including fire, police, medical and health, welfare, sanitation, and transit services. Also, the argument goes, cities provide many services that benefit residents of surrounding areas. These include airports, museums, athletic facilities, and institutions of higher education that draw much of their support from local property taxes. City advocates contend that even when user fees are imposed for such services, they must be subsidized by local tax revenues.

Proof of municipal overburden is taken from comparative tax figures. The National Urban Coalition study examined the 1969-70 ratio of city expenditures to state expenditures for public services such as police, fire, refuse, sewers, and health. On the average, comparing city expenditures per capita with state expeditures per capita, city costs for such municipal services were often twice as high.[59]

The added public services supported by city residents indeed not only cost more money per capita, but also require higher total tax payments. Results of several studies are remarkably consistent in this regard. The National Urban Coalition study compared city and state total local property tax rates per $1,000 of personal income for 1969-70. On the average, city residents paid $71 per $1,000 of personal income for municipal services, while the state average was only $59—20 percent more by this measure.[60] Netzer used 1971-72 data to perform a similar analysis. He compared local taxes as a percent of personal income for eight cities and the remaining jurisdictions within their standard metropolitan statistical area. In every instance, the city taxpayer was committed to a higher proportion of personal income than were surrounding residents.[61]

The fact that per capita tax payments, or even tax payments relative to

---

[59] Ibid., p. 29.

[60] *Ibid.*, p. 31.

[61] Dick Netzer, "State Education Aid and School Tax Efforts in Large Cities," in *Selected Papers in School Finance, 1974,* ed. Esther O. Tron (Washington, D.C.: U.S. Office of Education, 1974), p. 157.

personal income, are higher for cities than for other areas should not be taken immediately as evidence that city residents themselves actually pay higher taxes. Many cities contain substantial amounts of nonresidential property. Taxes on parcels such as stores, factories, warehouses, and restaurants are to some degree shifted forward to consumers. Frequently, particularly in the case of large commercial enterprises, the consumers reside outside city boundaries. Under such circumstances, city property taxes are being "exported." The real tax payments are not being made by the city dweller. In order accurately to estimate the burden of taxes upon city residents, one must separate taxes paid by residential and nonresidential property owners.[62]

What is clear from the foregoing is that cities spend more for municipal services of all kinds, not simply schools, and tax themselves more heavily to support such services. What is not immediately evident is who pays the taxes and whether or not such a condition constitutes an "overburden." The economist Harvey E. Brazer cast a critical eye toward the overburden argument, and in a 1971 report to New York's Fleischmann Commission he posed the following questions of those who would contend that cities should be awarded compensation for "overburden" conditions:[63]

1. How does one distinguish "municipal overburden" from a community's greater taste for public goods?

2. How does one adjust for the fact that in some jurisdictions certain services such as fire protection, sanitation, and even schooling are for the most part provided privately, while in others these are provided publicly?

3. How does one account for the alternative costs to public service incurred by those living in uncongested areas? The city dweller may pay taxes for police protection, but the suburban commuter pays for equivalent protection by driving two hours a day to get to and from an area inaccessible to criminals.

4. Should society compensate or subsidize persons who choose to live in jurisdictions with excessively high social costs? Some part of the high public service costs of cities may simply reflect the inefficiencies of too dense concentrations of population. The cities will never thin out if these excess costs are subsidized by higher levels of government.

Whereas it is relatively clear that cities have unusual school expenses, it is not so obvious that they are handicapped in raising revenues. Where one stands

[62] For an example of an analytic effort to separate the incidence of property taxes upon residential and nonresidential property, see Stephen J. Scheier, "Equalizing Educational Expenditures in California by Implementation of a Statewide Property Tax on Commercial and Industrial Property," unpublished M.A. Thesis, School of Education, University of California, Berkeley, 1976.

[63] Harvey Brazer et al., "Fiscal Needs and Resource," an unpublished consultant's report to the New York State Commission on the Cost, Quality and Financing of Elementary and Secondary Education, 1971, as cited by Reischauer and Hartman, *Reforming School Finance,* p. 71.

on this issue depends upon one's responses to the preceding list of questions posed by Harvey Brazer. Regardless of what is "true" or where one stands on particular issues of city school finance, it generally is conceded that city school problems call for exceptional treatment in school finance plans if for no other reason than political reality. In the next section we describe and analyze various plans that have been suggested to assist cities in meeting their school dollar needs.

Solving City School Finance Problems

Proposals to provide added financial assistance to city schools generally possess one or both of two attributes: (1) they attempt to shift a larger portion of the finance burden to the state level, or (2) they rely more heavily on revenues other than the property tax for school support. The advantages and disadvantages of property taxation as a means of generating school revenues have been assessed in detail in Chapter Six. Consequently, we concentrate here only upon suggested means for shifting a greater proportion of city school support to the state.

PROMOTING A GREATER STATE SHARE

Suggestions for increasing state school aid to cities typically fall into one or a combination of three categories: (1) increased state support for high-cost pupils; (2) computational mechanisms for masking the true property wealth of cities so as to entitle them to greater state equalization aid, and (3) proposals for the state to assume the full costs of schooling.

PROVISIONS FOR SPECIAL PUPIL NEED

We have already described the enormous financial burdens imposed on city school districts by the high incidence of low-income, low-achieving, handicapped, and vocationally oriented pupils. Legislators and other state officials frequently are impressed with the validity of this argument and many states have already enacted appropriations to assist cities in the instruction of such high-cost students. As of 1977, 18 states provided added funds for disadvantaged students; six of these did so by using special weights in their distribution formulas.

A variant of the extra-cost student solution to city school finance problems is comprised of state formula adjustments for population. In 1977 three states had such aid factors in their distribution formulas. The assumption here is that a high concentration of students within a geographical area entails added expenses. Consequently, distribution formula components are constructed to allocate added funds per pupil to districts in which either total population or pupil population density exceeds a specified threshold. By adroitly drawing the cutoff point, the legislature has the ability to direct such aid precisely to city school districts. This tactic has its counterpart in so-called "sparsity aid," intended to compensate for the higher costs in small and sparsely settled rural districts. In 1977, 25 states had such distribution factors. Frequently, state aid formulas have both sparsity and density aid factors. The politics of such an arrangement should be obvious.

The planning necessary to incorporate funding for special students in aid formulas is technically simple. The political negotiations to bring such a plan to fruition may be brutal. The incidence of various categories of disadvantaged and handicapped students can be entered as data items in a state school finance computerized simulation model (see Chapter Twelve). Once such data are available, it is possible to adjust weighting and attached funding amounts until the total dollar appropriation for city school districts achieves a "desirable" level. "Desirable" in this instance is likely to be the outcome of political negotiations between a state's urban and nonurban interests.

TAX EFFORT AND WEALTH ADJUSTMENTS

A second urban school aid strategy consists of proposals for manipulating the fiscal capacity of city school districts. Generally this is attempted under the rationale of adjusting for "municipal overburden." There exist two major means for compensating an urban school district for the fact that its total (school and other municipal services) tax rate is high. One way is by using a "total tax effort equalization plan."[64] Such plans function similarly to percentage equalizing arrangements explained in Chapter Eight. Schools are subsidized by the state in areas where total tax rate is high. The major difference is that here state aid is not based on district school tax rate but on total local property tax rate. A total tax equalization plan effectively rewards school districts taxing themselves above the state average for all services. In this way the plan benefits high taxing cities and other above average tax rate districts.

The total tax equalization concept suffers from at least one drawback from a public finance perspective. It acts as an incentive for municipalities to shift services into the public sector. As such it is not a neutral taxing mechanism. In a city in which refuse collection is conducted by a private firm, citizens pay a monthly charge for the service out of their own pockets. Under a total tax equalization plan, however, this city would receive added subsidies from the state if it took over refuse collection and charged for the service through the property tax.

---

[64]This finance plan is explained in detail in Lawrence C. Pierce, Walter I. Garms, James W. Guthrie and Michael W. Kirst, *State School Finance Alternatives: Strategies for Reform* (Eugene, Ore.: Center for Educational Policy and Management, University of Oregon, 1975), pp. 45–49.

A second municipal overburden adjustment strategy consists of what is termed an "available wealth equalization plan."[65] This strategy involves computing the proportion of school taxes to total property taxes. Total assessed valuation is then adjusted in keeping with this proportion. If, for example, a city's total property tax rate was $12.00, of which school taxes were $4.00, then the total assessed valuation per pupil would be reduced by two-thirds. State aid eligibility whether under the foundation, percentage equalizing, or full state assumption plan, would then become a function of the "available wealth" to be taxed for school purposes.

"Available wealth" equalization plans also have flaws. They penalize school districts whose residents have chosen to spend their property tax revenues on schools rather than on other services. Unlike total tax effort equalization plans, they encourage localities to shift expenses from the school district budget to the municipal budget. This reduces "available wealth" and renders the school district eligible for more aid.

Redrawing "fiscal" boundaries can also be used as a strategy for increasing state aid to local school districts. For example, in 1969, the New York State legislature enacted a statute permitting New York City to be considered as five separate districts for purposes of calculating state aid. Manhattan Island contains awesome wealth when measured in terms of assessed value per pupil. In fact, the wealth of this one borough was sufficient to raise the average assessed valuation per pupil across all five New York City boroughs high enough to lose substantial state aid. By calculating state aid for each borough separately, as though it were a distinct school district, the impact of Manhattan's high property values was cushioned. Under the new system, the other city boroughs had sufficiently low assessed valuation per pupil to qualify for $60 million in added state aid.[66]

Large cities frequently have a commercially developed sector with many high-rise buildings and few school children. Proposals to isolate such geographic areas for purposes of calculating city school aid are intended to have the same effect as the New York City borough aid plan.

FULL STATE ASSUMPTION

City advocates frequently propose full state assumption of school costs as a means of aiding urban school districts. Such proposals are a mixed blessing for cities. On one hand, expenditure levels can be established to advantage city districts. For example, the Fleischmann Commission, in New York State, constructed its Full State Assumption (FSA) finance plan around New York City.

[65] *Ibid.*, pp. 50–56.
[66] See Charles S. Benson, "The Transition to a New School Finance System," in *School Finance in Transition,* ed. John Pincus (Cambridge, Mass.: Ballinger Publishing Co., 1974), pp. 151–75.

The Commission's finance proposals would have elevated spending in all New York State school districts to the spending level of the school district at the 67th percentile. That level was selected because it was New York City's per pupil expenditure level. By building a proposed system around the largest district in the state, and a politically powerful one at that, the plan's architects hoped to make it attractive to the state legislature. The Fleischmann recommendations contained a high weighting for low-achieving students (1.5), a feature also intended to benefit New York City and the state's other urban districts.[67]

On the taxation side, however, full state assumption contains risks for cities. Typically, FSA proposals specify a statewide property tax at the average tax rate among the state's school districts. As described previously, cities tend to have higher than average overall tax rates, but less than average taxes for school purposes. Consequently, a statewide property tax aimed at bringing all districts up (or down) to the state average generally spells an increase in city school tax rates. The change can be graduated over several years so as not to have an abrupt impact, but an eventual tax increase must be acknowledged. The impact upon city tax rates of full state assumption was a significant factor in discouraging the New York State legislature from adopting the Fleischmann Commission finance proposals.

DISTRICT POWER EQUALIZING

The genus of school finance plans described in Chapter Nine as "percentage equalizing" and its variant, district power equalizing (DPE), contain the potential to work hardships on city school districts. Because city districts tend to have lower than average school tax rates, most DPE proposals would necessitate school tax rate increases merely to enable city districts to spend at an average rate. This would entail particularly high city taxes when municipal service tax rates were added. Also, if a DPE plan had an "excess" revenue recapture provision, given the high level of assessed value in cities, it would mean that the city tax base would be subsidizing lower wealth areas in a state. For these reasons, city advocates frequently look upon DPE with some disfavor.

Our View

From our perspective, city school districts constitute the largest single problem in America's educational system. We have no higher priority than the eventual restoration of city schools to their past positions of excellence. The

[67]*Report of the New York State Commission to Study the Cost, Quality and Financing of Elementary and Secondary Education* (New York: Viking Press, Inc., 1972), Vol. 1, chap. 1.

question, as always, is how best to accomplish such an objective. On balance, we believe the general school finance reform plan explained in detail in Chapter Nine is an excellent vehicle for alleviating financial problems of city school districts. Several features of that plan are worthy of emphasis in this context.

MUNICIPAL OVERBURDEN

Our proposed finance reforms contain no special consideration of municipal overburden because we are not yet persuaded that such reforms make sense. Put another way, we do not believe the answers to Harvey Brazer's questions justify aiding school districts by manipulating fiscal capacity. Without question overall city tax rates are higher than surrounding areas. However, why should the state give added funding to a city school district because, for example, its residents subsidize an urban transit system with tax proceeds while the suburban commuter pays for transportation out of his or her own pocket? Similarly, the city may levy property taxes to pay for garbage collection; yet a farmer may have to spend time (time equals money) to bury or burn garbage. The fact that the city pays for its garbage through tax levies does not justify its receiving more state school aid than the farmer's school district.

PUPILS WITH SPECIAL NEEDS

On this dimension we are extraordinarily sympathetic to the condition of city school districts. The facts are incontrovertible; city schools serve highly disproportionate concentrations of students in need of costly school services. The continued neglect of such students portends not only unnecessary lifelong hardships for the individuals themselves, but also added welfare, health, and criminal justice costs for all of society. Schools can be one of the important institutions in attempting to alleviate social malaise. Consequently, we strongly advocate added urban aid based on students with special needs.

HUMAN CAPITAL

While acknowledging the potential significance of schooling, we do not believe that schools by themselves are sufficiently powerful as "social engines" to correct society's and individual students' ills single-handedly. The motivational and achievement problems of many city school students can be assisted only if a broader range of support services is brought into play. For example, children, from an early age, must be assured adequate nutrition and health care. We are not persuaded that schools in every instance are the correct setting for all the remediation that may be necessary. For this reason we believe that the educational coupon plan we explain in Chapter Nine can be adapted in cities to enable households to obtain a wide range of services which, though not directly connected with schools, will enhance the education of city students. In so doing we would hope to replenish the account of human capital for cities.

Summary

City schools once served as the nation's educational "lighthouses" by which other systems were guided in their efforts to offer high quality school services. However, the social and economic ills besetting urban America during the middle of the twentieth century imposed a heavy burden upon city schools. While the calibre of city schools was widely perceived as declining, their costs increased. Middle-class families moved to the suburbs, in part to obtain better schooling, and their places were filled by low-income households whose children badly needed high-priced bilingual, remedial, and special education services. High-cost municipal services aggravated the situation by draining city property tax bases. Resulting high tax rates frequently induced commercial and industrial interests to move to the suburbs, thereby eroding further the fiscal condition of many cities.

Solutions to city school problems do not come easily. Cities seldom enjoy parity in political power when pitted against suburban and rural interests. Distribution formula remedies intended to generate greater statewide equity frequently jeopardize the position of cities, either by threatening to reduce their expenditure levels or by raising their tax rates. Moreover, it is unlikely that schools by themselves are sufficiently powerful to address all the problems of city youth. Other institutions will have to be involved.

In general, we believe the school finance reforms proposed in Chapter Nine will be of great assistance in solving city school problems. However, we acknowledge quickly that such general solutions will have to be carefully tailored to the individual circumstances of each state.

16

HIGHER EDUCATION FINANCE ISSUES

Postsecondary Education

This book is concerned primarily with elementary and secondary education, yet it would not be complete without a brief overview of the issues involved in financing higher education. The problems of higher education are inseparable from those of elementary–secondary education: each sector affects the other's standards and requirements and, equally important, competes for the same funds.

COLLEGIATE SECTOR

The sector of education termed "higher education" in this chapter has been called the "collegiate sector" of postsecondary education by the National Commission on the Financing of Postsecondary Education.[1] In 1972–73, the collegiate sector consisted of 2,948 public and private institutions of higher education, including community colleges, four-year liberal arts colleges, major re-

---

[1] The National Commission on the Financing of Postsecondary Education, *Financing Postsecondary Education in the United States* (Washington, D.C.: U.S. Government Printing Office, 1973), p. 13.

search universities, and professional schools, all of which enrolled over nine million students. The breakdown of these institutions by type is shown in Table 16-1. Of the public institutions, 70 percent were operated by the states and were predominantly local institutions. Only nine were federal institutions. The "collegiate sector" of education does not include occupational or recreational postsecondary schools.

Elementary–Secondary and Higher Education Differences and Relationships

There are a number of important differences between elementary-secondary and higher education. There is much more diversity in higher education. Whereas about 9 percent of elementary and secondary students attend private schools, fully 31 percent of higher education students in four-year colleges and universities are in private institutions,[2] and the institutional diversity is even greater than these percentages would imply. Approximately 85 percent of the enrollment in private elementary and secondary schools is in Catholic schools. On the other hand, private colleges and universities are about 23 percent Protestant, 19 percent Catholic, 2 percent other religions, and over 50 percent independent of religious affiliation.[3]

There are also differences in institutional form and purpose in higher education that are not evident in lower education. Most elementary and secondary schools are comprehensive in nature, teaching substantially the same curriculum at the same grade levels to students all over the country. The curriculum in the many different kinds of institutions making up higher education is, on the contrary, extremely diversified, ranging from community college courses in the trades, to liberal arts studied through the Great Books, to graduate specializations in engineering and medicine, to colleges devoted exclusively to music.

The richness of institutional forms and curricula of higher education is matched by its diversity of financing. Elementary and secondary schools receive almost all of their funding from local taxes and state grants, with less than 10 percent from the federal government and less than 5 percent from other sources. Institutions of higher learning get significant amounts of money from tuition, state grants, federal aid, philanthropy, research contracts, endowment income, and sales of services. This diversity complicates any analysis of higher education finance and has both advantages and disadvantages. A major advan-

[2]National Center for Educational Statistics, *The Condition of Education, 1976* (Washington, D.C.: U.S. Government Printing Office, 1976), Table 1.18, p. 187; and, National Center for Educational Statistics, *Projections of Educational Statistics to 1984-85* (Washington, D.C.: U.S. Printing Office, 1976), Table 3, p. 19.

[3]National Center for Educational Statistics, *Digest of Educational Statistics, 1973* (Washington, D.C.: U.S. Government Printing Office, 1974), Table 85, p. 72.

TABLE 16-1

Collegiate Sector of Postsecondary Education: Institutions and Enrollment, by Type of Institution, 1972–73

Institutional Type	Institutions			Enrollment†		
	Public	Private	Total	Public	Private	Total
Leading research universities	26	20	46	809,701	230,056	1,039,757
Other research universities	30	18	48	602,475	156,769	769,244
Large doctorate granting institutions	23	12	35	299,662	135,762	435,424
Small doctorate granting institutions	22	14	36	279,612	109,270	388,882
Comprehensive colleges with substantial program offerings	214	92	306	1,787,193	421,618	2,208,811
Comprehensive colleges with limited program offerings	114	57	171	471,327	129,258	600,585
Highly selective liberal arts colleges	1	144	145	2,246	190,144	192,390
Other liberal arts colleges	31	537	568	57,271	467,305	524,576
Two-year colleges and institutions	882	251	1,133	2,671,377	129,278	2,800,655
Divinity schools	0	219	219	0	65,989	65,989
Medical schools and centers	30	15	45	54,940	9,675	64,615
Other health professions schools	6	21	27	3,585	9,734	13,319
Schools of engineering and technology	7	32	39	20,829	52,212	73,041
Schools of business and management	1	26	27	13,821	41,168	54,989
Schools of art, music, and design	4	48	52	2,525	32,891	35,506
Schools of law	1	10	11	1,525	9,302	10,827
Teachers colleges	1	7	8	1,063	8,360	9,423
Other specialized institutions	17	15	32	38,392	8,526	46,918
Total	1,410	1,538	2,948*	7,127,544	2,207,407	9,334,951

*Branch campuses are treated as separate institutions. The Higher Education General Information Survey (HEGIS) total, which does not count branch campuses separately, is 2,686.

†Individuals.

Source: National Commission on the Financing of Postsecondary Education, *Financing Postsecondary Education in the United States* (Washington, D.C.: Government Printing Office, 1973), p. 15.

tage is that no single source is able to dictate how resources will be used, as it is possible for state agencies to do with public school districts. If one source will not fund a new building or program, another source may be tapped. On the other hand, a diversity of sources makes for a diversity of regulations imposed on the use of money.

A fourth difference between elementary–secondary and higher education is voluntary attendance. The fact that students may choose their college and need not attend unless they wish produces competition among schools that is not present in elementary–secondary education except in the very small private sector. Colleges constantly vie for students through the provision of attractive environment and programs.

In spite of the differences, higher and elementary–secondary education are dependent upon each other. Of course, secondary schools furnish the students for higher education. Also, to judge the value of grades from each high school, college associations established accrediting agencies which have had an important influence on the curriculum, staff, and facilities of high schools. These agencies have both upgraded and standardized high schools and are thus responsible for both improvements and lack of experimentation. Too, colleges train teachers for elementary and secondary schools, and training programs are in turn affected by the certification requirements of the state department of education. Finally, colleges offer many courses taken by elementary and secondary teachers after graduation.

In spite of these relationships, there has been very little communication between the educational levels. In petitioning legislatures for funds, each level has tended to think of itself as having no relation to the other and as competing for funds with all segments of government. On the other hand, legislators are increasingly thinking in terms of education as an entity when estimating the educational budget, which means that competition between levels will tend to be aggravated.[4]

RATIO OF EXPENDITURE

One line of research has been concerned with what it is that determines the ratio of public expenditure for higher education to that for elementary–secondary education in a state. This ratio varies from .05 in Massachusetts to .20 in North Dakota. A study by Garms hypothesizes that the political decisions regarding the ratio of expenditures in a state are the result of measurable environmental factors.[5] The states were the unit of analysis. Those variables which were believed to contribute to an explanation of the ratio were:

[4] The best work on the subject of increasing competition between the levels of education is Michael D. Usdan, David W. Minar, and Emanuel Hurwitz, Jr., *Education and State Politics* (New York: Columbia University, Teachers College Press, 1969).

[5] Walter I. Garms, *State-Local Governmental Support for Education: The Balance Between Higher and Lower Education* (unpublished, 1972). A portion of the study

1. Ability to support education, measured by personal income per capita.
2. Demand for higher education, measured by three variables:
   a. Proportion of the population aged 18 through 20, as a measure of the number eligible for higher education.
   b. Percentage of adults who had some college training, as a measure of relative demand for quality as well as quantity of higher education.
   c. Density of population in 1860, the reason for which is explained below.
3. Demand for elementary–secondary education, measured by two variables:
   a. Proportion of the population aged five through 17, as a measure of the number eligible for elementary–secondary education.
   b. Percentage of the population which is Catholic. (Private elementary–secondary schools are about 85 percent Catholic.)
4. Government factors, measured by three variables:
   a. Dollars of state and local general revenue raised through taxation per $1,000 of personal income, as a measure of the extractive capability of the government.
   b. The ratio of state taxes to local taxes, as a measure of relative extractive capability, since higher education is funded mostly from state sources.
   c. Elasticity of the state tax structure, as a measure of ability to keep up with demands.

Rather surprisingly, the best predictor of the ratio of public higher education expenditure to elementary-secondary expenditure was density of population in 1860. This variable was used to measure the force of tradition. It was hypothesized that those states having a sufficiently high population density before a large amount of governmental money was put into higher education nevertheless felt a need for colleges, and established private ones. Less densely populated states did not. When the federal government began putting money into public higher education, the less densely populated states clamored to take advantage, and soon developed a system of public higher education that prevented private higher education from gaining a foothold. Public expenditures per capita for higher education in these states should be high. In states that had been densely populated and had developed a system of private higher education, the federal money did not stimulate the development of a system of public higher education. If this reasoning was correct, the "more established" states should spend relatively less on public higher education. The year 1860 was chosen for the measure of population density because the Morrill Act of 1862 provided money to the states for the establishment of land grant colleges.

An interesting thing about this variable measuring tradition is that it is not just a proxy for present density of population. Density of population in 1860 is a better predictor than density in 1900, 1930, or 1960, the three other census years that were tried.

----

has been published as "The Prediction of State–Local Expenditures for Higher and Lower Education in the United States," in Robert Leiter, ed., *Costs and Benefits of Education* (Boston: Twayne Publishers, 1975), pp. 14–30.

Sources of Revenue for Higher Education

Institutions of higher learning receive revenue from a number of sources. A brief discussion of each of these follows.

TUITION

Tuition has been an important source of income for private higher education from its beginning yet it does not begin to pay the total cost of education. In private institutions tuition has normally paid about half the cost of education; in public institutions it has usually paid less than one-fifth. Tuition has been increasing at a higher percentage rate in public higher education than in private higher education, but because private tuitions are so much higher, the absolute dollar spread between public and private tuition has been widening rather than narrowing.

The level of tuition in public higher education has been a source of contention for many years. Private institutions maintain, with some justification, that low-tuition public institutions are unfair competition. Indeed, it is difficult to understand why parents would send their children to expensive private institutions instead of low-tuition public colleges. Of course, many believe that highly endowed private colleges offer better student–teacher ratios, facilities, and teachers and a more prestigious degree, yet if something is not done to improve the desperate financial situation of some private colleges, they may someday be able to provide little more than the opportunity to meet other students rich enough to afford their high tuition.

In any case, it is obvious that the enrollment of the public college has been increasing relative to that of the private one. In 1950 the enrollment in public and private institutions was about equal. By the mid-1970s more than three out of four college students were in public institutions.

Low tuition in public institutions has been stoutly defended as a necessary equity measure to enable students from poor as well as rich families to attend college. City University of New York (CUNY) and the California state system of higher education are outstanding examples of institutions founded on this belief. Both systems not only were substantially tuition-free but also guaranteed any student with a high school diploma admission to some part of the system. The financial problems of both New York City and New York State caused CUNY to abandon both tuition-free and open enrollment postures in 1976. California continues its program only at the community college level; its university and state college systems imposed tuition in 1968.

It can be argued that low or no tuition is an inefficient way of providing access to all, for it subsidizes the rich as well as the poor. It appears to be a more efficient use of available money to charge tuition comparable to that of private institutions of equivalent quality, and offer scholarships based on need. We agree with this position, and note that it is consistent with our proposals for elementary and secondary education. We have proposed that a basic education through grade 14 be offered to all students free, and that additional education be obtained with educational coupons purchased, like food stamps, at a discount by poor families. All states provide some tuition assistance for needy students in public colleges, and about 35 of the states also provide some for students in private colleges. However, the amount is much smaller than it could be if a higher tuition were charged in the public institutions.

W. Lee Hansen and Burton A. Weisbrod carried this principle to its logical conclusion by suggesting that the state of Wisconsin provide higher education money to students only, through tuition vouchers.[6] The vouchers could be spent at any institution of higher education, public or private, and this would constitute the sole source of funding for public institutions. It should be noted that the position taken by Hansen and Weisbrod assumes that the external benefits of higher education are negligible, and that therefore the principal purpose of state aid should be to further equity. A case can be made for equal subsidies to all if the main purpose is to promote increased consumption of education rather than to promote equity. Actually, the choice of what to do depends also upon the elasticity of demand for higher education by each income group. If the demand by higher income groups is relatively inelastic, and that by lower income groups is relatively elastic, then graduated subsidies can achieve both equity and efficiency goals. We have insufficient data on whether this view of elasticity is true. A reasonable way of compromising would be to provide a uniform grant for all students, and provide an additional subsidy based on income. Such a program is also politically more acceptable, for it gives something to everyone.

STATE AND LOCAL AID

Except for community colleges in some states, and a few municipal colleges, public higher education receives little assistance from local governments. It gets half or more of its income for educational and general purposes from state sources. Some legislatures simply make a direct appropriation to each public college or university in the state. The appropriation is usually based on a budget proposed by each institution, and the appropriations are often on a line-item basis, which makes adapting to changed conditions or poor estimates difficult.

As the number of public institutions of higher education in a state increased,

[6]W. Lee Hansen and Burton A. Weisbrod, "A New Approach to Higher Education Finance," in M. D. Orwig, *Financing Higher Education: Alternatives for the Federal Government* (Iowa City, Iowa: American College Testing Program, 1971), pp. 117–42.

legislators discovered that each was lobbying against the others for its piece of the appropriations pie; thus the price of increased appropriations often became a coordinating agency. By now more than half of the states have such agencies. Some of them replace individual governing boards, thus exerting intra- as well as inter-institutional control. Most, however, merely coordinate otherwise separately governed institutions. The coordinating board usually develops a consolidated budget proposal, which is agreed upon beforehand by each institution and presented to the legislature as a unified document.

The natural result of such enforced cooperation was the development of formulas for determining the allocation to each institution, to reduce the areas of disagreement on a consolidated budget. Such formulas are now in use in at least a dozen states. Examples include:

1. Determination of faculty size by use of student–faculty ratios. These range from a simple ratio applicable to all institutions for all programs (as in Kentucky and Tennessee) to the extreme case of California, where in the formula estimates the ratio of students to faculty on a course-by-course basis that considers subject field and type and level of instruction.

2. Cost per unit of workload. In Florida, allocations for instruction other than faculty salaries are based on a specified amount per student credit-hour, and in Texas custodial service allowances are based on an amount per square foot of building area.

3. Average of actual practice. In Florida, Kentucky, Oklahoma, Tennessee, and Texas an average salary per faculty position is determined by comparing actual practice in adjoining states and in private institutions.

Besides a proposed budget and formulas, costs analysis procedures are another way to determine state appropriations. These differ from formulas in attempting to assess past costs in a scientific rather than an arbitrary way. In New Mexico, for example, the method gives a historical cost per full-time equivalent student for administration, instruction, organized research, extension and public service, libraries, and operation and maintenance. These figures are inflated by an appropriate amount and then multiplied by the full-time equivalent enrollment to determine the allocation for each institution.

Some states also provide money to private institutions, although the amounts are generally small. Two states provide substantial amounts. Pennsylvania has blurred the line between public and private institutions by granting unrestricted general support to 16 private colleges and universities. However, it has insisted on putting public members on the governing boards of some of them. New York has, since 1968, provided money to private institutions in the state based on degrees granted. It provides $940 for each bachelor's degree granted, $650 for each master's, and $3100 for each doctorate. The money is for unrestricted use by the private institutions. This system has helped private institutions to remain financially healthy.

FEDERAL AID

The federal government has provided aid for colleges, as for elementary and secondary schools, for specific purposes, the most important of which has been research. The relationship has been mutually beneficial, with the government benefiting from the research and the universities receiving a subsidy. This research money proved a bonanza for research universities in the 1960s, but a cutback in federal funding in the late 1960s and 1970s resulted in financial strains for some of the most prestigious universities in the country. What happened was that they hired faculty on this "soft" money and allowed many of them to acquire tenure. When the grants came to a halt, it was necessary to support these faculty members on "hard" money, which the university received from more certain sources. To make things worse, increasing costs were putting a squeeze on the hard money, and funds used to construct buildings and laboratories designed specifically for federal programs seemed to be wasted as these programs were phased out.

Of course, large federal grants to colleges and universities were also aimed at construction of buildings and training programs in specific areas. Much federal money in support of higher education has gone to individual students in the form of grants, including the "G.I. Bill" and Educational Opportunity Grants.

The federal government has increasingly applied regulations to all activities of colleges, including those not financed by federal funds. Institutions must obey the regulations or forfeit all federal monies. For most, this is not a reasonable alternative, and the institution is forced to comply with complicated guidelines regarding such things as equal employment opportunity, affirmative action, age discrimination, the Occupational Safety and Health Act, pensions, environmental protection, and experimentation on human subjects. Some of these guidelines were originally written for industry and are not readily applicable to colleges; others are overcomplicated, and the regulations associated with one law sometimes conflict with those of another. The result is a maze of "Catch-22" regulations, in which the university is damned if it complies and damned if it doesn't. The amount of administrative time spent in complying with federal regulations has become an important cost to higher education. Federal support of higher education is discussed in greater detail later.

ENDOWMENT EARNINGS

Income from endowment is a small part of total income of higher education, but it is important to a few institutions. Endowment is money that has been given to the college to be held in perpetuity. The principal usually may not be spent, but the income may. Occasionally the endowment income may be used for any college purpose; frequently it is restricted to use for particular purposes.

Harvard University has by far the largest endowment of any university, with holdings worth $1.3 billion in 1975. It has been able to pursue a policy of not granting tenure to a faculty member unless it has endowment from which it can reasonably expect to pay the faculty member's salary indefinitely.

For private institutions, income from endowment in the 1930s and 1940s averaged about 25 percent of educational and general income. By 1950, it had slipped to 14 percent, and by 1972 it was only 6 percent.[7] Since the majority of all endowment is held by a relatively small number of prestigious private institutions, endowment income is usually only a small percentage of operating income for private, postsecondary education. For public institutions, endowment is even less important. In the 1930s and 1940s it constituted about two percent of income; it is now less than half of one percent.[8]

The main reason endowments have declined as a percentage of income is that income (and expenditures) have been increasing so rapidly. Actually, total dollars of endowment income have been increasing, from about $70 million per year in the 1930s and 1940s to over $500 million now.[9] Costs, though, have been rising faster. Colleges have tried to combat this with campaigns for additional operating money. However, they have found that appeals for money for steel and concrete are much more visible signs of a donor's generosity.

Colleges have also tried to increase the income from endowment. Some years ago, because endowment managers are risk-averse, almost all endowment was conservatively invested in government bonds and mortgages, both of them fixed-income securities. In times of rapid inflation, however, these become relatively unattractive. Gradually, some institutions began to invest in other types of securities, including stocks and corporate bonds. Even though they are fixed-income securities, corporate bonds are relatively attractive for endowment funds because their higher coupon rate results from a taxable status inapplicable to tax-exempt schools and colleges. Stocks carry much more risk, but have provided spectacular capital gains for some endowment funds. The University of Rochester, an owner of large blocks of Eastman Kodak and Xerox, saw its endowment more than double during the 1960s.

A problem with investing in stocks is that there is a tradeoff between income and capital gains. A corporation may either pay out its income in dividends, or may retain the earnings to increase the total worth of the company, thus raising the stock's value per share. Endowment managers in the past have, often without judicial precedent, assumed that capital gains received on sale of a stock constitute part of the endowment principal, and are unavailable to be spent as income. The result has been a pressure to invest in stocks that pay regular and sizable dividends, ignoring possibilities for capital gain in other

---

[7]National Center for Educational Statistics, *Digest of Educational Statistics, 1974* (Washington, D.C.: U.S. Government Printing Office, 1975), Table 122, p. 107.

[8]*Ibid.*

[9]*Ibid.,* Table 125, p. 110.

stocks. Some institutions, however, have adopted a method that enables port-folio managers to invest without this restriction. The college takes each year as income a percentage of the value of the portfolio (usually a moving three- to five-year average of the value is used). The money for this may come either from dividends or capital gains. The remainder above this is reinvested.

PRIVATE GIFTS AND GRANTS

Private gifts and grants have been an important source of income for private higher education since its founding. A distinction must be made among giving for endowment, giving for capital purposes, and giving for current purposes. As already mentioned, colleges have found it easiest to raise money for capital purposes. Increasingly, however, private colleges have had to ask donors for money for current expenditures. Income from gifts for all purposes has increased manyfold over the years, from about $40 million in 1940 to over $2 billion in 1970.[10] As a percentage of total educational and general income, it has constituted a remarkably constant 12 to 14 percent of the educational and general income of private institutions and two to three percent of that of public institutions.[11] Along with money from endowment, gifts constitute a valuable source of money colleges can use for special expenditures.

There are all sorts of regulations on the different types of support that come to institutions of higher education. Usually, the regulations apply only to the use of the money from one particular source. A donor, for example, will specify that money donated is to be used only for construction of a new chemistry building, or for student aid. The institution must then properly account for how the money is spent. The result is "fund accounting," widely used in higher education. This means a separate account is established for each fund of money on which there are separate restrictions.

SALE OF SERVICES

Sale of services and products is a minor source of income for higher education, but is important for some departments. Agricultural schools sell their crops and the milk from their cows. Some departments contract to do research for governmental agencies and private concerns. Departments of education operate testing services for local school districts. All of these furnish money which can be used to give the department a degree of autonomy from the general budget.

[10]Council for Financial Aid to Education, *Voluntary Support of Education, 1969–70* (Washington, D.C., 1971), p. 64.

[11]National Center for Educational Statistics, *1974 Digest,* Table 126, p. 111.

Proposals to Aid Higher Education

Income of institutions of higher education from all sources has not risen as fast as costs have risen, and the result has been a retrenchment for many colleges. It is difficult to measure the extent to which this has happened, however. Higher education does not operate at a profit, and it does not help, therefore, to examine the "bottom line." The case is clear-cut when an institution is forced to close its doors, but in most cases the problem must be measured subjectively. Colleges can usually manage to balance their budgets, adjusting to an increase in costs by a reduction in what they attempt to do. The problem, then, must be measured in terms of reduced vigor of the institution, maintenance deferred, and opportunities foregone. These things are intangible, but the problem is real.

The question of the most appropriate finance methods for higher education is being discussed concurrently at state and national levels. However, the issues receive different emphasis at the two levels because of the unique relationships of federal versus state governments to colleges.

AT THE STATE LEVEL

Public colleges and universities are operated by state governments, and most state money for higher education goes into general institutional support. As a result, the greatest controversies at the state level have been over the total amount of the state higher education budget and the share of this to which each public college and university is entitled. In conjunction with this has been a debate over the appropriate level of tuition at public institutions. Many legislators have favored increased tuition, to ease the demands on the public purse. Many college administrators have supported low tuition, to increase access by low-income students and at the same time improve the competitive position of the public institutions over and against the private, high-tuition colleges. This argument has ended in a compromise in most states, whereby public tuition has increased but the dollar spread between public and private tuition has also continued to increase.

Lesser battles have been waged in various states over the suggestion that state support ought to take the form of scholarships to all students rather than institutional grants. Whether provided on the basis of academic merit or financial need, such scholarships are a way of providing state aid for private education. For this reason, they are resisted by public institutions. Until the 1960s little state aid went directly to students. New York, with many private institutions, was an exception, and for many years it provided more aid to students than all other states combined. By now, most of the states provide at least a minimal amount of scholarship aid.

The question of direct aid to private colleges and universities has also arisen in many states, but has been looked upon with less favor than student aid. Nine states provide some form of general institutional support to one or more private colleges and universities. Pennsylvania and New York have been the leaders in such efforts.

AT THE FEDERAL LEVEL

At the federal level, five major types of aid to higher education have been advocated, each with its supporters. These are:

1. Categorical aid: money provided for specific purposes usually related to national goals such as manpower development or research.
2. Student aid: money provided directly to students in the form of grants or loans.
3. Grants to institutions: money to colleges and universities for broad or undesignated purposes.
4. Tax relief: assistance to taxpayers for educational expenses in the form of exemptions, deductions, or tax credits.
5. Revenue sharing: return to the states of certain tax monies collected by the federal government.

Federal aid to higher education has been primarily in the first two categories, the most important of the categorical aids being federal research grants. Although many institutions argue that these are not aid at all, but payment for services rendered, they have certainly aided particular institutions to attract faculty and students. Federal monies for research are provided for two categories of expenditure: direct costs and indirect costs. Direct costs are those incurred by the very nature of the project, for example, expenditures for personnel, travel, supplies, and computer time. Indirect costs are those that cannot be allocated directly but are presumed to increase as a result of the research. Examples are costs of libraries and of administration. Direct costs are estimated in a budget for each project, and are paid by the government on receipt of proof of actual expenditures. Indirect costs are usually calculated as a percentage of total direct costs paid on the project. Each institution has an indirect cost rate established each year as a result of a detailed accounting of the university's total indirect costs, direct costs allocable to government research, and all other direct costs. Indirect costs are shared by the federal government on the basis of the ratio of the two categories of direct costs. The indirect cost paid by the government, which is frequently greater than 50 percent of total direct costs, goes directly to the university and can be used for any institutional purpose. It has often been transferred to departments not so favored by federal research grants, in an attempt to maintain an academic balance.

Second in importance to categorical grants have been those for construction of facilities. The Higher Education Facilities Construction Act of 1963 provided public and private institutions matching construction grants that reached a peak of $527 million 1965-66. As the demand for new facilities to house college and university students has declined, this program has been phased out. The Office of Education's principal activity in this area now is to administer an interest subsidy program for privately financed construction.

There have been several kinds of objections to categorical aid. Institutions receiving it complain that the provision of such monies tends to distort institutional goals. Colleges that receive little categorical aid would prefer institutional grants of unrestricted aid, for these would presumably be distributed on a formula basis and would result in a greater dispersion of funds. Currently, 85 percent of all research grants go to the top 100 universities. Still others feel that aid should be apportioned directly to students.

AID TO STUDENTS

Federal aid to students has been almost as important as categorical grants. The "G.I. Bill" has provided educational benefits for about 15 million veterans, five million of them at the college level, in the 30 or more years of its existence since the end of World War II. Of more recent impact is the Educational Opportunity Grant program that provides grants for students with exceptional financial need. A third type of student aid is federally guaranteed student loans. There has been a sharp division of opinion over whether student aid should be in the form of grants or loans. Those favoring grants emphasize equality of educational opportunity, and particularly the fact that poor students are often unwilling to commit themselves to large long-term loans. Those favoring loans emphasize the private benefits of higher education, and the fact that more students can be subsidized with the same amount of money in loans than in grants. A compromise that has often been suggested but never implemented by the government is called the "income-contingent" loan. The student agrees to pay a stipulated percentage of future income for a given number of years for each $1,000 borrowed. Those whose earnings are not substantially increased by their college education would not pay back as much as they had borrowed, whereas high earners would pay back more than they had borrowed. Yale University has such a plan.

INSTITUTIONAL AID

Institutional aid for general purposes has been favored by many institutions, particularly those receiving little in categorical aid. The federal government has provided little of such general aid because a majority of the members of Congress feel that they can retain greater control over federal funds by allocating federal aid only for specific purposes. In addition, economists have argued that federal aid should be channeled through students to encourage the operation of the marketplace in higher education.

TAX RELIEF

Those championing the cause of tax relief have been principally concerned with the problems of the middle-income parent sending children to college. Such relief would come in the form of deductions or tax credits. The deduction method consists of deducting educational expenses from income. The tax credit method allows such expenses to be deducted from taxes paid. Low-income individuals using the standard deduction would not benefit from the deduction method. Although tax credits would benefit them, it is unlikely that the credits would offset the full amount of the cost, and they might prove insignificant. For high-income individuals, the tax saving under either the deduction or tax credit method would be a relatively small part of the total tax. Thus the benefit of either method would accrue primarily to middle-income individuals. It is alleged by some that these are the persons most hurt by the present system, in which high-income individuals can afford to send their children to college and low-income families are helped by various programs of student aid. However, thus far Congress has not seen fit to pass such a tax relief bill.

REVENUE SHARING

Federal sharing of revenue with states and localities (counties and cities) seems now to be well established. It is based on the fact that the federal tax system is more elastic than that of the states. Revenue sharing money has enabled some localities to stave off financial disaster while others have been able to reduce local taxes. Although school districts are specifically exempted from receiving revenue sharing money directly, revenue sharing money is used by some states for schools and colleges.

Financing Community Colleges[12]

In some states the community college developed as an extension of the public school system, an opportunity for an additional two years of education for graduates of a local high school. In others, it originated with higher education as a way of taking the burden of the first two years of undergraduate education from the universities. The fact that community colleges have antecedents in both higher education and elementary–secondary education has resulted in many kinds of community colleges as well as many ideas about what a community college should do or be. Those colleges developing from higher edu-

---

[12] This section on community colleges borrows heavily from *Financing Community Colleges,* by Walter I. Garms (New York: Colombia University, Teachers College Press, 1977) which should be seen for amplification of this discussion and additional topics regarding community college finance.

cation emphasized transfer programs preparatory to full-fledged university work. Those growing out of elementary–secondary education emphasized terminal programs—courses that prepare community college students to take their places in the world of work. Tension between these two curricular goals, transfer and terminal programs, is still present in community colleges today.

Just as the curriculum of a community college reflects its origins in either higher or lower education, so also does its governance. Some are governed as extensions of public school districts, others as branches of the state university system, still others as independent entities. Two, or even three, of these patterns may occur in the same state.

This duality is also reflected in the financing of community colleges. Some are financed as if they were institutions of higher education, others as if they were part of elementary–secondary education, and a third group has the mixed blessing of a combination of finance methods. As a result, both the issues that face the financing of higher education and those facing the public schools are, at least potentially, issues in the financing of community college education.

The double origin of community colleges also manifests itself in the fact that there is consensus neither on what the community colleges are nor about what they should be doing. No uniform definition of a community college exists, and the American Association of Community and Junior Colleges has been forced, in its *Junior College Directory,* to accept as junior or community colleges those that the state says are such. For example, a few states list area vocational institutes as community colleges, while most do not.

This confusion is an example of the problems faced by a new concept struggling to establish an identity and a mission. In a sense, one of the strengths of the community college movement is the thing that makes it hard to analyze— i.e., that it has not been hidebound by traditional forms easily categorized and counted. But this diversity has also made it difficult for community colleges to band together as a powerful force to influence legislation, as other segments of education have been able to do.

The same problem arises when one talks about the function of the community college. Most community colleges offer programs that can be categorized as transfer, terminal, or community service (vocational, avocational, and academic courses for those who are past the usual college age). But community colleges are not the only ones to offer such programs. Four-year institutions offer the first two undergraduate years. High schools and the area vocational centers offer vocational courses. And both high schools and university extension programs offer adult education courses. What is the unique function of community colleges?

Despite the difficulty in defining the identity of the community college or its mission, one can conceive of three functions that characterize most of these institutions and justify their existence.

The first special function is that community colleges provide entry to postsecondary education for those who find access to traditional institutions difficult or impossible, and thus encourage social mobility. Among the students who can be put into this category are those who find the cost of traditional institutions too high, those whose academic ability and performance have not yet been proven, those who live too far from a four-year institution, and those beyond the usual college age.

The second function is that community colleges provide courses and programs that are not provided, or are insufficiently provided, by four-year institutions: vocational courses, avocational courses, short-term programs, non-degree programs, and other similar offerings.

The third function served by community colleges is the provision of those programs most needed in the local community, as determined by that community. The special needs of the community in which it is located are often of little concern to a four-year institution, which likes to think of itself as having a statewide, regional, or even national appeal. Conversely, the very name "community college" emphasizes its commitment to meeting local needs.

It is on the basis of these special capabilities that community colleges should be able to justify their separate existence. Prominent on the list of criteria for judging the value of any community college program should be the extent to which it enhances or impedes the college in meeting these special capabilities.

MODELS OF COMMUNITY COLLEGE FINANCING

There are many ways to finance community colleges if we take into account all the varying percentages of income from a wide range of sources and the ways in which these amounts are determined. But the number of theoretical models of finance plans are limited. Each of those discussed in the following sections represents a more or less "pure" method, though possibly none is suitable for adoption in that pure form. Most of them have been used with modifications in one or more states.

Financing methods can be broadly categorized into three groups: market economy models, planned economy models, and mixed models. Each group contains specific variations of these models. Only one of the models, that of power equalizing, does not currently exist in some form in the United States at the community college level.

MARKET ECONOMY MODELS

The completely private system. A completely private system would reflect the market economy in its purest sense. All institutions would be private, and would neither be controlled nor subsidized in any way by a governmental body. In addition, there would be no indirect subsidies through grants to students. There are at present a few private nonprofit institutions operating in the United States that would fit this model, as would most of the proprietary (profit-making) institutions. However, the model does not work as it would in its pure form because these institutions are in competition with institutions that receive substantial government subsidization. A private system is favored by free-market economists who believe that the external values of higher education are small or nonexistent, and that private values are paramount. If this is true, higher education should be in the private sector, with people free to purchase as much or little as they see fit, and government limited to the regulation necessary to prevent fraud and monopoly.

Such a system would tend to promote greater variety in instituions and programs than would a state-supported system. Automatic regulation of the amount of education provided (by the market, through the price system) would encourage more efficient operation and reduce the burden on taxpayers. One major drawback is the lack of equity for students, since the rich can buy as much education as they wish, while the poor may be unable to afford any. Another is the danger that the profit motive would encourage the proliferation of educational programs that only appeared to meet students' and society's needs. The modifications discussed below might alleviate these problems somewhat.

Private system with government grants to students. In this model, institutions would receive no direct government aid. Instead subsidies to students, if allocated on a selective basis, could be used to promote certain social goals, such as providing access to higher education for needy students. If done on a nonselective basis, the system would approximate what has been called a "social security" type plan: a payroll tax used to entitle each person to a certain number of years of postsecondary education, with the education to be acquired all at one time, or in bits and pieces throughout an individual's life. In either case, one would be free to use one's grant at any educational institution desired (including proprietary ones), as was done with the "G.I. Bill." This model currently applies to a number of proprietary schools. Flight schools, for example, can receive payment from the federal government for the cost of flight training for veterans under the "G.I. Bill." This model would provide more equity to students than the first one, by guaranteeing an education to all on an equal basis. It has important similarities to the proposals we made in Chapter Nine for financing secondary education. However, in its pure form, with only private institutions, it is not clear that it would serve us adequately as a nation. The benefits of education are diverse and often difficult to evaluate. The profit motive does not necessarily coincide with social perceptions of needs, as evidenced by the offerings of television.

Private system with government grants to institutions. In this model, all institutions would still be private, but there would be some direct government subsidization. This is essentially the system used to support New York State colleges. One problem with such a system is that distribution of money will be limited predominantly to existing institutions, and new institutions offering substantially different programs will find it particularly difficult to receive approval for grants. This discourages experimentation. The other problem is that there is bound to be significant governmental control, for the government will be unwilling to distribute money without accounting for its usage. Finally, this plan would not necessarily serve the cause of equity, unless easier access for low-income students were made a condition of the grant (thus imposing further controls). Although this model is in use, it appears to offer no important advantages. It could probably be termed a stopgap measure, since it merely maintains existing private institutions as an alternative to having to provide space for their students in public institutions.

PLANNED ECONOMY MODELS

These models are so called because the system of financing so strongly resembles the economic system of socialist countries. It is characterized by centralized planning, absence of the profit motive as a regulator of the kind and quality of services to be furnished, and a consequent lack of diversity. Such models may well sacrifice efficiency on the altar of equity, just as the completely private system sacrifices equity for efficiency.

State financing with centralized control. In this system, individual colleges would be, in effect, branch campuses of a centrally controlled, statewide, community college system. The budget would be established by a state board on a line-item basis. There would be no local financial contributions, and no mechanism for local decision making on programs. Major program decisions would be made centrally. Students could be assigned to any branch of the institution in order to achieve optimum use of facilities. This model exists, with minor variations, in 11 states.[13] This centralized system tends, more than most models, to provide equity to students and taxpayers, to keep the monetary demands of community colleges on the state treasury in bounds, and to prevent wasteful duplication of programs and facilities. However, it does this at the expense of being less responsive to local needs, and of having inadequate mechanisms for promoting efficient operation.

State financing with some decentralization of control. In this model, as in the previous one, there is little or no local financial contribution to community colleges, but problems are ameliorated by allowing individual colleges to have some say in how they spend their money. Rather than centrally controlled budgets, this approach would emphasize formula budgeting, based on criteria such as number of students, complexity of course offerings, and square feet of building to be maintained. Such a system, with more or less complicated budgeting formulas, is in use in six states.[14] The main difference between this model and the completely centralized model is that the first, by allowing schools to

---

[13] Alaska, Colorado (the six state-supported colleges), Georgia, Iowa, Kentucky, Massachusetts, Montana, Oklahoma, Utah, Virginia, and Rhode Island.

[14] Connecticut, Florida, North Carolina, South Carolina, Tennessee, and Washington.

spend money as they see fit, fosters innovation and increases the ability of the college to respond to the needs of the local community. Conversely, decentralized control obscures the demands of the system as a whole upon the state treasury and increases the possibility of wasteful duplication.

MIXED MODELS

The market economy model and the planned economy model represent extremes. While examples of both exist in the United States (one in the private sector and one in the public), it is evident that in most states the public has been unwilling to accept either extreme. The mixed models represent a middle ground. The thing that characterizes them all is the existence of a financial (and control) partnership between the state government and a local government. The four models discussed below are distinguished from one another by the manner in which the amounts of the state and local shares are determined.

Percentage matching. This system allows the local community college to set its own budget as desired. The state then agrees to provide a percentage of this budget, say one-third. The percentage provided is uniform throughout the state, rather than varying with the wealth of the community. This model should not, therefore, be confused with percentage equalizing plans discussed in Chapter Eight. Five states have such a system.[15] The intent of the model is to have the state shoulder part of the cost, while encouraging community colleges to provide what is needed in their localities without interference from the state. This tends to work well, for the amount of money received from the state depends only upon the budget adopted, and not on number of students or credit-hours of approved programs. However, it is actually an anti-equalizing model. Those communities that are rich in taxable wealth find it easy to budget large expenditures and thus receive more money from the state; poor communities can support only small expenditures, and consequently receive less from the state. In addition, unless strict limits are imposed upon total state payments, this model constitutes a blank check on the state treasury.

Flat grant. In this model the state gives each college a set number of dollars per full-time equivalent student. The college raises the rest of its budget as it can, through such things as local taxation or tuition. Eight states have a flat grant system.[16] As was noted in Chapter Eight in connection with the financing of elementary and secondary education, if the flat grant constitutes most of the cost of education, it has a strong equalizing effect. However, it is usually a much smaller percentage of the cost, and is thus less equalizing than other methods using the same amount of money.

[15] Maryland, Missouri, New Jersey, New York, and Pennsylvania.

[16] Colorado (the six locally operated colleges), Kansas, Mississippi, New Mexico, North Dakota, Oregon, Texas, and Wisconsin.

Foundation program. This method of financial support comes directly from elementary–secondary education. While it is in use at this level in 35 states, it is used at the community college level in only California, Illinois, Michigan, and Wyoming. The state specifies a number of dollars per full time equivalent student (FTE) as representing the amount necessary for an adequate community college program (different numbers of dollars may be set for different programs). The state also specifies a local tax effort that must be made (usually in terms of a required tax rate), and may specify a tuition rate. The amount of the budget guaranteed by the state is equal to the foundation amount per FTE times the FTE of the college. From this is deducted the amount raised by the required local tax rate and the income from tuition, if any. The remainder is supplied by the state.

As with the foundation program in elementary–secondary education, if the foundation amount is set sufficiently high, and the required tax rate sufficiently low, it is highly equalizing. However, the foundation is usually set too low, and colleges in property-rich areas can easily raise more than the foundation at the required tax rate. In addition, this plan (and some of the others) is more complicated at the community college level because community colleges do not all offer the same general mix of courses. In order to be fair, the foundation program must set a different guarantee for different courses, and the cost accounting involved can be complicated.

Power equalizing. Although power equalizing has been adopted by a number of states at the elementary–secondary level, no state yet uses this method for community colleges. In essence, the state guarantees that the college will have a guaranteed amount of assessed valuation per FTE student. The college can decide the tax rate to be levied, and any two colleges that decide to levy the same tax rate will have the same amount per student to spend. A full discussion of the advantages and disadvantages of power equalizing is contained in Chapters Eight and Nine.

A disadvantage of the power equalizing plan is the difficulty of guaranteeing, in essence, a greater assessed valuation per student in high-cost programs than in low-cost programs. This is most easily taken care of by weighting the FTE by factors that represent the relative cost of the programs.

A problem with both the foundation plan and the power equalizing plan at the community college level is that, up to the level of the guarantee, additional students are completely subsidized by the state. That is, the amount raised by the required tax rate (for the foundation program) or the levied rate (for power equalizing) is deducted from the amount per FTE guaranteed times the total FTE, and the remainder is paid by the state. If the college increases its FTE, neither the guarantee per FTE nor the amount raised by the district in local taxes is changed. Thus, the entire guarantee per FTE is paid by the state for the additional students. If the guarantee is sufficiently high to be strongly equalizing, it will also be high enough to encourage colleges to pull in many additional students who will be fully supported by the state. The problem is not evident at the elementary-secondary level where mandatory attendance in the local public schools makes it infeasible for a district to change its number of pupils voluntarily.

This chapter concludes with our own recommendations for financing higher education, but before outlining them we present several views on the theoretical issue of equity versus efficiency.

Equity Versus Efficiency

Much of the debate on the financing of higher education has centered on the question of equity versus efficiency, a problem discussed in relation to elementary-secondary education in Chapter Two. In higher education, voluntary enrollment and the existence of tuition have set the confrontation in sharper relief. Those for whom efficiency is most important would probably subscribe to the following statements:

1. Not all students are smart or motivated, and we should not be wasting taxpayers' money on those who will not profit from advanced material.

2. Economic returns to a college education are almost entirely private, and thus individuals who benefit from education should pay its cost.

3. Through the action of the marketplace, private institutions are forced to be more efficient than public institutions, and therefore we should not put private institutions at a competitive disadvantage by creating public subsidized institutions.

On the other hand, those who believe equity is more important would tend to make statements like the following:

1. While it is true that some students are smarter than others, we have no effective way of measuring how much students can benefit from college, either before they enroll or while they are in college. The proof comes only after college, and even then should be judged by the individuals who received the education, rather than by others. This means that anyone who wishes to enroll in college should be allowed to do so. This would not preclude different colleges from having different entry and retention standards, but there should be institutions available for all.

2. The returns to a college education are external as well as private. They include the additional income that an educated person can help others achieve through supervision, and the improved operation of our democracy through the contributions of educated people. Because this is so, higher education should not only be made possible for those of all abilities, but should be made available to all by means of low tuition or grants to the needy.

3. Private higher education, because it is not regulated by the government, cannot be trusted to provide education to all equitably, and we must therefore have many public institutions of higher education.

There is at present no scientific way of resolving these value positions. There is no question that some people are smarter than others. However, the benefits of higher education are broader than can be measured by an intelligence or achievement test, and it will undoubtedly remain difficult to determine in advance who will benefit most from college. Second, economists do not agree about the external benefits of higher education nor about how to measure them. Third, it may well be true that private higher education can operate more efficiently but less equitably than public higher education, but that does not resolve the dispute in favor of either side.

The result is that the problem of equity versus efficiency will continue to be fought on an ideological basis. The research we review below contributes important information, but the clash of values involved must ultimately be settled through the political process.

HIGHER EDUCATION SUBSIDIES VS. FAMILY INCOME

An important component of the equity–efficiency debate is the question of the optimal method(s) of college financing. W. Lee Hansen and Burton A. Weisbrod, professors of economics at the University of Wisconsin, examined the equity of the California system at a time when no tuition was charged for this state's higher education. Hansen and Weisbrod attempt to examine whether free tuition was in fact the most equitable method of financing.

They showed statistically that students attending community colleges received the lowest subsidy from the state; those attending the state colleges received a higher subsidy, and those attending the University of California received the highest subsidy.[17] They also discovered that those attending the university came from higher income families than those attending state colleges, who in turn came from more prosperous families than those attending the community colleges. Thus, it appeared that, on the average, the poor were being subsidized less heavily than the rich through the California higher education system. Hansen and Weisbrod went on to compare the subsidies received by each class of families participating in the California public higher education system with the total state and local taxes paid by those families. The results, shown in Table 16-2, indicated that the net subsidy (benefits less taxes) increased as one went from users of the junior college system to users of the university system.

This study provoked a great deal of interest, primarily because of its policy implications. Hansen and Weisbrod recommended that the inequity they had shown be remedied by the use of substantial tuition at the public institutions plus subsidies for poor students. Because many educators believe strongly in the

[17]W. Lee Hansen and Burton A. Weisbrod, "Distribution of Costs and Direct Benefits of Public Higher Education: The Case of California," *The Journal of Human Resources*, 4, No. 2 (Spring 1969), 176-91.

TABLE 16-2

Average Family Incomes, Average Higher Education Subsidies, and Average State and Local Taxes Paid by Families, by Type of Institution, California, 1964

Item	All Families	Families Without Children in California Public Higher Education	Families with Children in California Public Higher Education			
			Total	Junior College	State College	University of California
1. Average family income	$8,000	$7,900	$9,560	$8,800	$10,000	$12,000
2. Average higher education subsidy per year	–	0	880	720	1,400	1,700
3. Average total state and local taxes paid*	620	650	740	680	770	910
4. Net transfer (Line 2 – Line 3)	–	-650	+140	+40	+630	+790

*Total state and local tax rates were applied to the median incomes for families in each column.

Source: W. Lee Hansen and Burton A. Weisbrod, *Benefits Costs, and Finance of Public Higher Education* (Chicago: Markham Publishing Company, 1969), Table IV-12.

principle of free tuition as the great leveler, it was inevitable that a counter-attack on the Hansen-Weisbrod recommendations should be mounted.

Joseph Pechman, director of economic studies at the Brookings Institution, reanalyzed the Hansen-Weisbrod data.[18] Instead of merely including those families whose children were attending public institutions of higher education in California, Pechman separated all families into income classes. For each income class, he estimated the percentage of families who would have children in each of the higher education systems of California, as well as the percentage without children in any one of the three systems. He could then estimate the average subsidy per family for each income class. He performed a similar calculation for the average taxes paid by each income class in support of higher education. His results are shown in Table 16-3. It appears, on the basis of this analysis, using the same data, that the redistribution of money is from rich to poor, the opposite of the Hansen-Weisbrod finding. Based on his findings, Pechman recommended a system of free tuition as being preferable to the recommendations of Hansen and Weisbrod.

Robert Hartman, also of the Brookings Institution, then demonstrated that the analyses of both Hansen-Weisbrod and Pechman were correct; they simply represent different ways of looking at the data.[19] Hansen and Weisbrod considered, for each of the three systems of public education in California, the "average" family with a son or daughter in the system. Pechman looked at people by income class. The better way of looking at things depends upon the questions one wishes to ask.

Hartman goes on to point out that neither analysis of the data really addresses the important policy issues.

> The basic principles are that public higher education should be seeking to achieve two goals: (1) Equalization of opportunity. This goal clearly implies that subsidies be targeted on lower-income students. (2) The provision of below-cost higher education to ensure that both public and private benefits are accounted for in the enrollment decision. This goal need not imply that subsidies be targeted on children from low-income families. Indeed, it seems to me that a good starting point for developing criteria for the appropriate distribution of subsidies to ensure that public benefits are preserved is that all students in post-secondary education should receive approximately equal subsidies. Advocates of public-supported institutions should tell us why a Berkeley student is more productive of social benefits than a Stanford student or than a junior college student.
>
> The third basic principle is that nature and legislatures are niggardly, and there is a tradeoff between the two public policy goals. We cannot avoid asking whether we are willing to risk a little less assurance of public

[18] Joseph A. Pechman, "Distributional Effects of Public Higher Education in California," *The Journal of Human Resources,* 5, No. 3 (Summer 1970), 361-70.

[19] Robert W. Hartman, "A Comment on the Pechman-Hansen-Weisbrod Controversy," *The Journal of Human Resources,* 5, No. 4 (Fall 1970), 519-23.

TABLE 16-3

Average Net Subsidy or Tax Payment
for the Higher Education System By Income Class, California, 1965

Adjusted Gross Income Class	Average Tax Payment Using Taxes Selected by Hansen- Weisbrod	Average Higher Education Subsidy	Net Subsidy (+) or Net Tax Payment (-)
A. *Assuming the Subsidy Is Distributed on the Basis of Distribution of Families with Parent-Supported Students*			
$ 0- 3,999	$ 66	$ 56	$ -10
4,000- 5,999	77	122	+45
6,000- 7,999	88	129	+41
8,000- 9,999	112	126	+14
10,000-11,999	142	179	+37
12,000-13,999	175	167	-8
14,000-19,999	229	229	0
20,000-24,999	348	271	-77
25,000 and over	974	291	-683
B. *Assuming the Subsidy Is Distributed on the Basis of All Families, Including Those with Self-Supporting Students*			
$ 0- 3,999	$ 66	$ 83	$ +17
4,000- 5,999	77	139	+62
6,000- 7,999	88	143	+55
8,000- 9,999	112	122	+10
10,000-11,999	142	160	+18
12,000-13,999	175	155	-20
14,000-19,999	229	181	-48
20,000-24,999	348	252	-96
25,000 and over	974	235	-739

Source: Joseph Pechman, "The Distributed Effects of Public Higher Education in California," *The Journal of Human Resources* V, No. 3 (Summer 1970), p. 366.

benefits in exchange for a little more equalization of opportunity. And that means that we have to talk about how much we value . . . social benefits of higher education as well as debating the value of opportunity equalization.[20]

The consideration of public benefits goes to the heart of the efficiency question, for if there were only private benefits, efficiency would be best assured

[20]*Ibid.*, pp. 522–23.

by making higher education entirely private. Thus we have in this exchange again the confrontation of equity and efficiency.[21]

THREE CONCEPTIONS OF EQUITY

Another way of looking at the equity–efficiency controversy is to examine three conceptions of equity in educational expenditures, and ask which contributes most to efficiency. Figure 16-1 illustrates these three conceptions. On the average, under the present educational system, the lower the socioeconomic status (SES) of a group, the lower its average educational achievement. This does not tell us anything about the ability of these students, but only what happens under the present system of education. Many of the differences may have to do with the students' background. Figure (a) shows three curves relating achievement, however measured, to educational expenditure. With very low expenditure, achievement for all three groups is correspondingly low. After a certain point is reached (perhaps the point at which a competent teacher can be hired), the achievement increases rapidly, with that of the high SES groups increasing fastest. At some point, achievement levels off, and additional expenditures serve no further function. This happens sooner with high SES groups than with low ones.

The concept of equity illustrated by (a) is equal expenditures per student. A_1 represents a relatively low expenditure, and A_2 a higher one. At either level of expenditure, the achievement of high SES students is higher than that of lower SES students.

Some argue that this concept of equity is actually inequitable, since it does not take into account differences in need, and propose a concept that would require equal attainment by all students. This is shown by (b), with B_1 representing a low level of attainment and B_2 a higher level. The difficulty with this concept of equity should be evident: it implies that the achievement of low SES students should be almost as great as their potential (given the present educational system), while that of high SES students should be held down. To raise the level of attainment of high SES students to accord more with their potential, we may have to raise the attainment level to above the present potential of the low SES group.

Neither of these conceptions of equity take economic efficiency into account. The economist would argue that efficiency demands that *marginal* outputs for the last dollar of expenditure should be equal. This implies that expen-

[21] The Hansen-Weisbrod article generated additional comments. The following are all from *The Journal of Human Resources:* Elchanon Cohn, "Comment" (Spring 1970), pp. 222-26; Adam Gifford, "Comment" (Spring 1970), pp. 227-29; Ira Sharkansky, "Comment" (Spring 1970), pp. 230-36; W. Lee Hansen and Burton A. Weisbrod, "Reply" (Summer 1971), pp. 363-74; and Joseph A. Pechman, "Further Comments" (Summer 1971), pp. 375-76.

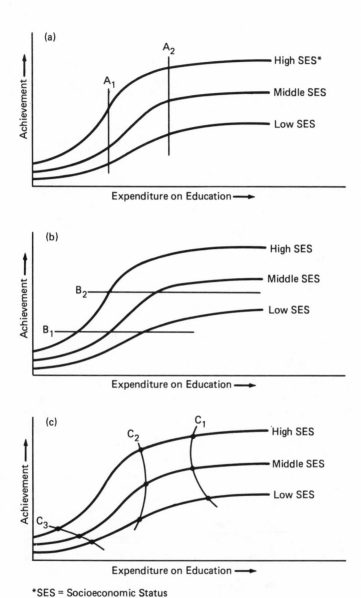

(a)

A_2

A_1

Achievement →

High SES*

Middle SES

Low SES

Expenditure on Education →

(b)

Achievement →

B_2

B_1

High SES

Middle SES

Low SES

Expenditure on Education →

(c)

C_2 C_1

C_3

Achievement →

High SES

Middle SES

Low SES

Expenditure on Education →

*SES = Socioeconomic Status

FIG. 16-1. Equity in Expenditures for Education

ditures on each group should be such that the rate of increase in achievement is the same. Part (c) of the figure shows this, with C_1, C_2, and C_3 revealing entirely different expenditure patterns. C_1 is a rather high rate, and C_2 is a somewhat lower rate. Both of them look more like part (a) of the figure than part (b). However, C_3 also places expenditures at equal slopes of the curve, albeit at low slopes, and looks more like part (b) of the figure. Any of these would be efficient in the economist's sense; whether any would be politically acceptable is an open question. In any case, we do not have data sufficient to construct such curves in the detail needed to make actual allocation decisions, and there is thus no way in which we can achieve such a concept of economic efficiency.

Note that the reason this discussion has been couched in terms of SES groups is that equity is usually discussed in terms of wealth. However, the argument would be the same if, instead, one spoke of high, average, and low intelligence or achievement groups. It is in these terms, as a matter of fact, that many people are thinking when they question large expenditures for the higher education of students who show limited achievement.

Our Recommendations

Our recommendations for financing elementary–secondary education can be applied to the financing of higher education. We have indicated our belief that there is a public interest in providing a basic education allowing children to become literate adults. Such an education would provide the basic tools necessary to cope with our complex society and to participate in a democratic government. We have also indicated our belief that this basic education can be imparted through mandatory education to end with the eighth grade. Aside from this basic "citizenship training," we feel that people should be encouraged to partake of the kinds of education they want, in the amounts and at the times they choose. Earlier in this chapter, we quoted Robert Hartman to the effect that the equity aims in financing higher education could be met through a system of grants keyed to ability to pay, while public and private benefits might be better guaranteed through a system of equal subsidies. We feel that both these aims can be met. Our educational coupons are indeed grants keyed to ability to pay, whereas our six-year portable grant for education above the eighth-grade level is an equal subsidy to all.

Our system of financing higher education, then, is a simple one, employing both state grants and educational coupons. Both would be keyed to the decisions of individuals, those exercising their portable grant entitlement and those purchasing educational coupons. For courses taken by students using a portable grant entitlement, the college would apply to the state for its legal allowance. Any excess in tuition over the amount of the state grant would be charged to the student, who could pay for it with educational coupons. The coupons would, of course, be turned in to the state for reimbursement in cash. Besides providing colleges with reimbursements, the state could continue to fund research and public service activities of public colleges and universities.

We do not anticipate that states will soon dismantle their systems of public higher education in order to adopt our program. However, we also have less far-reaching recommendations for the reform of higher education financing, and these assume the maintenance of our present system of publicly supported institutions. First, we note a disturbing tendency for those in higher education to turn to the federal government for the solution of their money problems. We do not believe this is either desirable or necessary, and we suspect that in any case there will be little additional federal money available for higher education in the foreseeable future. The solution is up to each state. We recommend the following procedures, which the states could enact now, to ensure a more equitable and efficient system of higher education with minimum dislocation.

1. Institute tuition at the public colleges and universities that is at least half of that at the average private institution. This would help to reduce the unfair competition with the private colleges that public higher education has engaged in for many years.

2. Adopt a system of aid to low-income students similar to that used in New York State. This would mitigate the effect of the tuition increase for poor students, while still having rich students come closer to paying their own way.

3. Provide state monies to public four-year colleges and universities based on a formula system such as that in use in California, where sophisticated formulas adjust state aid fairly closely to the needs of the colleges.

4. For community colleges, adopt a modified power equalizing scheme. This is preferred to the foundation, flat grant, or percentage matching models described earlier because it leaves to the local community the decision of how heavily it should tax itself for community colleges, while putting all communities on an equal footing with regard to the amount raised for a given tax effort. However, in order to prevent the finance plan from putting a heavy and unpredictable burden on the state treasury, it is necessary to formulate the model in terms other than a guaranteed assessed valuation per student. Otherwise, colleges will be encouraged to expand indefinitely, with the entire cost of additional students paid by the state. The solution to this is to specify power equalizing in terms of a guaranteed assessed valuation *per capita*. Colleges in different communities that set the same tax rate will have the same number of dollars to spend per resident of the community college district, regardless of local wealth. They can then choose to spend this money for community colleges in the way they see fit. In addition to reducing the temptation to raid the state treasury, this plan has the further advantage of dissociating the amount of money received from the number of students. This would encourage the offering of innovative programs for which it is difficult to define FTE students.

Summary

The interrelationships between the financing of elementary-secondary education and the financing of our colleges and universities are so important that a book on school finance cannot ignore higher education. Yet, because it is impossible to do justice to such a large topic in a single chapter, this chapter has only mentioned briefly many of the important issues of higher education finance.

We have reviewed the small amount of research that has been done on the relationship between the public financing of elementary-secondary education and that of higher education. It appears that the most important determinant of the relative emphasis given to higher education over elementary-secondary education is the force of tradition. Those states that developed a strong private higher education sector early in time have continued to be less concerned with public expenditure on higher education than other states.

The chapter has also discussed each of the principal sources of revenue for higher education: tuition, state and local aid, federal aid, endowment earnings, private gifts and grants, and sale of services. The problems and potential of each are reviewed. Proposals to aid higher education at the state and federal levels are also discussed, including direct aid to students, institutional aid, tax relief, and revenue sharing.

An important section of the chapter examines the financing of community colleges. There are a number of models in use by the various states; some of them are similar to the systems used for elementary-secondary finance, others resemble the ways in which the systems of four-year institutions are financed, and some are like neither system. Eight models currently in use are discussed, as well as a power-equalizing analogue of the equivalent elementary-secondary system, which has not yet been tried at the community college level.

A brief discussion is included of the problem of equity versus efficiency, which is even more strikingly presented at the higher education level than in elementary-secondary education. A review of the research on the subject makes it clear that the issue is one that will be with us for some time.

Finally, we have presented our own recommendations for the financing of higher education. Our ultimate recommendations are tied to our suggestions in Chapter Nine for a completely new way of financing and organizing education. Recognizing that these sweeping reforms will not soon be adopted, we also recommend four steps that would improve the present system:

1. Increase tuition at the public colleges and universities.
2. Adopt a comprehensive system of aid to low-income students, whether attending public or private institutions.
3. Provide state money to public four-year institutions on the basis of a sophisticated formula that suits revenue to needs.
4. Adopt a modified power-equalizing system for financing community colleges.

17

WHERE DOES
THIS LEAVE US?

I want to offer a few comments that are generally related to this broad problem of the gap between the policy analyst and planner on the one hand and the implementer, political leader, administrator on the other. Within the bounds of the problem I include the tendency of the practitioners of policy science to develop their own mystique and the parallel tendency of politicians and administrators to act as if they understood it. Nothing confers status like seeming to be a participant in the newest and most fashionable mysteries!

Harold Howe[1]

As policy analysts and planners who have been involved intimately with the process of policy formation and implementation, we recognize the tendencies referred to in the quote above, and hope this book, rather than becoming a part of the problem, will make a modest contribution to its solution.

In the opening chapter, we indicated some of the dilemmas currently facing education in the United States. Declining enrollments and changing budget priorities have transformed education from a growing to a stable industry, introducing many new problems. Disagreement over whether and to what

[1] Harold Howe, II, "Policy Studies: Blueprints for Progress—Or Social Security for Social Scientists," remarks at a meeting of the Association for Institutional Research, Washington, D.C. May 6, 1974. Unpublished.

extent education should pass on old values to the new generation, or inculcate new values, has made agreement on goals more difficult than in the past. New programs and techniques for improving education have had only moderate success. Disadvantaged groups, hoping for a bigger slice of the educational pie, have fought with established groups struggling to keep theirs. All this has contributed to a concern that is sometimes expressed by citizens as a feeling that "the schools are not doing their job."

Yet it is clear that education is vitally important to the functioning of our society and the individuals in it. We cannot abandon education because of its alleged lack of performance, for a competent educational system is at the very center of our complex society. The only reasonable alternative is to seek ways to improve education. Of course, a book concerned primarily with the financing of education cannot hope to solve all education's problems. We believe, though, that we have made some suggestions worthy of further thought, and that these proposals will be attractive to politicians and administrators.

Chapter Two discussed three strongly held values that have influenced American education as well as all American public policy: equality, efficiency, and liberty. It is impossible to achieve all three of these values completely and simultaneously, yet there are ways to attain more of each than we have presently. We have made policy proposals that we believe promote all three goals, and achieve a reasonable balance among them. We recognize, of course, that determining a "proper balance" is itself a matter of values, and that this choice can only be made through the political process.

The Organization and Financing of Elementary-Secondary Education

Perhaps our most sweeping recommendation is the proposed method for financing and organizing schools discussed in Chapter Nine. Briefly, we call for a system of state-supported, community-operated public schools that aim toward producing students who, on completing the eighth grade, can read, write, do ordinary arithmetic, and have a basic understanding of the operation of our government. Attendance would be compulsory for only as long as necessary to complete this basic program, and the program would be free to all children. The cost would be paid for through uniform state taxes, and the amount allocated to school districts per student would be adjusted for differences in pupil need and cost of education. Parents would be free to send their child to any public school (or, as now, to any private one, if they wished to pay the tuition). Transportation to any school within 15 miles of home would be provided by the local district.

All supplemental education, i.e., areas of study other than reading, writing, arithmetic, and citizenship, would be financed through a system of educational coupons and provided by public schools, private schools, or individual tutors. The coupons, like food stamps, would be for sale at a price adjusted to parents' income, with the poorest paying only a few cents on the dollar, and rich parents paying almost full price. The coupons would pay for all or part of the educational services furnished by any teacher or school, depending on tuition. Public schools would have the choice of furnishing such educational services on a tuition basis, or through local unequalized taxation approved by voters. Parents could purchase as many or as few educational coupons as they wished, and spend them for any kind of supplementary education including such things as music, swimming, science, or dancing.

After the eighth grade, all individuals would be provided with a portable grant that could be used at any time during the remainder of their lives. It would entitle them to an additional six years of basic and vocational education, to be taken whenever they desired. In addition, they would be entitled to purchase educational coupons for supplementary education throughout their lives.

In Chapter Nine, we discuss the proposal and its possible difficulties in greater detail. Here we are concerned with examining the extent to which it promotes equality, efficiency, and liberty. Equality is promoted in two ways. First, this basic education would be fully funded by the state, and thus made available to all on a basis independent of the wealth of the community in which the student lives, and the decisions of neighbors. The allocation to local schools, being adjusted to take care of differences in educational need and cost, would provide sufficient resources to assure equal educational opportunity in all districts. Second, since the price of educational coupons would be scaled according to family income, families would make approximately equal sacrifices to purchase additional education for their children. The cost to the state of the coupons would be raised by uniform (and we hope progressive) statewide taxation.

In Chapter Two we noted that the goals of efficiency and liberty stem from different concerns, and in Chapter Ten we pointed out the difficulties of achieving efficiency in public schools through industrial models involving production functions, or other accountability systems. Briefly, there is insufficient agreement on the goals of schooling, no consensus on a technology of education, and no completely adequate system of measuring accomplishment. We have thus chosen to recommend a type of efficiency that at the same time maximizes liberty in the form of choice by individual parents. In essence, this is a free market approach to efficiency. It is no coincidence that this way of promoting efficiency also promotes liberty. Essentially, instead of specifying the methods by which efficiency is to be achieved, we leave this determination to those who supply education, with the free market ensuring the elimination of those who do not supply it efficiently.

One way of providing such choice is embodied in our plan for basic education through grade eight. Parents may send a child to any school, public or private. This allows families to choose schools and teachers they feel will fill their child's needs. No longer would children be sentenced to attend schools they disliked, with teachers unsympathetic to their problems. Although most parents would undoubtedly choose to send their children to neighborhood schools, the opportunity to transfer would defuse much local controversy. This might cause overcrowding at some schools and empty classrooms at others, but we have offered some suggestions for alleviating that problem. We recognize that our plan will probably not achieve racial balance in the schools. There is no obvious way around this aspect of equality, and we have elected to provide freedom of choice rather than mandatory busing. We suspect the majority of Americans agree with us.

This freedom of choice would also promote efficiency in public schools because some schools would be favored over others. Principals of depopulated schools would have a strong incentive to find ways of increasing their attendance, if for no other reason than to save face. In addition, the local electorate would probably favor remunerating principals partially on the basis of number of teachers supervised. With such incentives, we could expect both a general upgrading of basic education and the evolution of specialized schools to deal with particular learning problems.

The value of liberty would also be nurtured by eliminating compulsory education beyond the elementary level. Instead students would be encouraged to come back for secondary education when they saw a need for it. Uninterested students would not be forced to attend high school, and their absence would substantially improve the instructional climate for those attending.

There is an even greater liberty in the concept of educational coupons, for the decisions of how many to purchase, what subjects to study, and with what teachers would be purely individual. Our proposal provides, we believe, as much liberty as is compatible with the social interest of ensuring that all individuals are provided with the basic tools to enable them to be functioning adults in the labor market and participants in the democratic process.

The Governance of Public Education

We realize that our proposals for financing and organizing education will not be adopted overnight. Those with vested interests will resist such changes and the sheer size and cumbersomeness of public education makes any reform difficult. We must, therefore, ask if education as it is now organized and financed can be improved with only modest changes in its present framework. We have recognized the complaint that schools are too resistant to change, too unresponsive to the desires of their clients, too secretive about what is actually happening behind classroom and administrative office doors. Thus one of our most important recommendations is embodied in the "school site management" concept discussed in Chapter Eleven. These proposals have met with a measure of success singly but have never been presented as a package. To recapitulate briefly;

1. The basic unit of educational management would be the individual school. This means that most of the decisions about educational programs, teachers, and students would be made at the local school level. Principals would thus assume their full range of duties as educational managers, with power to hire and fire teachers (within state guidelines), to establish courses of study (while meeting minimum state requirements), and to operate the building as they see fit. We feel this emphasis on the principal puts the power and the responsibility where they belong in the educational system.

2. In order to make sure that principals consider the feelings and desires of parents, each school would have a Parent Advisory Council. Its most important functions would be to participate in the selection of a principal and to approve or reject the principal's reappointment at the end of a three- to five-year contract. In addition, the Parent Advisory Council would endorse school site budgets and participate in negotiations with the school's teachers on details of the educational program.

3. An important facet of the concept is school site budgeting. The school district would allocate funds to each of its schools and develop an accounting procedure to ensure that funds are used legally. The amount to be allocated to each school might be a flat sum per student, modified by differing educational needs. Funds should be allocated to the school in a single lump sum, to be used as the principal, in consultation with the Parent Advisory Council and teachers, deems best. In addition to this legal accounting, a separate accounting, in a program accounting format, would be made for control and decision-making purposes.

4. The interests of the state in an adequate education in reading, writing, and arithmetic would be safeguarded through a system of statewide testing in these basic skills. This information would also help families to evaluate local schools.

5. An annual performance report would be required of each school, giving information on school and staff characteristics, student performance, areas of strength and areas needing improvement, and separate parent, teacher, and (for secondary schools) student assessments of school performance. The performance report would be widely disseminated in the local school area.

This school site management proposal does not specifically aim toward greater equality, except insofar as each school's monetary allocation is based on number of students adjusted for pupils with special needs. Our concern has been more with efficiency and liberty, for these values, we feel, have been neglected in the push for professionalization and unionization in the last quarter century. As was evident in our finance proposal, our belief is that efficiency can best be promoted by ensuring parent choice. The proposal for school site management provides as much choice as seems feasible within the limits of the present system of public school organization. By making the principal educational manager, responsible for all that goes on at the school, we place the responsibility at the level where parents may have the greatest influence. Provision of the Parent Advisory Council institutionalizes this influence. The annual performance report helps parents decide whether and to what extent to bring influence to bear. We recognize that many principals, because of their training, or because they have been selected on the basis of other criteria, will not be prepared to assume the kinds of responsibility implied by school site management. This problem is not insurmountable, however, for those principals who cannot grow into their jobs will be replaced by those who can.

We also recommend changes in state collective bargaining statutes to give citizens—parents, taxpayers, and students—a stronger voice in collective bargaining negotiations. Under most current state laws representatives of school boards and teacher unions are required to negotiate an agreement on a variety of financial and operational matters affecting local schools. The signed agreement, which is negotiated secretly, becomes the law for the two parties involved. The public, in most instances, is not consulted or informed about the progress of the negotiations. They are also virtually excluded from influencing the negotiations through the marketplace by withdrawing their children from school. If the people are to control their public institutions, they must exercise that control by participating directly in the collective bargaining process. Parent unions, bargaining in open public sessions, public notice and prior public discussions of bargaining positions by management and labor, and consultative or third-party bargaining are possible ways of restoring public influence over educational decision-making.

Finally, we recognize that decisions affecting the governance and financing of public schools are made politically. This is as it should be. Contrary to the views of many educators, we interpret the increasingly frequent rejection of school budgets and bonds as a normal and expected result of a democratic fiscal system. Given the inability of educators to agree on a definition of an adequate education, or to agree on the costs of providing such an education, the decision on how much education is enough should be made politically. A guarantee of the state's average annual expenditure per pupil, for example, leaves the choice of how much is enough to the public through their votes for local school board members and school budgets. We recommend maximum public participation in decision-making and reliance on volunteerism, rather than compulsion, whenever possible. Both sharpen the ability of citizens to make better choices, and also increase their incentive to take advantage of educational opportunities.

Higher Education

Our recommendations for the financing of higher education parallel those for elementary-secondary education. We have suggested that direct appropriations to public colleges and universities be limited to those for research and public service. The bulk of the money colleges and universities would receive, whether public or private institutions, would be from two sources: the two years of portable grants remaining to each student after finishing secondary school, and educational coupons. This, for most purposes, puts all colleges on an equal financing basis and encourages the operation of the marketplace. Because portable grants would be equally available to all, and educational coupons would be sold on the basis of ability to pay, equality would also be served. Our proposal achieves efficiency through the market and simultaneously fosters liberty through expanded freedom of choice.

Since we doubt that most states will immediately adopt these measures, we also make some interim recommendations:

1. Require tuition at public colleges and universities to equal at least half the average at private institutions in the state, in order to reduce present unfair competition.

2. Adopt a system of student aid to enable even the poorest students to attend the college they choose, regardless of level of tuition.

3. Provide state money to public four-year colleges and universities on a formula basis such as that in use in the California state college system.

4. Adopt a modified power equalizing scheme for community colleges in which the college is guaranteed an assessed valuation per capita (rather than per student). This would allow the local district to decide the scale of its operation while equalizing the ability of all community colleges to raise money. By using the per capita measure, the state would not have to bear the entire cost of additional students, and state aid would be divorced from the method of counting students, thus encouraging innovative programs.

We do not pretend to have the only answers to all problems of school finance, nor even necessarily the best answers. We are also painfully aware of the fact that an attempt to solve a social problem usually creates a new one. However, we do believe that our proposals are reasonable and worthy of careful consideration, because they balance not only equity, efficiency, and liberty, but also political feasibility.

INDEX

A

Accountability, 25, 248–61, 349–50
  methods, 248–61
  movement, 248–49
  resistance to, 258–59
Achievement tests, 255–56, 283
  scores (*table*), 26
Advisory councils, parent (*see* Parent
  advisory councils)
AFDC, 173
AFL-CIO, 106, 176
AFT (*see* American Federation of
  Teachers)
Aid for Families with Dependent
  Children, 173
Aid ratio, 193, 194
Allocative efficiency, 89
Alternative schools, 155
Alum Rock, California, Voucher ex-
  periment, 223
American Association of Community
  and Junior Colleges, 429

American Farm Bureau Federation,
  177
American Federation of State,
  County, and Municipal Employees, 106
American Federation of Teachers,
  107–8, 177
Annual performance reports, 283–84,
  285, (*table*) 285
Anti-government sentiment, 10–11
Appropriations, federal, 168
Arbitration, binding interest, 105
Architects, 366–67
Assessed value, 136, 313–15
  projection, 313–15
Assessment of property:
  agricultural reserve, 135
  Arizona, 138–39
  businesses, 134
  determining, 136
  economic effects of, 135
  factories, 134
  farm land, 134